W9-BIB-273

Windows Server® 2008 Hyper-V™ Resource Kit

Robert Larson and Janique Carbone
with the Windows Virtualization Team at Microsoft

PUBLISHED BY
Microsoft Press
A Division of Microsoft Corporation
One Microsoft Way
Redmond, Washington 98052-6399

Library of Congress Control Number: 2009927477

Printed and bound in the United States of America.

2 3 4 5 6 7 8 9 WCT 4 3 2 1 0

Distributed in Canada by H.B. Fenn and Company Ltd.

A CIP catalogue record for this book is available from the British Library.

Microsoft Press books are available through booksellers and distributors worldwide. For further information about international editions, contact your local Microsoft Corporation office or contact Microsoft Press International directly at fax (425) 936-7329. Visit our Web site at www.microsoft.com/mspress. Send comments to rkinput@microsoft.com.

Acquisitions Editor: Martin DelRe
Developmental Editor: Karen Szall
Project Editor: Melissa von Tschudi-Sutton
Editorial Production: Custom Editorial Productions, Inc.
Technical Reviewer: Randall Galloway; Technical Review services provided by Content Master, a member of CM Group, Ltd.
Cover: Tom Draper Design
Cover Illustration: Todd Daman

Body Part No. X15-58116

This book is dedicated to my family, both near and far, who continue to support my endeavors.

—JSC

I dedicate this book to my two children, Alex and Xavier. They continue to inspire me every day.

—REL

Contents at a Glance

Contents

What do you think of this book? We want to hear from you!

Microsoft is interested in hearing your feedback so we can continually improve our
books and learning resources for you. To participate in a brief online survey, please visit:

microsoft.com/learning/booksurvey

Chapter 2   Hyper-V Overview   27

Chapter 18   Virtual Desktop Infrastructure   617

Chapter 23 Server Virtualization Project: Pilot Phase   721

What do you think of this book? We want to hear from you!

Microsoft is interested in hearing your feedback so we can continually improve our
books and learning resources for you. To participate in a brief online survey, please visit:

microsoft.com/learning/booksurvey

Acknowledgments

Principal Authors

Janique Carbone, Robert Larson

Contributing Authors

Tim Mueting, Vijay Tewari, Jim Collins, Arno Mihm, Paul Despe, Bryon Surace, Rob Hefner, Shane Burton, Michael Michael, Ed Reed, Tony Voellm, Tony Soper, Matthijs ten Seldam, Keith Mange, John Howard, Mike Williams, Jeff Woolsey, Gregoire Guetat, Justin Braun, Max Herrmann, Teresa Lewandowski, Tom Pisello, Mark Lunday, Ken Durigan, Dave Hamilton, Will Martin, Rakesh Malhotra, David Ziembicki, James O'Neil, Tom Acker, Chuck Timon

Microsoft Press

Acquisitions Editor: Martin DelRe

Contract Specialist: Heather Stafford

Developmental Editor: Karen Szall

Project Editor: Melissa von Tschudi-Sutton

Project Manager: Megan Smith-Creed

Copy Editor: Julie Hotchkiss

Technical Editor: Randall Galloway

Microsoft Product Team Reviewers

Bryon Surace, John Howard, Michael Michael, Arno Mihm, Shai Ofek, Jeff Woolsey, Peter Fitzsimon, Jason Fulenchek, Hector Linares, Bill Scheidel, Kerim Hanif, Alan Goodman, Shadi El Hajj Sleiman, Vijay Tewari, Paul Despe, Ed Reed, Keith Mange, Taylor Brown

Microsoft Consulting Services Reviewers

Ken Durigan, Alexander Ortha, Mike Williams, Keith Carey, Nicholas DiCola, David Ziembicki

Microsoft Customer Support Services Reviewers

Tom Acker, Joseph Conway, Ken Grainger, Rob Hefner, Jim Collins, Chuck Timon

Microsoft Technical Specialist Reviewers

Tim Cerling, Matthijs ten Seldam, James O'Neill

Acknowledgments

As was the case with the *Virtual Server 2005 R2 Resource Kit*, the development of this book represents the collective effort of many individuals that shaped, wrote, reviewed, and prepared the content so that it is useful, accurate, and worth the time and investment that you make in it. Therefore, once again, we have many individuals to thank, as without their help, this book would been a lesser work.

Martin DelRe from Microsoft Press worked to make the *Windows Server 2008 Hyper-V Resource Kit* project a reality shortly after the completion of the *Microsoft Virtual Server 2005 R2 Resource Kit*. Martin, we thank you again for the opportunity that you provided to us and your assistance throughout this project.

Another thank you goes to Heather Stafford, who helped us with all contract and billing processes.

We had wonderful Microsoft Press editors that helped to guide our efforts and make certain that the book content was consistent and of high-quality. Many thanks go to Karen Szall for getting us started on the right track. Julie Hotchkiss and Megan Smith-Creed were wonderful copy editors. They did a great job in making the text clearer and more concise, as well as challenging our assumptions. Finally, we want to thank Randall Galloway, the technical editor, for his work on this book.

Melissa von Tschudi-Sutton was our main project editor and a pleasure to work with throughout the process. Melissa had her hands full keeping the project on-track and her suggestions were invaluable. Melissa, we appreciate all of your help and commitment to this book project and very much enjoyed working with you again.

We would like to thank the Windows Virtualization product team for helping us in the effort to create a worthwhile *Windows Server 2008 Hyper-V Resource Kit*. Many members of the product team reviewed and contributed input to the book outline and the content. They answered emails and questions while working on the Windows Server 2008 R2 Hyper-V release. We thank each and every one of you for your cooperation and support during this time.

In particular, we owe a special thanks to Arno Mihm and Jeff Woolsey, our main points of contact in the product team. Several developers also assisted us to ensure that we could get code-level questions answered. These developers were crucial in helping us document information concerning Hyper-V that will be of great interest and assistance to the readers of this book. Thank you one and all for the extra effort!

In addition to the product team, we wanted to ensure that each chapter in this book was reviewed by Microsoft team members "in the field." Many field reviewers volunteered from the Microsoft Consulting Services and Customer Support Services teams, as well as Microsoft Sales. Each individual that participated in chapter reviews worked above and beyond their daily responsibilities to provide feedback and suggestions that greatly improved the book content. Thank you again for giving up some of your own time to help us and adding significant value to the resultant product.

We also had great support from Donna Becker and Tim Mueting from AMD, John Porterfield, Shane Burton, and Justin Brown from Compellent Technologies, and Trevor McGill from Sun Microsystems. As indicated in the Introduction section of this book, they provided us with hardware, their expertise, and content that allowed us to test and validate technical scenarios on real enterprise-class devices. Thank you so much for working with us under an extended timeline. We very much appreciate your support and cooperation!

And to you, the reader, thank you for purchasing this book. We have worked hard to compile and organize the content of this book such that it might be a valuable resource to help you deploy successful solutions based on Hyper-V technology. We are very interested in your comments, suggestions, and questions. Please send book-related emails to *askme@doingITvirtual.com*. We will generally respond to you within 24 hours. For additional information regarding Microsoft virtualization technology, join the Doing IT Virtual community at *http://doingitvirtual.com* and keep up with our blogs at *http://doingitvirtual.com/blogs/virtualzone/default.aspx* and *http://blogs.technet.com/roblarson*.

Best Regards,

Janique S. Carbone
Managing Member, Infrastructor Group
http://www.doingitvirtual.com

Robert E. Larson
Architect, Microsoft Consulting Services
http://blogs.technet.com/roblarson

Introduction

Welcome to the *Windows Server 2008 Hyper-V Resource Kit*!

The *Windows Server 2008 Hyper-V Resource Kit* is a comprehensive technical resource for planning, deploying, and managing virtualization infrastructures based on Windows Server 2008 Hyper-V and Microsoft Hyper-V Server 2008.

Virtualization technology continues to evolve and change the options and speed at which IT departments can react to changing business needs by creating the basis for a powerful, flexible, and adaptable computing environment. Many organizations can draw benefits from the implementation of Hyper-V technology, including potential cost savings that can result from workload virtualization. Server consolidation, test and development infrastructure, business continuity, and branch office environments in enterprise settings are some of the principal targets of Hyper-V technology solutions. However, small and medium businesses also benefit from workload virtualization. Therefore, our purpose for this book was to provide information and tools that could be useful to a broad spectrum of IT professionals and organizations.

Within this Resource Kit, you will find in-depth information and procedures to help you manage all aspects of Windows Server 2008 Hyper-V and Hyper-V Server 2008, including manual and automated installation, security configuration, virtual machine and host-level failover clustering, virtual machine creation and migration processes, monitoring, and backup and recovery techniques. In addition, we have included guidance to assist you with all aspects of a virtualization project from the early vision and scope setting phase through the project pilot phase.

In this book, you will find numerous sidebars contributed by members of the Windows Virtualization product team, Microsoft Consulting Services, Microsoft Support Services, Microsoft Sales, and Microsoft Partners that explain Hyper-V design details, feature highlights, and best practices and optimization tips to assist you in getting the most from a Hyper-V deployment. Finally, the companion media includes sample scripts and job aids that you can use and customize to help you automate various aspects of managing Hyper-V environments.

Microsoft Partner Support

Many of the technical scenarios presented in this book were configured and tested on hardware that was provided by AMD, Compellent Technologies, Sun Microsystems, and the Microsoft Partner Solutions Center. All of these Microsoft partners repeatedly extended the loan of their equipment to accommodate our changes in schedule, and they were all very forthcoming in answering questions and providing support when it was needed.

AMD provided us with enterprise-class hardware to support installation, failover clustering, and configuration test procedures. Donna Becker, Tim Mueting, and John McCrae from AMD worked diligently to provide us with two Dell PowerEdge 2970 servers configured with dual quad-core Opteron 2356 processors, 16 gigabytes (GB) of RAM, a Dell PERC 5/I Integrated RAID controller, and 300 GB of internal storage. The configuration was enhanced with an additional 300 GB of external, iSCSI-based storage.

Compellent Technologies, Sun Microsystems, and the Microsoft Partner Solutions Center dedicated hardware and remote access to enterprise-class servers connected to a Compellent Storage Center storage area network (SAN). John Porterfield, Shane Burton, and Justin Braun of Compellent Technologies provided their time, expertise, and assistance in assembling a hardware configuration that could be used to test additional failover clustering scenarios remotely. The configuration of the Compellent Storage Center SAN was configured with 10 terabytes of Tier-1 storage and 41 terabytes of Tier-3 storage.

John Porterfield of Compellent Technologies coordinated with Trevor McGill of Sun Microsystems to secure several servers for the duration of our tests. In particular, Sun Microsystems provided a Sun X4450 server with four quad-core Intel X7350 processors, 64 GB of RAM, four 146-GB SAS drives, and four Gigabit Ethernet network adapters, and two Sun X4150 servers with two quad-core Intel E5345 processors, 16 GB of RAM, four 146-GB SAS drives, and four Gigabit Ethernet network adapters.

Overview of Book

The four parts of this book cover the following topics:

Part I Getting Started with Windows Server 2008 Hyper-V   Provides an in-depth look at the features of Windows Server 2008 Hyper-V and Microsoft Hyper-V Server 2008, as well as product architecture details.

Part II Understanding Windows Server 2008 Hyper-V   Provides in-depth information and guidance on installing Window Server 2008 Hyper-V and Microsoft Hyper-V Server 2008 using advanced product features, configuring security, tuning performance, and moving from Virtual Server 2005 R2 to Hyper-V. There is also a comprehensive preview of the new features that are included in Windows Server 2008 R2 Hyper-V.

Part III Managing a Windows Server 2008 Hyper-V Infrastructure   Describes how to monitor and maintain the health of a Hyper-V infrastructure using tools such as System Center Virtual Machine Manager 2008, Windows Backup Server, System Center Data Protection Manager SP1, and the Windows Server 2008 Hyper-V Management Pack for System Center Operations Manager 2007. This part of the book also contains information to help you develop scripts using the Windows Management Instrumentation (WMI) application programming interface (API) and Windows PowerShell scripting tool.

Part IV Server Virtualization Project Methodology   Defines common server virtualization scenarios, basic concepts and components that compose a VDI solution, and comprehensive guidance on how to manage a virtualization project from the initial vision and scope setting phase to the pilot deployment phase.

Document Conventions

The following conventions are used in this book to highlight special features or usage.

Reader Aids

The following reader aids are used throughout this book to point out useful details.

READER AID	MEANING
Note	Underscores the importance of a specific concept or highlights a special case that might not apply to every situation.
Important	Calls attention to essential information that should not be disregarded.
Caution	Warns you that failure to take or avoid a specified action can cause serious problems for users, systems, data integrity, and so on.
On the Companion Media	Calls attention to a related script or job aid on the companion media that helps you perform a task described in the text.
Best Practice	Provides advice that the authors or the Windows Virtual Team have gained from using and deploying the products.
More Info	Contains cross-references to other critical reference material, such as the product documentation, relevant Web sites, other books, or to other sections of this book.

Sidebars

The following sidebars are used throughout this book to provide added insight, tips, and advice concerning different Hyper-V features.

SIDEBAR	MEANING
Direct from the Source	Contributed by Windows Virtualization product team experts at Microsoft to provide "from-the-source" insight into how Hyper-V works, best practices, and troubleshooting tips.
Direct from the Field	Contributed by field experts from Microsoft Consulting Services, Microsoft Customer Support Services, Microsoft Sales, and Microsoft Partners to provide "from-the-source" insight into how Hyper-V works, best practices, and troubleshooting tips.
How It Works	Provides unique glimpses of technology features and how they work.

NOTE Sidebars are provided by individuals in the industry as examples for informational purposes only and may not represent the views of their employers. No warranties, express, implied, or statutory, are made as to the information provided in sidebars.

Command-Line Examples

The following style conventions are used in documenting command-line examples throughout this book.

STYLE	MEANING
Bold font	Used to indicate user input (characters that you type exactly as shown).
Italic font	Used to indicate variables for which you need to supply a specific value (for example, *file_name* can refer to any valid file name).
`Monospace font`	Used for code samples and command-line output.
%SystemRoot%	Used for environment variables.

Companion Media

The companion media is a valuable addition to this book and includes the following items:

Scripts and Job Aids   Sample scripts written in Visual Basic Scripting Edition (VBScript) or Windows PowerShell for the administration of different aspects of Hyper-V infrastructures. These scripts can be used either as-is or customized to meet your administrative needs. Also included are job aids referenced in the book text.

Bonus Content and Links to Resources   In the Bonus Content folder, you'll find an electronic version of the Microsoft Press title *Understanding Microsoft Virtualization*. On the Links to Resources and Tools page, you'll find numerous links to helpful resources and tools identified by the authors of this resource kit.

eBook   An electronic version of the entire *Windows Server 2008 Hyper-V Resource Kit* is also included on the companion media.

Full documentation of the contents and structure of the companion media can be found in the Readme.txt file on the media.

> **Digital Content for Digital Book Readers:** If you bought a digital-only edition of this book, you can enjoy select content from the print edition's companion CD.
> Visit **http://go.microsoft.com/fwlink/?LinkId=149827** to get your downloadable content. This content is always up-to-date and available to all readers.

System Requirements

The following are the minimum system requirements to run the companion media provided with this book:

- Windows Server 2008 or Windows Vista Service Pack 1
- Windows PowerShell 1.0 or later version (for scripts)
- Microsoft Office 2003 or later version (for job aid worksheets)
- DVD drive
- Internet connection
- Display monitor capable of 1024 × 768 resolution
- Microsoft Mouse or compatible pointing device
- Adobe Reader or PDF reader for viewing the eBook

Using the Scripts

Scripts on the companion media must be run using Cscript.exe or Windows PowerShell as the script host. You can do this in several ways:

- Type **cscript *script_name*.vbs <parameters>** at a command prompt. For a list of available parameters, type **cscript *script_name*.vbs /?** at a command prompt, or open the script using Notepad and read the comments in the script.

- Configure the default script host on the local computer to Cscript.exe so that you can run scripts by typing **script_name.vbs <parameters>** at a command prompt. To set the default script host to Cscript.exe, type **cscript //h:cscript //nologo //s** at a command prompt.

- For Windows PowerShell 1.0, open a PowerShell command window. To do this from the Run box, click Start, click Run, type powershell, and click OK. You can also start Windows PowerShell 1.0 from the Start menu. Just click Start, click All Programs, click Windows PowerShell 1.0, and then click Windows PowerShell.

- For Windows PowerShell 2.0, from the Start menu, click Start, click All Programs, click Windows PowerShell, and then click Windows PowerShell V2. Alternatively, you can click Windows PowerShell V2 ISE to open the Windows PowerShell V2 Integrated Scripting Environment.

To function as intended, most scripts on the companion media must also be run using elevated privileges. To open an admin-level command prompt in Windows Vista, click the Start button and select All Programs. Select Accessories, right-click on Command Prompt, and select Run As Administrator. (As an alternative, create a shortcut to an elevated command prompt and save the shortcut on your Quick Launch toolbar.)

Resource Kit Support Policy

Every effort has been made to ensure the accuracy of this book and the companion media content. Microsoft Press provides corrections to this book through the Web at the following location:

http://www.microsoft.com/learning/support/search.aspx

If you have comments, questions, or ideas regarding the book or companion media content, or if you have questions that are not answered by querying the Knowledge Base, please send them to Microsoft Press by using either of the following methods:

E-mail:

rkinput@microsoft.com

Postal Mail:

Microsoft Press
Attn: *Windows Server 2008 Hyper-V Resource Kit* editor
One Microsoft Way
Redmond, WA 98052-6399

Please note that product support is not offered through the preceding mail addresses. For product support information, please visit the Microsoft Product Support Web site at the following address:

http://support.microsoft.com

## PART I

Getting Started with Windows Server 2008 Hyper-V

Introducing Virtualization

The objective of this book is to provide an in-depth look at the new Microsoft virtualization technology named Windows Server 2008 Hyper-V. Hyper-V represents the evolution of Microsoft virtualization technology from the hosted architecture of Microsoft Virtual Server 2005 R2 that runs on top of a Windows operating system to a hypervisor-based architecture. Within Hyper-V, the Windows hypervisor is a software layer that runs directly on physical hardware, enables the execution of multiple, isolated environments (or partitions) with separate sets of virtualized resources, and arbitrates access to underlying physical hardware resources. In short, the Windows hypervisor is the foundation piece that makes Hyper-V a secure and scalable virtualization solution that you can use to support a wide variety of deployment scenarios.

Before jumping directly into all the technical details that you need to plan, deploy, and manage a virtualized infrastructure founded on Hyper-V, this chapter provides you with an overview of the major types of virtualization methodologies to help you understand where Hyper-V fits in the current technology spectrum. In addition, you will gain a more detailed understanding of the various business and technical scenarios that are addressed with a Hyper-V deployment solution, to help you build and present a clearer case for a server virtualization project to technical peers and management.

Understanding Virtualization

Over the last few years, many organizations have turned to virtualization technology to consolidate physical servers and reverse the trend of server sprawl, as well as lower data center power, cooling, and space costs to contend with smaller budgets. More recently, desktop and application virtualization technologies have also emerged and have been adopted in an effort to simplify the deployment and management of end-user infrastructures. Increasingly, information technology (IT) departments find that virtualized infrastructures provide more flexible environments to operate and help to more quickly adapt to changing business needs.

Virtualization Background

Virtualization, in the context of software such as Microsoft Hyper-V Server and Virtual Server 2005 R2, can be described as the abstraction of physical systems resources such that multiple logical partitions can be created to host a heterogeneous set of operating systems, each running simultaneously on a single server. Each logical partition, also referred to as a *virtual machine*, is the software environment that exposes resources (using hardware emulation or other devices), on top of which an operating system and one or more applications can be installed and executed. Even though virtualization has become aggressively adopted in x86-based IT environments only in the current decade, the technology itself was actually first introduced over 40 years ago.

Commercial-grade virtualization technology was conceived by IBM in the mid-1960s to allow the System/360 Model 67 hardware to support multiple, concurrent guest virtual machines, each able to run a single-user operating system. IBM accomplished this by developing two individual operating systems, Virtual Machine (VM) and Conversational Monitor System (CMS), commonly referred to as VM/CMS. VM created and controlled virtual machines, and CMS—a single-user operating system—ran inside the virtual machine, delivering access to underlying system resources to each user. To this day, IBM continues to develop and market VM (rebranded as z/VM), having evolved it to even run itself within a virtual machine in multiple nested levels.

x86-Based Virtualization

In the last decade, virtualization technology research and product development has resurged with a focus on the x86 (32-bit and 64-bit) platform. In 2006, both AMD and Intel released x86 processor revisions with new instructions and extensions specifically targeted to enable hardware-assisted virtualization. Although differing in implementation details, AMD Virtualization (AMD-V) and Intel Virtualization Technology (VT) provide hardware virtualization features that can be leveraged by software vendors to simplify their virtualization software code and extend their virtualization solution architectures.

In 2007 and 2008, enhancements to AMD-V and Intel VT in the release of 64-bit dual-core and quad-core AMD processors and 64-bit dual-core and quad-core Intel processors have had an impact by facilitating the code development for Hyper-V. In fact, Microsoft and other virtualization software vendors continue to work with AMD and Intel to define areas of optimization and improvements for future processor releases.

AMD-V Architecture Highlights

AMD-Virtualization (AMD-V) provides a Secure Virtual Machine (SVM) processor architecture that allows software vendors to implement secure virtualization solutions and reduce software code complexity. The following list includes AMD-V SVM architecture highlights that are most commonly mentioned with reference to virtualization software like Hyper-V:

- Host Mode allows a hypervisor, or more generically, a Virtual Machine Monitor (VMM), to execute with the highest level of privilege. This execution mode is sometimes referred to as Ring −1 mode.

- Guest Mode allows a guest operating system to execute in privileged mode (Ring 0) and the application stack running in user mode (Ring 3).

- Eight SVM instructions support virtualization, including VMRUN, which enables the context switch, or world switch, from Host Mode to Guest Mode to load and execute a new guest operating system.

- A Virtual Memory Control Block (VMCB) data structure contains guest state information, including settings that define intercepts and instructions that cause transitions from Guest Mode to Host Mode.

- An Address Space Identifier (ASID) is a unique identifier assignment in a Translation-Lookaside Buffer (TLB) to distinguish between coexisting host and guest entries and help to improve the performance of a context switch. A TLB is a processor cache that holds virtual-to-physical memory address mappings. Each processor core has an individual TLB.

- Simultaneous support is provided for 16-bit, 32-bit, and 64-bit guest operating systems.

- Rapid Virtualization Indexing, also referred to as Nested Paging, provides processor-powered translation of the guest memory address space to the host virtual address space, and finally to the host physical address space.

- I/O Memory Management Unit (IOMMU) is a virtualization technology that allows guest operating systems running in virtual machines to make direct use of peripheral devices attached to the host server.

The Rapid Virtualization Indexing and IOMMU features of the AMD-V SVM architecture are not leveraged in the initial release of Hyper-V, but they may be considered for use in a future release.

MORE INFO For more in-depth information on AMD-V, you can consult the AMD64 Architecture Tech Docs at *http://www.amd.com/us-en/Processors/DevelopWithAMD /0,,30_2252_739_7044,00.html.*

AMD-V Rapid Virtualization Indexing

Tim Mueting, Virtualization Solutions Manager
Advanced Micro Devices, Inc.

System Virtualization Basics

To properly virtualize and isolate a virtual machine, the hypervisor must control or mediate all privileged operations performed by the virtual machine. One of the techniques that the hypervisor can use to accomplish this is called hardware-assisted virtualization. With hardware-assisted virtualization, the hypervisor uses processor extensions such as AMD-V Technology to intercept and emulate privileged operations in the guest. In certain cases, AMD-V technology allows the hypervisor to specify how the processor should handle privileged operations in the guest itself without transferring control to the hypervisor.

Virtualizing x86 Paging

To provide protection and isolation between guests, the hypervisor must control address translation on the processor by essentially enforcing another level of address translation when guests are active. This additional level of translation maps the guest's view of physical memory to the system's view of physical memory.

For unmodified guests, the hypervisor must completely virtualize x86 address translation, which can result in significant overhead.

Software Techniques for Virtualizing Address Translation

Software-based techniques maintain a *shadow* version of the page table derived from the *guest page table* (gPT). When the guest is active, the hypervisor forces the processor to use the *shadow page table* (sPT) to perform address translation. The sPT is not visible to the guest.

Shadow paging can incur significant additional memory and performance overheads with SMP guests. In an SMP guest, the same gPT instance can be used for address translation on more than one processor. In such a case, the hypervisor must either maintain sPT instances that can be used at each processor or share the sPT between multiple virtual processors. The former results in high memory overheads; the latter could result in high synchronization overheads.

It is estimated that, for certain workloads, shadow paging can account for up to 75 percent of overall hypervisor overhead.

AMD-V Rapid Virtualization Indexing

To avoid the software overheads under shadow paging, AMD64 quad-core processors contain an AMD-V feature called Rapid Virtualization Indexing (RVI). RVI uses an additional or *nested page table* (NPT) to translate guest physical addresses to system physical addresses and leaves the guest in complete control over its page tables. Unlike shadow paging, after the nested pages are populated, the hypervisor does not need to intercept and emulate the guest's modification of gPT.

RVI is designed to reduce the overhead associated with shadow paging. However, because RVI introduces an additional level of translation, the TLB miss cost could be larger. RVI has shown to deliver performance improvements for memory-intensive workloads with high context–switch frequency with higher TLB hit rates.

The Details

Using nested page tables, both the guest and the hypervisor have their own copy of the processor state affecting paging.

The gPT maps guest linear addresses to guest physical addresses. Nested page tables (nPT) map guest physical addresses to system physical addresses.

Guest and nested page tables are set up by the guest and hypervisor respectively. When a guest attempts to reference memory using a linear address and nested paging is enabled, the page walker performs a two-dimensional walk using the gPT and nPT to translate the guest linear address to system physical address.

When the page walk is completed, a TLB entry containing the translation from guest linear address to system physical address is cached in the TLB and used on subsequent accesses to that linear address.

AMD processors supporting RVI and nested page tables maintain a *nested TLB* that caches guest physical to system physical translations to accelerate nested page table walks. Nested TLB exploits the high locality of guest page table structures and significantly improves TLB hit rates.

Memory Savings with NPT

Unlike shadow paging, which requires the hypervisor to maintain an sPT instance for each gPT, a hypervisor using nested paging can set up a single instance of nPT to map the entire guest physical address space. Since guest memory is compact, the nPT will typically consume considerably less memory than an equivalent shadow-paging implementation.

Conclusion

Rapid Virtualization Indexing reduces the virtualization overheads associated with traditional software-based shadow-paging algorithms. Together with other architectural and micro-architectural enhancements in AMD64 quad-core processors, RVI can deliver performance improvements to virtual environments, specifically for memory intensive workloads with high context-switch frequency.

AMD I/O Virtualization Technology

Tim Mueting, Virtualization Solutions Manager
Advanced Micro Devices, Inc.

AMD's I/O virtualization technology helps increase the performance, security, and reliability of device virtualization. First published in February 2006, AMD's IOMMU (I/O Memory Management Unit) specification for I/O virtualization defines a methodology for abstracting devices in virtual environments and enables virtualization software to map devices directly to VMs. I/O Virtualization is implemented primarily in the chipset-I/O bridges and other system core logic.

IOMMUs provide device isolation by restricting the access of an adapter to the specific area of memory that the IOMMU allows. Without isolation, an adapter could corrupt memory in a buggy or malicious manner, compromising the security or availability of the system.

IOMMUs support virtualization by providing peripherals with address translation like that in the processor. This helps improve performance by moving the added address translations needed by virtualization software into hardware. An IOMMU can create a unique translated address space, independent of any address space instantiated by the Memory Management Unit (MMU) of the processor, which can map the addressable range of a device to anywhere in system memory.

AMD's I/O Virtualization Technology defines an IOMMU that is designed to translate and protect memory from any DMA transfers by peripheral devices. Devices are assigned into a protection domain with a set of I/O page tables defining the allowed memory addresses. For each DMA transfer, the IOMMU intercepts the access for that device, using its cache or IOTLB for efficient translation. Similarly, each device interrupt can be intercepted and remapped to the processor best prepared to handle the interrupt.

The translation and isolation functions of the IOMMU may be used independently of hardware or software virtualization; however, these facilities are a natural extension of virtualization.

Intel VT Architecture Highlights

ntel Virtualization Technology (Intel VT) provides a processor architecture that supports virtualization software applications through a set of extensions referred to as Virtual Machine Extensions (VMX). The following list includes Intel VT VMX highlights that are most commonly mentioned with reference to virtualization software like Hyper-V:

- VMX Root operating mode allows a hypervisor or VMM to execute in fully privileged mode.

- VMX Non-Root operating mode allows a guest operating system to execute in Ring 0 and the application stack in Ring 3.

- Ten VMX instructions support virtualization, including VMLAUNCH, which enables the context switch to load and execute a new guest operating system.

- A Virtual Memory Control Data Structure (VMCS) contains guest and host state information, as well as VMX control fields used to manage the transitions between VMX Root and VMX Non-Root operating modes.

- A Virtual Processor Identifier (VPID) is a unique identifier assignment stored in the VMCS to distinguish between coexisting host and guest entries. TLB entries are tagged with the appropriate VPID value, reducing the impact during context switches by not requiring a flush and reload of the TLB.

- Simultaneous support is provided for 16-bit, 32-bit, and 64-bit guest operating systems.

- Extended Page Tables (EPT) provide processor-powered translation of the guest physical memory address space to the host physical address space.

- Virtualization Technology for Directed I/O (VT-d) enables direct assignment and use of devices connected to the host server by guest operating systems running in virtual machines.

As in the case of AMD-V Rapid Virtualization Indexing and IOMMU, Hyper-V does not leverage the Intel VT Extended Page Tables or VT-d features in the initial release. You can see that Intel VT and AMD-V architectures offer much similar functionality to virtualization software application developers, although their feature implementation and nomenclature differ from each other.

MORE INFO For more detailed information on the Intel VT, you can consult the Intel 64 and IA-32 Architectures Software Developer's Manuals at *http://www.intel.com /products/processor/manuals/*.

The shortcomings of the legacy x86 processor platform with respect to virtualization features did not stop software vendors from developing solutions prior to the release of Intel VT and AMD-V. In fact, several types of virtualization technologies were created to run on the original x86 processor architecture, using diverse methodologies that differ in their level of abstraction and address specific problem spaces.

What Is Software Virtualization?

Software virtualization includes various techniques to enable a single physical system to host multiple secure, isolated partitions, simultaneously sharing resources. Accordingly, these different approaches vary in partition density (the number of concurrent partitions), scalability, performance, and breadth of operating systems that can be simultaneously supported on a given platform.

Machine-Level Virtualization

At the foundation of a machine-level virtualization solution is a Virtual Machine Monitor (VMM). The VMM is responsible for the creation, isolation, and preservation of the virtual machine state, as well as the orchestration of access to system resources. VMM design is tied to a specific processor architecture; although it allows various and unmodified operating systems to run inside a virtual machine, you are usually limited to operating systems that can run natively on the physical system processor.

Figure 1-1 illustrates three different VMM implementations: Type-2 VMM, the "hybrid" model, and Type-1 VMM. A Type-2 VMM runs above a host operating system, such as the Java VM. In the "hybrid" model, the VMM runs as a peer to the host operating system. This is the implementation in Virtual Server 2005 R2. In contrast, a Type-1 VMM, or "hypervisor," runs directly on the hardware below all virtual machine partitions. Microsoft Hyper-V is a hypervisor-based solution.

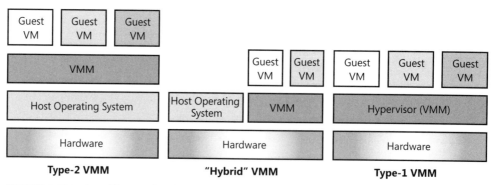

FIGURE 1-1 Virtual machine monitor types

In terms of performance, the Hypervisor (Type-1 VMM) is generally capable of achieving higher levels of efficiency and therefore greater virtual machine density. The other types of VMMs depend on the host operating system for access to resources, which results in more expensive context switches and greater performance overhead.

Taking a step further into VMM implementations, three major variants are used to create an interface between the virtual machines and the virtualized system resources. These methods are full virtualization, native virtualization, and paravirtualization.

Full Virtualization

In this method, a complete virtual system is created and maintained by the VMM to abstract the real hardware from the virtual machine. This approach allows an operating system to execute in a virtual machine without any modification. Virtual Server 2005 R2 uses this technique along with binary translation, a process that allows the VMM to handle nonvirtualizable x86 instructions to provide system virtualization on the pre-Intel VT and AMD-V x86 processor architectures.

A benefit of full virtualization and the approach of decoupling the physical hardware from the virtual machine is the ability to move virtual machines easily between servers with different physical configurations. This flexibility comes with a performance hit because of the overhead associated with the maintenance of each virtual machine state and latency introduced with binary translation.

Native Virtualization

Native virtualization depends on a virtualizable processor architecture, such as is available with the AMD-V and Intel VT series. These processors implement new execution modes, instructions, and data constructs in hardware that are designed to reduce the complexity of the VMM.

With native virtualization, the VMM is no longer required to maintain virtual machine resource characteristics and state in software; these functions now belong to the processor hardware and logic. Just as in the case of full virtualization, operating systems can run unmodified inside the virtual machines. Hyper-V uses this method to run legacy operating systems.

This type of implementation has many potential benefits, ranging from the simplification of the VMM architecture to significant performance improvements as a result of the reduction of software-based overhead. By lowering the virtualization overhead, a greater partition density can be achieved on any single system.

Virtual Server 2005 R2—A Hosted Virtualization Solution

Within Microsoft, two categorizations are used for virtualization solutions: hosted and hypervisor. Virtual Server 2005 R2 is a hosted virtualization solution because it runs on top of a Windows operating system. In a standard (nonvirtualized) Windows software stack, the operating system runs at the highest x86 privilege level (Ring 0, or "privileged" mode), while applications run in the lowest x86 privilege level (Ring 3, or "user" mode). In Virtual Server 2005 R2, the VMM is installed as a kernel-level driver that runs at the same level as the Windows operating system kernel, Ring 0.

When a virtual machine needs to execute, the operating system kernel yields control, and the VMM is switched onto the processor to run the virtual machine guest operating system. Although the guest operating system thinks it is running at Ring 0, it is actually running in an intermediate mode, Ring 1. The applications layered on the guest operating system continue to run in Ring 3. This method is called *ring compression*.

Use of the ring compression method is required because of 17 instructions in the x86 that cannot be fully virtualized but that could result in a fault state, crashing the system. So, to preserve the integrity of the system state, the VMM intercepts and translates the guest operating system instructions to host operating system instructions (binary translation process), handing control back to the Windows operating system kernel when hardware resource access is required or a condition occurs that the VMM cannot handle. Virtual Server 2005 R2 SP1 adds support for hardware-assisted (native) virtualization available with AMD-V and Intel VT, but it remains a hosted virtualization solution because it runs on top of a host Windows operating system.

Paravirtualization

Paravirtualization was developed as an alternative to using binary translation to handle x86 nonvirtualizable instructions. In this approach, guest operating systems require modification to enable "hypercalls" from the virtual machine to the hypervisor. Instead of having the hypervisor (or VMM) translate a potentially unsafe instruction from a guest operating system to guarantee system state integrity, a structured hypercall is made from the guest to the hypervisor to manage the system state changes.

A strict paravirtualization implementation offers greater performance on standard x86 hardware by eliminating the need for costly operations incurred using full virtualization and binary translation. However, it does so at the cost of limiting unmodified guest operating system support and migration of virtual machines back to a physical server. Recognizing these limitations, virtualization products based on paravirtualization implementations also leverage hardware virtualization to host unmodified operating systems. This approach allows a broader range of support, extending to legacy operating systems that are unlikely to be modified, and it allows newer operating systems to be updated, taking advantage of enhancements and performance gains offered through paravirtualization.

Paravirtualization was pioneered and implemented by XenSource (recently acquired by Citrix), which produced the open-source virtualization solution, Xen. Initial releases of Xen supported only a few modified operating systems. With the release of Xen 3.0, which leveraged the hardware virtualization functionality of AMD-V and Intel VT, an unmodified Windows XP operating system could execute in a guest virtual machine.

In July 2006, Microsoft and XenSource entered into an agreement to support a level of interoperability that would allow Xen-modified Linux virtual machines to be migrated seamlessly to Hyper-V and Windows virtual machines to a Xen solution. Microsoft and Citrix are continuing the virtualization partnership started with XenSource. In fact, Citrix developed an adaptation layer that maps the Citrix hypercall Application Programming Interface (API) to the Hyper-V hypercall API, as well as storage and network drivers for supported Linux distributions. These drivers provide enhanced performance when installed in a Linux guest operating system running in Hyper-V.

> **NOTE** Citrix XenServer is the current server virtualization product developed from a Xen-Source code base. Citrix also offers an application virtualization product named XenApp and a desktop virtualization product named XenDesktop. For more detailed information on Citrix virtualization products, you can consult *http://www.citrix.com/English/ps2/category.asp*.

HOW IT WORKS

Hyper-V—A Hypervisor Virtualization Solution

Microsoft uses two categories to describe virtualization solutions: hosted and hypervisor. In contrast to Virtual Server 2005 R2, Hyper-V is a hypervisor solution because it loads and runs directly above the hardware level. This implementation is also commonly referred to as a "bare metal virtualization." Hyper-V requires a 64-bit (x64) AMD-V or Intel VT hardware processor platform. As explained previously, AMD-V and Intel VT add two new processor modes: one for execution of a hypervisor with full privilege (sometimes referred to as Ring –1), and another mode for execution of the guest operating system and application stack in Ring 0 and Ring 3, respectively. This implementation eliminates the need for the ring-compression mechanism used in Virtual Server 2005 R2. Hyper-V does not run on 32-bit x86 or 64-bit Itanium processor architectures. Essentially, the Windows hypervisor controls and arbitrates access to physical hardware resources from isolated execution environments called partitions. Each partition represents a virtual machine that provides a virtualized set of hardware resources to a guest operating system and applications.

Hyper-V supports native virtualization to support legacy Windows operating systems prior to and including Windows Server 2003 running without Integration Services, and it also implements paravirtualization. A hypercall interface allows guest virtual machines to make action or informational requests to the Windows hypervisor. Windows Vista and Windows Server 2008 are the first Windows operating systems to include paravirtualization modifications, which Microsoft calls "enlightenments." Initial enlightenments allow Windows Vista and Windows Server 2008 to determine if they are running in a virtual machine, as well as provide optimizations in memory management to enhance performance.

MORE INFO For a detailed description of the Hyper-V architecture including enlightenments and Integration Components, refer to Chapter 3, "Hyper-V Architecture."

Operating System–Level Virtualization

Operating system–level virtualization is based on the abstraction of the operating system layer to support multiple, isolated partitions or to support virtual environments (VEs) on a single-instance host operating system. The virtualization is accomplished by multiplexing access to the kernel while ensuring that no single VE is able to take down the system. Figure 1-2 shows the basic architecture implemented with this approach.

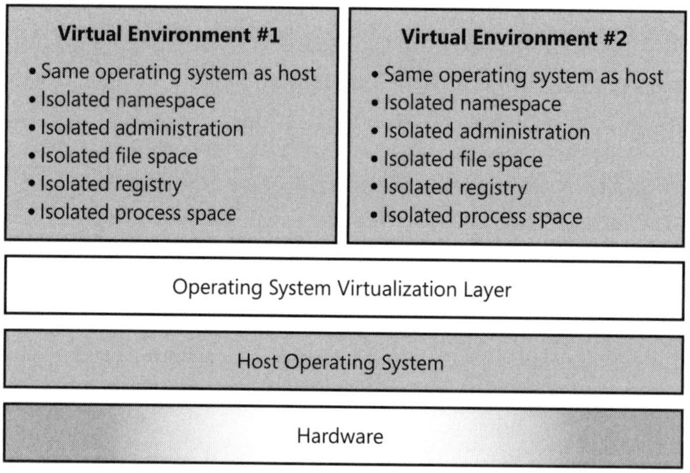

Virtual Environment #1	**Virtual Environment #2**
• Same operating system as host • Isolated namespace • Isolated administration • Isolated file space • Isolated registry • Isolated process space	• Same operating system as host • Isolated namespace • Isolated administration • Isolated file space • Isolated registry • Isolated process space

Operating System Virtualization Layer

Host Operating System

Hardware

FIGURE 1-2 Basic operating system–level virtualization architecture

This technique results in very low virtualization overhead and can yield high partition density. However, there are two major drawbacks with this type of solution. The first drawback is the inability to run a heterogeneous operating system mix on a given server because all partitions share a single operating system kernel. The second drawback, also caused by the shared kernel model, is the lack of support for running a mixed 32-bit and 64-bit workload. In addition, any operating system kernel update affects all virtual environments. For these reasons, operating system–level virtualization tends to work best for largely homogeneous workload environments. Virtuozzo Containers from Parallels, formerly SWsoft, is an example of a product that uses operating system–level virtualization. Virtuozzo Containers has been extensively adopted and deployed by the Web hosting industry to build high-density infrastructures, offering isolated Web services.

Application-Level Virtualization

All the virtualization techniques discussed to this point have the same objective—increase the number of secure, isolated partitions executing concurrently on physical hardware to maximize use of CPU, storage, network, memory, and other resources. Although they can be applied in a desktop setting, they are mainly geared toward solving resource management problems in server-class environments. They do not address specific client desktop application management issues.

Application-level virtualization is a technology that is geared toward partitioning and isolating client-side applications running on the local operating system. As shown in Figure 1-3, applications are isolated in a virtual environment layered between the operating system and application stack. The virtual environment loads prior to the application, isolates the application from other applications and the operating system, and prevents the application from modifying local resources such as files and registry settings. Applications can read information from the local system registry and files, but writable versions of these resources are maintained inside the virtual environment. In fact, the application might never be locally installed on the desktop; instead, the code bits can be dynamically streamed and cached in the virtual environment as new portions of the application are needed

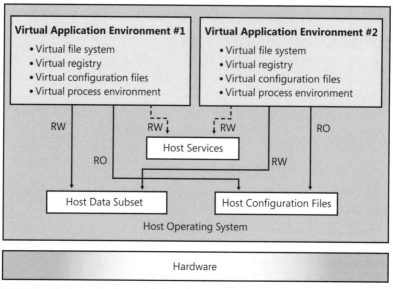

FIGURE 1-3 Basic application-level virtualization architecture

Application-level virtualization provides several benefits. The most important of these in-clude increased stability of the local desktop; simple application removal without changes to the local environment that could negatively affect other applications; and seamless, conflict-free, side-by-side execution of multiple instances of an application. One or more additional servers might be required to maintain application distributions, application streaming to the desktop, and other enterprise-wide functions.

> **NOTE** In 2006, Microsoft entered the application-level virtualization market with the acquisition of Softricity and the SoftGrid product line. Microsoft SoftGrid Application Virtualization for Desktops runs on the local desktop and maintains the virtual registry, file system, and other data or configuration components needed by the application as it is executing. Microsoft SoftGrid Virtual Application Server maintains the application store and streams the application code on demand to the desktop. Other major components included in the Microsoft SoftGrid Application Virtualization solution include Microsoft SoftGrid Sequencer to package and virtualize applications; Microsoft SoftGrid Manage-ment Web Service to centralize application policy services; and Microsoft SoftGrid Man-agement Console to deliver provisioning, access, and reporting for virtualized applications. Finally, Microsoft SoftGrid Application Virtualization for Terminal Services allows Terminal Servers to offer virtualized application services to clients. In 2008, Microsoft released an update to the SoftGrid application line, Microsoft Application Virtualization 4.5.

Desktop Virtualization

Desktop virtualization is focused on changing the provisioning, deployment, and management of end-user computing resources by virtualizing desktops and consolidating them on centralized servers. Desktop virtualization is commonly implemented using a Virtual Desktop Infrastructure (VDI), a term that actually describes a combination of hardware, virtualization software, and management tools that comprise a desktop virtualization solution. The following list includes some of the most common objectives of desktop virtualization:

- Reduction of IT end-user computing resources capital and operational costs

- Reduction in time to provision or decommission a new end-user virtual desktop

- Increase in utilization of system resources

- Increase in accessibility of end-user computing resources

- Centralization of confidential or sensitive information on more secure and available storage devices

- Centralization of virtual desktop operating system upgrades, patching, backup and restore, and other desktop management functions

Desktop virtualization can be implemented as either static virtual desktops or dynamic virtual desktops. In a static virtual desktop scenario, a physical desktop is replaced with a virtual counterpart, usually dedicated to one particular end user. In the dynamic virtual desktop scenario, end users are dynamically connected to one of a pool of virtual desktops on demand. In Figure 1-4, you can see a representation of a basic VDI solution.

Whereas a static virtual desktop scenario may be more applicable in an environment that requires individual customization of the virtual desktop to perform specific duties, the dynamic virtual desktop scenario may satisfy the requirements for an environment with a large number of users that all perform similar functions using a common set of tools, such as might be the case in a call center. With the addition of application virtualization solutions to provide streamed applications on demand to dynamic virtual desktops, more flexible desktop virtualization environments are possible, although they involve more complex architectures and sophisticated management infrastructure.

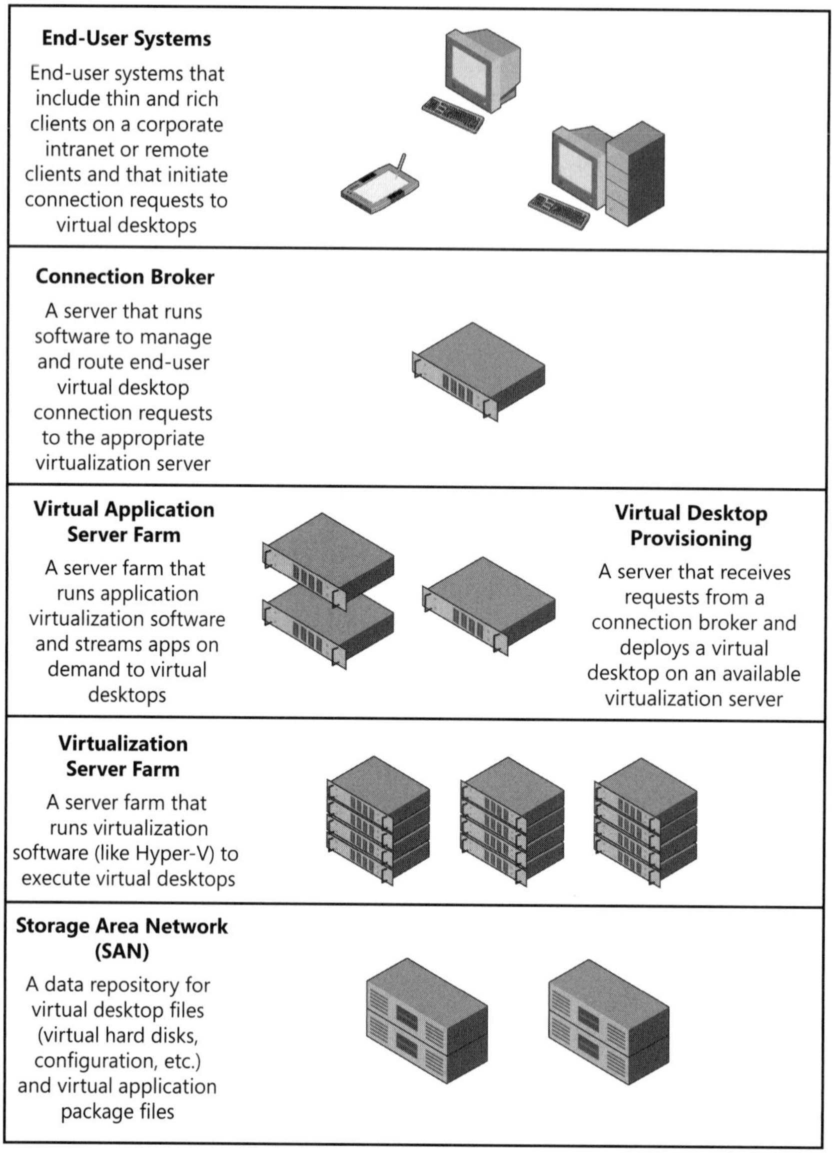

End-User Systems End-user systems that include thin and rich clients on a corporate intranet or remote clients and that initiate connection requests to virtual desktops	
Connection Broker A server that runs software to manage and route end-user virtual desktop connection requests to the appropriate virtualization server	

Virtual Application Server Farm A server farm that runs application virtualization software and streams apps on demand to virtual desktops	**Virtual Desktop Provisioning** A server that receives requests from a connection broker and deploys a virtual desktop on an available virtualization server

Virtualization Server Farm A server farm that runs virtualization software (like Hyper-V) to execute virtual desktops	
Storage Area Network (SAN) A data repository for virtual desktop files (virtual hard disks, configuration, etc.) and virtual application package files	

FIGURE 1-4 A basic Virtual Desktop Infrastructure (VDI) solution

> **MORE INFO** For additional information on desktop virtualization, refer to Chapter 18, "Virtual Desktop Infrastructure."

Making a Business Case for Server Virtualization

In today's information technology (IT) shops, the core of any business case made for the adoption of a new technology is minimizing cost while increasing the capacity, security, reliability, availability, and flexibility of the infrastructure to rapidly adapt to changing business needs. Server virtualization technology is the foundation that can enable an enterprise to accelerate achievement of the following goals:

- Reduction of IT capital and operational costs
- Implementation of a simplified, dynamic enterprise infrastructure
- Increase in availability of computing resources
- Reduction in time needed to provision or distribute new services
- Reduction in management complexity

Understanding how a virtualized infrastructure can deliver these benefits will clarify the business case to be made for rapid adoption of the technology.

Reducing Capital and Operational Costs

Over the last 15 years, the physical server inventory of mainstream businesses grew extensively as new applications and computing capacity were rolled out to meet organizational growth. To provide application and server management isolation, the majority of deployments resulted in single-server, single-application configurations. The main consequence of this approach was that an increasing portion of the IT budget was allocated to operational costs to cover space, power, cooling, administrative personnel, and associated management tools. In tandem, many businesses have experienced one or more data center relocations, outgrowing facilities that could not accommodate an expansion of controlled floor space, additional power requirements, or cooling units to provision the computing environment. Making matters worse, estimates of average server utilization are between 5 percent and 15 percent. So not only are IT shops dealing with server sprawl and a rise in overhead costs, but they are unable, with a traditional server architecture, to maximize the return on capital investment from their servers because of the predominant single-server, single-application deployments in their enterprise.

Virtualization of production servers, from the departmental level up to the data center, can help reduce new capital costs because fewer physical servers need to be purchased as new workloads need to be rolled out. If one or more deployed servers have spare computing capacity, the new workloads can simply be deployed as new virtual machines. Because virtual machines present a standard, emulated hardware configuration to the operating system and applications running within them, they are also easily moved between servers with different hardware configurations. This flexibility allows for the rebalancing of existing server workloads to dissimilar but available server hardware, creating the required capacity for a new deployment while avoiding new capital budget expenditures. In addition, physical servers are operating at much higher utilization levels when hosting multiple workloads, so the return on investment (ROI) per server is improved.

With processor power ratings and server density rising in traditional infrastructures, space, power, and cooling requirements become major problems for IT organizations. Even with new techniques for power management that balance server power consumption to utilization rates and more efficient power supplies coming onto the market, additional solutions are needed to address the issue. Here again, virtualization of the computing environment can help to reduce operational costs. By consolidating workloads to a smaller number of servers, physical plant footprint, cooling, and power consumption can be significantly reduced. As the computing capabilities of servers grow with multiprocessor, multicore density leaps, workload consolidation ratios will continue to trend upward in the future, leading to a greater downward impact on these operational costs.

Implementing a Simple, Flexible, and Dynamic Server Infrastructure

Businesses today are only as flexible as their computing infrastructure and processes allow. A traditional infrastructure is complex, somewhat inflexible, and rarely dynamic. IT staff members face the challenging task of creating and maintaining hardware standards while hardware and software technology is continually changing. Economic factors are also driving IT managers to maximize the life span of server hardware, extending server refresh cycles to reduce capital expenditures. Unfortunately, this strategy tends to increase facilities management complexity and support issues.

Reducing the complexity of the infrastructure helps to reduce costs. A virtualized environment reduces complexity because a virtual machine is designed to provide a standard hardware solution that is compatible with many operating systems. Because the virtualized hardware is decoupled from the actual physical server devices that it runs on, you will also be able to achieve compatibility across different physical servers. This flexibility allows you to build a virtual machine on a server using a certain hardware configuration and transfer it to a server using a different hardware configuration, without modification. This eliminates time-consuming tasks for IT staff people, who no longer have to work through the lengthy server certification process that currently takes place to validate that a workload will execute as expected on new hardware.

Furthermore, traditional deployments of applications using a single workload per server to meet service level agreements (SLAs) and eliminate workload compatibility issues can be transformed through virtualization. The core problem is that a traditional deployment method wastes server resources, often making the infrastructure too rigid. Virtualization creates a more flexible server infrastructure that can be optimized for higher efficiency and server utilization levels and even enables you to host heterogeneous workloads on a single physical machine.

Test and development environments also can benefit from virtualization. In this setting, virtualization can enable virtual machines to be provisioned quickly to create complex application environments across single or multiple servers. A virtualized environment also can be leveraged to reproduce bugs uncovered during testing very simply, without requiring reinstallation of a system, as is often the case when operating a traditional testing infrastructure. Specifically, bug reproduction is accomplished by leveraging the ability to create virtual machine snapshots that capture point-in-time virtual machine configuration and state information. Virtual machine snapshots provide testing personnel the option to revert to one of the previously captured states in just a few seconds, simply by choosing to reload a saved snapshot.

Virtualized infrastructures are also much more dynamic than traditional infrastructures when it comes to relocation of workloads. There is no simple, streamlined process in a traditional environment to move a workload on the fly from one server to another. In a virtualized environment, rebalancing of workloads can be automated easily and is accomplished with much less risk, because the virtual machines abstract away any hardware dependencies.

Increasing the Availability of Computing Resources

One of the great challenges faced by IT organizations, whether they are in a small business or large multinational corporation, is planning for single recovery events such as a server hardware failure, in conjunction with negative impacts to a larger percentage of computing resources. The process of providing business continuity after a massive natural disaster that causes significant or total loss of capital equipment to local facilities and then instantiating the affected services in alternate locations is not simple when dealing with workloads that are tightly coupled to hardware. Apart from software stack dependencies on hardware configuration, there is complexity and high cost involved in keeping data synchronized between physical locations separated by large distances. There is also significant complexity in testing and validating recovery procedures to ensure that they are successful and effective.

Virtualization technology can assist with increasing the availability of computing resources through integration with high-availability services, such as clustering, that provide failover features. The fine-grained control provided by virtualization solutions gives you the ability to cluster single virtual machines across servers, cluster servers themselves, or dynamically reallocate workloads to different servers. This greater degree of control allows traditional single points of failure to be eliminated, making the recovery process simpler and easier.

Dealing with events that can cause a large number of servers and workloads to go offline is also simplified by adopting a virtualized infrastructure. Virtual machine encapsulation into a few portable and easily replicated files can greatly reduce planning, testing, and time to recovery for larger scale outages. Because virtual machine configuration settings are contained in small files, when they are replicated to a recovery site along with the data files, recovery is a simple matter of registering the virtual machine with the new host and booting the operating system. The abstraction of hardware inherent in virtualization solutions is a key element in making recovery and business continuity less complex and streamlining processes.

Decreasing Time to Provision or Distribute Services

To gain a business advantage, you must find ways to make business processes and core infrastructures able to respond to change quickly. A business advantage could potentially mean a market-share increase, a rise in profit, new market penetration, or other return leading to business growth. If your business can reduce the time to market with a new idea or line of business applications, it can also obtain a faster return on its investment.

The implementation of a new application in a corporate environment is dependent on a complex life cycle, typically involving envisioning, planning, development, test, quality assurance, deployment, and operational phases. With a traditional infrastructure, many of these phases require provisioning or deploying new computing resources, or even the purchase of new hardware before the project can effectively begin. Each purchase takes time going through project approval, budgeting, vendor bidding, order placement, delivery, testing, and physical deployment. This timeline can vary widely from one company to the next, ranging anywhere from a few weeks to several months. If multiple hardware resources are required from different vendor sources, additional time impacts can further delay development of the new solution. Minimizing the time from project conception to deployment is crucial to gaining a business edge.

A virtualized computing infrastructure can drive project timeline compression by reducing the need to acquire and deploy new servers for each new project. Instead, using virtualized server pools and pre-created virtual machine libraries, the process of provisioning project computing resources can be reduced to minutes, and configuration changes to virtual resources such as storage, network cards, or memory can be done in seconds. Virtualization does not provide this benefit without proper capacity planning efforts. It also does not completely eliminate the need for hardware purchases; instead, new servers are added to increase the capacity to host multiple new workloads and projects instead of single ones. The significant gain provided by virtualization is that when the virtual infrastructure is established, you can literally accomplish new workload provisioning in minutes or hours rather than weeks or months.

Decreasing Management Complexity

Typical IT infrastructures are composed of various vendor hardware components that require regular maintenance and management to ensure that they are up to date with firmware upgrades and patches, and that they are free of hardware faults. When virtualizing a physical infrastructure, the reduction in the number of physical servers is a key benefit that leads to a simplification of the environment and a reduction in the time required for management. By also reducing the number of unique brand servers, you can reduce the variety of unique tools required, further driving down management complexity.

Another significant IT management task is the backup process. Backup management typically consists of administering the backup software, backup agents, server backup process, and backup media for each server. Backup management in a virtualized infrastructure is much less complex. Storage snapshot technologies, available to support backup of complete virtual machine workloads from the physical server level, drive the reduction in management complexity of the backup process. There is no longer a need to install, update, and maintain agents in each guest operating system to perform backups, resulting in faster backups in addition to simplified management.

Defining Server Virtualization Scenarios

Now that we have examined the business case for server virtualization, it is time to consider the four major scenarios that stand out as prime opportunities for a server virtualization solution. Using Hyper-V, these are the areas where you can experience the most immediate benefits, while addressing areas that have high pain points and a significant impact on business. The four scenarios are as follows:

- Data center consolidation
- Branch office consolidation
- Virtualization of test and development infrastructure
- Implementation of business continuity and recovery plans

Consolidating the Data Center

This scenario addresses the need of most customers to resolve the power, cooling, and physical space crises currently taking place in data centers. Many workloads running in a data center these days are good candidates for consolidation, which will enable IT managers and administrators to make fuller use of machine capacity while decreasing the number of physical units to manage. Achieving a consolidated data center can involve a couple of approaches:

- **Homogeneous consolidation**   Combining on a single platform servers with similar applications or workloads
- **Mixed workload**   Combining on a single platform servers with different workloads

Homogeneous and mixed workload consolidations can use virtualization as a method to achieve objectives. In these cases, virtualization provides the following benefits:

- Establishment of a simple physical-to-virtual machine migration process that minimizes the design and testing required to ensure compatibility of workloads on a single platform
- Reduction in the number of physical servers, leading to lower IT costs
- Elimination of duplicate services, decreasing the need for management
- Availability of dynamic tuning to maximize server capacity usage

Consolidating the Branch Office

This scenario addresses the need that a majority of customers have to minimize hardware deployments to a large number of small field offices. Implementation of a virtualized environment in the branch office allows customers to avoid the support and security issues that exist when combining domain controller, file and print, Exchange Server, and additional workloads directly atop a host operating system. Using virtualization to accomplish the branch office consolidation also has the following benefits:

- Implementation of individual SLAs for each virtualized workload
- Establishment of a simple physical-to-virtual machine migration process that minimizes the design and testing required to ensure compatibility of workloads on a single platform
- Reduction in the number of physical servers, leading to lower IT costs
- Separation of management for each virtualized workload while securing physical server access

Virtualizing Test and Development Infrastructure

This scenario addresses the implementation of a virtualized test and development infrastructure. Maintaining and provisioning traditional test and development environments can be a drain on budgets and a huge management challenge. Using virtualization in this scenario provides the following benefits:

- Reduction in the hardware needed to host complex application architectures that include multiple workloads. A single server with appropriate capacity is often sufficient because each workload can run in a separate virtual machine.
- Reduction in time to provision new test and development scenarios and automation of virtual machine deployment to servers with available capacity.
- Positive impact on test and development life-cycle management. For example, the time needed to accomplish a migration of new applications from the development and test environment to the production environment is greatly reduced by the portability and ease of replication of virtual machine files.
- Simple creation of a virtual machine library to store and retrieve testing scenarios.
- Simple migration of a production environment from physical servers into a test and development virtual machine library.
- Simpler bug reproduction process by using virtual machine state preservation and snapshot features.

Implementing Business Continuity and Recovery

This scenario addresses the implementation of a business recovery process in the event of a single point of failure or major disaster. The challenge for customers when planning for business continuity is defining a simple, low-risk, and fast recovery approach that can be validated to meet business continuity requirements. Using virtualization to accomplish business continuity and recovery has the following benefits:

- Support for clustering of individual virtual machines across servers and clustering of virtualization servers and workloads to achieve high availability
- Reduced dependencies on expensive, complex hardware to maintain data in sync between physical locations
- Ability to establish a physical-to-virtual machine business continuity solution
- Ability to establish a virtual-to-virtual machine business continuity solution
- Ability to use low-cost file replication technologies to replicate virtual machine files between servers and reduce time to recovery

> **MORE INFO** For additional information on server virtualization, refer to Chapter 17, "Server Virtualization Scenarios."

Summary

In this chapter, you learned about the different types of software virtualization technologies and how they relate to the development and basic architecture of Hyper-V. You were exposed to the key motivators to consider when developing a business case for virtualization technology adoption. The chapter concluded with a review of core technical virtualization scenarios targeted with Hyper-V solutions and the associated benefits of those solutions.

Additional Resources

The following resources contain additional information related to the topics in this chapter.

- Microsoft Virtualization Web site available at *http://www.microsoft.com/virtualization/default.mspx*
- White paper, "Virtualization from the Datacenter to the Desktop," available at *http://www.microsoft.com/virtualization/datacenter.mspx*
- AMD64 Architecture Tech Docs available at *http://www.amd.com/us-en/Processors/DevelopWithAMD/0,,30_2252_739_7044,00.html*

- Technical Document, "AMD64 Architecture Programmer's Manual Volume 2: System Programming," available at *http://www.amd.com/us-en/assets/content_type /white_papers_and_tech_docs/24593.pdf*

- Technical Document, "AMD64 Architecture Programmer's Manual, Volume 3: General-Purpose and System Instructions," available at *http://www.amd.com/us-en/assets /content_type/white_papers_and_tech_docs/24594.pdf*

- Intel 64 and IA-32 Architectures Software Developer's Manuals available at *http://www.intel.com/products/processor/manuals/*

- Technical Document, "Intel 64 and IA-32 Architectures Software Developer's Manual Volume 1: Basic Architecture," available at *http://download.intel.com/design/processor /manuals/253665.pdf*

- Technical Document, "Intel 64 and IA-32 Architectures Software Developer's Manual Volume 2B: Instruction Set Reference, N-Z," available at *http://download.intel.com /design/processor/manuals/253667.pdf*

- Technical Document, "Intel 64 and IA-32 Architectures Software Developer's Manual, Volume 3B: System Programming Guide, Part 2," available at *http://download.intel.com /design/processor/manuals/253669.pdf*

- Technical Document, "Intel Virtualization Technology for Directed I/O – Architecture Specification," available at *http://download.intel.com/technology/computing/vptech /Intel(r)_VT_for_Direct_IO.pdf*

Hyper-V Overview

This chapter contains an overview of the Hyper-V features available as a role in a full installation of Windows Server 2008, as a Server Core role, and in Microsoft Hyper-V Server 2008. In order to provide a robust virtualization platform that abstracts physical hardware dependencies and scales to support numerous concurrent workloads, Hyper-V is based on a hypervisor-based architecture that enables standard services and resources to create, manage, and execute virtual machines. Hyper-V offers a standard virtual hardware environment, virtual hard disks (VHD), and virtual networks that enable virtual machine execution, storage, and communications, respectively. Integration Services (IS) and Integration Components (IC) support critical processes and enhance the performance of virtual machines. Hyper-V Manager, a Microsoft Management Console (MMC) snap-in, is available to perform Hyper-V management and virtual machine configuration functions. The Hyper-V Manager provides a primary interface to create, inspect, and configure virtual machines, virtual hard disks, and virtual networks, as well as to assign virtual machine memory and processor allocations. Hyper-V properties are also modified through the Hyper-V Manager. Virtual Machine Connection (VMC) is integrated into the Hyper-V Manager to provide remote access to virtual machines from within the console and is also available as a stand-alone application. In addition, Hyper-V offers an extensive Windows Management Instrumentation (WMI) interface that you can leverage using various scripting and development languages, including PowerShell, to programmatically and remotely control the deployment, administration, and configuration of virtual machines.

Hyper-V Background

In February 2003, Microsoft entered the virtualization arena with the acquisition of Connectix software virtualization technology. In October 2004, Microsoft released Virtual Server 2005, an enterprise infrastructure virtualization solution for the x86 platform with support for 32-bit virtual machines. Virtual Server 2005 represents a hosted virtualization architecture because it runs in conjunction with a host Windows operating system and depends on it to arbitrate hardware resource access. In November 2005, Virtual Server 2005 Release 2 (R2) was released with several performance-enhancing features, as well as support for x64 host operating systems, iSCSI connectivity, Non-Uniform Memory Access (NUMA), Pre-Execution Environment (PXE) booting, and Virtual Server host clustering. The last major release, Virtual Server 2005 R2 Service Pack 1 (SP1), occurred in June 2007. In this release, Microsoft added support for Intel VT and AMD-V processors and provided the ability to control hardware virtualization on an individual virtual machine (VM) basis. Finally, in May 2008, an update was released (KB948515) to extend Virtual Server 2005 R2 SP1 support to Windows XP SP3, Windows Vista SP1, and Windows Server 2008, both as host and guest operating systems.

In parallel with Virtual Server 2005 R2 SP1, Microsoft worked on the development of its next generation enterprise virtualization product, Windows Server 2008 Hyper-V, released in June 2008. Figure 2-1 shows the basic Hyper-V architecture, which is based on a 64-bit microkernel hypervisor, the Windows Hypervisor. The Windows Hypervisor runs directly above the hardware, enables multiple operating systems to run concurrently within partitions, and ensures strong isolation between the partitions by enforcing access policies for critical system resources such as memory and processors. Unlike Windows operating systems such as Windows Server 2003 and earlier versions, the Windows Hypervisor does not contain any third-party device drivers or code, which minimizes its attack surface and provides a more secure architecture.

> **NOTE** Based on the microkernel architecture of the Windows Hypervisor, including the fact that it does not encompass Windows drivers, the Windows Hypervisor is less than 1 megabyte (MB) in size.

In addition to the Windows Hypervisor, there are two other major elements in Hyper-V: a parent partition and child partitions. The parent partition is a special virtual machine that runs Windows Server 2008, controls the creation and management of child partitions, and maintains direct access to hardware resources. This requires that device drivers for physical devices be installed in the parent partition. Finally, the role of a child partition is to provide a virtual machine environment for the installation and execution of guest operating systems and applications.

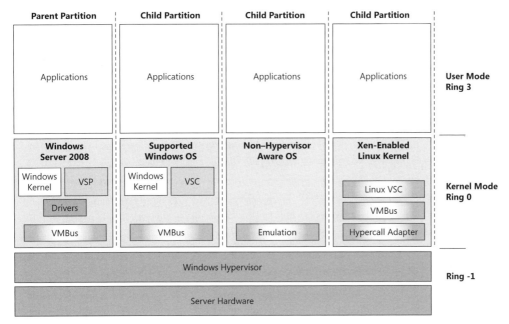

FIGURE 2-1 Basic Hyper-V architecture

Hyper-V allows high-speed communication between the parent and child partitions through the VMBus. The VMBus supports dedicated point-to-point channels for secure interpartition communications between Virtualization Service Providers (VSP) in the parent partition and Virtualization Service Clients (VSC) in the child partitions. VSPs are software components that manage input/output (I/O) requests from the VSCs in the virtual machines and channel the requests to physical hardware through the device drivers. VSCs are synthetic drivers, basically software components without physical counterparts that provide high-performance access to networking, video, storage, and human-interface devices in virtual machines. In the current release of Hyper-V, VSCs are available for a subset of Windows operating systems and for Suse Linux Enterprise Server 10, which has a Xen hypervisor-aware kernel. When running on Hyper-V, Suse Linux Enterprise Server 10 uses a Hypercall Adapter to translate Xen hypervisor calls (hypercalls) into Hyper-V hypervisor calls, enabling high-performance execution.

> **MORE INFO** For a complete list of the Windows operating systems that support VSCs, refer to Chapter 5, "Hyper-V Advanced Features."

Virtual machines that run guest operating systems without VSC support use emulation (or legacy) drivers to provide access to virtualized hardware devices. The parent partition monitors and intercepts I/O requests to virtualized hardware devices and channels the requests to physical hardware.

MORE INFO For a detailed description of the Hyper-V architecture, refer to Chapter 3, "Hyper-V Architecture."

Hyper-V Core Features

Table 2-1 summarizes the basic features found in Windows Server 2008 Hyper-V editions and Hyper-V Server 2008. Hyper-V VMs support both 32-bit and 64-bit guest operating systems and the allocation of up to four virtual processors and 64 gigabytes (GB) of memory for Hyper-V servers running on Windows Server 2008 Enterprise or Datacenter edition. In its original release, Hyper-V supported 16 processor cores and 128 virtual machines. However, a subsequent update (KB956710) increased Hyper-V support to 24 logical processors and a maximum of 192 concurrent virtual machines.

TABLE 2-1 Hyper-V Basic Features Comparison

FEATURES	MICROSOFT HYPER-V SERVER 2008	WINDOWS SERVER 2008 STANDARD	WINDOWS SERVER 2008 ENTERPRISE	WINDOWS SERVER 2008 DATACENTER
x86 Support	Guest OS Only	Guest OS Only	Guest OS Only	Guest OS Only
x64 Support	Host and Guest	Host and Guest	Host and Guest	Host and Guest
# of VMs—x64 Host	192 (Max)	192 (Max)	192 (Max)	192 (Max)
Host Memory Support	32 GB	32 GB	1 terabyte	1 terabyte
Host Processor Support	24 Cores (Max) (See Note)	24 Cores (Max) (See Note)	24 Cores (Max) (See Note)	24 Cores (Max) (See Note)
Virtual Networks	Unlimited	Unlimited	Unlimited	Unlimited
Guest VM Memory	32 GB (Max)	32 GB (Max)	64 GB (Max)	64 GB (Max)
Guest Virtual Processor	4 per VM	4 per VM	4 per VM	4 per VM
Guest Virtual NICs	4 Legacy 8 Synthetic	4 Legacy 8 Synthetic	4 Legacy 8 Synthetic	4 Legacy 8 Synthetic
Guest Storage Adapters	2 IDE 4 SCSI	2 IDE 4 SCSI	2 IDE 4 SCSI	2 IDE 4 SCSI
Guest Storage Devices	4 IDE 256 SCSI	4 IDE 256 SCSI	4 IDE 256 SCSI	4 IDE 256 SCSI
Cluster Support	N	N	Y	Y
Quick Migration	N	N	Y	Y
Included Use Licenses	None	1 Physical 1 VM	1 Physical 4 VMs	1 Physical Unlimited VMs

AMD-V and Intel VT Support

Hyper-V requires an x64 AMD-V or Intel VT processor that supports hardware-assisted virtualization and hardware-based Data Execution Prevention (DEP). You must ensure that both of these options are enabled in the Basic Input/Output System (BIOS), as they may be disabled by default. Specifically for DEP, you must enable the AMD No-Execute (NX) bit, or Intel Execute-Disable (XD) bit, which assists in preventing buffer overflow exploits. Other advantages of running on an AMD-V or Intel VT x64 platform include access to a larger address space and a higher partition density. Hyper-V does not support Itanium or x86-based systems.

Full Installation and Server Core Installation Support

Hyper-V can be installed as a role in either a full installation or a Server Core installation of 64-bit Windows Server 2008 Standard, Enterprise, and Datacenter editions. In a full installation of Windows Server 2008, you can use the Initial Configuration Tasks or the Server Manager to add the Hyper-V role to your system. The Windows Hypervisor is present and enabled only after the Hyper-V role is installed on Windows Server 2008. Furthermore, when you select and add the Hyper-V role, all of the Hyper-V components are installed on your system. This also includes Hyper-V management tools such as the Hyper-V Manager MMC snap-in and the Virtual Machine Connection application, which allows you to remotely access virtual machines. Installing the Hyper-V role in a full installation of Windows Server 2008 requires that you restart the computer before it will boot the Windows Hypervisor.

Windows Server 2008 Server Core is a new feature that allows you to install a minimal server configuration that includes only the subset of binaries that are required to run one of the supported roles. A key advantage of Server Core is the reduction in operating system maintenance (i.e., fewer updates) and management requirements based on the smaller number of files and services included in the installation.

There are nine Server Core roles: Hyper-V, File Services, Active Directory Domain Services, Active Directory Lightweight Directory Services, DHCP Server, DNS Server, Print Services, Streaming Media Services, and Web Server. The default management interface for a Windows Server 2008 Server Core installation is a command prompt, since it does not install the Explorer shell graphical user interface (GUI). Therefore, you must rely on command-line options to enable the Hyper-V role in a Server Core installation. However, a Windows Server 2008 Server Core installation can be managed remotely using the standard MMC tools from a server with a full installation of Windows Server 2008. You can also use the Remote Server Administration Tools (RSAT) to manage your Server Core installations from 32-bit and 64-bit editions of Windows Vista Business with Service Pack 1 (SP1), Windows Vista Enterprise with SP1, and Windows Vista Ultimate with SP1.

> **NOTE** If you are going to install and use RSAT to manage a Windows Server 2008 Server Core installation, you must download and install KB941314 from *http://support.microsoft.com/kb/941314.*

> **MORE INFO** For detailed installation procedures of the Hyper-V role in either a full installation or Server Core installation of Window Server 2008, refer to Chapter 4, "Hyper-V Installation and Configuration."

Microsoft Hyper-V Server 2008

Microsoft Hyper-V Server 2008 is a stand-alone product based on the same virtualization architecture available in Windows Server 2008 Hyper-V. However, it has been simplified and optimized to run Hyper-V only. Similar to a Server Core installation of Windows Server 2008, it provides only a command-line user interface and can be administered remotely using the Hyper-V management tools and RSAT.

Microsoft Hyper-V Server 2008 is available as a free download from the Microsoft Web site. It is a good choice for single virtualization host deployments that do not require enterprise-class features such as high availability, and for virtual machines that need less than 32 GB of memory. You may also want to consider using Windows Hyper-V Server 2008 in non-production, development, and test environments. There is no software upgrade path from Microsoft Hyper-V Server 2008 to Windows Server 2008 Hyper-V. However, virtual machines are compatible between the two products and can be migrated using Hyper-V virtual machine export and import features, which will be discussed later in this chapter.

Microsoft Hyper-V Server 2008 includes a command-line, menu-driven configuration tool called HVConfig.cmd to permit the configuration of basic connectivity and features required to use it in a managed environment. HVConfig.cmd supports the following configuration and actions:

- Domain or workgroup membership
- Computer name
- Network settings
- Local administrators
- Windows Update settings
- Download and install Windows Updates
- Remote Desktop
- Regional and language options
- Date and time
- Log Off User
- Restart Server
- Shut Down Server
- Exit To Command Line

HVConfig.cmd actually executes a Visual Basic Script file called HVConfig.vbs that contains all the functionality. HVConfig.cmd launches every time that you log on to the system.

Access Control Using Authorization Manager

Hyper-V leverages Authorization Manager (AzMan) to provide role-based access control to Hyper-V and virtual machines. This allows you to create job definitions and translate them into a role with a limited set of operations and tasks. You can assign individual users or groups to appropriate roles, allowing them to fulfill their job responsibilities while restricting their access to only the required Hyper-V resources, operations, and tasks.

MORE INFO For more details on how to use AzMan with Hyper-V and the types of roles that might be useful to define for Hyper-V and virtual machine management, refer to Chapter 6, "Hyper-V Security."

Live Backup with Volume Shadow Copy Service

Volume Shadow Copy Service (VSS) support in Hyper-V provides stateful, host-side backups, eliminating the need to load an agent in each virtual machine. Any VSS-aware application, such as System Center Data Protection Manager (DPM) 2007 SP1, can leverage this functionality to provide VSS snapshot backup services if it utilizes the VSS writer interface implemented in Hyper-V. Any virtual machine running a VSS-aware guest Windows operating system (Windows Server 2003 and later) can be backed up in a live state. Any other guest operating system (Windows 2000, Linux, and so on) will need to be in saved state prior to the VSS snapshot. Because VSS snapshots are performed through an extremely fast process (they take seconds), virtual machine downtime is minimized. Additionally, with VSS support, the number of steps involved in archive or restore operations is reduced and the consistency of the data is ensured.

> **MORE INFO** For more details on performing live backups using VSS, refer to Chapter 13, "Hyper-V Backup and Recovery."

High Availability Using Failover Clustering

Hyper-V supports Windows Failover Clustering to implement a high-availability strategy that can manage both unplanned and planned downtime. There are two levels at which you can implement a failover cluster with Hyper-V: at the guest operating system level, and at the virtualization host level. A guest operating system failover cluster requires cluster-aware applications running in virtual machines. In addition, you have to run an operating system in the virtual machine that supports failover clustering, such as Windows Server 2003 (for up to an 8-node cluster) or Windows Server 2008 Enterprise or Datacenter edition (for up to a 16-node cluster). The second failover cluster option consists of two or more Windows Server 2008 Hyper-V servers, each configured as a cluster node. This type of configuration allows you to provide a high-availability solution for both non-cluster-aware guest operating systems and applications that run in virtual machines.

> **MORE INFO** For more details on how to configure guest and host failover clusters, refer to Chapter 5.

Quick Migration

Hyper-V also supports Quick Migration, the ability to move a virtual machine across cluster nodes without data loss and with minimal service interruption. To accomplish this, a virtual machine is placed in saved state, active memory and processor state are captured to disk, and storage resources ownership is transferred to another node in the cluster. On the new node, the virtual machine active memory and processor state are reloaded and processing is resumed. Depending on the underlying storage and the size of the state data, the entire process can take place in a matter of seconds or minutes.

> **MORE INFO** For more details on Quick Migration, refer to Chapter 14, "Server Migration Using System Center Virtual Machine Manager."

Integration Services

In Hyper-V, Integration Services (IS) provide support for five unique components that require a secure interface between a parent and child partition. These functions are:

- Time synchronization
- Heartbeat
- Shutdown
- Key/value pair exchange
- Volume Shadow Copy Service (VSS)

Integration Services target very specific areas that enhance the functionality or management of supported guest operating systems. In addition to these services, Integration Services provide the synthetic or high-performance drivers for networking, video, storage, and human-interface devices. If you install Windows Server 2008 in a virtual machine, the Integration Services are pre-installed. However, you should update them to the latest version. For other operating systems, you should install the Integration Services after the operating system installation is complete. It is important to note that only a subset of Integration Services may be supported for some legacy or non-Windows guest operating systems.

> **MORE INFO** For more details on Integration Services, refer to Chapter 3 and Chapter 5.

Virtual Machine Import and Export

The import and export features in Hyper-V are meant to move and copy virtual machines between Hyper-V servers. These features do not provide a solution to export or import virtual machines between other virtualization applications like Virtual Server 2005 R2. In addition, you can export only a virtual machine that is in saved state or that is shut down.

Virtual Hard Disk Management

Hyper-V provides several options to manage virtual hard disks (VHD), accessible through the Hyper-V Manager console. The VHD management options include:

- **Compact**   Provides the ability to shrink the size of a VHD by removing blank space that remains after data is deleted from the VHD file
- **Convert**   Provides the ability to transfer a dynamically expanding VHD to a fixed-size VHD or vice versa
- **Expand**   Provides the ability to increase the storage capacity of a dynamically expanding VHD or fixed-size VHD
- **Merge**   Provides the ability to combine the content of a child differencing disk with the parent differencing disk
- **Reconnect**   Provides the ability to reconnect a child differencing disk to the parent disk

The options that are available depend on the type of VHD that you select and also on the status of that VHD.

> **MORE INFO**   For more details on the VHD management options, refer to Chapter 5.

Virtual Machine Snapshots

The Hyper-V snapshot feature allows you to capture the configuration and state of a virtual machine at any particular point in time, and provides you with the ability to reload any existing snapshot within a matter of seconds. Hyper-V snapshots can be extremely useful in scenarios for which you need to make incremental changes to a virtual machine with the ability to roll back to a previous state. The Hyper-V snapshot feature is principally designed for use in test and development environments, not in a production infrastructure.

> **MORE INFO**   For more details on virtual machine snapshots, refer to Chapter 5.

Virtual Machine Connection

Virtual Machine Connection (VMC) is a remote administration tool provided with Hyper-V. VMC uses the Widows Remote Desktop Protocol to allow remote access to the guest operating system running in a virtual machine. It is embedded in the Hyper-V Manager MMC and is available as a stand-alone application. VMC provides access to the video frame buffer of the video machine from the moment a virtual machine is powered on so that you have access during the boot process.

> **MORE INFO**   For more details about using VMC, refer to Chapter 11, "Hyper-V Single Server Management."

Windows Server 2008 R2 Hyper-V Features

Vijay Tewari, Principal Program Manager
Windows Virtualization

Microsoft has made a big investment in developing Windows Server 2008 Hyper-V, a virtualization platform that provides flexibility and performance for IT organizations to consolidate their workloads. Although this book provides an excellent in-depth look at various aspects of the Hyper-V platform, Microsoft continues to enhance and evolve Hyper-V with features and capabilities. Here is a sneak peek at some capabilities of Windows Server 2008 R2 Hyper-V, the next release of the Windows Server Virtualization platform.

Live Migration of Virtual Machines

Windows Server 2008 provides Quick Migration to move VMs between hosts in a cluster with minimal service interruption. However, this capability requires pausing the virtual machine momentarily while the saved state is moved from the source to the destination node. A virtual machine in saved state does not run during this period (called the "blackout" period), in effect causing downtime for the virtual machine. In today's IT environment, downtime even for short periods is problematic. In order to address this issue, Microsoft is enhancing the Hyper-V product with the Live Migration capability. With Live Migration, there is no perceived downtime in the workloads running in the VM, and network connections to and from the migrated VM stay connected. As with Quick Migration, Live Migration will be possible between nodes within a failover cluster. In effect, the infrastructure investment made in order to use Quick Migration will be enhanced through Live Migration. In addition, Microsoft is adding Clustered Shared Volumes to failover clusters, which allow multiple VHDs for different VMs to be stored on a single Logical Unit Number (LUN). This not only simplifies management of shared storage for a cluster, it also provides a significant reduction in the blackout period for VMs moved through Live Migration.

Support for Enhanced Hardware Virtualization Features

Over the years, hardware vendors such as AMD and Intel have made significant enhancements (such as AMD-V and Intel VT) to processors and chipsets with capabilities specifically targeting virtualization. Continuing with these enhancements, AMD and Intel support Nested Page Tables (NPT) and Extended Page Tables (EPT), respectively. These capabilities improve the performance of memory address translations. Without these hardware enhancements, each time a guest page faults, it requires a context switch to the hypervisor to handle the page fault. With NPT and EPT, a guest can handle page faults directly, eliminating the need for a costly context switch to the hypervisor and reducing virtualization overhead for memory translations.

Addition and Removal of Virtual Storage

Virtualization decouples the software running on a system from the hardware and makes it convenient for IT organizations to deploy and manage their environments. With this flexibility, it is inevitable that customers also seek the ability to expand and reduce storage coupled with virtual machines. With Windows Server 2008 R2 Hyper-V, Microsoft is adding the ability to add and remove virtual hard disks from a virtual machine while it is in operation. This capability opens up a range of possibilities for backup storage solutions and so on.

Networking Enhancements

Networking vendors have also made enhancements to hardware that benefit virtualized platforms. Two such key technologies are TCP Offload Engine (TOE) and Virtual Machine Queues (VMQ).

TCP Offload Engine refers to the offloading of TCP/IP processing to the network interface card (NIC). This technology is not specific to virtualized platforms, as non-virtualized operating systems and applications can also benefit by using it. A generally well-accepted rule of thumb is that 1 Hertz (Hz) of CPU processing is required to send or receive 1 bit of TCP/IP data. For high speed NICs, the overhead associated with processing TCP/IP traffic can be substantial. Windows Server 2008 R2 Hyper-V will support offloading the TCP/IP processing from virtual machines onto supported NICs, reducing the overhead for network processing. This has the benefit to free up processor cycles for additional work.

VMQ provides multiple queues and sorting algorithms in the NIC. One or more queues can be assigned by the hypervisor to individual virtual machines. The NIC sorts incoming network traffic and places it in the appropriate queues for the virtual machines. Since this processing happens in the NIC hardware, it reduces the hypervisor overhead and again frees up processor cycles for other work.

In addition, Microsoft is also adding support for jumbo frames that enable large send and receive payloads. A jumbo frame is an Ethernet frame with up to 9000 bytes of data payload as opposed to the traditional 1500 bytes. This reduces the overhead incurred per transferred byte. Coupled with large send offload (LSO), which is the ability of the operating system to transfer large chunks of data to the NIC to create Ethernet frames, and large receive offload (LRO), which allows the creation of a single large data buffer from multiple incoming Ethernet frames, this provides additional reductions of network processing overhead.

Power Management Enhancements

Recognizing the fact that data center power distribution and cooling infrastructure for the computing infrastructure are uppermost in IT staff minds, the next generation of the Windows Hypervisor has enhancements to reduce the power footprint of virtualized workloads. These capabilities include the use of "core parking," which allows the hypervisor to proactively consolidate idle workloads onto fewer cores. The unused processors can then be put into a deep sleep state, effectively reducing the power consumption of the server. In addition, the virtual management infrastructure, more specifically System Center Virtual Machine Manager (SCVMM), also can assist through optimal workload placement that reduces the overall power consumption of workloads.

Remote Desktop Connection Broker

The Remote Desktop Connection Broker creates a unified administrative experience for traditional session-based (i.e., Terminal Services) remote desktops and for virtual machine-based remote desktops in a Virtual Desktop Infrastructure (VDI). The two key deployment scenarios supported by the Remote Desktop Connection Broker are persistent (permanent) VMs and pooled VMs. Using a persistent VM, a user is assigned a dedicated VM that can be personalized and customized, and that preserves any changes made by the user. With a pooled VM, a single VM image is replicated as needed for users. User state can be stored using profiles and folder redirection, but it does not persist on the VM after the user logs off.

Host Operating System Support

The following list includes all the currently supported 64-bit host operating systems for Hyper-V:

- Windows Server 2008 Standard Edition
- Windows Server 2008 Enterprise Edition
- Windows Server 2008 Datacenter Edition
- Microsoft Hyper-V Server 2008

Guest Operating System Support

The following list includes all the supported x86 guest operating systems that can be used with Windows Server 2008 Standard, Enterprise, and Datacenter editions, as well as Microsoft Hyper-V Server 2008:

- Windows 2000 (support for one virtual processor)
  - Windows 2000 Server with SP4
  - Windows 2000 Advanced Server with SP4
- Windows Server 2003 x86 (support for one or two virtual processors)
  - Windows Server Web Edition with SP2
  - Windows Server Standard Edition with SP2

- Windows Server Enterprise Edition with SP2
- Windows Server Datacenter Edition with SP2

- Windows Server 2003 R2 x86 (support for one or two virtual processors)
  - Windows Server Web Edition with SP2
  - Windows Server Standard Edition with SP2
  - Windows Server Enterprise Edition with SP2
  - Windows Server Datacenter Edition with SP2

- Windows Server 2003 x64 (support for one or two virtual processors)
  - Windows Server Standard Edition with SP2
  - Windows Server Enterprise Edition with SP2
  - Windows Server Datacenter Edition with SP2

- Windows Server 2003 R2 x64 (support for one or two virtual processors)
  - Windows Server Standard Edition with SP2
  - Windows Server Enterprise Edition with SP2
  - Windows Server Datacenter Edition with SP2

- Windows Server 2008 x86 (support for one, two, or four virtual processors)
  - Windows Server 2008 Standard Edition
  - Windows Server 2008 Enterprise Edition
  - Windows Server 2008 Datacenter Edition
  - Windows Web Server 2008 Edition
  - Windows Server 2008 Standard Edition without Hyper-V
  - Windows Server 2008 Enterprise Edition without Hyper-V
  - Windows Server 2008 Datacenter Edition without Hyper-V

- Windows Server 2008 x64 (support for one, two, or four virtual processors)
  - Windows Server 2008 Standard Edition
  - Windows Server 2008 Enterprise Edition
  - Windows Server 2008 Datacenter Edition
  - Windows Web Server 2008 Edition
  - Windows Server 2008 Standard Edition without Hyper-V
  - Windows Server 2008 Enterprise Edition without Hyper-V
  - Windows Server 2008 Datacenter Edition without Hyper-V

- Windows HPC Server 2008 (support for one, two or four virtual processors)
- Suse Linux Enterprise Server 10 x86 (support for one virtual processor)
  - SUSE Linux Enterprise Server 10 with SP1

- SUSE Linux Enterprise Server 10 with SP2
  - Suse Linux Enterprise Server 10 x64 (support for one virtual processor)
    - SUSE Linux Enterprise Server 10 with SP1
    - SUSE Linux Enterprise Server 10 with SP2
  - Windows XP Professional x86
    - Windows XP Professional with SP2 (support for one virtual processor)
    - Windows XP Professional with SP3 (support for one or two virtual processors)
  - Windows XP Professional x64
    - Windows XP Professional with SP2 (support for one or two virtual processors)
  - Windows Vista x86 (support for one or two virtual processors)
    - Windows Vista Business Edition with SP1
    - Windows Vista Enterprise Edition with SP1
    - Windows Vista Ultimate Edition with SP1
  - Windows Vista x64 (support for one or two virtual processors)
    - Windows Vista Business Edition with SP1
    - Windows Vista Enterprise Edition with SP1
    - Windows Vista Ultimate Edition with SP1

Reviewing Hyper-V

Windows Server 2008 Hyper-V and Microsoft Hyper-V Server 2008 are both hypervisor-based virtualization platforms. Hyper-V is multithreaded and concurrently runs one or more virtual machines (workloads), each in its own thread of execution. Each virtual machine presents a set of virtualized or synthetic devices to the guest operating system and applications that abstracts the underlying physical hardware, providing workload portability between dissimilar physical servers running Hyper-V.

Virtual Machine Hardware Environment

Table 2-2 lists the standard set of virtualized components that a virtual machine exposes to a guest operating system and application stack. These devices are detected and appear to be the physical hardware resources available to the running workload. When a virtual machine workload requests access to the virtualized resources, Hyper-V works in conjunction with the parent partition to translate the requested operation from the virtual hardware environment to the physical hardware, and access is achieved via the standard kernel device drivers installed in the parent partition. This approach provides virtual machine workloads the ability to run across a wide variety of server hardware without requiring any modifications to the workload configuration.

TABLE 2-2 Virtualized Hardware Components

COMPONENT	VIRTUALIZED HARDWARE
Basic input/output system (BIOS)	American Megatrends (AMI) BIOS with Intel 440BX chip set and PIIX4 ACPI including: ■ Complementary metal oxide semiconductor (CMOS) ■ Real-time clock ■ RAM and video RAM (VRAM) ■ Memory controller ■ Direct memory access (DMA) controller ■ PCI bus ■ ISA bus ■ SM bus ■ Power management ■ 8259 programmable interrupt controller (PIC) ■ Programmable interrupt timer (PIT)
Floppy disk drive	Single 1.44-MB floppy disk drive that maps to a floppy drive image.
Serial (COM) port	Dual serial ports that can be connected to local named pipes.
Printer (LPT) port	None
Mouse	Standard PS/2 Microsoft IntelliMouse pointing device mapped to the PS/2 device on the physical computer. Synthetic mouse device (requires Integration Services installation).
Keyboard	Standard PS/2 101-key Microsoft keyboard that can be mapped to a PS/2 keyboard on the physical computer. Synthetic keyboard device (requires Integration Services installation).
Network adapter (multifunction)	Up to four legacy Multiport DEC/Intel 21140 Ethernet network adapters. Up to eight synthetic network adapters (requires Integration Services installation).
Processor	Up to four processors that are the same as the physical computer processors.

COMPONENT	VIRTUALIZED HARDWARE
Memory	Up to 32 GB of RAM per virtual machine for Windows Server 2008 Hyper-V Standard Edition and Microsoft Hyper-V Server 2008. Up to 64 GB of RAM per virtual machine for Windows Server 2008 Hyper-V Enterprise and Datacenter editions.
Video card	VESA compatible emulated graphics adapter with 4 MB of VRAM, VGA, and SVGA support compliant with VESA 1.2, 2-D graphics accelerator and hardware cursor, and support for DirectX. Synthetic video adapter (requires Integration Services installation).
IDE/ATAPI storage	Dual IDE channels that support hard drives, CD-ROM or DVD-ROM drives, and ISO images. Each IDE channel supports two disks.
SCSI storage	Up to four synthetic SCSI adapters, each supporting 64 disks (requires Integration Services installation).
Sound card	None

A few limitations are imposed on virtual machine workloads based on the virtual hardware environment. Operating systems or applications that require direct access to a hardware device that is not listed in Table 2-2 cannot execute in a virtual machine. Because virtual machines expose only four CPUs to a hosted workload, applications that require symmetric multiprocessing (SMP) can be assigned one, two, or four processors in a virtual machine.

Virtual Hard Disks

Virtual hard disks (VHDs) are single file representations of a physical hard disk that encapsulate virtual machine data. Virtual hard disks reflect the same internal structure as a physical hard disk, including block allocation tables, data blocks, and sectors. Table 2-3 provides a list of virtual hard disk types available in Hyper-V.

TABLE 2-3 Virtual Hard Disk Types

DISK TYPE	DESCRIPTION
Fixed	Virtual hard disk file with all data blocks allocated on the host disk subsystem at creation time. A 10-GB fixed disk consumes 10 GB on the host physical disk where it is created.

DISK TYPE	DESCRIPTION
Dynamically Expanding	Virtual hard disk file that is preallocated with no data blocks reserved and grows as data is written until it reaches full size. A 10-GB dynamically expanding disk takes less than 2 MB initially and grows to 10 GB in 2-MB data block increments. In Hyper-V, the maximum size for this VHD type is 127 GB.
Differencing	Virtual hard disk file that is tied to an existing "parent" virtual hard disk file as an overlay. All writes are made to the differencing disk, the "child," whereas reads come from the parent and the child. Differencing disks are created as dynamically expanding disks.
Linked	A physical disk volume that you want to convert to a virtual hard disk. Linked disks exist only to perform the migration from physical to virtual hard disk.

Within a virtual machine, a virtual hard disk is represented as a physical disk. On a Hyper-V server physical disk, a virtual hard disk is stored as a file with a .vhd extension. Virtual machines connect to a virtual hard disk through a virtualized Integrated Drive Electronics (IDE) or Small Computer System Interface (SCSI) adapter. Hyper-V is responsible for mapping the virtual hard disk to the .vhd file on the physical disk. A VHD can be stored on any IDE, SCSI, iSCSI, storage area network (SAN), or Network-Attached Storage (NAS) storage system supported by the Windows Server 2008 operating system.

Virtual hard disks are created using either the Hyper-V Manager or through the WMI application programming interface (API). A virtual machine can support a maximum of 260 virtual hard disks through a combination of IDE and SCSI-connected VHDs.

NOTE Virtual hard disk specifications are independent of the bus type used to connect to the virtual machine. However, the bus type does impose a size limitation on virtual hard disks. Virtual hard disks connected via IDE cannot exceed 127 GB. Virtual hard disks connected via SCSI cannot exceed 2040 gigabytes.

Pass-Through Disks

Using Hyper-V, you can expose a disk to a virtual machine that is connected to the physical server without creating a volume on it. This is referred to as a pass-through disk. Pass-through disks can be physically connected to the Hyper-V server or as a LUN on a SAN. One of the advantages of pass-through disks is that they are not subject to the 2040-gigabyte size limitation that is imposed on VHDs. In contrast, pass-through disks do not support dynamically expanding VHDs, differencing VHDs, or Hyper-V snapshots.

Virtual IDE Interface

A virtual machine provides built-in primary and secondary virtual IDE interfaces. In Hyper-V, you can boot a virtual machine only from a virtual hard disk that is connected through the virtual IDE interface. Each virtual IDE interface can support two devices attached to it, for a total of four IDE devices for every virtual machine. Either virtual hard disks or virtual CD-ROMs can be connected to an IDE interface. By default, the first virtual CD-ROM is attached to the secondary interface as the master device.

Virtual SCSI Interface

Contrary to the built-in virtual IDE interfaces exposed within the virtual machine environment, virtual SCSI interfaces are optional components that must be installed in a virtual machine before they can be used. A virtual machine supports up to four virtual SCSI adapters. Each virtual SCSI adapter can have up to 64 devices attached, for a total of 256 SCSI devices for every virtual machine.

Because virtual SCSI adapters are implemented as synthetic devices that load after the guest operating system loads, SCSI-attached VHDs cannot be used to boot a virtual machine.

iSCSI Disks

Another option to expose storage devices to a virtual machine is to install an iSCSI initiator in the guest operating system and connect directly to an iSCSI target. However, Hyper-V does not support booting from iSCSI-connected disk; therefore, you will still need to connect your boot disk through the virtual IDE interface. Using iSCSI-connected disks requires that you dedicate a NIC in the Hyper-V server for iSCSI communications.

Virtual Networks

A virtual network is a software emulation of a Layer 2 network switch with unlimited ports and a switched uplink that can connect to an external physical network through a physical network adapter or remain disconnected to create an isolated internal network. For each virtual network that you create in Hyper-V, a new software-based switch is created. In addition, each virtual network port simulates a 10-gigabit Ethernet port. Hyper-V supports an unlimited number of virtual networks with an unlimited number of ports for virtual machine connections.

Hyper-V provides three types of virtual networks: External, Private, and Internal. An external virtual network is used to provide connectivity to a physical network. When you create a new external virtual network, a virtual NIC is created in the Hyper-V parent partition with all the basic network bindings. The virtual NIC connects to a new virtual network switch, and the virtual network switch connects to the physical NIC that you select. If there are multiple physical NICs installed in a Hyper-V server, you can choose the one to bind to the new external virtual network. The physical NIC will have all network bindings removed with the exception of the Microsoft Virtual Network Switch Protocol. When a new virtual machine is connected to the external virtual network, a new network port is added to the virtual network switch.

An internal virtual network provides a means to allow virtual machines to communicate with the Hyper-V server, but it does not provide access to physical networks. In this case, a virtual NIC is again created in the Hyper-V parent partition and is connected to a port on a new virtual network switch. However, the new virtual network switch is not connected to any of the physical NICs installed in the Hyper-V server. When a new virtual machine is connected to the internal virtual network, a new network port is added to the virtual network switch.

A private virtual network allows multiple virtual machines to communicate with each other, but not with the Hyper-V server or with any host connected on an external physical network. Essentially, when you create a new private virtual network, a new virtual network switch is created, but no virtual NIC is created in the Hyper-V parent partition. As you add new virtual machine connections to the new virtual network switch, additional network ports are added to it.

All three types of virtual network can be created through the Hyper-V Manager MMC or using WMI.

Virtual Network Adapters

There are two types of supported virtual network adapters in Hyper-V: legacy (emulated) and synthetic. A legacy network adapter emulates a virtual Multiport DEC 21140 network adapter. Using a legacy network adapter will increase the processor overhead because device access requires context switching that is not required with the synthetic network adapter. A synthetic network adapter provides higher performance because virtual machine device access requests are made through the high-speed VMBus to the parent partition. In order to use a synthetic network adapter, the guest operating system in the virtual machine must support the installation of Integration Services.

Virtual machines support a maximum of four virtual legacy network adapters and eight synthetic network adapters. Only the legacy network adapter supports the Pre-boot Execution Environment protocol (PXE), allowing virtual machines to be provisioned using standard image-deployment tools such as Windows Deployment Services (WDS) or other third-party applications. This is the case because the synthetic network adapter is loaded only after the virtual machine has booted.

When a legacy network adapter is added to a virtual machine, you can define the virtual network to connect it to or leave the virtual machine disconnected from any virtual network. Hyper-V allocates a new dynamic media access control (MAC) address to the new virtual network adapter from its pool of available addresses. It is also possible to provide a virtual network adapter with a static MAC address that is manually configured. With Hyper-V, both legacy and synthetic network adapters provide support for virtual LAN (VLAN) identification.

> **IMPORTANT** Although the virtual Multiport DEC 21140 network adapter defines a 10/100 megabit Ethernet interface, there is no network bandwidth limitation imposed on virtual machine workloads. If the underlying physical network adapter is capable of achieving higher network performance (for example, gigabit speed), the virtual machine workload has the ability to exceed the 100-megabit specification.

Using the Hyper-V Manager Console

The Hyper-V Manager MMC is installed when the Hyper-V role is configured in a full instal-lation of Microsoft Windows Server 2008. It is the default graphical user interface that allows you to manage and configure Hyper-V servers and virtual machines. It is also available for Microsoft Vista with SP1 (x86 and x64) as a download from the Microsoft Web site.

> **NOTE** If you are interested in running Hyper-V Manager on Microsoft Vista with SP1, it is available for download from *http://support.microsoft.com/kb/952627*.

The Hyper-V manager allows an administrator to manage multiple Hyper-V servers; however, it is meant to be the primary management tool only for small virtualization deploy-ments. If you are deploying Hyper-V in a large or complex environment, you should use an enterprise-class management application like System Center Virtual Machine Manager.

You can launch Hyper-V Manager from the Start menu by selecting Hyper-V Manager from the Administrative Tools menu as shown in Figure 2-2. In a default full installation of Windows Server 2008, you can also invoke it using the Start menu Run option or from a com-mand prompt by typing **C:\Program Files\Hyper-V\virtmgmt.msc**.

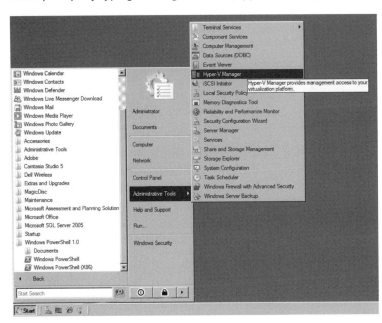

FIGURE 2-2 Launching Hyper-V Manager from the Start menu

As shown in Figure 2-3, the Hyper-V Manager console is divided into three sections. The left pane displays the tree view of managed Hyper-V servers. The center pane displays existing virtual machines and their state, as well as a tree view of existing snapshots and a minimized view of the virtual machine console when a virtual machine is selected. The right pane contains the list of actions available to manage the Hyper-V servers and virtual machines. The list of virtual machine actions is displayed only after a virtual machine is created or added on the Hyper-V server.

FIGURE 2-3 Hyper-V Manager default view

Managing Multiple Hyper-V Servers

Although the Hyper-V Manager allows only a single Hyper-V server to be managed at a time, it is a simple matter to connect to and switch the management focus to a different Hyper-V server. Figure 2-4 shows the Select Computer dialog box that is displayed when you right-click Hyper-V Manager in the left tree view pane and select Connect To Server. This dialog box is where you can specify the name or IP address of a Hyper-V server that you would like to manage.

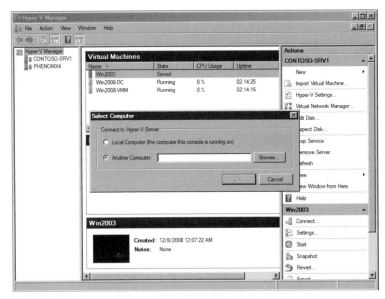

FIGURE 2-4 Hyper-V Manager server selection

In this dialog box, you also have the option to select Another Computer and browse for Hyper-V servers that you want to manage from your console.

Managing Virtual Machines

The Hyper-V Manager allows you to create, delete, export and import, or configure virtual machines on the managed Hyper-V server. You manage the virtual machines by selecting the desired management option and then providing or changing information through simple wizards.

Creating Virtual Machines

In order to create a new virtual machine, you can select the New option directly under the Hyper-V server name in the Actions pane and then choose the Virtual Machine menu option, as shown in Figure 2-5.

FIGURE 2-5 Creating a new virtual machine in Hyper-V Manager

Hyper-V provides the New Virtual Machine Wizard, shown in Figure 2-6, to guide you through the process of configuring and creating a new virtual machine.

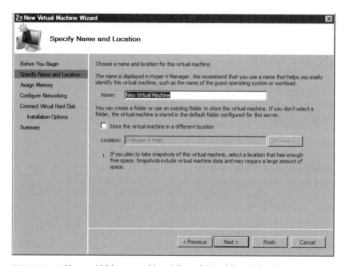

FIGURE 2-6 Hyper-V Manager New Virtual Machine Wizard

The wizard gathers basic information about the new virtual machine configuration, including the virtual machine name and storage location, memory to assign to the virtual machine, the virtual network to connect to the virtual machine, and whether you want to create a new virtual hard disk, use an existing virtual hard disk, or attach a virtual hard disk at a later time. Finally, you can specify the guest operating system installation options that include installing the guest operating system later, installing the guest operating system from a boot CD or DVD-ROM, installing the guest operating system from a boot floppy disk, or installing a guest operating system from a network-based installation server. When you have made your selections, you will have an opportunity to review the settings and select whether or not to start the virtual machine after it is created.

When the information in the wizard is submitted to Hyper-V, a new virtual machine configuration file (.xml) that contains the settings information is created. The new virtual machine is registered and visible in the Hyper-V Manager; a new virtual hard disk is created, if specified; and a virtual network adapter is connected to the virtual machine. The new virtual machine is then ready to boot and install a new operating system or load an existing operating system.

Virtual Machine Export and Import

If you want to export a virtual machine, right-click the virtual machine in Hyper-V Manager or select the Export option from the Actions pane. You will then see the Export Virtual Machine dialog box shown in Figure 2-7. It is important to note that you can export only a virtual machine that is in a saved state or is powered off.

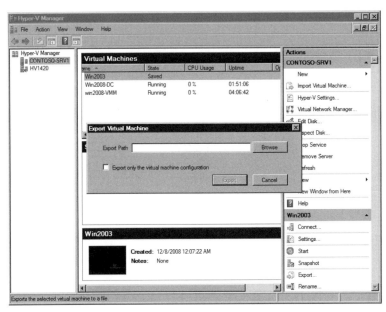

FIGURE 2-7 The Export Virtual Machine dialog box in Hyper-V Manager

In the Export Virtual Machine dialog box, you can browse to specify the location to save the virtual machine export files. There is also an option to export only the virtual machine configuration file (.exp), but not other files, such as saved state files or VHDs.

After you have moved or copied the virtual machine export files and you are ready to import the virtual machine into Hyper-V, select the Import Virtual Machine option from the

Actions pane under the server name. As shown in Figure 2-8, you must enter the path to the export files in the Import Virtual Machine dialog box or browse to select it.

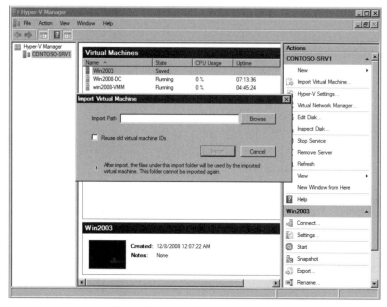

FIGURE 2-8 The Import Virtual Machine dialog box in Hyper-V Manager

You also need to decide whether or not to reuse the VM ID, which is the Global Unique Identifier (GUID) assigned when a new VM is created. If you are making a copy of an existing virtual machine, you should generate a new virtual machine ID and will leave this option unchecked. If you are moving a virtual machine or restoring a backup copy of a virtual machine, then you should reuse the old virtual machine ID.

> **NOTE** If you select to reuse the old virtual machine ID and the original virtual machine is still present on the Hyper-V server, the import operation will fail because the virtual machine ID has to be unique.

When you import a virtual machine, it will be left in the import path location, and it will not be possible to move the virtual machine after import. Therefore, you should ensure that you move the exported virtual machine files to the destination storage location before you import the virtual machine.

Virtual Machine Snapshots

The Hyper-V snapshot feature allows you to capture the configuration and state of a virtual machine at any point in time and return it to that state without noticeable interruption. Hyper-V allows you to create a snapshot whether the virtual machine is running, in saved state, or powered off.

In order to create a snapshot of a virtual machine in Hyper-V Manager, right-click the virtual machine and select the Snapshot option from the menu, as shown in Figure 2-9.

FIGURE 2-9 Creating a virtual machine snapshot using the Hyper-V Manager console

Figure 2-10 illustrates the changes in the Hyper-V Manager console when the snapshot completes. The Snapshots section in the center pane now displays a tree structure that reflects the virtual machine snapshot hierarchy. The root node of the tree is the snapshot that was just created and includes the creation time stamp. Under the root node, there is a child named Now that represents the running version of the virtual machine.

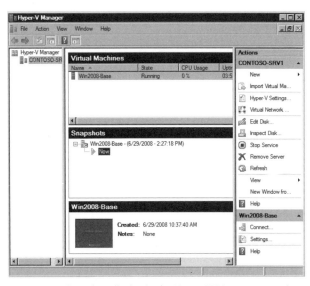

FIGURE 2-10 Snapshot display in the Hyper-V Manager console

As you make changes to the configuration of a virtual machine, you can create and save additional snapshots. Figure 2-11 shows that another snapshot was generated after the initial one, and they are displayed in a parent and child hierarchy that also reflects the relationship of the differencing disks that are created for each snapshot to capture changes to the virtual machine operating system, applications, and data.

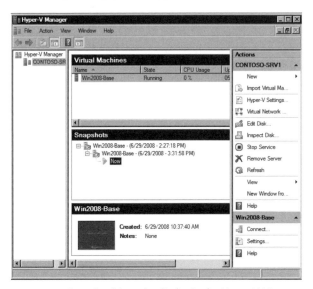

FIGURE 2-11 Snapshot hierarchy display in the Hyper-V Manager console

If after making a series of changes to a virtual machine, you decide that you want to reload the previous snapshot, use the Hyper-V Revert option, as shown in Figure 2-12. After the Revert option is applied to a virtual machine, the resulting configuration and state of the virtual machine are returned to the settings saved in the snapshot files.

If you want to reload a snapshot that is two or more levels higher than the running virtual machine (represented by the Now marker in the Snapshot pane), you can right-click the snapshot and choose the Apply option from the menu, as shown in Figure 2-13.

FIGURE 2-12 The Snapshot Revert Option in the Hyper-V Manager console

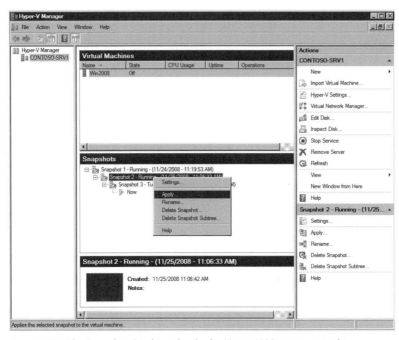

FIGURE 2-13 The Snapshot Apply option in the Hyper-V Manager console

If you decide that you no longer need a snapshot or snapshot subtree, Hyper-V provides two different Delete options (shown in Figure 2-14) to permanently remove one or more snapshots from the snapshot hierarchy.

FIGURE 2-14 The Delete Snapshot and Delete Snapshot Subtree options in the Hyper-V Manager console

You can choose to delete a single snapshot or a snapshot subtree, as you can see in the shortcut menu shown in Figure 2-14. Deleting a single snapshot will not affect other snapshots in the hierarchy; however, it will immediately delete the configuration file and save state files associated with the snapshot. Deleting a snapshot subtree immediately deletes the configuration and save state files associated with all the snapshots in the subtree.

Virtual Machine State

Virtual machine state can be changed through the Hyper-V Manager. Figure 2-15 shows the menu options that are available after you right-click a running virtual machine. The menu options will differ based on the state of a virtual machine. For example, if a virtual machine is in the Off or Saved state, the Start option will appear on the menu.

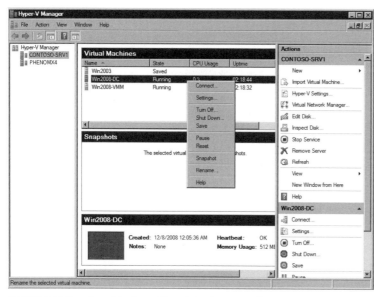

FIGURE 2-15 Running virtual machine state change options

The virtual machine state options that you can change through the Hyper-V Manager are:

- **Start**   Power on and boot a virtual machine
- **Turn Off**   Noncontrolled power-off of a virtual machine (equivalent to pulling the power cord on a physical computer)
- **Shut Down**   Controlled power-off of a virtual machine (requires Integration Services support)
- **Save**   Stop virtual machine processing and save the memory and processor state to file
- **Pause**   Suspend virtual machine processing
- **Resume**   Restart virtual machine processing after pausing it
- **Reset**   Noncontrolled restart of a virtual machine (equivalent to pushing the reset button on a physical computer)

Managing Virtual Machine Configurations

As shown in Figure 2-16, you can right-click a virtual machine and select Settings from the menu options to access the virtual machine settings in Hyper-V Manager.

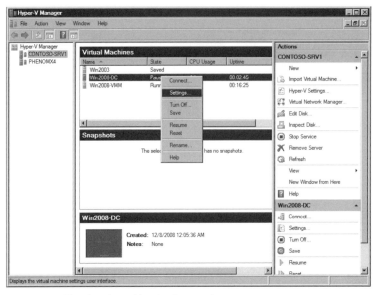

FIGURE 2-16 The virtual machine Settings option

Figure 2-17 shows an example of the virtual machine settings dialog box. The virtual machine hardware and management settings are displayed in the pane at left, divided by major component. The pane on the right displays the options that are available for each virtual machine hardware and management component.

FIGURE 2-17 An example of the virtual machine settings dialog box

Table 2-4 provides a list of virtual machine hardware configuration options and a description of the changes associated with each component.

TABLE 2-4 Virtual Machine Hardware Configuration Options

CONFIGURATION OPTION	DESCRIPTION
Add Hardware	Allows the addition of synthetic SCSI controllers, synthetic network adapters, and legacy (emulated) network adapters to a virtual machine.
BIOS	Allows the configuration of the Num Lock state (on or off), and the startup order of the devices (CD, IDE, legacy network adapter, floppy) at boot time.
Memory	Allows the specification of the virtual machine memory allocation.
Processor	Allows the specification of the virtual machine logical processor allocation, resource control, and processor functionality.
IDE Controller 0	Allows the addition of virtual hard drives or DVD drives attached to the virtual machine through IDE Controller 0.
Hard Drive	Allows the configuration of which virtual IDE or SCSI controller a hard drive is connected to and the position (location) where it is connected. Also provides access to the virtual hard drive management tools (compact, convert, expand, and so on), and allows the configuration of pass-through disks. Finally, allows removal of hard drives from the virtual machine.
IDE Controller 1	Allows the addition of virtual hard drives or DVD drives attached to the virtual machine through IDE Controller 1.
CD/DVD	Allows IDE-based CD/DVD drives to be attached to the virtual machine. The CD or DVD can be in the form of an ISO image or physical CD/DVD drive installed on the host. In addition, allows removal of CD/DVD drives from the virtual machine.
SCSI Controller	Allows the addition of virtual hard drives to the virtual machine that are connected using a SCSI Controller.
Legacy Network Adapter	Allows the addition, configuration, and removal of virtual network cards installed in the virtual machine. For each network adapter, you have options to specify the virtual network connection and whether the network adapter MAC address is assigned dynamically or statically. In addition, you can configure and enable virtual LAN (VLAN) identification.

CONFIGURATION OPTION	DESCRIPTION
Network Adapter	Allows the addition, configuration, and removal of synthetic network cards installed in the virtual machine. For each network adapter, you have options to specify the virtual network connection and whether the network adapter MAC address is assigned dynamically or statically. In addition, you can configure and enable virtual LAN (VLAN) identification.
COM 1 and Com 2 Ports	Allows for the connection of COM ports to or the disconnection of COM ports from the virtual machine. COM ports can connect to a named pipe on the local or remote computer.
Diskette Drive	Allows the virtual floppy disk drive to connect to an existing floppy disk image.

Table 2-5 provides a list of virtual machine management configuration options and a description of the changes that are associated with each component.

TABLE 2-5 Virtual Machine Management Configuration Options

CONFIGURATION OPTION	DESCRIPTION
Name	Allows the specification of a name for the virtual machine and a set of electronic notes about the virtual machine.
Integration Services	Allows the selection of the Integration Services components that Hyper-V will support for the virtual machine.
Snapshot File Location	Allows specification of the folder location used to store the snapshot files.
Automatic Start Action	Allows the configuration of the virtual machine start up action when the Hyper-V server starts. The action can be set to take no action, to start automatically if the virtual machine was running when the service stopped, or to always start the virtual machine automatically. In addition, there is an option to configure an automatic start delay to reduce resource contention between virtual machines.
Automatic Stop Action	Allows the configuration of the virtual machine stop action when the Hyper-V server shuts down. The action can be set to save the virtual machine state (saved state), turn off the virtual machine, or shut down the guest operating system. The Integrations Services component must be supported by the guest operating system.

Managing Virtual Hard Disks

The Hyper-V Manager allows you to create, inspect, and edit virtual hard disks and virtual floppy disks on the managed Hyper-V server. Just as a virtual hard disk is a single file representation of a physical hard disk, a virtual floppy disk is a single file representation of a physical floppy disk.

Creating Virtual Hard Disks

Virtual hard disk files are a main component of a virtual machine, encapsulating the guest operating system and application data. Within Hyper-V Manager, a virtual hard disk can be created separately from a virtual machine by clicking the New option in the Actions pane and selecting the Hard Disk option from the menu. Figure 2-18 shows the New Virtual Hard Disk Wizard that is launched. To create a virtual hard disk, you must define the virtual hard disk type (dynamically expanding, fixed size, or differencing), specify a name and storage location for the new VHD, and define the size of the new VHD. Optionally, you can specify to copy the contents of a physical disk to the new VHD.

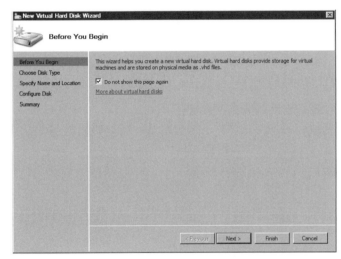

FIGURE 2-18 Creating a new virtual hard disk in Hyper-V Manager

> **NOTE** Details for each virtual hard disk type are provided in Chapter 3 and Chapter 5.

A virtual machine exposes a single virtual floppy drive to the guest operating system. A virtual machine does not allow the removal of the virtual floppy drive, nor does it support additional floppy drives to be connected. Hyper-V Manager allows only the creation of a 1.44-MB virtual floppy disk. The virtual floppy disk is created by clicking the New option in the Actions pane, selecting the Floppy Disk menu option, and then specifying the file name and storage location for the new virtual floppy disk.

Inspecting and Editing Virtual Hard Disks

If you select the Inspect Disk option in the Actions pane, Hyper-V Manager will prompt you to identify the targeted virtual hard disk. Hyper-V opens the virtual hard disk, obtains the current and maximum size settings as well as the virtual hard disk type, and displays the information, as shown in Figure 2-19.

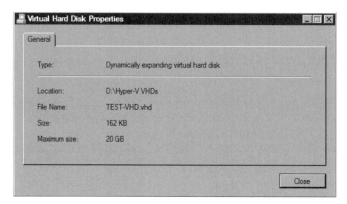

FIGURE 2-19 Inspecting a virtual hard disk in Hyper-V Manager

If you select the Edit Disk option in the Actions pane, Hyper-V Manager will launch the Edit Virtual Hard Disk Wizard shown in Figure 2-20.

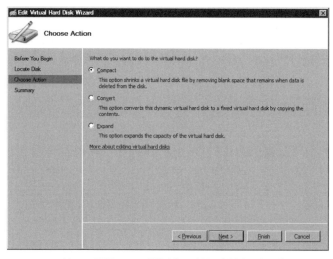

FIGURE 2-20 Hyper-V Manager Edit Virtual Hard Disk Wizard

After you select the targeted virtual hard disk and depending on the type of VHD that it is, a list of potential actions is displayed. Table 2-6 contains the list of potential actions that are available for each type of virtual hard disk.

TABLE 2-6 Virtual Hard Disk Edit Actions by VHD Type

ACTION	VHD TYPE	DESCRIPTION
Compact	Dynamically Expanding Differencing	Compact a dynamically expanding disk to re-gain unused space.
Convert	Dynamically Expanding Fixed Size	Convert a dynamically expanding disk to a fixed-size disk, or a fixed-size disk to a dynamically expanding disk.
Expand	Dynamically Expanding Fixed Size	Increase the storage size of the virtual hard disks.
Merge	Differencing	Merge the changes in a child disk into the parent disk or merge the parent and child disks into a new virtual hard disk.
Reconnect	Differencing	Reconnect a child differencing disk to a parent virtual hard disk.

Managing Virtual Networks

The Hyper-V Manager allows the creation, addition, and configuration of virtual networks on the managed Hyper-V server. Virtual networks allow virtual machines to connect to each other, the host, and other physical or virtual machines on a physical network.

Creating Virtual Networks

To create a new virtual network, click the Virtual Network Manager menu option in the Hyper-V Manager Actions pane. Hyper-V Manager launches the Virtual Network Manager shown in Figure 2-21.

To create a new virtual network, you must select one from the three types available: External, Internal, and Private. An external virtual network provides virtual machine connectivity to external physical networks. This type of virtual network must be bound to a physical network adapter installed in the Hyper-V server. An internal virtual network provides connectivity between virtual machines and the Hyper-V server but does not provide access to any physical networks. In other words, no packets from any attached virtual machines or the Hyper-V server are transmitted on a physical network. A private virtual network is even more restrictive than an internal one, as it provides connectivity only between virtual machines. There is no access to any physical networks or to the Hyper-V server.

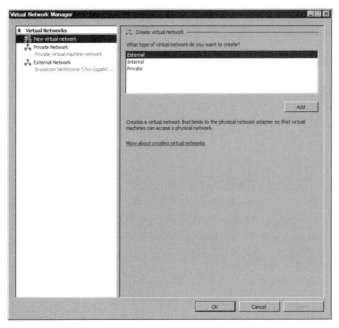

FIGURE 2-21 The Virtual Network Manager in Hyper-V Manager

If you choose to add a new External virtual network, you will have to specify a name for the new virtual network and select the physical network adapter to bind the virtual network. As shown in Figure 2-22, there is a drop-down menu in the New Virtual Network pane that allows you to choose the desired physical network adapter from the list of available adapters.

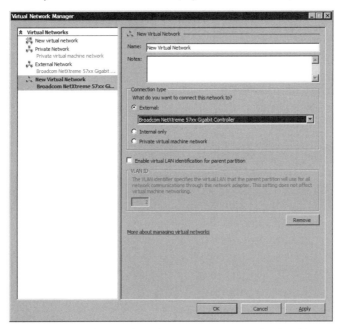

FIGURE 2-22 Virtual network configuration parameters in Virtual Network Manager

If you select a new Internal or Private virtual network, you would choose the Internal Only or Private Virtual Machine Network options in the Connection Type section, respectively.

If you select a new External or Internal virtual network, you can also choose to enable and configure a virtual LAN identifier (VLAN ID). A VLAN ID can be used to isolate the network traffic from different virtual machines connected to the same virtual network. Virtual machines with the same VLAN ID can communicate with each other but not with any other system configured with a different VLAN ID. VLANs are not supported for Private virtual networks.

Virtual Machine Connection Application

You can remotely access a virtual machine using the Virtual Machine Connection (VMC) application that is embedded in the Hyper-V Manager. As shown in Figure 2-23, to launch the VMC and connect to a virtual machine, double-click the thumbnail at the bottom of the Hyper-V Manager center pane or right-click the name of a virtual machine and select the Connect option from the shortcut menu.

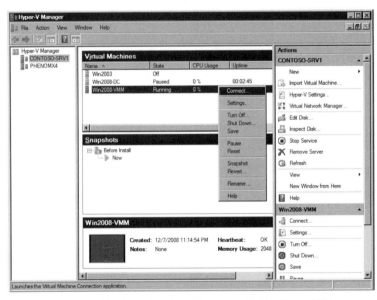

FIGURE 2-23 Connection to a virtual machine using VMC in Hyper-V Manager

VMC essentially frames a remote desktop session within a Hyper-V specific GUI and allows connection to a virtual machine for administrative or functional purposes. An example of a VMC is shown in Figure 2-24. The VMC GUI provides much of the functionality available in Hyper-V Manager to manage virtual machines. This includes providing actions to change the virtual machine state (e.g., Start, Turn Off, Save, and so on), access virtual machine settings, manage snapshots, manipulate the bindings of the virtual DVD and floppy disk drives to different media, and provide an option to install Integration Services.

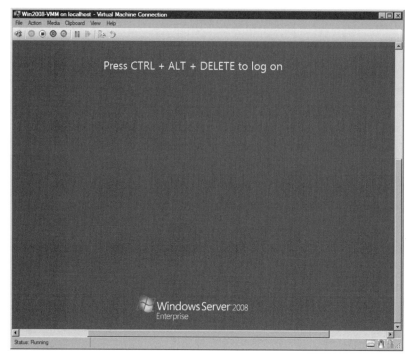

FIGURE 2-24 VMC view

The VMC allows client remote access and interaction with a virtual machine from the moment the virtual machine is powered on.

Managing Hyper-V Settings

The Hyper-V Manager also provides the ability to configure Hyper-V settings. Figure 2-25 shows the Hyper-V Settings dialog box that is displayed when you select the Hyper-V Settings option in the Actions pane menu.

There are two sets of Hyper-V settings that you can modify: Server and User. The Server settings allow you to specify the default folder location to store the virtual hard disk files and virtual machine configuration files. The User settings provide several options. The Keyboard component allows you to set the focus of Windows key combinations to either the physical server or a virtual machine. The Mouse Release Key provides you with a way to set the key combinations to use when Integration Services are not installed or supported in the guest operating system. The User Credentials allow you to specify whether the Virtual Machine Connection should automatically use your default credentials to connect to a running virtual machine. The Delete Saved Credentials component allows you to delete the credentials that you used to connect to a running virtual machine. Finally, the Reset Check Boxes feature allows you to restore default settings for Hyper-V confirmation messages and wizard pages hidden by selecting certain check boxes.

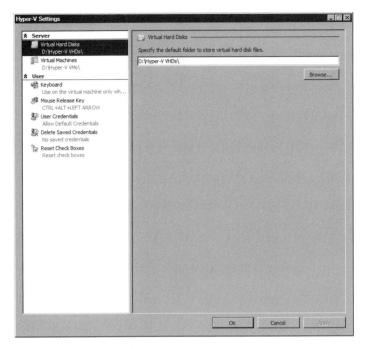

FIGURE 2-25 Hyper-V settings

Outlining the WMI API

Hyper-V provides an extensive and powerful WMI API that can be used to programmatically control and monitor Hyper-V as well as automate deployment and management of virtual machines. All of the features offered in Hyper-V Manager can be reproduced as scripts that leverage this development interface.

Scripts and self-developed applications can be created using a variety of languages, including C#, Perl, C++, or Visual Basic, to name just a few popular alternatives. Scripts can be executed using Microsoft Windows PowerShell, which provides you with the ability to run commands in a Windows Shell and immediately see the results.

> **NOTE** The Hyper-V WMI API is discussed in detail in Chapter 16, "Hyper-V Management Using Windows PowerShell." Chapter 16 contains many scripts that you can use or modify to use in your environment.

Summary

Hyper-V provides many features, including virtual machines that expose a standard virtual hardware environment to their guest operating system and applications. Becoming familiar with the virtual hardware environment and new synthetic device model in Hyper-V is crucial to making competent decisions concerning physical workloads that can successfully be redeployed as virtual machines.

Creation, inspection, and configuration of the main components of virtual machines, including virtual hard disks and virtual networks, can be accomplished through the Hyper-V Manager. You can also use the Hyper-V Manager to configure Hyper-V Settings.

Use the Virtual Machine Connection application from within Hyper-V (or as a stand-alone application) to access and manipulate virtual machines remotely from the moment they become active. If you anticipate having or already have a significant deployment of Hyper-V servers and virtual machines, leverage the WMI API to programmatically control the deployment, administration, and configuration of Hyper-V servers and virtual machines, or use System Center Virtual Machine Manager.

Additional Resources

The following resources contain additional information related to the topics in this chapter:

- Microsoft Technet Blog, "Can I run Hyper-V on my machine?" available at *http://blogs.technet.com/apawar/archive/2008/11/11/can-i-run-hyper-v-on-my-machine.aspx*

- Microsoft Technet Blog, Windows Virtualization Team Blog, available at *http://blogs.technet.com/virtualization/default.aspx*

- Microsoft Web site, "Virtualization with Hyper-V: Technical Resources," available at *http://www.microsoft.com/windowsserver2008/en/us/hyperv-technical-resources.aspx*

- Microsoft Web site, "Microsoft Hyper-V Server 2008 Configuration Guide," available at *http://www.microsoft.com/downloads/details.aspx?FamilyId=E1E111C9-FA69-4B4D-8963-1DD87804C04F&displaylang=en*

Hyper-V Architecture

Microsoft delivers Hyper-V in two forms: as a role in Windows Server 2008 or as a stand-alone product called Microsoft Hyper-V Server 2008. Windows Server 2008 can be installed with or without the Hyper-V role. Without Hyper-V, the operating system components and applications run directly on the underlying hardware. When Hyper-V is introduced, this behavior changes dramatically. Microsoft Hyper-V Server is a stand-alone product that enables machine virtualization based on technologies that are used in Windows Server 2008 and Hyper-V. Hyper-V Server has a very similar architecture to Hyper-V in Windows Server 2008; for example, it uses the same drivers that Windows does, which enables Windows Hyper-V Server to run on a wide variety of server hardware. This chapter describes the architecture of Hyper-V using the Hyper-V role in Windows Server 2008, but all discussions also apply to Microsoft Hyper-V Server 2008.

Windows Server 2008 Hyper-V role consists of a set of components that include a hypervisor (called the Windows hypervisor), kernel mode components, and user mode components. The Windows hypervisor was designed to be a microkernel-based type-1 hypervisor. This means that the Windows hypervisor runs directly on the hardware.

Processor rings define the privilege level of the instructions, with Ring 0 having the highest privilege, and Ring 3 having the lowest privilege. The kernel of an operating system runs in Ring 0, and user applications typically run in Ring 3. Ring −1 (minus one) was introduced with the hardware virtualization extensions that Intel and AMD made to their processor lines. This new ring allows the Windows hypervisor to run in its own context and at a privilege level higher than the Windows kernel, while allowing any Guest operating system kernel to remain running in processor Ring 0. User applications continue to run in processor Ring 3.

Figure 3-1 provides a graphical representation of the relationship between the user/kernel modes, the processor ring levels, and the components of Hyper-V. After the Hyper-V role is installed and the hypervisor loads, the hypervisor can create partitions. The root partition, called the parent partition, is the only partition created by default, and it contains the Windows Server 2008 operating system and drivers. There is a set of components installed with Hyper-V that provide management of partitions, hardware access, and programmatic interfaces.

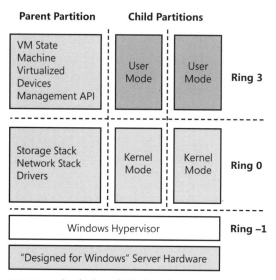

FIGURE 3-1 Stack view of Windows Server 2008 with the Hyper-V role enabled

Windows Hypervisor

The Windows hypervisor is a software interface that sits between the physical hardware and one or more operating systems. The Windows hypervisor controls access to a core set of hardware and defines isolated execution environments called partitions.

The primary tasks of the Windows hypervisor are to guarantee isolation between the partitions, enforce policy restrictions for hardware access, and monitor the partitions. The hypervisor maintains control over the set of hardware that allows it to guarantee isolation of each partition, while delegating access control to the remaining hardware to processes or drivers in the parent partition. The Windows hypervisor controls hardware like the advanced programmable interrupt controllers (APICs) for interrupt routing, physical processors for scheduled access to logical processors the virtual machines access, system counters, physical address space for controlling access to random access memory (RAM) and device memory, and other hardware. The parent partition controls RAM allocation, processor and system power management, PCI bus access, device access through device drivers, and so on.

A hypervisor must be simple and must perform its operations quickly and without interruption. One way that the Windows hypervisor achieves this is by not being pre-emptable. This is accomplished by disabling external interrupts and interprocessor interrupts while code is running within the hypervisor. Only system management interrupt (SMI) and nonmaskable interrupts (NMI) are allowed to occur while code is running in the hypervisor.

The Windows hypervisor is logically divided into two layers. The lower layer contains the microkernel that supports memory address space allocation, threads, signaling, and hardware abstraction mechanisms. The upper layer provides virtualization services interfaces using the hypercall Application Programming Interface (API). Virtualization services include the creation of partitions, virtual processors, and address translation.

DIRECT FROM THE SOURCE

Hypervisor Boot Process

Jim Collins, Senior Support Escalation Engineer
Windows Virtualization Support Team

You might wonder which gets loaded first, the hypervisor or Windows Server 2008. Windows Server 2008 boot loader boots the machine and loads a special driver called Hvboot.sys. Hvboot.sys performs the following steps to initialize the hypervisor:

- Detects whether a hypervisor is already loaded and, if so, aborts launching the hypervisor.

- Calls a platform detection routine to determine if the processor is an Intel processor or an AMD processor and if it has virtualization extensions. If the processor supports virtualization extensions, Hvboot.sys loads the hypervisor image that understands the architecture and virtualization extensions for the specific processor. The processor-specific hypervisor images are:

  - AMD-V: %SystemRoot%\System32\Hvax64.exe

  - Intel VT: %SystemRoot%\System32\Hvix64.exe

  - Invokes the hypervisor launch code on all processors known to the parent operating system to start the hypervisor.

- Initializes platform-specific per-processor structures and other hypervisor subsystems by using the processors' virtualization extensions. When these operations are completed, the hypervisor is fully initialized. A virtual processor is created for each physical processor and the parent operating system is isolated into the parent partition.

Control is returned to the parent operating system (in the parent partition) and the hypervisor is executing in de-privileged mode (Ring –1) at this point.

Partitions

Partitions are containers isolated from each other by the hypervisor. A partition consists of virtual memory address space, one or more virtual processors, worker processes, and communication interfaces. The virtual memory address space of a partition is mapped to the physical memory address space of the physical server. The number of virtual processors in a partition cannot exceed the number of hardware threads in the physical server.

A partition can be assigned or can obtain access to specific hardware resources (memory, devices, CPU cycles, and so on). Each partition has certain permissions and access right policy that is enforced by the Windows hypervisor.

There are two types of partitions in Hyper-V: parent and child. Hyper-V contains a single parent partition and one or more child partitions.

Parent Partition

The parent partition is the first partition that is created. Although it is technically a virtual machine, it has unique features. It owns all of the resources not owned by the hypervisor. It manages the creation and operations of the child partitions. It controls access to the resources and defines whether they can be shared by child partitions or is restricted to a single child partition. It is in charge of power management, plug and play, and hardware events. The parent partition is where all the device drivers for the physical hardware are loaded. Whereas a child partition sees the emulated or synthetic devices, the parent partition sees the real physical hardware.

Child Partition

Child partitions are software-based representations of physical hardware and are also referred to as virtual machines. Child partitions have no direct access to the real physical hardware of the server. All they see is virtual hardware and virtual devices presented to them. Each child partition sees the same exact base virtual hardware: motherboard, serial ports, video card, PCI bus, and so on. Additional virtual hardware can be "plugged into" the virtual motherboard. This hardware includes virtual network adapters, virtual SCSI adapters, virtual hard disks, virtual CD/DVD drives, and memory. Some of the virtual devices represent their physical counterparts in the physical world, and these are called emulated devices. Virtual devices that have no physical counterparts are called synthetic devices.

Figure 3-2 shows the relationship between the Windows hypervisor, the parent partition, and child partitions running different operating systems. The legend indicates which item provides which components.

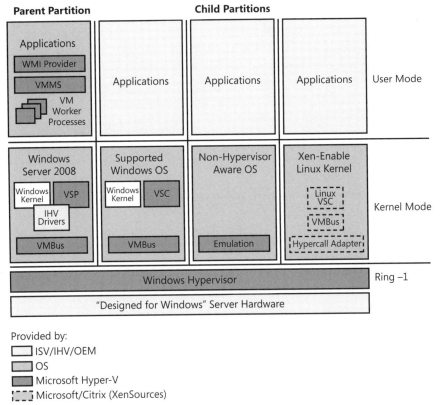

Parent Partition   **Child Partitions**

User Mode — Applications / WMI Provider / VMMS / VM Worker Processes / Applications / Applications / Applications

Kernel Mode — Windows Server 2008 (Windows Kernel, VSP, IHV Drivers, VMBus) / Supported Windows OS (Windows Kernel, VSC, VMBus) / Non-Hypervisor Aware OS (Emulation) / Xen-Enable Linux Kernel (Linux VSC, VMBus, Hypercall Adapter)

Ring −1 — Windows Hypervisor

"Designed for Windows" Server Hardware

Provided by:
- ISV/IHV/OEM
- OS
- Microsoft Hyper-V
- Microsoft/Citrix (XenSources)

FIGURE 3-2 Windows Server 2008 Hyper-V architecture stack view

Virtualization Stack

The Hyper-V virtualization stack is a collection of software components and virtual devices that work together to support the creation and management of virtual machines. The stack works in conjunction with the Hyper-V Management console and the hypervisor to provide the support. There are components of the stack that run in the parent and child partitions.

The virtualization stack includes the following major components. Some of the components are constructed of one or more subcomponents:

- Worker Processes
- Configuration Component
- Windows Management Instrumentation (WMI) Interfaces
- Virtual Machine Management Service (VMMS)
- Virtualization Service Provider (VSP)
- Virtualization Service Client (VSC)

- Virtualization Infrastructure Driver (VID)
- Virtualization Stack Memory Manager (VSMM)
- Virtual Machine Bus (VMBus)
- Emulated Devices
- Virtual Motherboard
- Integration Services

Figure 3-3 provides a view of the virtualization stack, including how the components are implemented in user or kernel mode and which components are implemented in the parent partition versus the child partition.

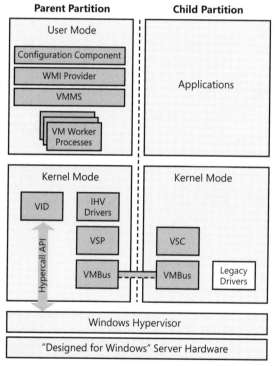

FIGURE 3-3 Virtualization stack

The following sections provide details on the virtualization stack components, what they do, and how they interact.

Virtual Machine Management Service

The Virtual Machine Management Service (VMMS) is a collection of components that work together to manage virtual machines. The VMMS is implemented as a single executable service module, VMMS.exe, under the name Hyper-V Virtual Machine Management.

The VMMS is responsible for providing the WMI virtual machine provider, managing virtual machines, managing worker processes, managing snapshots, providing the RDP listener for desktop redirection, registering and managing service connection points (SCP) in Active Directory, and providing the Volume Shadow Copy Service (VSS) writer interface for creating VSS snapshots of the parent partition and virtual machines.

Inside the VMMS are the following components:

- WMI Provider
- Virtual Machine Manager
- Worker Process Manager
- Snapshot Manager
- Single Port Listener for RDP
- Active Directory Service Marker
- VSS Writer
- Cluster Resource Control

Figure 3-4 provides a diagram that shows all of the subcomponents of the Virtual Machine Management Service.

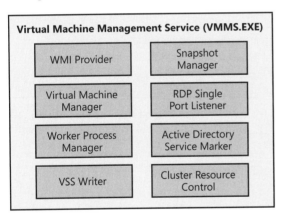

FIGURE 3-4 Virtual Machine Management Service component diagram

WMI Provider

The WMI Provider component allows remote management of virtual machines based on a defined object model. When the WMI provider receives a request to manage a virtual machine, it first determines if the virtual machine is running or offline. If the virtual machine is running, the WMI provider forwards the request to the worker process for the virtual machine. The worker process then forwards the request to the appropriate device or component and returns the result to the WMI provider to be returned to the calling application. If the virtual machine is offline, there is no worker process to forward the request to, so the VMMS handles the request itself. VMMS determines which device or component the request is for, loads the device or communicates with the component, and sends the request. When the response returns to the VMMS, it forwards it to the calling application.

> **MORE INFO** A link to the Virtualization WMI specification is provided in the "Additional Resources" section at the end of the chapter.

Virtual Machine Manager

The Virtual Machine Manager (VMM) maintains the list of virtual machines defined in Hyper-V, creates worker processes, manages the virtual machine configuration, and manages the addition or removal of devices. When the VMM launches, it builds the list of virtual machines registered on the Hyper-V server and maintains the state information as virtual machines are started, stopped, paused, or when their state is saved. If a virtual machine has an active worker process, all requests for changes to state, configuration, and devices are forwarded to the worker process. If the worker process does not exist, then the VMM handles the configuration change request or state change. Virtual Machine Manager works with the Worker Process Manager (WPM) to launch the worker processes that VMM creates.

For example, when a request is made to create a virtual machine, the VMM creates a default configuration for the virtual machine, manages any changes to that configuration before the virtual machine is started, and registers the newly created virtual machine in the list it maintains.

When a request is made to launch a virtual machine, the VMM searches the list of virtual machines, requests a new worker process be created, and then hands the worker process to the Worker Process Manager so that it can launch the worker process and monitor it.

When a request to stop a running virtual machine happens, the VMM searches its list for the virtual machine, finds the handle to the worker process, and then asks the worker process to stop the virtual machine.

Worker Process Manager

The Worker Process Manager (WPM) launches, maintains a list of all running work processes, and provides change notifications to subscribers on the state of the worker process. When WPM launches a new worker process, it adds the worker process to the list of running processes. After the worker process is started and registered in the list, WPM subscribes to change events for the worker process and allows internal components to subscribe to change notifications for the worker process. When changes in state (start, stop, pause, resume, and so on) or other events occur, WPM sends event notifications to all subscribers.

When the Worker Process Manager first starts, it contacts the Virtual Machine Manager and enumerates all of the registered virtual machines. From that point it maintains a list of any worker processes it starts and their current state. If the VMMS is restarted for some reason, WPM checks to see if any of the virtual machines already have a worker process, adds that virtual machine to the list of known worker processes, and subscribes for change events. When a state change occurs, the worker process list is updated (added or removed if required), and all subscribers are notified of the state change.

Snapshot Manager

Snapshots are allowed to occur when the virtual machine is offline or online. If the virtual machine is online, the worker process's state machine manages the snapshot process. For an offline machine, there is no worker process to manage the snapshot process, so the Snapshot Manager provides that functionality.

From a high level, the Snapshot Manager performs the following steps when a snapshot is requested for an offline virtual machine:

1. Creates a new differencing disk by using the current virtual hard disk as the parent
2. Creates a new snapshot configuration file and directory
3. Copies current VM configuration file to the snapshot configuration file
4. Copies the save state files (.vsv and .bin) to the snapshot configuration directory

Deleting a snapshot is a little more difficult because it involves investigating the differencing disk chain and dependencies, but from a high level the snapshot manager does the following when it receives a request to delete a snapshot and the virtual machine is offline:

1. Deletes the configuration file of the snapshot requested to be deleted
2. Deletes the snapshot save state files in the snapshot directory
3. Deletes the snapshot directory
4. Merges the current snapshot differencing disk if required

> **MORE INFO** More information on snapshots can be found in Chapter 5, "Hyper-V Advanced Features."

Single Port Listener for RDP

Remote Desktop Protocol (RDP) is the protocol that is used to send video, keyboard inputs, and mouse movements between a server and a client application. In Hyper-V, there are multiple components involved in a remote virtual machine management session over the RDP protocol on port 2179. The Single Port Listener (SPL) for RDP within VMMS manages the incoming connection requests from the virtual machine management client (Vmconnect. exe) and routes them to the appropriate worker process for handling. The worker process has a subcomponent called the RDP Encoder that accepts the connection and works with the input manager and the video monitor to provide the user experience over RDP for the virtual machine's console session.

Active Directory Service Marker

Active Directory Service Marker (ADSM) is a subcomponent of VMMS that provides registration and management of service connection points (SCP) in Active Directory. An SCP is an object published in Active Directory that allows clients to query for data that the service has published in the SCP. SCPs are stored in the global catalog, which makes them available across an Active Directory forest.

A service connection point is registered at installation of Hyper-V under the computer object. At every start of the Virtual Machine Management Service, the ADSM attempts to reregister the service connection point. If a valid Active Directory domain controller cannot be found within the timeout window, an error message will be written to the \Application and Services Log\Microsoft\Windows\Hyper-V VMMS\Admin event log with an event id of 14050.

Hyper-V does not require the SCP to be successfully registered to load or provide virtualization services. If an SCP record does not get successfully registered, a query of Active Directory will produce no results for that Hyper-V server.

The service connection point objects contain a multivalued item called *ServiceBindingInformation*. By default, ADSM registers the following binding information:

- ServiceBindingInformation[0] = the UNC for the server WMI connection
- ServiceBindingInformation[1] = the URL for the WS-Management connection
- ServiceBindingInformation[2] = the URL for the server RDP Connection
- ServiceBindingInformation[3] = the location of the AzMan store

VSS Writer

Volume Shadow Copy Service (VSS) uses three tiers of components to identify objects for backup, execute the backup operations, and restore previously backed-up objects:

- VSS Requestor gathers information about the objects and manages the process.
- VSS Framework is the interface between the VSS Requestor and the VSS Writer and also controls the snapshot process.
- VSS Writer performs specialized actions for the component it is designed for.

The VSS Requestor is the backup application that makes the request to perform the backup. In order to provide the best backup possible, it queries the parent partition to enumerate all the VSS writers that are registered on the system. The VSS requestor selects the appropriate VSS writers and queries them for all the components they support. The VSS Writer returns a metadata description of the component.

The Hyper-V VSS Writer treats each virtual machine as a separate component. A query by the VSS requestor to the Hyper-V VSS writer will return a metadata description of each VM separately. The metadata description tells the requestor what information it needs to back up to obtain a consistent backup. A virtual machine metadata description contains the following information:

- Virtual machine configuration files
- Snapshot files
- All virtual disk information (except pass-through disks)

The Hyper-V VSS writer can support online and offline backups of a virtual machine. In order to perform an online backup, the virtual machine must have the Hyper-V Integration

Services loaded so that the VSS Writer Integration Services service is installed and can be queried.

Cluster Resource Control

The cluster resource control is the interface in VMMS to the Vmclusres.dll user mode component that Windows 2008 Failover Clustering uses to create and manage a highly available virtual machine. The cluster resource control accepts commands to manage the state and the configuration of the virtual machine and passes them to the appropriate subcomponents or the worker process.

Configuration Component

The configuration component provides the creation, management, modification, and destruction of child partition configuration settings. Whenever a virtualization stack component needs to access a key-value pair from the virtual machine settings file, the request must be forwarded to the configuration component for processing. Configuration settings are stored in an XML file. By default, the configuration file is created at the root of the directory where the virtual machine is created and assigned the filename *GUID*.xml, where *GUID* is the Globally Unique Identifier of the child partition.

Virtualization Service Providers

Virtualization Service Providers (VSPs) are software components that run in the parent partition and handle input/output (I/O) requests on behalf of the virtual machines. VSPs provide the interface via the VMBus to Virtualization Service Clients (VSCs). VSPs also communicate to physical hardware, via the Windows driver stack or device driver, to handle I/O requests. They can exist in user or kernel mode and can be implemented as COM objects, services, or drivers. Each VSP communicates with one or more VSC using dedicated point-to-point channels. The parent partition contains a VSP for storage, video, network, and human interface devices. A single VSP can service multiple child partition VSCs using dedicated channels of communication over the VMBus.

DIRECT FROM THE SOURCE

Parent Partition Network I/O

Arno Mihm, Program Manager
Windows Virtualization Team

Although Virtualization Service Providers normally service only Virtualization Service Client I/O requests, a special case exists for the networking VSP and the parent partition. If a virtual network has been created and has been bound to a physical network adapter, by default the parent partition network I/O requests that are routed over that physical network adapter will communicate through the network VSP. To prevent parent partition network traffic from using that network adapter and therefore the parent partition from communicating through the network VSP, you can disable the parent partition Local Area Network connection to the physical network adapter under the Control Panel – Network Connections window.

Virtualization Service Clients

Virtualization Service Clients (VSCs) are synthetic drivers that run within the child partition and communicate across VMBus to corresponding Virtualization Service Providers in the parent partition. VSCs exist for networking, video, storage, and interface devices.

Virtualization Service Clients are installed when the Integration Services components are installed in a child partition. Until the VSCs are installed, the child partition sees emulated hardware and loads device drivers for those emulated devices if they exist.

VMBus

VMBus is a high-speed interpartition communications mechanism that is made up of multiple components or technologies:

- A protocol for transferring data between a child and parent partition
- A protocol for discovering or offering services to child partitions
- A protocol for managing guest physical addresses
- A bus driver that implements all of the protocols
- A data transfer library that provides user or kernel mode services

VMBus is designed to provide point-to-point communications between a child partition and a parent partition over a dedicated channel. Each VSP provides a separate channel for a child partition VSC. A single VSP can communicate with multiple VSCs.

The VMBus driver implements endpoints that allow reading and writing data through the VMBus. Channels consist of either two endpoints—one at the VSC and one at the VSP—or two ring buffers—one at the VSC and one at the VSP. Each channel also has a transfer page. A transfer page is a pre-allocated page of memory that is mapped into both partitions at the endpoints and is not part of a ring buffer. Transfer pages are used as a target for direct memory address (DMA) or other data transfer that might take a long time to complete. In order to facilitate DMA, a Guest Physical Address Descriptor List (GPADL) is used to provide a device in the parent partition direct memory address to or from the child partition. This is accomplished by the child partition placing Guest Physical Addresses pointing to data in the descriptor list and the parent partition using DMA to access the data.

Data is moved between partitions using different mechanisms:

- Commands are placed in ring buffers.

- Data that is small enough can be passed using ring buffers.
- Larger amounts of data use the transfer pages controlled by commands in the ring buffers.
- Data that is too large for transfer buffers uses GPADL addresses and DMA without copying the data.
- Packets are sent asynchronously over the VMBus.

The Windows hypervisor is involved in the VMBus channel setup between the child and parent partition and when signaling partitions are needed. Data transfer does not require hypervisor involvement.

Virtualization Infrastructure Driver (VID)

The Virtualization Infrastructure Driver (VID) is the parent partition kernel level interface to the Windows hypervisor using defined API interfaces called hypercalls. The VID provides services to the worker and administrative management interfaces running in user mode and communicates with the Windows hypervisor to coordinate execution of virtual machines.

The VID is implemented in two pieces: a kernel mode device driver, VID.sys, and a user mode client interface, VID.dll. The kernel mode driver contains a logical subcomponent called the Virtualization Stack Memory Manager (VSMM). The VID provides VSMM instruction completion services when a memory interrupt is received and the VSMM provides the VID interfaces to access child partition page tables and memory during instruction completion. Figure 3-5 shows the relationship between VID.dll and VID.sys.

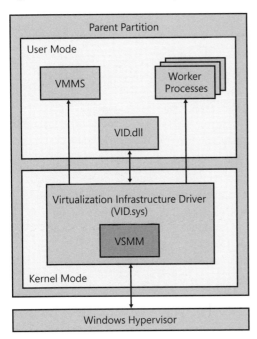

FIGURE 3-5 VID interface to the Windows hypervisor and user mode processes

The VID provides partition management, virtual processor management, memory management, and runtime support for virtualization services.

Partition Management

The VID provides the Virtual Machine Management Service (VMMS) and the worker processes provide the ability to create, delete, start, stop, save, restore, and manage partitions. The VID does not actually do any of these tasks but instead coordinates access to the hypervisor and other services for them to do the tasks. For example, when the worker process asks the VID to create a partition, the VID requests that the hypervisor create the child partition, the hypervisor creates the partition and returns a handle to the partition, and the VID then owns that handle and uses it to manage the partition.

During a partition save request, the VID saves the state of the running partition and all its virtual processors into a blob of data and returns that to the worker process. It is then the worker process's responsibility to store that blob to disk and to retrieve it and provide it back to the VID for restoration.

The VID also provides the ability to manage the CPU resource allocation settings for a single or multiple partitions that it owns. This includes modifying the partitions' relative weight, reservations, and maximum CPU usage. The VSMM is responsible for setting the limits on memory usage.

Virtual Processor Management

The VID provides the ability to manage the number of virtual processors assigned to a partition. During partition creation, the number of virtual processors is set to 1 by default. After it is created, the child partition must be in a powered-off state to change the number of virtual processors.

The VID also provides the ability to initialize, start, stop, provide state information, and handle interrupts to a partition. During initialization, the VID sets the CPUID information for each virtual processor. This allows CPUID interrupts to be handled without child partition involvement. The VID provides the ability to start and stop an individual virtual processor and notify the child partition when the action is completed. The VID provides the ability for the state machine in the worker process to read and write the state of the virtual processors that it owns while the virtual processor is in a suspended state. This includes all general purpose registers, control registers, floating point registers, segment registers, debug registers, and descriptor tables. This provides one part of the ability to save the state of the child partition.

Memory Management

The Virtualization Stack Memory Manager (VSMM) provides both user mode and kernel mode interfaces to provide child partition memory management. The user mode interface is an input/output control (IOCTL) API interface, and the kernel mode interface is a Plug and Play (PnP) Device Interface. VSMM interfaces with the Windows hypervisor through the hypercall API provided by the WINHV.sys kernel mode driver. VSMM interfaces with the worker processes using the IOCTL interface and with the VSPs using the kernel mode PnP device interface.

The VSMM receives notification from the Windows hypervisor when memory intercepts occur. VSMM then handles the memory intercept and notifies the Windows hypervisor that the intercept has been properly handled.

Runtime Support

The VID provides interrupt handling services (IN/OUT instructions) and instruction completion services to support the operation of partitions. The VID provides interrupt handling services by implementing internal handlers to receive intercepts from the Windows hypervisor. The VID handles guest processor exceptions, model specific register (MSR) access requests, and I/O port access requests. The VSMM handles all memory interrupt intercepts from the hypervisor. The VID provides instruction completion by acting as an external monitor and intercepting requests to access memory that have been marked by the hypervisor for intercept.

The VID provides the ability to parse x86 and x64 instructions and complete instructions that Windows hypervisor does not. In order for the VID to parse an instruction, it must be able to use its knowledge of the Guest page tables and the current guest physical address to system physical address mappings and access data in memory of the child partition directly. Or to state it more simply, the VID must be able to do direct memory access.

WMI Interfaces

Windows Management Instrumentation (WMI) interfaces exist to allow for the remote management and operations of Hyper-V. WMI interfaces consist of a WMI service, WMI clients, and WMI providers. The WMI Service (SVCHost.exe) provides the interface between the WMI clients and the WMI providers. The WMI clients are applications and components that need to consume data from the WMI providers or issue well-defined commands to the providers to accomplish a task. Figure 3-6 provides a high-level diagram that shows the WMI interfaces.

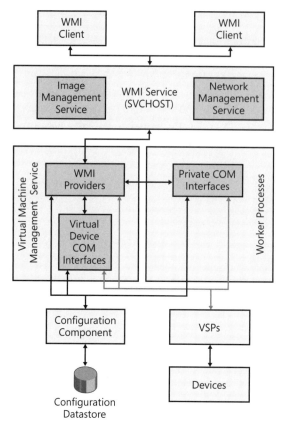

FIGURE 3-6 WMI interfaces

The Hyper-V Virtual Machine Management Service (VMMS) implements the primary WMI providers that allow the management of child partitions. The VMMS providers interface with COM objects in the virtual devices, worker processes, configuration component, and VSPs to manage the complete configuration and state.

Two special services have been implemented to provide WMI interfaces to manage storage and networking. The Hyper-V Image Management Service (IMS) provides the WMI interfaces to manage the virtual hard disks (VHD). Whereas the VMMS manages WMI interfaces for the connections of the VHDs to the virtual machines, the IMS provides the WMI interfaces for the management of the VHDs themselves (inspecting the disk, merging, and compacting). The Hyper-V Networking Management Service (NMS) provides the WMI interfaces to manage virtual networks and virtual switches. Whereas the VMMS manages WMI interfaces for the connections of the virtual network adapters in child partitions to the virtual networks, the NMS provides the WMI interfaces for the management of the virtual networks themselves (configuration, binding to physical network adapters, and VLAN settings). The IMS and the NMS are implemented as plug-in interfaces to the SVCHost.exe WMI Service.

The primary WMI client that comes with Hyper-V is the Hyper-V Manager MMC. It uses all the WMI interfaces to manage the virtual machines, the virtual storage, and the virtual networking.

Worker Process

A worker process is created for every virtual machine that is running or being configured. The job of the worker process is to manage the running state of the virtual machine, manage the configuration and state of the virtual machine and its devices, manage remote RDP sessions, and communicate with the integration services running in the child partition. To accomplish this, the worker process consists of a series of subcomponents that handle various aspects of these tasks:

- Virtual Motherboard
- Memory Manager
- Virtual Devices
- State Machine
- Virtual Devices Plug-in Interface
- Integration Services (core virtual device)
- RDP Encoder (core virtual device)

The worker process works with other external components of the virtualization stack to accomplish the required management tasks, as shown in Figure 3-7.

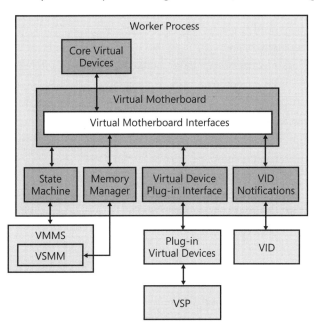

FIGURE 3-7 Worker process components and interfaces

Virtual Motherboard

The virtual motherboard provides the definition of the default motherboard virtual devices and interfaces, the ability to insert additional emulated or synthetic virtual devices, and BIOS management. The virtual motherboard is separated into two components. The first component maintains a manifest of all of the devices configured for the motherboard. The manifest is stored in a repository maintained by the worker process. The second component is a set of interfaces that provide memory access, virtual device plug-in and removal, I/O ports, interrupts, and timers. The interfaces component also communicates with the virtualization infrastructure driver via notifications.

By default, the virtual motherboard manifest contains all of the nonremovable core virtual devices and the BIOS, except for the synthetic video and mouse controllers, which are plug-in virtual devices that cannot be removed. Using the functions, additional virtual devices like virtual network cards or virtual SCSI cards can be "plugged in" to the virtual motherboard or removed from the virtual motherboard. The action of adding or removing a virtual device requires that the virtual machine be powered down. The plug-in virtual devices are implemented as synthetic devices that act as proxies to the Virtual Service Providers (VSP) for video, network, and storage.

Memory Manager

The memory manager is responsible for managing the memory resources for a virtual machine. The memory manager implements the memory management, and the virtual motherboard is responsible for exposing the interfaces to the memory manager to the virtual devices. The requests for memory management come to the virtual motherboard from virtual devices, and the virtual motherboard routes them to the memory manager. The memory manager then manages the multiple requests for memory and interfaces with the Virtualization Stack Memory Manager (VSMM) for the actual implementation of memory access and management.

The memory manager is responsible for allocating and de-allocating memory blocks and mapping subsections of memory blocks into the virtual machines' guest physical addresses (GPA). When a new worker process is created, the memory manager queries the configuration component for the amount of allocated RAM and calls the VID to create a memory block with the specified size. After the memory block has been allocated, the memory manager can create a GPA mapping for the entire memory block.

> **MORE INFO** Refer to the section titled "Virtual Memory" later in this chapter for a detailed discussion on guest physical addresses.

Core Virtual Devices

The worker process contains core virtual devices that provide endpoint interfaces for virtual motherboard functionality. These include BIOS, serial communication ports, IDE, integration services, RDP, timers, and others. The core virtual devices are created automatically when the worker process and virtual motherboard are created. Additional virtual devices are designed as plug-in DLLs so that they can be added when desired. These devices include the network adapter, legacy network adapter, and SCSI adapter. The plug-in virtual devices act as proxies for communications with the Virtualization Service Providers (VSPs).

State Machine

The state machine instantiates and manages the virtual machine, the state transitions, save and restore functionality, and snapshots. The state machine never communicates directly with the virtual devices; it always communicates through the virtual motherboard. All interfaces with the state machine are performed via the state management API using WMI.

Table 3-1 provides the valid states for a virtual machine and the description of each state.

TABLE 3-1 Virtual Machine States

STATE	DESCRIPTION
Not Active	Initial state when the worker process is created
Starting	State when the virtual machine is being powered on
Stopping	State when the virtual machine is being powered off
Paused	State when the virtual processors are not running
Running	State when the virtual machine has finished its Starting state initialization
Saving	State when the virtual machine is saving the state to disk
Snapshotting	State when the virtual machine is taking a snapshot of the virtual machine

Integration Components Virtual Device

The Integration Services core virtual devices provide the communication interface between the integration services running in the child partitions to the worker process via the VSPs running in the parent partition. The Integration Services core virtual devices are implemented as DLLs and include heartbeat (Vmicheartbeat.dll), time synchronization (Vmictimesync.dll), key-value pair exchange (Vmickvpexchange.dll), shutdown (Vmicshutdown.dll), and VSS integration (Vmicvss.dll). All communications between the child partition and the VSP are transmitted over the VMBus.

RDP Encoder Virtual Device

The RDP Encoder is a core virtual device that is responsible for creating and enumerating remote RDP connections, managing the data flow between the RDP components and the virtual machine, and encoding the video, mouse, and keyboard into a single RDP data stream. The RDP encoder accomplishes this by providing the connection establishment interface to an RDP client through the VMMS Single Port Listener for RDP, communicating with the video VSP for video data, and communicating with the input VSP for the keyboard and mouse data.

Virtualization Stack in Action

We have discussed the major components and subcomponents of the Hyper-V architecture and explained what each one does. Now we can demonstrate how they all work together to complete a task like powering on a virtual machine defined in the Hyper-V MMC interface. Figure 3-8 provides a flow diagram of the virtual machine boot process.

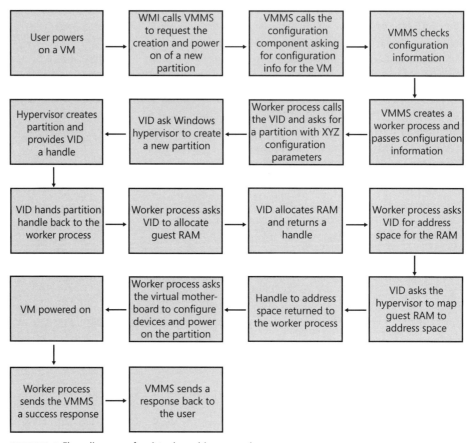

FIGURE 3-8 Flow diagram of a virtual machine powering on

Virtual Devices

Virtual devices can be of two types: emulation and synthetic. Device emulation allows the virtual machine to see virtualized physical hardware. That means that the device driver providing the emulation interacts in most cases the same way it would with the physical counterpart. So an emulated device can provide near or perfect compatibility with existing software. Selection of which device to emulate is typically driven by a common denominator across all the operating system versions that you want to support. Emulated devices require the parent partition to provide a "monitor" to intercept requests for direct hardware access and redirect them to the correct location. Synthetic virtual devices do not attempt to emulate physical hardware but instead provide device capabilities that can be optimized for a virtual environment.

Virtual Memory

Let's start with the basics in our discussion of virtual memory. A physical computer has physical memory and virtual memory. The physical memory has a defined number of address blocks based on the amount of physical memory in the computer. The computer maintains a set of addresses to each block that allow programs to find each block. Virtual memory allows the computer to have more addresses—a larger address space—than it has physical memory. The operating system kernel maintains a mapping between the virtual memory address space and the physical memory address space. This is typically done in chunks called memory pages. Because the physical memory address space is smaller than the physical memory space, pages of virtual memory must be mapped to physical memory pages and swapped in and out when needed. Any virtual pages that do not have a current mapping to a physical page must be stored somewhere else, typically on a hard disk. This is called paging, and most operating systems use a page file for this storage. Figure 3-9 shows a representation of this concept.

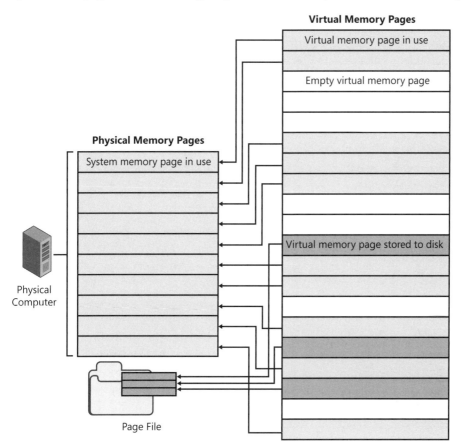

FIGURE 3-9 Physical memory to virtual memory mapping

Virtualization complicates the mapping between physical and virtual memory address spaces because each guest assumes it is running on a physical computer with a physical address space and the operating system running in the guest assumes there is a virtual address space. To address this, the Windows hypervisor architecture defines three independent memory address spaces:

- System physical addresses (SPAs)
- Guest physical addresses (GPAs)
- Guest virtual addresses (GVAs)

System physical addresses are the physical memory address space of the physical computer. There is only one SPA for the Hyper-V server computer. Guest physical addresses are the physical memory address space of the child partition. Each child partition has a single GPA just like every physical computer has a single SPA. To the child partition, the GPA is the equivalent of the SPA. Inside each child partition, there is a virtual address space referred to as the guest virtual address space. This is used just like a physical machine to provide a virtual address space that is much larger than the physical amount of memory, and pages of memory that are not mapped to a GPA location are paged to disk.

The parent partition is treated as a special child partition in that it owns the physical system memory. Although the parent partition can page its virtual memory pages out to disk, the child partitions cannot page to disk. Figure 3-10 shows a representation of how the SPA, GPA, and GVA relate to each other.

Windows Server 2008 Hyper-V uses only available physical memory to load and run virtual machines. The amount of RAM configured and used by a virtual machine is defined at creation and stored in the virtual machine settings. The Windows hypervisor performs the allocation from physical RAM when the virtual machine is powered on, and the amount of virtual machine system RAM cannot be modified while the virtual machine is running. Hyper-V does not allow page sharing between virtual machines.

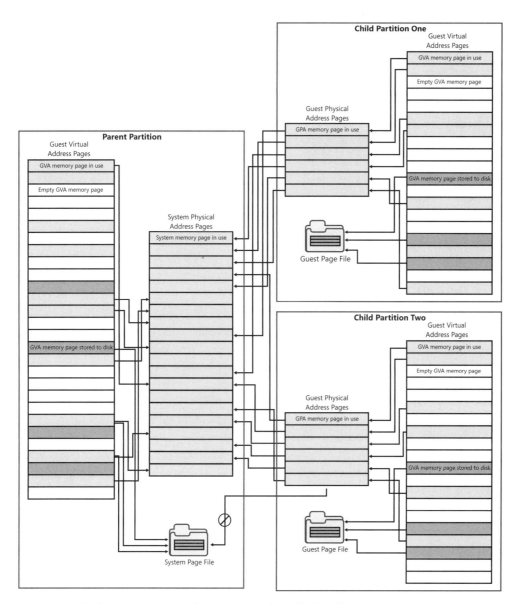

FIGURE 3-10 Physical memory to virtual memory mapping with virtualization

Virtual Processors

Prior to the introduction of hardware virtualization support in the Intel and AMD processor line, the x86-processor architecture was hard to virtualize because it has poor privileged and user state separation, and some instructions that access privileged state were nontrappable. Although emulation was possible, the overhead associated with complete emulation was not acceptable. Virtual Server 2005 R2 SP1 used a combination of direct execution and emulation to obtain the best performance, with direct execution as the preferred execution method.

Today the physical computer has physical processors that can contain one or more logical processors called cores or hyperthreads. Windows hypervisor creates one virtual processor in the parent partition for every logical processor that exists in physical hardware at boot time. Unlike virtual processors within child partitions, the virtual processors within the parent partition have hard affinities, or are bound, to the specific physical processor cores they represent. The parent and child partitions will always have one or more virtual processors.

Virtual processors can be in one of four states:

- **RUNNING**   Currently consuming processor cycles of a logical processor
- **READY**   Ready to consume processor cycles, but other virtual processors are running
- **WAITING**   Put on hold by the hypervisor scheduler for various reasons
- **SUSPENDED**   Stopped on a guest instruction boundary

Child partition virtual processors that are currently executing threads are in the RUNNING state. Child partition virtual processors that currently have running processes that need processor cycles and in which the child has not exceeded its threshold boundary for virtual processor cycles are in the READY state. Child partition virtual processors that have no current running processes, have running processes but have exceeded their threshold boundary for virtual processor cycles, or are put on hold by the Windows hypervisor scheduler are in the WAITING state. Child partition virtual processors that were running but have been stopped by the hypervisor to process an instruction that requires support from other virtualization stack components are in the SUSPENDED state. Child partition virtual processors can be explicitly or implicitly suspended.

Virtual Networking

Virtual networking in Hyper-V provides the ability for the parent and child partitions to build virtual networks that can either be isolated within the physical system or take advantage of installed physical network adapters to connect to an external/physical network. This requires components in both the parent and child partitions. Figure 3-11 shows the components and how they interact.

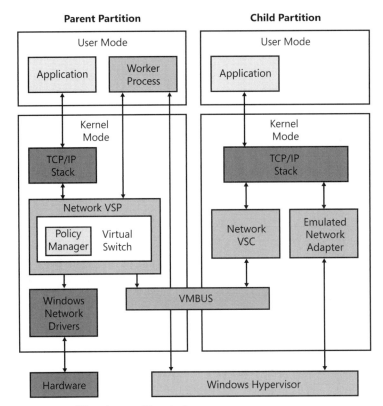

FIGURE 3-11 Virtual networking stack

The networking VSP component consists of two pieces: the virtual switch and the policy manager. The virtual switch is a multiport Layer 2 network switch implemented in software. The policy manager controls who can create and delete virtual switches and ports in addition to who can access what port on the virtual switch.

Each child partition implements two possible interfaces to the virtual switch. The first is a network VSC that implements synthetic network adapter drivers and communicates over VMBus to the parent partition. The second is an emulated network adapter card that does not communicate over the VMBus.

There are three types of virtual networks available in Hyper-V:

- **External** The virtual switch is bound to a physical network adapter, connected to the parent network stack, and potentially connected to a child partition.

- **Internal** The virtual switch is connected to the parent partition networking stack in a loopback mode and is potentially connected to a child partition.

- **Private** The virtual switch has no connection to the parent partition networking stack and is potentially connected to a child partition.

Virtual Switch

The virtual switch is implemented as a Layer 2 switch based on the 802.1D standard using a NDIS intermediate MUX driver. The virtual switch provides routing based on MAC address or VLAN tag ids as defined in the 802.1Q standard. Each switch can have an unlimited number of ports, and the ports can be dynamically added and removed from a switch. The virtual switch also provides TCP/IP checksum and large segment offloading support.

The virtual switch requires the ability to modify MAC addresses so that it can transport packets with different MAC addresses than its own. This allows the virtual switch to bind to any physical 802.3 Ethernet network adapter. The virtual switch cannot bind to 802.11 wireless adapters because the 802.11 standard does not support sending packets with source MAC address different than its own MAC address.

Virtual Network Adapter

The child partition requires a network adapter to communicate outside the partition. There are two types of adapters available for a child partition: synthetic and emulated (also called legacy). The synthetic network adapter is what is implemented as a VSC and is installed when you install the integration services in a guest operating system. The emulated adapter can be installed with or without the integration services installed in the guest operating system.

One difference between emulated network adapters and synthetic adapters is that the synthetic adapter does not exist until the guest operating system is booted and dependent services like the VMBus are loaded. This means that a synthetic network adapter cannot support PXE boot. The emulated network adapter does not have dependencies on VMBus.

Child Partition Integration Services

Integration Services are software components that may be installed within selected guest operating systems running in child partitions. Integration services also provide the components that allow child partitions to communicate with other partitions through the Virtualization Services Providers via the VMBus.

Integration Services are packaged in the following mountable .ISO file on the parent partition on a Windows Server 2008 server with the Hyper-V server role:

%SystemRoot%\System32\VMGuest.iso

When Integration Services are installed in supported guest operating systems, the system components listed in Table 3-2 are installed and configured. The components may be viewed in Device Manager by looking under the appropriate device node and finding the device name. Table 3-2 lists the drivers that should be installed under each device.

TABLE 3-2 Integration Services Components

DEVICE	DEVICE NAME	INTEGRATION SERVICES
Display Adapter	Microsoft VMBus Video Device	C:\Windows\system32\drivers\VMBusVideoM.sys C:\Windows\system32\VMBusVideoD.dll
Human Interface Devices	Microsoft VMBus HID Miniport	C:\Windows\system32\drivers\hidclass.sys C:\Windows\system32\drivers\hidparse.sys C:\Windows\system32\drivers\hidusb.sys C:\Windows\system32\drivers\VMBusHID.sys
Network Adapters	Microsoft VMBus Network Adapter	For Windows Server 2008 and Windows Vista SP1: C:\Windows\system32\drivers\netvsc60.sys For Windows Server 2003 SP2 and Windows XP SP2 and SP3: C:\Windows\system32\drivers\netvsc50.sys
Storage Controllers	Storage miniport driver	C:\Windows\system32\drivers\storvsc.sys
System Devices	Disk VMBUS Acceleration Filter Driver	C:\Windows\system32\drivers\storflt.sys C:\Windows\system32\VmdCoinstall.dll
	Microsoft Emulated S3 Device Cap	C:\Windows\system32\s3cap.sys
	VMBus	C:\Windows\system32\drivers\vmbus.sys C:\Windows\system32\drivers\winhv.sys C:\Windows\system32\vmbuspipe.dll

The components in Table 3-3 are also installed with Integration Services as system services, and they are implemented in Vmicsvc.exe. After installing the Integration Services, the services are registered and configured to autostart. Table 3-3 lists the required files for each service.

TABLE 3-3 Integration Services System Services

SERVICE NAME	INTEGRATION SERVICES
Hyper-V Data Exchange Service	C:\Windows\system32\IcCoinstall.dll C:\Windows\system32\vmicsvc.exe
Hyper-V Guest Shutdown Service	C:\Windows\system32\IcCoinstall.dll C:\Windows\system32wmicsvc.exe
Hyper-V Heartbeat Service	C:\Windows\system32\IcCoinstall.dll C:\Windows\system32\vmicsvc.exe

SERVICE NAME	INTEGRATION SERVICES
Hyper-V Time Synchronization Service	C:\Windows\system32\lcCoinstall.dll
	C:\Windows\system32\vmicsvc.exe
	C:\Windows\system32\vmictimeprovider.dll
Hyper-V Volume Shadow Copy Service	C:\Windows\system32\lcCoinstall.dll
	C:\Windows\system32\vmicsvc.exe

The configuration for these services is defined in the registry keys listed in Table 3-4.

TABLE 3-4 System Services Configuration Registry Location

SERVICE NAME	REGISTRY KEY
Hyper-V Data Exchange Service	HKEY_LOCAL_MACHINE\System\CurrentControlSet\Services\Vmickvpexchange
Hyper-V Guest Shutdown Service	HKEY_LOCAL_MACHINE\System\CurrentControlSet\Services\Vmicshutdown
Hyper-V Heartbeat Service	HKEY_LOCAL_MACHINE\System\CurrentControlSet\Services\Vmicheartbeat
Hyper-V Time Synchronization Service	HKEY_LOCAL_MACHINE\System\CurrentControlSet\Services\Vmictimesync
Hyper-V Volume Shadow Copy Service	HKEY_LOCAL_MACHINE\System\CurrentControlSet\Services\Vmicvss

Virtual Hard Disks

Virtual machines require the same basic hardware that physical machines need to boot and operate: a motherboard, BIOS, memory, network adapter, keyboard, mouse, display, and a hard disk. Hyper-V architecture ensures that virtual machines have the highest portability possible. One portability design challenge was how to make a virtual machine hard disk accessible and portable while also providing acceptable performance. Microsoft addressed this issue with the concept of a virtual hard disk (VHD). VHDs are single-file representations of a physical hard disk that are stored in a file on a physical machine's hard disk. Because they are self-contained single files, they are easy to migrate from one system to another.

There are five types of virtual hard disks:

- Fixed hard disk
- Dynamically expanding hard disk
- Differencing hard disk
- Undo hard disk (not used by Hyper-V)
- Automatic virtual hard disk

A fixed virtual hard disk is one for which the disk size on the server's physical disk is pre-allocated based on the size of the drive specified at creation. When creating a 100-gigabyte (GB) fixed virtual hard disk, for example, Hyper-V will immediately allocate all 100 GB of data block storage and the additional overhead for the disk headers and footers.

A dynamically expanding virtual hard disk is one for which the initial size of the virtual hard disk contains no data blocks and which will grow as data blocks are allocated, up to the maximum size of the specified virtual hard disk.

Differencing virtual hard disks are special versions of a dynamically expanding virtual hard disk and differ primarily by disk header content.

Automatic virtual hard disks (.avhd) are differencing disks that are automatically created when a snapshot is taken of a virtual machine.

VHDs can be stored on locally attached physical hard disks or any volume presented to the parent partition. Any disk that stores a VHD must be formatted with the NTFS file system to provide the security access controls required.

Pass-Through Disks

Pass-through disks are a new feature of Windows Server 2008 Hyper-V. Pass-through disks are virtual hard disks that are not stored as a single file representation. Instead of creating a VHD file, pass-through disks use offline volumes attached to the parent partition. Pass-through disks can be used as system or data volumes in a child partition. When used as a system volume, pass-though disks allow the child partition to boot directly from the pass-though disk. The underlying concept of the pass-through disk is fully transparent to the VM itself.

The volume used for a pass-through disk can be a locally attached disk, an iSCSI Logical Unit Number (LUN) connected to the parent partition, or a Storage Area Network (SAN) LUN connected to the parent partition. In the parent partition, the volume that will be used must be offline and not used by the parent partition.

> **MORE INFO** For more information on pass-through disks, refer to Chapter 5.

How Is a Virtual Hard Disk Structured?

Virtual hard disks share a basic structure, as shown in Figure 3-12. Each virtual hard disk file contains a hard disk footer, a block allocation table (BAT), the actual data blocks, and an optional disk header that varies for each virtual hard disk drive type. Data blocks are 2 megabytes (MB) in size and contain 4096 × 512 byte sectors. A copy of the hard disk footer is maintained in the beginning of the file for redundancy purposes.

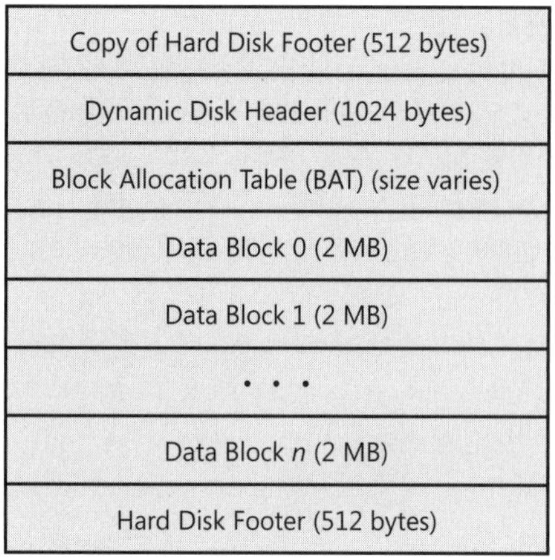

FIGURE 3-12 Virtual hard disk structure

NOTE The complete Virtual Hard Disk Image Format Specification can be downloaded from Microsoft's Web site at *http://www.microsoft.com/downloads /details.aspx?FamilyID=c2d03242-2ffb-48ef-a211-f0c44741109e&DisplayLang=en.*

HARD DISK FOOTER DEFINITION

The hard disk footer contains the information that defines the size, type, geometry, and features defined in the virtual hard disk. Table 3-5 provides the specification of the field information and size for the 512-byte hard disk footer. The disk footer format is consistent across all the virtual hard disk types.

TABLE 3-5 Hard Disk Footer Specification

FIELD NAME	SIZE (BYTES)	DESCRIPTION
Cookie	8	Used to identify the original creator of the virtual hard disk and is set to "connectix" by default.
Features	4	Used to indicate specific feature support within the virtual hard disk.
File Format Version	4	File specification version of the virtual hard disk file.
Data Offset	8	Contains the absolute byte offset, from the beginning of the file, to the next disk header structure. This field is used for dynamic disks and differencing disks, but not fixed disks. For fixed disks, this field is set to 0xFFFFFFFF.

FIELD NAME	SIZE (BYTES)	DESCRIPTION
Time Stamp	4	Stores the original creation time of the virtual hard disk file. It is stored as the number of seconds since January 1, 2000, 12:00:00 AM in UTC/GMT.
Creator Application	4	Used to document which application created the virtual hard disk file. It is set to "vs" if the virtual server created the file and "vpc" if Virtual PC created the file.
Creator Version	4	Major/minor version of the application that created the virtual hard disk file.
Creator Host OS	4	Contains a value that indicates the host operating system that created the virtual hard disk file. It is set to "Wi2k" (0x5769326B in hexadecimal) for Windows.
Original Size	8	Size of the virtual hard disk in bytes specified at creation.
Current Size	8	Current size of the virtual hard disk in bytes.
Disk Geometry	4	Value that contains the cylinder, heads, and sectors per track for the hard disk. It is stored as 2 bytes for the cylinder, 1 byte for the heads, and 1 byte for sectors per track.
Disk Type	4	Defines the type of disk this virtual hard disk file contains (fixed, dynamic, or differencing).
Checksum	4	Checksum of the hard disk footer using ones' complement algorithm.
Unique Id	16	128-bit universally unique identifier (UUID) used by a differencing virtual hard disk header.
Saved State	1	Flag that indicates if the virtual machine is in a saved state.
Reserved	427	Reserved fields are currently not used and contain zeros.

NOTE   You can use a HEX file editor to open a VHD file and walk the fields in the disk footer to verify the definition.

DYNAMIC DISK HEADER DEFINITION

The Data Offset field in the hard disk footer points to an additional disk header that specifies the information needed to define a dynamic or differencing disk. The header provides the details of the dynamic disk layout and the data it references. For a differencing disk, the header provides the location of the parent virtual hard disk in the form of a locator entry. Table 3-6 provides the definition of the dynamic disk header.

TABLE 3-6 Dynamic Disk Header Definition

DYNAMIC DISK HEADER FIELDS	SIZE (BYTES)	DESCRIPTION
Cookie	8	Identifies the header, and holds the value "cxsparse" by default.
Data Offset	8	Contains the absolute byte offset to the next structure in the hard disk image. It is currently unused by existing formats and should be set to 0xFFFFFFFF.
Table Offset	8	Stores the absolute byte offset of the BAT in the file.
Header Version	4	Stores the version of the dynamic disk header. Currently, this field must be initialized to 0x00010000.
Max Table Entries	4	The maximum number of entries present in the BAT. This should be equal to the number of blocks in the disk (disk size divided by the block size).
Block Size	4	A block is a unit of expansion for dynamic and differencing hard disks stored in bytes, and it represents only the data section block size. The sectors per block must always be a power of two. The default value of 2 MB is 0x00200000.
Checksum	4	Holds a basic checksum of the dynamic header. The checksum value is a ones' complement of the sum of all the bytes in the header without the checksum field.
Parent Unique ID	16	Used for differencing hard disks. A differencing hard disk stores a 128-bit UUID of the parent hard disk.
Parent Time Stamp	4	This field stores the modification time stamp of the parent hard disk. This is the number of seconds since January 1, 2000, 12:00:00 AM in UTC/GMT.

DYNAMIC DISK HEADER FIELDS	SIZE (BYTES)	DESCRIPTION
Reserved	4	Not used, and should be set to zeros.
Parent Unicode Name	512	Contains a Unicode string (UTF-16) of the parent hard disk filename.
Parent Locator Entry 1	24	Each Parent Locator Entry stores an absolute byte offset in the file where the parent locator for a differencing hard disk is stored. This field is used only for differencing disks and should be set to zero for dynamic disks.
Parent Locator Entry 2	24	
Parent Locator Entry 3	24	
Parent Locator Entry 4	24	
Parent Locator Entry 5	24	
Parent Locator Entry 6	24	
Parent Locator Entry 7	24	
Parent Locator Entry 8	24	
Reserved	256	Currently unused and must be set to zeros.

BLOCK ALLOCATION TABLE

The block allocation table (BAT) is a table of absolute sector offsets to the data blocks in the virtual hard disk. The size of the BAT is determined during the creation of the virtual hard disk. Each data block entry is 2 MB in size, and each BAT entry is 4 bytes in size. Each data block consists of a sector bitmap and data. The sector bitmap usage depends on whether the VHD is for a dynamic or differencing disk.

For a dynamic disk, each sector bitmap value indicates which sectors contain valid data. If a sector contains valid data, the corresponding location on the sector bitmap contains a value of "1". If a sector contains no data, the sector bitmap location will contain a "0". For a differencing disk, the sector bitmap value indicates which sectors contain data in the differencing disk (1) versus data in the parent disk (0).

Virtual Floppy Disks

Virtual floppy disks are single-file representations of physical floppy disks. Hyper-V reads and writes to 1.44-MB and 720-KB virtual floppy disk images, but it will create only 1.44-MB virtual floppy disk images. A physical 1.44-MB floppy disk has two sides of 80 tracks, with 18 sectors per track and 512 bytes per sector for a total of 1,474,560 bytes per disk. A virtual floppy disk format is the same as that of a physical floppy disk, but it maps the two sides of the physical floppy disk into a single flat file representation.

Each virtual machine has a single floppy drive available in the virtual hardware. At any one time, a single virtual floppy disk image can be attached to the virtual floppy disk drive. Unlike

Virtual Server 2005 R2, Hyper-V does not allow you to mount a physical floppy disk to the virtual floppy disk drive; only virtual floppy disk images are supported.

> **NOTE**   Hyper-V does not provide a way to access the contents of a virtual floppy image (.vfd) file unless it is attached to a running virtual machine. There are third-party applications that can mount a .vfd file and allow read and write access without attaching a virtual floppy image file to a virtual machine.

Summary

Windows Server 2008 Hyper-V provides a microkernel-based hypervisor that runs directly on the hardware. Hyper-V consists of multiple components that include the Windows hypervisor, user mode components, and kernel mode components. These components work in conjunction to allow the creation and management of child partitions, or virtual machines. User mode components such as worker processes, virtual machine management services, and WMI interfaces allow the Hyper-V MMC and other applications using the WMI APIs to remotely manage the Hyper-V server settings and the virtual machines running on the server. Kernel mode components such as the virtualization service providers, virtual machine bus services, and the virtualization infrastructure driver provide services to the user mode components, allow the child partitions to access the hardware, and implement the policy that the Windows hypervisor sets.

Additional Resources

The following resources contain additional information related to this chapter.

- Virtual Hard Disk Image Format Specification available at *http://www.microsoft.com /windowsserversystem/virtualserver/techinfo/vhdspec.mspx*
- Hypervisor Functional Specification available at *http://www.microsoft.com/downloads /details.aspx?FamilyID=91E2E518-C62C-4FF2-8E50-3A37EA4100F5&displaylang=en*
- Virtualization WMI Provider and class definition in MSDN available at *http://msdn2.microsoft.com/en-us/library/cc136992(VS.85).aspx*
- Publishing Service Connection Points (SCP) available at *http://msdn2.microsoft.com /en-us/library/ms677638(VS.85).aspx*

Understanding Windows Server 2008 Hyper-V

Hyper-V Installation and Configuration

The previous chapters explained the hypervisor, the Hyper-V architecture, and an overview of the Hyper-V product. Now it is time to install it and see what it can do. This chapter will explain the prerequisites and installation options for installing the Hyper-V role on Windows Server 2008 and for installing Microsoft Hyper-V Server 2008. The chapter provides step-by-step installation procedures for each option, and we'll also discuss additional post-installation configuration steps that should be done to prepare the Hyper-V server for your environment.

Installation Overview

Windows Server 2008 can be installed with either a full graphical interface (default installation option) or just a command-line interface (Server Core installation option). The Hyper-V role can be installed using either Windows Server 2008 installation option.

Hyper-V is available only in 64-bit editions of Windows Server 2008 Standard, Windows Server 2008 Enterprise, and Windows Server 2008 Datacenter. Microsoft Hyper-V Server 2008 is available only as a 64-bit version. The Hyper-V role will not install on 32-bit (x86) editions of Windows Server 2008 or Windows Server 2008 for Itanium-based systems. The Hyper-V Manager MMC can be installed on all x32 and x64 versions of

Windows Server 2008 except for Itanium. In addition, the Hyper-V Manager MMC can be installed on Windows Vista SP1 or later.

Before installing the Hyper-V role, you must decide which installation option to use for Windows Server 2008—Server Full or Server Core. Windows Server 2008 Server Full allows Hyper-V to be managed directly from the server using a graphical user interface (GUI). Server Core provides less overhead and better performance but requires all Hyper-V management to occur over the network.

Installation Prerequisites

Before you can install Hyper-V, you must complete some prerequisite tasks that help streamline the process. Windows Server 2008 with the Hyper-V role or Microsoft Hyper-V Server 2008 requires the correct hardware and BIOS settings to ensure that the hypervisor will start. Hyper-V requires server hardware that supports 64-bit processor instructions and hardware-assisted virtualization technology in the processor of the server. This is available in processors with Intel Virtualization Technology (Intel VT) or AMD Virtualization (AMD-V) technology. In addition, Hyper-V requires that hardware-enforced Data Execution Prevention (DEP) be available and enabled in the BIOS. Specifically, you must enable Intel XD bit (execute disable bit) or AMD NX bit (no execute bit).

> **NOTE** After the virtualization and DEP processor options are configured in the BIOS of the server, the server must be powered off for the options to take effect.

Integrate Hyper-V RTM into Windows Server 2008

Windows Server 2008 shipped prior to Hyper-V releasing to manufacturing (RTM). Although Hyper-V is included with Windows Server 2008, it is the beta version of the Hyper-V role. In order to get the RTM version of Hyper-V, you must download and install an update. Microsoft Knowledge Base (KB) article 950050 provides the information and download package for updating a Windows Server 2008 installation to the RTM version of Hyper-V.

Although you can use Windows Update or can download and manually install the KB 950050 update, having to do that on every Hyper-V host will result in additional reboots and wasted time. A better way is to slipstream KB 950050 into the Windows Server 2008 ISO image so that it is installed by default. By slipstreaming the Hyper-V update, the RTM code will be installed automatically every time you create a new Hyper-V host. An additional benefit is that every time you create a Windows Server 2008 virtual machine using the ISO, the updated Integration Services will be installed automatically.

Windows Server 2008 uses the Windows Imaging (WIM) format to install the operating system quickly. The Windows Server 2008 DVD media has two WIM images: Boot.wim and Install.wim. Boot-level drivers and tools are stored in the Boot.wim image and are used during the boot process to start the install process. Install.wim contains six installation images: Standard, Enterprise, and Datacenter using Server Full Install, and Standard, Enterprise, and

Datacenter using Server Core Install. Windows Server 2008 provides a new servicing model that allows you to integrate update patches and drivers directly into Install.wim so they can be installed as part of the primary installation routine.

Microsoft provides a toolkit called Windows Automated Installation Kit (WAIK) that allows you to mount and manage the WIM images. The toolkit provides some key tools to allow you to service the WIMs. ImageX.exe allows you to mount a WIM image file for access and modification, including copying or deleting files. Pkgmgr.exe allows you to integrate updates into the WIM image and makes the required changes so the WIM knows that the new files exist. Oscdimg.exe allows you to create an updated bootable DVD ISO that can be burned to a blank DVD disk.

The steps required to create a new Windows Server 2008 ISO that can be used to install either a Hyper-V host or a Windows Server 2008 virtual machine are as follows:

1. Install the WAIK on your machine.

2. Copy the Windows Server 2008 x64 DVD to a subdirectory.

3. Make a copy of Install.wim for modification.

4. Mount the Install.wim copy with ImageX.

5. Integrate the Hyper-V RTM update with Pkgmgr.

6. Replace the original Install.wim.

7. Create a new ISO using Oscdimage.

DIRECT FROM THE SOURCE

Windows Server 2008 SP2 Includes Hyper-V RTM

Paul Despe, Program Manager
Windows Virtualization

Windows Server 2008 SP2 includes the latest version of Hyper-V integrated into the service pack. If you use media that has Service Pack 2 already slipstreamed, then you will not have to create slipstream media or import the KB950050 update into Microsoft Deployment Tookit 2008 Deployment Workbench.

Required Software and Tools

In order to perform the slipstream process, you will need to have the following software and hardware available:

- Windows Automated Installation Kit (WAIK)

- Windows Server 2008 x64 DVD in physical or ISO format

- Hyper-V RTM update file KB950050 x64 version

- DVD burner (if you want to create a new physical DVD)

Install the WAIK

The WAIK for Windows Server 2008 is available from the Microsoft download site. The downloaded file is an ISO that needs to be burned to disc, or else you can use a tool that will allow you to mount the ISO as a drive letter for installation. Install WAIK by inserting the disk in your machine and then clicking the Windows AIK Setup option on the welcome screen. Installation is a quick three-step process that involves accepting the EULA, accepting the default installation folder, and clicking Install. After it is installed, you can exit the dialog box by selecting the Exit option on the WAIK welcome screen.

Prepare for Slipstreaming

Slipstreaming the Hyper-V update requires creating a copy of the original Windows Server 2008 installation files from the DVD to a hard disk and making a working copy of Install.wim that will be used to slipstream the Hyper-V update.

To prepare for slipstreaming the update, do the following:

1. Insert the Windows Server 2008 x64 DVD into the DVD drive.
2. Create a C:\NewWin2008ISO folder on your machine.
3. Copy all the contents of the Windows Server 2008 DVD to C:\NewWin2008ISO.
4. Create a C:\WIM folder on your machine.
5. Copy the C:\NewWin2008ISO\Sources\INSTALL.WIM to C:\WIM.

The WIM format allows for multiple installation images to exist in a single .wim file. Each image is referenced by an index number. Table 4-1 shows the images and index numbers that are contained within the Windows Server 2008 Install.wim file.

TABLE 4-1 Installation Images and Index

INDEX NUMBER	NAME
1	Windows Longhorn SERVERSTANDARD
2	Windows Longhorn SERVERENTERPRISE
3	Windows Longhorn SERVERDATACENTER
4	Windows Longhorn SERVERSTANDARDCORE
5	Windows Longhorn SERVERENTERPRISECORE
6	Windows Longhorn SERVERDATACENTERCORE

Since each image is independent in Install.wim, the update will need to be applied to each image. This is accomplished by mounting Install.wim with the image index reference using ImageX.exe, installing the update into that image, and committing those changes to the Install.wim during the dismount operation. You then repeat the process for each index in the image.

When the WAIK is installed, it provides a link to a custom command prompt that makes the WAIK command-line tools available. The command prompt will need to be elevated using Run As Administrator for ImageX to operate correctly.

ImageX has the following syntax to mount a .wim file:

Imagex /mountrw <path to WIM> <WIM image Index> <mount folder>

To prepare to slipstream the Hyper-V update into the first image in Install.wim, perform the following steps:

1. Open an elevated Windows PE Tools Command Prompt from the Microsoft Windows AIK program menu. You must right-click the Windows PE Tools Command Prompt option and select Run As Administrator.

2. Create a folder called C:\MNT by typing **MD C:\MNT** and then press Enter.

3. Run the following command to mount the first image in Install.wim, Windows Server 2008 Server x64 Standard Edition, using the following syntax:

    imagex /mountrw C:\WIM\INSTALL.WIM 1 C:\MNT

Now the first image within Install.wim is ready for the Hyper-V update to be slipstreamed.

Extract the Hyper-V RTM Update

In order to integrate the update into Install.wim, you need the cab file from the KB950050 Windows Update installation package. This involves downloading the update package and using the Expand.exe command-line tool to extract all of the files.

Follow these steps to extract the files:

1. Download the Hyper-V RTM update for x64 (KB950050).

2. Make a directory called C:\EXTRACT.

3. Expand the Hyper-V RTM update by typing the following command line:

    expand <download folder>\Windows6.0-KB950050-x64.msu -F:* C:\EXTRACT

The extracted file that is required for slipstreaming is Windows6.0-KB950050-x64.cab, located in the C:\EXTRACT folder.

Slipstream the Hyper-V RTM Update

You are now ready to use Pkgmgr.exe to slipstream the Hyper-V RTM update into the first image of Install.wim. Pkgmgr.exe is a command-line tool that uses a series of command-line parameters to control the package installation options. Pkgmgr has the following syntax:

Pkgmgr <options> /m:<path to package> /o:<path to mounted wim>;<path to Windows directory in wim> /s:<temp directory>

The only option required for slipstreaming a package is

/ip – install a single package

For the procedures so far, the paths would be

/m:C:\EXTRACT\Windows6.0-KB950050-x64.cab

/o:C:\MNT;C:\MNT\WINDOWS

/s:%temp%

Follow these steps to integrate the extracted Hyper-V update cab:

1. Using Pkgmgr, integrate the KB950050 update into the mounted image by typing the following command line:

   start /w pkgmgr /ip /m:C:\EXTRACT\Windows6.0-KB950050-x64.cab /o:C:\MNT;C:\MNT\WINDOWS /s:%temp%

2. To check for success, type the following on the command line:

   Echo %errorlevel%

   If the returned error level is zero, then there were no errors in the update integration.

3. To save the modified image into Install.wim, unmount Install.wim and commit the changes by typing the following command line:

   imagex /unmount /commit C:\MNT

Unfortunately, this process updated only one out of the six images in the Install.wim file. To update each image, the following process must be repeated for each image index:

1. Mount Install.wim using a new image index value.

2. Slipstream the Hyper-V update using the Pkgmgr tool.

3. Unmount and commit the changes.

Build a New ISO

After all of the images within Install.wim file have been updated, it is time to build a new ISO file that can be burned to DVD to install a physical server or mounted by a virtual machine for installation. The WAIK provides the command-line tool Oscdimg.exe to create bootable ISO images. Oscdimg.exe has the following command-line syntax:

oscdimg [options] Source Location TargetFile

The list of options is long, but the main options required for creating a bootable ISO image are the following:

- **-b Location**   Specifies the location of the boot sector file. Do not use any spaces, as shown in the following example:

   -bC:\TEMP\Etfsboot.com

- **-m**   Ignores the maximum size limit of an image.

- **-n**   Enables long file names.

Based on the previous procedures, the C:\NewWin2K8ISO folder has all the required files to build a new ISO.

Follow this procedure to create an updated ISO:

1. Copy the updated C:\WIM\Install.wim to C:\NewWin2008ISO\Sources\, overwriting the existing copy.

2. Open an elevated Windows PE Tools Command Prompt from the Microsoft Windows AIK program menu. To do this, you must right-click the Windows PE Tools Command Prompt option and select Run As Administrator.

3. Use Oscdimg.exe from the WAIK to create a new ISO. Type the following command line and press Enter:

   Oscdimg −n −m −bC:\NewWin2K8ISO\BOOT\ETFSboot.com C:\NewWin2K-8ISO C:\Win2008Hyper-V-RTM.ISO

4. Burn the ISO to DVD or place the ISO where you can mount it when creating virtual machines.

Installation Options: Hyper-V Role

Installing the Hyper-V role on Windows Server 2008 can be accomplished using multiple methods. The methods available depend on the version of Windows Server 2008 you have installed. Table 4-2 details the different installation methods available on a Windows Server 2008 Full or Server Core install.

TABLE 4-2 Hyper-V Role Installation Methods

INSTALLATION METHOD	FULL INSTALLATION	SERVER CORE INSTALLATION
Server Manager MMC	X	
ServerManagerCMD.exe	X	
OCSetup.exe		X
Unattend.xml	X	X
Task sequence	X	X

Install Using Server Manager MMC

Server Manager provides a graphical interface to manage the configuration of Windows Server 2008, including install and uninstall of roles and features. Using Server Manager, the Hyper-V role can be installed easily. Start Server Manager by clicking the Server Manager icon in the system tray and then right-clicking Computer and selecting Manage, or by selecting Server Manager in the Administrative Tools menu. Use the following steps to install the Hyper-V role.

1. After you have launched Server Manager, select Roles in the left pane. This will display the Roles Summary screen in the right pane (see Figure 4-1) that details the roles that are currently installed on the server and provides options to add and remove roles.

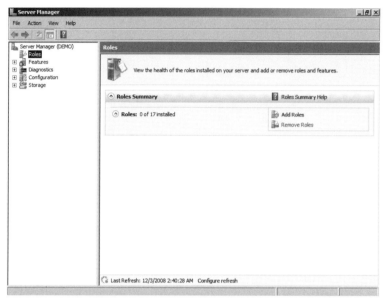

FIGURE 4-1 The Roles Summary screen

2. Click Add Roles to provide a list of roles to choose from.

3. Click Next to bypass the Before You Begin page.

4. On the Select Server Roles page, select the box next to Hyper-V (see Figure 4-2) and click Next.

5. If the server you are trying to install the Hyper-V role on does not detect the required processor extensions, the Add Roles Wizard will prompt you with an information dialog box (see Figure 4-3) that says that Hyper-V role cannot be installed.

6. You will be presented with a Hyper-V Cannot Be Installed dialog box. Review the information displayed, resolve the BIOS issues, and then resume the role installation at step 1 in this procedure.

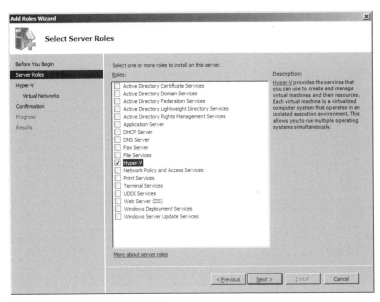

FIGURE 4-2 Select the Hyper-V role

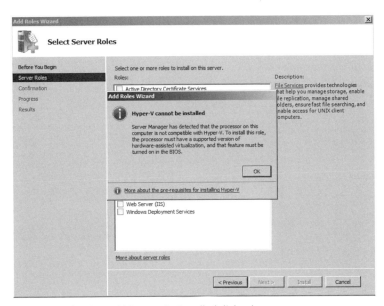

FIGURE 4-3 The Hyper-V Cannot Be Installed dialog box

7. If there are no processor issues, the wizard enumerates the network interfaces on the server and presents a dialog box (see Figure 4-4) asking if you want to define a virtual network with any of these interfaces. You are not required to select an interface at this time. Selecting an interface will create an external virtual network automatically during Hyper-V role installation. Make your selection and click Next.

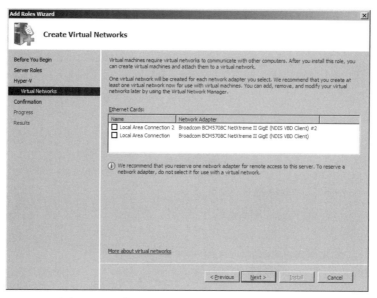

FIGURE 4-4 Select an interface for a virtual network.

> **NOTE**   If you are installing the Hyper-V remotely over a Remote Desktop connection, be careful not to select the network interface that the Remote Desktop session is currently using. During the creation of the virtual network, the TCP/IP stack is reset and the remote desktop session will be interrupted. The remote desktop should reconnect after the network stack is reset.

8. You have now completed all the installation choices. Click Install to install the Hyper-V role and administrative tools. After the files are installed, you will be prompted to reboot the computer to finish the installation of the role on the server. When the server has rebooted, the hypervisor should be running and the Hyper-V Manager MMC will be an option under Administrative Tools in the Start menu.

Install Using ServerManagerCmd.exe

ServerManagerCmd.exe provides a command-line interface to manage the configuration of Windows Server 2008. Almost anything you can do using the Server Manager MMC you can accomplish with ServerManagerCmd.exe with command-line options. It is possible to install the Hyper-V role using ServerManagerCmd.exe, although it is not possible to select a network adapter to be configured as a virtual network. After the Hyper-V role is installed, the virtual network can be created using the Hyper-V MMC.

1. To add the Hyper-V role using the command line, type the following command from an elevated command prompt and press Enter.

   ServerManagerCmd.exe –install Hyper-V

2. If the server that you are attempting to install Hyper-V on does not meet the hardware requirements, the following error will be presented.

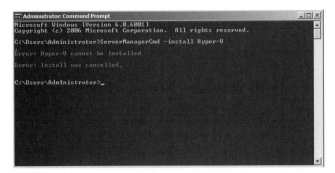

3. If there are no hardware requirement issues, the installation will begin immediately, and during installation the percent complete status will be displayed in the form <*xxx*/100>, where *xxx* is the percent complete. When the installation is complete, a reminder will be displayed that a reboot is required to finish the installation. Reboot the server with no wait time by typing **Shutdown –r –t 0**.

Using OCSetup.exe

When installing the Hyper-V role on a Server Core installation of Windows Server 2008, it is not possible to use ServerManagerCmd.exe because Server Manager is not available on a Server Core installation. Microsoft provides another tool called OCSetup.exe that can be used to install roles or features on Server Core.

During installation on Server Core with OCSetup.exe, there are two approaches you can take. The first is to just use OCSetup.exe to install Hyper-V. The second involves an additional step to enable the hypervisor to run automatically and then install with OCSetup. The difference in the approaches involves the number of reboots. If you use just OCSetup, the installation will require an additional reboot cycle to ensure that all the options are enabled. If you manually enable the hypervisor automatic launch before installing the Hyper-V role with OCSetup, then one reboot will be eliminated.

To prepare the current installation of Windows Server 2008 to launch the hypervisor automatically at boot, before you install the Hyper-V role, type the following command:

Bcdedit /set HypervisorLaunchType Auto

When you have the hypervisor launch type set to automatic, the Hyper-V role can be installed using OCSetup.exe.

1. From the command window, type the following and press Enter:

    Start /w OCSetup Microsoft-Hyper-V

> **NOTE** The role "Microsoft-Hyper-V" is case sensitive. You must enter it as shown.

2. To verify that Hyper-V was installed, you can use the OCList tool. Type **OCList** and then press Enter.

    You will see a list of all the installable packages on the server in alphabetic order. Scroll through the list looking for Microsoft-Hyper-V. If it was properly installed, it should be listed as Installed:Microsoft-Hyper-V.

Installation Options: Microsoft Hyper-V Server 2008

Microsoft Hyper-V Server 2008 is a stand-alone hypervisor solution based on Windows Server 2008 and Hyper-V technology. Unlike Windows Server 2008, where you must install the Hyper-V role, installing Microsoft Hyper-V Server 2008 does not require an additional configuration after installation to get hypervisor virtualization support.

Installing Microsoft Hyper-V Server 2008 is very similar to installing any other Windows Server product and uses the standard wizard installation approach. The following list provides the steps for installing Microsoft Hyper-V Server 2008:

1. Insert the Microsoft Hyper-V Server 2008 installation CD.

2. Power on the server and select to boot from the CD.

3. The main installation screen displays and prompts you for the language you are using for installation screens. Select the language you prefer.

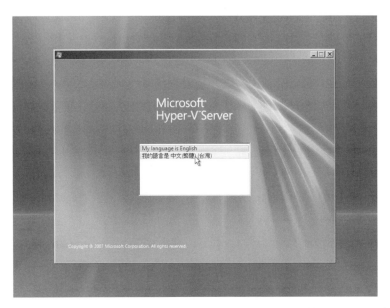

4. The next screen allows you to select the language to install, the time and currency format, and the keyboard language. When you have finished making these choices, click
Next.

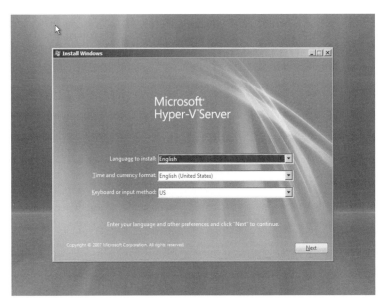

5. You are now ready to start the installation. Click Install Now.

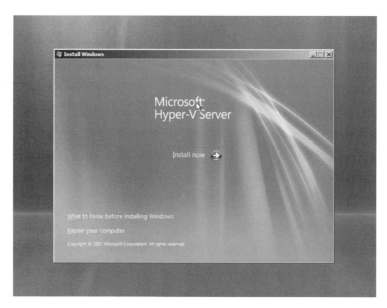

6. Review the license terms and select I Accept The License Terms if you agree, and then click Next.

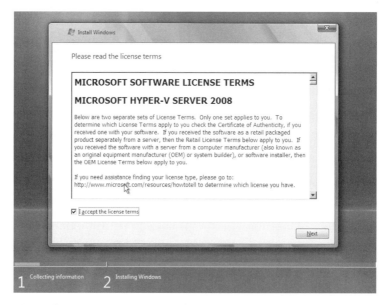

7. Microsoft Hyper-V Server 2008 does not support an upgrade from another version of Windows, so the only option is to perform a custom installation. Click Custom.

8. Select the disk and partition to install and optionally use the options to create, delete, or modify existing partitions. Click Next when you are ready to continue.

9. Installation will start and will be fully automated.

10. When installation is complete, you will see the logon screen. Microsoft Hyper-V Server 2008 is now fully installed and awaiting further configuration.

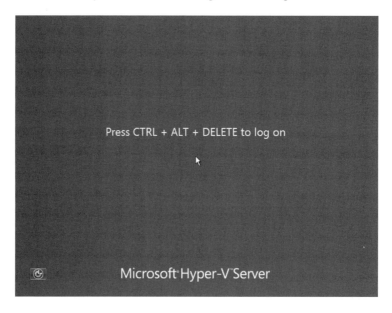

Additional Installation Methods

In addition to installing Hyper-V manually, there are options for installing it using automated methods. The first method—unattended installation using Unattend.xml—installs the operating system as well as the Hyper-V role in a single process. The Unattend.xml file answers all of the questions during the deployment. The second method—Microsoft Deployment Toolkit 2008—provides a way to install the operating system and the Hyper-V role in a single automated step but without the development of the Unattend.xml file. MDT will automatically create an Unattend.xml file and utilize post-install scripts to configure other specified options and settings. The third method—System Center Virtual Machine Manager (SCVMM) 2008—provides a way to install the Hyper-V role as part of the process of adding a host to the management console.

Using Unattend.xml to Install Hyper-V

Using unattended setup based on an Unattend.xml file and the updated ISO version that has the Hyper-V RTM update slipstreamed will allow you to fully automate the installation of the Windows Server 2008 operating system and the Hyper-V role. The unattended installation method will also work for Microsoft Hyper-V Server 2008, although Hyper-V is already installed by default, and the unattended installation is used only to install the server operating system.

Unattended installation involves creating an Unattend.xml file with all the options and settings you want, placing it on a floppy drive, and booting a server with a WinPE boot disk. Then, from the WinPE command prompt, you change to the CD-ROM drive letter and run the following command from a command prompt to start the installation using the Unattend.xml file in the floppy drive:

```
Setup /unattend:A:\unattend.xml
```

Unattended Installation of Hyper-V Role

Modifying an existing Windows Server 2008 Unattend.xml file to enable the Hyper-V role is a simple process. It involves adding a foundation package, the KB950050 update, and specifying that the Hyper-V role and the Hyper-V management clients are enabled for installation.

To modify an existing Windows Server 2008 Enterprise Edition Unattend.xml file, perform the following steps:

1. Launch the Windows System Image Manager (WSIM) (see Figure 4-5).

2. Select a Windows Server 2008 Install.wim file using the Select Windows Image option under the File menu.

3. Open the existing Unattend.xml file for editing using the File\Open Answer File option from the File menu.

4. Under Packages, expand the Foundation node.

5. Right-click the entry called amd64_Microsoft-Windows-Foundation_Package_6.0.6001.18000 and select Add To Answer File.

6. In the Answer File panel, select the entry called amd64_Microsoft-Windows-Foundation_Package_6.0.6001.18000, and you will see the properties of the package in the pane on the right.

7. Under the section called Windows Features Selection, use the drop-down list to change the Microsoft-Hyper-V and Microsoft-Hyper-V-Management-Clients from Disabled to Enabled.

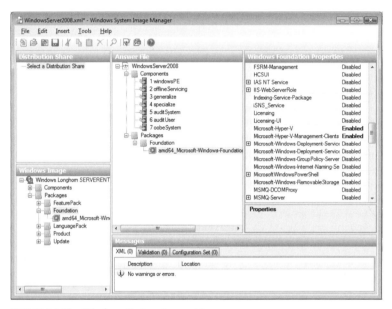

FIGURE 4-5 The Windows System Image Manager

8. Now save the answer file and use it to install a server. You should find the Hyper-V role installed.

Unattended Installation of Microsoft Hyper-V Server 2008

Performing an unattended installation of Microsoft Hyper-V Server 2008 involves creating a Unattend.xml answer file using Install.wim from the Microsoft Hyper-V Server 2008 media and using that answer file to install the server. Microsoft Hyper-V Server 2008 is based on the same technologies as Windows Server 2008, but it is optimized to be a hypervisor only–based virtualization server. Hyper-V virtualization support is installed by default, so there is no need to specify a role to install. There is also no need to slipstream the KB950050 update because Microsoft Hyper-V Server comes with the latest version of Hyper-V. In this case, you would use the Unattend.xml file only to customize options such as computer name, domain join, and IP addresses.

Microsoft Deployment Toolkit 2008

Microsoft Deployment Toolkit 2008 is a solution accelerator that has developed over time to perform operating system installation with minimal interaction. This is referred to as Lite Touch. The current version of Microsoft Deployment Toolkit 2008 (MDT) is the fourth generation of the technology. MDT allows you to customize the deployment of the operating system to a high degree, using the concept of a task sequence. A task sequence is a step-by-step set of scripted instructions that allows MDT to install the operating system; inject drivers and updates; configure the network; join a domain; download and apply updates; install roles, features, and applications; and much more. All of these tasks are controlled and configured at the MDT console called the Deployment Workbench.

Using Microsoft Deployment Toolkit to Install the Hyper-V Role

Using MDT eliminates the requirement to create a slipstreamed version of Windows Server 2008 with the Hyper-V Update. Instead of forcing you to integrate the update manually, MDT allows you to import the update into the Deployment Workbench Operating System Packages node. MDT automatically expands the package and extracts the cab file. During installation, MDT automatically injects the update as part of the deployment process, eliminating the need to slipstream it into the OS image.

The following procedures explain the process for integrating the KB950050 into MDT Deployment Workbench and deploying a Windows Server 2008 server with the Hyper-V role automatically installed.

To add the KB950050 update to the Deployment Workbench, follow these steps:

1. Download the KB950050 x64 update from Microsoft Downloads and place it in the C:\Updates directory on the MDT server.
2. Launch Deployment Workbench.
3. In the left pane, right-click the Distribution Share\OS Packages node and select New.
4. The New Package Wizard will start. On the Specify Directory page of the wizard, enter C:\Updates as the directory you want the wizard to check for packages, and then click Finish.
5. The KB950050 update package will be expanded and added to the OS Packages node.
6. After the package add is complete, you will see a package listed as Package_for_ KB950050 listed in the OS Packages list.

To create a task sequence to install Windows Server 2008, follow these steps:

1. After the package is installed, create a new Task Sequence by highlighting the Task Sequences node in the left pane of the Deployment Workbench. Right-click the node and select New.
2. On the General Settings page of the New Task Sequence Wizard (see Figure 4-6), provide a unique Task Sequence ID and a Task Sequence Name that you will use to refer to the task sequence, and then click Next.

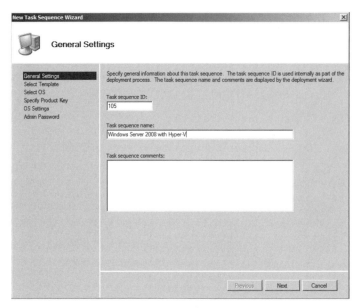

FIGURE 4-6 The General Settings page of the New Task Sequence Wizard

3. On the Select Template page (see Figure 4-7), select the Standard Server Task Sequence option from the drop-down list, and then click Next.

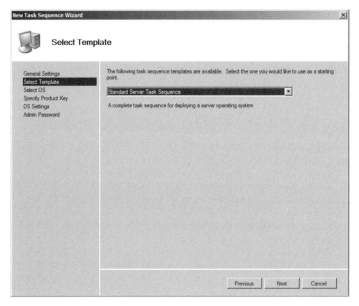

FIGURE 4-7 The Select Template page of the wizard

4. On the Select OS page of the wizard (see Figure 4-8), select the Windows Server 2008 operating system version to install. For example, select Windows Longhorn SERVER-ENTERPRISE to install Windows Server 2008 Enterprise Edition with full install, and then click Next.

NOTE If you do not already have the Windows Server 2008 operating system available in the Deployment Workbench, you must use the New OS Wizard to load Windows Server 2008. Refer to the Microsoft Deployment Toolkit Quick Start Guide for step-by-step instructions.

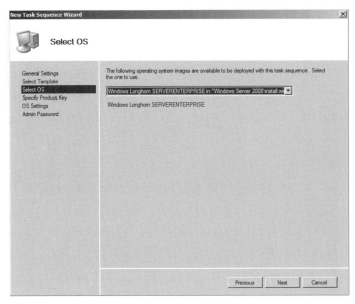

FIGURE 4-8 The Select OS page of the wizard

5. On the Specify Product Key page (see Figure 4-9), chose to specify a product key or not, and then click Next.

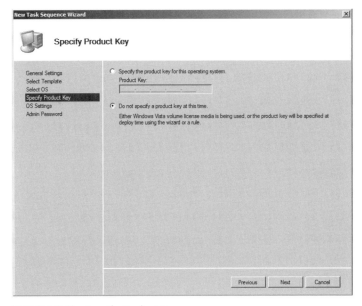

FIGURE 4-9 The Specify Product Key page

6. On the OS Settings page (see Figure 4-10) provide the correct information in the Full Name, Organization, and Internet Explorer Home Page text boxes, and then click Next.

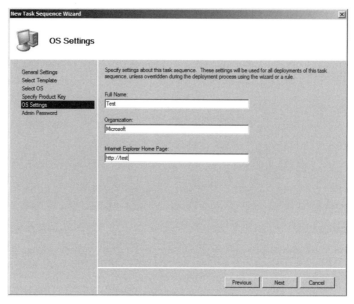

FIGURE 4-10 The OS Settings page

7. On the Admin Password page (see Figure 4-11), chose whether to specify an Administrator Password. Enter the password if desired, and then click Finish.

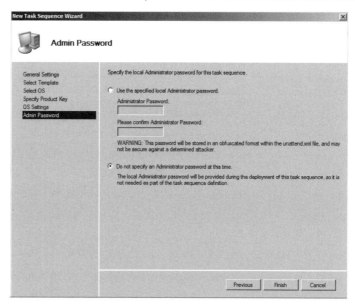

FIGURE 4-11 The Admin Password page

To edit the task sequence to specify to install the Hyper-V role, follow these steps:

1. Select the Task Sequences node so that the center pane of the Deployment Workbench displays all of the existing task sequences. Double-click the task sequence just created to see the properties.

2. Select the Task Sequence tab (shown in Figure 4-12) to display the task sequence flow.

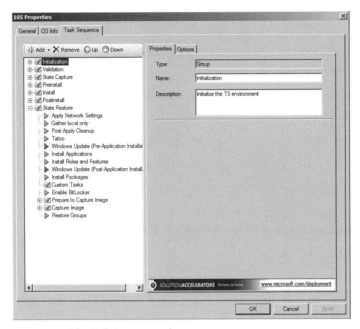

FIGURE 4-12 The Task Sequence tab

3. Under the State Restore node, highlight the Install Applications step and click Add, select the Roles option, and then select Install Roles And Features (see Figure 4-13).

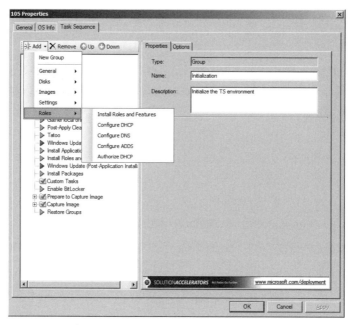

FIGURE 4-13 Select Install Roles And Features on the Task Sequence tab.

4. Highlight Install Roles And Features in the task sequence, and then in the right pane find the Hyper-V role and select the box next to it to install the role (see Figure 4-14). Then click OK. The task sequence is now configured to install the Hyper-V role.

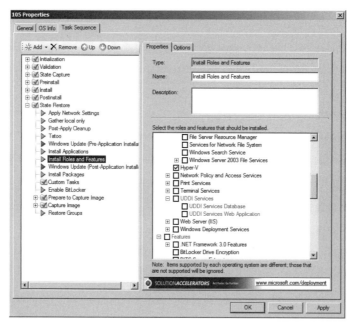

FIGURE 4-14 Select the Hyper-V role.

5. Follow MDT standard deployment process for installing a task sequence using PXE boot to Windows Deployment Services or using the Lite Touch WinPE ISO image.

Using Microsoft Deployment Toolkit to Install Microsoft Hyper-V Server

Microsoft Hyper-V Server 2008 comes with Hyper-V virtualization technology installed by default. To utilize MDT to install Microsoft Hyper-V Server 2008, the operating system files from the installation media must be loaded into Deployment Workbench as a valid operating system image on the distribution share. This is a wizard-driven process and requires the installation media to be available on the MDT server.

To load a new operating system image into the Deployment Workbench, follow these steps:

1. Launch the Deployment Workbench console.

2. In the left pane, under Distribution Share, right-click the Operating Systems node, and then select New.

3. On the OS Type page shown in Figure 4-15, select from the options of Full Set Of Source Files, Custom Image File, or Windows Deployment Services Images. For this procedure, accept the default of Full Set Of Source Files and then click Next.

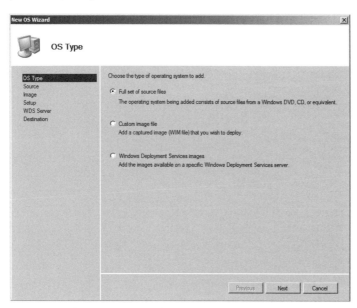

FIGURE 4-15 The OS Type page of the Deployment Workbench console

4. On the Source page (see Figure 4-16), insert the installation media into the DVD drive and specify the drive in the Source Directory box (D:\), and then click Next.

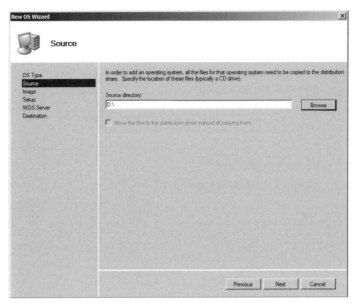

FIGURE 4-16 The Source page

5. On the Destination page (see Figure 4-17), in the Destination Directory Name text box, specify the name of the directory to store the operating system media files, and then click Finish.

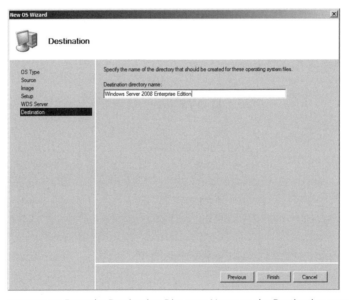

FIGURE 4-17 Enter the Destination Directory Name on the Destination page.

6. The Deployment Workbench will copy the files to the distribution share in the folder specified (shown in Figure 4-18), and when finished, it will provide an entry in the Operating System list for each image found within Install.wim.

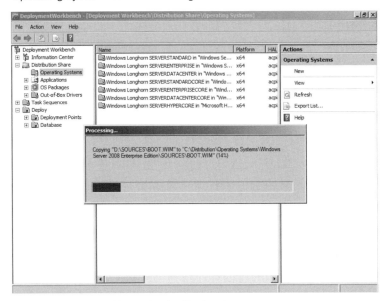

FIGURE 4-18 Copying files to the distribution share

NOTE You can obtain more information on Microsoft Deployment Toolkit 2008 and the forthcoming Microsoft Deployment Toolkit 2010 from *http://www.microsoft.com /deployment*.

Install the Hyper-V Role Using System Center Virtual Machine Manager 2008

System Center Virtual Machine Manager (SCVMM) 2008 is the Microsoft solution to managing Hyper-V servers from a central console. SCVMM can manage a Windows Server 2008 host that does not have the Hyper-V role installed, one that already has the Hyper-V role installed, or one that has an installed Microsoft Hyper-V Server 2008 host. If the Hyper-V role is not enabled, SCVMM can remotely enable the role during the process of adding the host to the management console.

Use the following steps to add a host to the SCVMM management console and automatically enable the Hyper-V role:

1. Launch the SCVMM Administration Console, shown in Figure 4-19.

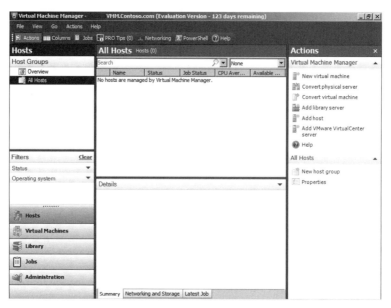

FIGURE 4-19 Launching the SCVMM Administration Console

2. From the Actions menu, select Add Host to launch the Add Hosts Wizard.

3. On the Select Host Location page (see Figure 4-20), there are three possible options to identify the host. Only two are acceptable options for a Hyper-V server:

   ■ If the server is a member of the same domain or a trusted domain, select the option Windows Server–Based Host On An Active Directory Domain. Also provide the password and credential information to connect to the domain, and then click Next.

   ■ If the server is a member of a perimeter network or is not attached to any domain, select the option Windows Server–Based Host On A Perimeter Network, and then click Next.

4. On the Select Host Servers page (see Figure 4-21), select the servers to add to the SCVMM console. In the Computer Name text box, specify the name of the server to add, and then click Add. After you have added all the servers to the SCVMM console, click Next.

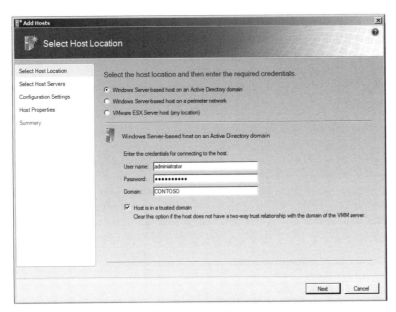

FIGURE 4-20 Options for identifying a Hyper-V host

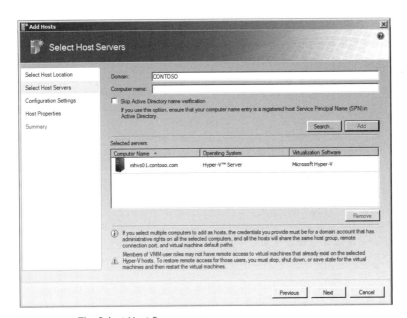

FIGURE 4-21 The Select Host Servers page

5. If any of the hosts that were selected are Hyper-V servers, SCVMM displays a warning box (shown in Figure 4-22) explaining that the Hyper-V role will be deployed if it is not already installed. Click Yes.

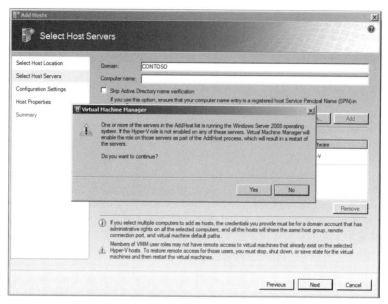

FIGURE 4-22 VMM warning message

6. On the Configuration Settings page (see Figure 4-23), select the Host Group for the Hyper-V server to be placed. The default is All Hosts. click Next.

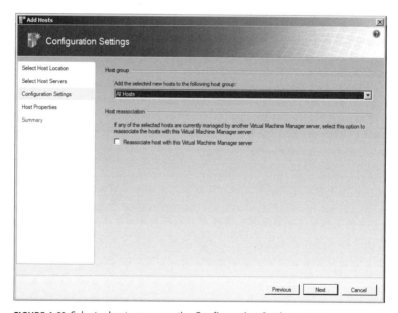

FIGURE 4-23 Select a host group on the Configuration Settings page.

7. On the Host Properties page (see Figure 4-24), specify any additional paths for virtual machine storage and modify the default port for Remote Desktop if required. Then click Next.

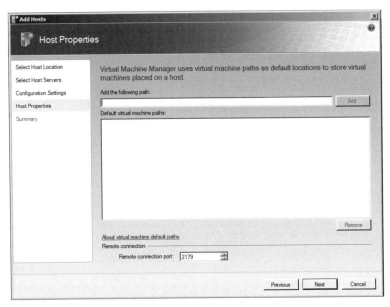

FIGURE 4-24 The Host Properties page

8. On the Summary page (Figure 4-25), review the actions that will be taken. Then click Add Hosts.

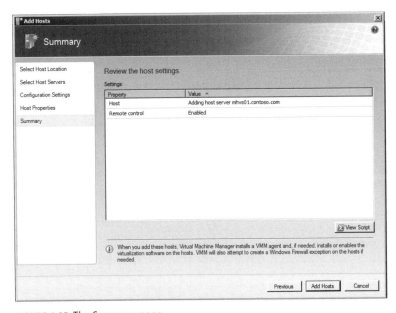

FIGURE 4-25 The Summary page

9. The Jobs dialog box will display (see Figure 4-26). Select the current running job to see the execution status.

> **NOTE** If the firewall is blocking access to the ADMIN$ share on the host, the Add Hosts job will fail. Configure the firewall to allow the File And Print Sharing exception and try again.

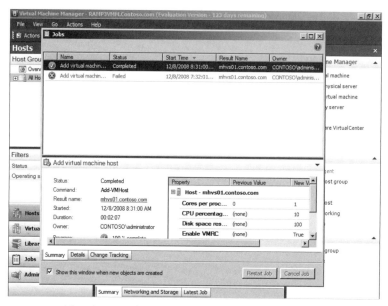

FIGURE 4-26 View the execution status on the Jobs page.

Post-Install Configuration Considerations

After you have the Windows Server 2008 Hyper-V role enabled or the Microsoft Hyper-V Server 2008 installed, you will need to complete some post-configuration steps. These steps include configuring the server identity, enabling Remote Desktop, applying updates, config- uring firewall rules, and many other tasks. Performing these actions on a full install of Win- dows Server 2008 with the graphical interface is a familiar process. Most individuals are not familiar with performing these actions on a Server Core install or on Microsoft Hyper-V Server 2008 using the command-line interface, however.

Microsoft has provided a step-by-step guide for Windows Server 2008 Server Core to document the common configuration actions and tools. For Microsoft Hyper-V Server 2008, Microsoft provides a command-line tool that combines the common configuration actions that need to be performed to enable a Hyper-V server to be managed remotely. The tool does not necessarily perform all the configuration options required, but it does get the Hyper-V Server configured and accessible so that standard remote management GUI tools can be used.

Commands for Modifying a Server Core Installation

The following sections cover some common tasks and the corresponding commands for configuring a Server Core installation. This list of tasks is not comprehensive.

Domain Configuration

Table 4-3 provides a list of the command tasks and corresponding commands for modifying the domain and workgroup membership of a Hyper-V server.

TABLE 4-3 Domain and Workgroup Configuration Commands

TASK	COMMAND
Join a computer to a domain	netdom join %computername% /domain:<domain> /userd:<domain>\username> /password:*
Remove a computer from a domain	netdom remove
Change the name of a domain-joined computer	netdom renamecomputer %computername% /NewName:<new computer name> /userd:<domain \username> /password:*
Change the name of a computer in a work group	netdom renamecomputer <currentcomputername> /NewName:<newcomputername>

Local Administrators Group Configuration

Table 4-4 provides a list of the command tasks and corresponding commands for modifying the local administrator's password and the local administrator's membership of a Hyper-V server.

TABLE 4-4 Local Administrators Configuration Commands

TASK	COMMAND
Set the local administrative password	net user administrator *
Add a user to the local Administrators group	net localgroup Administrators /add <domain>\<username>
Remove a user from the local Administrators group	net localgroup Administrators /delete <domain\username>

Networking Configuration

Table 4-5 provides a list of the command tasks and corresponding commands for modifying the network configuration of a Hyper-V server.

TABLE 4-5 Networking Configuration Commands

TASK	COMMAND
Change to a static IP address	netsh interface ipv4 set address name <ID from interface list> source=static address=<preferred IP address> gateway=<gateway address>
Set a static DNS address for Primary DNS server	netsh interface ipv4 add dnsserver name=<name of primary DNS server> address=<IP address of the primary DNS server> index=1
Set a static DNS address for Secondary DNS server	netsh interface ipv4 add dnsserver name=<name of secondary DNS server> address=<IP address of the secondary DNS server> index=2
Change to a DHCP-provided IP address from a static IP address	netsh interface ipv4 set address name=<IP address of local system> source=DHCP

Activation

Table 4-6 provides a list of the command tasks and corresponding commands for activating a Hyper-V server.

TABLE 4-6 Activation Configuration Commands

TASK	COMMAND
Activate the server locally	slmgr.vbs -ato
Activate the server remotely	cscript slmgr.vbs -ato <servername> <username> <password>

Firewall

Table 4-7 provides a list of the command tasks and corresponding commands for modifying the firewall configuration of a Hyper-V server.

TABLE 4-7 Firewall Configuration Commands

TASK	COMMAND
Enable remote administration of the firewall	netsh advfirewall firewall set rule group="Windows Firewall Remote Management" new enable=yes
Disable the firewall	netsh firewall set opmode=disable
Enable the firewall	netsh firewall set opmode=enable
Enable File and Print firewall exceptions	netsh firewall set service fileandprint mode=enable
Enable remote management	netsh firewall set service remoteadmin enable

Event Logs

Table 4-8 provides a list of the command tasks and corresponding commands for listing, querying, and managing the event log of a Hyper-V server.

TABLE 4-8 Event Log Commands

TASK	COMMAND
List event logs	wevtutil el
Query events in a specified log	wevtutil qe /f:text <log name>
Export an event log	wevtutil epl <log name>
Clear an event log	wevtutil cl <log name>

Microsoft Hyper-V Server 2008 Configuration Tool

Microsoft Hyper-V Server 2008 comes with a menu-driven command-line configuration tool called HVConfig.cmd that allows you to configure basic connectivity and features required to use Hyper-V Server in a managed environment. HVConfig.cmd actually calls a Visual Basic Script file called HVConfig.vbs, which provides all the functionality. HVConfig.cmd launches at every login and allows you to do the following:

- Configure domain or workgroup membership
- Set computer name
- Configure network adapter settings
- Add domain accounts to local administrators group
- Configure Windows Update for automatic or manual updates
- Download and install Windows updates
- Configure Remote Desktop

- Set regional and language options
- Set data and time

Additionally, the Hyper-V Configuration menu allows you to perform the following actions:

- Log off
- Restart
- Shut down

Figure 4-27 shows the Hyper-V Configuration menu that launches after the installation of Hyper-V Server.

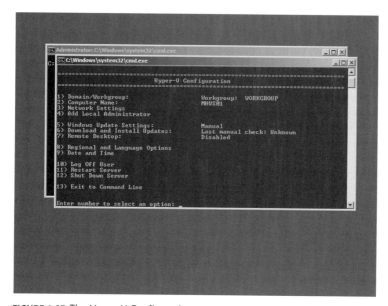

FIGURE 4-27 The Hyper-V Configuration menu

Domain or Workgroup Configuration

Selecting option 1 from the menu will allow you to configure Hyper-V Server for a domain or a workgroup as shown in Figure 4-28. By default, after installation, the server is in a workgroup.

Follow these steps in the Hyper-V Configuration command window to add the server to a domain:

1. Type **1** to select the option to configure the domain or workgroup.

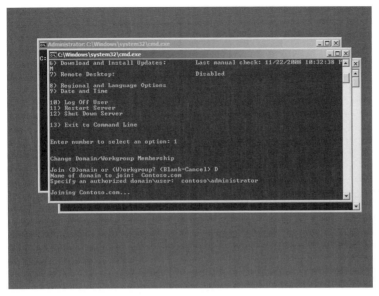

FIGURE 4-28 Configuring Hyper-V Server for a domain or workgroup

2. Type **D** to configure domain membership.

3. Enter a domain name (example: contoso.com), and then press Enter.

4. Enter a userid in the domain provided that has credentials to add a computer to the domain (example: contoso\administrator), and then press Enter.

5. The domain join will be attempted. When it is successful, you will be prompted with the message You Must Restart Your Computer To Apply These Changes, Restart Now? Click Yes to reboot.

Computer Name

Select option 2 in order to change the name of the Hyper-V Server. The current name is displayed on the screen.

To change the name of the server, follow these steps in the Hyper-V Configuration command window:

1. Type **2** to select the option to change the server's name.

2. Enter the new computer name, and then press Enter.

3. The options will change depending on whether the server is currently in a domain or in a workgroup.

    ■ For a workgroup-joined machine, the name change will be made, and if it is successful, you will be prompted with a dialog box that says The Computer Needs To Be Restarted In Order To Complete The Operation. The command completed successfully, so click OK.

- For a domain-joined machine, you will be prompted for a domain and a userid that has local rights to change the computer's name. Enter the domain\userid and then press Enter. You will then be prompted for the password for the provided domain\ userid. Enter the password, and then press Enter.

4. You will now be prompted with the message You Must Restart Your Computer To Apply These Changes, Restart Now? Click Yes to reboot.

Network Settings

Select option 3 to change the configuration of the network adapters in the Hyper-V Server, as shown in Figure 4-29. You can chose to configure IP addresses for static or DHCP assignment, configure DNS servers for name resolution, or clear current DNS server settings.

To configure the network adapters of the server, follow these steps in the Hyper-V Configuration command window:

1. Type **3** to select the option to change the server's network adapter configuration.

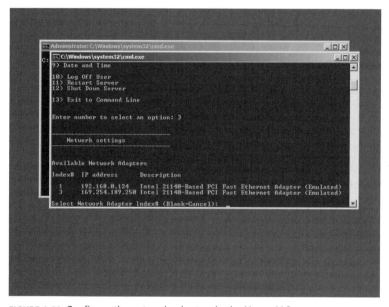

FIGURE 4-29 Configure the network adapters in the Hyper-V Server.

2. You will be prompted with a list of network adapters. Select the adapter by entering the index number, and then press Enter.

3. The current configuration of that network adapter will be displayed (see Figure 4-30), including the IP address, the subnet mask (if the adapter is DHCP enabled), the default gateway, and the preferred and secondary DNS servers. You are provided with four new menu options: Set Network Adapter IP Address, Set DNS Servers, Clear DNS Server Settings, and Return To Main Menu.

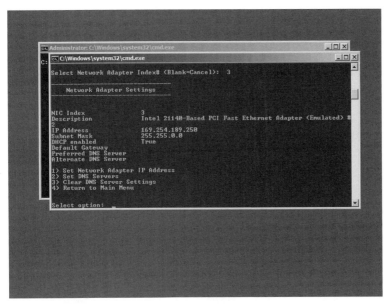

FIGURE 4-30 The network adapter's current configuration and menu options

4. Select menu option 1 to set the IP address, and then press Enter.

5. You will be prompted with a choice to specify a DHCP or Static IP address. Type **D** to select a DHCP address and **S** to specify a static IP address.

   If you entered D, then the server is configured to get an IP address, subnet mask, and gateway from the DHCP server.

   If you entered S, then you will be prompted for the static address to assign to this network adapter. Enter the desired static IP address in dotted decimal form (example: 10.10.1.22), and then press Enter.

6. Enter the desired subnet mask in dotted decimal form (example: 255.255.0.0), and then press Enter.

7. Enter the desired default gateway in dotted decimal form (example: 10.10.1.1), and then press Enter. You are now back at the Network Settings menu.

To configure DNS IP addresses for the preferred and secondary DNS servers, follow these steps:

1. Type **2** and press Enter.

2. Enter the IP address of the preferred DNS server and press Enter.

3. The preferred DNS server will be configured and a dialog box will display that says Preferred DNS Server Set. Click OK.

4. Enter the IP address of the alternate DNS server and press Enter.

5. The alternate DNS server will be configured and a dialog box will display that says Alternate DNS Server Set. Click OK.

If there is a need to change from Static to DHCP configuration, the preferred and alternate static DNS server entries need to be reset for the DHCP DNS entries to be applied.

To clear the static DNS server entries, follow these steps:

1. Type **3** and then press Enter.

2. You will see a dialog box with a message that says DNS Servers Removed. DNS servers will be automatically obtained from the network. Click OK.

After you have made all the changes to the network settings that are required, type **4** to return to the main menu, and then press Enter.

Add Local Administrator

Selecting option 4 will allow you to add a local or domain user to the local administrators group on the Hyper-V server. The server must be a member of a domain to add domain users or must be a member of a domain that has a trust relationship with a domain with a user you would like to add. To simplify the process, you should be logged in with local administrative rights for this option.

To add a user to the local Administrators group of the server, follow these steps in the Hyper-V Configuration command window:

1. Type **4** to select the option to add a user to the local Administrators group.

2. If you want to add a domain user to the local Administrators group, type the domain\ userid of the user you want to add and press Enter.

3. If you want to add a local user to the local administrators group, type the userid of the user you want to add and press Enter.

4. Regardless of whether you add a local or domain user, you will be prompted with the message User Added To Local Administrators Group, and the userid that you success-fully added will be displayed. Click OK.

Windows Update Settings

Selecting option 5 will allow you to configure the Hyper-V server to manually receive Windows Updates or automatically receive Windows Updates at the default time of 3:00 AM daily, as shown in Figure 4-31.

To configure Windows Update configuration, follow these steps from the Hyper-V Configuration command window:

1. Type **5** to select the option to change the Windows Update setting.

2. If the Hyper-V server is configured for Automatic Windows Updates, type **M** to config-ure the server for manual updates, and then press Enter.

   You will be prompted with the message Windows Update Set To Manual. System Will Never Check For Updates. Click OK.

3. If the Hyper-V server is configured for Manual Windows Updates, type **A** to configure the server for automatic updates, and then press Enter.

You will be prompted with the message Windows Update Set To Automatic. System Will Check For And Install Updates Every Day At 3:00 AM. Click OK.

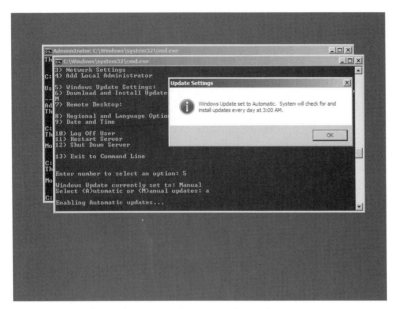

FIGURE 4-31 Configure the Hyper-V host to receive updates.

4. The Hyper-V Configuration menu will display the current configuration for Windows Update.

Download and Install Updates

Selecting option 6 will allow you to interactively download updates from Windows Update. To use this option, the Hyper-V server must have Internet connectivity. Selecting this option will run a script that uses the local Windows Update client to communicate to the Windows Update servers and determine the missing updates on the server. A list will be presented and the option to install all the updates or to cancel the update will be provided. If All Updates is selected, the updates will be downloaded from Windows Update and installed. If a reboot is required after the updates, a dialog box will notify you of the required reboot.

To download and install Windows Updates to the Hyper-V server interactively, follow these steps from the Hyper-V Configuration command window:

1. Type **6** to select the option to download and install Windows Updates. A new command window will be launched running the Windows Update script (see Figure 4-32).

2. The script will determine any missing Windows Updates and provide a list of all the critical and recommended updates, as shown in Figure 4-33. You will be prompted with the message Download And Install Updates Now? If you type **Y**, all the updates in the list will be downloaded and installed on the local machine.

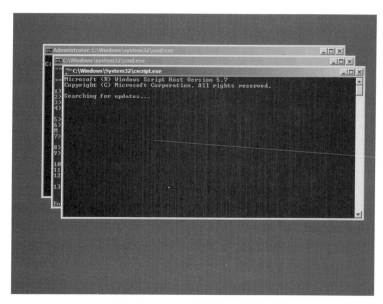

FIGURE 4-32 Download and install updates to the Hyper-V host.

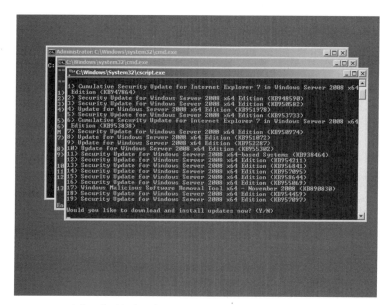

FIGURE 4-33 A list of critical and recommend updates

3. You may be prompted with a message that says A Restart Is Required To Complete Windows Updates. Restart Now? Click Yes to initiate a restart.

Remote Desktop

Selecting option 7 will allow you to enable or disable Remote Desktop on the Hyper-V server, as shown in Figure 4-34. Windows Server 2008 supports different remote desktop clients. By default, Windows Server 2008 supports clients that use a version of Remote Desktop Connection client 6.0 or later. These clients support network-level authentication and other advanced features. By default, Windows Vista and Windows Server 2008 use Remote Desktop Connection client version 6.0. Windows XP SP2 and Windows Server 2003 SP1 or SP2 use an earlier version of Remote Desktop Connection client but can download and install an update to the Remote Desktop Connection client to bring them to version 6.0.

To configure Remote Desktop on the Hyper-V server, follow these steps from the Hyper-V Configuration command window:

1. Type **7** to select the option to configure Remote Desktop on the Microsoft Hyper-V Server 2008.

2. By default, Remote Desktop is disabled. To enable Remote Desktop, type **E**.

3. You will be prompted with two options:

    ■ Type **1** to enable Remote Desktop for clients running Remote Desktop Connection client version 6.0 or higher using the more secure network level authentication.

    ■ Type **2** to enable Remote Desktop for clients running Remote Desktop Connection clients lower than version 6.0 using less secure authentication.

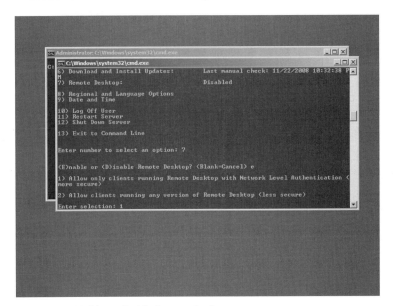

FIGURE 4-34 Enable or disable Remote Desktop

4. You will be prompted with a dialog box that indicates your selection. Click OK.

If you need to disable Remote Desktop on the Microsoft Hyper-V Server 2008 host, follow these steps from the Hyper-V Configuration command window:

1. Type **7** to select the option to configure Remote Desktop on the Microsoft Hyper-V Server 2008.

2. To disable Remote Desktop, type **D**.

3. You will be prompted with the message Remote Desktop Disabled. Click OK.

Regional and Language Options

Selecting option 8 will allow you to configure regional and language options on the Hyper-V server, as shown in Figure 4-35. The regional and language options include the language in which numeric data is displayed, the location of the server, the keyboard and display language, and managing the administrative options for storing and retrieving language settings.

To configure regional and language options on the Hyper-V server, follow these steps from the Hyper-V Configuration command window:

1. Type **8** and press Enter to configure or modify the Hyper-V server regional and language options.

2. You will be presented with the Hyper-V server Regional And Language Options dialog box.

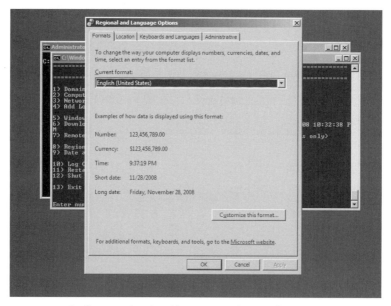

FIGURE 4-35 Configure regional and language options on the Hyper-V server.

3. When you are finished configuring regional and language options, click OK or Apply to commit the changes or click Cancel to discard them.

Date and Time

Selecting option 9 will allow you to configure date and time options on the Hyper-V server, as shown in Figure 4-36. The date and time options include the date, time, time zone, and additional clocks. While the tab is displayed to configure additional clocks, the additional clocks are not displayed on the screen.

To configure date and time options on the Microsoft Hyper-V Server, follow these steps from the Hyper-V Configuration command window:

1. Type **9** and press Enter to configure or modify the Hyper-V server date and time options.

2. You will be presented with the Hyper-V Server Date And Time options dialog box.

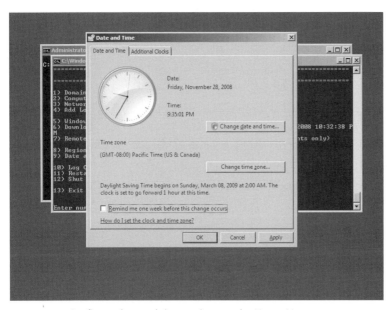

FIGURE 4-36 Configure date and time options on the Hyper-V server.

3. When you are finished configuring date and time options, click OK to commit the changes or click Cancel to discard them.

Log Off User

Selecting option 10 will allow you to end the current configuration session and log off the current user on the Hyper-V server. This will return the Microsoft Hyper-V Server host to the standard Windows login screen. This option will result in the same action as when a user presses Ctrl+Alt+Delete and selects the option to log off from the menu.

To log off the current user on the Microsoft Hyper-V Server host, follow these steps from the Hyper-V Configuration command window:

1. Type **10** and press Enter to log off the current user.

2. You will be prompted with the message Are You Sure You Want To Log Off? Click Yes.

Restart Server

Selecting option 11 will allow you to restart the Microsoft Hyper-V Server host. This option will result in the same action as when a user presses Ctrl+Alt+Delete and selects the option to restart from the menu. If there are any running virtual machines on the Hyper-V Server, they will be automatically saved before the Hyper-V host is restarted.

To restart the Microsoft Hyper-V Server host, follow these steps from the Hyper-V Configuration command window:

1. Type **11** and press Enter to restart the Hyper-V Server.

2. You will be prompted with the message Are You Sure You Want To Restart? Click Yes.

Shut Down Server

Selecting option 12 will allow you to shut down the Microsoft Hyper-V Server host. This option will result in the same action as when a user presses Ctrl+Alt+Delete and selects the option to shut down from the menu. If there are any running virtual machines on the Hyper-V Server, they will be automatically saved before the Hyper-V server is shut down.

To shut down the Microsoft Hyper-V Server host, follow these steps from the Hyper-V Configuration command window:

1. Type **12** and press Enter to shut down the Hyper-V server.

2. You will be prompted with the message Are You Sure You Want To Shut Down? Click Yes.

Exit to Command Line

Selecting option 13 exits the Hyper-V configuration tool to the command prompt. You can manually restart the Hyper-V configuration tool, or when you log out and then log back in, it will restart automatically.

To exit and restart the Hyper-V configuration tool, follow these steps from the Hyper-V Configuration command window:

1. Type **13** and press Enter to exit to the command line.

2. If you need to restart the Hyper-V Configuration tool, type **hvconfig** and press Enter.

Summary

This chapter described the options for installing the Hyper-V role on the full and server core installs of Windows Server 2008 64-bit Standard, Enterprise, and Datacenter editions as well as Microsoft Hyper-V Server 2008. Hyper-V requires a 64-bit processor with hardware virtualization support and Data Execute Protection enabled before Hyper-V will install. A slipstreamed version of Windows Server 2008 and the Hyper-V role was created so that the Hyper-V RTM version and Integration Services would be available. The chapter discussed how using Microsoft Deployment Toolkit 2008 can eliminate the requirement to pre-create slip-stream media and provides an easy-to-use deployment tool. You learned that System Center Virtual Machine Manager installs the Hyper-V role automatically during the Add Host process if the server does not already have Hyper-V loaded. This chapter also covered post-installation steps and tools that can streamline the process.

Additional Resources

The following resources contain additional information related to this chapter.

- Microsoft Deployment Toolkit 2008, a resource that provides information on downloading and using the Microsoft Deployment Toolkit 2008, available at *http://www.microsoft.com/deployment*

- Netsh Commands for Windows Firewall, a resource that provides all the command-line options for the netsh firewall command, available at *http://technet.microsoft.com /en-us/library/cc771046.aspx*

- Microsoft Hyper-V Server 2008, a resource that provides information about the Microsoft Hyper-V Server 2008 product and documentation on installation and configuration, available at *http://www.microsoft.com/HVS*

- Windows Imaging File Format, a resource that describes the Windows Imaging file format, available at *http://go.microsoft.com/fwlink/?LinkId=92227*

## CHAPTER 5

Hyper-V Advanced Features

This chapter describes advanced features in Hyper-V and explains how you can use them in the virtualization process. You will learn about virtual hard disks, virtual machine (VM) snapshots, Integration Services (IS), virtual networks, pass-through disks, and clustering options that you can use to deploy broad virtualization infrastructure solutions. The information in this chapter provides technical descriptions and configurations along with common usage scenarios.

Using Virtual Hard Disk Advanced Features

Hyper-V uses the virtual hard disk (VHD) format to encapsulate virtual machine data into one or more files that are equivalent to physical drives associated with a traditional server. Using the VHD format as a basic building block, Hyper-V provides advanced virtual hard disk features that enable the creation of virtualized environments that are more functional and flexible than physical equivalents, particularly for disciplines such as development, testing, training, and support. Table 5-1 lists the advanced virtual hard disk features covered in this section.

TABLE 5-1 Virtual Hard Disk Advanced Features

FEATURE	DESCRIPTION
Differencing disks	A special type of dynamically expanding virtual hard disk that stores virtual machine data changes while isolating them from the base virtual hard disk.
Automatic differencing disks	A special type of dynamically expanding virtual hard disk that stores virtual machine data changes while isolating them from the base virtual hard disk. These are similar to differencing disks, but there are differences in options and applicable scenarios. Automatic differencing disks are created when a virtual machine snapshot is taken.
Physical disk to VHD copy	The process to copy the contents of a physical hard disk into a virtual hard disk file. The process associated with copying the data of a physical disk to a virtual hard disk is potentially time consuming, depending on the size of the physical disk.
Convert VHD	The process to convert a dynamically expanding disk to a fixed-size disk or vice versa. The process associated with the conversion is potentially time consuming, depending on the size of the virtual hard disk. A VHD must be offline during this process.
Compact VHD	The process to regain unused space allocated to a virtual hard disk. The compaction process works only for dynamically expanding and differencing virtual hard disks. No other type of virtual hard disk can be compacted. A VHD must be offline during this process.
Expand VHD	The process to increase the maximum storage capacity of dynamically expanding or fixed-size virtual hard disks. A VHD must be offline during this process.

Differencing Disks

A virtual machine running within Hyper-V has its data encapsulated in one or more base virtual hard disks. When data changes occur to the guest operating system or the applications running in it, modifications are committed to the virtual hard disks. The changes made to the virtual hard disks are permanent, paralleling the process that would occur with a standard physical system. However, a variety of compelling scenarios are enabled by preserving a base virtual hard disk in an unchanged state, while still capturing and storing ongoing virtual machine changes.

A differencing disk is a special type of dynamically expanding disk that stores changes to virtual machine data in a separate file from a base virtual hard disk. The association of the base virtual hard disk to the differencing disk is defined as a parent-child relationship. In this parent-child relationship, each child differencing disk can derive from only one parent disk, but parent disks can be used as the basis to create multiple, distinct child differencing disks.

Figure 5-1 shows that differencing disks can be created in very simple or very complex parent-child hierarchies. A multilevel differencing disk hierarchy is commonly referred to as a *chain* of differencing disks, reflecting that a child differencing disk can have a parent disk that is also a differencing disk. The chain can consist of several levels, but it always stems from either a standard dynamically expanding or fixed-size virtual hard disk at the top of the hierarchy. This concept is important because data changes in a differencing disk are simply represented as modified blocks in relation to the parent disk. Therefore, a differencing disk is never used independently, but in conjunction with all parent disks in its hierarchy. (See Figure 5-1.)

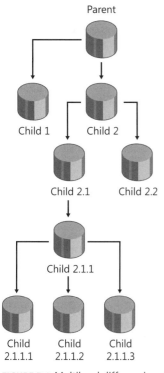

FIGURE 5-1 Multilevel differencing disk hierarchy

If you examine a Hyper-V server file system, you will see each differencing disk stored as an individual file. Within the virtual machine file system, you see only a single disk, independent of how many levels of differencing disks are actually associated with a specific virtual hard disk.

> **BEST PRACTICES** To identify parent-child differencing disk relationships in a complex chain quickly and easily, adopt a standardized virtual hard disk naming convention. The Hyper-V Manager allows you to inspect a differencing disk and discover its parent disk, but it does not report any child differencing disks related to it.

Creating a Differencing Disk

When you create a new differencing disk, the location of the base virtual hard disk that will be the parent for the new differencing disk must be specified. The parent disk can be either a fixed-size or dynamically expanding virtual hard disk. A differencing disk grows as needed, up to the size specified for the parent virtual hard disk.

To create a differencing disk, follow these steps:

1. Open the Hyper-V Manager console.

2. In the Actions pane, under the server name, click New and select Hard Disk from the menu to launch the New Virtual Hard Disk Wizard.

3. On the Before You Begin page, click Next.

4. On the Choose Disk Type page, select Differencing and then click Next.

5. On the Specify Name And Location page, type a name for the new differencing disk in the Name text box and then type a fully qualified path to the storage folder in the Location text box, or click the Browse button to use Windows Explorer to select the storage folder. After you complete these actions, click Next.

6. On the Configure Disk page, type the fully qualified path to the parent virtual hard disk in the Location text box, or click the Browse button to use Windows Explorer to select the parent virtual hard disk and then click Next.

7. On the Completing The New Virtual Hard Disk Wizard page, review your selections.

8. Click Finish.

> **NOTE** By default, differencing disks use the .vhd file extension, which makes them difficult to distinguish from standard virtual hard disks.

Examining Parent-Child Differencing Disk Relationships

Every dynamic disk contains a standard virtual hard disk header that embeds a specific dynamic disk header. The dynamic disk header format is identical for both standard dynamically expanding and differencing disks. However, several fields in this header are relevant only to differencing disks, as they identify parent disk attributes. A list of the dynamic disk header fields is provided in Table 5-2, with those relating only to differencing disks appearing in boldface type.

TABLE 5-2 Dynamic Disk Header

DYNAMIC DISK HEADER FIELDS	DESCRIPTION
Cookie	A set field that identifies the header
Data Offset	Absolute byte offset to next hard disk image structure (currently unused)
Table Offset	Absolute byte offset of the block allocation table (BAT) in the file

DYNAMIC DISK HEADER FIELDS	DESCRIPTION
Header Version	Dynamic disk header version
Max Table Entries	Maximum number of entries in the BAT
Block Size	Size of unit that is used to expand the dynamic disk incrementally
Checksum	Checksum of the dynamic disk header
Parent UUID	**128-bit universally unique identifier (UUID) of the parent disk (used only for differencing disks)**
Parent Time Stamp	**Modification time stamp of the parent disk (used only for differencing disks)**
Reserved	Field is set to zero
Parent Unicode Name	**Unicode string for file name of the parent disk (used only for differencing disks)**
Parent Locator Entry 1	**Platform-specific format containing the absolute byte offset in the file where the parent locator is stored (used only for differencing disks)**
Parent Locator Entry 2	**Platform-specific format containing the absolute byte offset in the file where the parent locator is stored (used only for differencing disks)**
Parent Locator Entry 3	**Platform-specific format containing the absolute byte offset in the file where the parent locator is stored (used only for differencing disks)**
Parent Locator Entry 4	**Platform-specific format containing the absolute byte offset in the file where the parent locator is stored (used only for differencing disks)**
Parent Locator Entry 5	**Platform-specific format containing the absolute byte offset in the file where the parent locator is stored (used only for differencing disks)**
Parent Locator Entry 6	**Platform-specific format containing the absolute byte offset in the file where the parent locator is stored (used only for differencing disks)**
Parent Locator Entry 7	**Platform-specific format containing the absolute byte offset in the file where the parent locator is stored (used only for differencing disks)**
Parent Locator Entry 8	**Platform-specific format containing the absolute byte offset in the file where the parent locator is stored (used only for differencing disks)**
Reserved	Field is set to zero

A differencing disk uses the parent UUID and Unicode file name information stored in its dynamic disk header to locate and open the parent disk. Because a parent disk can also be a differencing disk, it is possible that the entire hierarchy of parent disks will be opened, up to the base virtual hard disk.

Portability of parent and child differencing disks across server platforms is provided by the Parent Locator entries listed in Table 5-2. Parent Locator entries store platform-specific information to locate the parent differencing disk on the physical drive.

> **IMPORTANT** For the Microsoft Windows platform, both the absolute (for example, C:\parent\parent.vhd) and relative (for example, .\parent\parent.vhd) paths of the parent disk are stored in the Parent Locator entry of a differencing disk. If you use the virtual machine export feature to move to a new server, you will be able to import the virtual machine on that Hyper-V server and turn it on without having to make any additional changes.

> **MORE INFO** To learn more about the Hyper-V virtual machine export and import features, refer to Chapter 2, "Hyper-V Overview."

When a virtual machine using differencing disks issues a write operation, the data is written only to the child differencing disk. As part of the process, an internal virtual hard disk data structure is updated to reflect changes that supersede data in the parent disk. During read operations, the same internal virtual hard disk data structure is checked to determine which data to read from the child differencing disk. Unchanged data is read from the parent disk.

DIRECT FROM THE SOURCE

Configure Parent Disks as "Read-Only"

Bryon Surace, Program Manager
Windows Virtualization

A child differencing disk stores the parent disk modification time stamp when it is created. Any modifications made to the parent disk after creation of the child differencing disk will be detected and will invalidate the child differencing disk. To ensure that nothing can be written to the parent disk that will corrupt the parent-child disk relationship, configure the parent disk as "read-only."

Reconnect Differencing Disks

If one or more virtual hard disks in a chain of differencing disks cannot be located, virtual machines that are associated with any disconnected child differencing disk will be unable to run. If you try to start a virtual machine with a disconnected differencing disk, Hyper-V will generate an error similar to the one shown in Figure 5-2. In addition, you are unable to add a disconnected child differencing disk to a virtual machine.

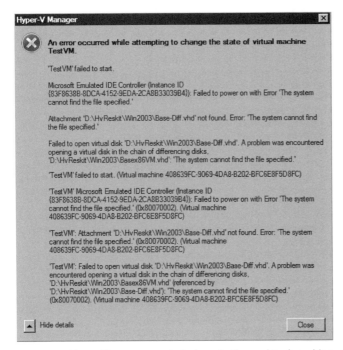

FIGURE 5-2 Hyper-V error generated when starting a virtual machine with a disconnected differencing disk

In order to resolve this problem, you must reconnect a child differencing disk to its parent disk. If the parent disk was accidentally deleted or moved, you can simply move it back to its original location. If the parent disk was purposefully moved to a different folder, you have to update the child differencing disk Parent Locator entry with the new path. Fortunately, Hyper-V provides an option for you to inspect a child differencing disk and reconnect it to its parent disk. Using this option, you specify the new location of the parent disk and Hyper-V updates the absolute and relative paths stored in the Parent Locator entry of the child differencing disk.

To reconnect a child differencing disk to its parent disk using the Inspect Disk option, follow these steps:

1. Open the Hyper-V Manager console.

2. In the Actions pane, under the server name, click Inspect Disk.

3. In Windows Explorer, navigate to the folder that contains the child differencing disk, click the appropriate VHD file, and then click Open.

4. In the Virtual Hard Disk Properties dialog box, click Reconnect to launch the Edit Virtual Hard Disk Wizard.

5. On the Reconnect Virtual Hard Disk page, click Next.

6. On the Reconnect To Parent Virtual Hard Disk page, type the fully qualified path and name of the parent virtual hard disk, or click Browse to use Windows Explorer to navigate to the folder and select the VHD file. After these actions are complete, click Next.

7. On the Completing The Edit Virtual Hard Disk Wizard page, review your selections.

8. Click Finish.

9. Ensure that the Virtual Hard Disk Properties dialog box reflects the correct fully qualified path to the parent virtual hard disk.

10. Click Close.

> **NOTE** As an alternative, you can bypass the Inspect Disk option and select Edit Disk from the Actions pane in the Hyper-V Manager. After you select the disconnected differencing disk, the Edit Virtual Hard Disk Wizard will automatically recognize that it needs to be reconnected and will present the Reconnect Virtual Hard Disk page of the Edit Virtual Hard Disk Wizard, as indicated in step 5 of the previous procedure.

Merging Differencing Disks

Although a differencing disk can be used to permanently store virtual machine data changes, you might need to combine the child differencing disk with the parent disk. Hyper-V provides two ways to accomplish this. You can either merge the differencing disk into the parent disk or merge the differencing disk and the parent disk into a new virtual hard disk. If you merge a differencing disk into the parent disk, the differencing disk is deleted upon completion of the process, and any other differencing disk that points to the original parent disk is invalidated. If you need to retain the differencing disk, you should choose to merge the differencing disk and parent disk into a new virtual hard disk. This approach is recommended to lower the risk of data loss. You can verify that the merge operation is successful prior to deleting the original files.

> **IMPORTANT** Prior to merging a differencing disk and parent disk into a new virtual hard disk, make sure there is enough space on the physical disk to perform the operation.

To merge a differencing disk into a new virtual hard disk, follow these steps:

1. Open the Hyper-V Manager console.

2. In the Actions pane, under the server name, click Edit Disk to launch the Edit Virtual Hard Disk Wizard.

3. On the Before You Begin page, click Next.

4. On the Locate Virtual Hard Disk page, type the fully qualified path to the differencing disk that you want to merge, or click Browse to use Windows Explorer to select it. Then, click Next.

5. On the Choose Action page, select Merge and then click Next.

6. On the Merge Changes From Differencing Disk page, select the To A New Virtual Hard Disk option. You must type the fully qualified path and the name of the new virtual hard disk, or click Browse to use Windows Explorer to select the folder and then type the name. Then, you must select the new hard disk type (dynamic or fixed). After these actions are complete, click Next.

7. On the Completing The Edit Virtual Hard Disk Wizard page, review your selections.

8. Click Finish.

Using Differencing Disks

Functionality gains from using differencing disks become evident when you consider a typical support scenario. A support engineer often needs to troubleshoot server configurations for different operating system update levels or with different applications. Using one or more physical test servers, even with preconfigured build images, the setup and testing of multiple server configurations is a lengthy, complex process that results in protracted problem response time. Using Hyper-V with differencing disks, a support engineer can quickly create a virtual machine for each unique server configuration. Starting with a common parent virtual hard disk that contains the base operating system, each individual server configuration is created as a new virtual machine with one or more differencing disks to capture incremental operating system patches and application stacks.

> **IMPORTANT**   Differencing disks should not be used with cluster configurations.

As shown in Figure 5-3, implementing a virtualized support environment using differencing disks can help significantly reduce the setup and test cycles associated with problem resolution response time. Even with a single physical server constraint, a Hyper-V server can run multiple virtual machines (VMs) concurrently, allowing parallel testing of distinctive server configurations. In addition to creating an environment that can lead to faster support response time, this solution also has the benefit of saving significant amounts of physical disk space for any scenario that requires multiple complex configurations sharing a large common software base.

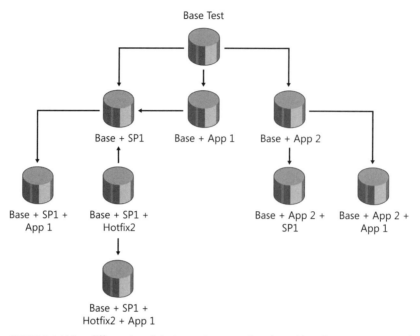

FIGURE 5-3 Using differencing disks to create guest virtual machines for concurrent testing

Automatic Differencing Disks

Automatic differencing disks are similar to differencing disks. Like a differencing disk, an automatic differencing disk is used to isolate virtual machine data changes from a base virtual hard disk. Automatic differencing disks also share the special dynamic disk characteristics previously defined for differencing disks. However, automatic differencing disks are used to support the Hyper-V virtual machine snapshot feature when data changes need to be quickly discarded or a rapid rollback to the base virtual machine state is required.

> **NOTE** Unlike a differencing disk, which has a .vhd file name extension, an automatic differencing disk uses an .avhd file name extension. By default, automatic differencing disks are stored in the same directory as the virtual machine in a subdirectory named Snapshots.

> **MORE INFO** To learn more about the Hyper-V virtual machine snapshot feature, refer to the section titled "Using Virtual Machine Snapshot Features" later in this chapter.

One major distinction between differencing disks and automatic differencing disks is in the configuration process. A differencing disk is created at an individual virtual hard disk level and usually is associated with the creation of a new virtual machine. In contrast, an automatic differencing disk is created by Hyper-V when a virtual machine snapshot is generated. An automatic differencing disk is created for every virtual hard disk associated with the virtual machine. In other words, you do not have the ability to individually choose the virtual hard disks for which automatic differencing disks are generated.

> **IMPORTANT**   If you need to move a virtual machine from one Hyper-V server to another, use the Hyper-V virtual machine export feature to ensure that virtual machine configuration files, parent virtual hard disks, child differencing disks, and automatic differencing disks associated with snapshots are saved in a single export directory.

Physical Disk to VHD Copy

Hyper-V allows you to duplicate the contents of a physical drive into a new virtual hard disk. There are several requirements to consider when using this method to migrate the contents of the physical disk into a virtual hard disk. The limitations are as follows:

- VHD copy is limited to converting a physical disk, not a volume or a partition.
- VHD copy must be used only to migrate a data disk; operating system disk migration is not supported.
- VHD copy should be used to convert a physical disk that is not being accessed by the host operating system or applications during the conversion process.
- VHD copy requires that if the physical disk that is being converted is larger than 127 gigabytes (GB), you must attach the virtual hard disk into which the disk contents will be copied to a virtual SCSI adapter.

Depending on the size of the physical disk that you select to copy to a VHD, this process can take a considerable amount of time.

> **BEST PRACTICES**   Prior to starting the VHD copy, you should use the Disk Management Microsoft Management Console (MMC) or other similar tool to remove the drive letter for the target drive. This will make the drive inaccessible to the host operating system, preventing disk corruption during the conversion process.

Converting a Physical Disk to a Virtual Hard Disk

The process to create a new virtual hard disk from a physical disk is simple. To begin the process and copy the physical drive content to a new virtual hard disk, follow these steps:

1. Open the Hyper-V Manager console.
2. In the Actions pane, under the server name, click New and then select Hard Disk from the menu to launch the New Virtual Hard Disk Wizard.

3. On the Before You Begin page, click Next.

4. On the Choose Disk Type page, select the type of disk to create (Dynamically Expanding or Fixed Size) and then click Next.

5. On the Specify Name And Location page, type a name for the new virtual hard disk in the Name text box and then type a fully qualified path to the storage folder in the Location text box, or click Browse to use Windows Explorer to select the storage folder. After you complete these actions, click Next.

6. On the Configure Disk page, select Copy The Contents Of The Specified Physical Disk and then click the physical hard disk that you want to convert from the list that is presented. After you complete these actions, click Next.

7. On the Completing The New Virtual Hard Disk Wizard page, review your selections.

8. Click Finish.

NOTE You should use a fixed-size disk as the target for the VHD conversion unless you have a requirement for dynamic expansion of the virtual hard disk.

Converting a VHD

In Hyper-V, you can convert a dynamically expanding VHD to a fixed VHD or convert a fixed-size VHD to a dynamically expanding VHD. A dynamically expanding VHD makes the most efficient use of physical disk space, but with a performance penalty caused by file fragmentation. If you create a 1-GB dynamically expanding VHD, its initial size on the physical disk is about 10 kilobytes (KB), whereas a maximum size 2040-GB dynamically expanding VHD initially uses approximately 16 megabytes (MB) of disk space. Since a new dynamically expanding VHD does not yet contain data, the initial size reflects the VHD file header and footer information and block allocation table. As new data is written within the virtual machine, Hyper-V expands the VHD size up to its preset limit.

In contrast, a fixed-size VHD provides better performance because the entire physical disk allocation for a fixed-size VHD occurs when it is initially created, generally resulting in contiguous block allocation. Similar to a dynamically expanding VHD, a fixed-size VHD initially contains a file header, footer, and block allocation table, as well as a data segment with empty blocks. As the virtual machine writes new data to the VHD, the empty blocks are replaced with the data.

During the process to convert a dynamically expanding VHD to a fixed-size VHD and vice versa, Hyper-V creates a new VHD of the type specified and copies the contents from the original VHD into it. To use the VHD convert option, follow these steps:

1. Open the Hyper-V Manager console.

2. In the Actions pane, under the server name, click Edit Disk to launch the Edit Virtual Hard Disk Wizard.

3. On the Before You Begin page, click Next.

4. On the Locate Virtual Hard Disk page, type the fully qualified path to the virtual hard disk that you want to compact, or click Browse to use Windows Explorer to select it and then click Next.

5. On the Choose Action page, select Convert and then click Next.

6. On the Convert Virtual Hard Disk page, type the fully qualified path of the converted virtual hard disk that you want to create, or click Browse to use Windows Explorer to select the location, type in the VHD name, and then click Next.

7. On the Completing The Edit Virtual Hard Disk Wizard page, review your selections.

8. Click Finish.

 CAUTION Converting a VHD requires that you have enough disk space to concurrently store the original virtual hard disk file and the new virtual hard disk. Hyper-V checks the storage space on the target disk prior to starting the process to convert the VHD and returns an error if there is insufficient space available. After a successful conversion, the original virtual hard disk is retained on the source disk.

Compacting a VHD

VHD compaction is a process that reduces the size of a virtual hard disk file on a physical disk. Hyper-V includes a compaction option that removes blocks that are physically all zeros or blocks that are marked as unused space in dynamically expanding or differencing virtual hard disks if they are NTFS formatted. Fixed-size virtual hard disks have to be converted to a dynamically expanding disk prior to being compacted. Although it is possible to use the Hyper-V compaction option by itself, a better approach is to use a two-step process that includes defragmentation prior to compaction. In order to use the Hyper-V compaction option, a virtual hard disk must not be in active use by a virtual machine.

NOTE Prior to virtual hard disk file defragmentation, remove temporary files and folders, delete any other unwanted data, and empty the recycle bin.

If a dynamically expanding or differencing virtual hard disk is not NTFS formatted, then you must use a three-step process that includes defragmentation, precompaction, and compaction. Defragmentation and precompaction prepare the virtual hard disk file for the compaction process. Precompaction replaces blank spaces in a virtual hard disk file with zeros. This allows Hyper-V to remove sectors that contain only zeros during compaction, resulting in greater reductions in file size. VHD compaction requires that a virtual hard disk be offline; therefore, any virtual machine that may access a virtual hard disk must be powered off prior to compaction.

Compacting a VHD After Deleting a Partition in the Guest Operating System

Rob Hefner, Support Escalation Engineer
Microsoft Enterprise Platforms Support

If you delete a partition in a guest operating system, you may find that Hyper-V compaction may not completely compact the associated VHD. For example, consider a 100-GB VHD that originally had two partitions defined in the guest operating system: a 10-GB partition, and another 90-GB partition. If you delete the 90-GB partition, the VHD could still be larger than 10 GB, even though it now contains only a single 10-GB partition. Hyper-V compaction will not fully compact the VHD because it operates only on active partitions. In order to perform a full compaction in this type of scenario, you should run a disk defragmention utility inside the guest operating system, then create an NTFS partition using the unallocated space, and finally, power off the virtual machine and run the Hyper-V compaction using the Edit Disk Wizard in Hyper-V Manager. If you follow this process, the VHD will be fully compacted.

BEST PRACTICES Because of processor and disk resource requirements, you should use a nonproduction server, when possible, to perform the virtual hard disk compaction process. In Hyper-V, you can perform the defragmentation and precompaction step within a virtual machine or by mounting a virtual hard disk on a Hyper-V server while the virtual hard disk is offline. It is recommended that you perform defragmentation, precompaction, and compaction with the virtual hard disk offline.

Defragmenting the Virtual Hard Disk File

The first step in the process to reduce the size of a virtual hard disk file is defragmentation. As new information is written to disk, data might not be saved in contiguous disk blocks. In time, as you delete data on the disk, empty blocks will be randomly filled with file fragments. Performance is adversely affected when the disk fragmentation is excessive because it takes longer to retrieve related data spread across a disk than if it were located in a contiguous set of blocks. Defragmentation reduces or eliminates the number of fragmented files on a disk, resulting in larger areas of empty contiguous blocks.

To defragment a virtual hard disk offline, you first have to mount the virtual hard disk file on a Hyper-V server and bring it online. Following is a simple example of using a PowerShell script to mount a VHD file, assign it a drive letter, and bring it online.

```
#Specify the fully qualified path for the VHD file to be mounted
$VHDFilename = "D:\HVResKit\Win2003\BaseX86VM.vhd"

#Get a pointer to the MSVM_ImageManagementService WMI object
$IMGMgtSvc = get-wmiobject -class "Msvm_ImageManagementService"
      -namespace "root\virtualization" -computername "."

#Mount the VHD file
$Result = $IMGMgtSvc.Mount($VHDFilename)

#Check result of VHD mount action and get disk index
if ($Result.returnValue -eq 4096)
      {$Job = [WMI]$result.job
      while ($job.jobstate -eq 4) {Start-Sleep -seconds 1 ; $Job.PSBase.Get() }
      Start-sleep 2
      $MountedDiskImage= Get-WmiObject -NameSpace "root\virtualization"
      -query ("Select *
      from Msvm_MountedStorageImage where name ='"+
      $VHDFilename.replace("\","\\")  +"'")
      $diskIndex=(Get-WmiObject -Query "Select * From win32_diskdrive Where Model='Msft
      Virtual Disk SCSI Disk Device' and ScsiTargetID=$($MountedDiskImage.TargetId) and
      ScsiLogicalUnit=$($MountedDiskImage.Lun) and
      ScsiPort=$($MountedDiskImage.PortNumber)").index

#Bring the VHD online using Dispart
      if ($diskIndex -ne $null) {@("select disk $diskIndex", "online disk" ,
      "attributes disk clear readonly", "exit")  | Diskpart | Out-Null}
      }
```

After the virtual hard disk file is mounted, use the Windows Defrag utility on the server system to defragment the virtual hard disk file. The time required to defragment the virtual hard disk file depends on several factors, including the degree of fragmentation, file size, and disk characteristics.

> **NOTE** In Windows Server 2008, use "Defrag *DriveLetter* –w" from the command line, where *DriveLetter* is the drive letter associated with the mounted virtual hard disk, and –w specifies that all file fragments should be consolidated, regardless of size.

Precompacting the Virtual Hard Disk File

For virtual hard disk files that are not NTFS formatted, the second step in the process is precompaction. Hyper-V does not provide a precompaction tool. However, Virtual Server 2005 R2 includes the Virtual Disk Precompactor, which is designed to overwrite any unallocated disk blocks in a virtual hard disk file with zeros. You can use it to prepare the virtual hard disk and ensure that the Hyper-V compaction tool can make a non-NTFS virtual hard disk file as small as possible.

The Virtual Disk Precompactor is contained in the Precompact.iso disk image that is included with Virtual Server 2005 R2. If you have Virtual Server 2005 R2 installed on a system, copy the Precompact.iso file to the Hyper-V server and use your favorite virtual CD tool to mount the image and retrieve the Precompact.exe tool. Table 5-3 lists the options that are available when you invoke the Virtual Disk Precompactor tool from the command line.

TABLE 5-3 Virtual Disk Precompactor Command-Line Options

COMMAND-LINE OPTION	DESCRIPTION
–Help	Displays the help dialog box that lists the command-line options, product version, and syntax examples.
–Version	Displays the help dialog box that lists the command-line options, product version, and syntax examples.
–Silent	Executes the precompactor in unattended mode and suppresses all dialog boxes.
–SetDisks:<*list*> *<list>* is an optional parameter that represents one or more drive letters.	Defines the list of virtual hard disks to precompact. If this option is not specified, all virtual hard disks attached to a virtual machine are compacted.

For example, the following command precompacts virtual hard disks mounted to drive letters F and G, in unattended mode:

```
Precompact –Silent –SetDisks:FG
```

> **NOTE** Hyper-V also allows precompacting virtual hard disk files from within a virtual machine. After you capture the Precompact.iso image on the virtual machine CD or DVD drive, you can double-click the drive to launch Virtual Disk Precompactor. Using this process, you cannot specify which virtual hard disk to precompact. Instead, Virtual Disk Precompactor precompacts all virtual hard disks attached to the virtual machine.

Compacting the Virtual Hard Disk File

The final step in the process to reduce the virtual hard disk size is disk compaction. The Hyper-V compaction tool finds disk blocks that are empty and removes them, reducing the virtual hard disk file size.

Before you use the Hyper-V compaction tool, you should unmount the virtual hard disk from the Hyper-V server. Here is a simple example of using a PowerShell script to unmount a VHD file.

```
#Specify the fully qualified path for the VHD file to be unmounted
$VHDFilename = "D:\HVResKit\Win2003\BaseX86VM.vhd"


#Get a pointer to the MSVM_ImageManagementService WMI object
$ImgMgtSvc = Get-WmiObject -NameSpace  "root\virtualization" -Class
"MsVM_ImageManagementService"


#Unmount the VHD file
$Result=$ImgMgtSvc.Unmount($VHDFilename)
```

To compact a virtual hard disk, follow these steps:

1. Open the Hyper-V Manager console.

2. In the Actions pane, under the server name, click Edit Disk to launch the Edit Virtual Hard Disk Wizard.

3. On the Before You Begin page, click Next.

4. On the Locate Virtual Hard Disk page, type the fully qualified path to the virtual hard disk that you want to compact, or click Browse to use Windows Explorer to select it. After this action is complete, click Next.

5. On the Choose Action page, select Compact and then click Next.

6. On the Completing The Edit Virtual Hard Disk Wizard page, review your selections.

7. Click Finish.

The VHD compaction process can also be scripted using the Hyper-V WMI API. This API allows you to create scripts and compact the virtual hard disk files outside of the Hyper-V Manager console.

 ON THE COMPANION MEDIA   On the book's companion media, you will find a directory called \Chapter Materials\Scripts\Chapter 5\Compact. Inside the directory, there are three files: a PowerShell script named CompactVHD.ps1, the PowerShell Management Library for Hyper-V named Hyperv.ps1, and an XML file named Hyperv.format.ps1xml. All three files must be stored in the same directory on your Hyper-V server. The CompactVHD.ps1 script uses functions in Hyperv.ps1 to mount the virtual hard disk file and run the defragmenter before invoking the Hyper-V compaction tool to compact the virtual hard disk offline. For more information on the Hyperv.ps1 management library, refer to *http://pshyperv.codeplex.com*.

Expanding a VHD

Another Hyper-V VHD feature is the ability to expand the maximum size of a dynamically expanding or fixed-size VHD. When Hyper-V expands the VHD, it adds the additional storage space at the end of the VHD file. After the VHD file has been expanded, you must create a new partition or expand a volume to use the additional storage space. It is important to note that a VHD cannot be expanded unless the virtual machine that it is connected to is powered off. To expand the size of a dynamically expanding or fixed-size VHD, follow these steps:

1. Open the Hyper-V Manager console.

2. In the Actions pane, under the server name, click Edit Disk to launch the Edit Virtual Hard Disk Wizard.

3. On the Before You Begin page, click Next.

4. On the Locate Virtual Hard Disk page, type the fully qualified path to the virtual hard disk that you want to compact, or click Browse to use Windows Explorer to select it. After this action is complete, click Next.

5. On the Choose Action page, select Expand and then click Next.

6. On the Expand Virtual Hard Disk page, type the new size for the VHD and then click Next.

7. On the Completing the Edit Virtual Hard Disk Wizard page, review your selections.

8. Click Finish.

 CAUTION It is important to note that you should not expand a VHD if it is connected to a virtual machine for which snapshots exist, or if it is the parent of a child differencing disk. Any modification made to a VHD in a differencing disk chain can invalidate all child differencing disks in the chain.

Using Virtual Machine Snapshot Features

Hyper-V virtual machine snapshots allow you to capture the configuration and state of a virtual machine at any point in time and return a virtual machine to that state without noticeable interruption. When you take a snapshot of a running virtual machine, Hyper-V briefly pauses the virtual machine to create a new automatic virtual hard disk (.avhd), attaches it to the virtual machine to capture changes to any virtual machine data from that point in time, saves the processor state into a file (.vsv), and then resumes the virtual machine. Hyper-V also makes a copy of the virtual machine configuration file (.xml), and saves the contents of the virtual machine memory into a file (.bin). Snapshots can also be created when a virtual machine is turned off, in which case Hyper-V does not need to capture virtual machine memory or processor state data.

In Hyper-V, the parent partition creates and manages child partitions through a set of components referred to as the *virtualization stack*. One of the components in the virtualization stack is the Virtual Machine Management Service (VMMS). The VMMS includes many critical subcomponents, including the Worker Process Manager (WPM) and the Snapshot Manager (SM). The WPM creates a Virtual Machine Worker Process (VMWP) for each virtual machine when it is started. The VMWP manages the creation of snapshots for a virtual machine that is in an online state (started and running). If a virtual machine is offline, and therefore does not have an active VMWP, the Snapshot Manager handles the snapshot creation process.

> **MORE INFO** To learn more about the role of each of these components in the creation of a virtual machine snapshot, refer to Chapter 3, "Hyper-V Architecture."

The Hyper-V virtual machine snapshot feature is principally for use in test and development environments, not in a production infrastructure. You must not use snapshots as a recovery mechanism for transactional applications like Microsoft Exchange Server or Active Directory Domain Services. However, snapshots can be extremely useful in scenarios in which you need to make incremental changes to a virtual machine with the ability to roll back to a previous state. An image build lab, help desk, and application testing lab represent excellent candidates for environments that can heavily leverage Hyper-V virtual machine snapshots to improve their functional efficiency.

Before delving more deeply into the creation and use of Hyper-V virtual machine snapshots, it is important to understand the file structure of a virtual machine on a Hyper-V server. As shown in Figure 5-4, the virtual machine folder and file structure on a default installation of Hyper-V includes:

- A Virtual Hard Disks folder that stores one or more virtual hard disks that contain the guest operating system files, application files, and data.

- A Snapshots folder that initially does not contain any files.

- A Virtual Machines folder that contains an XML-based virtual machine configuration file named using a globally unique identifier (GUID), and a folder named with the same GUID that contains two files. The first file is a saved state file (named using the same GUID as the XML file and with a .vsv extension) that is used to store virtual machine state information, such as processor register data. The second file is a binary file (also named with the same GUID as the XML file and with a .bin extension) that is used to store the virtual machine memory contents.

```
C:\ProgramData\Microsoft\Windows\Hyper-V
    Snapshots
    Virtual Machines
        6A88A1EC-7B39-4CCA-9890-0BA917A11773
            6A88A1EC-7B39-4CCA-9890-0BA917A11773.bin
            6A88A1EC-7B39-4CCA-9890-0BA917A11773.vsv
        6A88A1EC-7B39-4CCA-9890-0BA917A11773.xml
    .
    .
    .
C:\Users\Public\Documents\Microsoft Hyper-V\Virtual Hard Disks
    Basex86VM.VHD
```

FIGURE 5-4 Virtual machine folder and file structure on a default Hyper-V installation

For a virtual machine without snapshots, all changes made to the virtual machine guest operating system files, application files, and data are contained within the virtual hard disk associated with the virtual machine. Any state information is stored in the .vsv and .bin files. When you make any changes to the virtual machine settings, the modifications are stored in the associated .xml configuration file.

Creating a Virtual Machine Snapshot

The Hyper-V Manager console allows you to create, view, and manipulate virtual machine snapshots. As shown in Figure 5-5, Hyper-V Manager includes a Snapshots pane that is empty if a virtual machine does not have any associated snapshots. In order to create a snapshot in Hyper-V Manager, right-click a virtual machine and select the Snapshot option from the menu.

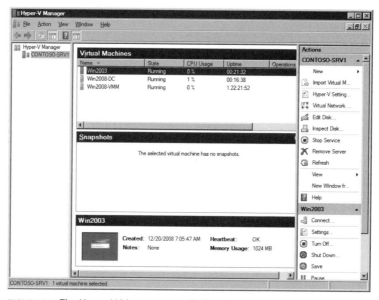

FIGURE 5-5 The Hyper-V Manager console Snapshot pane

Essentially, the snapshot creation process generates several new folders and files that contain the virtual machine snapshot information. As shown in Figure 5-6, the following folders and files are created in the virtual machine Snapshots folder:

- A new folder named with the original virtual machine GUID. In this folder, a new automatic differencing disk is created for each virtual hard disk associated with the virtual machine. The new automatic differencing disk is named using the original virtual hard disk name appended with a new GUID and an .avhd extension.

- A copy of the original virtual machine configuration file named using a new GUID and .xml extension.

- A new folder named using the same GUID as the new .xml file. This folder contains the saved state file (.vsv) and binary file (.bin) that are created during the virtual machine snapshot. Both files are named with the same GUID as their folder.

In addition, the original virtual machine configuration file is updated to replace the original virtual hard disk file name with that of the new automatic differencing disk.

- C:\ProgramData\Microsoft\Windows\Hyper-V
  - Snapshots
    - 30B05E02-C23C-4963-AD7C-36EE63516D1C
      - 6A88A1EC-7B39-4CCA-9890-0BA917A11773.bin
      - 6A88A1EC-7B39-4CCA-9890-0BA917A11773.vsv
    - 6A88A1EC-7B39-4CCA-9890-0BA917A11773
      - Basex86VM_676E5888-060A-40CF-B19B-40928836DB34.AVHD
    - 30B05E02-C23C-4963-AD7C-36EE63516D1C.xml
  - Virtual Machines
    - 6A88A1EC-7B39-4CCA-9890-0BA917A11773
      - 6A88A1EC-7B39-4CCA-9890-0BA917A11773.bin
      - 6A88A1EC-7B39-4CCA-9890-0BA917A11773.vsv
    - 6A88A1EC-7B39-4CCA-9890-0BA917A11773.xml

  .
  .
  .

- C:\Users\Public\Documents\Microsoft Hyper-V\Virtual Hard Disks
  - Basex86VM.VHD

FIGURE 5-6 Virtual machine Snapshots folder file structure after the first snapshot

If a virtual machine is offline or powered off when a snapshot is created, then there is no virtual machine state or memory contents to save, and those files (.vsv, .bin) are not generated. After a snapshot is created, all guest operating system, application, and data changes made during the execution of the virtual machine are stored in the associated automatic differencing disk. The original virtual hard disk is retained, as it is the parent of the automatic differencing disk, and is needed to return the virtual machine to the state of the first snapshot.

As shown in Figure 5-7, for each subsequent snapshot that is created, a new set of folders and files is generated to capture the virtual machine state and configuration. One important item to note is that automatic differencing disks that are created for every subsequent snapshot are related in a parent and child hierarchy with the original virtual hard disk as the top-level node.

- C:\ProgramData\Microsoft\Windows\Hyper-V
  - Snapshots
    - 30B05E02-C23C-4963-AD7C-36EE63516D1C *(Snapshot #1)*
      - 6A88A1EC-7B39-4CCA-9890-0BA917A11773.bin
      - 6A88A1EC-7B39-4CCA-9890-0BA917A11773.vsv
    - 6A88A1EC-7B39-4CCA-9890-0BA917A11773 *(Snapshot #1)*
      - Basex86VM_676E5888-060A-40CF-B19B-40928836DB34.avhd *(Snapshot #1)*
      - Basex86VM_623A3350-6CC8-4BBD-81BB-3E1800C0C634.avhd *(Snapshot #2)*
    - F8FAF91E-4008-4718-9B24-BA41F76F41C5 *(Snapshot #2)*
      - 6A88A1EC-7B39-4CCA-9890-0BA917A11773.bin
      - 6A88A1EC-7B39-4CCA-9890-0BA917A11773.vsv
    - 30B05E02-C23C-4963-AD7C-36EE63516D1C.xml *(Snapshot #1)*
    - F8FAF91E-4008-4718-9B24-BA41F76F41C5.xml *(Snapshot #2)*
  - Virtual Machines
    - 6A88A1EC-7B39-4CCA-9890-0BA917A11773
      - 6A88A1EC-7B39-4CCA-9890-0BA917A11773.bin
      - 6A88A1EC-7B39-4CCA-9890-0BA917A11773.vsv
    - 6A88A1EC-7B39-4CCA-9890-0BA917A11773.xml

.
.
.

- C:\Users\Public\Documents\Microsoft Hyper-V\Virtual Hard Disks
  - Basex86VM.VHD

FIGURE 5-7 Virtual machine Snapshots folder file structure after the second snapshot

Figure 5-8 illustrates the changes in the Hyper-V Manager console after two virtual machine snapshots. The Snapshots pane displays a tree structure that reflects the virtual machine snapshot hierarchy. The root node of the tree is the first snapshot that was created and includes the creation time stamp. Under the root node, there is the second snapshot, and following it is an object named Now that represents the running (or active) version of the virtual machine. The snapshot hierarchy also reflects the relationship of the automatic differencing disks that are created for each snapshot. Within a snapshot hierarchy, when a new snapshot is created, the active automatic differencing disk is disconnected from the virtual machine and becomes the parent of a new child automatic differencing disk that is in turn connected to the virtual machine. The new child automatic differencing disk captures changes to the virtual machine operating system files, application files, and data until the next snapshot is taken.

As you make changes to the configuration of a virtual machine, you can create and save multiple snapshots. For example, if you want to load and test multiple applications on a particular virtual machine, you can load one application at a time, test it, and take a snapshot of the virtual machine before proceeding to load and test the next application.

> **IMPORTANT** There is a limit of 50 snapshots for each virtual machine. By design, if you attempt to create another snapshot after you have reached this limit, you will receive an error reporting that the snapshot failed.

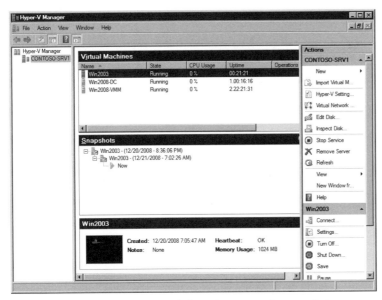

FIGURE 5-8 Hyper-V Manager console Snapshots pane after snapshots

If you right-click a virtual machine that has one or more snapshots, a Revert option appears in the menu that allows you to return quickly to the immediately preceding virtual machine state.

If you right-click a snapshot in the Hyper-V Manager, several menu options are available. These options include:

- **Settings** Opens the virtual machine settings dialog box and allows review of the virtual machine configuration when the snapshot was created. None of the hardware or management settings can be changed, with the exception of the snapshot name and associated notes.

- **Apply** Changes the state of the active virtual machine to that of the selected snapshot.

- **Rename** Edits the name of the snapshot displayed in the Hyper-V Manager Snapshots pane.

- **Delete Snapshot** Deletes the selected snapshot files, with the exception of the automatic differencing disk if it is the parent of another automatic differencing disk in the snapshot hierarchy. The automatic differencing disk may have to be merged with a child differencing disk to allow the active virtual machine or a subsequent snapshot to maintain data state. Automatic differencing disks are merged the next time that the virtual machine is powered off.

- **Delete Snapshot Subtree** Deletes the selected snapshot and any snapshot that is in the hierarchy beneath it.

All of these options are discussed in more detail in the following sections.

Using the Revert Snapshot Option

If, after making a series of changes to a virtual machine, you decide that you need to return to the state of the previous snapshot, Hyper-V provides a Revert option to perform this action. After the Revert action is applied to a virtual machine, the configuration and state of the virtual machine are returned to the settings saved in the snapshot that immediately precedes the running virtual machine in the snapshot hierarchy. This means that any and all configuration changes made since the snapshot was created, including virtual hardware modifications to RAM, number of processors, virtual hard disk adapters, and so on, will be lost.

When a Revert is performed, the running virtual machine is stopped and the active differencing disk (.avhd) is deleted. A new differencing disk is created and named using a new GUID. The virtual machine configuration saved during the snapshot is reinstated and the name of the new active differencing disk is updated. The virtual machine is then restarted and the save state files (.vsv and .bin) are loaded. If the snapshot was created when the virtual machine was powered off, then there are no save state files to load, and the virtual machine remains powered off.

Using the Apply Snapshot Option

In order to change the state of the active virtual machine to a snapshot that is more than one level higher in the snapshot hierarchy, you must right-click the snapshot in the Hyper-V Manager and select the Apply option from the menu, as shown in Figure 5-9.

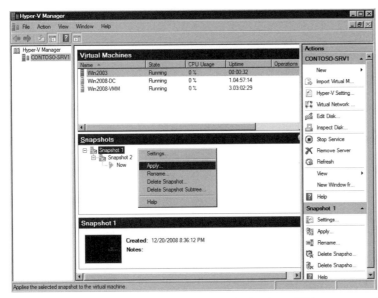

FIGURE 5-9 Selecting the Apply snapshot option in the Hyper-V Manager console

Figure 5-10 shows the dialog box that prompts you to create a snapshot of the active virtual machine prior to performing the Apply operation, or you can choose to continue and apply the selected snapshot without saving the current configuration and state. As in the case of the Revert option, if you don't take a snapshot prior to the Apply operation, the running virtual machine configuration and state is lost.

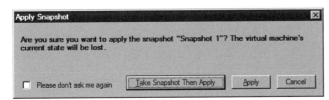

FIGURE 5-10 Hyper-V Manager console prompt after selecting the Apply snapshot option

The snapshot Apply action is similar to the Revert action. The active virtual machine is stopped, the automatic differencing disk is deleted, and a new automatic differencing disk is created. The snapshot virtual machine configuration is restored and the name of the new automatic differencing disk is updated in the virtual machine configuration file. The virtual machine is then restarted, and the save state files (.vsv and .bin) are loaded.

As shown in Figure 5-11, the Now marker moved right under the applied snapshot to indicate that the active virtual machine is based on it.

FIGURE 5-11 Hyper-V Manager console showing the Now marker position after the Apply snapshot option

At this point, if a new snapshot is created, it will create a new subtree in the snapshot hierarchy, as shown in Figure 5-12.

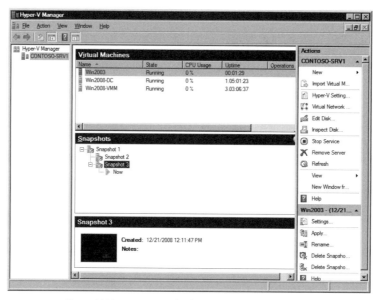

FIGURE 5-12 Hyper-V Manager console showing a new snapshot subtree

Using the Delete Snapshot Option

If you decide that you no longer need a snapshot, Hyper-V provides the Delete Snapshot option to permanently remove a single snapshot from the snapshot hierarchy. To delete a single snapshot, right-click the snapshot in the Hyper-V Manager console and select the Delete Snapshot option from the menu.

Deleting a single snapshot will not affect other snapshots, but it will immediately delete the configuration file and save state files associated with the snapshot. If you recall, in a snapshot hierarchy, snapshot automatic differencing disks are related to each other through a parent-child relationship. Therefore, a snapshot automatic differencing disk is immediately deleted only if it is not the parent of a child automatic differencing disk. If there is only one child automatic differencing disk, it is merged into the parent automatic differencing disk the next time that the virtual machine is powered off. If a parent automatic differencing disk has multiple children, then it is retained until only one of the child automatic differencing disk remains. The child automatic differencing disk is then merged into the parent automatic differencing disk the next time that the virtual machine is powered off.

Using the Delete Snapshot Subtree Option

Deleting a snapshot subtree immediately deletes the configuration and save state files associated with all the snapshots in the subtree. If the active virtual machine automatic differencing disk is not a child of any snapshot in the subtree, then all of the automatic differencing disks in the subtree will also be deleted. If the active virtual machine automatic differencing disk depends on a chain of automatic differencing disks in the subtree that is deleted, then the automatic differencing disk chain will be merged into the automatic differencing disk that is one level above the deleted subtree the next time that the virtual machine is powered off.

Using Integration Services Features

In a virtualized environment, processes that require an interface between a parent and child partition must do so in a manner that does not compromise the secure operation or isolation of resources in either partition. In Hyper-V, Integration Services (IS) provide support for five unique components that require a secure interface between a parent and child partition. These components include:

- Time synchronization service
- Heartbeat service
- Shutdown service
- Key/value pair exchange service
- Volume Shadow Copy Service (VSS)

Hyper-V Integration Services are available in a child partition after they are installed in a supported guest operating system. Integration Services communicate with components in the parent partition virtualization stack that are implemented as virtual devices (VDEVs). Communication between the parent and child partition components takes place over the Hyper-V VMBus. The VMBus supports high-speed, point-to-point channels for secure inter-partition communication that enhance virtual machine performance. A separate, dedicated VDEV manages each of the parent partition Integration Services functions. Correspondingly, a separate, dedicated service manages each of the Integration Services functions in the child partition.

> **MORE INFO**   To learn more about the Hyper-V Integration Services architecture, refer to Chapter 3.

Integration Services target very specific areas that enhance the functionality or management of supported guest operating systems. It is important to note that only a subset of Integration Components may be supported for some legacy or non-Windows guest operating systems. For example, since VSS is supported only in Windows operating systems beginning with Windows Server 2003, the VSS Integration Component will not be available for Windows 2000 Server, Windows XP, or supported Linux distributions.

Time Synchronization Service

An operating system running directly on a physical server usually relies on a combination of hardware and network-based protocols to maintain time accuracy. In Hyper-V, Integration Services provide an alternate solution to traditional hardware and network-based procedures and ensure that a virtual machine running in a child partition can use the parent partition as a consistent and reliable time synchronization source. In particular, Integration Services time synchronization addresses two specific situations:

- Keeping time synchronized in the guest operating system to account for time-drift in the virtual machine
- Restoring a virtual machine from a snapshot or saved state when a significant amount of time has passed since the guest operating system last synched time

Parent partition-based time synchronization makes it possible to deal with the following issues:

- Lack of network connectivity that makes traditional network-based protocols unusable
- Need for quicker time synchronization than network-based protocols can provide to allow fast virtual machine startup after a saved state or in the case of restoring a snapshot
- Need for successful time synchronization in the event that significant time has passed since the virtual machine was last online, as after a saved state or for a snapshot

In the last case, a standard network-based protocol could fail to successfully synchronize as the maximum time difference allowed could commonly be exceeded for virtual machine snapshots or even after a saved state.

Heartbeat Service

The Integration Services heartbeat functionality provides a mechanism for the parent partition to detect whether a guest operating system running in a child partition has become unresponsive. Essentially, the parent partition sends regular heartbeat requests to a child partition and logs an event if a response is not received within a defined time boundary. If a heartbeat response is not received within the expected delay, the parent partition will continue to send heartbeat requests and generate events for missing responses.

Shutdown Service

In order to cleanly shut down a virtual machine without needing to interact directly with the guest operating system through a virtual machine connection or remote desktop protocol (RDP) session, Integration Services provides a virtual machine shutdown function. The shutdown request is initiated from the parent partition to the child partition using a Windows Management Instrumentation (WMI) call.

Key/Value Pair Exchange Service

The purpose of the Integration Services key/value pair exchange functionality is to provide a means to set, delete, and enumerate specific information about the virtual machine and guest operating system configuration running in a child partition. In this way, the parent partition can request to set specific data values in the guest operating system or retrieve the data to expose it to third-party management or other tools.

Key/value pair data is stored in the following guest operating system registry locations:

- HKLM\Software\Microsoft\Virtual Machine\Auto
- HKLM\Software\Microsoft\Virtual Machine\External
- HKLM\Software\Microsoft\Virtual Machine\Guest\Parameters

By default, the child partition exposes the data stored in HKLM\Software\Microsoft\Virtual Machine\Auto to the parent partition upon request. Table 5-4 lists the information contained in this section of the registry.

TABLE 5-4 Registry Parameters in HKLM\Software\Microsoft\Virtual Machine\Auto

PARAMETER	DESCRIPTION
OSMajorVersion	The major version number of the guest operating system.
OSMinorVersion	The minor version number of the guest operating system.
OSBuildNumber	The build number of the guest operating system.
OSVersion	The version of the guest operating system (e.g., 5.0.2195).
OSPlatformId	The guest operating system platform (Win9x, NT4, or later).
CSDVersion	The latest Service Pack installed in the guest operating system.
ServicePackMajor	The major version number of the latest Service Pack installed in the guest operating system.
ServicePackMinor	The minor version number of the latest Service Pack installed in the guest operating system.
SuiteMask	The product suites available on the system.
ProductType	The product type installed on the system (Workstation, Server, DC).
OSName	The name set in HKLM\Software\Microsoft\Windows NT\CurrentVersion\ProductName.
ProcessorArchitecture	A processor architecture identifier (Intel, Itanium, AMD, unknown).
FullyQualifiedDomainName	The fully qualified DNS name that uniquely identifies the guest operating system. This name is a combination of the DNS host name and the DNS domain name. If this is a node in a cluster, then it is the fully qualified DNS name of the cluster virtual server.

If the guest operating system in the child partition has key/value pair information that needs to be shared with the parent partition, it will be located in the HKLM\Software\Microsoft\Virtual Machine\External registry section.

The parent partition provides the values in HKLM\Software\Microsoft\Virtual Machine\Guest\Parameters to the child partition. Table 5-5 lists the information contained in this section of the registry.

TABLE 5-5 Registry Parameters in HKLM\Software\Microsoft\Virtual Machine\Guest\Parameters

PARAMETER	DESCRIPTION
HostName	The domain name system (DNS) name set in the parent partition operating system. If the system is a cluster node, then this is the DNS name of the cluster virtual server.
PhysicalHostName	The non–fully qualified name set in the parent partition operating system.
PhysicalHostNameFullyQualified	The fully qualified name set in the parent partition operating system.
VirtualMachineName	The name of the virtual machine used by the virtualization stack.

Volume Shadow Copy Service (VSS)

For guest operating systems that support VSS, Integration Services allow the parent partition to request the synchronization and quiescence of a virtual machine running in a child partition. If all guest operating systems support VSS, a backup of the entire Hyper-V server, including all offline and online virtual machines, can be accomplished using a VSS snapshot.

> **MORE INFO** To learn more about VSS and the options available to perform Hyper-V host-level and virtual machine backups, refer to Chapter 13, "Hyper-V Backup and Recovery."

Integration Services Supported Guest Operating Systems

As mentioned previously, only a subset of Integration Services components may be installed on legacy Windows operating systems and Linux distributions. Table 5-6 contains the Integration Services matrix for guest operating systems supported in Hyper-V.

TABLE 5-6 Integration Services Guest Operating System Support Matrix

OPERATING SYSTEM	TIME SYNCHRONIZATION	HEARTBEAT	SHUTDOWN	KEY/VALUE PAIR EXCHANGE	VSS
Windows Server 2008 x64	Y	Y	Y	Y	Y
Windows Server 2008 x86	Y	Y	Y	Y	Y
Windows Server 2003 x64 with SP2	Y	Y	Y	Y	Y

OPERATING SYSTEM	TIME SYNCHRONIZATION	HEARTBEAT	SHUTDOWN	KEY/VALUE PAIR EXCHANGE	VSS
Windows Server 2003 x86 with SP2	Y	Y	Y	Y	Y
Windows 2000 Server with SP4	Y	Y	Y	Y	N
Windows 2000 Advanced Server with SP4	Y	Y	Y	Y	N
Windows Vista x64 with SP1	Y	Y	Y	Y	Y
Windows Vista x86 with SP1	Y	Y	Y	Y	Y
Windows XP x86 with SP2 or SP3	Y	Y	Y	Y	N
Windows XP x64 with SP2	Y	Y	Y	Y	N
Suse Linux Enterprise Server 10 x64	N	N	N	N	N
Suse Linux Enterprise Server 10 x86	N	N	N	N	N

Using Virtual Network Advanced Features

The Hyper-V network architecture allows virtual machine network traffic to be isolated from other virtual machines, the Hyper-V server, and external networks. It also allows virtual machines to be connected to each other, the Hyper-V server, corporate networks, and the Internet. Many configuration options are available and some depend on the implementation of advanced network settings.

Understanding Virtual Network Traffic Flow

There are three basic virtual network types in Hyper-V: external, internal, and private. When you create an external virtual network, you have the ability to connect virtual machines to it that require access to your corporate LAN or to the Internet. An internal network allows virtual machines to communicate with the Hyper-V server and other virtual machines that are connected to it but does not provide access to external physical networks. A private network restricts virtual machines that are connected to it to communicate only with each other.

As shown in Figure 5-13, the Network Connections window for the Hyper-V server (i.e., the parent partition) before the first virtual network is created includes only the network adapters installed in the physical machine. Furthermore, the physical network adapter properties show that the default items are bound to the network adapter, and that there is an additional Microsoft Virtual Network Switch Protocol that it is not bound to the network adapter.

In the Device Manager, shown in Figure 5-14, the physical network adapters are the only items listed, as expected.

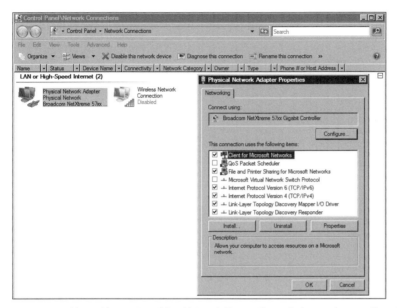

FIGURE 5-13 Hyper-V parent partition Network Connections window and properties with no virtual networks

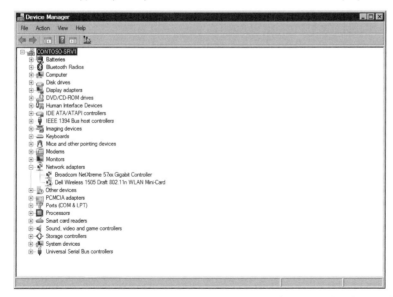

FIGURE 5-14 Hyper-V parent partition Device Manager without any virtual network adapters

External Virtual Network

As shown in Figure 5-15, when you create an external virtual network, Hyper-V creates two new components in the parent partition. The first component is a software-based or virtual network switch with the ability to add or remove network ports dynamically. Network ports are added to the virtual network switch as virtual machines are connected to the associated virtual network, and they are removed when virtual machines are disconnected from that virtual network. The second component is a virtual network adapter that is connected to the virtual network switch, and that allows the parent partition to directly communicate through that virtual network.

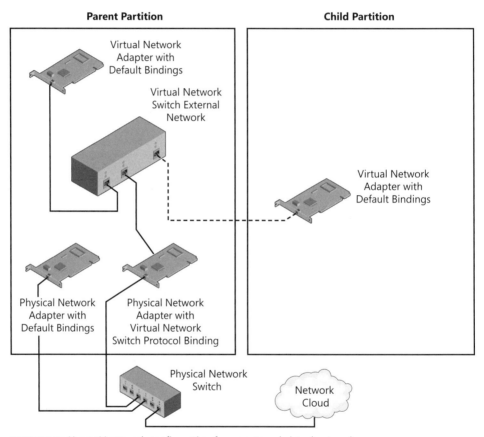

FIGURE 5-15 Hyper-V network configuration for an external virtual network

The virtual network adapter appears as a new component (in this case, Local Area Connection 2) in the Network Connections window, as shown in Figure 5-16. In addition, examining the properties reveals that the default items are bound to the network adapter.

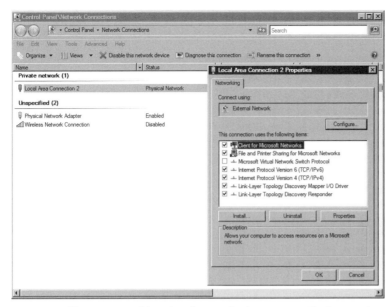

FIGURE 5-16 The parent partition virtual network adapter properties for an external virtual network

As shown in Figure 5-17, the physical network adapter has been reconfigured to unbind all the default items and is now bound only to the Microsoft Virtual Network Switch Protocol.

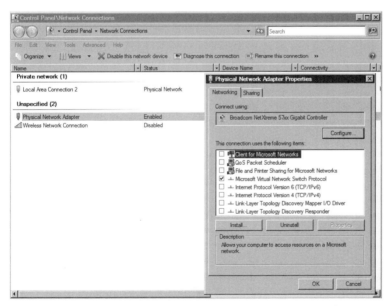

FIGURE 5-17 The parent partition physical network adapter properties for an external virtual network

In the Device Manager, shown in Figure 5-18, the virtual network adapter is now listed, and the device description in the properties defines that it is a Microsoft Virtual Network Switch adapter.

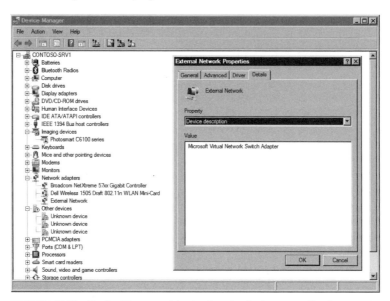

FIGURE 5-18 The Device Manager virtual network adapter properties for an external virtual network

When a virtual machine in a child partition needs to communicate through an external virtual network, the network traffic flow includes the following major steps:

- The data is sent through the guest operating system network stack bound to the virtual machine virtual network adapter (assuming there is only one virtual network adapter, as reflected in Figure 5-15).

- In the case of a synthetic network adapter, the data is sent to the virtual network switch in the parent partition through a VMBus connection. In the case of a legacy network adapter, the Windows Hypervisor intercepts the request and instructs the virtualization stack in the parent partition to retrieve the data from a preset memory buffer, which then sends it to the virtual network switch.

- The virtual network switch determines how to route the data to its destination.

- If the data destination is an external device on a physical network, the virtual network switch sends the data to the physical network adapter that is bound to the external virtual network, which transmits the data on the physical network.

- If the data destination is the parent partition, the virtual network switch sends the data to the network port to which the parent partition virtual network adapter is connected.

- Any return data or communication destined for the virtual machine follows the same path in reverse.

If a Hyper-V server is configured with a single physical network adapter, all data with a destination on the physical network is forced through the virtual network switch. As shown in Figure 5-15, it is recommended to configure at least two physical network adapters on the Hyper-V server and reserve one of these for its exclusive use.

> **NOTE** It is possible that network traffic from the parent partition with a destination on an external physical network can be routed through the virtual network switch instead of directly through the dedicated physical network adapter. In general, this should be the case only until the least-cost route to the physical network has been calculated by the parent partition network algorithms.

Internal Virtual Network

As shown in Figure 5-19, when you create an internal virtual network, Hyper-V also creates a virtual network switch and a virtual network adapter in the parent partition. However, in this scenario the virtual network switch is not connected to any physical network adapters installed in the Hyper-V server. This has the effect of restricting network communications between the Hyper-V server and virtual machines connected to the internal network. Internal network traffic is never transmitted through a physical network.

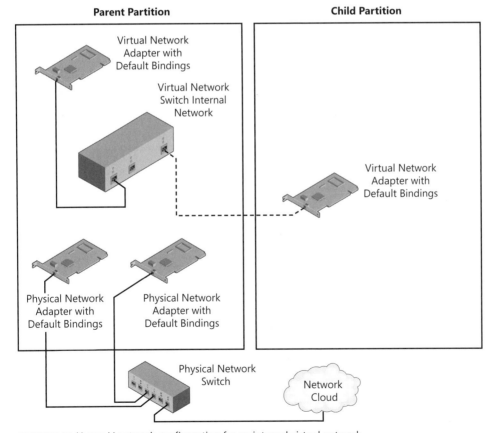

FIGURE 5-19 Hyper-V network configuration for an internal virtual network

The virtual network adapter appears as a new component (in this case, Local Area Connection 3) in the Network Connections window, as shown in Figure 5-20. Similar to the external virtual network scenario, examination of the virtual network adapter properties reveals that all the default items are bound to the virtual network adapter.

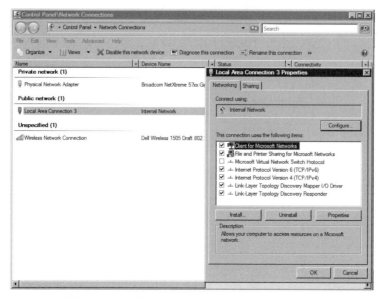

FIGURE 5-20 The parent partition virtual network adapter properties for an internal virtual network

In the internal virtual network configuration scenario, Figure 5-21 shows that the physical network adapter configuration remains unchanged, and all default bindings are maintained.

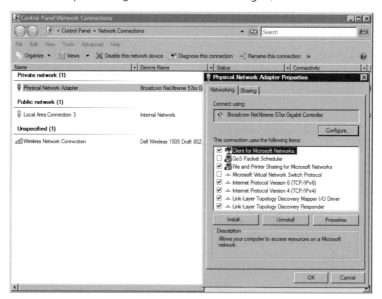

FIGURE 5-21 The parent partition physical network adapter properties for an internal virtual network

In the Device Manager, shown in Figure 5-22, the virtual network adapter is also listed and the device description in the properties defines that it is a Microsoft Virtual Network Switch adapter.

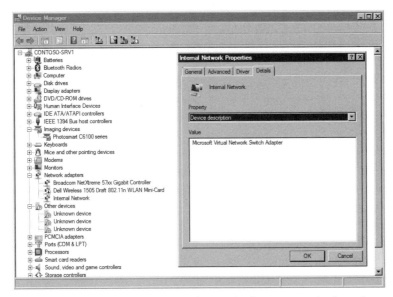

FIGURE 5-22 The Device Manager virtual network adapter properties for an internal virtual network

When a virtual machine in a child partition needs to communicate through an internal virtual network, the network traffic flow includes the following major steps:

- The data is sent through the guest operating system network stack bound to the virtual machine virtual network adapter.

- In the case of a synthetic network adapter, the data is sent to the virtual network switch in the parent partition through a VMBus connection. In the case of a legacy network adapter, the Windows Hypervisor intercepts the request and instructs the virtualization stack in the parent partition to retrieve the data from a preset memory buffer, which then sends it to the virtual network switch.

- The virtual network switch determines how to route the data to its destination.

- If the data destination is another virtual machine, the virtual network switch sends the data to the network port to which the virtual machine is connected and transmits the data across a separate VMBus connection, or with assistance of the Windows Hypervisor, to the emulated network adapter in the destination virtual machine.

- If the data destination is the parent partition, the virtual network switch sends the data to the network port to which the parent partition virtual network adapter is connected.

- Any return data or communication destined for the virtual machine follows the same path in reverse.

Private Virtual Network

As shown in Figure 5-23, when you create a private virtual network, Hyper-V creates only a virtual network switch in the parent partition. Therefore, network communication is restricted to virtual machines connected to the private virtual network. The Hyper-V server cannot transmit any data through a private virtual network.

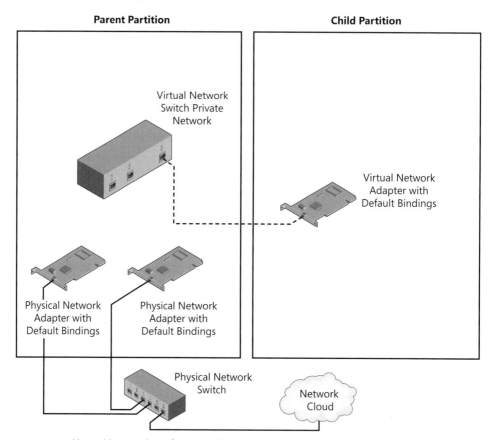

FIGURE 5-23 Hyper-V network configuration for a private virtual network

In the private virtual network configuration scenario, Figure 5-24 shows that the physical network adapter configuration remains unchanged, and all default bindings are maintained.

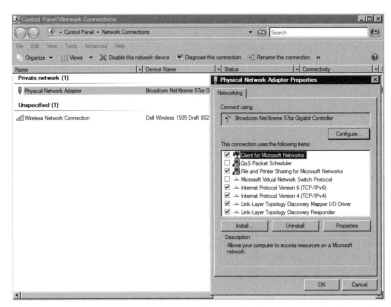

FIGURE 5-24 The parent partition physical network adapter properties for a private virtual network

In the Device Manager, shown in Figure 5-25, only the physical network adapters are listed.

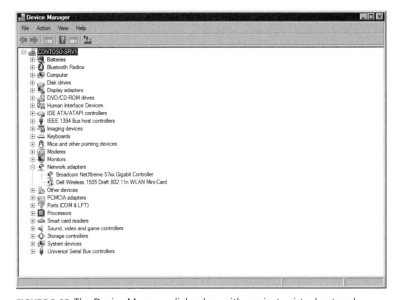

FIGURE 5-25 The Device Manager dialog box with a private virtual network

When a virtual machine in a child partition needs to communicate through an private virtual network, the network traffic flow includes the following major steps:

- The data is sent through the guest operating system network stack bound to the virtual machine virtual network adapter.

- In the case of a synthetic network adapter, the data is sent to the virtual network switch in the parent partition through a VMBus connection. In the case of a legacy network adapter, the Windows Hypervisor intercepts the request and instructs the virtualization stack in the parent partition to retrieve the data from a preset memory buffer, which then sends it to the virtual network switch.

- The virtual network switch determines how to route the data to the destination virtual machine either by sending the data to the network port on the virtual network switch to which the virtual machine is connected and transmitting the data across a VMBus connection, or with assistance of the Windows Hypervisor, to the emulated network adapter in the destination virtual machine.

- Any return data or communication destined for the virtual machine follows the same path in reverse.

IMPORTANT Because the Hyper-V virtual network switch operates at Layer 2 of the Open Systems Interconnection (OSI) model, it cannot route network traffic. If IP routing between virtual networks (OSI model Layer 3) is required, you must implement a software-based router (e.g., Internet Security & Acceleration Server 2006) in a virtual machine.

Understanding Virtual LANs

Windows Server 2008 Hyper-V provides support for using Virtual LANs (VLANs) in both the parent (Hyper-V server) and child partitions (virtual machines). The Institute of Electrical and Electronics Engineers (IEEE) defined the 802.1Q standard for VLAN tagging in order to transmit multiple network traffic streams across a single physical network connection. Each network stream is virtually isolated from the others such that machines on separate VLANs cannot see each other's packets unless routing is performed between VLANs. Figure 5-26 shows that a single physical network trunk can have network data from multiple VLANs flowing through it as well as non-VLAN data. This is referred to as "trunking." The diagram shows that different VLAN packets are part of a single network traffic stream and that only the server that is a member of the VLAN can see the packets tagged for that VLAN. A server that is not a member of a VLAN cannot see packets that are tagged for a VLAN.

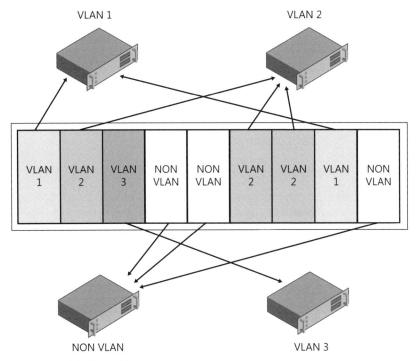

FIGURE 5-26 VLAN trunking

There are two different methods to implement a VLAN. The first method involves statically configuring a VLAN at the network switch port level. In this configuration, you assign the VLAN to the switch port and any traffic that flows through that port is tagged with a VLAN identification number (VLAN ID). This method prevents the device connected to the port from changing the VLAN ID value. However, if the device moves from one network switch port to another, then the new port must be configured for the correct VLAN. This method also prevents multiple devices connected to a network switch port to be members of different VLANs.

The second method requires that a device connected to a network port dynamically assign the VLAN ID before transmitting a packet. With this method, a device can be easily moved from one VLAN to another without requiring modification to the configuration of network switch ports. However, this method requires that a device fully support IEEE 802.1Q VLAN tagging. The device must be able to tag a packet, transmit a tagged packet, and open a tagged packet.

The first method, static VLAN configuration, is more secure than dynamic VLAN tagging because a network device cannot easily switch VLANs without moving network switch ports, and network switches are generally located in security-controlled areas.

Here is a list of requirements to support VLAN tagging (static or dynamic) in complex network environments:

- The Hyper-V server must have physical network adapters with IEEE 802.1Q support. For dynamic tagging, the physical network adapters must support VLAN tagged packets even if the driver is not configured for VLAN support.
- Network switches must include IEEE 802.1Q support.
- Network routers must include IEEE 802.1Q support to route tagged packets.

Configuring the Parent Partition to Use a VLAN

It is possible to make the Hyper-V parent partition a member of a VLAN. Usually this is done to separate Hyper-V management network traffic from child partition network traffic. In the case of a physical network adapter that is not bound to an external virtual network, the configuration of a VLAN ID is performed by changing the network driver Advanced settings, as shown in Figure 5-27. By default, the VLAN ID is set to zero. Changing this setting will tag all packets from the parent partition that flow through that physical network adapter with the new VLAN ID.

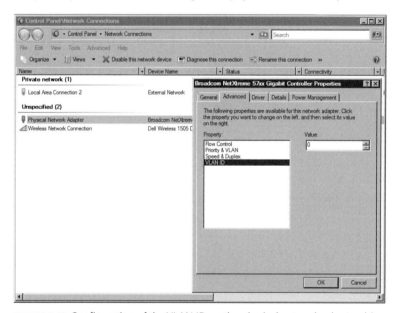

FIGURE 5-27 Configuration of the VLAN ID on the physical network adapter driver

If a physical network adapter is connected to an external virtual network, the configuration of the VLAN ID can be performed using the Virtual Network Manager in the Hyper-V Manager console. In order to configure the VLAN ID using the Virtual Network Manager, follow these steps:

1. Open the Hyper-V Manager console.
2. In the Actions pane, under the server name, click Virtual Network Manager.

3. In the Virtual Network Manager, select the target External Network from the Virtual Networks list displayed in the left pane.

4. In the right pane, under Virtual Network Properties, select Enable Virtual LAN Identification For Parent Partition.

5. In the VLAN ID text box, type the value of the VLAN ID.

6. Click OK to apply the changes.

After you have changed the VLAN ID, all parent partition traffic that flows through the selected network adapter will be tagged with the VLAN ID.

You can also change the settings of an internal virtual network to allow VLAN tagging in the parent partition. The process is identical to the steps used to configure the VLAN ID, with the exception that you must select the target internal virtual network in Virtual Network Manager.

NOTE Private virtual networks do not support VLAN tagging.

Configuring a Child Partition to Use a VLAN

Child partitions, or virtual machines, also support VLAN tagging. Configuration of a VLAN ID must be performed individually for each target virtual network adapter installed in the virtual machines. This allows you to connect a single virtual machine to multiple VLANs. Since a virtual machine can have a maximum of 12 virtual network adapters (8 synthetic and 4 legacy), it can be connected to a maximum of 12 VLANs concurrently.

In order to configure the VLAN ID for a virtual network adapter in a virtual machine, follow these steps:

1. Open the Hyper-V Manager console.

2. Right-click the virtual machine and select Settings from the menu options.

3. In the virtual machine Settings dialog box, select the target network adapter.

4. In the right pane, under Network Adapter, select Enable Virtual LAN Identification.

5. In the VLAN ID text box, type the value of the VLAN ID.

6. Click OK to apply the changes.

After you have changed the VLAN ID, all child partition traffic that flows through the selected virtual network adapter will be tagged with the VLAN ID.

If you have a requirement for a virtual machine to communicate using two or more VLANs, just configure additional virtual network adapters in the child partition, connect them to the target virtual network, assign them VLAN IDs, configure the IP addresses appropriately, and then make sure that the traffic that you want to flow across a particular VLAN is using the correct IP address or name of the target so the traffic flows across the right virtual network adapter.

Using VLANs to Configure Isolated Test Scenarios

VLANs can provide additional benefits to configure isolated test scenarios. For example, suppose that you have two Hyper-V servers connected to the same network switch and you need to configure a scenario that requires a service like DHCP to troubleshoot a problem. Furthermore, proper troubleshooting requires that virtual machines on different Hyper-V servers communicate with each other across the network. Configuration of a VLAN to isolate the network traffic can help to avoid the following issues:

- Offering competing DHCP services on a network
- Setting up a single Hyper-V server test configuration to eliminate DHCP service problems
- Complex test configurations such as adding an additional network adapter to each Hyper-V server, connecting the Hyper-V servers to an isolated network switch, configuring a new virtual network, and configuring virtual machines to use the new virtual network to perform the tests

VLAN tagging is a perfect solution to isolate the virtual machine network traffic for this type of test scenario. All that is required is to configure all the virtual machines needed for the test to connect to the target external virtual network and set the same VLAN ID on each virtual network adapter. This allows you to isolate a subnet across two servers, and only those machines configured with the same VLAN ID will see the network traffic and be able to communicate with each other.

Understanding MAC Address Pools

Hyper-V allows a virtual network adapter to be assigned either a static or dynamic Media Access Control (MAC) address. A static MAC address is one that a Hyper-V administrator assigns to a virtual machine. A dynamic MAC address is one that Hyper-V automatically assigns from its MAC address pool. After a dynamic MAC address has been assigned, it is not changed.

When Hyper-V is installed, a MAC address pool is created and stored in the registry at HKLM\Software\Microsoft\Windows NT\CurrentVersion\Virtualization. It is stored as a range of 256 values defined by two registry key values: MinimumMacAddress and MaximumMacAddress.

A MAC address is composed of two parts, an original equipment manufacturer (OEM) identifier and a unique value. To provide valid MAC addresses, Microsoft registered to obtain its own OEM identifier (00-15-5d); therefore, all Hyper-V MAC address ranges start with these three octets. The next two octets are generated by converting the last two octets of the IP address of the first enumerated physical network adapter installed in the Hyper-V server to hexadecimal values. For example, if the IP address of the first enumerated physical network adapter was 192.168.0.97, the last two octets are converted to hexadecimal such that 0.97 becomes 00-61, and they are used as the next two octets in the MAC address. This gives 00-15-5d-00-61 as the first five octets. To provide a range of 256 addresses, the last octet ranges from the MinimumMacAddress with a value of 00 to the MaximumMacAddress with a value of FF. As shown in Figure 5-28, the MAC address pool for this example ranges from 00-15-5d-00-61-00 to 00-15-5d-00-61-ff.

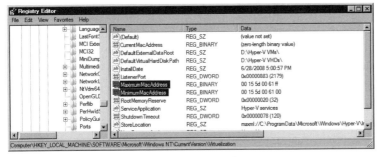

FIGURE 5-28 MAC address range in the registry of a Hyper-V server

The first time a virtual machine is powered on and it is configured to use a dynamic MAC address, it is assigned the next available value in the MAC address pool range. If the virtual machine has multiple virtual network adapters, then each adapter receives a MAC address from the pool. In addition, when an external or internal virtual network is generated, the virtual network adapter created in the parent partition receives a MAC address from the Hyper-V server pool.

By default, there can be a total of only 256 devices assigned a dynamic MAC address on a single Hyper-V server. This could represent 256 virtual machines with a single virtual network adapter, 128 virtual machines with two virtual network adapters, 126 virtual machines with two virtual network adapters and four internal virtual networks defined, or any other combination that equals 256 devices.

As MAC addresses are assigned, eventually the MAC address pool can be exhausted. If a virtual machine is deleted, the MAC addresses assigned to its virtual network adapters become available to recycle. If Hyper-V assigns all 256 MAC addresses, the search for an available MAC address starts back at the first MAC address in the pool. If the MAC address is actively being used, it will be skipped and the next available MAC address is used. If the search for a MAC address goes through a complete cycle without finding an available address, an error will be displayed stating that there are no available MAC addresses.

Modifying the MAC Address Pool on a Hyper-V Server

Having a range of 256 MAC addresses available on a single Hyper-V server will meet most deployment requirements. However, you can modify the registry values to extend the MAC address pool. In particular, you can use an octet or part of an octet to increase the number of available MAC addresses. To use a partial octet, modify the MinimumMacAddress and MaximumMacAddress values to use the last three hex digits for the address range:

MinimumMacAddress = 00-15-5d-00-61-00

MaximumMacAddress = 00-15-5d-00-6**F-FF**

For this example, this modification will provide a pool of 3839 MAC addresses. You should adjust the MAC address pool before you create any virtual machines or internal virtual networks.

CAUTION Back up the registry before you attempt any modifications. Editing the registry directly can have serious, unexpected consequences that can prevent the system from starting up.

Using a Pass-Through Disk

Hyper-V allows virtual machines to access a physical disk mapped directly to the Hyper-V server, but without a volume configured on it. This is referred to as a pass-through disk. Pass-through disks can be physically connected to the Hyper-V server or through a logical unit number LUN on a Storage Area Network (SAN). One of the advantages of pass-through disks is that they are not subject to the 2040-gigabyte size limitation that is imposed on virtual hard disks. In contrast, pass-through disks do not support dynamically expanding virtual hard disks, differencing disks, or virtual machine snapshots. In order to ensure that a virtual machine has exclusive access to the physical disk, it must be configured as offline on the Hyper-V server.

Configuring a Pass-Through Disk

Figure 5-29 shows a physical disk (Disk 2) that is attached to a Hyper-V server in an offline state. The disk should be initialized before it is connected to a virtual machine. To initialize the disk, follow these steps:

1. Open the Disk Management console.

2. Right-click the disk and select Initialize Disk from the menu options.

3. In the Initialize Disk dialog box, select the Master Boot Record (MBR) or GUID Partition Table (GPT) option and then click OK.

4. After the disk initializes, right-click the disk and select Offline.

5. Close the Disk Management console.

NOTE If a physical disk is not in an offline state on the Hyper-V server, it will not be available to select in the virtual machine configuration settings.

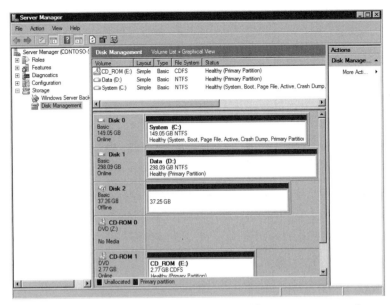

FIGURE 5-29 Physical disk in an offline state in the Disk Management console

In order to attach a pass-through disk to a virtual machine, follow these steps:

1. Open the Hyper-V Manager console.

2. Right-click the virtual machine and select Settings from the menu options.

3. In the virtual machine Settings dialog box, select the target storage controller for the pass-through disk in the Hardware pane on the left.

4. In the right pane, select Hard Drive and then click Add.

5. In the Hard Drive Properties dialog box, review and change the Controller and Location settings as appropriate for your configuration.

6. In the Media section, select Physical Hard Disk and then select the target physical disk from the drop-down menu.

7. Click OK.

You may have to assign a drive letter to the pass-through disk in the virtual machine before it appears in Windows Explorer. At this point, the pass-through disk is configured, and the virtual machine can begin to use it to store data.

If you plan to use a pass-through disk to boot the virtual machine guest operating system, the virtual machine configuration file must be stored in a different storage location. In contrast to virtual hard disks that are only files stored on physical disks, the entire pass-through disk is dedicated to the virtual machine guest operating system.

> **IMPORTANT** If a pass-through disk will be used to boot the virtual machine guest operating system, it must be attached to a virtual IDE controller. A data disk can be connected to either a virtual IDE controller or virtual SCSI controller.

Using Failover Clustering Features

Although server virtualization provides a solution for organizations to implement a dynamic, flexible core infrastructure that minimizes the number of deployed physical servers, increases utilization of physical resources, and reduces long-term operating costs, the migration of multiple physical servers onto a common virtualization server requires a broader high-availability strategy than in a traditional infrastructure. If one or more virtualization servers experience downtime, many users can be affected and can lose access to services and applications, translating into a loss in productivity and financial impact to the organization. At the hardware level, deploying virtualization servers on platforms that incorporate redundant or hot-swappable components (i.e., power supplies, processors, and memory) reduces the risk of unplanned downtime. Windows Server 2008 with Hyper-V provides an opportunity to leverage integrated failover clustering to manage both unplanned and planned downtime of virtualization servers and guests.

High Availability

High-availability solutions provide ways to manage both planned and unplanned downtime. Some examples of planned downtime include the installation of operating system or application upgrades that require taking a server offline. Unplanned downtime can be the result of a simple hardware component failure or loss of physical servers because of a natural disaster. On a large scale, building a high-availability strategy includes an end-to-end examination of all the interlinked components that provide users with access to services and may require the implementation of more than one solution to meet availability targets.

Windows Server 2008 Failover Clustering

Failover Clustering has been a component of Microsoft Windows server products beginning with NT 4.0. In the intervening years, the failover cluster component has evolved, especially in terms of ease of configuration and supported applications. A Windows Server 2008 failover cluster consists of at least two servers (nodes) that are connected through multiple network links, one of which enables communications between the nodes. Each failover cluster node is connected to a common storage array such as a SAN or iSCSI-based disk system, and only one node in a cluster can own the set of network and disk resources associated with an application or service at any one time. In terms of scale, a Windows Server 2008 failover cluster can contain up to 16 nodes. The nodes monitor each other using a network heartbeat to determine if nodes are responsive. If a node becomes unresponsive, the application or service running on the failed cluster node will be restarted on another cluster node after it has taken ownership of resources. Beginning with Windows Server 2008, geographically dispersed (or stretch) clusters also can be implemented without requiring custom or specialized hardware. This provides you with the ability to implement a failover cluster that can manage unplanned downtime by failing over to another local node in the case of a single server failure, or to a node in another geographical region in the event of a more severe local disruption such as might be caused by an extended power outage, natural disaster, or other large-scale problem.

Using Failover Clustering with Windows Server 2008 and Hyper-V provides the ability to implement a high-availability strategy that can manage both unplanned and planned downtime in a virtualized infrastructure. There are two different levels at which you can implement a failover cluster in a Hyper-V environment: at the virtualization server level and at the guest operating system level. In the following sections, you will learn how to configure virtual machines and Hyper-V servers to implement the failover clustering scenarios listed in Table 5-7.

TABLE 5-7 Hyper-V Common Failover Cluster Configurations

FEATURE	DESCRIPTION
Hyper-V Server Failover Cluster	A cluster based on Windows Server 2008 Failover Clustering that consists of two or more Hyper-V cluster nodes.
Virtual Machine Failover Cluster	A cluster based on Windows Server 2008 Failover Clustering that consists of two or more virtual machine cluster nodes supporting a cluster-aware application. Virtual machine cluster nodes can be located across Hyper-V servers, but they require iSCSI-based disks.

Implementing a Hyper-V Server Cluster

A Hyper-V server failover cluster model is illustrated in Figure 5-30. This failover cluster configuration allows you to achieve high-availability for non–cluster-aware applications running in virtual machines, and it addresses planned and unplanned downtime for Hyper-V servers. Hyper-V server clusters are commonly deployed using Fibre-Channel or iSCSI-based shared storage. Hyper-V server clusters can range from two-node to 16-node active clusters. It is important to understand that in this configuration, you are clustering the Hyper-V servers, not the applications running in the virtual machines. If one of the Hyper-V cluster nodes fails, virtual machines in the cluster configuration are restarted on other Hyper-V cluster member nodes. In contrast, a failure or crash of either the guest operating system or application will not result in a failover event.

> **IMPORTANT** The complete set of hardware used to implement a Hyper-V server cluster must be listed in the Windows Server Catalog as a qualified cluster solution for Windows Server 2008. You can find the catalog at *http://www.windowsservercatalog.com /results.aspx?&bCatID=1291&cpID=0&avc=10&ava=0&avq=0&OR=1&PGS=25.*

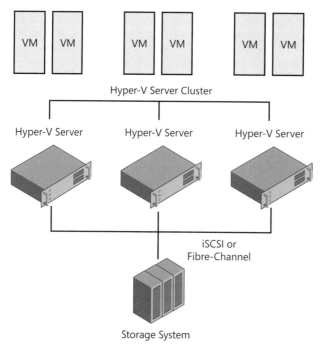

FIGURE 5-30 A Hyper-V server failover cluster using shared storage

> **NOTE** A Hyper-V server failover cluster is not limited to using iSCSI for connection to the shared storage system. In this configuration, you are able to leverage either iSCSI or Fibre-Channel connected shared storage. There are different storage configurations that you can implement depending on the requirements of your environment.

There are many scenarios in which you can apply a Hyper-V server cluster solution. Table 5-8 lists the most common scenarios that benefit from a Hyper-V server cluster implementation.

TABLE 5-8 Hyper-V Server Cluster Scenarios

SCENARIO	HYPER-V SERVER CLUSTER BENEFITS
Server hardware planned downtime	Prior to performing hardware maintenance on a Hyper-V cluster node, virtual machines can move over to other nodes in the cluster with minimal impact on application availability.
Server software updates	Before applying potentially disruptive software updates to a Hyper-V server, virtual machines can fail over to other nodes in the cluster with minimal impact on application availability.

SCENARIO	HYPER-V SERVER CLUSTER BENEFITS
Non–cluster-aware applications	Non-cluster–aware applications running in virtual machines on a Hyper-V server cluster node are protected from unplanned downtime caused by a server failure. If the Hyper-V server cluster node fails, the virtual machine can fail over to other nodes in the cluster with minimal impact on application availability.
Workload rebalancing	Virtual machine performance might dictate a need to rebalance the workload on a Hyper-V cluster node. If there is another cluster node with the required resources available, the virtual machine can be quickly failed over with minimal impact on application availability.

During planned downtime, a virtual machine is placed in a saved state, migrated to another cluster node, and restarted in a matter of a few seconds or minutes (depending on the size of the virtual machine memory allocation). Applications running in a virtual machine do not experience any data loss because the virtual machine state is loaded as it is restarted on the new cluster node. Unplanned downtime is usually caused by an unexpected power failure, failed hardware component, or software failure, resulting in application data loss and service disruption because it is not possible to save the state of the virtual machine prior to the event. Windows Server 2008 Failover Clustering ensures that applications experience minimal service disruptions, in either planned or unplanned downtime scenarios.

Table 5-9 lists implementation requirements prior to the creation of a Hyper-V server cluster that is supported in a production deployment.

TABLE 5-9 Hyper-V Server Cluster Requirements

REQUIREMENT	DESCRIPTION
Physical Hardware	Creation of a Hyper-V server cluster supported in production requires two or more identical physical servers that are listed in the Windows Server Catalog.
Operating System	Windows Server 2008 Enterprise Edition. Windows Server 2008 Datacenter Edition.
iSCSI or Fibre-Channel Storage	Microsoft iSCSI Software Initiator 2.8 (or later version) or Fibre-Channel storage system.
Witness and Shared Disks	Witness and Shared Disks targets must be created prior to configuring the cluster nodes. The Witness disk must be larger than 500 MB to satisfy requirements. The Shared disk must be sized to contain virtual machine VHD files.

REQUIREMENT	DESCRIPTION
Network Adapters	Network adapters should be added and configured for the public traffic and heartbeat traffic on each Hyper-V server cluster node. An additional network adapter should be added if using an iSCSI-based shared storage system.
Virtual Networks	Virtual networks should be created for public traffic and heartbeat traffic.
Integration Services	Integration Services should be installed on each virtual machine.

The deployment of a two-node Hyper-V server failover cluster on a Fibre-Channel SAN includes the following major steps:

- Create and map Witness and data storage volumes on the Fibre-Channel SAN.
- Configure volumes on each Hyper-V server.
- Install the Failover Clustering feature on each Hyper-V server.
- Configure Failover Clustering on each Hyper-V server and join it to the cluster.
- Configure a virtual machine for high availability.

NOTE The Hyper-V server cluster installation described in the following sections was performed on Sun Microsystems servers attached to a Compellent Technologies Storage Center system hosted in the Microsoft Partner Solution Center (MPSC). The Hyper-V server cluster configuration consisted of the following components:

Active Directory Domain Controller Configuration

Sun X4450 Server

Four (4) Intel X7350 Processors (2.93 GHz, Quad Core) for a total of 16 cores

Thirty-two (32) 2-GB FB DIMMs, for a total of 64 GB

Four (4) 146-GB SAS Drives

Four (4) Gigabit Ethernet Network Adapters

Hyper-V Server Cluster Configuration

Two (2) Sun X4150 Servers

Two (2) Intel E5345 Processors (2.33 GHz, Quad Core) for a total of 8 cores

Eight (8) 2 GB FB DIMMs for a total of 16 GB

Four (4) 146-GB SAS drives

Four (4) Gigabit Ethernet Network Adapters

Storage Area Network Configuration

Single Compellent Storage Center System

Ten (10) terabytes of Tier-1 storage

Forty-one (41) terabytes of Tier-3 storage

If you are interested in more details concerning the configuration of the Hyper-V server cluster test environment, refer to the description included in the Introduction of this book.

The steps shown in the following section that detail how to create and assign the Witness and data storage disks to cluster nodes are specific to the Compellent Storage Center, and the procedure will vary depending on your SAN vendor. However, these steps are included to give you a sense of the type of procedure that you will have to follow to prepare shared storage to support a Hyper-V server failover cluster.

Creating and Mapping Witness and Data Storage Volumes on a Compellent Storage Center SAN

Before you can configure the Hyper-V server cluster, you have to create and map Witness and virtual machine data storage volumes on the SAN. Figure 5-31 shows the Compellent Storage Center Web-based management interface and the Create Volume option.

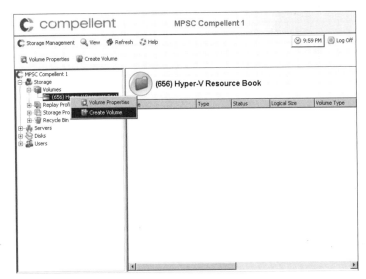

FIGURE 5-31 Compellent Storage Center volume creation

There are several parameters that must be defined, starting with the volume size, as shown in Figure 5-32. You must ensure that the size of the Witness volume is greater than 500 MB. On the Compellent Storage Center, volume storage is dynamically allocated as new data is written to the volume. Thus, the actual size of the volume on the Compellent Storage Center unit may be less than 1 GB when it is initialized, but it is presented as a 1-GB volume to the Hyper-V server.

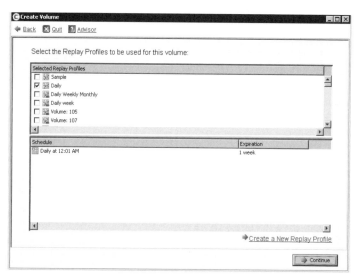

FIGURE 5-32 Compellent Storage Center volume size definition

The next step is to define the Replay profile for the volume, as shown in Figure 5-33. The Compellent Storage Center provides a Data Instant Replay feature that supports taking point-in-time snapshots of volumes.

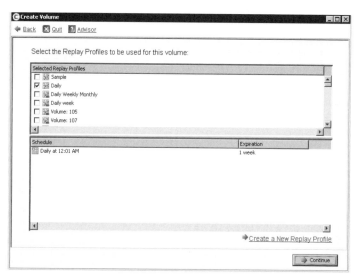

FIGURE 5-33 Compellent Storage Center Data Instant Replay configuration

After defining the Data Instant Replay profile for the volume, you must specify the volume name. As shown in Figure 5-34, specify Witness as the new volume name.

FIGURE 5-34 Compellent Storage Center volume name definition

Compellent Storage Center Data Instant Replay Feature

Shane Burton, Microsoft Product Specialist
Compellent Technologies

Compellent Storage Center Data Instant Replay provides the ability to take unlimited, space-efficient replays of any volume on the Compellent Storage Center. Unlike traditional snapshots, a Data Instant Replay simply "freezes" the original blocks as read-only. The blocks do not get copied or moved, so there is no additional overhead to this process. If the server needs to update a block, it will simply write a new block.

One advantage of Data Instant Replay is that it does not require any pre-allocation of storage space. A replay is not a complete clone of the volume; rather, it contains only blocks that have changed since the last replay.

As shown in Figure 5-35, the Compellent Storage Center has all the necessary information to create the new Witness volume and allows you to review the volume specifications prior to initiating the volume creation.

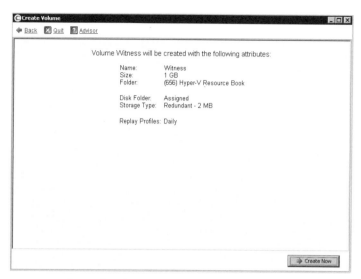

FIGURE 5-35 Compellent Storage Center volume specifications

While it creates the volume, you can view the progress of the operation, as shown in Figure 5-36.

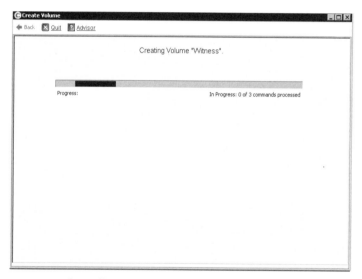

FIGURE 5-36 Compellent Storage Center volume creation progress

After the new volume is created, it must be mapped to a Hyper-V server. Using the Compellent Storage Center Web-based management interface, you must specify the mappings individually, as shown in Figure 5-37 and Figure 5-38. Upon completion, a process confirmation displays as shown in Figure 5-39. The process is repeated to map the Witness volume to each Hyper-V server that will become a node in the failover cluster.

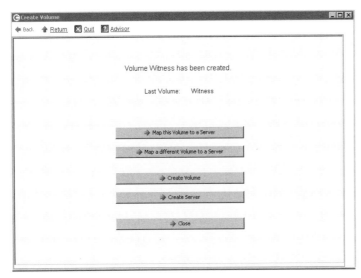

FIGURE 5-37 Compellent Storage Center volume mapping

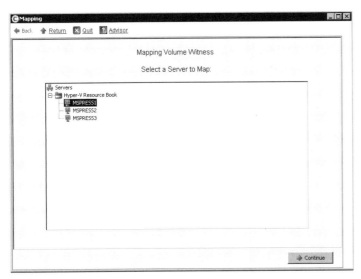

FIGURE 5-38 Compellent Storage Center volume mapping server selection

FIGURE 5-39 Compellent Storage Center volume mapping confirmation

After mapping the Witness volume to each Hyper-V server, the virtual machine data storage volume (named VmStorage in this example) is created and mapped to each Hyper-V server.

Figure 5-40 and Figure 5-41 show the Witness volume and VmStorage volume mapped to two Hyper-V servers, MSPRESS1 and MSPRESS2, respectively.

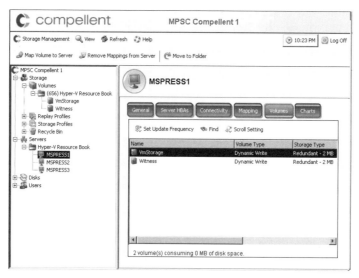

FIGURE 5-40 Compellent Storage Center volume mappings to Hyper-V server MSPRESS1

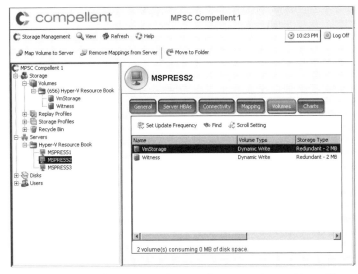

FIGURE 5-41 Compellent Storage Center volume mappings to Hyper-V server MSPRESS2

Configuring the Witness and Data Storage Volumes on the Hyper-V Servers

1. Open the Disk Management MMC on the first Hyper-V server.

2. Right-click the Witness disk (left pane) and select Online from the menu options.

3. Right-click the Witness disk again (left pane) and select Initialize Disk from the menu options.

4. In the Initialize Disk dialog box, select the appropriate partition style (MBR or GPT) and then click OK.

5. Right-click the Witness disk once more (right pane) and select New Simple Volume from the menu options.

6. On the first page of the New Simple Volume Wizard, click Next.

7. On the Specify Volume Size page, click Next.

8. On the Assign Drive Letter Or Path page, select drive letter W in the Assign The Following Drive Letter drop-down box and then click Next.

9. On the Format Partition page, select Format This Volume With The Following Settings, enter a new volume name in the Volume Label text box, and then click Next.

10. On the Completing The New Simple Volume Wizard page, review your selections and then click Finish.

11. Repeat steps 2 through 10 for the data storage disk and select drive letter S for the drive letter assignment.

12. Open the Disk Management MMC on the second Hyper-V server.

13. In the Disk Management MMC, right-click the Witness disk (left pane) and select On-line from the menu options.

14. Right-click the Witness disk once more (right pane) and select Change Drive Letter And Paths from the menu options.

15. In the Change Drive Letter And Paths For dialog box, click Change.

16. In the Change Drive Letter Or Path dialog box, select drive letter W in the Assign The Following Drive Letter drop-down box and then click OK.

17. Repeat steps 13 through 16 and select drive letter S for the data storage volume.

Adding the Failover Clustering Feature to the Hyper-V Servers

Before you can create a cluster, you have to add the Failover Clustering feature to each Hyper-V server. Follow these steps to add the Failover Clustering feature to the Hyper-V servers:

1. Log in to the first Hyper-V server with an account that has Domain Administrator credentials.

2. Open the Server Manager and click Features in the left pane.

3. In the right pane, click Add Features to open the Add Features Wizard.

4. On the Select Features page, select Failover Clustering and then click Next.

5. On the Confirm Installation Selections page, click Install.

6. On the Installation Results page, click Close.

7. Repeat steps 1 through 6 for the second Hyper-V server.

Configuring Failover Clustering on the Hyper-V Servers

When you create the first node in a cluster, you specify all parameters that define the cluster configuration. The Cluster Configuration Wizard guides you through the installation and completes the cluster setup when you have entered all the required information.

Follow these steps to configure Failover Clustering on the first Hyper-V server cluster node:

1. Click Start, click All Programs, click Administrative Tools, and then click Failover Cluster Management.

2. Select Validate A Configuration in the Management pane to launch the Validate A Configuration Wizard.

3. On the Before You Begin page, click Next.

4. On the Select Servers Or A Cluster page, type each Hyper-V server name in the Enter Name text box and click Add. After these actions are completed, click Next.

5. On the Testing Options page, select Run All Tests (Recommended) and then click Next.

6. On the Confirmation page, review the test list, ensure that there are no errors, and then click Next.

7. Correct any errors found during the validation process and then revalidate the configuration.

8. On the Summary page, click Finish.

9. Select Create A Cluster in the Management pane to launch the Create Cluster Wizard.

10. On the Before You Begin page, click Next.

11. On the Select Servers page, type each Hyper-V server name in the Enter Server Name text box and click Add. After these actions are completed, click Next.

12. On the Validation Warning page, select the appropriate option and then click Next.

13. On the Access Point For Administering The Cluster page, type the name of the cluster in the Cluster Name text box. You may also have to type the IP addresses to use for each configured network. After you complete these actions, click Next.

14. On the Confirmation page, review the cluster information and then click Next.

15. On the Summary page, click Finish.

After you complete these steps, each Hyper-V server will be a node in the failover cluster. To quickly verify that the failover cluster is functioning, you can shut down the first Hyper-V cluster node. When you open Failover Cluster Management on the second Hyper-V cluster node, you will see that it owns all cluster resources. After you have tested that cluster failover is successful, you can proceed with the configuration of the virtual machine.

> **IMPORTANT** After the Hyper-V server cluster is configured and before you create a new, highly available virtual machine, you have to configure and connect an identically named external virtual network on each Hyper-V server joined to the failover cluster.

Creating a Virtual Machine on a Hyper-V Server Failover Cluster

After the Hyper-V server cluster is configured, the next step is to create a virtual machine on one of the Hyper-V cluster nodes:

1. Open the Hyper-V Manager console on the first Hyper-V cluster node.

2. In the Actions pane, under the server name, click New and select Virtual Machine from the menu options to launch the New Virtual Machine Wizard.

3. On the Before You Begin page, click Next.

4. On the Specify Name And Location page, type the name of the new virtual machine. Then, select Store The Virtual Machine In A Different Location and click Browse to use Windows Explorer to select the data storage volume (drive letter S). After these actions are performed, click Next.

5. On the Assign Memory page, type the memory allocation for the virtual machine and then click Next.

6. On the Configure Networking page, select the external virtual network created for the non-cluster network traffic.

7. On the Connect Virtual Hard Disk page, select Create A Virtual Hard Disk and type the default Name, Location, and Size information for the new virtual machine. After these actions are performed, click Next.

8. On the Installation Options page, select the appropriate method to install the guest operating system in the virtual machine and then click Next.

9. On the Completing The New Virtual Machine Wizard page, clear the option to Start The Virtual Machine After It Is Created.

10. Click Finish.

Making a Virtual Machine Highly Available

With the virtual machine in the powered-off state, you can make it highly available. In order to configure the new virtual machine and make it highly available, follow these steps:

1. Open the Failover Cluster Management console on the first Hyper-V server cluster node.

2. In the left pane, right-click Services And Applications under the cluster name and select Configure A Service Or Application from the menu options to launch the High-Availability Wizard.

3. On the Before You Begin page, click Next.

4. On the Select Service Or Application page, select Virtual Machine from the list of options.

5. On the Select Virtual Machine page, select the appropriate virtual machine and then click Next.

6. On the Confirmation page, check the information and click Next.

7. On the Summary page, review the report and click Summary.

8. After these actions are complete, open the Hyper-V Manager and select Start under the virtual machine name to bring the new virtual machine online.

Verifying Virtual Machine High Availability

In order to verify that the high-availability virtual machine fails over to the second Hyper-V cluster node, follow these steps:

1. Open the Failover Cluster Management console on the first Hyper-V server.

2. In the left pane, right-click the virtual machine, select Move Virtual Machine(s) To Another Node, and select Move Virtual Machine(s) To Node 2. The entire process takes only a few moments, and the length of time it takes depends on the memory allocation for the virtual machine, how long it takes to save the state information, and the time needed to restore the state information on the new node using the saved state data.

IMPORTANT If you want to create and fail over multiple virtual machines independently, you have to store each one on a different volume.

Solving Drive Letter Restrictions with Mountpoints

Jeff Woolsey, Senior Program Manager
Windows Virtualization

Hyper-V server Failover Clustering is a great solution for scheduled downtime, such as when you need to migrate a virtual machine quickly from one node to another in order to perform maintenance (e.g., applying a BIOS update or adding memory or storage to the Hyper-V server). Hyper-V server Failover Clustering is also a great solution for unscheduled downtime, when a hardware failure occurs and you want the virtual machines to *automatically* failover over to another node.

When the migration or failure occurs, the entire drive or LUN moves to a new node. For a single virtual machine to migrate to another cluster node, the drive or LUN can contain only the files associated with that virtual machine. Typical installations of Windows Server 2008 Failover Clustering assign a drive letter to each LUN, but with only 26 drive letters available, this is a limitation. The solution is to place more than one virtual machine on a drive or find a way to have more LUNs accessible to the Hyper-V cluster nodes. Mountpoints allow you to create an unlimited number of LUNs and provide a way for Windows Server 2008 clusters to access them. For more information on how to create mountpoints to physical disks and configure them as disk resources in a failover cluster, refer to *http://support.microsoft.com/kb/280297*.

When designing your server-clustering solution, the number of nodes in the cluster and the failure scenario can affect the required hardware configurations. With a two-node cluster configuration, you must design a single node to handle the workload of both servers in the event of failure. To do this, you must determine the hardware requirements for the workload of a single node and double it. For example, if a single node workload for running 20 virtual machines requires two quad-core processors and 24 GB of memory, the hardware requirements for the node should be doubled to four quad-core processors and 48 GB of memory to support the failure of the second node.

As you add nodes to the cluster, the workload of the failed node can be distributed across other nodes and the hardware requirement of each node decreases from the two-node scenario. Alternatively, you can plan for a warm standby node in the cluster running no workload. When a cluster node fails, all the workload from that node resumes on the warm standby node. Using a warm standby node simplifies the design process, reduces the hardware requirements of each node (therefore reducing the cost of each node), and ensures that the failover process does not affect the workloads on the remaining nodes in the cluster.

Implementing a Virtual Machine Failover Cluster

As shown in Figure 5-42, a virtual machine failover cluster is implemented between two or more virtual machines running on separate Hyper-V servers that are connected to a shared storage system. In order to implement this option, you have to run an operating system in the virtual machine that supports failover clustering, such as Windows Server 2003 (up to eight nodes) or Windows Server 2008 Enterprise or Datacenter (up to 16 nodes) editions. In addition, the application that you intend to make highly available must be "cluster-aware." This means that the application has been developed with specific features that allow it to interact with the cluster service and enable it to fail over and restart with all required resources on a different cluster node.

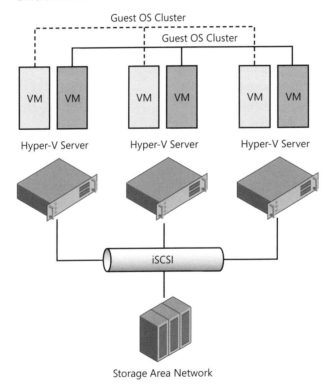

FIGURE 5-42 A virtual machine failover cluster using iSCSI-connected storage

If you are planning a virtual machine failover cluster, iSCSI is the only shared storage access protocol that is supported for this configuration. Using iSCSI to deploy a failover cluster eliminates the need for the specialized hardware that was previously required to configure clustering. The requirements for an iSCSI-based solution are network adapters to connect the storage to the cluster nodes and a storage unit that supports the iSCSI protocol. The iSCSI protocol defines the rules and processes for transmitting and receiving block storage data over TCP/IP networks. iSCSI-based implementations consist of an iSCSI initiator and an iSCSI target with an interconnecting network.

In order to use iSCSI and maximize performance, you must dedicate a virtual network adapter in each virtual machine for iSCSI communication. You should also dedicate one or more physical network cards and configure individual virtual networks on each Hyper-V server for iSCSI storage access. An iSCSI initiator is required in each virtual machine to access the iSCSI-based targets on the shared storage. An iSCSI initiator is a software component that enables the connection of a Windows server to an external iSCSI storage array over a TCP/IP network. It is important to note that this configuration does not support directly attaching an iSCSI target to the virtual machine as a boot device.

> **NOTE** The Microsoft iSCSI initiator is included in Windows Server 2008, but it must be downloaded for Windows Server 2003 and earlier versions. You can download the iSCSI initiator from *http://go.microsoft.com/fwlink/?linkid=44352*.

A virtual machine failover cluster is capable of supporting planned and unplanned downtime for cluster-aware applications. In fact, this configuration will manage unplanned downtime caused by a failure or crash that occurs within the virtual machine, as well as a failure or crash that occurs at the Hyper-V server platform level.

Table 5-10 lists implementation requirements prior to creating a two-node virtual machine cluster based on an iSCSI storage device.

TABLE 5-10 Requirements for an iSCSI-Based Virtual Machine Failover Cluster

REQUIREMENT	DESCRIPTION
Operating System	Windows Server 2003 Enterprise or Datacenter Edition, or Windows Server 2008 Enterprise or Datacenter Edition must be installed on each virtual machine cluster node.
Integration Services	Integration Services should be installed on each virtual machine node.
iSCSI Witness and Shared Disks	iSCSI Witness and Shared disks targets must be created prior to configuring the cluster nodes. The Witness disk must be larger than 500 MB in size to satisfy failover cluster requirements.
Virtual Networks	Virtual networks should be created for non-cluster traffic, heartbeat traffic, and iSCSI traffic.

REQUIREMENT	DESCRIPTION
Network Adapters	Three virtual network adapters should be added and connected to the non-cluster, heartbeat, and iSCSI virtual networks on each virtual machine cluster node, respectively.
Active Directory	Virtual machine cluster nodes must be members of an Active Directory domain.

To deploy a two-node virtual machine cluster using iSCSI, you must perform the following major steps:

- Create shared disk for the Witness and data storage volumes using the iSCSI Initiator.
- Configure shared disks on each virtual machine cluster node.
- Install the Failover Clustering feature on each virtual machine.
- Configure Failover Clustering on each virtual machine cluster node and join it to the cluster.

Configuring the iSCSI Shared Disks

After you build your Windows Server 2008 virtual machines, you can configure the cluster shared disks. Follow these steps to configure virtual machine cluster node access to iSCSI shared disks:

1. In the first virtual machine, open the Control Panel in Classic View, double-click the iSCSI Initiator icon, and click Yes in the Microsoft iSCSI dialog box to start the Microsoft iSCSI service. If prompted, click Yes to unblock the Microsoft iSCSI service to allow it to communicate through the Windows Firewall.

2. In the iSCSI Initiator Properties dialog box, click the Discovery tab, and in the Target Portals section, click Add Portal.

3. Enter the name or IP address of the server where the target iSCSI drive is defined and then click OK.

4. Click the Targets tab to display a list of disk targets.

5. Select the appropriate target name and click Log On.

6. Select Automatically Restore This Connection When The Computer Starts and then Enable Multipath if you have multipath software installed.

7. Click OK to connect to the iSCSI target.

8. Click OK to close the iSCSI Initiator Properties dialog box.

9. Open the Disk Management MMC.

10. Right-click the Witness disk (left pane) and select Online from the menu options.

11. Right-click the Witness disk again (left pane) and select Initialize Disk from the menu options.

12. In the Initialize Disk dialog box, select the appropriate partition style (MBR or GPT) and then click OK.

13. Right-click the Witness disk once more (right pane) and select New Simple Volume from the menu options.

14. On the opening page of the New Simple Volume Wizard, click Next.

15. On the Specify Volume Size page, click Next.

16. On the Assign Drive Letter Or Path page, select drive letter W from the Assign The Following Drive Letter drop-down list and then click Next.

17. On the Format Partition page, select Format This Volume With The Following Settings, enter a new volume name in the Volume Label text box, and then click Next.

18. On the Completing The New Simple Volume Wizard page, review your selections and then click Finish.

19. Repeat steps 11 through 18 for the Shared disk and select drive letter S for the drive letter assignment.

20. Repeat steps 1 to 9 for the second virtual machine.

21. In the Disk Management MMC, right-click the Witness disk (left pane) and select Online from the menu options.

22. Right-click the Witness disk once more (right pane) and select Change Drive Letter And Paths from the menu options.

23. In the Change Drive Letter And Paths For dialog box, click Change.

24. In the Change Drive Letter Or Path dialog box, select drive letter W from the Assign The Following Drive Letter drop-down list and then click OK.

25. Repeat steps 21 through 24 and select drive letter S for the Shared drive.

Adding the Failover Clustering Feature to the Virtual Machines

Before you can create a cluster, you have to add the Failover Clustering feature to each virtual machine.

Follow these steps to add the Failover Clustering feature to each virtual machine:

1. Log in to the first virtual machine with an account that has Domain Administrator credentials.

2. Open the Server Manager and click Features in the left pane.

3. In the right pane, click Add Features.

4. On the Select Features page of the Add Features Wizard, select Failover Clustering and then click Next.

5. On the Confirm Installation Selections page, click Install.

6. On the Installation Results page, click Close.

7. Repeat steps 1 through 6 for the second virtual machine.

Configuring Failover Clustering on the Virtual Machines

When you create the first node in a cluster, you specify all parameters that define the cluster configuration. The Cluster Configuration Wizard guides you through the installation and completes the cluster setup when you have entered all the required information.

Follow these steps to configure Failover Clustering on the first virtual machine cluster node:

1. Click Start, click All Programs, click Administrative Tools, and then click Failover Cluster Management.

2. Select Validate A Configuration in the Management pane to launch the Validate A Configuration Wizard.

3. On the Before You Begin page, click Next.

4. On the Select Servers Or A Cluster page, type each virtual machine name in the Enter Name text box and click Add. After these actions are completed, click Next.

5. On the Testing Options page, select Run All Tests (Recommended) and then click Next.

6. On the Confirmation page, review the test list and then click Next.

7. Correct any errors found during the validation process and then revalidate the configuration.

8. On the Summary page, click Finish.

9. Select Create A Cluster in the Management pane to launch the Create Cluster Wizard.

10. On the Before You Begin page, click Next.

11. On the Select Servers page, type each virtual machine name in the Enter Server Name text box and click Add. After these actions are completed, click Next.

12. On the Validation Warning page, select the appropriate option and then click Next.

13. On the Access Point For Administering The Cluster page, type the name of the cluster in the Cluster Name text box. You may also have to type the IP addresses to use for each configured network. After these actions are completed, click Next.

14. On the Confirmation page, review the cluster information and then click Next.

15. On the Summary page, click Finish.

 CAUTION When performing cluster validation, you may encounter an error that is related to duplicate IP addresses for the Teredo IPv6 Tunneling Protocol. To resolve this problem, open Device Manager, select Show Hidden Devices in the View menu, right-click the Teredo Tunneling Pseudo-Interface in Network Adapters, and select Disable.

After you complete these steps, each virtual machine will be a node in the failover cluster. To quickly verify that the failover cluster is functioning, you can shut down the first virtual machine cluster node. When you open Failover Cluster Management on the second virtual machine cluster node, you see that it now owns all cluster resources. After you have tested that cluster failover is successful, you can proceed with the installation of the cluster-aware application.

Summary

There are many advanced features in Hyper-V that you can leverage to optimize virtualization infrastructure deployments. If you are going to create complex testing, support desk, or user-training scenarios, use differencing disks and virtual machine snapshots to enable quick provisioning of new virtual machine configurations with the ability to roll back to the baseline state. When you need to reduce the size of NTFS-formatted dynamically expanding disks, use defragmentation prior to using the VHD compaction tool to minimize the size of compacted virtual hard disks. You must use a precompactor before compaction for a non-NTFS formatted VHD. Hyper-V provides external, internal, and private networks to enable a wide-range of network configurations and provide virtual machines with the appropriate connectivity scope. In addition, Hyper-V supports VLAN configuration at the server and virtual machine level. For cluster-aware applications running within virtual machines, use a virtual machine cluster to minimize downtime from virtual machine failures. In the case of non–cluster-aware applications, deploy high-availability Hyper-V server clusters to manage planned and unplanned downtime.

Additional Resources

The following resources contain additional information related to the topics in this chapter.

- Technet Blog of Jose Barreto, "Windows Server 2008 Hyper-V Failover Clustering Options," available at *http://blogs.technet.com/josebda/archive/2008/06/17 /windows-server-2008-hyper-v-failover-clustering-options.aspx*

- Technet Blog of Jose Barreto, "Failover Clustering for Windows Server 2008 Hyper-V with File Server Storage," available at *http://blogs.technet.com/josebda/archive /2008/07/16/failover-clustering-for-hyper-v-with-file-server-storage.aspx*

- Technet Blog of Jose Barreto, "More on Storage Options for Windows Server 2008 Hyper-V," available at *http://blogs.technet.com/josebda/archive/2008/03/06 /more-on-storage-options-for-windows-server-2008-s-hyper-v.aspx*

- Microsoft Knowledge Base Article, "Parallel SCSI Support in Windows Server 2008 Failover Clusters," available at *http://support.microsoft.com/kb/947710*

- Microsoft AskCore Blog, "Cluster Resource Type Options for Hyper-V," available at *http://blogs.technet.com/askcore/archive/2008/07/27/cluster-resource-type-options-for-hyper-v.aspx*

- Microsoft Technet Web Site, "Hyper-V Step-by-Step Guide: Hyper-V and Failover Clustering," available at *http://technet.microsoft.com/en-us/library /cc732181.aspx#BKMK_Install*

Hyper-V Security

This chapter describes the security features in Windows Server 2008 Hyper-V. You will learn about the Hyper-V files, services, and firewall rules that are installed in conjunction with the Hyper-V role, including how to create and configure Authorization Manager (AzMan) settings to delegate management of Hyper-V servers, virtual machines, virtual disks, and virtual networks and how to help secure virtual machine resources.

Reviewing Hyper-V Files

During a default installation of the Hyper-V role on Windows Server 2008, several folders are created on the file system, each of which contains critical application files. Tables 6-1 through 6-16 contain lists of these folders, the location in which they are created during a default installation of an English version of Hyper-V, and the files contained in each folder. You must be familiar with the Hyper-V folder and file structure so that you can develop, implement, and manage a successful, robust security model for your Hyper-V infrastructure.

TABLE 6-1 Hyper-V Management Client Files

FOLDER	FILES	OTHER DETAILS
%SystemDrive% \Program Files \Hyper-V		This folder contains Hyper-V management client files.
	InspectVhdDialog.exe	This is the dialog box that displays when you select Inspect Disk in Hyper-V Manager. It displays VHD properties such as file location, file name, file size, and maximum VHD size.
	Microsoft.Virtualization.Client.dll	
	Microsoft.Virtualization.Client.Management.dll	
	Microsoft.Virtualization.Client.RdpClientAxHost.dll	
	Microsoft.Virtualization.Client.RdpClientInterop.dll	
	Microsoft.Virtualization.Client.Settings.dll	
	Microsoft.Virtualization.Client.VMBrowser.dll	
	Microsoft.Virtualization.Client.Wizards.dll	
	SnapInAbout.dll	
	Virtmgmt.msc	This is the Hyper-V Manager MMC file.
	Vmconnect.exe	This is the Virtual Machine Connection application file.

TABLE 6-2 Hyper-V Management Client Resource Files

FOLDER	FILES	OTHER DETAILS
%SystemDrive% \Program Files \Hyper-V\en-US		This folder contains Hyper-V management client resource files.
	InspectVhdDialog.resources.dll	
	Microsoft.Virtualization.Client.Management.resources.dll	
	Microsoft.Virtualization.client.resources.dll	
	Microsoft.Virtualization.Client.Settings.resources.dll	
	Microsoft.Virtualization.Client.VMBrowser.resources.dll	
	Microsoft.Virtualization.Client.Wizards.resources.dll	
	SnapInAbout.dll.mui	
	Virtmgmt.msc	
	Vmconnect.resources.dll	

TABLE 6-3 Hyper-V Event Viewer Files

FOLDER	FILES	OTHER DETAILS
%SystemDrive%\ProgramData \Microsoft\Event Viewer\Views \Server Roles		This folder contains Hyper-V event viewer files.
	Virtualization.Events.xml	This file contains system events for Hyper-V services.

TABLE 6-4 Hyper-V Default Authorization Manager Store

FOLDER	FILES	OTHER DETAILS
%SystemDrive%\ProgramData \Microsoft\Windows\Hyper-V		This folder contains Hyper-V authorization Manager files.
	InitialStore.xml	This is the Hyper-V default Authorization Manager store file.

TABLE 6-5 Hyper-V Virtual Machine Snapshots Default Folder

FOLDER	FILES	OTHER DETAILS
%SystemDrive%\ProgramData\Microsoft\Windows\Hyper-V\Snapshots		This is the default folder that Hyper-V uses to store virtual machine snapshot files. It is initially empty.

TABLE 6-6 Hyper-V Virtual Machines Default Folder

FOLDER	FILES	OTHER DETAILS
%SystemDrive%\ProgramData\Microsoft\Windows\Hyper-V\Virtual Machines		This is the default folder that Hyper-V uses to store virtual machine files. It is initially empty.

TABLE 6-7 Hyper-V Virtual Floppy Disk Default Folder

FOLDER	FILES	OTHER DETAILS
%SystemDrive%\Users\Public\Public Documents\Hyper-V\Blank Floppy Disk		This is the default folder that Hyper-V uses to store a blank virtual floppy disk file.
	Blank.vfd	This is the default blank virtual floppy disk file.

TABLE 6-8 Hyper-V Virtual Hard Disks Default Folder

FOLDER	FILES	OTHER DETAILS
%SystemDrive%\Users\Public\Public Documents\Hyper-V\Virtual Hard Disks		This is the default folder that Hyper-V uses to store virtual hard disk files. It is initially empty.

TABLE 6-9 Hyper-V Driver Information Files

FOLDER	FILES	OTHER DETAILS
%SystemDrive%\Windows\Inf		This folder contains Hyper-V information files.
	Wnetvsc.inf, wnetvsc.pnf	These are the information file (.inf) and precompiled information file (.pnf) for the installation of the Hyper-V network VSC miniport driver.

FOLDER	FILES	OTHER DETAILS
	Ws3Cap.inf, Ws3Cap.pnf	These are the .inf and .pnf files for the installation of the Hyper-V VGA Cap driver.
	Wstorflt.inf, wstorflt.pnf	These are the .inf and .pnf files for the installation of the Hyper-V virtual disk acceleration filter driver.
	Wstorvsc.inf, wstorvsc.pnf	These are the .inf and .pnf files for the installation of the Hyper-V storage VSC miniport driver.
	Wstorvsp.inf, wstorvsp.pnf	These are the .inf and .pnf files for the installation of the Hyper-V storage VSP miniport driver.
	Wvid.inf, wvid.pnf	These are the .inf and .pnf files for the installation of the Hyper-V virtualization infrastructure driver.
	Wvmbus.inf, wvmbus.pnf	These are the .inf and .pnf files for the installation of the Hyper-V VMBus driver.
	Wvmbushid.inf, wvmbushid.pnf	These are the .inf and .pnf files for the installation of the Hyper-V VMBus HID miniport driver.
	Wvmbusvideo.inf, wvmbusvideo.pnf	These are the .inf and .pnf files for the installation of the Hyper-V synthetic video driver.
	Wvmic.inf, wvmic.pnf	These are the .inf and .pnf files for the installation of the Hyper-V Integration Services.
	Wvms_mp.inf, wvms_mp.pnf	These are the .inf and .pnf files for the installation of the Hyper-V VM switch miniport edge driver.

FOLDER	FILES	OTHER DETAILS
	Wvms_pp.inf, wvms_pp.pnf	These are the .inf and .pnf files for the installation of the Hyper-V VM switch protocol edge driver.

TABLE 6-10 Hyper-V Compiled HTML Help Files

FOLDER	FILES	OTHER DETAILS
%SystemDrive%\Windows\Help\Mui\0409		This folder contains Hyper-V help files.
	Virtual_help.chm	This is a compiled HTML help file for Hyper-V.

TABLE 6-11 Hyper-V Compiled Help Files

FOLDER	FILES	OTHER DETAILS
%SystemDrive%\Windows\Help\en-US		This folder contains Hyper-V help files.
	Virtsrv_start.h1s	This is a compiled help file for Hyper-V.
	Virtual_help.h1s	This is a compiled help file for Hyper-V.

TABLE 6-12 Hyper-V Windows Hypervisor and Integration Services Files

FOLDER	FILES	OTHER DETAILS
%SystemDrive%\Windows\System32		This folder contains Hyper-V executable files, DLL files, and other files related to Integration Services.
	Hvax64.exe	This is the AMD version of the Hyper-V Windows Hypervisor.

FOLDER	FILES	OTHER DETAILS
	Hvix64.exe	This is the Intel version of the Hyper-V Windows Hypervisor.
	Hypervisor.mof	This is the managed object format (MOF) file that describes the diagnostic trace events that the Windows Hypervisor logs to the Event Tracing for Windows (ETW).
	IcCoinstall.dll	This is the Hyper-V Integration Services Coinstaller DLL file.
	Nvspwmi.dll	This is the Virtual Network Switch WMI provider DLL file.
	Rdp4vs.dll	This is the Virtual Machine Remoting Services API DLL file.
	RemoteFileBrowse.dll	This is the Hyper-V remote file browser data source DLL file.
	Removehypervisor.mof	This is the managed object format (MOF) file that is used to unregister the diagnostic trace events that the Windows Hypervisor logs to ETW.
	Synthnic.dll	This is the synthetic network card support DLL file.
	Synthstor.dll	This is the synthetic storage adapter support DLL file.
	Vhdsvc.dll	This is the VHD management service support DLL file.
	Vid.dll	This is the infrastructure library driver support DLL file.

FOLDER	FILES	OTHER DETAILS
	Vmbuspipe.dll	This is the VMBus user mode pipe support DLL file.
	Vmbusvdev.dll	This is the virtual machine bus device support DLL file.
	Vmclusex.dll	This is the virtual machine failover cluster administrator extension support DLL file.
	Vmclusres.dll	This is the virtual machine failover cluster resource support DLL file.
	VmdCoinstall.dll	This is the Integration Services coinstaller support DLL file.
	Vmguest.iso	This is an image file that is used to install Integration Services in guest virtual machines.
	Vmicheartbeat.dll	This is the Integration Services heartbeat virtual device support DLL file.
	Vmickvpexchange.dll	This is the Integration Services heartbeat key value parameters support DLL file.
	Vmicshutdown.dll	This is the Integration Services shutdown virtual device support DLL file.
	Vmicsvc.exe	This file is the Integration Services service.
	Vmictimeprovider.dll	This is the Integration Services time synchronization provider library support DLL file.

FOLDER	FILES	OTHER DETAILS
	Vmictimesync.dll	This is the Integration Services time synchronization virtual device support DLL file.
	Vmicvss.dll	This is the Integration Services VSS writer virtual device support DLL file.
	Vmms.exe	This file is the virtual machine management service.
	Vmprox.dll	This is the Hyper-V component proxy support DLL file.
	Vmsntfy.dll	This is the virtual machine switch notify support DLL file.
	Vmwp.exe	This file is the virtual machine worker process.
	Vmwpctrl.dll	This is the virtual machine moniker support DLL file.
	Vsconfig.dll	This is the virtual machine configuration support DLL file.
	WindowsVirtualization.mof	This is the managed object format file with directives to add all classes and instances in the Virtualization namespace.
	WindowsVirtualizationUninstall.mof	This is the managed object format file that contains the uninstallation directives for all classes and instances in the Virtualization namespace.

TABLE 6-13 Hyper-V Driver Files

FOLDER	FILES	OTHER DETAILS
%SystemDrive%\Windows\System32\Drivers		This folder contains Hyper-V driver files.
	Hvboot.sys	This is the Windows Hypervisor boot driver file.
	Isoparser.sys	This is the ISO image parser driver file.
	Passthruparser.sys	This is the pass-through disk parser driver file.
	S3Cap.sys	This is the Microsoft S3 emulated device Cap driver file.
	Storflt.sys	This is the virtual storage filter driver file.
	Storvsc.sys	This is the storage VSC miniport driver file.
	Storvsp.sys	This is the storage VSP miniport driver file.
	Vhdparser.sys	This is the VHD parser driver file.
	Vid.sys	This is the Hyper-V infrastructure driver file.
	Vmbus.sys	This is the VMBus driver file.
	Vmswitch.sys	This is the network VSP driver file.
	Winhv.sys	This is the Windows Hypervisor interface driver file.

TABLE 6-14 Hyper-V Driver Localization Files

FOLDER	FILES	OTHER DETAILS
%SystemDrive%\Windows\System32\drivers\en-US		This folder contains localization files for Hyper-V driver files.
	Isoparser.sys.mui	
	Hvboot.sys.mui	
	Vmbus.sys.mui	
	Netvsc50.sys.mui	
	Netvsc60.sys.mui	

FOLDER	FILES	OTHER DETAILS
	Passthruparser.sys.mui	
	Storflt.sys.mui	
	Storvsp.sys.mui	
	Vhdparser.sys.mui	

TABLE 6-15 Hyper-V Information Localization Files

FOLDER	FILES	OTHER DETAILS
%SystemDrive%\Windows\System32\DriverStore\en-US		This folder contains localization files associated with Hyper-V information files.
	Wnetvsc.inf_loc	
	Ws3cap.inf_loc	
	Wstorflt.inf_loc	
	Wstorvsp.inf_loc	
	Wvid.inf_loc	
	Wvmbus.inf_loc	
	Wvmbushid.inf_loc	
	Wvmbusvideo.inf_loc	
	Wvmic.inf_loc	
	Wvms_mp.inf_loc	
	Wvms_pp.inf_loc	

TABLE 6-16 Hyper-V Integration Services Localization Files

FOLDER	FILES	OTHER DETAILS
%SystemDrive%\Windows\System32\en-US		This folder contains localization files for Hyper-V Integration Services.
	Nvspwmi.dll.mui	
	RemoteFileBrowse.dll.mui	
	SynthNic.dll.mui	
	SynthStor.dll.mui	
	Vhdsvc.dll.mui	
	Vmclusex.dll.mui	
	Vmclusres.dll.mui	

FOLDER	FILES	OTHER DETAILS
	Vmicheartbeat.dll.mui	
	Vmickvpexchange.dll.mui	
	Vmicshutdown.dll.mui	
	Vmictimesync.dll.mui	
	Vmicvss.dll.mui	
	Vmms.exe.mui	
	Vmwp.exe.mui	
	Vsconfig.dll.mui	
	WindowsVirtualization.mfl	
	WindowsVirtualizationUninstall.mfl	

As shown in Tables 6-5 through 6-8, there are several default folders that Hyper-V creates during installation to store virtual machine–related files. In particular, these are:

- %SystemDrive%\ProgramData\Microsoft\Windows\Hyper-V\Snapshots
- %SystemDrive%\ProgramData\Microsoft\Windows\Hyper-V\Virtual Machines
- %SystemDrive%\Users\Public\Public Documents\Hyper-V\Virtual Hard Disks
- %SystemDrive%\Users\Public\Public Documents\Hyper-V\Blank Floppy Disk

You should modify the location of these folders to avoid storing virtual machine files on your system drive. In most cases, it is a best practice to modify the location of these folders to avoid input/output (I/O) and capacity-related problems from occurring on the server system volume. You can modify the Hyper-V server settings in Hyper-V Manager to specify new paths for the virtual machine and virtual hard disk folder locations. The virtual machine snapshot folder location and path to a virtual floppy disk are specified for each individual virtual machine using the virtual machine settings in Hyper-V Manager.

 CAUTION The virtual machine snapshot folder location cannot be changed if a virtual machine has at least one snapshot.

BEST PRACTICES A security best practice is to add the Hyper-V role to a Windows Server 2008 Server Core installation. On Windows Server 2008 Server Core, the Hyper-V management client files are not installed, which reduces the Hyper-V file attack surface. In addition, this approach has the benefit of also reducing the Hyper-V server footprint and should result in less downtime because fewer updates are required to maintain the system.

Reviewing Hyper-V Services

As discussed in detail in Chapter 3, "Hyper-V Architecture," there are three services installed with Hyper-V in the parent partition. The services are as follow:

- **Hyper-V Image Management Service (IMS)**   The IMS service supports management of virtual hard disks through WMI interfaces. VHD management includes actions such as inspecting virtual hard disks, as well as VHD compaction and merging differencing disks.

- **Hyper-V Networking Management Service (NMS)**   The NMS service supports management of virtual networks through WMI interfaces. Virtual network management includes actions such as physical network adapter bindings and VLAN configuration.

- **Virtual Machine Management Service (VMMS)**   The VMMS service supports management of child partitions through WMI interfaces. This includes VHD connection to virtual machines, virtual network adapter connection to a virtual network, creation of virtual machine worker processes, snapshot management, and many other critical functions.

The Hyper-V services are configured to start automatically, have dependencies to the Remote Procedure Call (RPC) service and the Windows Management Instrumentation (WMI) service, and run under the context of system accounts with the lowest possible privilege level. The IMS executes with the credentials and rights of the Network Service account (NT AUTHORITY \Network Service). The Network Service account has limited access to local computer resources and uses the computer account for authenticated access to network resources. The NMS and VMMS execute in the context of the Local System account (NT AUTHORITY\LocalSystem). The Local System account has extensive privileges on the local computer and acts as the computer on the network. Because the Local System security token includes the NT AUTHORITY \SYSTEM and BUILTIN\Administrators security identifiers (SID), this account has access to many system objects.

 CAUTION   You should never change the system account settings for the Hyper-V services. Altering the settings or the context in which the Hyper-V services execute can cause them to stop functioning.

Reviewing Hyper-V Firewall Rules

In order to enable network traffic that is required to access or manage Hyper-V and virtual machine resources, several firewall rules are configured during the installation of Hyper-V. Table 6-17 contains a list of these firewall rules and the associated network ports.

TABLE 6-17 Windows Server 2008 Hyper-V Firewall Rules

FIREWALL RULE	DESCRIPTION	PROTOCOL	NETWORK PORTS
Hyper-V – WMI (Async-In)	Inbound rule for Hyper-V to allow asynchronous WMI traffic	TCP	Local – Any Remote – Any
Hyper-V – WMI (DCOM-In)	Inbound rule for Hyper-V to allow WMI management using DCOM	TCP	Local – 135 Remote – Any
Hyper-V – WMI (TCP-In)	Inbound rule for Hyper-V to allow remote WMI traffic	TCP	Local – Any Remote – Any
Hyper-V (RPC)	Inbound rule for Hyper-V to allow remote management using RPC/TCP	TCP	Local – Dynamic RPC Remote – Any
Hyper-V (RPC-EPMAP)	Inbound rule for the RPCSS service to allow RPC/TCP traffic for Hyper-V	TCP	Local – RPC Endpoint Mapper Remote – Any
Hyper-V (SPL-TCP-In)	Inbound rule for Hyper-V to allow remote connections to virtual machines	TCP	Local – 2179 Remote – Any
Hyper-V Management Clients – WMI (Async-In)	Inbound rule for Hyper-V management clients to allow asynchronous WMI traffic	TCP	Local – Any Remote – Any
Hyper-V Management Clients – WMI (DCOM-In)	Inbound rule for Hyper-V management clients to allow WMI management via DCOM	TCP	Local – 135 Remote – Any
Hyper-V Management Clients – WMI (TCP-In)	Inbound rule for Hyper-V management clients to allow remote WMI traffic	TCP	Local – Any Remote – Any
Hyper-V – WMI (TCP-Out)	Outbound rule for Hyper-V to allow remote WMI traffic	TCP	Local – Any Remote – Any
Hyper-V Management Clients – WMI (TCP-Out)	Outbound rule for Hyper-V management clients to allow remote WMI traffic	TCP	Local – Any Remote – Any

As shown in Figure 6-1, you can use the Windows Firewall With Advanced Security Microsoft Management Console (MMC) in Windows Server 2008 to view and manage both inbound and outbound firewall rules. Follow these steps to open the Windows Firewall with Advanced Security MMC:

1. On the Windows taskbar, click Start.

2. Select Administrative Tools from the menu.

3. Click the Windows Firewall With Advanced Security menu option.

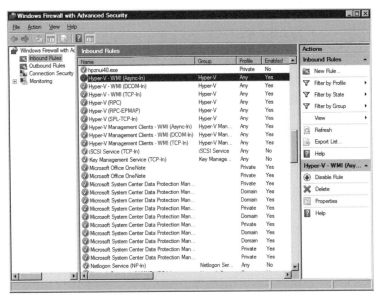

FIGURE 6-1 The Windows Firewall With Advanced Security MMC

> **NOTE** You must be logged in with an account that is a member of the Administrators group or the Network Operators Group to use the Windows Firewall With Advanced Security MMC.

Securing Hyper-V Resources

In Virtual Server 2005 R2, the ability to provide access rights to a Virtual Server host, virtual machine, virtual hard disk, and virtual network resources was implemented as a modification of Discretionary Access Control Lists (DACLs) for specific Virtual Server 2005 R2 file and folder objects. In this type of model, administrative tasks are translated into permissions on individual objects, and users and groups are granted the required access rights to each object to perform their job functions.

In contrast, Hyper-V defines a set of operations that can be used to create role-based access controls (RBAC) that do not require direct modification of permissions on each individual object affected, but rather assign permissions to a set of resources to enable pertinent job functions to be performed. Using RBAC, a role is the basic unit that allows management of permissions and assignments. Specifically, permissions are granted to a role, and users or groups are assigned to the role that allows them to perform their job functions.

Using Authorization Manager with Hyper-V

Hyper-V leverages the Authorization Manager (AzMan) framework to define role-based access controls. Authorization Manager allows you to define administrative roles tailored to individual jobs in your environment, to grant permissions that are needed to perform the functions related to a specific role, and to assign users and groups to the defined roles. Following are some basic AzMan concepts that you should understand before attempting to modify the baseline Hyper-V security model:

- **Operation** This is a low-level permission that defines a particular action allowed by an application. Hyper-V related examples are starting a virtual machine, connecting to a virtual network switch port, and creating a virtual machine.

- **Task** This is a collection of operations that is used to define a basic administrative action. Tasks can also contain other tasks. For example, in Hyper-V, you could create a task named Manage VMs that could consist of the operations to start a virtual machine, stop a virtual machine, pause a virtual machine, and restart a virtual machine.

- **Role** This is a collection of operations and tasks that a user needs to perform a particular job. A role is applied to a set of application-related objects, and users or groups are assigned to roles. For example, in Hyper-V, you could define a VM User role, a VM Administrator role, and so on.

- **Scope** This is the boundary of objects to which a role can apply. For example, a scope can include objects such as files or folders, an Active Directory container, or any object exposed by an application. In Hyper-V, scopes can apply to virtual machines, virtual switches, and virtual switch ports.

- **Authorization Policy** This describes the relationships between operations, tasks, roles, and scopes that are contained in an Authorization Manager store.

As opposed to a file or folder ACL that is stored with the object, the definitions of roles, tasks, and operations, and the assignment of users and groups to the roles are saved separately from the objects they affect in an authorization store that can be managed through the Authorization Manager MMC. By default, Hyper-V creates a file-based authorization store (%SystemDrive%\ProgramData\Microsoft\Windows\Hyper-V\InitialStore.xml) when it is installed. An authorization store can also be maintained in Active Directory. In addition to the Authorization Manager MMC, you also can manage an authorization store through Authorization Manager APIs that support scripting languages such as Visual Basic Scripting (VBScript).

> **NOTE** An XML-based authorization store does not support delegation of administration because access to an XML-based authorization store is controlled by the DACL on the file, which controls access to the entire contents of the file.

If an Active Directory database is used for the authorization store, Active Directory Domain Services (AD DS) must be at the Windows Server 2003 functional level. It is crucial that you include the authorization store in your Hyper-V backup strategy. The Hyper-V VSS writer can back up an authorization store on a Hyper-V server.

CAUTION An XML-based file authorization store can be edited simultaneously by two administrative applications. Therefore, you must ensure through procedural steps that only a single administrator makes changes to the XML-based file at any particular time.

Using Authorization Manager, Hyper-V queries the authorization policy at run time to confirm that a user is authorized to perform a requested operation on a Hyper-V resource.

 CAUTION Before you make any modifications to the Hyper-V Authorization Store, you should back it up using Windows Backup Server or other backup application. If the Hyper-V Authorization Store is missing or corrupt, Hyper-V services will fail to start.

MORE INFO If you would like more details about the Authorization Manager framework, refer to *http://technet.microsoft.com/en-us/library/cc732077.aspx*.

Creating an Authorization Store in Active Directory

If you want to implement an Authorization Store in Active Directory, you typically create it under the Program Data container. This is not a requirement, and you can adapt this based on your Active Directory design and management policies. However, an authorization store must be contained within the Active Directory domain naming context; therefore, you cannot store one in an application partition.

 ON THE COMPANION MEDIA On the companion media, you will find a directory called \Chapter Materials\Scripts\Chapter 6\AzMan. Inside the directory there is a script named CreateAzStore.js. You must run the script using an elevated command prompt. The script creates a new authorization store in Active Directory given the path to the initial authorization store (InitialStore.xml), as well as the name and location in Active Directory for the new authorization store. In addition, the operations and the default Administrator role are created in the new authorization store based on the information contained in the initial store. However, the Administrator role is not assigned to any users or groups.

```
cscript CreateAzStore.js msxml://C:\ProgramData\Microsoft\Windows
\Hyper-V\InitialStore.xml "msldap://CN=AzStoreRK,CN=Microsoft,
CN=Program Data,DC=contoso,DC=com"
```

In this example, the path to the initial store is C:\ProgramData\Microsoft\Windows \Hyper-V\InitialStore.xml, the new authorization store name is AzStoreRK, and the location to create the new authorization store in Active Directory is CN=Microsoft,CN=Program Data, DC=contoso,DC=com.

After you run the CreateAzStore.js script, follow these steps to open the Authorization Manager MMC and view the new authorization store in Active Directory:

1. In the parent partition, click Start, type **azman.msc** in the Start Search text box, and then press Enter.

2. In the left pane of the Authorization Manager console, right-click the Authorization Manager root and select Open Authorization Store.

3. In the Open Authorization Store dialog box, select Active Directory or Active Directory Application Mode (ADAM) and then click Browse.

4. In the next dialog box, select the authorization store that was created using the CreateAzStore.js script and then click Open.

5. In the Open Authorization Store dialog box, ensure that the right authorization store appears in the Store Name text box and then click OK.

6. In the left pane of the Authorization Manager console, expand the new authorization store, then the Hyper-V Services node, and finally the Definitions node.

7. Select Role Definitions and you should see the Administrator role in the right pane.

8. Close the Authorization Manager console.

In order for the Hyper-V server to use the Authorization Manager store in Active Directory, follow these steps to change the location value of the authorization store in the registry:

1. In the parent partition, click Start, type **regedit** in the Start Search text box, and then press Enter.

2. In the Registry Editor, navigate to the HKEY_Local_Machine\SOFTWARE\Microsoft \Windows NT\CurrentVersion\Virtualization key.

3. In the left pane, right-click the key and select Export.

4. In the Export Registry File dialog box, enter a file name to save the key and then click Save.

5. In the left pane, right-click the StoreLocation entry and select Modify.

6. In the Edit String dialog box, enter the new location of the authorization store in Active Directory (such as msldap://CN=AzStore*RK*,CN=Microsoft,CN=Program Data,DC=contoso,DC=com) and then click OK.

Additionally, you should grant the Hyper-V server computer account Read access to the authorization store in Active Directory. Follow these steps to grant the appropriate permissions to the Hyper-V server computer account:

1. In the parent partition, click Start, type **azman.msc** in the Start Search text box, and then press Enter.

2. In the left pane of the Authorization Manager console, right-click the new authorization store and select Properties.

3. In the authorization store Properties dialog box, click the Security tab.

4. In the Authorization Manager User Role drop-down list, select Reader.

5. In the authorization store Properties dialog box, click Add.

6. In the Select Users, Computers, Or Groups dialog box, enter the Hyper-V server computer account name, click Check Names, and then click OK.

7. In the authorization store Properties dialog box, click OK.

8. Close the Authorization Manager console.

9. Open the Services console and restart the Hyper-V Virtual Machine Management Service (VMMS) and the Hyper-V Networking Management Service (NVSPWMI).

10. Close the Services console.

Follow these steps to restore the Hyper-V server configuration to use the initial store file:

1. In the parent partition, open the Services console and stop the Hyper-V Virtual Machine Management Service and the Hyper-V Networking Management Service.

2. Open the Registry Editor and navigate to the HKEY_Local_Machine\SOFTWARE \Microsoft\Windows NT\CurrentVersion\Virtualization key.

3. In the left pane, right-click the StoreLocation entry and select Modify.

4. In the Edit String dialog box, enter the location of the initial authorization store (such as msxml://C:\ProgramData\Microsoft\Windows\Hyper-V\InitialStore.xml) and then click OK.

5. Close the Registry Editor.

6. In the Services console, restart the Hyper-V Virtual Machine Management Service and the Hyper-V Networking Management Service.

7. Close the Services console.

8. Open the Authorization Manager console and verify the Authorization Policy configuration.

9. Close the Authorization Manager console.

> **NOTE** If you use System Center Virtual Machine Manager (SCVMM) to manage Hyper-V servers, SCVMM creates and uses its own authorization store. SCVMM does not import any data from the authorization store used by a Hyper-V server before the SCVMM agent is installed, nor does it export any data to it. When a Hyper-V server is removed from SCVMM management, you must configure the local initial authorization store (or an Active Directory–based authorization store) to implement additional roles for finer control and management of the Hyper-V server.

Understanding Hyper-V Security

By default, Hyper-V defines a single scope, 33 operations, and a single role. You can view and modify the default Hyper-V authorization policy using the Authorization Manager MMC. To use the Authorization Manager MMC, you must be using an account that is a member of the administrators group in the parent partition.

Follow these steps to open the Authorization Manager MMC and view the Hyper-V authorization policy:

1. In the parent partition, click Start, type **azman.ms**c in the Start Search text box, and then press Enter.

2. In the Authorization Manager console, right-click Authorization Manager in the left pane and select Open Authorization Store from the menu.

3. In the Open Authorization Store dialog box, select XML File, type **%ProgramData% \Microsoft\Windows\Hyper-V\InitialStore.xml** in the Store Name text box, and then click OK.

4. Expand the Hyper-V Services node under InitialStore.xml to view role and task definitions, as well as role assignments.

As shown in Figure 6-2, Hyper-V Services represents the default scope that applies to all Hyper-V objects. Additional scopes can be defined, and they inherit role definitions, task definitions, and role assignments from the default scope. However, new scopes can be created and applied only to virtual machines, virtual switches, virtual switch ports, and VMMS objects.

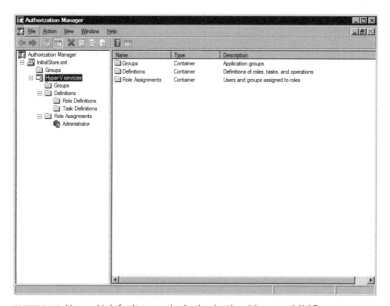

FIGURE 6-2 Hyper-V default scope in Authorization Manager MMC

Tables 6-18 through 6-20 list the Hyper-V operations grouped into services, network, and virtual machine categories, respectively. When defining new roles using Authorization Manager, these are the operations available to provide permissions to Hyper-V objects and define tasks that are then assigned to a role.

TABLE 6-18 Hyper-V Services Operations

OPERATION	DESCRIPTION
Read Service Configuration	Authorizes reading the configuration of the Virtual Machine Management Service
Reconfigure Service	Authorizes the reconfiguration of the Virtual Machine Management Service
View Virtual Switch Management Service	Authorizes viewing the Virtual Switch Management Service

TABLE 6-19 Hyper-V Network Operations

OPERATION	DESCRIPTION
Bind External Ethernet Port	Authorizes binding to an external Ethernet port
Change VLAN Configuration on Port	Authorizes modifying VLAN settings
Connect Virtual Switch Port	Authorizes connecting to a virtual switch port
Create Internal Ethernet Port	Authorizes creating an internal Ethernet port
Create Virtual Switch	Authorizes creating a new virtual switch
Create Virtual Switch Port	Authorizes creating a new virtual switch port
Delete Internal Ethernet Port	Authorizes deleting an internal Ethernet port
Delete Virtual Switch	Authorizes deleting a virtual switch
Delete Virtual Switch Port	Authorizes deleting a virtual switch port
Disconnect Virtual Switch Port	Authorizes disconnecting from a virtual switch port
Modify Internal Ethernet Port	Authorizes modifying the internal Ethernet port settings
Modify Switch Port Settings	Authorizes modifying the switch port settings
Modify Switch Settings	Authorizes modifying the switch settings
Unbind External Ethernet Port	Authorizes unbinding from an external Ethernet port
View External Ethernet Ports	Authorizes viewing the available external Ethernet ports

OPERATION	DESCRIPTION
View Internal Ethernet Ports	Authorizes viewing the available internal Ethernet ports
View LAN Endpoints	Authorizes viewing the LAN endpoints
View Switch Ports	Authorizes viewing the available switch ports
View Switches	Authorizes viewing the available switches
View VLAN Settings	Authorizes viewing the VLAN Settings

TABLE 6-20 Hyper-V Virtual Machine Operations

OPERATION	DESCRIPTION
Allow Input to Virtual Machine	Authorizes a user to give input to a virtual machine
Allow Output from Virtual Machine	Authorizes viewing the output from a virtual machine
Change Virtual Machine Authorization Scope	Authorizes changing the scope of a virtual machine
Create Virtual Machine	Authorizes creating a virtual machine
Delete Virtual Machine	Authorizes deleting a virtual machine
Pause and Restart Virtual Machine	Authorizes pause and restart of a virtual machine
Reconfigure Virtual Machine	Authorizes reconfiguring a virtual machine
Start Virtual Machine	Authorizes starting a virtual machine
Stop Virtual Machine	Authorizes stopping a virtual machine
View Virtual Machine Configuration	Authorizes viewing a virtual machine configuration

 CAUTION In Windows Server 2008 Hyper-V, a single operation to provide the permissions to create virtual machine snapshots is not included. However, such an operation (Allow Virtual Machine Snapshots) is included in Windows Server 2008 R2 Hyper-V.

There is only a single default role defined in Hyper-V. It is the Administrator role that is shown in Figure 6-3. Since all 33 Hyper-V operations are assigned to the Hyper-V Administrator role, it is capable of viewing and modifying all Hyper-V objects, including virtual machines, virtual hard disks (with appropriate ACLs), virtual networks, and Hyper-V settings.

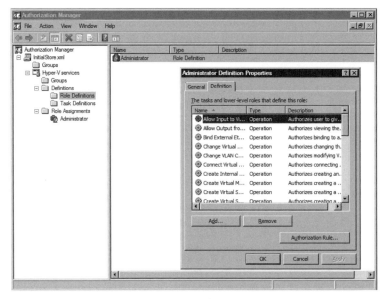

FIGURE 6-3 Hyper-V Administrator Role Definition in Authorization Manager MMC

In a default installation of Windows Server 2008 Hyper-V, only members of the local administrators group (in the parent partition) are granted access to manage the Hyper-V configuration as well as virtual machine, virtual hard disk, and virtual network objects. As shown in Figure 6-4, the local administrators group is the only group that is assigned to the Administrator role. Additional roles and role assignments must be specifically added to grant other users or groups permissions to access and manage Hyper-V resources.

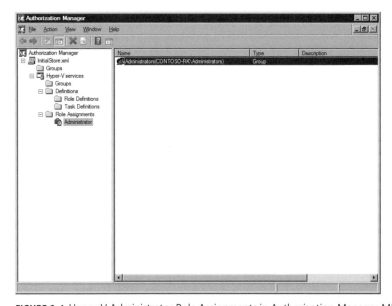

FIGURE 6-4 Hyper-V Administrator Role Assignments in Authorization Manager MMC

The next several sections describe potential Hyper-V management roles in conjunction with the new role definitions and assignments required to enable specific role-based access rights. To implement one or more of these roles, define a group that corresponds to the role, add the appropriate individual users as members of the group, and assign the group to the target role.

In organizations where there is a very strict separation of duties, the roles represented by the individual groups are populated with various teams and individuals. In organizations with multifunction teams, teams or individuals can be easily granted multiple roles by being assigned to more than one of the defined groups.

Configuring a Hyper-V Monitor Role

The Hyper-V monitor role is one that you might want to implement in your Hyper-V environment to use the Hyper-V Manager MMC and examine Hyper-V configuration settings without allowing any modification rights. For example, you might have an individual or team responsible for monitoring Hyper-V or virtual machine performance and settings. Table 6-21 lists the operations to assign to this role. This role can be defined using the default Hyper-V Services scope.

TABLE 6-21 Hyper-V Monitor Role Definition

ACCESS RIGHTS	OPERATIONS
Hyper-V Services	Read Service Configuration
	View Virtual Switch Management Service
Virtual Machines	Allow Output from Virtual Machine
	View Virtual Machine Configuration
Virtual Networks	View External Ethernet Ports
	View Internal Ethernet Ports
	View LAN Endpoints
	View Switch Ports
	View Switches
	View VLAN Settings

Follow these steps to open the Authorization Manager MMC, create the Hyper-V Monitor role, and assign users or groups to the role:

1. Log into a Hyper-V server using an account with administrator rights.

2. In the parent partition, click Start, type **azman.msc** in the Start Search text box, and then press Enter.

3. In the Authorization Manager console, right-click Authorization Manager in the left pane and select Open Authorization Store from the shortcut menu.

4. In the Open Authorization Store dialog box, select XML File, type **%ProgramData%\ Microsoft\Windows\Hyper-V\InitialStore.xml** in the Store Name text box, and then click OK.

5. Expand the Hyper-V Services node (the default scope) under InitialStore.xml.

6. Expand Definitions to view role and task definitions, as shown in Figure 6-5.

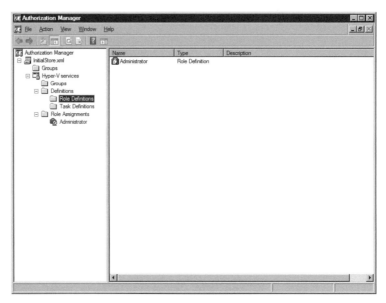

FIGURE 6-5 Role and task definitions in Authorization Manager

7. Right-click Role Definitions and select New Role Definition from the shortcut menu.

8. In the New Role Definition dialog box, shown in Figure 6-6, type **Hyper-V Monitor** in the Name text box. Optionally, you can also type a short description of the role in the Description text box.

FIGURE 6-6 The New Role Definition dialog box

9. After you have entered the role definition name and description, click Add.

10. In the Add Definition dialog box, click the Operations tab (see Figure 6-7).

11. In the Operations tab, select each of the operations listed in Table 6-21 and then click OK.

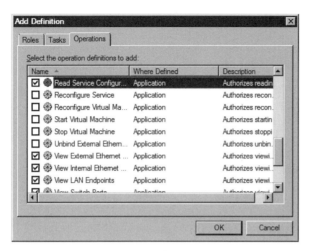

FIGURE 6-7 The Operations tab of the Add Definition dialog box

12. In the New Role Definition dialog box, verify that the required operations are listed (shown in Figure 6-8) and then click OK.

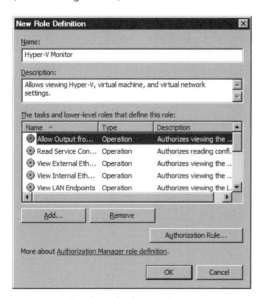

FIGURE 6-8 List of required operations

13. In the left pane, expand Role Assignments.

14. Right-click Role Assignments and select New Role Assignment from the shortcut menu, as shown in Figure 6-9.

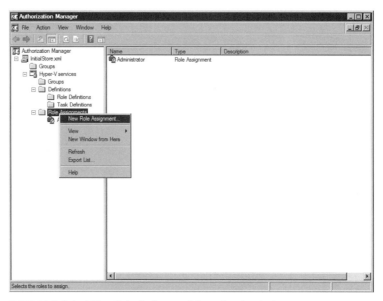

FIGURE 6-9 Select New Role Assignment from the shortcut menu.

15. In the Add Role dialog box, select Hyper-V Monitor (see Figure 6-10) and then click OK.

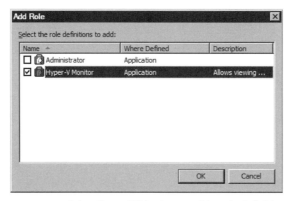

FIGURE 6-10 Select Hyper-V Monitor to add a role definition.

16. In the right pane, right-click Hyper-V Monitor, select Assign Users And Groups, and then select From Windows And Active Directory, as shown in Figure 6-11.

FIGURE 6-11 Select From Windows And Active Directory.

17. In the Select Users, Computers, Or Groups dialog box, enter the name of the security group that contains the users that need to monitor Hyper-V (see Figure 6-12) and then click OK.

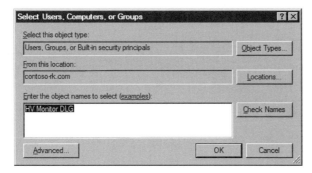

FIGURE 6-12 Enter the name of the security group.

18. In the Authorization Manager MMC, verify that the security group is included in the Hyper-V Monitor role assignment, as shown in Figure 6-13.

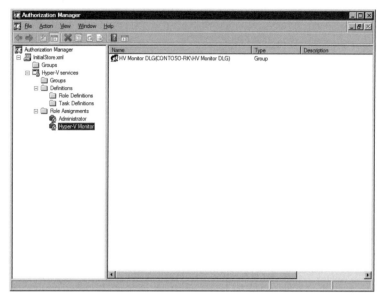

FIGURE 6-13 Verify the security group.

19. Close the Authorization Manager MMC.

You can log into the Hyper-V server with an account that is a member of the security group assigned to the Hyper-V Monitor role and use the Hyper-V Manager to view Hyper-V, virtual machine, and virtual network configuration. However, if you attempt to modify any settings, you will receive an error message similar to the one shown in Figure 6-14, stating that you do not have the required permissions.

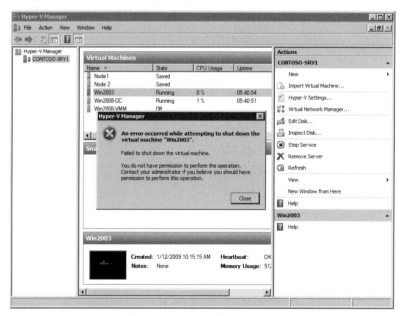

FIGURE 6-14 Error returned when using the Hyper-V Monitor role to modify virtual machine state

Configuring a Virtual Network Manager Role

The Virtual Network Manager role provides the ability to create, add, and modify virtual networks. Virtual networks can also be removed from Hyper-V. Table 6-22 lists the operations to assign to the Virtual Network Manager role definition. This role can be defined using the default Hyper-V Services scope. The Virtual Network Manager role might be implemented if a specific team is designated to maintain a strict virtual network structure.

TABLE 6-22 Virtual Network Manager Role Definition

ACCESS RIGHTS	OPERATIONS
Hyper-V Services	Read Service Configuration
	View Virtual Switch Management Service
Virtual Networks	Bind External Ethernet Port
	Connect Virtual Switch Port
	Create Internal Ethernet Port
	Create Virtual Switch
	Create Virtual Switch Port
	Delete Internal Ethernet Port
	Delete Virtual Switch
	Delete Virtual Switch Port
	Disconnect Virtual Switch Port
	Modify Internal Ethernet Port
	Modify Switch Port Settings
	Modify Switch Settings
	Unbind External Ethernet Port
	View External Ethernet Ports
	View Internal Ethernet Ports
	View LAN Endpoints
	View Switch Ports
	View Switches
	View VLAN Settings

Using the procedure described in the section titled "Configuring a Hyper-V Monitor Role" earlier in this chapter, create a new role definition named Hyper-V Virtual Network Manager, assign it the operations listed in Table 6-22, create a new role assignment, and assign the appropriate security group to the role.

Configuring a Virtual Machine Manager Role

The Virtual Machine Manager role provides the ability to delegate the management of virtual machines using the Hyper-V Manager MMC. The Virtual Machine Manager role might be implemented in a test lab or production environment in which a specific team needs to access only a subset of the virtual machines running on a Hyper-V server.

In order to implement the Virtual Machine Manager role, you must also provide access rights to the Hyper-V Manager MMC at the default scope level. To do this, use the procedure described in the section titled "Configuring a Hyper-V Monitor Role" earlier in this chapter to create a new role definition named Hyper-V Manager, assign it the operations listed in Table 6-23, create a new role assignment, and assign the appropriate security group to the role.

TABLE 6-23 Hyper-V Manager Role Definition

ACCESS RIGHTS	OPERATIONS
Hyper-V Services	Read Service Configuration
	View Virtual Switch Management Service

To delegate management to only a subset of the virtual machines running on a Hyper-V server, you must create a new AzMan scope and apply it to the target set of virtual machines. Then you can create the Virtual Machine Manager role definition (using the operations listed in Table 6-24) and the role assignment under the new scope.

TABLE 6-24 Virtual Machine Manager Role Definition

ACCESS RIGHTS	OPERATIONS
Virtual Machines	Allow Input To Virtual Machine
	Allow Output From Virtual Machine
	Pause And Restart Virtual Machine
	Start Virtual Machine
	Stop Virtual Machine
	View Virtual Machine Configuration

Follow these steps to use the Authorization Manager MMC to create a new scope, role definition, and role assignment for the Virtual Machine Manager role:

1. Log into a Hyper-V server using an account with administrator rights.

2. In the parent partition, click Start, type **azman.msc** in the Start Search text box, and then press Enter.

3. In the Authorization Manager console, right-click Authorization Manager in the left pane and select Open Authorization Store from the menu.

4. In the Open Authorization Store dialog box, select XML File, type **%ProgramData% \Microsoft\Windows\Hyper-V\InitialStore.xml** in the Store Name text box, and then click OK.

5. Expand the Hyper-V Services node under InitialStore.xml.

6. Right-click Hyper-V Services and select New Scope from the menu (see Figure 6-15).

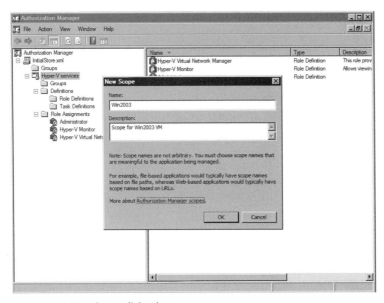

FIGURE 6-15 New Scope dialog box

7. Under the new scope, right-click Role Definitions and select New Role Definition from the menu.

8. In the New Role Definition dialog box, type **Hyper-V Virtual Machine Manager** in the Name text box (see Figure 6-16). Optionally, you can also type a short description of the role in the Description text box.

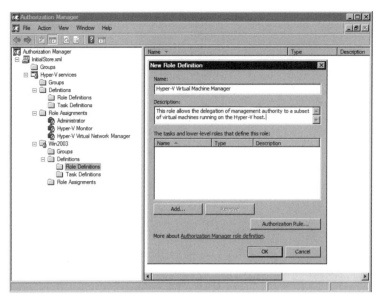

FIGURE 6-16 New Role Definition dialog box

9. After you have entered the role definition name and description, click Add.

10. In the Add Definition dialog box, click the Operations tab.

11. On the Operations tab, select each of the operations listed in Table 6-24 and then click OK.

12. In the New Role Definition dialog box, verify that the required operations are listed and then click OK.

13. Under the new scope, right-click Role Assignments and select New Role Assignment from the menu.

14. In the Add Role dialog box, select Hyper-V Virtual Machine Manager and then click OK.

15. In the right pane, right-click Hyper-V Virtual Machine Manager, select Assign Users and Groups, and then select From Windows And Active Directory.

16. In the Select Users, Computers, Or Groups dialog box, enter the name of the security group that needs to manage the virtual machines and then click OK.

17. In the Authorization Manager MMC, verify that the security group is included in the Hyper-V Virtual Machine Manager role assignment.

18. Close the Authorization Manager MMC.

After the new scope is created, you have to apply it to the subset of virtual machines. To apply the new scope, you must set each virtual machine object *ScopeOfResidence* property to the new scope name. You must use a script to modify the virtual machine *ScopeOfResidence* property because a graphical user interface is not provided to perform this action.

Following is a sample VBScript that allows you to assign a new scope to a virtual machine.

```
Option Explicit

Dim WMIService
Dim VM
Dim VMManagementService
Dim VMSystemGlobalSettingData
Dim VMName
Dim VMScope
Dim Result

'Enter the VM name and the name of the scope to assign it to
VMName = InputBox("Specify the virtual machine to change scope on:")
VMScope = InputBox("Specify the new scope to be used:")

'Get an instance of the WMI Service in the virtualization namespace
Set WMIService=GetObject("winmgmts:\\.\root\virtualization")

'Get a VMManagementService object
Set VMManagementService = WMIService.ExecQuery("SELECT * FROM
Msvm_VirtualSystemManagementService").ItemIndex(0)

'Get the VM object that we want to modify
Set VM=(WMIService.ExecQuery("SELECT * FROM Msvm_ComputerSystem WHERE ElementName='" &
VMName & "'")).ItemIndex(0)

'Get the VirtualSystemGlobalSettingsData of the VM to be modified
Set VMSystemGlobalSettingData = (VM.Associators_("MSVM_ElementSettingData",
"Msvm_VirtualSystemGlobalSettingData")).ItemIndex(0)

'Change the ScopeOfResidence property
VMSystemGlobalSettingData.ScopeOfResidence = VMScope

'Update the VM with ModifyVirtualSystem
Result = VMManagementService.ModifyVirtualSystem(VM.Path_.Path,
VMSystemGlobalSettingData.GetText_(1))
```

After the new scope is applied to the subset of virtual machines, the users in the security group assigned to the Virtual Machine Manager role will have the ability to use the Hyper-V Manager MMC and manage the designated virtual machines.

 ON THE COMPANION MEDIA On the book's companion media, you will find a directory called \Chapter Materials\Scripts\Chapter 6\Scopes. Inside the directory, there are three scripts: ChangeVMScope.vbs, ClearVMScope.vbs, and DisplayVMScope.vbs. The ChangeVMScope.vbs script allows you to change the *ScopeOfResidence* property for a virtual machine. The DisplayVMScope.VBS script allows you to view the scope applied to each virtual machine. Finally, the ClearVMScope.vbs script allows you to reset the virtual machine *ScopeOfResidence* property to the default scope.

Reviewing Hyper-V Security Best Practices

As you develop a security plan for your Hyper-V infrastructure, you must consider securing the parent partition as well as each of the guest virtual machines. The following sections define best practices that you should consider to secure your Hyper-V virtualization infrastructure.

Minimize the Hyper-V Parent Partition Attack Surface

Deploying Hyper-V on a Windows Server Core installation allows you to achieve the smallest attack surface for your Hyper-V servers. Because a Server Core installation installs only the components needed for a specific role (such as Hyper-V) and does not install any graphical user interface (GUI) management tools, not only is the attack surface minimized, but maintenance cycles are reduced because fewer updates are needed, and uptime potential increases.

MORE INFO To learn how to perform a Server Core installation of Window Server 2008 Hyper-V, refer to Chapter 4, "Hyper-V Installation and Configuration."

Because a Server Core installation of Hyper-V does not install the Hyper-V management tools, you will have to manage these Hyper-V servers remotely from other Windows Server 2008 or Windows Vista SP1 workstations.

MORE INFO To learn how to remotely manage a Server Core installation of Window Server 2008 Hyper-V, refer to Chapter 12, "Server Farm Management."

Run Applications Only in Child Partitions

The Hyper-V parent partition should be dedicated to the management of child partitions, and you should not run any applications (such as Exchange Server or SQL Server) in it. An application installed in the parent partition could potentially cause it to deadlock or become unresponsive, which would affect all child partitions. Therefore, run applications only in child partitions that are isolated from the parent partition and other child partitions. In this way, if an application running on a guest operating system in a child partition becomes unresponsive, it will not affect the execution or performance of applications in any other partition.

Define Virtual Machine Security Levels

The security framework required for each virtual machine depends on the requirements of the workload (applications and data) running on it. Therefore, you should use security policy requirements to define security levels (i.e., high, medium, low) and group virtual machines with similar levels onto common Hyper-V servers. This allows you to define and implement more stringent security measures for Hyper-V servers with highly sensitive virtual machine workloads, and fewer security measures for Hyper-V servers with less sensitive virtual machine workloads.

Define a Least-Privilege Authorization Policy

Because a virtualization platform can host multiple virtual machines with possibly different administrative teams, it is crucial that you define an authorization policy that adheres to the principle of least privilege. Therefore, you should neither grant local administrator rights to a Hyper-V server nor use the default Hyper-V Administrator role in Authorization Manager to assign permissions to groups and users that require access only to a subset of virtual machines. Instead, you should extend the default Hyper-V Authorization Policy by defining new roles and scopes that reflect the administrative model in your organization, and provide only the least privilege to any new role that allows fulfilling the defined job functions.

> **IMPORTANT** Remember that accounts with administrative permissions in the parent partition can make configuration changes to Hyper-V settings that can affect all child partitions on the Hyper-V server, whereas accounts with administrative permissions in a child partition have administrative privileges for that partition only.

Implement a Rigorous Update Strategy

One of the advantages of converting physical server workloads into virtual machines is that a virtual machine consists of a set of portable files that can be easily deployed and migrated between Hyper-V servers. In addition, with the ability to deploy new virtual machines more quickly based on a set of template files, it is essential that you implement a rigorous update strategy for ongoing maintenance of both running and offline template virtual machines. If you use System Center Configuration Manager, Windows Update Services, or other software update applications, ensure that you extend your current plan to incorporate your virtualization infrastructure.

You might also consider deploying one or more Hyper-V servers as *maintenance hosts*. A maintenance host is a Hyper-V server that you dedicate to the creation, staging, and update of virtual machines before you deploy them into your production environment. When the virtual machine is fully updated, you can use Quick Migration to move it onto a production Hyper-V server. Alternatively, you can use System Center Virtual Machine Manager to move a virtual machine between Hyper-V servers, based on a set of defined criteria that includes server load.

Dedicate a Physical Network Adapter to the Parent Partition

For both performance and security reasons, you should dedicate a network adapter to the parent partition on Hyper-V servers that you deploy in your production environment. In addition, use one or more additional physical network adapters to isolate the network traffic of virtual machines running in child partitions. This strategy will also provide you with the most flexibility in terms of securing network traffic using VLAN, IPSEC, or other protocols implemented based on virtual machine requirements.

Use Windows BitLocker Drive Encryption in the Parent Partition

If you need to safeguard your Hyper-V servers against physical or data theft, you should consider implementing Windows BitLocker Drive Encryption technology in the Hyper-V parent partition to help secure the system boot process and virtual machine files on shared storage systems. Because of the complex nature of this technology, you should carefully plan and design its deployment strategy.

> **MORE INFO** To learn more about Windows BitLocker Drive Encryption planning and design, refer to the BitLocker Design Guides that you can download from *http://go.microsoft.com/fwlink/?LinkId=134201*.

Implement or Extend Your Audit Strategy

Prior to deployment of your Hyper-V infrastructure, you should extend your current audit strategy to include the collection, analysis, and reporting of Hyper-V security-related events. If you are in the planning stage and developing an audit strategy, you can use any third-party auditing tool or System Center Operations Manager 2007 Audit Collection Services (ACS). ACS collects, consolidates, and generates reports on Windows security log data in real time.

Securing Virtual Machine Access

As described in Table 6-1, Hyper-V creates several folders in %ProgramData%\Microsoft\Windows\Hyper-V as the default location for virtual machine files (.xml, .vhd, .avhd, .vsv, and .bin). By default, VHD files are stored in %Users%\Public\Public Documents\Hyper-V\Virtual Hard Disks, and a blank floppy disk is stored in %Users%\Public\Public Documents\Hyper-V\Blank Floppy Disk.

When a new virtual machine is created, a corresponding folder is generated in the default folder hierarchy and the virtual machine files are placed in it. However, virtual machine files are not typically stored in the default location in enterprise environments. Instead, architecture, performance, and file size requirements commonly drive virtual machine folders to be located on one or more centrally managed storage systems or file servers.

IMPORTANT   If you specify different storage locations for virtual machine files, ensure that the System account and the Administrators groups have Full Control permissions for the new folders.

Each virtual machine folder hierarchy should be secured by direct application of NTFS permissions based on organizational needs. This will prevent unauthorized users from creating, copying, replacing, or deleting virtual machine files. However, since each virtual machine runs in the context of a virtual machine worker process, users who have been granted appropriate access rights to Hyper-V in Authorization Manager can perform management tasks (for example, stop and start virtual machines) despite restricted NTFS permissions on the virtual machine files. Therefore, securing virtual machine access requires a strategy that combines setting appropriate NTFS permissions on virtual machine files with adopting a rigorous authorization policy to restrict virtual machine management capabilities.

Hyper-V Virtual Machine SIDs

Ed Reed, Senior Software Design Engineer
Windows Virtualization

Hyper-V implements a role-based authorization policy using Authorization Manager. However, it still needs to access resources from a virtual machine's worker process, like virtual hard disk files, that are protected by discretionary access control lists (DACL). One possible solution to this issue would be to run the worker processes under the SYSTEM service user account like the Virtual Machine Management Service (VMMS). However, the SYSTEM account has complete and unrestricted access to the parent partition. This is undesirable because if a child partition could somehow compromise its worker process, the child would gain complete control of the parent partition.

To protect against this scenario, the VMMS creates and manages a special security identifier (SID) that is unique to each virtual machine. This SID is called the virtual machine SID or VM SID. From Windows Explorer, the VM SID appears in the form "NT VIRTUAL MACHINE\<VMID>" where <VMID> is the virtual machine's unique GUID identifier. When a DACL-protected resource is attached to the virtual machine, the VMMS modifies the resource's DACL to grant access to the VM SID. The VMMS creates a special access token using the NETWORK SERVICE account as the primary account identity and includes the VM SID in the token's list of SIDs. The virtual machine's worker process is then run using this special token. This allows Hyper-V to grant a specific virtual machine's worker process access to resources, and reduces the risk of a compromised worker process. Using the VM SID also improves isolation between virtual machine worker processes because no two worker processes have the same VM SID.

To allow all virtual machine worker processes access to common DACL-protected resources, the VMMS also creates and maintains another special SID called the VM Group SID. From Windows Explorer, the VM Group SID appears as "NT VIRTUAL MACHINE\VirtualMachines." When the VMMS creates the special access token to run the virtual machine worker process, it adds the VM Group SID to the SID list in addition to the VM SID. Using the VM Group SID helps improve isolation between the collection of virtual machine worker processes and other services running as NETWORK SERVICE in the parent partition.

In a typical production environment, there is likely a requirement to accommodate different administrators that manage different virtual machines on the same Hyper-V server. Some common scenarios include core business workloads administered by a central administrator group, line of business workloads administered by departmental or business groups, and test and development workloads administered by project teams or individual team members.

Configuring Centrally Managed Virtual Machine Folders

Several critical business workloads are commonly managed by a central administration team. Workloads that usually fall in this category are core infrastructure services such as Active Directory, Domain Name Service (DNS), and Dynamic Host Configuration Protocol (DHCP). Enterprise-wide applications, such as Microsoft Exchange Server, encompass another category of workloads that is often centrally managed. Figure 6-17 depicts how to organize and manage permissions on a virtual machine folder hierarchy in a scenario in which there is a centralized administration team (which can be composed of subteams) with responsibilities to manage core workloads.

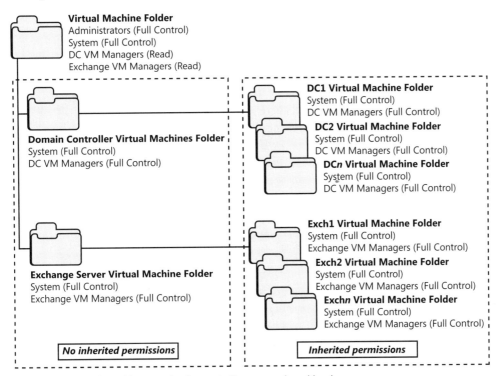

FIGURE 6-17 Virtual machine security for centrally managed workloads

In this model, workload folders are created to contain individual virtual machine folders. NTFS permissions applied to the workload and virtual machine folders are strictly configured to restrict access to the virtual machine manager group responsible for the workload. Furthermore, permission inheritance is implemented only at the virtual machine folder level.

Configuring Organizationally Managed Virtual Machine Security

In most environments, line of business workloads are managed using a decentralized administration model. These workloads are typically administered at a departmental, business unit, or other organizationally based level. In this scenario, it is crucial to apply the appropriate permissions to the virtual machine folders on shared storage and ensure that only the appropriate administrative team is assigned access rights. Figure 6-18 depicts how you can organize and manage permissions for a folder hierarchy in an environment in which one or more virtual machines are departmentally managed.

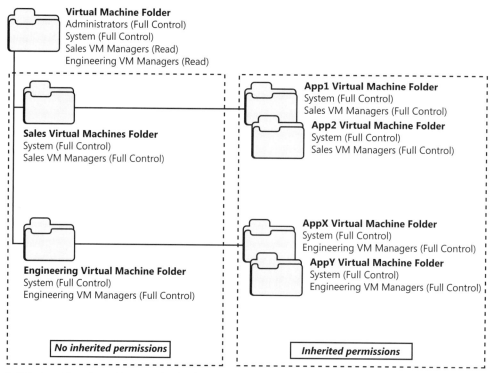

FIGURE 6-18 Virtual machine security for departmentally managed workloads

In this model, departmental folders are created to contain individual virtual machine folders. NTFS permissions applied to the departmental and virtual machine folders are strictly configured to restrict access to the departmental virtual machine manager group. Again, permission inheritance is implemented only at the virtual machine folder level.

Configuring Project-Managed Virtual Machine Security

In test and development environments, there are usually multiple, concurrent projects in progress. Each project has a defined team, and individual responsibilities are assigned to team members. In this scenario, both project-level and individual-level virtual machines are needed throughout the project life cycle. Here again, it is crucial to apply the appropriate permissions to virtual machine folders on shared storage and ensure that only the appropriate team or individual is assigned access rights to specific virtual machines. Figure 6-19 depicts how you can organize and manage permissions for a folder hierarchy in a test and development environment.

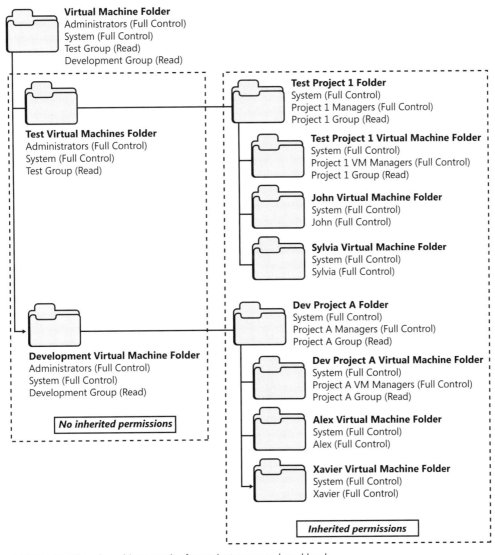

FIGURE 6-19 Virtual machine security for project-managed workloads

In this model, high-level test and development group folders are defined for individual project subfolders. Within each of the project subfolders, discrete virtual machine folders are created, and access is restricted to each team member. There is also a project-level virtual machine folder that can be accessed by individual team members to refresh their environment, but it can be modified only by the project virtual machine managers groups. Inherited permissions are not enabled in this folder hierarchy.

Summary

To properly secure access to Hyper-V resources, it is critical to understand the components that need protection. You must provide access rights to Hyper-V and virtual machine resources through a combination of authorization policy and NTFS permissions. In all cases, identify the management roles needed in your environment, create role definitions and role assignments in Authorization Manager, create corresponding security groups, place the appropriate members in the groups, and assign these groups to the appropriate roles. Virtual machine folder hierarchies should be clearly defined and secured based on the virtual machine management requirements in your environment. It is important to review and apply security best practices to secure access to Hyper-V and virtual machines.

Additional Resources

The following resources contain additional information related to the topics in this chapter.

- Microsoft Web site, "Windows Server 2008 Security Guide," available at *http://www.microsoft.com/downloads/details.aspx?FamilyID=fb8b981f-227c-4af6-a44b-b115696a80ac*

- Microsoft Technet Web site, "Authorization Manager," available at *http://technet.microsoft.com/en-us/library/cc726036.aspx*

- Microsoft Technet Blog, Windows Virtualization Team Blog, available at *http://blogs.technet.com/virtualization/default.aspx*

- Microsoft Technet Blog, "Hyper-V How To: Plan Security," available at *http://blogs.technet.com/tonyso/archive/2008/11/20/hyper-v-how-to-plan-security.aspx*

Hyper-V Best Practices and Optimization

This chapter provides recommendations and best practices to configure a Hyper-V host and virtual machines to optimize performance. The chapter covers modifying the default configuration of the Hyper-V Manager settings, host and virtual machine performance considerations and best practices, and operational considerations. Performance tuning recommendations are included for processor, memory, networking, and storage components.

Modifying the Default Hyper-V Installation

The default installation of the Hyper-V role on Windows Server 2008 or Microsoft Hyper-V Server 2008 assumes that only the system volume exists (drive C). The default storage location for virtual hard drives and virtual machine files is therefore the C drive, where they are stored in two separate folder locations:

- **Default Virtual Machine Storage Path**
  C:\ProgramData\Microsoft\Windows\Hyper-V

- **Default Virtual Hard Disk Storage Path**
  C:\Users\Public\Documents\Hyper-V\Virtual Hard Disks

Using the defaults allows virtual machines to be created quickly, simply by specifying the virtual machine name, but creating virtual machines this way does cause the virtual machine files to be stored on the system volume. If you use the default, dynamically expanding virtual hard disks, or if you take snapshots of the virtual machine, you have the potential to exhaust the available disk space on the system volume quickly. Before the first virtual machine is created, the default storage locations should be changed to a volume other than the system volume.

To change the default storage locations, follow these steps on a local Hyper-V server or remotely using the Hyper-V Manager MMC:

1. Launch the Hyper-V Manager MMC.

2. If you are managing a remote Hyper-V server, right-click Hyper-V Manager in the top of the tree on the left pane and select Connect To Server. Figure 7-1 shows the Select Computer dialog box that displays. Select the Another Computer option and type the Hyper-V server or browse for a Hyper-V server to manage and then click OK.

3. When you are managing the correct Hyper-V server, select the Hyper-V Settings option in the Actions menu on the right side.

4. Figure 7-2 shows the Hyper-V Settings dialog box. The first two options allow you to change the default storage locations. To modify the options, use the Browse button for each storage option to select a different folder on the machine.

5. After you have reset the storage options to a location other than the system volume, click OK.

> **BEST PRACTICE**   Although it's a good idea to change the default storage locations, when you create a new virtual machine, you should also utilize the check box option Store The Virtual Machine In A Different Location and specify a path for the virtual machine files. This will create a subdirectory using the name of the virtual machine at the path provided and will store the virtual hard disk, the configuration file, and the save state files in this subdirectory.

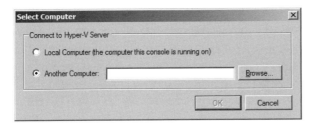

FIGURE 7-1 Select the Hyper-V server to manage remotely.

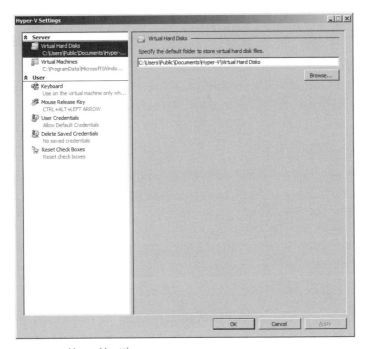

FIGURE 7-2 Hyper-V settings

Rename the First External Virtual Network

When you create the first external virtual network, it is given the name of the physical network interface card. This will happen automatically on installation for the Hyper-V role if you
selected a network adapter during the installation wizard. (This will not happen if the Hyper-V
role is installed from the command line or on Microsoft Hyper-V Server 2008.) The problem
is that most server hardware comes with dual network adapter interfaces that use the same
chipset and are usually denoted differently only in the adapter name by appending a "#2."
This means that the virtual network adapter will be hard to distinguish in the user interface
when it uses the default network adapter name.

To resolve this issue, you should rename the default virtual network name, using something that makes sense in your environment. For example, you can use something simple, such as "Intranet," or something more descriptive, such as "1Gb link connected 10.10.1.0 network." The point is to use a name that is unique, that identifies the network to which it is connected, and that allows you to confidently select the correct virtual network in the New Virtual Machine Wizard.

BEST PRACTICE Distinguish between *internal* versus *external* virtual networks. You can establish a naming standard to prefix the virtual network name with the same standard on all internal networks. This is beneficial because if you use the same prefix, then all the internal networks will be displayed in the drop-down list together.

Use Common Virtual Network Names

Hyper-V virtual networks are defined by a GUID and a friendly name. When a virtual machine is exported or migrated from one Hyper-V server, the import process attempts to connect the virtual network adapters to the same virtual networks as before. Typically, the GUID does not match between Hyper-V hosts, so the friendly name is used. If a virtual network is found with the same friendly name, the import process connects the virtual network adapter to that virtual network. If a virtual network cannot be found with the same GUID or friendly name, then the virtual network adapter is not connected to any virtual network. A host cluster configured without common virtual network names will result in a migrated virtual machine with no network connectivity.

BEST PRACTICE Standardizing on common virtual network names for virtual networks connected to the same subnets will allow virtual machines that are migrated from one Hyper-V server to another to be automatically connected to the correct virtual network.

Back Up the Authorization Store

Hyper-V uses an authorization store that controls which roles have access to perform allowable actions. By default, there is a single role defined, named Administrators. This role has complete access to all allowable operations in Hyper-V. The authorization store is named InitialStore.xml and is stored at the default location C:\ProgramData\Microsoft\Windows\Hyper-V\.

If the authorization store becomes corrupt or unavailable, you will not be able to do common tasks such as start a virtual machine, edit virtual networks, or create new virtual machines. To back up the InitialStore.xml file, just copy the file from the default location to another location on the system, to a remote server, or to removable media.

Reinitializing the InitialStore.xml File

Mike Williams, Senior Consultant II
Microsoft Services

Although you can use the developer mode of Authorization Manager MMC to create a new store, create the Hyper-V Services application, add the Administrators role, add all the operation definitions, and create the role assignment, these are all wasted efforts because Hyper-V relies on specific GUIDs in the original InitialStore.xml file.

If for some reason you did not back up the original IntitialStore.xml authorization store on your Hyper-V server and it gets corrupted, never fear. There is an easy solution to get it back. All you need is another Hyper-V server with an unmodified InitialStore.xml file. Copy InitialStore.xml from the other server to your Hyper-V server and replace the corrupted version.

Microsoft Services Enable Remote Desktop

Virtual machines do not have a physical console that you can sit down at and interact with, and therefore all interaction is done from a remote console. Hyper-V uses a dedicated client called VMConnect.exe to provide the remote interface to the virtual machine. VMConnect uses the Remote Desktop Protocol (RDP) to provide this interface using the Single Port Listener on TCP port 2179. This port is enabled as a firewall exception by default when Hyper-V is installed on the machine.

VMConnect allows you to connect to the Hyper-V server and redirect the remote desktop of any virtual machine to which you have access. VMConnect uses resources on the Hyper-V server to establish the remote connection and transfer the screen refreshes. If VMConnect is used locally on the Hyper-V server to connect to virtual machines, it launches a separate copy of VMConnect for each remote session. Each VMConnect session uses approximately 20 megabytes (MB) of RAM.

Establishing too many VMConnect sessions on the Hyper-V server console can use valuable RAM that could be used to run another virtual machine. The better approach is to enable Remote Desktop in the virtual machine and use that to connect to and manage the virtual machine.

NOTE For non-Windows guest operating systems, Remote Desktop is not available, so VMConnect is the best option to manage the virtual machine remotely from a Windows operating system.

> **BEST PRACTICE** If you prefer to use VMConnect to manage virtual machines, you should do so from another Windows Server 2008 server, Windows Vista, or Windows 7 desktop running the Remote Server Administration Tools (RSAT). This way the memory overhead is not affecting the Hyper-V server.

Optimizing Server Performance

Configuring your Hyper-V server to obtain the best performance requires focusing on four main configuration areas: processor, memory, disk subsystem, and network adapters. Using the fastest hardware components available is a good beginning, but how you combine them to obtain the optimum configuration is not always obvious. In this section, you will learn more about the four main configuration areas and best practices to obtain the optimum performance from your Hyper-V server.

Maximizing Processor Performance

Hyper-V requires 64-bit processors from Intel or AMD with hardware virtualization support—Intel VT or AMD-V. Utilizing multiple processors does not provide linear scaling on performance, but a multithreaded application such as Hyper-V can take full advantage of multiple processors.

Server virtualization performs best on servers that have multiple processors, since the prime focus is to consolidate workloads from multiple physical servers to hypervisor-based servers that share processors. This allows you to take a group of servers that are operating at low utilization (processor capacity) and combine them on a single server to maximize capacity. Because the number of simultaneous threads is directly related to the number of processor cores that are available to execute them, the best host configuration is one that has multiple cores. To maximize the number of processors available and minimize the footprint of the server you are using, purchasing servers with the latest multicore processors will provide you with the best price-to-performance solution.

Hyper-V supports up to 24 logical processors (LPs) on a physical server and eight virtual processors (VPs) per logical processor. Hyper-V also supports a maximum of 192 virtual machines per server. This means that Microsoft has tested only to this scaled configuration, not that Hyper-V cannot expand to a higher number. This is also driven by the typical server that is available in the marketplace. Most servers today are dual or quad processor with two, four, or six cores per processor. If you purchase a server that has more than 24 total processors or cores, you can hardware-partition the server to 24 core increments and run a separate copy of Hyper-V on the partition to take full advantage of the hardware.

Choosing a processor with larger L2 or L3 processor cache can increase performance. This comes from workloads that have large working set in memory and can benefit from it being pre-cached for quick access. Having larger cache also helps with Hyper-V servers that have a high ratio of virtual processors to logical processors.

To obtain the best processor performance for Hyper-V, it is recommended that you run the Server Core installation of Windows Server 2008 and the Hyper-V role or Microsoft Hyper-V Server 2008. Windows Server 2008 with only the Hyper-V role loaded on the parent partition will minimize the amount of processing power the parent partition requires, providing more processing power to the child partitions.

Maximizing Memory Performance

Available memory is a critical requirement in a Hyper-V environment because Hyper-V uses only physical RAM to load and run virtual machines. If you properly plan the memory requirements and configuration of a Hyper-V server, you will have positive performance results for a virtual machine.

Understanding Memory Types

Most motherboards can use different types of memory, depending on the processor and chipset in use. Memory choices typically involve a tradeoff between speed and capacity. By choosing the faster memory chips, you can potentially reduce the maximum capacity of memory available in the system. This reduction could be a bus performance issue or just the fact that the faster memory is not available in larger density chips. For example, the same motherboard might support both 667-MHz and 800-MHz memory. The motherboard might support up to 64 gigabytes (GB) of RAM using 8-GB memory modules in each slot. These modules might be available in 667-MHz speed but not in 800 MHz. By choosing 800-MHz memory for speed, you might be limiting the maximum amount of memory that you can install in the server until the higher density modules are available.

BEST PRACTICE Determining the best practice configuration for memory in a Hyper-V server is really driven by the goals of the system. If the goal is to obtain the fastest memory performance possible on the Hyper-V server, use the fastest memory available. If the goal is to obtain the best performance possible but run the maximum number of virtual machines possible on the server, use the memory that gives you the highest capacity and compensate with other components, such as faster processors or a faster speed disk subsystem.

Understanding Memory Configuration

Memory chip performance is not the only consideration when evaluating the performance of virtual machines. Virtual machines that have too little memory allocated to them suffer from excessive amounts of memory paging to disk. Disk access is typically measured in milliseconds (10^{-3} seconds), whereas memory access is measured in nanoseconds (10^{-9} seconds). That makes memory access one million times faster than disk systems in retrieving data. Because disk access in a virtual environment has additional overhead, the actual impact on performance is even higher. Reducing the amount of memory paging to disk will increase the performance of the virtual machines.

The parent partition requires memory to provide services such as input/output (I/O) virtualization, snapshots, remote access, and general management tasks. Operating systems inside virtual machines require no less memory than on their physical counterparts. Child partitions incur memory overhead for communication and management interfaces to the parent partition, whereas purely physical environments do not require these additional interfaces and therefore do not have the additional overhead. Memory overhead varies, but typical values are 32 MB of additional space for the first gigabyte of RAM in the virtual machine, and an additional 8 MB of RAM for each additional gigabyte of RAM in the virtual machine.

Physical servers are typically purchased based on a standard configuration. In the case of memory, many physical servers are purchased with more memory than workloads require. The base configuration for a physical server might be 4 GB of RAM even though a specific workload might never utilize more than 2 GB of RAM. Hyper-V virtual machines can be allocated memory in 1 MB slices so child partitions can be allocated memory in precise amounts if desired.

Understanding Non-Uniform Memory Access

Another memory consideration involves the architecture of the processor and motherboard. Non-Uniform Memory Access (NUMA) is an architectural feature of modern multiprocessor platforms. NUMA architecture combines the processor, I/O bus, and memory into a "node" that is tuned for performance. These nodes are interconnected by a high-speed bus system. The processor has faster access, with lower latency and greater bandwidth, to the memory contained within the node. When the server needs to access memory on another node using the system interconnect, the performance will be affected by increased latency and reduced bandwidth. Proper configuration of a NUMA-based machine allows for maximizing local memory access while minimizing memory access using the system interconnect. An improperly configured NUMA-based server can suffer from significant performance issues.

Configuration of a NUMA architecture server requires understanding the memory requests of the virtual machines that will be running in the system. To properly configure the memory on a NUMA system, you need to evenly distribute the memory assigned to each processor. This gives each processor the same size of local cache and minimizes the memory requests between nodes. Figuring out how much memory to put in the system depends on a combination of factors, including the largest memory block a virtual machine requires, the number of processors in the system, and the size of the memory sticks that the system will accept.

If you have a virtual machine that is assigned 4 GB of memory, you need to ensure that you have at least 4 GB of memory installed on each processor node in the NUMA system so that the virtual machine thread running on a processor will be able to have all of its memory loaded in the local node. If you have four processor nodes, the minimum amount of memory you should be placing in the server is 16 GB, or 4 GB per node.

DIRECT FROM THE SOURCE

NUMA Ratio

Rob Hefner, Microsoft Services Support Engineer
Virtualization

NUMA vendors have established a NUMA ratio value that describes the amount of time it takes for a node to access "remote" memory, or memory that is assigned to another node, versus its own "local" memory. Generally, performance is not affected if the NUMA ratio is between 1.0 and 1.5. When the ratio is 3.0 or greater, however, performance will degrade.

On NUMA systems running the Hyper-V role or Microsoft Hyper-V Server that have one or more headless nodes (nodes with just memory and no CPUs), Hyper-V will not allocate memory from the node. Although this is typically seen when using the NUMPROC parameter in the boot configuration data store, we recommend that you check with your hardware vendors regarding their specific NUMA configurations to understand how to configure the memory properly.

BEST PRACTICE For optimum performance, determine the largest amount of memory that will be assigned to a virtual machine memory on the NUMA system and then purchase at least that much memory per processor. You should evenly distribute the memory to each processor to maximize local node use of memory and reduce the number of memory calls to another node. Because a virtual machine in Hyper-V can have a maximum of 64 GB of RAM, it may not be possible to allocate the maximum amount of memory and have it all reside on a single processor node.

BEST PRACTICE Utilize Windows Server 2008 Server Core Installation option and the Hyper-V role over the full installation option for your Hyper-V servers. This will give you approximately 80 MB more RAM on the server for child partition usage.

Maximizing Host Storage Performance

A Hyper-V server requires storage for the parent partition, the child partitions, and virtualization-specific overhead storage. The parent partition requires space for operating system files, page file, log files, and shadow copies for backup. Each child partition requires storage for operating system files, page file, log files, application files, application data storage, and shadow copies for backup. Although it is not required, it is recommended to also reserve space for a memory dump file on both the parent partition and the child partitions. The child partition storage is encapsulated in either a virtual hard disk (VHD) or a pass-through disk. Virtualization-specific overhead storage includes storage for virtual machine save state files, virtual machine configuration files, and automatic virtual hard disk files.

Hyper-V server scalability is heavily dependent on the disk subsystem. As you add more virtual machines to a host, the disk I/O workload increases. A single virtual machine performing heavy disk I/O can adversely affect the performance of other running virtual machines.

Evaluating Host Applications That Are Affecting Disk Performance

Applications that can affect a Hyper-V server disk performance should be eliminated or reconfigured to minimize the effects on disk performance. Antivirus software is an example of a common application that is installed on Hyper-V servers in the parent partition. Antivirus software is typically implemented as a disk filter driver that intercepts all calls for read access and writes to the hard disk and that scans the information for viruses before allowing the operation to complete. Antivirus software typically targets executables and other file types that can present a threat to the host operating system.

Hyper-V services and associated file extensions are not excluded by default from most antivirus applications. Most antivirus applications allow you to exclude file extensions or processes from virus scans. If you exclude the file extension, you exclude any application that might be reading and writing to those files, which might include a virus or Trojan horse. However, if you exclude processes, any other application that attempts to open the files would be scanned and the potential for catching a virus or Trojan horse is much higher.

BEST PRACTICE Configure the antivirus application to exclude file extensions or processes. Using the process exclusion method rather than the file exclusion method is recommended because it provides better protection. When configuring the antivirus software to exclude the Hyper-V management processes, you should exclude the Hyper-V Virtual Machine Management service (VMMS.exe) and the Virtual Machine Worker Process service (Vmwp.exe).

If your antivirus application does not support excluding processes, you should add .vhd, .avhd, .vfd, .vsv, and .xml file extensions to your antivirus file exclusion list so that they are not scanned.

Understanding Disk Hardware Performance

Obtaining the best disk performance for your virtual machines requires the use of high-speed disks and spreading the disk I/O load over as many spindles as possible. The speed of the disk is directly related to how fast data can be read from and written to the disk. Hard drives typically come in speeds of 4200, 5400, 7200, 10,000, and 15,000 revolutions per minute (RPM). The most common drive speed today is the 7200-RPM.

Hard disk platters are arranged in concentric circles called tracks. Each track is divided into sectors that look like smaller arcs. As the platter spins, the read/write head is positioned over the track where sectors are located. The faster the platter spins, the faster the read/write head can access the sector, increasing throughput.

BEST PRACTICE Use 10,000-RPM or faster drives in the Hyper-V server to minimize the data read/write times for virtual machines. Using a 10,000-RPM drive rather than a 7200-RPM drive significantly increases the number of read and write operations performed per minute.

Understanding How Disk Types Affect Performance

Disk speed is only one part of the equation. The type of drive is also very important. Drive types available today include Serial-ATA, Serial Attached SCSI (SAS), and SCSI. All drive types have different performance specifications, and most even have different grades of drives, with higher throughput capabilities as the grades and prices increase. Table 7-1 shows a comparison of the performance ratings of standard SATA, SAS, and SCSI drives currently available.

TABLE 7-1 Drive Performance Comparison

DRIVE TYPE	THROUGHPUT	QUEUING
SATA	2.4 gigabits/second per drive	NCQ
SAS	6 gigabits/second per drive	TCQ
SCSI	2.5 gigabits/second per shared bus	none

Drives also operate using different protocols. Serial Advanced Technology Attachment (SATA), Small Computer System Interface (SCSI), and Serial Attached SCSI (SAS) drives can queue multiple requests and make intelligent decisions about which sequence the operations should be performed in. The latest SATA drives use a method called Native Command Queuing (NCQ), whereas SAS drives use a similar method called Tagged Command Queuing (TCQ). Both methods are designed to increase performance by allowing an individual hard disk to queue more than one I/O request at a time and dynamically modify the order in which the operations are performed. Without command queuing, the drive would have to complete additional revolutions and head movement to perform operations using the first-in-first-out approach, decreasing efficiency. With command queuing, operations can be reordered to minimize the head movement and optimize the read/write head idle time. This flexibility reduces disk latency.

> **BEST PRACTICE** Use the SATA or SAS drive type in the Hyper-V server to obtain the benefits of command queuing. Although 10,000-RPM or faster drives are recommended, the exact drive type and speed you choose will depend on your available budget and, potentially, the original equipment manufacturer (OEM) contracts or standards that are in place.

Understanding Disk Drive Configuration

Storage performance is defined by the components that are used and the configuration of those components. The components include the type of hard drives, the number of hard drive spindles, and the speed and number of storage controllers. The configuration includes the arrangement of the hard drives in an array. Performance is also affected by the workload on the host and the number and placement of virtual machines on the storage system.

Running one virtual machine on a single dedicated spindle will provide great performance. But as the number of virtual machines increases, so will the disk activity, and a single drive will no longer be able to provide acceptable read/write performance. Increasing the number of hard drive spindles will increase the available storage bandwidth, and placing a single virtual machine per spindle will maximize the performance. With many spindles connected to a single controller, the controller becomes the bottleneck and the largest single point of failure. Creating a disk array is the best way to spread the disk I/O load across multiple spindles without having to dedicate a spindle per virtual machine. Most storage arrays provide redundancy at some level so that a disk failure does not affect the array. This is accomplished using a Redundant Array of Inexpensive Disks (RAID). Common RAID levels are shown in Table 7-2.

TABLE 7-2 RAID Configurations

RAID TYPE	DESCRIPTION
RAID 0 (striping)	RAID 0 is a data layout scheme in which sequential logical blocks of a defined size (the stripe unit) are laid out in a round-robin manner across multiple disks. It presents a logical disk that stripes disk access over a set of physical disks. The overall storage load is balanced across all physical drives. Because no capacity is allocated for redundant data, RAID 0 does not provide data recovery mechanisms such as those in other RAID levels. The loss of any disk results in data loss.
RAID 1 (mirroring)	RAID 1 is a data layout scheme in which each logical block exists on at least two physical disks. It presents a logical disk that consists of a disk mirror pair. RAID 1 often has worse bandwidth and latency for write operations than RAID 0. This is because data must be written to two or more physical disks. Request latency is based on the slowest of the two (or more) write operations that are necessary to update all copies of the affected data blocks. RAID 1 can provide faster read operations than RAID 0 because it can read from the least busy physical disk from the mirrored pair. RAID 1 can survive the loss of any single physical disk.
RAID 0+1 (striped mirrors)	The combination of striping and mirroring provides the performance benefits of RAID 0 and the redundancy benefits of RAID 1. This option is also known as RAID 1+0 and RAID 10. RAID 0+1 is typically configured as a RAID 1 mirrored set of two RAID 0 stripes. RAID 0+1 can survive the loss of one or more drives within a stripe.
RAID 5 (rotated parity)	RAID 5 presents a logical disk composed of multiple physical disks that have data striped across the disks in sequential blocks (stripe units). However, the underlying physical disks have parity information scattered throughout the disk array. For read requests, RAID 5 has characteristics that resemble those of RAID 0. However, small RAID 5 writes are much slower than those of RAID 0 because each parity block that corresponds to the modified data block requires three additional disk requests. Because four physical disk requests are generated for every logical write, bandwidth is reduced by approximately 75%. RAID 5 provides data recovery capabilities because data can be reconstructed from the parity. RAID 5 can survive the loss of any one physical disk.

RAID TYPE	DESCRIPTION
RAID 6 (double-rotated redundancy)	RAID 6 is basically RAID 5 with additional redundancy built in. Instead of a single block of parity per stripe of data, two blocks of redundancy are included. The second block uses a different redundancy code (instead of parity), which enables data to be reconstructed after the loss of any two disks. Or, disks can be arranged in a two-dimensional matrix, and both vertical and horizontal parity can be maintained.

Storage area networks (SANs) are disk systems that have high-speed connections to drive arrays. SANs have software interfaces that allow the disk space to be combined into logical unit numbers (LUNs) and quickly reconfigured. Host bus adapters (HBAs) provide the high-speed connection between the host and the disk array. Most HBAs use fiber-optic cable connections called fiber channel.

Internet SCSI (iSCSI) is a network protocol that allows data transfer using the SCSI protocol over TCP/IP networks. iSCSI requires only an Ethernet network adapter to operate. iSCSI does not require expensive HBAs or storage protocols such as Fibre-Channel, and it does not require SCSI disks to be used on the target system. This allows iSCSI to provide inexpensive access to centralized storage. Some newer Gigabit Ethernet network adapters provide iSCSI offloading to accelerate the placement and removal of SCSI packets on the wire.

iSCSI uses a client/server metaphor for communication. The iSCSI client is called an *initiator*, and the iSCSI server is called a *target*. An iSCSI initiator is a client device that connects to an iSCSI target, providing block-level access to its disk storage. One limitation of an iSCSI initiator/target system is that only one iSCSI initiator can talk to a specific iSCSI target at a time. The iSCSI target handles heavy load by using a buffer to queue inbound requests.

BEST PRACTICE For Hyper-V servers that boot using internal hard drives, utilize RAID 1 to provide fault tolerance for the parent partition and the Hyper-V configuration settings.

BEST PRACTICE For virtual machines storage, utilize a SAN that provides the redundancy of RAID 0+1 configurations, iSCSI target capability, and the ability to use high RPM command-queued I/O hard drives. Selecting one that supports SATA and SAS hard drives in the same enclosure will provide you with the most flexibility. When creating the RAID 0+1 disk array, you should use as many spindles as feasible to distribute the I/O load.

Maximizing Network Performance

The parent partition provides access to the physical network adapters in the Hyper-V server for applications running in the parent partition and for the operating systems and applications running in the child partitions. Network traffic is required for both the Hyper-V server and the virtual machines running on the server. Host-based traffic can include remote management, agent communications, iSCSI communications, and clustering communications. Virtual machine traffic can include remote management, agent communications, iSCSI communications, clustering communications, and application-specific network traffic. Separating the host traffic from the virtual machine traffic will reduce any issues of not being able to communicate to the host and manage a virtual machine that might be experiencing network issues. If the host and the virtual machines share a single network adapter, it is possible for a single virtual machine to be the target of a denial of service (DOS) attack, therefore making the host unreachable.

> **BEST PRACTICE**   Dedicate at least one physical network adapter to Hyper-V management and backup. Dedicating a network adapter to Hyper-V management means that the Hyper-V server management and backup network traffic will not affect the virtual machine traffic.

Having multiple types of network traffic on a single adapter can be a bad idea. For example, if the Hyper-V parent partition uses iSCSI-based LUNs, disk performance can be adversely affected by an overloaded network adapter. If a Hyper-V server is a member of a cluster, it is very important that the cluster communications and heartbeat signal are not on a network adapter that could be overloaded with additional traffic and impact the cluster communications.

> **BEST PRACTICE**   Dedicate a network adapter for iSCSI communications and utilize an adapter that provides iSCSI processing support in hardware.

> **BEST PRACTICE**   Dedicate a network adapter for cluster communications.

Windows Server 2008 networking stack can offload one or more tasks to a network adapter that has the appropriate task-offload capabilities. Table 7-3 provides more details about each offload.

TABLE 7-3 Offload Capabilities for Network Adapters

OFFLOAD TYPE	DESCRIPTION
Checksum calculation	The networking stack can offload the calculation and validation of both Transmission Control Protocol (TCP) and User Datagram Protocol (UDP) checksums on sends and receives for both IPv4 and IPv6.
IP security authentication and encryption	The TCP/IP transport can offload the calculation and validation of encrypted checksums for authentication headers and Encapsulating Security Payloads (ESPs). The TCP/IP transport can also offload the encryption and decryption of ESPs.
Segmentation of large TCP packets	The TCP/IP transport can offload the segmentation of large TCP packets. Large Send Offload (LSO) version 1 and 2 are supported.
TCP stack	The TCP offload engine (TOE) enables a network adapter that has the appropriate capabilities to offload the entire network stack.

By default, all of the offloading features are available for a physical network adapter, but they may not be enabled by default. Additional features such as jumbo frames, send/receive buffer adjustments, and receive side scaling also are supported in Windows Server 2008.

Windows Server 2008–based Hyper-V servers that have external virtual networks bound to physical network adapters limit the supported offload features available to virtual machines using that external virtual network to Large Send Offload (LSOv1) and TCPv4 checksum offload. Communications from the parent partition through the parent partition TCP/IP stack are not affected by these limitations.

NOTE Windows Server 2008 R2–based Hyper-V servers add TCP Chimney, Large Send Offload v2, and jumbo frame support to virtual machines.

Enabling TCP Chimney Offload

TCP Chimney Offload will work only if it is enabled in the operating system and the advanced properties of the network adapter. In Windows Server 2008, TCP Chimney Offload is disabled by default in both of these locations.

To manually enable TCP Chimney Offload on a Windows Server 2008 server running the Hyper-V role or a Microsoft Hyper-V Server 2008 host, follow these steps:

1. Use administrative credentials to open a command prompt.

2. At the command prompt, type the following command and then press Enter:

```
netsh int tcp set global chimney=enabled
```

To configure TCP Chimney Offload on the network adapter, follow these steps:

1. Open Device Manager.

2. Under Network Adapters, double-click the network adapter that you want.

3. On the Advanced tab, select Enabled in the list box next to the TCP offload entry.

NOTE Different manufacturers may use different terms to describe TCP Chimney Offload on the Advanced tab of the Network Adapter page.

After you have enabled TCP Chimney offload, you can determine which connections have been offloaded by using the *netstat –t* command. The output will include a column named Offload State. If the TCP connections have been offloaded, the state will show Offload. If the TCP connection have not been offloaded, the state will show InHost.

BEST PRACTICE Do not enable TCP Chimney offload on Hyper-V host clusters. Failover Clustering in Windows Server 2008 does not take advantage of TCP Chimney offload features.

BEST PRACTICE Enable TCP Chimney offload on non-clustered Hyper-V servers. Even though physical network adapters bound to external virtual networks will not take advantage of the TCP offloading engine, other adapters will.

BEST PRACTICE Test application performance before and after TCP Chimney is enabled. Not all applications can take advantage of TCP Chimney offload, and some network adapters are not powerful enough to handle the additional load that comes from TCP Chimney offloading. In either case, enabling TCP Chimney offload can negatively affect networking performance of some applications.

Increasing Network Adapter Resources

Some network adapters allow transmit and receive buffers to be configured manually. By default, the vendor might use low values for transmit and receive buffers to conserve memory utilization on the server, but low values can reduce performance and cause dropped packets. For improved performance, you can configure the transmit and receive buffers to larger values.

To configure transmit and receive buffers on the network adapter, follow these steps:

1. Open Device Manager.

2. Under Network Adapters, double-click the network adapter that you want.

3. On the Advanced tab, click Receive Buffers in the Property list and increase the available buffers to the maximum value.

4. In the Property list, click Transmit Buffers and increase the available buffers to the maximum value.

> **NOTE** If the adapter does not expose manual resource configuration, then it either dynamically configures the resources, or it is set to a fixed value that cannot be changed.

Enabling Jumbo Frames

Jumbo frames allow for the payload size of a packet to exceed the default Ethernet size of 1500 bytes. Jumbo frames allow for the payload to be as large as 9000 bytes. This allows more data to be sent at a time, therefore reducing the number of packets that need to be sent, which can reduce the processor overhead and increase the throughput by allowing less processing of frame headers. In order to utilize jumbo frames, the operating system, network adapters, network switches, and routers all must support jumbo frames.

Jumbo frames can provide a significant increase in performance for applications or protocols that attempt to transmit large amounts of data across the network. Two prime examples are server message block (SMB) file transfers and iSCSI.

To configure jumbo frames on the network adapter, follow these steps:

1. Open Device Manager.

2. Under Network Adapters, double-click the network adapter that you want.

3. On the Advanced tab, click Jumbo Frames in the list and set the value in the drop-down list to Enabled or to the defined value of the network card.

Network Adapter Teaming

Teaming of physical network adapters in a single computer enables increased availability of servers through the failover feature and the increased throughput with load-balancing feature. There are two ways to implement load balancing and failover (LBFO): switch-independent and switch-dependent. A switch-independent approach provides greater failure independence, but not all functionalities are available in all scenarios.

Hyper-V technology enables virtual machines to communicate on the local area network using external virtual networks bound to physical network adapters. Figure 7-3 shows a typical external virtual network configuration of the host, virtual machines bound to the external virtual network, the virtual switch, and computers on the local area network.

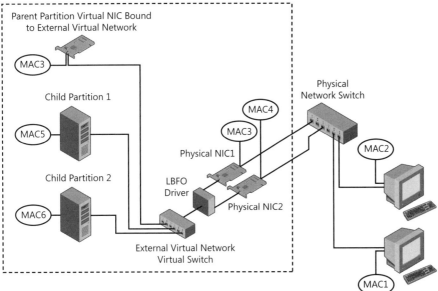

FIGURE 7-3 Example of a Hyper-V network configuration for an external network using network adapter teaming

In Figure 7-3, each client has one network adapter, whose respective Media Access Control (MAC) addresses are MAC1 and MAC2. The Windows 2008 Server with Hyper-V role has two physical network adapters with MAC addresses MAC3 and MAC4. They are teamed together in an LBFO team. The server has two child partitions with MAC addresses MAC5 and MAC6. The parent partition has an external virtual network that is bound to the network team and has a MAC address of MAC3.

Child partitions use their MAC addresses for communication between each other and with other clients. The external virtual network virtual switch takes care of communication between partitions connected to the switch. The LBFO driver is installed below the Hyper-V virtual switch in the networking stack. Therefore, internal communications between partitions over internal virtual networks should not be affected in any way by the LBFO driver.

All communications between the server and the clients go through the LBFO driver. In this case, a virtual switch can be considered equal to a real switch. The difference in the Hyper-V environment is that the LBFO driver does not actually implement teaming between a server and a switch, but between two (or more) switches.

Switch-Dependent Approach

Computers and switches in a subnet operate using MAC addresses. The translation between Internet Protocol (IP) and MAC addresses is done through Address Resolution Protocol (ARP). A switch-dependent implementation based on IEEE 802.3AD does not modify MAC addresses in incoming or outgoing packets. The implementation also does not require any ARP assistance. Therefore, all switch-dependent implementations should work with Hyper-V technology. In this approach, an LBFO driver does not have to be aware that it is installed below the Hyper-V virtual switch.

Switch-Independent Send-Side Load Balancing

Switch-independent send-side load balancing is typically implemented by sending modified outgoing traffic through all available team members. The LBFO driver modifies each outgoing packet's source MAC address to match the MAC address of the adapter that it uses to transmit it. This is required because if all team members try to send packets using the same MAC address, the switch will indefinitely reassign that MAC address from one port to another.

In the scenario from Figure 7-3, the outgoing packets from all child partitions have the source MAC address equal to the MAC address of the physical adapter transmitting it (MAC3 or MAC4) and the destination MAC address equal to the actual destination. Physical switches, operating at the MAC layer, would not be able to distinguish between the child partitions. The switches see two MAC addresses, MAC3 and MAC4, but not the actual MAC addresses of the child partitions MAC5 or MAC6. The clients on the LAN fill their ARP cache with values from ARP responses. For send-side load balancing, the LBFO driver does not modify ARP responses. Therefore, the clients receive the actual MAC5 or MAC6 addresses from the ARP request for the child partitions and the MAC3 address from the parent partition.

This approach results in performance and security issues. Since the clients on the LAN see the child partition MAC addresses MAC5 and MAC6, but the switches do not see them, traffic destined for these two MAC addresses cannot be sent to the correct switch port. The switch will therefore send any packet destined for either of these MAC addresses to all ports on all switches on the subnet. This will affect the performance of the network switches, the response time of packets to the child partitions, and any machine attached to the network switch can sniff the child partitions traffic easily.

Switch-Independent Receive-Side Load Balancing

Switch-independent receive-side load balancing is typically implemented by responding with different MAC addresses to the ARP requests coming from different clients. This is actually client balancing, instead of traffic balancing. This load balancing can be static or dynamic. In the dynamic implementation, unsolicited directed ARP packets are sent to specific clients to change a receive NIC.

This feature is highly affected by the Hyper-V network implementation. In Figure 7-3, LBFO drivers operating in this mode modify all ARP responses coming from child partitions. The child partition source MAC addresses MAC5 and MAC6 are replaced with the teamed network adapter MAC address MAC3 or MAC4. Therefore, clients on the LAN receive frames with a source MAC address of MAC3 or MAC4 instead of MAC5 or MAC6. When a client on the LAN wants to communicate with a child partition, the packet is sent with a destination MAC address of MAC3 or MAC4. When the external virtual network virtual switch receives this packet, it forwards it to the parent partition (because it is associated with these MAC addresses). The child partition never receives any responses, since the child partition's MAC address is not present in the packet.

> **BEST PRACTICE**   Disable receive-side load balancing on all teamed network adapters. If you do not, virtual machines connected to external virtual networks bound to teamed network adapters will not be able to communicate externally to the Hyper-V server.

Installation of Teamed Network Adapters

Even though teamed network adapters are not supported by Microsoft, if they are installed correctly, it is possible to get them to work. To make them work, the LBFO driver must be installed below the Hyper-V virtual switch protocol driver in the networking stack.

To properly install the LBFO driver, follow these general steps:

1. Add the Hyper-V role on Windows Server 2008.
2. Use Windows Update to install the latest updates on the server.
3. Download and install the latest version of the LBFO solution from the vendor.
4. Configure the LBFO solution by setting the desired features and disabling receive-side load balancing.
5. Create a Hyper-V external network using the virtual teamed adapter miniport.

> **NOTE**   Load balancing and failover solutions are implemented differently by vendors. Some vendors implement changes in the LBFO configuration by restarting or reloading the LBFO driver. This will result in the loss of network connectivity and any existing connections.

> **NOTE**   The Microsoft support position on NIC teaming for Windows Server 2008 (deployed either in a physical environment or in a virtualized environment with Hyper-V) is that hardware and driver support is provided by the hardware manufacturer.

Optimizing Virtual Machine Performance

Optimizing a virtual machine's performance involves tuning the processor, memory, network, and storage configuration. Tuning options will vary based on the type of workload, Hyper-V server configuration, interactions with other virtual machines, and the guest operating systems. This section discusses the options available and best practices for tuning the processor, memory, network, and storage of a virtual machine. Each section also presents guidance on monitoring each component to determine if the configuration is correct.

Maximizing Processor Performance

Hyper-V virtual machines can be configured with one, two, or four processors. To obtain the maximum processor performance, there are a series of actions that you should undertake to configure and then evaluate the configuration of each virtual machine to ensure that it is running and using processors efficiently.

Use Enlightened Guests

Windows Vista SP1, Windows Server 2008, and later Windows releases contain kernel modifications that optimize their operation for virtual machines when the kernel detects that it is running in a Hyper-V–based hypervisor environment. The kernel modifications decrease the CPU overhead of Windows by optimizing the processor calls to take advantage of the hardware virtualization features in the processor.

Earlier versions of Windows do not contain these kernel modifications and will require the hypervisor to interrupt processor and I/O operations that are invalid for the virtual environment. These interruptions reduce the performance of the virtual machines and add additional overhead to the Hyper-V server processor and I/O systems.

> **BEST PRACTICE**   Use Windows Server 2008 or newer versions of server operating systems to obtain the best performance in the Hyper-V child partitions. Migrate any Windows 2000 Server or Windows Server 2003 virtual machines to Windows Server 2008 to improve performance of the virtual machine and reduce the load on the Hyper-V server.

Install Integration Services

Integration Services is a set of enlightened drivers and services that provide optimized disk, network, processor, and memory interfaces. The enlightened drivers are for synthetic devices that are tuned specifically for a virtualized Hyper-V child partition. Integration Services synthetic devices reduce the processor overhead required to accomplish a task. They can significantly improve performance and throughput over emulated devices.

For more information on Integration Services, refer to Chapter 5, "Hyper-V Advanced Features."

Virtual Processors

Hyper-V supports a maximum of four virtual processors per virtual machine (VM). VMs that have workloads that are not processor intensive should be configured with a single virtual processor. Configuring additional processors for a virtual machine that are not used will result in additional overhead, such as additional synchronization costs in the guest operating system. If the virtual machine's workload requires additional processors, the number of virtual processors should be increased to two or four virtual processors (depending on the operating system used).

For more information on guest operating systems and supported number of processors, refer to Chapter 2, "Hyper-V Overview."

Remove Unused Emulated Devices

Virtual machines have the ability to install removable emulated (legacy) devices. The two supported devices are the virtual CD/DVD drive and the legacy network adapter. Even when not in use, these devices can add overhead and processing cycles during idle checks.

The virtual CD/DVD drive is installed by default on every virtual machine when it is created. The virtual CD/DVD provides access to the physical CD/DVD drive and ISO images of CDs or DVDs. Legacy network adapters must be installed using the Add Hardware option. Legacy adapters provide support for older operating systems and the ability to boot from the network over pre-execution environment (PXE). Unless you are using an operating system that does not have Integration Services support or you need to boot the virtual machine from a PXE device, you should be using standard synthetic network adapters.

> **BEST PRACTICE** Remove the virtual CD/DVD drive from the virtual machine. The CD/ DVD drive must be checked on a regular basis for the insertion of media, and this uses CPU cycles even if you are not using the drive.

> **BEST PRACTICE** Utilize the legacy network adapter for PXE boot or for operating systems that do not have integration services support for the synthetic network adapter. Legacy network adapters require a higher level of host processor time to process the packets through the virtual machine worker process. Legacy network adapters have lower through-put capability than synthetic adapters because of the path through the virtualization stack.

> **BEST PRACTICE** Virtual machines that require the legacy networking adapter in order to communicate on a daily basis should be isolated to a separate Hyper-V server. This prevents additional processor overhead of the legacy adapters from affecting the per-formance or scalability of Hyper-V servers running virtual machines using the synthetic network adapter.

Configuring Screen Saver for Virtual Machines

Screen savers were designed for the physical world to prevent images from burning into the monitor screen and to lock the computer console automatically if the user forgets and walks away leaving a physical computer unattended for a set amount of time. In the virtual machine world, there is no monitor screen to worry about, but locking the keyboard is still important if the console access is not restricted. Screen savers also utilize a small amount of processor time to keep the image changing and to monitor the keyboard for key sequences.

> **BEST PRACTICE** On machines that have the console access restricted to a trusted set of individuals, disabling the screen saver can save idle processor cycles. For machines that need the screen saver to lock the console to prevent unauthorized access, a blank screen saver that shows no images minimally checks for key sequences.

Optimize Workload Coexistence

Hyper-V allows you to run multiple virtual machines on a single physical server and share the resources of that server between the virtual machines. If you combine a series of virtual ma-chines that have performance and I/O timeline signatures that overlap, the I/O services of the

Hyper-V server could be overtaxed and the performance of the virtual machines could suffer. For example, if the virtual machines on a single Hyper-V server are all configured to perform backups at 1:00 AM across the LAN to a central backup system, the processor, network, and disk storage systems in the Hyper-V server will all be fighting for the same set of resources. To optimize performance, schedule the backups for virtual machines with minimal or no overlap.

BEST PRACTICE Perform an analysis of the workload profile of processor, networking, and disk I/O of a virtual machine to understand what the affects of adding that virtual machine will have on the existing workload profile.

Understanding Processor Resource Control

Hyper-V manages processor allocation to each virtual machine through the Processor Resource Control Settings accessible from the virtual machine Settings dialog box, shown in Figure 7-4.

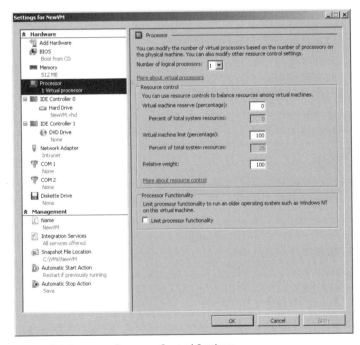

FIGURE 7-4 Processor Resource Control Settings

Processor resource control configuration provides three options: reserve capacity, limit capacity, and relative weight. Table 7-4 defines the three resource control settings and the allowed ranges of the values.

TABLE 7-4 Resource Control Settings

CONTROL SETTING	RANGE	DESCRIPTION
Reserve Capacity	0–100	Reserved capacity is the percentage of a logical processor that Hyper-V will guarantee is available for a virtual machine. The maximum percentage is 100.
Limit Capacity	0–100	Maximum capacity is the percentage of a logical processor that Hyper-V will not allow a virtual machine to exceed.
Relative Weight	1–10,000	Relative values assigned to virtual machines that define the amount of processing power a virtual machines receives. A virtual machine with a high relative weight obtains more processing power than a virtual machine with a low relative weight.

By default, all virtual machines have a relative weight of 100 and a maximum logical processor capacity set to 100 percent so that the resource requirements of each virtual machine are equal and none is given preference over another.

Resource control has two aspects: the values that you can set on the virtual machines for relative weight, limited capacity, and reserved capacity; and the available capacity of the host when you attempt to turn on a virtual machine. It is possible to set the reserved capacity for every virtual machine to 100 percent. Although it seems that you can oversubscribe the capacity of the processing power of the host, processor resource allocation manages the available capacity automatically for you. As you start a virtual machine that has reserved capacity set, the amount of available capacity on the system is reduced. When you attempt to start a virtual machine that has a reserved capacity allocation that is larger than the available capacity left on the system, Hyper-V will return an error and will not power on the virtual machine.

The reserved and limited capacity is calculated based on the number of logical processors in the host and the number of virtual processors assigned to the virtual machine. In Figure 7-4, the host has four logical processors and one virtual processor assigned to the virtual machine, so the capacity limit of the system that can be allocated to a single virtual machine is 25 percent. This value is calculated by taking 100 percent, dividing it by the number of logical processors in the host, and multiplying by the number of virtual processors assigned to the virtual machine.

When you actually set the value for reserved capacity of the virtual machine, you are setting a percentage of the logical processor that you want to reserve. So if you want to reserve an entire logical processor for a virtual machine, you enter 100 percent for the setting, and the system will calculate the amount of system capacity that will be allocated from the available pool of capacity when you turn on the virtual machine—in this case, that would be one logical processor, or 25 percent of the system capacity. If you set the reserved capacity of a virtual machine to 50 percent, the reserved capacity of the system would display as 12 percent.

Resource control should always be part of the planning process for the placement of virtual machine workloads on a Hyper-V server. You should also revisit the current allocation on a host on a regular basis to ensure that the addition or removal of virtual machines on the host has not upset the balance of the system. When you modify the default resource control configuration for a virtual machine, you risk starving other virtual machines for processing power.

> **BEST PRACTICE** Use resource control as a last resort. Unless you are going to manage the resource control settings of every virtual machine, you should maintain the default configuration of load-balanced processor resources. If you have virtual machines that need a guarantee that processing power is available when needed, use the reserved capacity setting. If you have a Hyper-V server that has virtual machines that experience spikes in processor activity and are affecting other virtual machines on the host, use capacity limits to curb those virtual machines and get predictive performance.

Monitor Processor Performance

Monitoring processor performance of virtual machines to determine if they are getting enough processing power requires a combination of monitoring the logical processors of the host and the virtual processors of the virtual machines. Best-case configuration of logical to virtual processors is a one-to-one mapping. This means that every virtual machine would have an entire logical processor available. For certain applications, this is the right thing to do, and you can either limit the number of virtual machines running on the host to the number of logical processors in the host, or you can leverage resource control to accomplish that configuration on a per virtual machine basis.

If the goal of the system is to maximize the consolidation ratio, then the number of virtual processors allocated will exceed the number of logical processors in the host, but they will not all be operating at full capacity.

To monitor processor performance of guest operating systems on a Hyper-V environment, there are a few main performance counters to monitor from the host and guest operating systems:

\Hyper-V Hypervisor Logical Processor(_Total)\% Total Run Time – (LPTR)

\Hyper-V Hypervisor Virtual Processor(_Total)\% Total Run Time – (VPTR)

\Hyper-V Hypervisor Virtual Processor(*)\%Guest Run Time – (VPGRT)

LPTR gives you an indication of how busy the logical processors in the host are. VPTR shows you how busy the virtual processors in the host are. VPGRT indicates how busy the virtual processors in the guest are.

Use the following thresholds to evaluate the performance monitor counters:

- Less than 60% consumed = Healthy
- 60% to 89% consumed = Monitor or Caution
- 90% to 100% consumed = Critical, performance will be adversely affected

If VPTR is high on the host, but LPTR is low, then there are virtual machines that do not have enough processing power allocated. Use VPGRT counters in each virtual machine to determine which virtual machine is running at high processor utilization and then add an additional virtual processor to that virtual machine. If the guest operating system does not support additional virtual processors, then scale out the application by adding an additional virtual machine and balancing the workload between the virtual machines.

If LPTR is high and VPTR is low, then there are many virtual machines running light loads. The context switching between virtual machines is causing a bottleneck in the host processors. If a virtual machine running on the host has a spike in processor utilization, then there are two possible outcomes. Either the virtual machine will get the additional processing power at the expense of other running virtual machines, or the VM will not get the additional processing power and its performance will be affected. Neither outcome is desirable if it is occurring on a regular basis. Consider adding an additional Hyper-V server and moving virtual machines to that host.

If both VPTR and LPTR are high, the Hyper-V server processors are oversubscribed. You should add an additional Hyper-V servers and balance the existing virtual machines between the servers.

> **BEST PRACTICE**   Understand the workload configuration of each host before you start monitoring for performance issues. If you monitor a Hyper-V server and you do not know if the server's workload is configured to maximize server consolidation or to maximize workload performance, you will not know what to look for in performance counters.

Maximizing Memory Performance

The hypervisor virtualizes the child partitions' memory to isolate partitions from each other and provide a contiguous, zero-based memory space for each guest operating system. Memory pages are tracked in tables that map the virtualized memory space to the physical memory space of the Hyper-V server. Memory virtualization can increase the cost of accessing memory, especially when applications frequently allocate and deallocate memory in the virtual address space.

Windows Server 2008 and newer Windows operating systems include kernel enlightenments and optimizations to the memory manager to reduce the processor overhead from Hyper-V memory virtualization. Workloads that have a large working set in memory can benefit from using Windows Server 2008 or newer versions as the guest operating system.

These enlightenments reduce the processor cost of context switching between processes and accessing memory.

Windows is not the only operating system to include kernel enlightenments. SUSE Linux Enterprise Server 10 also has the similar kernel enlightenments to optimize memory allocation and performance under Hyper-V.

To maximize the advantage of the enlightenments in the Windows Server 2008 or SUSE Linux Enterprise Server 10, you must install Integration Services in the guest operating systems.

Allocate the Right Amount of Memory

Virtual machines require no less memory than their physical counterparts do. One advantage they have, however, is that the granularity of memory allocation is in 1-MB chunks. This allows you to optimize the memory allocation to just the amount you need, but be careful when you do this. Virtual machines page content to disk just like physical machines do, and paging to disk in a virtual machine can have a major impact on performance, and so it should be minimized if at all possible.

Memory allocation is a process of tradeoffs. If memory was infinite, you could give each virtual machine enough memory to not require paging to disk at all. This would maximize performance, but it would also greatly reduce the number of virtual machines you could place on a single Hyper-V server. Your goal should be to allocate enough memory to minimize the paging to disk during normal operations, but not to eliminate it. The best way to accomplish this goal is to allocate memory to a virtual machine and then monitor the memory performance and modify as needed.

> **NOTE** Starving the Hyper-V parent partition for memory can also have adverse effects on the performance of virtual machines. Be sure to reserve a minimum of 1 GB of memory for the parent partition.

Monitor Memory Performance

After you have virtual machines configured and running, you need to understand if the virtual machine is allocated the proper amount of memory. You can use a series of performance monitor counters to measure the impact of available memory on the performance of a guest operating system installed on a Hyper-V virtual machine. Measuring the amount of available memory in the virtual machine can provide you with an indication of the percentage of memory that is available to processes running in the virtual machine as a percentage of the amount of memory installed in the virtual machine. Use the performance monitor counter *\Memory\Available Mbytes* inside the virtual machine to monitor the health of memory usage. The following guidelines apply when measuring the value of this performance monitor counter:

- 50% of free memory available or more = Healthy

- 25% of free memory available = Monitor

- 10% of free memory available = Warning

- Less than 5% of free memory available = Critical, performance will be adversely affected

Measuring the rate at which pages are read from or written to disk to resolve hard page faults can give you an indication if the operating system has to swap the contents of memory to disk. A high number of page faults with a low percentage of free memory available indicate that the virtual machine does not have enough allocated RAM. Use the performance monitor counter \Memory\Pages/sec inside the virtual machine to monitor the health of pages to disk. The following guidelines apply when measuring the value of this performance monitor counter:

- Less than 500 = Healthy

- 500 to 1000 = Monitor or Caution

- Greater than 1000 = Critical, performance will be adversely affected

BEST PRACTICE   If the \Memory\Available Mbytes counter is consistently showing lower than 10 percent free memory available, and the \Memory\Pages/sec counter is showing greater than 1000, you should allocate additional RAM to the virtual machine. If the \Memory\Available Mbytes counter is consistently showing higher than 50 percent free memory available, and the \Memory\Pages/sec counter is consistently showing less than 250, you should consider reducing the RAM allocated to the virtual machine.

DIRECT FROM THE SOURCE

Get Maximum Performance by Assigning VM Memory to a NUMA Node

Tony Voellm, Principal Software Design Engineer
Windows Kernel Test

Keeping virtual processors and virtual machine memory on the same NUMA node will provide the best performance, but there is no guarantee that it will happen automatically. Unless the processor is using local memory from the same node, the processor has a different path to memory, and those paths can have various lengths. For example, CPU 0 on Node 0 when accessing memory on Node *X* might take 10 ns, whereas CPU 0 on Node 0 accessing memory on Node *Y* will take 20 ns. It's this difference in memory access times that can affect overall VM performance. The worst case would be for a virtual machine's virtual processor (VP) to be running on a node that is farthest from where the memory for the virtual machine is allocated.

In order to improve performance, you can assign a virtual machine's memory on different nodes. In addition to placing the memory, the hypervisor scheduler will attempt to run the virtual machine's virtual processor(s) near where the memory of the virtual machine is allocated. This creates a dual affinity that can be very beneficial.

It is possible to assign a virtual machine memory to a specific NUMA node using a PowerShell script. You only need to know the name of the virtual machine and the NUMA node that you want to assign the node. An example script is included here:

```
# This script will set the Virtual Machine to run
# on a specific NUMA node
# Check command line arguments
if (($args.length -lt 1) -or
    (($args[0] -ne "/list") -and
    ($args[0] -ne "/set") -and
    ($args[0] -ne "/clear")) -or
    (($args[0] -eq "/set") -and ($args.length -lt 3)) -or
    (($args[0] -eq "/clear") -and ($args.length -lt 2))) {
    Write-Host "numa.ps1 /list [<Hyper-V host>]"
    Write-Host "numa.ps1 /set <vm machine name> <required node> [<Hyper-V host>]"
    Write-Host "numa.ps1 /clear <vm machine name> [<Hyper-V host>]'n"
    Write-Host "Options:"
    Write-Host "'t/list - show configured VM's"
    Write-Host "'t/set <vm machine name> <required node> - set the NUMA node for
the VM"
    Write-Host "'t/clear <vm machine name> - clear NUMA node setting for the VM"
    exit;
  }
# just display VM's
if ($args[0] -eq "/list") {
  if ($args.length -gt 1) {
    $HyperVHost = $args[1];
  }
  Get-WmiObject -Namespace 'root\virtualization' -Query "Select *
From Msvm_ComputerSystem" | select ElementName
  exit;
}
# Set or clear
$HyperVHost = '.';
if ($args[0] -eq "/set") {
  if ($args.length -gt 3) {
    $HyperVHost = $args[3];
  }
  $VMName = $args[1];
  $RequiredNode = $args[2];
} elseif ($args[0] -eq "/clear") {
```

```
      if ($args.length -gt 2) {
        $HyperVHost = $args[2];
      }
      $VMName = $args[1];
    }
    #Main Script Body
    $VMManagementService = Get-WmiObject -Namespace root\virtualization
    -Class Msvm_VirtualSystemManagementService -ComputerName $HyperVHost
    $Query = "Select * From Msvm_ComputerSystem Where ElementName='" + $VMName + "'"
    $SourceVm = Get-WmiObject -Namespace root\virtualization -Query $Query
    -ComputerName $HyperVHost
    $VMSettingData = Get-WmiObject -Namespace root\virtualization -Query "Associators
    of {$SourceVm} Where ResultClass=Msvm_VirtualSystemSettingData
    AssocClass=Msvm_SettingsDefineState" -ComputerName $HyperVHost
    if ($args[0] -eq "/set") {
      $VMSettingData.NumaNodesAreRequired = 1
      $VMSettingData.NumaNodeList = @($RequiredNode)
    } else {
      $VMSettingData.NumaNodesAreRequired = 0
    }
    $VMManagementService.ModifyVirtualSystem($SourceVm$VMSettingData.PSBase.
    GetText(1))
```

After you have the script saved as NUMA.PS1, you can use it to assign a virtual machine to be created on a specific NUMA node. Follow these examples:

Example 1: List currently configured VMs.

```
C:\> .\numa.ps1 /list
```

Example 2: Set NUMA affinity to node 1. Node numbering starts at node 0.

```
C:\> .\numa.ps1 /set testvm 1
```

Example 3: Clear NUMA affinity.

```
C:\> .\numa.ps1 /clear testvm
```

Maximizing Network Performance

Hyper-V supports network adapters (synthetic) and legacy network adapters (emulated) in virtual machines. Synthetic network adapters offer significantly better performance and reduced processor overhead. A network adapter can be connected to four types of networks:

- **Not Connected**   Network adapter is not plugged in to the network

- **Private Virtual Network**   Network switch that provides only virtual machine to virtual machine communications within a single Hyper-V server
- **Internal Virtual Network**   Network switch that provides communications between virtual machines and the Hyper-V server
- **External Virtual Network**   Network switch that is bound to a physical network adapter in the Hyper-V server and provides communications to any network-attached device on that network or routed network

The Hyper-V server can create an unlimited number of external virtual network switches, and each switch can be bound to a single physical network adapter. This poses a practical limit on the number of external network switches, depending on the number of physical adapters in the Hyper-V server.

Synthetic Network Adapter

Installing Integration Services in a virtual machine allows for the use of a synthetic network adapter. Synthetic network adapters are designed specifically for virtual machines to achieve higher network throughput while using less processor cycles. The synthetic network adapter communicates between the child and parent partition through a dedicated channel in the virtual machine bus (VMBus). Synthetic network adapters are available only for supported guest operating systems that have Integration Services.

> **BEST PRACTICE**   Load Integration Services and use synthetic network adapters to maximize network performance.

A virtual machine can have up to eight synthetic network adapters installed. The number of network adapters that are installed is based on the number of different subnets that the virtual machine needs connectivity to and the network workload on each subnet. It is possible for a virtual machine to generate enough network traffic to overload a physical adapter. Therefore, it is feasible that a virtual machine might need more than one network adapter connected to the same subnet to service the required network workload.

Legacy Network Adapter

Legacy network adapters are emulated network adapters. The emulation is based on a common industry-available network adapter and allows for most operating systems to use a standard driver. Because legacy network adapters use emulation, the performance is not on par with synthetic network adapters. Two virtual machine scenarios require the use of legacy network adapters: PXE boot and operating systems that do not have available versions of Integration Services.

PXE boot is required for a network-based installation of the guest operating system in the virtual machine using technology like Windows Deployment Services, Microsoft Deployment Services, Remote Installation Services, and others.

Operating systems that do not have Integration Services are not supported on Hyper-V, but as long as the operating system supports the emulated network adapter, network communications is possible.

> **BEST PRACTICE**   Use legacy network adapters for loading virtual machines via PXE, then switch to synthetic network adapters (assuming the guest operating system has a supported version of Integration Services).

For more information on legacy network adapters, refer to Chapter 5.

Offload Hardware

Hyper-V virtual machines support Large Send Offload (LSO) version 1 and IPv4 TCP checksum offload features provided by some physical network adapters. These features reduce the processor cycles required for packet processing in the parent partition and increase the throughput of virtual machines. The recovered processor cycles can be used to provide more processing power to virtual machines.

> **BEST PRACTICE**   Purchase physical network adapters that provide Large Send Offload and IPv4 TCP checksum offload features for Hyper-V servers. Be sure to properly enable and configure the options in the driver settings of the parent partition.

VLAN Performance

Both legacy and synthetic network adapters support virtual local area network (VLAN) tagging. This is configured at the virtual machine per network adapter by specifying the VLAN identifier. In order for VLAN tagging to provide the maximum performance possible, the physical network adapter should support large send and TCP checksum offload. The best performance is obtained when the physical network adapter NDIS 6.0 miniport driver supports NDIS_ENCAPSULATION_IEEE_802_3_P_AND_Q_IN_OOB encapsulation for both large send and checksum offload. Without this support, Hyper-V cannot use hardware offload for packets that require VLAN tagging and network performance will not be optimized.

Wireless Networks

Hyper-V external virtual networks cannot be bound to wireless network adapters directly. Hyper-V virtual machines need to have a unique MAC address identity, and since the IEEE 802.11 standard does not allow for the MAC address of a wireless network to be modified, virtual machines cannot have a unique identity. It is possible for a Hyper-V virtual network to be bound to an Ethernet network adapter and for that adapter to be connected to a wireless router so that all traffic is transmitted over wireless.

> **NOTE** The Hyper-V parent partition can use wireless network adapters. The wireless network adapter driver must be loaded and the Windows Server 2008 Wireless LAN Service feature must be installed.

Testing Network Performance

If you are experiencing poor network performance, see Table 7-5 for some tests that can be performed to assist in identifying the source of the problem.

TABLE 7-5 Network Performance Tests

TEST	DESCRIPTION
Network latency	Ping each virtual machine to ensure adequate network latency.
	Perform this test from the local host, from virtual machines on the same host, and from other physical or virtual machines on the subnet. On local area networks, expect to receive less than 1-ms response times.
Packet loss	Use the Pathping.exe utility to test packet loss between virtual machines on the same host and other physical or virtual machines on the subnet.
	Pathping.exe measures packet loss on the network. It sends out a burst of 100-ping requests to each network node and calculates how many pings are returned. On local area networks, there should be no loss of ping requests.
Network file transfer	Copy a 100-MB file between virtual machines on the same host and other physical or virtual machines on the subnet.
	Measure the length of time required to complete the copy. On a healthy 100-Mbit (megabit) network, a 100-MB file should copy in 10 to 20 seconds. On a healthy 1-Gbit network, a 100-MB file should copy in about 3 to 5 seconds. Copy times outside of these parameters are indicative of a network problem.

Monitoring Network Performance

Monitoring network performance allows you to determine if the virtual machine network adapters are properly configured, if the workload is being balanced properly, and if additional network adapters are needed in the virtual machine.

You can use a series of performance monitor counters to measure the network utilization of a guest operating system installed on a Hyper-V virtual machine. Measuring the network utilization can provide an indication of network performance issues. Use the performance monitor counter \Network Interface(*)\Bytes Total/sec inside the virtual machine to monitor the throughput of network interfaces. After you have these values, you need to convert them to percent of bandwidth utilization by multiplying Bytes Total/sec by 8 to convert it to bits, multiplying the result by 100, and then dividing by the network adapter's current bandwidth.

The following guidelines apply when measuring the value of this performance monitor counter:

- Less than 40% of the interface consumed = Healthy
- 41% to 74% of the interface consumed = Monitor or Caution
- 75% to 100% of the interface consumed = Critical, performance could be adversely affected

Use the performance monitor counter \Network Interface(*)\Output Queue Length inside the virtual machine to monitor the number of threads waiting on the network interface.

The following guidelines apply when measuring the value of this performance monitor counter:

- 0 = Healthy
- 1–2 = Monitor or Caution
- Greater than 2 = Critical, performance could be adversely affected

If there are more than two threads waiting on the network adapter, then there may be a bottleneck on the network. Common causes of this are poor network latency and/or high collision rates on the network.

> **BEST PRACTICE**   If a virtual machine network adapter output queue is higher than 2 on a regular basis, the virtual machine needs an additional network adapter to handle the network load. The additional network adapter can be bound to the same virtual network or to another virtual network.

> **BEST PRACTICE**   To determine if the existing virtual network can handle the additional traffic, measure the \Network Interface(*)\Output Queue Length performance counter on the host to determine the queue length. If the host network adapter queue length is higher than 2, you should add an additional physical network adapter, create a new external virtual network bound to it, and reallocate virtual machines to the new external virtual network to balance the network load.

> **BEST PRACTICE**   Configure all the physical and virtual network adapters on a Hyper-V server to the same maximum transmission unit (MTU).

Maximizing Storage Performance

Virtual machine storage performance is a key factor in the overall performance of a virtual machine. Disk I/O is the slowest component in a physical or virtual machine. Selecting the correct virtual hard disk and controller is very important to obtaining the best disk performance possible.

Virtual Hard Disk Types

There are four types of virtual hard disks available to a virtual machine in Hyper-V: dynamically expanding, fixed, differencing, and pass-through. Table 7-6 provides a comparison of the different types of virtual hard disks.

TABLE 7-6 Virtual Hard Disk Comparison

TYPE	DESCRIPTION
Dynamically expanding	A single file-encapsulated virtual hard disk. Initially created with a master boot record and a file table but no data space. Space for data storage is allocated on demand and stored in virtual tracks and sectors. When a block is first written to the file, the space must be allocated within the VHD file for the block and then the data can be written. Space is allocated in 2-MB chunks.
Fixed-size	A single file-encapsulated virtual hard disk. Initially created with a master boot record, a file table, and all data blocks with zeros. Performance is better because a write operation does not trigger a block allocation like a dynamic disk.
Differencing	A dynamically expanding virtual hard disk that acts as an overlay to an existing parent virtual hard disk. Any data block write is written to the overlay file. Any read is serviced from the parent if the overlay does not have an updated data block.
Pass-through	A virtual hard disk that is mapped directly to a physical disk or LUN instead of a VHD file. The physical disk or LUN must not be in use by the Hyper-V server. This is the only virtual hard disk that can be larger than 2 terabytes with a single disk.

From a disk I/O performance standpoint, the pass-through disk is the best-performing type of virtual hard disk. Pass-through disks do not support snapshots, and they are less portable than single file VHD, however. A fixed virtual hard disk is the next fastest with a very small loss in performance. They also are less prone to fragmentation since the space is pre-allocated at creation. Dynamic disks are slower than fixed virtual hard disks because of the block allocation overhead. Differencing disks are the slowest type of virtual hard disk, but they are the most efficient in disk space usage. Figure 7-5 provides a flowchart to assist you in the decision process to determine which virtual hard disk type to select for your virtual machine.

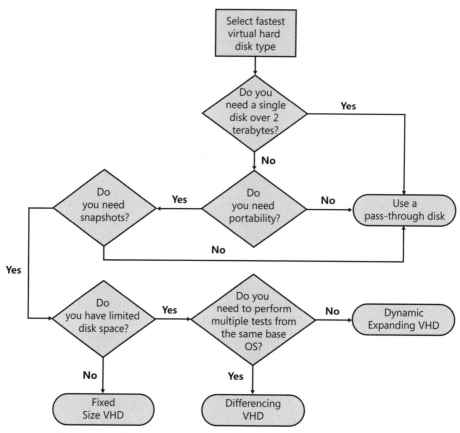

FIGURE 7-5 Virtual hard disk decision flowchart

> **BEST PRACTICE** Use fixed virtual hard disks for a balanced approach. They offer the fastest combination of performance, portability, and snapshot support.

Synthetic SCSI Controller

The SCSI controller in Hyper-V is a synthetic device that loads at boot time as an add-in card. Because the SCSI card is not present until the synthetic driver loads, the SCSI controller cannot be used to boot a virtual machine. The synthetic SCSI controller provides much higher expansion capabilities than the IDE controller, with 64 virtual hard disks per controller. The SCSI controller synthetic driver is installed as part of the Integration Services. Although the IDE and SCSI controllers in Virtual Server 2005 R2 provided a large difference in performance, the VMBus architecture of Hyper-V allows comparable performance with a single virtual hard disk connected. The synthetic SCSI controller provides additional optimization when multiple virtual hard disks are connected.

Monitoring Disk Performance

Measuring disk performance of virtual machines will tell you if any adjustments need to be made to the virtual hard disk type or controller configuration. You can use a series of performance monitor counters to measure the disk performance of a guest operating system installed on a Hyper-V virtual machine. Measuring the amount of time that read and write operations take to respond to the operating system can provide an indication of disk performance issues. Use the performance monitor counter \Logical Disk(*)\Avg. sec/Read and \ Logical Disk(*)\Avg. sec/Write inside the virtual machine to monitor the health of disk performance. The use of logical disk versus physical disk performance monitor counters is recommended because Windows applications and services utilize logical drives represented as drive letters wherein the physical disk (LUN) presented to the operating system can be comprised of multiple physical disk drives in a disk array.

The following guidelines apply when measuring the average response time value of this performance monitor counter:

- 1 ms to 15 ms = Healthy
- 16 ms to 25 ms = Warning or Monitor
- 26 ms or greater = Critical, performance could be adversely affected

Average response times greater than 25 ms indicate an issue with disk performance. This can be caused by a controller that is overloaded in the virtual machine or the host, the selection of a slower virtual disk format due to a storage requirement for portability or disk space limits, or a hard disk that is low on disk space.

If a single virtual machine is experiencing disk performance issues on a Hyper-V server running multiple virtual machines, then it will typically be a virtual machine–specific configuration or application problem. If multiple virtual machines are experiencing issues, it probably indicates an issue with a parent partition driver, the physical controller, or a physical hard disk.

Operational Considerations

Using Hyper-V in test, development, or production environments requires that operational standards be established to maintain efficiency. This section addresses establishing naming standards and creating and operating a library of virtual machines.

Establishing Standards

Establishing a set of configuration standards before you roll out virtualization on an enterprise basis will save you many hours of configuration changes. Standards are critical to minimizing virtual machine migration efforts between hosts, provisioning virtual machines, and making virtual machines and virtual networks easily identifiable.

Virtual machines are listed in the Hyper-V Manager according to the virtual machine name, and they are sorted in ascending alphabetical order. The virtual machine name is not required to match the actual computer name in the guest operating system, however. This approach provides both flexibility and confusion. You are allowed to specify a name for the virtual machine that is different from the guest operating system name, giving you flexibility for sorting and grouping in the user interface. However, you must maintain a mapping of the virtual machine name to the guest operating system name.

The virtual machine name is not required to be unique on a single host or even across hosts, but the location where it is stored must be unique on a host. Virtual machines are assigned a global unique identifier (GUID) at creation. This GUID is what provides the unique identity across Hyper-V servers.

> **BEST PRACTICE** Establish naming standards for virtual machine names as well as for the computer name of the guest operating system. Guest operating system computer names should use the company naming standard for servers. Virtual machine names should either match the guest operating system name, computer name, or provide a way to group the machines in the user interface while including the guest operating system computer name.
>
> For example, the company naming standard might be a three-letter location name followed by a server role designator, followed by a unique numeric value, such as the following name:
>
> HOUFS01
>
> Using the standard three-letter airport code designators provides a pre-existing recognized standard. The corresponding virtual machine name could be one of the following:
>
> HOUFS01
>
> F&P - HOUFS01
>
> Using F&P at the beginning of the virtual machine name groups all file and print servers together in the Hyper-V Manager user interface.

Sample VHD Naming Standard

A sample VHD naming standard includes computer name, drive type, and drive number combined together to form a name such as the following one:

```
ComputerName-Drivetype-drivenumber.vhd
```

Table 7-7 summarizes VHD sample naming standard components.

TABLE 7-7 Sample Naming Standard Components

NAMING STANDARD COMPONENT	DESCRIPTION
Computer name	Virtual machine computer name
Driver type	I = IDE disk
	S = SCSI disk
	ID = IDE differencing disk
	SD = SCSI differencing disk
Drive number	VHD drive number for multiple VHD drives attached to a single machine

Using this standard, a virtual machine called HOUFS01 with two SCSI disks would produce the following:

```
HOUFS01-S-01.vhd - Disk 1
HOUFS01-S-02.vhd - Disk 2
```

Summary

This chapter covered best practices to address common configuration, performance, and operational issues associated with deployments of Hyper-V. You can avoid configuration issues by modifying the default virtual machine and virtual hard disk storage folders, renaming the external virtual network, enabling remote desktop, and backing up the authorization store.

Host performance issues can be avoided by selecting appropriate memory configurations, selecting and correctly configuring the right network adapters, purchasing a SAN with high-RPM SATA or SAS hard disks and iSCSI support, and utilizing RAID 0+1 to provide the maximum performance and fault tolerance.

Virtual machine performance issues can be avoided by following best practices for your host hardware configuration, using proper resource control settings, installing virtual machine Integration Services, utilizing network adapters that support large send and TCP checksum offload, and using fixed-size virtual hard disks connected to synthetic SCSI controllers.

Finally, you can keep operational headaches to a minimum by establishing naming standards that allow you to quickly and easily identify and track virtual machines and virtual hard disks.

Additional Resources

The following resources contain additional information related to this chapter.

- "Performance Tuning Guidelines for Windows Server 2008," a resource that provides information on tuning Windows Server 2008 performance for multiple scenarios, available at *http://www.microsoft.com/whdc/system/sysperf/Perf_tun_srv.mspx*

- "Measuring Performance on Hyper-V," a resource that provides guidelines on how to measure processor, network, storage, and memory performance of Hyper-V, available at *http://msdn.microsoft.com/en-us/library/cc768535.aspx*

- "Troublehooting Hyper-V," a resource that provides guidelines on how to troubleshoot performance issues and other problems with Hyper-V, available at *http://technet.microsoft.com/en-us/library/cc742454.aspx*

- "Information about the TCP Chimney Offload, Receive Side Scaling, and Network Direct Memory Access features in Windows Server 2008," a resource that provides information and guidelines on configuring advanced networking features, available at *http://support.microsoft.com/kb/951037*

Moving from Virtual Server 2005 R2 to Hyper-V

M oving from Virtual Server 2005 R2 SP1 to Hyper-V involves migrating both the Virtual Server host and the virtual machines. Because of the change in architecture, it is not a simple process—you can't perform an upgrade in place to make this move. Rather, the host and virtual machine migrations must be done separately. It is not a terribly difficult process, but the multiple steps involved in the migration must be performed in the correct order. This chapter will provide you with guidance about what should be moved, how to move it, when to move it, and other important considerations you need to be aware of during the process.

Considerations Before Migrating a Virtual Server 2005 R2 Host to Hyper-V

Virtual Server 2005 R2 SP1 is a hosted virtualization solution that runs on top of the operating system, and Hyper-V is a hypervisor that runs under the operating system. Because this is a significant change in architecture between Virtual Server 2005 R2 SP1 and Hyper-V, there is no option to perform an in-place upgrade of a Virtual Server 2005 R2 SP1 to Hyper-V.

The goal of the migration should be to get the Virtual Server host and virtual machines migrated with minimum impact and downtime. The best way to accomplish this is to migrate to new server hardware. This allows you to install Windows Server 2008 and the Hyper-V role or Microsoft Hyper-V Server 2008, configure the machine for the migration, and properly optimize the configuration following the guidelines provided in Chapter 7, "Hyper-V Best Practices and Optimization." After you have optimized the installation, the virtual machines can be migrated from the Virtual Server 2005 R2 SP1 server to the new Hyper-V server.

Maintaining Virtual Server 2005 R2 Hosts

Although you might be tempted to migrate off all Virtual Server 2005 R2 SP1 hosts, it is a good idea to keep Virtual Server around for certain guest operating systems. Virtual Server 2005 R2 SP1 provides support for the following guest operating systems that Hyper-V does not support:

- Windows NT Server 4.0 with Service Pack 6a
- Windows XP SP2 (for Virtual Server 2005 R2 only)
- OS/2 4.5
- Red Hat Enterprise Linux 2.1 (update 7)
- Red Hat Enterprise Linux 3.0 (update 8)
- Red Hat Enterprise Linux 4.0 (update 4)
- Red Hat Enterprise Linux 5.0
- Red Hat Linux 9.0
- SuSE Linux 9.3
- SuSE Linux 10.0
- SuSE Linux 10.1
- SuSE Linux 10.2

If you have virtual machines running any of these guest operating systems, we would recommend keeping them on Virtual Server instead of moving them to Hyper-V.

Wireless Networking Support

Virtual Server 2005 R2 SP1 provides support for wireless networks to be used for binding virtual networks. Hyper-V does not implement direct attachment of external virtual networks to wireless network adapters because Hyper-V adheres strictly to the 802.11 specifications, and those specifications do not allow wireless networks to modify the MAC address.

Server Hardware Support

You must evaluate your hardware before upgrading to Hyper-V to manage your virtual machines. The hardware you are planning to use for the Hyper-V server must be 64-bit and must provide hardware virtualization extensions enabled for the Hyper-V installation to be completed successfully. Since you cannot upgrade an existing Virtual Server 2005 R2 SP1 server directly to Hyper-V, either you must provide new server hardware, or the existing hardware must meet the recommended minimum Hyper-V hardware specifications to be reused.

Minimizing Downtime

When you migrate virtual machines from Virtual Server to Hyper-V, the virtual machines must be powered off for the migration. This will cause a period of downtime for the individual virtual machines. In addition, depending on the approach you take during the migration of the Virtual Server host, the host also could experience downtime that will result in downtime for all the virtual machines. Therefore, you should determine how much downtime is acceptable for the host and the virtual machines before you choose the host migration approach.

Migrating a Virtual Server 2005 R2 Host to Hyper-V

Migrating from Virtual Server 2005 R2 SP1 to Hyper-V is a multistep process, but the steps may vary based on the current configuration of your Virtual Server host. From previous chapters, you know that to run Hyper-V, you must have either Windows Server 2008 64-bit or Microsoft Hyper-V Server 2008. Unless the current Virtual Server 2005 R2 SP1 installation is running on the Windows Server 2008 64-bit operating system, you will first need to create a new installation of Windows Server 2008 x64 or Microsoft Hyper-V Server 2008.

If the Virtual Server host is currently running on Windows Server 2008 x64, it is possible to back up the host, uninstall Virtual Server, install the Hyper-V role, and then migrate the virtual machines. This method allows you to use the same hardware during the migration without having to copy virtual machine files to another computer, but it requires the existing Virtual Server and the virtual machines to be taken offline, so users will experience downtime. It also means that if something goes wrong, the recovery process will not be quick or painless. To minimize downtime on the host and the virtual machines, a better approach is to build a new Hyper-V server and migrate the virtual machines to the new server. You will gain several advantages by using this approach:

- The flexibility to migrate virtual machines when needed
- The ability to size the hardware to meet the requirements
- No downtime for the existing Virtual Server host
- The consolidation of multiple Virtual Server hosts to a single Hyper-V server or cluster of hosts

In addition, if something goes wrong during the migration process, the virtual machines still exist on the Virtual Server host and can be rebooted quickly.

The host migration process discussed in the following sections focuses on the side-by-side migration approach versus the migrate-in-place approach. The steps in the process include developing the specification for the Hyper-V server hardware, building the Hyper-V servers, and migrating the configuration. When you have completed the migration, you will be able to add any new features or capabilities available in Hyper-V.

Developing the Hyper-V Server Specification

The first step in the process is discovering and documenting the configuration of the Virtual Server 2005 R2 SP1 environment so that you can determine the minimum required Hyper-V hardware configuration. This involves determining the current hardware specification for memory, disk storage, networking, and processor. In addition, collect the number of virtual networks currently configured on the Virtual Server host. When you have collected this information, you can start developing the Hyper-V server specification. Use the following guidelines to determine the specification.

Hyper-V memory configuration should include memory reserved for the parent partition—typically a minimum of 1 gigabyte (GB) of RAM, virtual machine memory—the size of the memory of each virtual machine plus overhead calculated by adding 32 MB for the first gigabyte (GB) of RAM and then 8 MB for each additional gigabyte of RAM, and memory for the predicted number of concurrent VMConnect.exe sessions on the host at 20 MB each. It is always a good idea to add additional memory for expansion for temporary purposes (1 to 2 GB of RAM). At a minimum, you should make sure the Hyper-V server has as much memory as the current Virtual Server host.

Disk storage can involve many choices, including disk drive speed, disk drive size, RAID configuration, controller cards, and so on. Focusing on just the amount of storage you will need, the server requires space for the parent partition operating system; space for each virtual machine's virtual hard disk (VHD), the maximum defined size of the VHD; space for saved-state files, which will vary based on the amount of RAM in the virtual machine; space for snapshots, which will vary based on the number of snapshots planned; and space for additional files such as CD or DVD images. At a minimum, you will need the amount of storage space that is currently used on the Virtual Server host, plus additional space for snapshots if you plan to use them.

Networking configuration involves the needs of the parent partition, interfaces for iSCSI communications, interfaces for clustering if the Hyper-V server is a member of a host cluster, and interfaces for the required number of virtual networks. The Hyper-V server should include a minimum of one 1-gigabit Ethernet card reserved for parent partition management purposes, one 1-gigabit Ethernet card for iSCSI communications (if iSCSI will be used), two 1-gigabit Ethernet cards for cluster communications (if a member of a host cluster), and one 1-gigabit Ethernet card for each required external virtual network.

> **NOTE** Virtual Server allowed multiple virtual networks to be configured to a single network interface card, but Hyper-V allows only a single virtual network to be bound to a network interface card.

Processor configuration involves the needs of the parent partition, each virtual machine, and reserve for unexpected peaks in performance. The Hyper-V parent partition should have a minimum of one processor core reserved for its use to manage shared parent partition resources; each virtual machine should have a minimum of a single processor core; and a reserve amount of processing (one or more cores) should be included for peaks in performance and possible expansion. Virtual machines in Virtual Server 2005 R2 SP1 could have only a single processor. With Hyper-V, each virtual machine can have up to four virtual processors (depending on the operating system). If any virtual machines currently running under Virtual Server are utilizing high amounts of processing power, there is an opportunity to add virtual processors during the migration. Be sure to account for any additional processors you may need during the sizing process.

Installing Hyper-V

When you have identified the Hyper-V configuration you will require and have purchased and assembled the hardware, you are ready to install Hyper-V on the system. Chapter 4, "Hyper-V Installation and Configuration," goes into detail about how to install Hyper-V on the hardware and outlines the post-installation configuration changes that you should make.

Migrating Virtual Networks

After you have completed the default installation and optimization, you are ready to migrate the current configuration of the Virtual Server 2005 R2 SP1 virtual networks to the Hyper-V server. This is a manual process and involves recreating the required virtual networks that existed on the Virtual Server host on the Hyper-V server. In order to do this, you must determine the mapping of the existing virtual networks to physical adapters or loopback adapters (in the case of internal networks). When you have identified the mapping, collect the TCP/IP settings for the network adapter so that the subnet can be identified. This will allow you to determine which physical network adapter must be used in the Hyper-V server when the external virtual networks are recreated or how many internal or private virtual networks must be created.

The next step is recreating the external virtual networks on the new Hyper-V server to the correct physical network adapter using the mapping you identified. Although the virtual network name does not have to be the same as it was on the Virtual Server host, it is a good idea to use the same name to minimize any confusion. After the external virtual networks are completed, recreate any required internal or private virtual networks.

> **NOTE** You no longer have to add a loopback adapter to get guest-to-parent partition communications internal to the Hyper-V server. An internal network provides this functionality. For each Virtual Server network that was created using a loopback adapter, create an internal virtual network in Hyper-V.

If the Hyper-V server was configured with additional physical network adapters to expand the number of available external virtual networks, now is the time to configure these. Remember to use the established naming convention for virtual networks.

Considerations Before Migrating Virtual Machines

Hyper-V does not provide the ability to import virtual machines that exist on a Virtual Server 2005 R2 SP1 host; you must migrate the virtual machines manually. The building blocks of a virtual machine in Virtual Server 2005 R2 SP1 and Hyper-V are basically the same, a virtual hard disk and a configuration file. The virtual hard disk has not changed and can be easily migrated from Virtual Server to Hyper-V. The configuration file has completely changed, however, and Microsoft does not provide a tool to migrate the settings from the old format to the new format.

Boot Disk Configuration

Virtual Server 2005 R2 SP1 virtual machines could be attached to the virtual SCSI adapter and the virtual machine would boot in this configuration (it was a recommended configuration for best performance). This was possible because the SCSI adapter was emulated and available at boot time. Hyper-V virtual machines cannot boot from the SCSI adapter, however, because it is synthetic, and synthetic devices are not available immediately at boot time. Therefore, virtual machines that are currently configured to boot from SCSI in Virtual Server must be converted to boot from IDE as part of the migration to Hyper-V.

> **NOTE**   Unlike Virtual Server IDE–attached virtual hard disks, IDE-attached virtual hard disks in Hyper-V perform almost on par with SCSI-attached virtual hard disks.

Virtual Machine Additions

Virtual Server 2005 R2 SP1 uses enhanced drivers to provide emulated devices and to improve performance in a virtual machine. Hyper-V uses something similar to provide synthetic devices and performance enhancements to virtual machines. The architecture and interfaces between these two technologies are not compatible; therefore, you must remove Virtual Machine Additions as part of the process of migration to Hyper-V. Although it is possible to remove the additions after you have migrated the virtual machines to Hyper-V, your ability to do this depends on the version of Virtual Machine Additions that is installed. The better approach, which will work regardless of the version installed, is to uninstall Virtual Machine Additions prior to migrating to Hyper-V.

Undo Disks

The Undo disk feature in Virtual Server 2005 R2 has been removed in Hyper-V and replaced with a more powerful feature called *snapshots*. You cannot migrate Undo disks to Hyper-V; they must be discarded or committed prior to migrating the virtual machine hard disk to Hyper-V.

Saved States

Virtual Server 2005 R2 SP1 and Hyper-V both have the ability to save the state of a running virtual machine to disk. The concept is similar to hibernation. In Virtual Server 2005 R2, the saved state file was a single file (.vsv) that contained the contents of memory and information on running processes, threads, and the processor stack. Hyper-V has split the save state file into two parts: the memory contents (.bin) and the stack and process information (.vsv). Because of this change, saved states cannot be migrated and must be merged or discarded before the migration can occur.

Hardware Abstraction Layer Differences

Virtual machines running in Virtual Server 2005 R2 can have only a single virtual processor. Hyper-V provides the ability for a virtual machine to be configured with up to four virtual processors. This presents an issue with hardware abstraction layer (HAL) compatibility. Hyper-V virtual machines require a multiprocessor Advanced Configuration and Power Interface (ACPI) HAL. Virtual Server 2005 R2 virtual machines can have APCI or non-ACPI HALs based on how they were created and what version of additions are loaded. Regardless of which HAL the existing virtual machine has, the HAL must be changed during the migration of the virtual machine to Hyper-V. For instructions on changing the HAL for Vista and Windows 2008 virtual machines, go to *http://technet.microsoft.com/en-us/library/dd296684.aspx*.

Differencing Disks

Both Hyper-V and Virtual Server 2005 R2 support differencing disks, and the technology has not changed. Differencing disks require that the parent and the child retain the same relative path when they are moved on the same machine or between machines. The relative path to the parent VHD is stored in the disk header of the child VHD. If a child VHD is copied and the parent is not, or if the relative path is not maintained between the two files, the child VHD will not have all the information it requires and the differencing disk will not be usable.

> **NOTE** During migration, you may want to modify the directory structure of how the virtual machines are stored. If the directory structure change breaks the differencing disk relative path, you can repair the virtual hard disk using the Inspect Disk feature in the Hyper-V Manager MMC console.

Shared SCSI Virtual Machine Clusters

Virtual Server 2005 R2 virtual machine–emulated SCSI controllers provided a mode called shared SCSI (a parallel SCSI bus). Enabling shared SCSI on the controller allowed a Windows Server 2003 cluster to be built between virtual machines. Hyper-V has switched to a synthetic SCSI controller and removed the ability to put the SCSI controller into parallel SCSI bus mode. You can still create a cluster between virtual machines in Hyper-V, but you must use an iSCSI Initiator to attach remote iSCSI LUNs to the virtual machines. Virtual Server–based virtual machine clusters must be manually migrated to Hyper-V.

Migrating Virtual Machines

The following sections will guide you through a process that will enable you to migrate virtual machines from Virtual Server 2005 R2 SP1 to Hyper-V. Not all of the steps provided in the process will be required for your Virtual Server installation, depending on what features you are using from Virtual Server. The process includes the following tasks:

- Determine compatibility with Hyper-V.
- Convert SCSI boot to IDE boot.
- Remove Virtual Server Additions.
- Remove network interface cards.
- Commit or discard all Undo drives.
- Merge or discard saved states.
- Merge all differential disks.
- Check the hardware abstraction layer (HAL).
- Copy the virtual hard disk to the new Hyper-V server.
- Create a new virtual machine using existing VHD.
- Install Integration Services.

Determine Compatibility

Before you migrate a virtual machine, you should determine if it contains a supported operating system, and if the applications running in the virtual machine are supported by the independent software vendor (ISV) for production use on Hyper-V. Compare the operating system with the Hyper-V–supported guest operating systems and be sure to match product versions and service pack levels.

Convert SCSI Boot to IDE Boot

We have already discussed that Hyper-V does not support booting from the synthetic SCSI controller. So before you can migrate a Virtual Server 2005 R2 virtual machine that currently boots from a SCSI adapter to Hyper-V, you must convert it to boot from the IDE controller. Follow these steps to migrate the boot disk from a SCSI controller to an IDE controller:

1. Launch the Virtual Server Administrative Web console.

2. Select Configure from the Virtual Machines menu and then select the virtual machine name from the list.

3. From the Configuration menu options, select Hard Disks to display the Virtual Hard Disk Properties page, which shows the current configuration of all the hard disks for the virtual machine (see Figure 8-1).

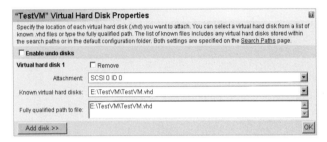

FIGURE 8-1 Virtual Hard Disk Properties page

4. To convert the virtual hard disk so that it boots from the primary IDE controller (ID 0) instead of the SCSI controller (ID 0), select Primary Channel (0) from the Attachment drop-down list, as shown in Figure 8-2.

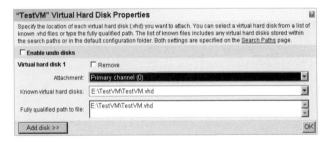

FIGURE 8-2 Virtual hard disk with Primary IDE channel (0) selected

5. To save the change, click OK.

Migrate VHD from SCSI to IDE Controller

Tony Soper, Senior Technical Writer
Windows Server Technical Writing Team

If you standardized attaching VHDs to SCSI controllers as most people did for performance reasons, manually migrating them to IDE controllers can be time-consuming. Following is a script that can help automate that process. Save this script as SCSI2IDE.vbs and run it with a command-line option to indicate the virtual machine for which you want to reconfigure the boot disk to use IDE instead of SCSI.

 ON THE COMPANION MEDIA This script is included on this book's companion media, in the \Scripts\Chapter 8 folder.

```
Option Explicit

dim id, rtn
dim objVS, objVM, objHardDisk
dim colArgs, colVMs
dim hdskConnections
dim objhdskConnection
dim strFile

Set objVS = CreateObject("VirtualServer.Application")
set colVMs = objVS.VirtualMachines
set colArgs = wscript.Arguments

id = 0

For Each objVM in colVMs
    If objVM.Name = colArgs.item(0) then
        set hdskConnections = objVM.HardDiskConnections
        For Each objhdskConnection In hdskConnections
            set objHardDisk = objhdskConnection.HardDisk
            strFile = objHardDisk.File
            wscript.echo "VM Disk File" & strFile
            If objhdskConnection.BusType = 1 Then
                rtn = objhdskConnection.SetBusLocation (0,0,id)
                id = id+1
            End If
        Next
    End if
Next
```

Remove Virtual Machine Additions

Virtual Server 2005 R2 SP1 Virtual Machine Additions are not compatible with the Hyper-V architecture and will not work properly with it. Although it is possible to remove Virtual Machine Additions version 13.813 or newer from within a migrated virtual machine, a less risky approach is to remove the additions prior to migrating the virtual machine.

Follow these steps to remove Virtual Machine Additions:

1. Power on the virtual machine and log in with administrative privileges.

2. In the virtual machine, open Control Panel and then double-click Add Or Remove Programs or Programs And Features (depending on the operating system version).

3. Select Virtual Machine Additions and then select Remove, or right-click and select Uninstall (depending on the operating system version).

4. Click Yes in the confirmation dialog box that appears.

5. After you have successfully removed Virtual Machine Additions, restart the virtual machine.

Remove Emulated Network Interface Cards

Virtual Server 2005 R2 SP1 virtual machines have a single network interface card installed inside the virtual machine by default. The network interface card emulates an Intel 21140 adapter. In Hyper-V, the default networking interface card is not the legacy network adapter (which also emulates an Intel 21140 adapter), but instead is the synthetic network adapter. If you attempt to move a virtual machine with the emulated Intel 21140 adapter still installed, the network adapter will become a hidden device. You can install Hyper-V Integration Services and all will seem to be fine, but if the emulated Intel 21140 adapter had a static IP address assigned, any attempt you make to reassign that static IP address to the new synthetic network adapter will result in a warning box that says the IP address is already in use.

Follow these steps to remove the network adapter from the virtual machine:

1. Power on the virtual machine.

2. Log in with administrative permissions.

3. Open Control Panel and double-click Device Manager.

4. Expand the Network Adapters node.

5. Right-click the Intel 21140 adapter listed and select Uninstall.

6. Shut down the virtual machine.

When you migrate the virtual machine to Hyper-V, a synthetic adapter will be installed. The network adapter might not function until you install the Integration Services, however.

NOTE The synthetic network adapter in Hyper-V does not support boot from pre-execution environment (PXE). To enable PXE boot, you must use a legacy adapter.

Commit or Discard Undo Disks

Virtual Server 2005 R2 provided a disk mode that would write all changes to a separate file. This mode, called Undo, allowed you to perform what-if changes to the disk without fear that the changes had to be permanent. Undo disks were not very flexible if you needed to perform multiple what-if scenarios, however, so in Hyper-V the technology was replaced with snapshots. This means that any Undo disks in Virtual Server virtual machines must be discarded or committed to the virtual hard disk prior to migrating it to Hyper-V.

If a virtual machine is configured to use Undo disks but does not currently have an active Undo disk, then you do not need to perform any additional steps. If you do need to commit or discard an Undo disk, the procedures are slightly different depending on whether the virtual machine is currently powered on or not.

Follow these instructions for committing or discarding the Undo disks for a virtual machine that is currently powered on:

1. Shut down the virtual machine.

2. Select Turn Off Virtual Machine And Commit Undo Disks to commit the Undo disk if you want to merge the current changes into the virtual hard disk, or select Turn Off Virtual Machine And Discard Undo Disks to discard the changes to the Undo disk if you do not want to merge the changes.

Follow these instructions for committing or discarding the Undo disks for a virtual machine that is currently powered off:

1. Launch the Virtual Server 2005 Administration Web site.

2. On the Master Status page, find the appropriate virtual machine in the list of virtual machines and click the arrow to display the actions menu.

3. Figure 8-3 displays the menu options available. Select Merge Undo Disks or Discard Undo Disks from the menu.

FIGURE 8-3 Undo Disk actions menu for a virtual machine

Restore or Discard Saved States

Virtual Server 2005 R2 saved states are not compatible with Hyper-V saved states, so the virtual machine must be powered on and shut down properly, or the saved state must be discarded. If the virtual machine is currently powered on, perform a shutdown from within the virtual machine and do not select to save the state.

Follow these instructions for discarding the saved state for a virtual machine that is currently powered off:

1. Launch the Virtual Server 2005 Administration Web site.

2. On the Master Status page, find the appropriate virtual machine in the list of virtual machines and click the arrow to the display the actions menu.

3. Figure 8-4 displays the menu options available. Select Restore From Saved State or Discard Saved State from the menu.

FIGURE 8-4 Saved State actions menu for a virtual machine

4. If you select to restore the saved state, after the virtual machine is restored, perform a shutdown.

5. If you select to discard the saved state, then no further actions are required.

Merge Differential Disks

Differential disks allow you to save space by creating a dependent chain of virtual hard disks. This eliminates the need to duplicate copies of data. If you are migrating all virtual machines that contain differencing disks from a Virtual Server 2005 R2 host to the same Hyper-V server, then you do not have to merge the differencing disks. You will need to maintain the same relative path on both hosts, however, or you will need to repair the parent-child links.

If you are planning to migrate virtual machines that depend on the same differencing disk to different Hyper-V servers, then you must merge the differencing disks to break the dependency.

Follow these instructions for merging a virtual machine differencing disk:

1. Shut down the virtual machine with the differencing disk.

2. Launch the Virtual Server 2005 Administration Web site.

3. On the Master Status page, select Inspect Disk from the Virtual Disks menu.

4. Specify the virtual hard disk that has a parent that needs to be merged (as shown in Figure 8-5) and click Inspect.

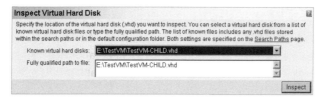

FIGURE 8-5 Inspect Virtual Hard Disk page

5. The Properties and Actions will be displayed as shown in Figure 8-6. Select Merge Virtual Hard Disk from the Actions menu to merge the parent and child virtual hard disks.

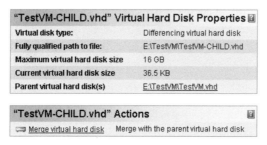

FIGURE 8-6 Differencing disk Properties And Actions page

6. The Merge Virtual Hard Disk page is displayed (as shown in Figure 8-7). Select Merge To New Virtual Hard Disk and specify the full path to the new virtual hard disk that will be created as a result of the merge operation. Optionally, you can specify the type of virtual hard disk to be created—dynamic or fixed.

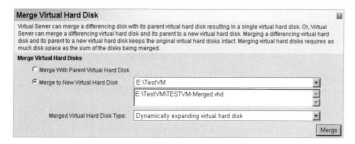

FIGURE 8-7 Merge Virtual Hard Disk options page

7. When you have selected all the appropriate options, click Merge.

The resulting merged virtual hard disk is the file that you will migrate to the Hyper-V server.

Check the Hardware Abstraction Layer

Hyper-V uses a multiprocessor APCI hardware abstraction layer (HAL). Although you would probably be prompted for the upgrade of HAL when you install Integration Services, it is best to prepare the machine for HAL detection prior to the migration so that it properly detects and updates the HAL.

Follow these steps to change the HAL prior to migrating the virtual machine:

1. Power on the virtual machine.

2. Log in with administrative permissions.

3. Run the System Configuration utility (MSConfig.exe) by clicking Start, clicking Run, typing **msconfig**, and then clicking OK.

4. Click the Boot tab and then select Advanced Options.

5. Select the Detect HAL check box, click OK, and then shut down the virtual machine.

Complete the Migration

After you have performed all the required pre-migration steps, the last tasks involve copying the virtual hard disk from the Virtual Server 2005 R2 server to the new Hyper-V server and creating a new virtual machine using that virtual hard disk.

Follow these steps to create a new virtual machine:

1. On the Hyper-V server, create a folder to hold the new virtual machine on a drive other than the system drive. Use the name of the virtual machine as the folder name (for example, D:\VMs\NEWVM).

2. Copy the virtual hard disk from the Virtual Server 2005 R2 host to the new directory.

3. Open the Hyper-V Manager MMC console.

4. Select New from the Actions menu and then select Virtual Machine. The New Virtual Machine Wizard will start. Click Next.

5. Specify the name of the virtual machine (use the same name as the directory you created) in the Name text box.

6. Select the check box that says Store The Virtual Machine In A Different Location and enter the path to the directory above the virtual machine folder you created (that is, enter D:\VMs for the example shown previously) in the Location text box, as shown in Figure 8-8. Click Next.

    This will allow the wizard to use the directory you created for all the virtual machine files.

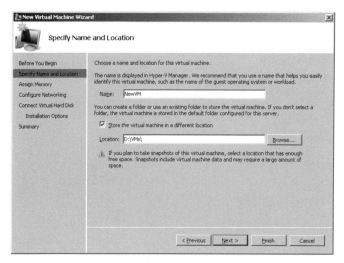

FIGURE 8-8 Specify name and location to store the new virtual machine

7. On the Assign Memory page, specify the amount of RAM the virtual machine requires and click Next.

8. On the Configure Networking page, select a virtual network to attach to the virtual machine and click Next.

9. On the Connect Virtual Hard Disk page (shown in Figure 8-9), select the Use An Existing Virtual Hard Disk option, and specify the path to the virtual hard disk (such as D:\VMs\NEWVM.VHD), and then click Next.

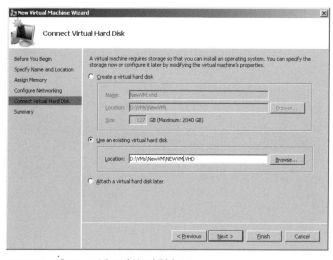

FIGURE 8-9 Connect Virtual Hard Disk page

10. On the Completing The New Virtual Machine Wizard page, click Start The Virtual Machine After It Is Created and then click Finish.

The virtual machine will power on.

11. At the login screen that will display after the virtual machine is booted, log in with administrative permissions.

12. On the VMConnect Actions menu, click Insert Integration Services Setup Disk. This should start the installation of Integration Services for the virtual machine. Complete the installation and reboot the virtual machine.

The virtual machine is now migrated to Hyper-V.

VMC to Hyper-V Migration Tool

Matthijs ten Seldam, Technology Specialist
Microsoft Sales

Migrating a virtual machine from Virtual Server to Hyper-V requires changes to the virtual machine prior to migration, migration of the virtual hard disk to the Hyper-V server, creation of a new virtual machine using the migrated virtual hard disk, and modification of the configuration of the virtual machine. Although you can perform the migration step manually, the VMC to Hyper-V tool, also called VMC2HV, is able to import the complete Virtual Server virtual machine configuration to Hyper-V, and it will allow you to modify the virtual machine configuration in one step.

VMC2HV can be used both locally and remotely. In the local scenario, the tool runs on the Hyper-V server, which limits its use to systems running Windows Server 2008 with graphical user interface, because it needs the .NET Framework to operate. For server core installations of Windows Server 2008 and Hyper-V Server 2008, it can be used from a remote installation of Windows Server 2008 or Windows Vista with the .NET Framework installed.

To use the tool with as little effort as possible, the recommendation is to copy the VMC and virtual hard disk file(s) to the Hyper-V server in a folder with the name of the new virtual machine. For example, you could copy the files Machine1.vmc and Machine1.vhd to a folder at D:\vm\machine1. When the tool imports the file Machine1 with a Virtual Machine Path to D:\vm, it will use the folder D:\vm\machine1 and will create the new virtual machine in that folder. This way, all the files belonging to Machine1 will be contained in the same folder.

Upon import, VMC2HV reads the configuration file and displays all properties. Properties that no longer exist in Hyper-V are ignored, and you can set new properties in Hyper-V manually. Figure 8-10 shows the tool with a remote connection after importing a VMC file.

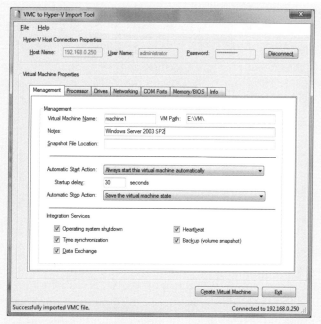

FIGURE 8-10 VMC2HV opening page

The tool shows several tabs related to the Virtual Machine Properties. The Processor tab allows you to specify the number of logical CPUs, the Resource Control, and Processor Functionality. The Drives tab (shown in Figure 8-11) shows the virtual disk drives such as floppy drives, CD/DVD ROM drives, and virtual hard disks, as well as their locations (IDE/SCSI and device ID).

In the case of a virtual machine that booted from SCSI under Virtual Server, the VMC2HV tool offers you the option to swap the SCSI disk at location 0 with IDE at location 0.

The Networking tab (shown in Figure 8-12) shows the number of network adapters and allows you to set them to Legacy; under Virtual Server, an adapter is always an emulated Dec/Intel adapter. By default, VMC2HV creates a synthetic adapter (which is also the default with Hyper-V). The tool also allows you to specify which virtual network and which VLAN you want the adapter to connect to.

Special features include recognizing the guest operating system and limiting the number of logical processors, if applicable (according to support policy), and warning you if the virtual hard disks cannot be found at the current location. Any new paths for virtual hard disks can be edited using the VMC2HV tool, which is available as a download from *http://blogs.technet.com/matthts/*.

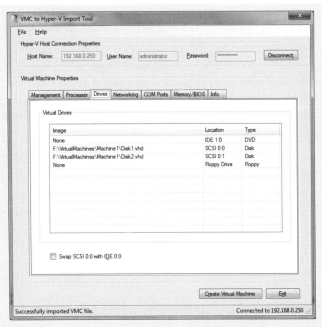

FIGURE 8-11 The Drives tab of Virtual Machine Properties in VMC2HV

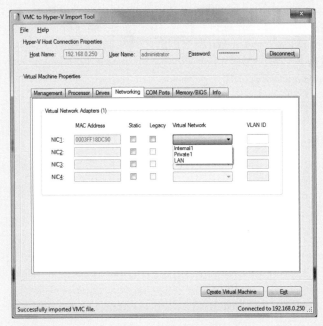

FIGURE 8-12 The Networking tab of Virtual Machine Properties in VMC2HV

Summary

Migrating virtual machines from Virtual Server 2005 R2 to Hyper-V involves migrating both the configuration of the host and the virtual machines themselves. In this chapter, we discussed what you need to consider prior to migrating the host and the virtual machines. A key decision you must make before migrating the host involves determining if there are any virtual machines using operating systems that are not supported on Hyper-V, in which case you should maintain a Virtual Server host.

The chapter provided you with the important considerations and the steps for preparing the virtual machine hard disk for migration. These included dealing with hardware differences (SCSI controllers, network adapters, and HAL), cleaning up the virtual hard disk (Undo, saved state, and differencing disks), and removing Virtual Machine Additions. After the host is migrated, you learned that you can create a new virtual machine using the existing virtual hard disk, and then you must install Integration Services to provide support for synthetic devices and improve performance.

Additional Resources

The following resources contain additional information related to the topics in this chapter.

- Virtual Machine Migration Guide, a resource with information about how to migrate Virtual Server 205 R2 virtual machines to Hyper-V, available at *http://technet.microsoft.com/en-us/library/dd296684.aspx*
- VMC2HV Migration Tool, a resource for simplifying the migration process, available at *http://blogs.technet.com/matthts/*

## CHAPTER 9

Taking a Look at Windows Server 2008 R2 Hyper-V

I n Chapter 2, "Hyper-V Overview," you were offered a high-level description of the major features that are implemented in the latest release of Hyper-V. In this chapter, you can find a more detailed preview of the new features and functionality that are delivered in Windows Server 2008 Release 2 (R2) Hyper-V and Hyper-V Server 2008 R2. Since the information presented in this chapter is based on beta versions of the software, you may find variations from what is presented here in the final release. However, with Windows Server 2008 R2 Hyper-V and Hyper-V Server 2008 R2, Microsoft continues to extend the Hyper-V feature set to increase the flexibility, scalability, and availability of the virtualization platform.

> **NOTE** Throughout the chapter, Hyper-V Version 1 (V1) refers to Windows Server 2008 Hyper-V, and Hyper-V R2 refers to Windows Server 2008 R2 Hyper-V.

Installing the Hyper-V Role on Windows Server 2008 R2

The quickest method to begin the evaluation of the new Hyper-V R2 features is to perform a full installation of Windows Server 2008 R2 and then use the Server Manager console to install the Hyper-V role.

Windows Server 2008 R2 Hyper-V requires that hardware-enforced Data Execution Prevention (DEP) is enabled in the BIOS. Specifically, you must enable the Intel XD bit (execute disable bit) or AMD NX bit (no execute bit).

Use the following steps to install the Hyper-V role on a full installation of Windows Server 2008 R2 using Server Manager:

1. On the lower-left corner of the taskbar, click the Server Manager icon (represented by a server with a toolbox, as shown in the lower-left corner of Figure 9-1).

FIGURE 9-1 The Server Manager icon

2. In Server Manager, select the Roles node in the left pane (see Figure 9-2). In the right pane, the Roles Summary lists the roles that are currently installed on the server and provides the option to add and remove roles.

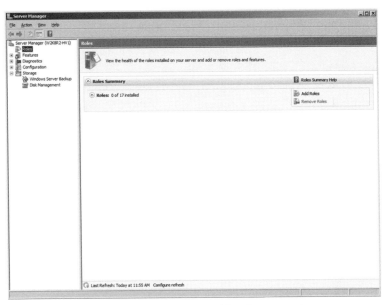

FIGURE 9-2 Installed roles and the option to add and remove roles

3. Click Add Roles to launch the Add Roles Wizard.

4. On the Before You Begin page (see Figure 9-3), click Next.

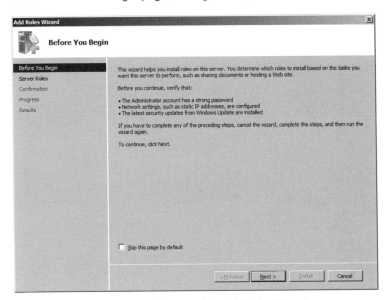

FIGURE 9-3 The Before You Begin page of the Add Roles Wizard

5. On the Select Server Roles page (see Figure 9-4), select the box next to the Hyper-V role and then click Next.

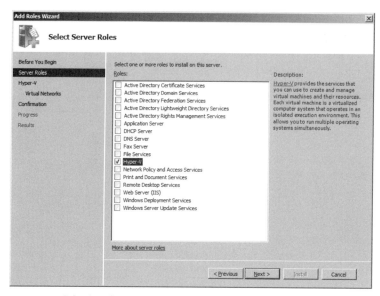

FIGURE 9-4 Selecting the Hyper-V role on the Select Server Roles page

6. On the Hyper-V role introduction page (see Figure 9-5), review the information and then click Next.

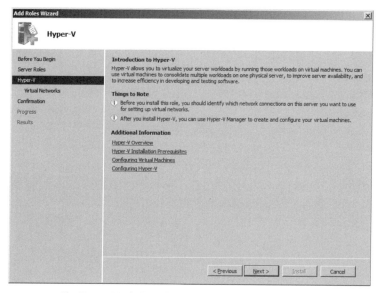

FIGURE 9-5 The Hyper-V role introduction page

7. On the Create Virtual Networks page, shown in Figure 9-6, you see a list of the network adapters installed on the server, and you have the option to select one or more adapters. Although you are not required to select any adapters, if you do, an external

virtual network is created for each selected adapter during the Hyper-V role installation. In addition, one network adapter is automatically reserved and dedicated to the management partition (parent partition) network traffic. After you make your selections, click Next.

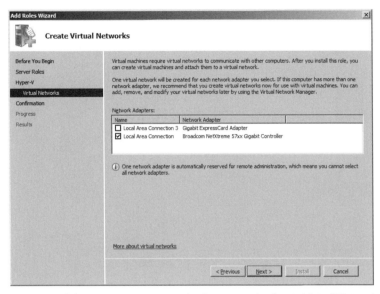

FIGURE 9-6 Select one or more network adapters on the Create Virtual Networks page.

8. On the Confirm Installation Selections page (see Figure 9-7), review the information and then click Install.

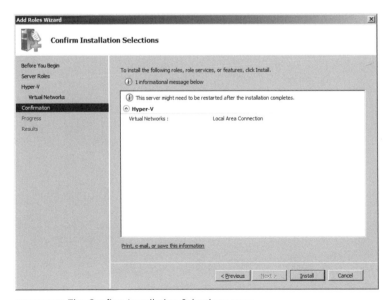

FIGURE 9-7 The Confirm Installation Selections page

9. After the Hyper-V files are installed, you are prompted to restart the server to finish the installation process, as shown in Figure 9-8. Click Close to restart the server.

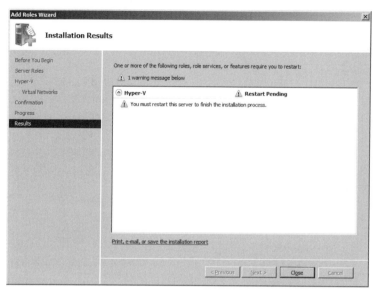

FIGURE 9-8 After installation, you are prompted to restart the server.

10. After the server restarts, the Resume Configuration Wizard launches and presents the results of the Hyper-V role installation process, as shown in Figure 9-9. Review the informational messages and then click Close.

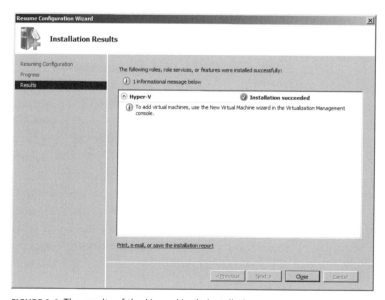

FIGURE 9-9 The results of the Hyper-V role installation process

Reviewing New Features in Hyper-V

Table 9-1 summarizes the basic features found in Windows Server 2008 R2 Hyper-V Enterprise and Datacenter editions, as well as in the free, stand-alone Hyper-V Server 2008 R2 product. Windows Server 2008 R2 Hyper-V Standard Edition is also available, but is not shown in this table. A significant change that comes with the R2 version of Hyper-V is the support for 32 processor cores to accommodate servers with up to eight quad-core physical processors. Windows Server 2008 Hyper-V supports 16 cores, and it can support 24 cores with the installation of an additional update (KB 956710).

TABLE 9-1 Hyper-V R2 Feature Comparison

FEATURES	MICROSOFT HYPER-V SERVER 2008 R2	WINDOWS SERVER 2008 R2 ENTERPRISE	WINDOWS SERVER 2008 R2 DATACENTER
x86 Support	Guest OS Only	Guest OS Only	Guest OS Only
x64 Support	Host and Guest	Host and Guest	Host and Guest
# of VMs—x64 Host	256 (Max)	256 (Max)	256 (Max)
Host Memory Support	1 terabyte	1 terabyte	1 terabyte
Host Processor Support	32 Cores (Max)	32 Cores (Max)	32 Cores (Max)
Virtual Networks	Unlimited	Unlimited	Unlimited
Guest VM Memory	64 GB (Max)	64 GB (Max)	64 GB (Max)
Guest Virtual Processor	4 per VM (Max)	4 per VM (Max)	4 per VM (Max)
Guest Virtual NICs	4 Legacy 8 Synthetic	4 Legacy 8 Synthetic	4 Legacy 8 Synthetic
Guest Storage Adapters	2 IDE 4 SCSI	2 IDE 4 SCSI	2 IDE 4 SCSI
Guest Storage Devices	4 IDE 256 SCSI	4 IDE 256 SCSI	4 IDE 256 SCSI
Cluster Support	Y	Y	Y
Quick Migration	Y	Y	Y
Live Migration	Y	Y	Y
Included Use licenses	None	1 Physical 4 VMs	1 Physical Unlimited VMs

In addition to Quick Migration, Windows Server 2008 R2 Hyper-V supports Live Migration. Live Migration enables you to move a virtual machine between cluster nodes without service interruption, extending the options available to manage both planned and unplanned down-time as well as load-balancing policy across Hyper-V server farms.

> **MORE INFO** Live Migration features and configuration are discussed in the next section, "Live Migration."

The Hyper-V Server 2008 R2 feature set has been substantially upgraded and is compa-rable to Windows Server 2008 R2 Enterprise Edition. Hyper-V Server 2008 R2 supports up to 1 terabyte of physical server memory, virtual machine memory allocation up to 64 gigabytes (GB), and up to 256 concurrent virtual machines (VMs), allowing deployment as a solution to a broad set of virtualization scenarios. Furthermore, Hyper-V Server 2008 R2 includes Failover Clustering, Quick Migration, and Live Migration support, features that are not available in Hyper-V Server 2008. In contrast to Windows Server 2008 R2 Hyper-V, Hyper-V Server 2008 R2 includes only a local command-line and text-based configuration utility for management, al-though it can be managed remotely using the Hyper-V Manager and Failover Cluster Manager.

> **IMPORTANT** As with Hyper-V Server 2008, Hyper-V Server 2008 R2 is not a Windows Server edition, and you do not receive any Windows licenses with it. Therefore, you must purchase a valid Windows license for each Windows-based virtual machine that you plan to run on it.

Live Migration

In Hyper-V (V1), Quick Migration uses Windows Server 2008 Failover Clustering to enable moving a virtual machine across cluster nodes *without data loss and with minimal service interruption*. The service interruption occurs because a virtual machine is placed in saved state to capture the active memory and processor state to disk and then transfer the data connec-tion to the destination cluster node. After the storage resources are moved to the destina-tion node and the virtual machine active memory and processor state are reloaded, service resumes.

With Live Migration, Hyper-V R2 provides the ability to move a virtual machine across cluster nodes *without data loss or service interruption*. Like Quick Migration, Live Migration is independent of the guest operating system running in a virtual machine. Further, cluster configurations that support Quick Migration also support Live Migration, if the following requirements are met:

- All Hyper-V cluster nodes must use processors from the same manufacturer and of the same type.

- All Hyper-V cluster nodes must be configured on the same TCP/IP subnet.
- All Hyper-V cluster nodes must have access to shared storage.

NOTE The same shared storage options that are supported in Hyper-V (V1) are also supported in Hyper-V R2.

A live migration of a virtual machine can be initiated through the Failover Cluster Manager, System Center Virtual Machine Manager (for Hyper-V servers that it manages), or a WMI or PowerShell script.

IMPORTANT If you use System Center Virtual Machine Manager, you will need System Center Virtual Machine Manager R2 to initiate and manage Live Migration of Windows Server 2008 R2 Hyper-V and Hyper-V Server 2008 R2 servers.

Live Migration Process

Live Migration consists of a multistep process that begins with the creation of a TCP connection from the Hyper-V source node to the destination node. Through this connection, the virtual machine configuration data is transferred to the destination node, and the data is used to create a new virtual machine with identical settings. This includes the definition of virtual storage adapters, virtual network adapters, virtual processor and memory allocations, and other virtual machine configuration parameters.

After the virtual machine configuration on the destination node is complete, the virtual machine memory pages on the source node are transferred to the destination node. Since the virtual machine on the source node continues to execute, Hyper-V tracks modifications to the memory pages and iteratively copies the modified pages to the destination node. This process continues until the iteration threshold is reached or all modified memory pages are copied to the destination node.

The next step is to pause the virtual machine, copy any remaining modified memory pages, and transfer the processor register and device state from the source node to the destination node. At this stage, you can no longer cancel the live migration process.

While the virtual machine is paused, control of the virtual machine storage, including virtual hard disks and pass-through disks, is also assigned to the destination node. Then, with the virtual machine in a consistent state, execution is resumed on the destination node.

Finally, the physical network switch is forced to update its tables with the new port to direct the network traffic for the virtual machine (this is the physical network switch port to which the destination node is connected), and the virtual machine is removed from the source node.

Live Migration Performance

In order to avoid service interruption, the time frame that the virtual machine pauses must be minimized to avoid exceeding application and TCP network connection timeout values. Therefore, an essential architectural element of a Hyper-V cluster is a high-speed network connection link (at minimum 1-gigabit Ethernet) to optimize memory and state data transfers between source and destination nodes. In addition, the amount of time needed to complete a live migration is dependent on the following variables:

- **Virtual machine memory size**   The larger the virtual machine memory size, the longer the live migration process may take.
- **Virtual machine activity level**   The higher the virtual machine activity level, the higher the potential for memory page modifications. This results in additional iterations to create a consistent memory state on the destination node.
- **Source and destination node load**   High utilization rates on the source and destination nodes will extend the time frame required to complete the live migration process.
- **Network bandwidth and throughput**   High-speed network bandwidth and throughput will decrease the amount of time required to copy the virtual machine memory page and state information from the source node to the destination node.
- **Shared storage configuration**   The transfer of a logical unit number (LUN) between the source and destination node is a factor in the migration timeline. It is possible to significantly reduce and even eliminate its impact using the new Cluster Shared Volumes (CSV) feature in Windows Server 2008 R2.

If you intend to use Live Migration in your environment and want to optimize the shared storage configuration, you should implement Cluster Shared Volumes. Cluster Shared Volumes reduce the complexity of your shared configuration and the time required to complete virtual machine live migrations.

> **IMPORTANT**   Each Hyper-V cluster node can participate only as the source or destination in a single live migration at a time. Therefore, a 16-node cluster can support a maximum of eight concurrent virtual machine live migrations.

Cluster Shared Volumes

Since Windows NT 4.0, Windows Server products have provided a high-availability solution through Failover Clustering, but they have allowed only one cluster node to have ownership of a LUN and, therefore, access to the data stored on it. In Windows Server 2008, when a virtual machine is transferred to another node in a Hyper-V cluster through Quick Migration, the time to perform the migration is partially dependent on the rapidity of the LUN ownership transfer. In addition, to migrate only one virtual machine between Windows Server 2008

Hyper-V cluster nodes, you have to store a single virtual machine on a LUN, unless you implement more complex mountpoints.

MORE INFO For more information on mountpoints, refer to the sidebar titled "Direct from the Source: Solving Drive Letter Restrictions with Mountpoints" in Chapter 5, "Hyper-V Advanced Features."

To address these limitations, Windows Server 2008 R2 introduces Cluster Shared Volumes. CSV implements and presents a consistent file namespace to all cluster nodes and allows multiple cluster nodes to concurrently access a LUN on a shared storage system. CSV volumes are created and stored as directories beneath a root folder named ClusterStorage. This is the default name for the root folder, but you can modify it to fit your folder naming convention. For example, you can attach a single LUN to drive S and, using CSV, you can create a volume for each virtual machine as follows:

- S:\ClusterStorage\Volume1\VM1
- S:\ClusterStorage\Volume2\VM2
- S:\ClusterStorage\Volume3\VM3
- S:\ClusterStorage\Volume*n*\VM*n*

To a virtual machine, a CSV volume appears as if it is stored on its own LUN. However, all of the virtual machine storage resides on a single LUN, and every cluster node can access the volumes using the same fully qualified path. Some of the other benefits of CSV include:

- Full compatibility with NTFS.
- Implementation does not require reformatting shared storage media.
- Reduction in the number of drive letters implemented to store multiple VMs.
- Support includes SAN or iSCSI-based storage devices.

The Cluster Shared Volumes feature is enabled at the cluster level through the Failover Cluster Manager. You do not need any other specialized management tools to support CSV.

MORE INFO In the section titled "Using Live Migration" later in this chapter, you will find a step-by-step procedure that describes how to configure a Hyper-V host cluster using Cluster Shared Volumes and initiate a virtual machine live migration from the Failover Cluster Manager.

Second Level Address Translation

As described in Chapter 3, "Hyper-V Architecture," the Windows Hypervisor manages two levels of address space translation for guest operating systems running in virtual machines. The first level of translation maps the guest operating system virtual address space into its physical address space. The second level of translation maps the guest operating system physical address space into the system physical address space. In order to do this, the Windows Hypervisor maintains a Shadow Page Table that combines the two levels of address space translation into a single page table. In the Hyper-V (V1) release, the overhead to maintain the Shadow Page Table can be up to 10 percent of the total processor time and require multiple megabytes (MB) for each virtual machine.

Hyper-V R2 eliminates the need to maintain a Shadow Page Table by leveraging Second Level Address Translation (SLAT) functionality that is implemented in AMD-V and Intel VT processor hardware architectures. AMD-V implements SLAT through a mechanism named Nested Page Tables (NPT), also referred to as Rapid Virtualization Indexing (RVI). The Intel VT SLAT technology is named Extended Page Tables (EPT). Using NPT or EPT, AMD-V and Intel VT processors can maintain and perform the two levels of address space translations required for each virtual machine in hardware, reducing the complexity of the Windows Hypervisor and the context switches needed to manage virtual machine page faults. As a result, the processor and memory overhead required to manage the Shadow Page Table is removed, and Hyper-V R2 can provide better scalability of Hyper-V servers. This technology provides specific advantages for Hyper-V servers that run a large number of virtual machines or virtual machine workloads that very frequently modify memory.

> **MORE INFO** For more details on the AMD-V NPT or RVI technology, refer to the sidebar titled "Direct from the Field: AMD-V Rapid Virtualization Indexing" in Chapter 1, "Introducing Virtualization."

Core Parking

The Advanced Configuration and Power Interface (ACPI) specification defines processor power states, also called C-states, that a processor or processor cores (for some multicore processors) may be placed into independently when idle. Depending on the C-state that an ACPI-compliant processor core enters, it may power off some of its components and suspend instruction execution, providing a reduction in core voltage and lower power consumption.

Windows Server 2008 R2 implements a new power management feature, *Core Parking*, that provides the ability to place processors into deep C-states (low power states) when the server workload can be managed by a fewer number of processor cores than are allocated to it. By default, Core Parking affects all processor cores and is not applied to individual cores. In Hyper-V (V1), the virtual machine workload is scheduled to optimize the use of available processor cores, but the introduction of Core Parking has resulted in modifications in the Hyper-V R2 Windows Hypervisor scheduler. Based on thresholds defined in server power policy, the management partition (parent partition) kernel determines the set of processor cores to park and provides the information to the Hyper-V R2 Windows Hypervisor. When the Windows Hypervisor schedules virtual machines for execution, it uses the Core Parking information to determine if it can avoid selecting processors that are parked. If the workload requires additional processor cores, processors are brought out of the C-state and back online to support virtual machine workloads.

> **NOTE** For most environments, you will probably not need to modify the power policy to fine-tune Core Parking–related parameters. However, it is possible to use Active Directory group policy settings or the Powercfg.exe utility that is provided with Windows Server 2008 R2 to view and modify power settings. You can view the default power policy processor parameters using the following command:

```
powercfg /qh SCHEME_CURRENT SUB_PROCESSOR
```

Dynamic Addition and Removal of Storage

In Hyper-V (V1), a virtual machine has to be powered off to add or remove virtual hard disks or pass-through disks. Hyper-V R2 supports adding and removing virtual hard disks and pass-through disks to a running virtual machine without requiring a reboot, if Integration Services are installed and the disks are attached to virtual SCSI controllers.

TCP Offload Support

The TCP Offload feature in Hyper-V R2 allows a virtual machine to push TCP/IP processing down to supported physical network adapters. Although this functionality is available in Windows Server 2008, it is not supported for virtual machines. With the increasing adoption of 10-gigabit Ethernet networks and the significant TCP/IP processing overhead increase that results from higher-speed networks, TCP Offload support at the virtual machine level is crucial. In most cases, the networking offload support in Hyper-V R2 reduces the load on processor cores, freeing processor time and improving overall virtual machine network performance.

Virtual Machine Queue Support

Hyper-V R2 also supports Virtual Machine Queue (VMQ) to help reduce the complexity and overhead associated with delivering network packets received by a physical network adapter to the target virtual machine. Specifically, a virtual machine queue is created on the network adapter for each virtual machine, and a VMQ identifier is assigned to each virtual machine. When a network packet arrives, the VMQ identifier is used for quick identification of the target virtual machine. Further, network packets can be directly copied into the target virtual machine memory, providing a significant reduction in processing overhead and an increase in performance when compared with Hyper-V (V1).

Jumbo Frames

Similar to the TCP Offload feature, support for TCP/IP jumbo frames in Windows Server 2008 is limited to physical network adapters. With Hyper-V R2, jumbo frame support is extended to virtual network adapters. A jumbo frame is an Ethernet frame with up to 9000 bytes of payload data, as opposed to the Ethernet standard of up to 1500 bytes. Using jumbo frames reduces the overhead incurred for each transferred byte of network data. The results are additional performance enhancements due to significant processor and TCP/IP overhead reduction.

MAC Address Range Configuration

Hyper-V (V1) automatically creates a MAC address pool for virtual network adapter assignments when it is installed. However, there is no option in the Hyper-V Manager to modify the MAC address pool. If you need to change the MAC address pool, you have to edit the registry.

In Hyper-V R2, you have the ability to manage the MAC address pool through the Virtual Network Manager. To manage the MAC address pool, open the Virtual Network Manager in the Hyper-V Manager console and select the MAC Address Range option under Global Network Settings. This allows you to modify the MAC address pool configuration on the Hyper-V server.

By default, there can be only 256 virtual network adapters concurrently assigned a dynamic MAC address. If you require more than 256 concurrent dynamic MAC address assignments on a single Hyper-V server, or you need to modify the MAC address pool to avoid duplicate MAC address assignments, you can use this new feature to make the changes, without resorting to a more risky registry manipulation.

DIRECT FROM THE SOURCE

MAC Address Spoofing

Keith Mange, Software Design Engineer
Windows Virtualization

In Windows Server 2008 R2 Hyper-V and Hyper-V Server 2008 R2, there is a new option (Enable Spoofing Of MAC Addresses) in the virtual network adapter settings to enable spoofing of MAC addresses. If you do not select this option and disallow MAC address spoofing, the following rules are enforced:

- The virtual switch port that connects the virtual network adapter sends and receives packets that contain any valid MAC address.

- The virtual network adapter MAC address cannot be moved or associated with another virtual switch port.

- The virtual switch port does not forward unicast flooded packets (packets that are forwarded to all switch ports if the destination MAC address is not found in the switch forwarding table) to the virtual network adapter.

- You cannot override the virtual network adapter MAC address configuration using the NetworkAddress key in the virtual machine registry.

NOTE   The configuration of a virtual network adapter, including the NetworkAddress key that contains the MAC address value, is found under HKEY_LOCAL_MACHINE\System\CurrentControlSet\Control\Class \{ 4D36E972-E325-11CE-BFC1-08002BE10318} key. Each of the four-digit numbers (0000, 0001, and so on) in the subkey tree represents a particular network adapter that you can easily identify through its DriverDesc value.

If you select the option to enable MAC address spoofing, the MAC address can be learned on other ports, and the following actions will be allowed:

- The virtual switch port that connects the virtual network adapter can send and receive packets that contain any MAC address.

- The virtual switch port dynamically learns of new MAC addresses and the virtual switch can add them in its forwarding table.

- The virtual switch port will receive and forward unicast flooded packets to the virtual network adapter.

- You can override the virtual network adapter MAC address configuration using the NetworkAddress key in the virtual machine registry.

If you place the virtual network adapter in promiscuous mode and enable MAC address spoofing, the virtual network adapter will be allowed to receive unicast flooded packets.

Virtual Machine Snapshot Operation

Hyper-V R2 includes a new operation, Allow Virtual Machine Snapshot, which can be used to delegate the permission to create virtual machine snapshots more granularly through Authorization Manager policy. In Hyper-V (V1), providing the permission to create virtual machine snapshots also requires the permission to start and stop a virtual machine, two operations that you may not want to delegate in tandem with the more innocuous ability to create virtual machine snapshots.

New Default Hyper-V Folders

There are two new default folders that Hyper-V R2 creates during installation to store virtual machine–related files. In particular, these are:

- %SystemDrive%\ProgramData\Microsoft\Windows\Hyper-V\Snapshots Cache

- %SystemDrive%\ProgramData\Microsoft\Windows\Hyper-V\Virtual Machines Cache

Hyper-V R2 uses these folders to store XML files that contain the globally unique identifier (GUID) and the common name associated with a specific virtual machine. This allows Hyper-V R2 to resolve and display the common name of a virtual machine, rather than just the GUID, even if the virtual machine storage location is offline or the virtual machine configuration file is not readily accessible.

> **NOTE** Hyper-V R2 also does not create a default floppy disk drive, which is a change from Hyper-V (V1).

Using Live Migration

Live Migration allows you to implement a high-availability solution for mission-critical virtual machines without the requirement for a cluster-aware guest operating system or application, and it enables enterprise management applications like SCVMM R2 to provide dynamic load balancing of virtual machines without service interruption.

In this section, you will learn how to configure the two-node Hyper-V host cluster configuration shown in Figure 9-10 to support Live Migration. The Hyper-V cluster will use an iSCSI-based shared storage device (such as a Windows Storage Server device) with Cluster Shared Volumes. When using iSCSI, you should dedicate a physical network adapter in each Hyper-V server for iSCSI storage access. An iSCSI initiator is required on each Hyper-V cluster node to access the iSCSI-based targets on the shared storage.

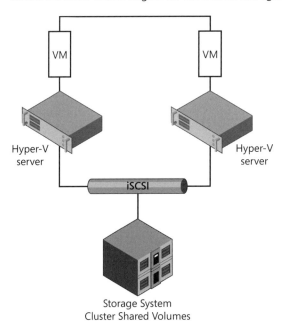

FIGURE 9-10 A Hyper-V host cluster using iSCSI shared storage and Cluster Shared Volumes

NOTE An iSCSI initiator is a software component that enables the connection of a Windows host to an external iSCSI storage array over a TCP/IP network.

After the configuration of the Hyper-V cluster, Cluster Shared Volumes, and virtual machine to support Live Migration, you will learn how to initiate a virtual machine live migration using the Failover Cluster Manager.

Creating a Two-Node Hyper-V Host Cluster

The procedure provided in this section assumes that you have installed Windows Server 2008 R2 on each physical server and also have installed the Hyper-V role using the steps outlined in the section titled "Installing the Hyper-V Role on Windows Server 2008 R2" earlier in this chapter. To create the two-node Hyper-V host cluster using an iSCSI-based shared storage device, you must complete the following major steps:

- Configure the Witness disk on each Hyper-V server using the iSCSI initiator.
- Add the Failover Clustering feature on each Hyper-V server.
- Configure Failover Clustering on each Hyper-V server.
- Validate the cluster configuration and create the cluster.

Configuring iSCSI Shared Disks

Before undertaking the following procedure, you have to coordinate the creation of an iSCSI target and disk devices with your storage management team. They must create a Witness disk (of at least 600 MB) and a virtual machine storage disk on the iSCSI storage system, as well as authorize both Hyper-V servers to access the iSCSI target. After the iSCSI target is created, follow these steps to configure the Witness disk on the Hyper-V servers using the iSCSI initiator:

1. Log into the first Hyper-V server with an account that has Domain Administrator credentials.

2. Click Start, select Administrative Tools, and then select iSCSI Initiator.

3. Click Yes in the Microsoft iSCSI dialog box to start the Microsoft iSCSI service.

4. In the iSCSI Initiator Properties dialog box, click the Discovery tab, and in the Target Portals section, click Discover Portal.

5. Enter the name or IP address of the server where the target iSCSI drive is defined, and then click OK.

6. Click the Targets tab to display a list of discovered targets. You may have to click Refresh to display the list.

7. Select the appropriate target name and click Connect.

8. Ensure that the Add This Connection To The List Of Favorite Targets check box is selected. This allows the Hyper-V server to automatically restore the connection to

the iSCSI target when the computer restarts. You may also need to select the Enable Multipath check box if you have multipath software installed.

9. Click OK to connect to the iSCSI target.

10. Click OK to close the iSCSI Initiator Properties dialog box.

11. Open Server Manager, expand Storage in the left pane, and select Disk Management.

12. In the Disk Management bottom pane, right-click the Witness disk (600 MB) in the left pane and select Online from the menu options.

13. Right-click the Witness disk again (in the left pane) and select Initialize Disk from the menu options.

14. In the Initialize Disk dialog box, select the appropriate partition style (MBR or GPT) and then click OK.

15. Right-click the Witness disk once more (in the right pane) and select New Simple Volume from the menu options.

16. On the opening page of the New Simple Volume Wizard, click Next.

17. On the Specify Volume Size page, click Next.

18. On the Assign Drive Letter Or Path page, select a drive letter (for example, W) from the Assign The Following Drive Letter drop-down list and then click Next.

19. On the Format Partition page, select Format This Volume With The Following Settings, enter a name (for example, Witness) in the Volume Label text box, and then click Next.

20. On the Completing The New Simple Volume Wizard page, review your selections and then click Finish.

21. Repeat steps 1 to 11 for the second Hyper-V server.

22. In the Disk Management console, right-click the Witness disk (in the left pane) and select Online from the menu options.

23. Right-click the Witness disk once more (in the right pane) and select Change Drive Letter And Paths from the menu options.

24. In the Change Drive Letter And Paths For dialog box, click Change.

25. In the Change Drive Letter Or Path dialog box, select the same drive letter (in this example, it is W) that was used for the first cluster node from the Assign The Following Drive Letter drop-down list, and then click OK.

Adding the Failover Clustering Feature to the Hyper-V Servers

Before you can create a cluster, you have to add the Failover Clustering feature to each Hyper-V server. Follow these steps to add the Failover Clustering feature to the Hyper-V servers:

1. On the first Hyper-V server, open the Server Manager and click the Features node in the left pane.

2. In the right pane, click Add Features to open the Add Features Wizard.

3. On the Select Features page, select Failover Clustering and then click Next.

4. On the Confirm Installation Selections page, click Install.

5. On the Installation Results page, click Close.

6. Repeat steps 1 through 5 for the second Hyper-V server.

Configuring Failover Clustering on the Hyper-V Servers

When you create the first node in a cluster, you specify all parameters that define the cluster configuration. The Cluster Configuration Wizard guides you through the installation and completes the cluster setup when you have entered all the required information.

Follow these steps to configure Failover Clustering on the first node of the Hyper-V host cluster:

1. Click Start, select Administrative Tools, and then click Failover Cluster Manager.

2. Select Validate A Configuration in the Management pane to launch the Validate A Configuration Wizard.

3. On the Before You Begin page, click Next.

4. On the Select Servers Or A Cluster page, type each Hyper-V server name in the Enter Name text box and click Add. After these actions are completed, click Next.

5. On the Testing Options page, select Run All Tests (Recommended) and then click Next.

6. On the Confirmation page, review the test list, ensure that there are no errors, and then click Next.

7. Correct any errors found during the validation process and then revalidate the configuration.

8. On the Summary page, click Finish.

9. Select Create A Cluster in the Management pane to launch the Create Cluster Wizard.

10. On the Before You Begin page, click Next.

11. On the Select Servers page, type each Hyper-V server name in the Enter Server Name text box and click Add. After these actions are completed, click Next.

12. On the Validation Warning page, select the appropriate option and then click Next.

13. On the Access Point For Administering The Cluster page, type the name of the cluster in the Cluster Name text box. You may also have to type the IP addresses to use for each configured network. After these actions are completed, click Next.

14. On the Confirmation page, review the cluster information and then click Next.

15. On the Summary page, click Finish.

After you complete these steps, each Hyper-V server will be a node in the failover cluster. To quickly verify that the failover cluster is functioning, you can shut down the first Hyper-V host cluster node. When you open Failover Cluster Management on the second Hyper-V host cluster node, you will see that it owns all cluster resources.

Configuring Cluster Shared Volumes

Before you configure a virtual machine for Live Migration, you have to enable Cluster Shared Volumes for the Hyper-V host cluster. Follow these steps to enable Cluster Shared Volumes using the Failover Cluster Manager:

1. On the first Hyper-V cluster node, open the Failover Cluster Manager, right-click the cluster name in the left pane, and select Enable Cluster Shared Volumes.

2. In the Enable Shared Volumes dialog box, select the I Accept These Terms And Restrictions check box and then click OK.

3. Open the Server Manager, expand Storage in the left pane, and select Disk Management.

4. In the Disk Management bottom pane, right-click the virtual machine storage disk in the left pane and select Online from the menu options.

5. Right-click the disk again (left pane) and select Initialize Disk from the menu options.

6. In the Initialize Disk dialog box, select the appropriate partition style (MBR or GPT) and then click OK.

7. Right-click the disk once more (right pane) and select New Simple Volume from the menu options.

8. On the opening page of the New Simple Volume Wizard, click Next.

9. On the Specify Volume Size page, click Next.

10. On the Assign Drive Letter Or Path page, select drive letter S from the Assign The Following Drive Letter drop-down list, and then click Next.

11. On the Format Partition page, select Format This Volume With The Following Settings, enter VMs in the Volume Label text box, and then click Next.

12. On the Completing The New Simple Volume Wizard page, review your selections and then click Finish.

13. In the Failover Cluster Manager, expand the cluster node in the left pane, right-click Storage, and select Add Disk.

14. In the Add Disks To A Cluster dialog box, select the check box next to the appropriate disk and then click OK. After the disk is added, you will see it in the Summary Of Storage list.

15. In the left pane, right-click Cluster Shared Volumes and select Add Storage.

16. In the Add Storage dialog box, select the check box next to the appropriate disk and then click OK.

If you open Windows Explorer, you can see that the new Cluster Shared Volume appears in %SystemRoot%\ClusterStorage on all nodes of the Hyper-V host cluster.

Creating a New Virtual Machine

After the Hyper-V host cluster is configured and before you create a new, highly available virtual machine, you should configure and connect an identically named external virtual network on each Hyper-V cluster node. After this is done, the next step is to create a virtual machine on one of the Hyper-V host cluster nodes.

1. On the first Hyper-V node, open the Hyper-V Manager console.

2. In the Actions pane, under the server name, click New and select Virtual Machine from the menu options to launch the New Virtual Machine Wizard.

3. On the Before You Begin page, click Next.

4. On the Specify Name And Location page, type the name of the new virtual machine. Then, select Store The Virtual Machine In A Different Location and click Browse to use Windows Explorer to select Volume1 in %SystemRoot%\ClusterStorage. After these actions are performed, click Next.

5. On the Assign Memory page, type the memory allocation for the virtual machine and then click Next.

6. On the Configure Networking page, select the external virtual network created for the non-cluster network traffic.

7. On the Connect Virtual Hard Disk page, select Create A Virtual Hard Disk and type the default Name, Location, and Size information for the new virtual machine. After these actions are performed, click Next.

8. On the Installation Options page, select the appropriate method to install the guest operating system in the virtual machine and then click Next.

9. On the Completing The New Virtual Machine Wizard page, click Finish.

10. Install the guest operating system and applications on the new virtual machine.

Making a Virtual Machine Highly Available

In order to configure the virtual machine and make it highly available, follow these steps:

1. On the first Hyper-V node, open the Hyper-V Manager console and power off the virtual machine.

2. Close the Hyper-V Manager and then open the Failover Cluster Manager console.

3. In the left pane, right-click Services And Applications under the cluster name and select Configure A Service Or Application from the menu options to launch the High-Availability Wizard.

4. On the Before You Begin page, click Next.

5. On the Select Service Or Application page, select Virtual Machine from the list of options.

6. On the Select Virtual Machine page, select the appropriate virtual machine and then click Next.

7. On the Confirmation page, check the information and click Next.

8. On the Summary page, review the report and click Summary.

9. After these actions are complete, open the Hyper-V Manager and select Start under the virtual machine name to bring it online.

Configuring Cluster Networks for Live Migration

The last (and optional) step before initiating a virtual machine live migration is the configuration and prioritization of cluster networks. Follow these steps to tune the configuration of cluster networks for live migration:

1. On the first Hyper-V node, open the Failover Cluster Manager and then select the cluster name in the left pane.

2. Expand Services And Applications and select the virtual machine in the left pane.

3. In the center pane, under the virtual machine summary, right-click the virtual machine resource and then select Properties.

4. Click the Network For Live Migration tab and select one or more cluster networks for live migration. You can also move the networks up and down in the list to define the most preferred network.

5. After you have made your selections, click OK.

Live Migration will use the cluster networks in the order specified in the list. If a connection to the destination cluster node through the first network fails, the next network in the list is used until all networks are exhausted or there is a successful connection through one of the listed networks.

Initiating a Live Migration

In order to initiate a virtual machine live migration using the Failover Cluster Manager, follow these steps:

1. On the first Hyper-V node, open the Failover Cluster Manager.

2. Expand Services And Applications and select the virtual machine in the left pane.

3. Right-click the virtual machine, select Live Migrate Virtual Machine To Another Node, and then select the second cluster node.

4. When the live migration completes, the virtual machine is running on the second cluster node.

Managing Hyper-V R2

Windows Server 2008 R2 Hyper-V can be managed locally or remotely from another Windows Server 2008 R2 server using the Hyper-V Manager console. Because Hyper-V Server 2008 R2 does not provide a graphical user interface, it is designed to be managed remotely.

> **NOTE** System Center Virtual Machine Manager 2008 does not support Windows Server 2008 R2 Hyper-V or Hyper-V Server 2008 R2. However, the next version, System Center Virtual Machine Manager 2008 R2, will fully support Hyper-V R2 as well as Hyper-V (V1) servers.

Another option to manage Windows Server 2008 R2 Hyper-V and Hyper-V Server 2008 R2 is to use the Remote Server Administration Tools (RSAT) for Windows 7. You can install the RSAT on either an x86 or x64 version of Windows 7. The Hyper-V Manager and Failover Cluster Manager are among the tools included in the RSAT for Windows 7.

> **NOTE** You can download the RSAT for Windows 7 from the Microsoft Web site at *http://www.microsoft.com/downloads/details.aspx?FamilyID=82516c35-c7dc-4652-b2ea-2df99ea83dbb.*

After you download and install the RSAT for Windows 7, you can enable all available tools or only a selection of tools using the Windows Features control panel applet, and you can access them from the Administrative Tools.

Summary

Windows Server 2008 R2 Hyper-V and Hyper-V Server 2008 R2 provide significant new features that include Live Migration, Cluster Shared Volumes, Second Level Address Translation, and Core Parking, as well as virtual hard disk and virtual network features and improvements that enhance Hyper-V R2 performance. To quickly start your evaluation of Hyper-V R2, you should begin with a full installation of Windows Server 2008 R2 and add the Hyper-V role using Server Manager. To test Live Migration, use the provided procedures to create a two-node Hyper-V host cluster, configure Cluster Shared Volumes, define a new virtual machine, make the virtual machine highly available, and initiate a Live Migration. In addition, ensure that you understand the current options to manage Hyper-V R2 using Windows Server 2008 R2 and Windows 7.

Additional Resources

The following resources contain additional information related to the topics in this chapter.

- Microsoft white paper, "Windows Server 2008 R2 Reviewers Guide," available at *http://www.microsoft.com/windowsserver2008/en/us/R2-Beta.aspx*

- Microsoft white paper, "Microsoft Hyper-V Server 2008 R2 (Beta) Overview," available at *http://www.microsoft.com/downloads/details.aspx?familyid=F81A38D2-A152-4DDE-96E6-2AA184FDF9B7*

- Microsoft white paper, "Microsoft Hyper-V Server 2008 R2 (Beta) Setup and Configuration Tool Guide," available at *http://www.microsoft.com/downloads/details.aspx?familyid=5C88B04D-2896-4FA4-9E59-7BC4442FF333*

- Microsoft white paper, "Windows Server 2008 R2 Hyper-V Live Migration," available at *http://www.microsoft.com/downloads/details.aspx?FamilyID=fdd083c6-3fc7-470b-8569-7e6a19fb0fdf&displaylang=en*

- Microsoft Technet Web site, "Hyper-V: Step-by-Step Guide to Using Live Migration in Windows Server 2008 R2," available at *http://technet.microsoft.com/en-us/library/dd446679.aspx*

Managing a Windows Server 2008 Hyper-V Infrastructure

Hyper-V Management Overview

Part III, "Managing a Windows Server 2008 Hyper-V Infrastructure," focuses on how to manage configurations of single or multiple Hyper-V servers. This chapter provides an overview of the products and technologies that can be combined to provide a comprehensive management solution for Hyper-V and virtual machines. The products are presented in three groups: management solutions, disaster recovery solutions, and monitoring solutions.

Management solutions focus on the products or tools that allow you to manage the configuration of the Hyper-V server or virtual machines running on the Hyper-V server. The section covering disaster recovery solutions introduces products or tools that allow you to back up and recover the Hyper-V server configuration and parent partition and the virtual machines. Monitoring solutions include products or tools that allow you to track the health of the Hyper-V server, the running virtual machines, and the applications running within the virtual machines.

The chapters that follow in Part III address the details of how to use the products and tools:

- Chapter 11, "Hyper-V Single Server Management," explains how the tools provided with Microsoft Hyper-V Server and Windows Server 2008 can be used to manage a single Hyper-V server.

- Chapter 12, "Server Farm Management," explains how System Center Virtual Machine Manager 2008 can be used to manage a farm of Hyper-V servers.

- Chapter 13, "Hyper-V Backup and Recovery," explains how Microsoft Server Backup and System Center Data Protection Manager 2007 SP1 are used as disaster recovery solutions.

- Chapter 14, "Server Migration Using System Center Virtual Machine Manager," explains how to perform physical to virtual and virtual to virtual server migrations.
- Chapter 15, "Server Monitoring with the Windows Server 2008 Hyper-V Management Pack for System Center Operations Manager 2007," explains how to set up and use System Center Operations Manager 2007 to monitor Hyper-V and running virtual machines.
- Chapter 16, "Hyper-V Management Using Windows PowerShell," explains how to use Windows PowerShell and the Hyper-V WMI interfaces to manage Hyper-V and virtual machines.

Management Solutions

Microsoft's management solutions for Hyper-V allow you to manage a single server configuration, a multiserver configuration, and a clustered configuration. The Hyper-V Manager MMC is a free tool that allows you to manage a single Hyper-V server at a time. Hyper-V Manager MMC is installable on any Windows Server 2008 version installed with the graphical user interface (GUI) or as part of the Remote Server Administration Tools (RSAT) available for Vista. System Center Virtual Machine Manager allows you to manage a farm of Hyper-V servers from a single console. Failover Cluster Manager MMC is a free tool available on Windows Server 2008 Enterprise or Datacenter editions for managing failover clusters.

The following section provides an overview of each tool and how it can be used to manage a Hyper-V server, farm of Hyper-V servers, or Hyper-V server cluster.

Hyper-V Manager MMC

Hyper-V Manager is the Microsoft Management Console (MMC) designed to provide a GUI to manage a Hyper-V server. Hyper-V Manager is automatically installed when the Hyper-V role is enabled on a full install of Windows Server 2008. On a server core install of Windows Server 2008 or with Microsoft Hyper-V Server 2008, the Hyper-V Manager MMC is not installed because there is no GUI. For these two configurations of Hyper-V, you must use the Hyper-V Manager from another machine. This can be either a full install of Windows Server 2008 that contains a GUI for the MMC to run, or a Windows Vista SP1 computer on which you install the Remote Server Administration Tools (RSAT). Regardless of how or where you install the Hyper-V Manager MMC, you can use it to remotely manage a Hyper-V server.

> **NOTE** Windows Server 2008 R2 and Windows 7 RSAT tools are currently available as a beta download from Microsoft Downloads at *http://www.microsoft.com/downloads*.

The Hyper-V MMC allows you to manage the configuration of the Hyper-V server, the configuration of registered virtual machines, and the state of registered virtual machines. Although the Hyper-V Manager MMC can connect to multiple Hyper-V servers, you can manage only a single server at a time.

By default, the Hyper-V Manager MMC allows the members of the local administrators group full control over the host and the virtual machines registered on the server. This allows the administrator to manage things like the default storage location of virtual machines, keyboard shortcuts, user credentials, virtual machine registrations, and the configuration of virtual machines. When virtual machines are registered on a Hyper-V server, the Hyper-V Manager MMC allows the administrator to manage the processor, storage, networking, memory, state, and operation of each virtual machine.

Although members of the local administrators group have full control by default, you are not required to be a local administrator to manage the Hyper-V server and registered virtual machines. Hyper-V uses Authorization Manager (AZMAN) to provide role-based security. Authorization Manager allows you to define roles, assign the operations that each role can perform, and limit the scope of the objects that the role can manage. Hyper-V provides a set of predefined operations, a single administrator role, and the default scope of the Hyper-V server and all virtual machines. If you want more granular security, you can define a new role that has limited operations assigned or a new scope that contains only a defined group of virtual machines. You can assign local or active directory domain users and groups to a role.

> **NOTE** Refer to Chapter 6, "Hyper-V Security" for more in-depth coverage of AZMAN.

Hyper-V Manager allows you to register, create, and manage virtual machines configurations, but it depends on another tool called VMConnect.exe to actually provide the remote video, keyboard, and mouse access to a virtual machine. VMConnect utilizes Remote Desktop Protocol (RDP) to allow a Hyper-V administrator or virtual machine manager to remotely connect to a virtual machine as if you were sitting at the console.

Figure 10-1 provides a view of the Hyper-V Manager MMC. The Hyper-V Manager MMC follows the standard layout of most Microsoft management consoles. The vertical pane on the left defines the Hyper-V servers you are managing, and the center panes allow you to pick a virtual machine to manage; it also provides details on the selected virtual machines state, any snapshots, and a thumbnail of the virtual machine video buffer. The right pane provides an actions menu for the currently managed Hyper-V server and the currently selected virtual machine. The actions pane is context sensitive and only displays actions that are available based on what is selected in the center pane.

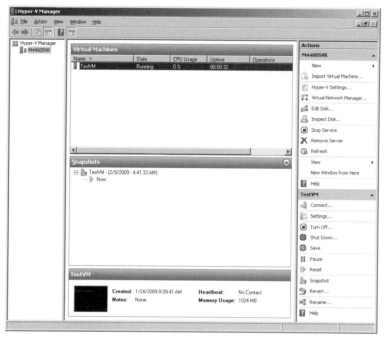

FIGURE 10-1 Hyper-V Manager MMC

Failover Cluster Manager

At some point in the deployment of server virtualization, you will want to provide high availability for the Hyper-V servers and the virtual machines running on the servers. Hyper-V utilizes Failover Clustering in Windows Server 2008 to provide high availability. Failover Clustering is an installable feature in Windows Server 2008.

Failover Clustering is managed by the Failover Cluster Manager MMC, which is installed automatically when the Failover Clustering feature is installed or can be installed manually as a feature administration tool option under the RSAT. Figure 10-2 provides a view of the default console of the Failover Cluster Manager MMC.

Failover Cluster Manager allows you to manage local cluster configuration or remote cluster configurations. In order to run Failover Cluster Manager, the computer that it is installed on must be a member of a domain, and the user account that you are logged in as must be a domain account with the correct privilege to run the MMC.

Failover Cluster Manager allows you to create and manage Hyper-V host clusters and virtual machine clusters. A host cluster is a cluster of up to 16 Hyper-V servers running highly available virtual machines. Neither the virtual machines nor the applications in the virtual machines need to be cluster-aware. A virtual machine cluster is a cluster of up to 16 virtual machine nodes running a cluster-aware application. Each node in a virtual machine cluster must be running on a different Hyper-V server to achieve proper high availability.

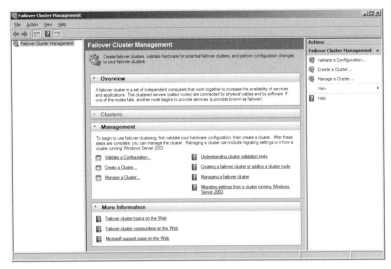

FIGURE 10-2 Failover Cluster Manager MMC

Building a cluster is a six-step process. The first step involves assembling the hardware and connecting the shared storage. In step two, you install Windows Server 2008 on each node of the cluster and enable the Hyper-V role. In step three, you install the Failover Cluster feature. Step four requires you to use the Failover Cluster Manager MMC to validate the cluster configuration. In step five, you use the Failover Cluster Manager MMC to create the cluster. In step six, you begin to use the Failover Cluster Manager MMC to manage the cluster and cluster resources.

To make a virtual machine highly available, first you must create a Hyper-V host cluster using shared disk storage. After the cluster has been built, you can create a virtual machine on the shared data storage. When it has been created, the virtual machine can be made highly available by using the Configure A Service Or Application option in the Failover Cluster Manager MMC and selecting Virtual Machine as the application type. Select the virtual machine that you want to make highly available and the resources will be added as cluster-managed resources. After all the resources are added, the virtual machine will show up as a highly available application. The last step you must take to make the virtual machine highly available is to right-click the application and bring it online. When it is online, the highly available virtual machine will be a cluster-managed resource, and any failure of a Hyper-V server will result in the virtual machine being restarted on another node of the host cluster.

System Center Virtual Machine Manager 2008

Whereas Hyper-V Manager MMC is designed to manage a single Hyper-V server at a time, System Center Virtual Machine Manager (SCVMM) 2008 is designed to manage a pool of Hyper-V servers from a single console. SCVMM consists of multiple components that work together to provide that single console interface. The components can be installed on a single server or distributed to multiple servers depending on load and requirements.

The SCVMM components include:

- Virtual Machine Manager (VMM) server
- Virtual Machine Manager Library
- Virtual Machine Manager Administrator Console
- Virtual Machine Manager Self-Service Portal
- Virtual Machine Manager database
- Virtual Machine Manager Agent

Virtual Machine Manager Server

The Virtual Machine Manager (VMM) server is the central management engine for SCVMM. It provides the commands, the command processing, and the ability to transfer files, and it controls communications between the other VMM components. It also communicates with all virtual machine hosts and VMM Library servers via the VMM installed agent.

Virtual Machine Manager Library

The VMM Library is a central repository for reusable objects (virtual hard disks, virtual floppy disks, ISO images, and scripts). These objects are represented by files and are maintained in a library share for download by Hyper-V servers. In addition, the VMM Library stores virtual machine templates, hardware profiles, and guest operating system profiles, which are used in creating virtual machines. These configurations are stored in the Virtual Machine Manager database but are not represented by physical configuration files in the library share. By default, an SCVMM installation must have a single VMM Library. This is installed with the VMM server. You can also create and register additional VMM Library servers.

Virtual Machine Manager Administrator Console

The VMM Administrator Console (shown in Figure 10-3) is the main GUI that you use to:

- Create, deploy, and manage virtual machines.
- Monitor and manage hosts and library servers.
- Manage global configuration settings.
- Manage security access

The VMM Administrator Console is installed after the VMM server and then connected to the VMM server to manage it. You can install the VMM Administrator Console on the same computer as the VMM server or on a different computer. The VMM Administrator Console can be used to connect to and manage any VMM server, but it can connect to and manage only one VMM server at a time. The VMM Administrator Console can manage a pool of individual Hyper-V servers and one or more Hyper-V host clusters running Failover Clustering (up to 16 nodes per cluster).

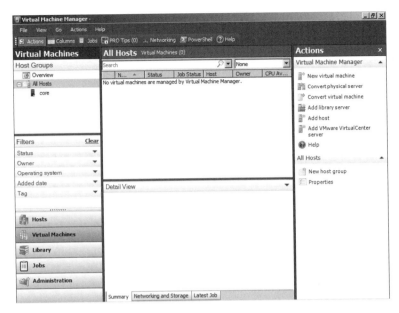

FIGURE 10-3 SCVMM Administrator Console

The VMM Administrator Console is built on top of a set of Windows PowerShell cmd-lets. When you install the VMM Administrator Console, the installation setup also installs a shortcut to a custom Windows PowerShell environment called the Virtual Machine Manager command shell. Using the VMM command shell, you can use the command line to enter commands that allow you to execute all management functions that you can perform within the VMM Administrator Console.

Virtual Machine Manager Self-Service Portal

The VMM Self-Service Portal is an optional Web portal that allows users to create and manage their own virtual machines. The Web portal utilizes administrator-defined user roles that determine the scope of the users' actions on their own virtual machines. In addition, the Web portal can be limited to only manage a set of Hyper-V servers. When a self-service user creates a virtual machine, the virtual machine is automatically placed on the most suitable host in the host group based on host ratings. A VMM administrator can set a virtual machine quota in a self-service user role and assign quota points to virtual machine templates to limit the number of virtual machines that a user or group can deploy.

Virtual Machine Manager Database

The Virtual Machine Manager database stores all VMM configuration information, library information, and job status information. The VMM database requires Microsoft SQL Server 2005 SP2 or newer. You can either specify a local or remote instance of an existing Microsoft SQL Server database or have the Setup Wizard install SQL Server 2005 Express Edition SP2 on the VMM server. Although VMM supports using SQL Server 2005 Express Edition SP2, it is recommended that for managing more than 150 hosts or integrating with Operations Manager 2007, you should use SQL Server 2005 SP2 Standard or Enterprise edition.

Virtual Machine Manager Agent

Every Hyper-V server or library server must have the VMM Agent installed in order for the VMM Administrator Console to manage the server. The VMM Agent can be installed from the VMM CD, or it can be pushed and installed as part of the registration process for a Hyper-V server. The agent provides the communications path between the Hyper-V server and the VMM Administrator Console.

Additional SCVMM Components

In addition to the main components described in the previous sections, SCVMM also provides the ability to perform physical to virtual (P2V) machine migrations or virtual machine to virtual machine (V2V) migrations. The physical to virtual machine migrations can be performed online or offline. When performed online, the source physical computer remains running and VSS snapshots are used to migrate the current state of the physical machine to a virtual machine. This restricts the online P2V migrations to operating systems that have VSS support.

Offline P2V migrations require the source physical machine to be powered off. The physical machine is then booted from a customized WinPE boot image and the migration is performed. This allows the WinPE image to have complete access to the disks on the physical computer. During the migration process, the changes in hardware from the physical machine to the virtual machine are made automatically. Offline P2V is the default mode for converting source machines with the Windows Server 2000 operating system. It is the only method to reliably convert an Active Directory domain controller or a source machine that contains FAT volumes.

Virtual to virtual migrations allow for migration of VMWare virtual machines to Hyper-V virtual machines. V2V migrations can be performed from a virtual machine managed by VMWare ESX server or from a VMWare virtual machine that is stored in the VMM library. VMWare virtual machines must be using the .vmdk storage format to be migrated. Virtual machines also must be running a Hyper-V–supported guest operating system for the migration to be successful.

New Features in SCVMM 2008 R2

Rakesh Malhotra, Principal Group Program Manager
System Center Virtual Machine Manager Team

System Center Virtual Machine Manager 2008 R2 provides features that enable new management scenarios, address customer and partner concerns, and enable support for Windows Server 2008 R2. New features include support for the following:

- **Live Migration** Management of the Live Migration feature of Hyper-V R2 for both planned and unplanned downtime scenarios.

- **Multiple virtual machines per LUN** Utilizing the Cluster Shared Volumes (CSV) feature of Windows Server 2008 R2, VMM R2 allows multiple virtual machines to reside on the same CSV-enabled logical unit number (LUN). In this configuration, a virtual machine can be migrated independently from the others residing on the same LUN.

- **SAN migration in and out of clusters** With VMM R2, you can migrate a virtual machine from one cluster to another, or from a stand-alone host into a cluster or vice versa.

- **Networking enhancements in Hyper-V R2** Hyper-V R2 provides support for TCP/IP chimney and Virtual Machine Queues (VMQ), reusing VMware port groups, and gives you the ability to enable/disable MAC spoofing on a per virtual machine basis.

- **Maintenance Mode** VMM R2 supports the concept of host maintenance mode. When a managed host is put into maintenance mode and the host supports live migration, then the virtual machines are live migrated off the server to another host. If the host does not support live migration, then the virtual machines can be placed in saved state.

- **Disjoint Domains** VMM 2008 R2 automatically creates custom SPN for DNS name when the host has a different fully qualified domain name in Active Directory and DNS.

Disaster Recovery Management Solutions

Disaster recovery management solutions provide the ability to back up and recover from planned or unplanned failure of the Hyper-V parent partition, the virtual machines, or both. Backing up or recovering the Hyper-V parent partition focuses on the configuration of the Hyper-V parent partition settings, InitialStore.xml security files, and system state. Backing up or restoring virtual machines involves the operating system, applications, and system state. Backing up or restoring the combination of the Hyper-V parent partition and the virtual machines involves the virtual machine configuration, save states, snapshots, dependent virtual hard drives, and the Hyper-V parent partition configuration.

Microsoft provides two primary disaster recovery management solutions: Windows Server Backup and System Center Data Protection Manager 2007 SP1.

Windows Server Backup

Windows Server Backup (WSB) is the backup disaster recovery solution provided with Windows Server 2008. Windows Server Backup uses an MMC user interface or a command-line tool (WBAdmin.exe) to provide access to the backup and restore features. Figure 10-4 shows the default console of the Windows Server Backup MMC.

FIGURE 10-4 Windows Server Backup

Windows Server Backup has the following restrictions:

- Backup is at the volume level.
- The volume being backed up must be locally attached.

- The volume must be formatted as NTFS.
- Backup to tape is not supported.
- Backups can be stored on internal or external disks, DVDs, and shared folders.
- Application-specific restore requires a custom VSS Writer.

Windows Server Backup only provides the ability to back up individual volumes or the entire system, but it allows you to restore files, folders, applications, entire volumes, or the complete system (as shown in Figure 10-5).

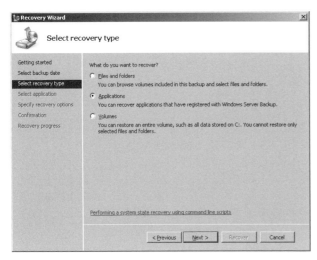

FIGURE 10-5 Windows Server Backup recovery options

The ability to restore files, folders, and volumes is included in Windows Server Backup as a standard feature. Restoring applications, however, requires a custom Volume Shadow Copy Service (VSS) Writer to provide specialized instructions on how to flush the contents of application memory to disk and back up the application state and files. This allows the application to ensure that there are no lost memory contents or pending disk writes.

Hyper-V installs a custom VSS Writer that understands how to back up and restore the Hyper-V configuration and virtual machines. In order to allow WSB to restore specific Hyper-V information and virtual machines, the Hyper-V VSS Writer must be registered with Windows Server Backup. After it is registered, WSB can restore the Hyper-V configuration, the Initial-Store.xml security file, and virtual machines.

Whereas a Hyper-V server must be backed up at the volume level, restoring the Hyper-V application will restore the Hyper-V InitialStore.xml security file and the virtual machines in the backup. During restore, you have an option to restore the files to the original location or an alternate location, as shown in Figure 10-6. If you restore to the original location, all existing files will be overwritten.

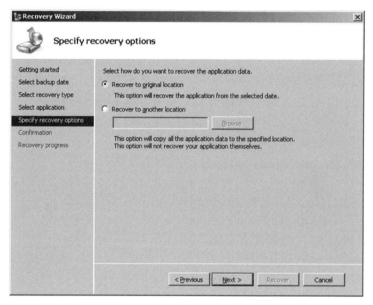

FIGURE 10-6 Recover location options

To restore individual files within a virtual machine, you must first restore the entire virtual machine to an alternate location, mount the virtual hard drive on the host file system, and then copy the desired individual files.

> **NOTE** Windows Server Backup snap-in is not included with Server Core installs of Windows Server 2008 or Microsoft Hyper-V Server 2008. You must use the command-line tool or back up the system remotely.

System Center Data Protection Manager 2007 SP1

System Center Data Protection Manager (DPM) 2007 SP1 is Microsoft's premier data backup and recovery application for Hyper-V. In addition, DPM also supports backup and recovery of file services, Windows SharePoint Services (WSS) and Microsoft Office SharePoint Server (MOSS), Exchange Server, SQL Server, workstations running Windows XP or Windows Vista, and Virtual Server 2005 R2 SP1. Figure 10-7 provides an overview diagram of the functionality in DPM SP1.

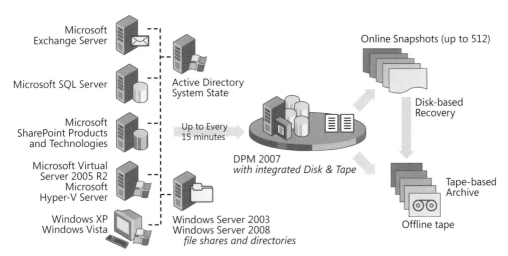

FIGURE 10-7 DPM backup functionality overview

DPM 2007 SP1 supports the following scenarios for Hyper-V when the DPM agent is installed on the Hyper-V server:

- Online backup of virtual machines running Windows operating systems that support VSS (Windows Vista, Windows Server 2003, and Windows Server 2008)

- Online backup of Hyper-V servers

- Offline backup of virtual machines running older Windows operating systems that do not support VSS (Windows 2000, Windows XP, Windows NT4), and Linux

- Online backup of clustered Hyper-V servers

For any of these backup scenarios, the virtual hard disks must be stored local to the Hyper-V server. Direct attached storage (DAS), Storage Area Networks (SAN), and iSCSI-based disks attached using the host iSCSI initiator are all supported. Virtual machines with storage attached using an iSCSI initiator, pass-through disks, or stored remotely on a share are not seen from the Hyper-V server and cannot be backed up using DPM.

DPM 2007 SP1 also supports the following scenario for Hyper-V when the DPM agent is installed in the virtual machine:

- Online backup of virtual machines files, folders, and applications

Using this scenario, virtual machine storage that is locally attached, connected via the iSCSI initiator in the virtual machine, pass-through disks, or stored on remote shares are all supported.

DPM can be deployed as an enterprise-wide backup solution or a local backup solution. DPM uses disk storage as the first level backup storage and then uses tape as the archival storage method. DPM must have complete control over the disk storage that it uses. Storage must be presented as initialized but offline storage to the DPM server. Storage is imported to the DPM console and automatically managed by DPM to create storage replicas. DPM uses single instance store technology to reduce the storage requirements of backed-up files.

DPM SP1 can be installed on a dedicated server to protect remote Hyper-V servers, or it can be installed directly on the Hyper-V server to protect it locally. Even though DPM uses delta change backup technology to reduce the amount of traffic it sends over the network during a backup, in very low bandwidth branch office situations, it might make more sense to install DPM SP1 on the local Hyper-V server. Having DPM installed locally allows all the backup data to be stored locally to the branch office, making disaster recovery a much faster process.

DPM SP1 can be used in a distributed fashion to protect itself. A central DPM SP1 server can be installed and used to back up and recover distributed DPM servers. This allows for DPM servers to be placed closer to the servers they protect, enabling faster backup and re-covery, while the DPM server is being protected from a central location.

Monitoring Solutions

Monitoring solutions provide you with the ability to investigate and obtain warnings about potential health issues with the physical host, the Hyper-V parent partition, and child parti-tions. Monitoring the physical host focuses on environmental issues such as temperature, power, and uptime. Monitoring the Hyper-V parent partition focuses on logical processors, system memory usage, system storage performance, system networking performance, the Windows hypervisor, and parent partition services. Monitoring the child partitions involves focusing on the allocated virtual hardware (virtual processors, memory, storage, and network adapters) and the services and applications running in the child partition.

Microsoft provides two primary monitoring solutions: the Reliability and Performance Monitor and System Center Operations Manager 2007.

Reliability and Performance Monitor

The Reliability and Performance Monitor comes standard with full installations of Windows Server 2008. It is an MMC-based application that can monitor the local system or a remote system. The Reliability and Performance Monitor is two tools in one. Reliability Monitor pro-vides information about system stability and the events that impact reliability, and Perfor-mance Monitor provides detailed real-time performance information on system components, services, and applications.

Reliability Monitor tracks the history of events like software installation, application failures, hardware failures, operating system failures, and many other miscellaneous failures. Data is presented in two forms, the System Stability Chart and the System Stability Report. As shown in Figure 10-8, the System Stability Chart displays events over the last 30 days and provides an index value that ranges from 1 (least stable) to 10 (most stable). The Stability Index is a weighted measurement derived from the number of specified failures seen over a rolling historical period. The System Stability Report provides the details on the actual events or failures, the activity that happened, the status, and the date that it occurred.

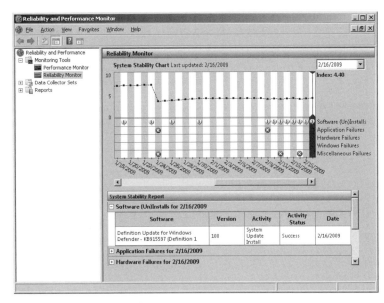

FIGURE 10-8 Reliability Monitor

Performance Monitor can operate in two modes: real-time data capture and logged data capture. As shown in Figure 10-9, real-time data capture allows you to see the real-time performance information on selected performance counters. Performance counters are defined by the operating system, application, or service.

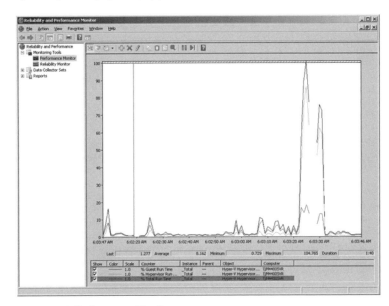

FIGURE 10-9 Performance Monitor

Counters are organized into groups, and a counter can provide a system performance number or it can consist of multiple instances. For example, if you look at the performance counter group called LogicalDisk, you will see a list of 23 counters defined. Figure 10-10 shows the LogicalDisk counter group in the Add Counters dialog box. If you select a counter in the list, an individual counter instance is created for each drive in your computer as well as one called Total and one called <All Instances>. In Figure 10-10, we selected the % Disk Read Time counter and the C: instance of that counter. In Performance Monitor, that counter would display the percentage of time that the system is reading data from drive C.

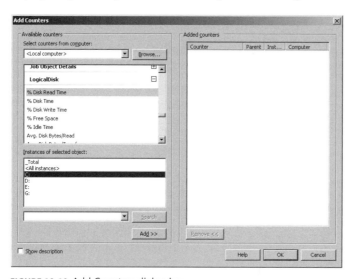

FIGURE 10-10 Add Counters dialog box

Hyper-V contains a long list of performance counter groups, each with selectable detailed counters. The following list provides the available performance counter groups for Hyper-V:

- Hyper-V Hypervisor
- Hyper-V Hypervisor Logical Processor
- Hyper-V Hypervisor Partition
- Hyper-V Hypervisor Root Partition
- Hyper-V Hypervisor Root Virtual Processor
- Hyper-V Hypervisor Virtual Processor
- Hyper-V Legacy Network Adapter
- Hyper-V Task Manager Detail
- Hyper-V Virtual IDE Controller
- Hyper-V Virtual Machine Bus
- Hyper-V Virtual Machine Health Summary
- Hyper-V Virtual Machine Summary

- Hyper-V Virtual Network Adapter
- Hyper-V Virtual Storage Device
- Hyper-V Virtual Switch
- Hyper-V Virtual Switch Port
- Hyper-V VM IO APIC
- Hyper-V VM Remoting
- Hyper-V VM Save, Snapshot, and Restore
- Hyper-V VM VID Driver
- Hyper-V VM VID Message Queue
- Hyper-V VM VID NUMA Node
- Hyper-V VM VID Partition
- Hyper-V VM Worker Process Manager

The data logging feature of Performance Monitor allows you to capture a historical view instead of a real-time view of available performance counters. In real-time collection mode, the data graph will overwrite the last set of data based on how fast you are collecting data. In order to maintain a history of the collected data, you must use the data logging mode.

System Center Operations Manager 2007

System Center Operations Manager 2007 is Microsoft's enterprise hardware, operating system, services, and application monitoring solution. Operations Manager 2007 uses an agent-based data collection mechanism to gather information from remote systems and store that data in a SQL database for analysis. Data collection configuration is based on the concept of a *management pack*. Management packs contain the rules, monitors, and tasks for a specific application, operating system, or hardware.

Rules define how to collect data from various sources, such as Perfmon, EventLog, SNMP, and log files. That data is then stored in the Operations Manager database and used for reporting purposes. Monitors are state machines that define the health of what is being monitored. Monitors can be in one of two states (green or red) or in one of three states (green, yellow, and red). The monitor's state changes in response to the monitoring information. Monitors can define thresholds to watch for in data that rules collect and then take actions based on the threshold being violated. For example, a monitor could be defined that looks at the network throughput of a virtual machine, and if it exceeds a specific throughput value, a yellow state (warning) is triggered and an alert is sent to the Operations Manager 2007 Operations Console. A task is a user-initiated action from the Operations Manager 2007 Operations Console that is run on a remote server via an Operations Manager agent. Pre-built tasks are defined in management packs and you have the ability to define additional custom tasks.

When monitoring a Hyper-V infrastructure with System Center Operations Manager 2007 SP1, your ability to maintain a healthy system will be based on the management packs that you import and utilize. At a minimum, you will need the latest Windows Server Base Operating System management pack that includes support for Windows Server 2008. This will allow you to monitor the availability and performance of the operating system, services, storage, networking, processor, and memory.

The tools you need to monitor Hyper-V servers, virtual machines, and SCVMM 2008 servers have been combined into a single management pack, the System Center Virtual Machine 2008 management pack. This management pack provides you with the ability to monitor and provide reports on Virtual Server 2005 R2, Hyper-V, and VMware ESX servers.

NOTE In order to monitor VMWare ESX servers, they must be SCVMM 2008 managed hosts.

The SCVMM 2008 management pack monitors Hyper-V server performance for storage, memory, processor, physical network, virtual network, and things like the number of virtual machines. The SCVMM 2008 management pack also monitors virtual machine performance for virtual processors, virtual hard disks and pass-through disks, virtual machine memory utilization, and virtual networks. This can be done with the Operations Manager 2007 agent loaded on the Hyper-V server. If you also install the Operations Manager 2007 agent inside the virtual machine, you can get application performance information if the associated management pack for the application has been imported into Operations Manager 2007.

The SCVMM 2008 management pack provides updated monitoring, rules, and reports:

- **VM Utilization Report**   Provides utilization information about your virtual machines. For the selected time period, this report shows average usage and total or maximums for virtual machine processors, memory, and disk space.
- **Host Utilization Report**   Displays the number of virtual machines running per host. For the selected time period and host group, this report shows average, total, and maximum utilization for host processors, memory, and disk space.
- **Virtualization Candidates Report**   Helps identify physical computers that are good candidates for conversion to virtual machines. The report displays average values for a defined set of performance counters for CPU, memory, and disk usage, along with hardware configuration, including processor speed, number of processors, and total RAM.
- **Host Utilization Growth Report**   Shows the percentage growth of host resources and the number of virtual machines running for the selected time period.
- **VM Allocation**   Provides information you can use to calculate chargeback to cost centers for virtual machines.

An advanced capability enabled by integrating System Center Virtual Machine Manager 2008 and System Center Operations Manager 2007 SP1 is Performance and Resource Optimization (PRO). Performance and Resource Optimization is a feature of Virtual Machine Manager that utilizes performance information from Operations Manager 2007 to help customers ensure that their virtual machine infrastructure is operating in an ideal and efficient manner. Extending the monitoring capabilities of System Center Operations Manager 2007, PRO enables administrators to respond to poor performance of failures of virtualized hardware, operating systems, or applications.

PRO provides two response options: The first involves surfacing alerts that a problem exists and providing a recommended mitigation solution. The administrator has the ability to implement the recommended mitigation with a single button click. The mitigation might involve a built-in action that migrates virtual machines from a Hyper-V server that has exceeded a defined processor utilization threshold to another Hyper-V server. PRO can be extended with custom actions that could, for example, use Wake-on-LAN to wake up a pre-built standby Hyper-V server, enabling you to dynamically expand the pool to meet new demand. The second response option is for the system to automatically implement the recommended action with no interaction from the administrator.

Summary

This chapter provided an overview of the products and technologies that can be combined to provide a comprehensive management solution for Hyper-V and virtual machines. The products were presented in three groups: management solutions, disaster recovery solutions, and monitoring solutions.

You saw that there are tools that ship with the operating system for each function as well as enterprise tools that greatly expand on the features and functionality available in the built-in tools. If you are going to manage a small number of Hyper-V servers or a small number of virtual machines, then the tools that come with the operating system can be great places to start. As your virtualization infrastructure grows, however, you will want to augment the built-in tools with the System Center suite of tools. The following chapters will provide a more in-depth look at managing a single server versus multiple servers, full disaster recovery scenarios, and monitoring.

Additional Resources

The following resources contain additional information related to the topics in this chapter.

- System Center Data Protection Manager 2007, a resource that provides access to the product, technical, and installation information for System Center Data Protection Manager 2007, available at *http://www.microsoft.com/systemcenter /dataprotectionmanager/en/us/default.aspx*

- System Center Virtual Machine Manager 2008, a resource that provides access to the product, technical, and installation information for System Center Virtual Machine Manager 2008, available at *http://www.microsoft.com/systemcenter /virtualmachinemanager/en/us/default.aspx*

- System Center Operations Manager 2007, a resource that provides access to the product, technical, and installation information for System Center Operations Manager 2007, available at *http://www.microsoft.com/systemcenter/operationsmanager/en/us /default.aspx*

- System Center Virtual Machine Manager 2008 Management Pack, a resource that provides information for the System Center Virtual Machine Manager 2008 management pack, available at *http://www.microsoft.com/downloads /details.aspx?FamilyID=d6d5cddd-4ec8-4e3c-8ab1-102ec99c257f&displaylang=en*

- Hyper-V Management Tools for Vista x86, a resource that provides access to the Vista 32-bit version of the Hyper-V administration client, available at *http://www.microsoft.com/downloads/details.aspx?familyid=BF909242-2125-4D06 -A968-C8A3D75FF2AA&displaylang=en*

- Hyper-V Management Tools for Vista x64, a resource that provides access to the Vista 64-bit version of the Hyper-V administration client, available at *http://www.microsoft.com/downloads/details.aspx?FamilyID=88208468-0ad6 -47de-8580-085cba42c0c2&DisplayLang=en*

Hyper-V Single Server Management

In this chapter, you will learn how to use the tools that are included with Windows Server 2008 Hyper-V to perform daily management tasks. We'll cover three main topics: Hyper-V and virtual machine management, disaster recovery, and performance monitoring. The tools include the Hyper-V Manager MMC (also referred to as the Hyper-V Manager or the Hyper-V Manager console), Windows Server Backup, and the Reliability and Performance Monitor. In particular, you will review Hyper-V and virtual machine configuration options and learn the step-by-step procedure to create and manage a new virtual machine using the Hyper-V Manager MMC. The procedure includes defining the virtual machine configuration, creating a virtual hard disk (VHD), connecting to a virtual network, tuning the virtual machine configuration, installing a guest operating system, and installing Integration Services to enhance performance and functionality. Additionally, you will learn the options and procedures to back up and recover Hyper-V as well as virtual machines using Windows Server Backup. Finally, you will gain an understanding of how to use the Reliability and Performance Monitor to collect information on the health and performance of your Hyper-V Server and virtual machine resources.

Managing Hyper-V

When you add the Hyper-V role on a full installation of Windows Server 2008, the Hyper-V Manager MMC is installed and provides the primary graphical user interface (GUI) to manage Hyper-V and virtual machines. On a Windows Server 2008 Server Core or Hyper-V Server 2008 installation, there is only a command-line interface, so the Hyper-V Manager MMC is not installed during the Hyper-V role setup. In order to manage Hyper-V on Windows Server 2008 Server Core or Hyper-V Server 2008, you must install the Hyper-V Manager MMC on another Windows Server 2008 system or on a Windows Vista Service Pack 1 (SP1) workstation.

Installing the Hyper-V Management Tools

Use the following steps to enable the Remote Server Administration Tools (RSAT) Hyper-V Tools feature on a Windows Server 2008 full installation without the Hyper-V role:

1. Open Server Manager.

2. In Server Manager, select the Features node in the left pane. In the right pane, the Features Summary lists features that are currently installed on the server and provides the option to add and remove features, as shown in Figure 11-1.

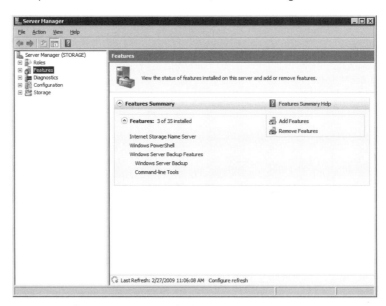

FIGURE 11-1 The Features Summary list in Server Manager

3. Click Add Features to launch the Add Features Wizard.

4. On the Select Features page, expand Remote Server Administration Tools (see Figure 11-2).

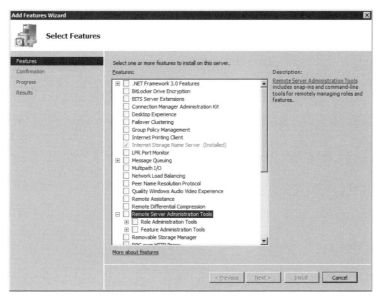

FIGURE 11-2 The Remote Server Administration Tools feature

5. Expand the Role Administration Tools, select Hyper-V Tools (see Figure 11-3), and then click Next.

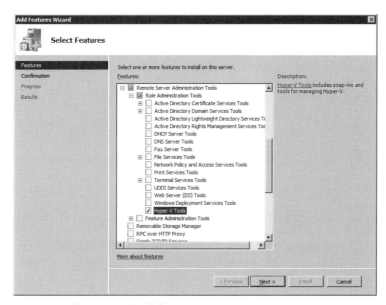

FIGURE 11-3 The Hyper-V Tools feature

6. On the Confirm Installation Selections page, shown in Figure 11-4, review the information, and then click Install.

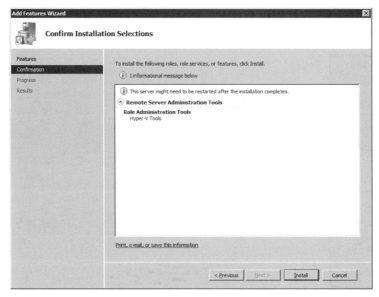

FIGURE 11-4 The Confirm Installation Selections page

7. On the Installation Results page, shown in Figure 11-5, click Close.

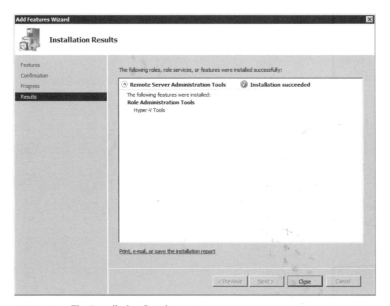

FIGURE 11-5 The Installation Results page

8. After the Add Features Wizard closes, the Features Summary reflects the availability of the Hyper-V Tools (see Figure 11-6).

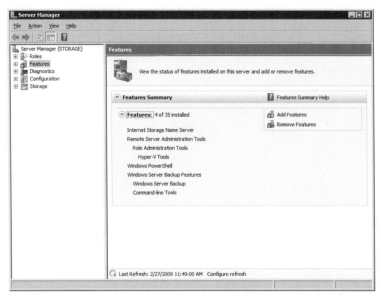

FIGURE 11-6 The Features Summary in Server Manager

The RSAT Hyper-V Tools are installed in the %SystemDrive%\Program Files\Hyper-V folder and include the Hyper-V Manager (Virtmgmt.msc) as well as the Virtual Machine Connection application (Vmconnect.exe).

> **NOTE** To install the RSAT Hyper-V Tools from the command line, type **ocsetup Microsoft-Hyper-V-Management-Clients**.

You can also install the Hyper-V Tools on an x86 or x64 version of a Windows Vista SP1 workstation. These are contained in a Hyper-V remote management package (KB 952627). Just like Windows Server 2008, the Windows Vista SP1 version of the tools supports remote management of one or more Hyper-V servers.

> **NOTE** You can download the Hyper-V remote management update for Windows Vista x64 SP1 from the Microsoft Web site at *http://www.microsoft.com/DownLoads /details.aspx?familyid=88208468-0AD6-47DE-8580-085CBA42C0C2*.

Use the following steps to install the Hyper-V remote management update on a Windows Vista SP1 workstation:

1. Launch the Hyper-V remote management update installation (see Figure 11-7).

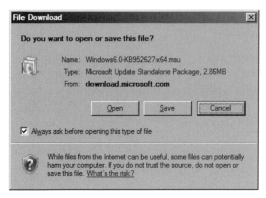

FIGURE 11-7 Download and launch the Hyper-V remote management update installation.

2. In the Windows Update Standalone Installer dialog box (Figure 11-8), click OK.

FIGURE 11-8 The Windows Update Standalone Installer dialog box

3. The update package installs the Hyper-V remote management update tools in the %SystemDrive%\Program Files\Hyper-V folder.

4. After the installation completes (shown in Figure 11-9), click Close.

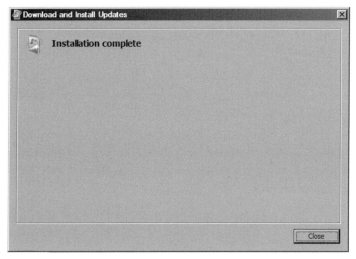

FIGURE 11-9 Hyper-V remote management update installation complete

A shortcut to the Hyper-V Manager MMC is added in the Administrative Tools menu and in the Administrative Tools control panel applet.

> **NOTE** By default, an Administrative Tools link is not included in the Windows Vista Start Menu. To enable the Start Menu links, right-click Start and select Properties. On the Start Menu tab, click Customize and select Display On The All Programs Menu And The Start Menu under System Administrative Tools, and then click OK twice to close the Taskbar And Start Menu Properties dialog box.

Enabling Remote Management

In addition to the installation of the Hyper-V management tools on a remote system, you have to configure the Hyper-V server to allow remote management. If you do not, you will be unable to connect to the Hyper-V server from your remote system. In particular, when you open the Hyper-V Manager MMC and try to connect to the server, you will get the following error: "You do not have the required permission to complete this task. Contact the administrator of the authorization policy for the computer 'COMPUTERNAME'."

Configuring remote management is a multistep process that involves modifying settings on the Hyper-V server that you want to manage as well as on the client workstation that hosts the management tools. One of the most common scenarios is managing a domain-joined Hyper-V server from a Windows Vista SP1 workstation that is joined to the same domain, without using an account with Domain Admin privileges. In this case, there are four major configuration steps:

- Create a domain account for Hyper-V management.
- Configure Authorization Manager policy.
- Configure Distributed Component Object Model (DCOM) settings.
- Configure Windows Management Instrumentation (WMI) settings.

Follow these steps to enable remote management of a Hyper-V server from a domain-joined Windows Vista SP1 workstation using an account without Domain Admin privileges:

1. Using a remote desktop connection to your domain controller, or Active Directory RSAT tools installed on your Windows Vista SP1 workstation, open the Active Directory Users And Computers console and create a domain account named HyperVMgr.

2. Log in to the Hyper-V server using an account with Domain Admin credentials and open the Authorization Manager console, as shown in Figure 11-10.

FIGURE 11-10 Opening the Authorization Manager console from the Start menu

3. In the Authorization Manager console, right-click Authorization Manager in the left pane and select Open Authorization Store, as shown in Figure 11-11.

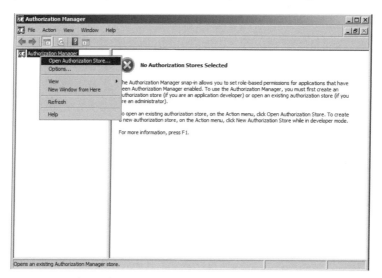

FIGURE 11-11 The Authorization Manager console

4. In the Open Authorization Store dialog box (shown in Figure 11-12), select XML File, type **C:\ProgramData\Microsoft\Windows\Hyper-V\InitialStore.xml** in the Store Name text box, and then click OK.

FIGURE 11-12 The Open Authorization Store dialog box

5. Expand the Hyper-V Services node in the left pane and then expand the Role Assignments node (see Figure 11-13).

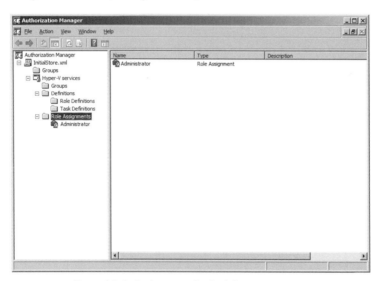

FIGURE 11-13 Expand Role Assignments in the left pane.

6. Right-click Administrator, select Assign Users And Groups, and then select From Windows And Active Directory, as shown in Figure 11-14.

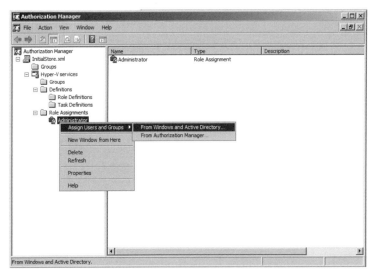

FIGURE 11-14 Users and Groups selection from Windows And Active Directory

7. In the Select Users, Computers, Or Groups dialog box (see Figure 11-15), type **HyperVMgr**, click Check Names, and then click OK.

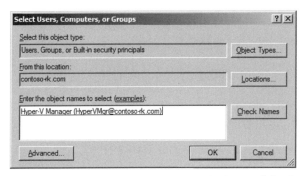

FIGURE 11-15 The Select Users, Computers, Or Groups dialog box

8. The HyperVMgr domain account is now a member of the Administrator role (see Figure 11-16), which allows it to manage Hyper-V and virtual machine resources. However, it does not provide the HyperVMgr any rights to manage other server resources, nor does it make HyperVMgr a member of the local administrator group.

> **NOTE** Based on your management and security policies, you may not want to add the HyperVMgr account to the default Administrator role. It is possible to create new role definitions and assignments in Authorization Manager. Refer to Chapter 6, "Hyper-V Security," to learn how to do this.

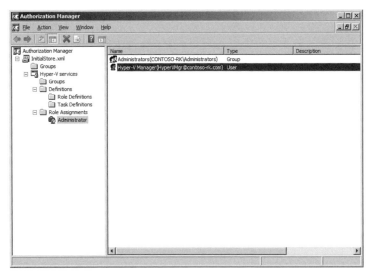

FIGURE 11-16 HyperVMgr domain account listed as a member of the Administrator role

9. Close the Authorization Manager console.

10. Open the Server Manager console, expand Configuration (left pane), expand Local Users And Groups, select Groups, and then select Distributed COM Users (see Figure 11-17).

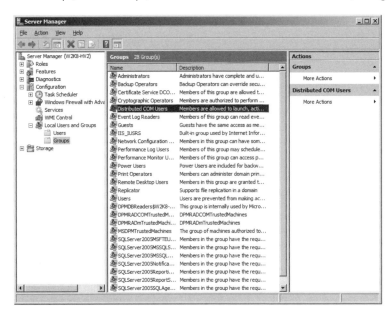

FIGURE 11-17 Select Distributed COM Users from Local Users And Groups

11. Right-click Distributed COM Users and select Add To Group.

12. In the Distributed COM Users Properties dialog box (shown in Figure 11-18), click Add.

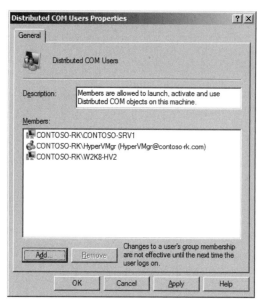

FIGURE 11-18 The Distributed COM Users Properties dialog box

13. In the Select Users, Computers, Or Groups dialog box, type **HyperVMgr**, select Check Names, and then click OK.

14. In the Distributed COM Users Properties dialog box, click OK.

15. In Server Manager, expand Configuration (in the left pane) and then select WMI Control (see Figure 11-19).

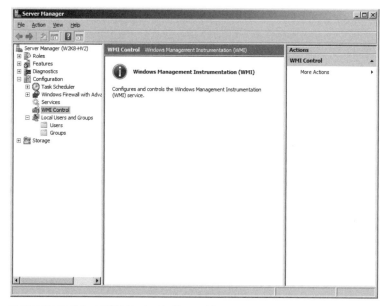

FIGURE 11-19 Select WMI Control in Server Manager.

16. Right-click WMI Control, select Properties, and then select the Security tab in the WMI Control Properties dialog box (see Figure 11-20).

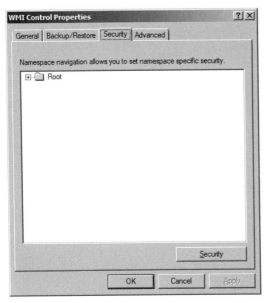

FIGURE 11-20 The Security tab of the WMI Control Properties dialog box

17. Expand Root, select CIMV2, and then click Security.

18. In the Security For ROOT\CIMV2 dialog box (see Figure 11-21), click Add and add the HyperVMgr domain account with default permissions.

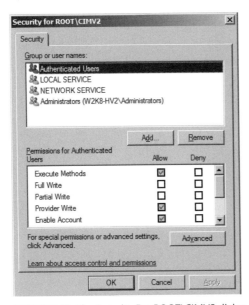

FIGURE 11-21 The Security For ROOT\CIMV2 dialog box

19. Back in the Security For ROOT\CIMV2 dialog box, select the HyperVMgr user name in the top pane and then click Advanced.

20. In the Advanced Security Settings For CIMV2 dialog box (see Figure 11-22), select the HyperVMgr user name and then click Edit.

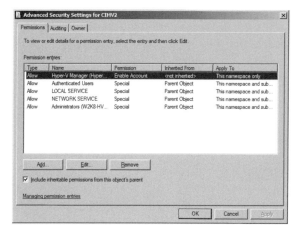

FIGURE 11-22 The Advanced Security Settings For CIMV2 dialog box

21. In the Permission Entry For CIMV2 dialog box, select This Namespace And Sub-namespaces from the Apply To drop-down box.

22. In Permissions, in the Allow column, select Remote Enable, and then select the option to Apply These Permissions To Objects And/Or Containers Within This Container Only (see Figure 11-23).

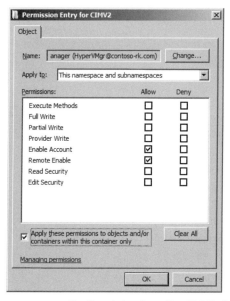

FIGURE 11-23 The Permission Entry For CIMV2 dialog box

23. Click OK three times to return to the WMI Control Properties dialog box.

24. In WMI Control Properties, under Root, select Virtualization and then click Security (see Figure 11-24).

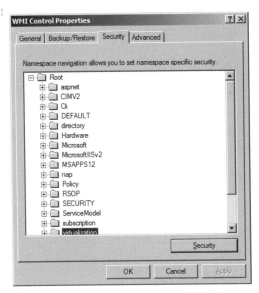

FIGURE 11-24 WMI Control Properties dialog box

25. Repeat steps 18 through 23 to allow remote management of the Virtualization namespace.

26. Click OK to close the WMI Control Properties dialog box.

27. Close Server Manager and then restart the Hyper-V server.

After the Hyper-V server restarts, you can log in to the Windows Vista SP1 workstation using the HyperVMgr user account, open the Hyper-V Manager MMC, and connect to the Hyper-V server with full rights to manage it as well as all virtual machines.

> **BEST PRACTICES** For the purpose of this example, a single domain account was assigned to the default Hyper-V Services scope Administrator role in Authorization Manager. However, you should create new Hyper-V roles tailored to the management job functions defined in your environment. Then, create new security groups and use the well-documented group nesting model for new Hyper-V role assignments. For example, within a single domain, create a new global group (such as Hyper-V Admins – GG to designate a global group) and add the target user accounts to the group. Then, create a domain local group (such as Hyper-V Local Admins – DLG to designate a domain local group) and nest the global group into it. Finally, use the domain local group in new Hyper-V role assignments.

HVRemote Configuration Script

John Howard, Senior Program Manager
Hyper-V Team, Windows Core Operating System Division

Setting up Hyper-V remote management when both the Hyper-V server and client are in the same domain is a relatively straightforward procedure. The steps involved become more complex when one or both machines are in workgroups. To simplify the configuration process, HVRemote is a script that applies the required settings to quickly configure the Hyper-V server and the client machine. It is written in VBScript, as this is a common scripting platform available on all Windows platforms.

HVRemote Server Support

HVRemote supports the following Hyper-V configurations:

- Windows Server 2008 with the Hyper-V role enabled, including Server Core and full installations
- Microsoft Hyper-V Server 2008
- Windows Server 2008 R2 with the Hyper-V role enabled, including Server Core and full installations
- Microsoft Hyper-V Server 2008 R2

HVRemote Client Support

HVRemote supports the following client operating systems:

- Windows Server 2008 x86 full installation
- Windows Server 2008 x64 full installations (both with and without the Hyper-V role enabled)
- Windows Vista SP1 (Business, Enterprise, and Ultimate editions)
- Windows 7 Client (Professional, Enterprise, and Ultimate editions)

HVRemote Configuration Support

HVRemote supports all combinations of workgroup and domain-joined Hyper-V server and client configurations. From a configuration perspective, if the Hyper-V server and client are in domains that do not trust each other, the procedure is the same as if they were in different workgroups.

HVRemote Configuration Steps

HVRemote modifies the following settings on the Hyper-V server when adding or removing users:

- Administrator role assignment in the default Authorization Store
- Distributed COM Users group membership
- WMI security permissions to the Root\CIMV2 namespace
- WMI Security permissions to the Root\Virtualization namespace
- Windows Firewall configuration to enable Hyper-V rules Windows Firewall configuration for WMI administration rules (optional)

HVRemote modifies the following settings on the client:

- Windows Firewall exception for Microsoft Management Console
- Windows Firewall exceptions for Hyper-V Management Clients
- Anonymous DCOM access (not needed in all scenarios)

HVRemote Support

HVRemote is not an official Microsoft tool, and therefore it is not supported by Microsoft. However, it is available under the Microsoft Public License and the Creative Common Attribution 3.0 license.

> **MORE INFO** You can download HVRemote and its documentation from *http://code.msdn.microsoft.com/HVRemote*.

Customizing the Hyper-V Manager View

The Hyper-V Manager allows you to customize the view that it presents to you. By default, the Hyper-V Manager contains three panes:

- **Console Tree Pane** This pane contains a tree view of each Hyper-V server that you have connected to the Hyper-V Manager MMC.
- **Virtual Machines Pane** This pane contains details of the registered virtual machines, virtual machine snapshots, and a thumbnail of the virtual machine display.
- **Actions Pane** This pane contains the list of actions that are allowed to manage the Hyper-V server and any highlighted virtual machine.

Follow these steps to customize the Hyper-V Manager view:

1. Open Hyper-V Manager MMC.

2. In the Actions pane, click View and then select Customize (see Figure 11-25).

FIGURE 11-25 Selecting the option to customize the Hyper-V Manager view

3. In the Customize View dialog box (Figure 11-26), select or clear the MMC and Snap-in options to show or hide items in the Hyper-V Manager MMC. As you select options, you will see the changes dynamically reflected in the Hyper-V Manager MMC.

FIGURE 11-26 The Customize View dialog box

4. After you have made your selections, click OK.

5. As shown in the Hyper-V Manager view in Figure 11-27, if you hide the Console Tree and Actions panes, only the Virtual Machines pane remains.

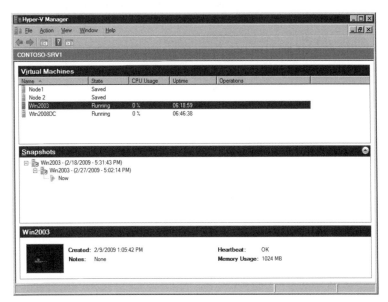

FIGURE 11-27 The Virtual Machines pane

Managing Hyper-V Settings

Table 11-1 contains a list of the Hyper-V settings that include server- and user-level configuration parameters. When you create a new virtual hard disk or virtual machine, you can override the default location defined in the Hyper-V settings.

TABLE 11-1 Hyper-V Settings

HYPER-V SETTING	DESCRIPTION
Virtual Hard Disks	This setting defines the default folder to store new virtual hard disk files.
Virtual Machines	This setting defines the default folder to store new virtual machine configuration files.
Keyboard	This setting defines how to apply Windows key combinations using the Virtual Machine Connection application. The selections are: ■ Use On The Physical Computer ■ Use On The Virtual Machine ■ Use On The Virtual Machine Only When Running Full-Screen

HYPER-V SETTING	DESCRIPTION
Mouse Release Key	This setting defines the key combination that you want to use to release the mouse if Integration Services are not installed in a virtual machine. The selections are: ■ Ctrl+Alt+Left Arrow ■ Ctrl+Alt+Right Arrow ■ Ctrl+Alt+Space ■ Ctrl+Alt+Shift
User Credentials	This setting specifies whether you want to present the credentials associated with your current Windows session by default when you create a new connection to a running virtual machine using the Virtual Machine Connection application.
Delete Saved Credentials	This setting allows you to delete credentials that were used to connect to a running virtual machine using the Virtual Machine Connection application.
Reset Check Boxes	This setting allows you to restore Hyper-V confirmation messages and wizard pages that you chose to hide previously.

Follow these steps to modify the Hyper-V settings:

1. Open the Hyper-V Manager MMC.

2. In the Actions pane, click Hyper-V Settings.

3. In the Hyper-V Settings dialog box, modify the settings that you want to configure and then click Apply.

4. After you have completed the modifications, click OK.

Changing the Virtual Machine Management Service State

From within the Hyper-V Manager, you can also choose to stop and start the Virtual Machine Management Service (VMMS). During the time that the VMMS is stopped, you will be unable to manage the Hyper-V server or any virtual machines. However, virtual machines continue to run, even though the VMMS service is stopped.

Follow these steps to stop and start the VMMS service:

1. Open the Hyper-V Manager MMC.

2. In the Actions pane, click Stop Service.

3. In the Stop Virtual Machine Management Service dialog box (see Figure 11-28), click Yes.

FIGURE 11-28 The Stop Virtual Machine Management Service dialog box

4. When the VMMS service stops, the Hyper-V Manager will refresh and indicate that the VMMS is not available, as shown in Figure 11-29.

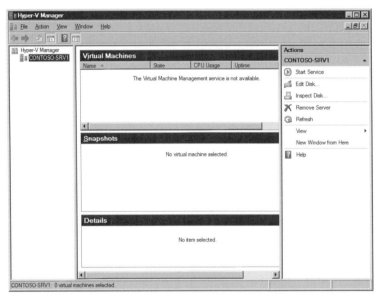

FIGURE 11-29 The VMMS is not available.

5. To restart the VMMS, in the Actions pane, click Start Service.
6. After the VMMS restarts, the Hyper-V Manager will refresh and redisplay Hyper-V resources, as shown in Figure 11-30.

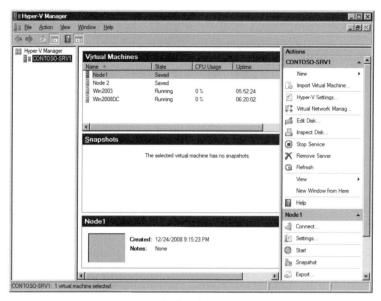

FIGURE 11-30 Hyper-V resources display after the VMMS restarts

> **NOTE** You can also stop and start the VMMS service from a command line by typing **net stop vmms** and **net start vmms**. Make sure that you execute these statements in a command window running with local administrator privileges.

Managing Virtual Machines Using the Hyper-V Manager

Creating a new virtual machine using the Hyper-V Manager is a straightforward process. However, before proceeding with the task, you should define the configuration items listed in Table 11-2. These are the basic parameters required to create a new virtual machine.

TABLE 11-2 Basic Parameters for New Virtual Machine Creation

PARAMETER	DESCRIPTION
Virtual machine name	The name to associate with the new virtual machine. This is the virtual machine name displayed in the Hyper-V Manager MMC.
Virtual machine folder	A new folder or an existing folder to store the virtual machine configuration file (.xml) as well as saved state files (.vsv and .bin). If you do not select a folder, the virtual machine is stored in the default folder specified in the Hyper-V settings.

PARAMETER	DESCRIPTION
Memory	The amount of memory to allocate to the new virtual machine, up to 32 GB (assuming Windows Server 2008 Standard Edition, otherwise the maximum memory allocation is 64 GB for the Enterprise and Datacenter editions). The memory allocation should take into consideration the amount of memory in the physical server in conjunction with the memory requirements of the parent partition and other running virtual machines.
Virtual network adapter	The virtual network to connect to the virtual machine network adapter.
	Alternatively, you can configure the virtual network adapter to remain disconnected.
Virtual hard disk	The name, storage location, and size for a new virtual hard disk. The maximum size of a virtual hard disk is 2040 GB.
	If an existing virtual hard disk should be connected to the new virtual machine, the virtual hard disk location is specified.
	Alternatively, virtual hard disk association to the new virtual machine can be deferred.
Installation options	The media to use to load a guest operating system on the new virtual machine. A guest operating system can be installed from a physical CD/DVD drive or an ISO image connected to the virtual DVD drive, using a boot floppy disk connected to the virtual floppy drive, or using a network-based installation server.
	Alternatively, installation of a guest operating system can be deferred.

After these basic parameters are defined, you can create a new virtual machine using the Hyper-V Manager MMC.

Creating a New Virtual Machine

The New Virtual Machine Wizard guides you through the process to create a new virtual machine. To create a new virtual machine, follow these steps:

1. In the Hyper-V Manager MMC Actions pane, click New and then select Virtual Machine.

2. On the Before You Begin page of the New Virtual Machine Wizard, click Next.

3. On the Specify Name And Location page, enter the virtual machine name. If you do not want to store the virtual machine in the default location, select Store The Virtual

Machine In A Different Location, enter the fully qualified path to the storage folder, and then click Next.

4. On the Assign Memory page, enter the virtual machine memory allocation in megabytes (MB). The default value reflects a minimum allocation that you should replace based on the factors listed in Table 11-2. When you are done, click Next.

5. On the Configure Networking page, select the virtual network to connect to the default virtual network adapter. If you do not want to connect the default virtual network adapter, select Not Connected. When you are done, click Next.

> **NOTE** If you plan to install an operating system that needs updates, you may want to select Not Connected or connect it to a private virtual network. This will help to ensure that the new virtual machine remains isolated until it is fully updated.

6. On the Connect Virtual Hard Disk page, you have the following choices:

   - Select Create A Virtual Hard Disk to create a new dynamically expanding virtual hard disk. Then, enter the fully qualified path to the storage folder. Finally, enter the size in gigabytes (GB) of the virtual hard disk. By default, the virtual hard disk will connect to a virtual IDE controller.

   - Select Use An Existing Virtual Hard Disk if you pre-created a virtual hard disk. Then, enter the fully qualified path and file name.

   - Select Attach A Virtual Hard Disk Later if you want to defer attaching a virtual hard disk.

7. After you have made your selection, click Next.

8. On the Installation Options page, you have the following choices:

   - Select Install An Operating System Later if you want to defer installing a guest operating system.

   - Select Install An Operating System From A Boot CD/DVD-ROM and then select the location of the installation media. This can be media in a physical CD/DVD drive or an ISO image that you connect to the default virtual DVD drive.

   - Select Install An Operating System From A Boot Floppy Disk and then specify the floppy disk image to connect to the default virtual floppy disk drive.

   - Select Install An Operating System From A Network-Based Installation Server if you want to install the guest operating system using a Pre-Execution Environment (PXE)–based method.

9. After you have made your selection, click Next.

10. On the Completing The New Virtual Machine Wizard page (shown in Figure 11-31), review your selections. If you want the virtual machine to start immediately after it is created, select Start The Virtual Machine After It Is Created, and then click Finish.

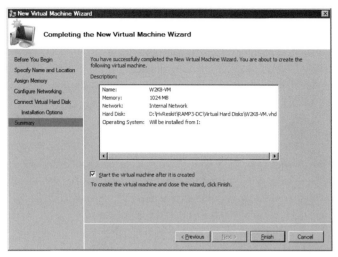

FIGURE 11-31 Hyper-V Manager New Virtual Machine Wizard summary page

The new virtual machine folder is created, as well as the virtual machine configuration file and virtual hard disk. When the new virtual hard disk is created, you will find that it is only a few kilobytes (KB) in size. Since the default new virtual hard disk type is dynamically expanding, the file contains only basic header information until an operating system is loaded. File space will be allocated to the virtual hard disk as required, up to the defined maximum size. When the configuration file and virtual hard disk are created, the virtual machine is registered, and its details appear in the Hyper-V Manager.

> **NOTE** In order to attach a fixed size or differencing virtual hard disk, use the New Virtual Hard Disk Wizard in the Hyper-V Manager (in the Actions pane, click New, then select Hard Disk) to create the virtual hard disk prior to generating the new virtual machine. Using the wizard, you can create any of the supported virtual hard disk types. When you create the new virtual machine, select the Use An Existing Virtual Hard Disk option and specify the pre-created virtual hard disk.

Tuning Virtual Machine Key Configuration Settings

When you create a new virtual machine, there are several virtual components such as the DVD drive, floppy drive, COM ports, and network adapter that are configured, some with default settings. However, you may want to tune one or more of these key components before proceeding with loading the operating system and applications in the virtual machine. In most cases when adding or removing components, the virtual machine must be powered off. Other configuration settings, such as changing a virtual DVD drive mapping or connecting a virtual network adapter to a different virtual network, can be modified even if the virtual machine is running. All of the configuration components are accessible from the virtual machine settings page in the Hyper-V Manager MMC.

Follow these steps to select and modify components using the virtual machine settings in the Hyper-V Manager MMC:

1. In the Hyper-V Manager Virtual Machines pane, right-click the virtual machine and select Settings.

2. On the Settings For page, select a component in the Hardware or Management sections to display the component details. If you want to add new virtual hardware components or modify components like the virtual machine memory or processor allocation, you can do so only if the virtual machine is powered off.

3. Click Apply to save your modifications, and then click OK to close the virtual machines settings page.

> **NOTE** It is also possible to script modifications to virtual machine configuration settings. In Chapter 16, "Hyper-V Management Using Windows PowerShell," you will learn how to develop scripts using Windows PowerShell.

Adding Virtual Hardware Devices

As workload requirements change, it may be necessary to modify or add new virtual hardware devices. Hyper-V supports adding SCSI controller and network adapter synthetic devices (ones that do not emulate a physical device), as well as legacy network adapters (a Multiport DEC 21140 emulation). Hyper-V supports up to four SCSI controllers, eight synthetic network adapters, and four legacy network adapters for each virtual machine. You can add new hardware only when a virtual machine is powered off.

Follow these steps to add virtual hardware devices to a virtual machine:

1. In the Hyper-V Manager Virtual Machines pane, verify that the virtual machine state is Off, right-click the virtual machine, and select Settings.

2. On the Settings For page, select Add Hardware.

3. In the right pane, select the virtual device and click Add.

4. Configure the device (attach a virtual hard disk to a SCSI controller, or configure the virtual network and other settings for a network adapter).

5. Click OK to close the virtual machines settings page.

> **NOTE** You can use synthetic devices only if Integration Services are supported and installed in the virtual machine guest operating system. When you install Integration Services, the synthetic device drivers for keyboard, mouse, video, storage, and network components are copied to the virtual machine driver store.

Configuring Virtual Machine BIOS Settings

In Hyper-V, there are only two virtual machine Basic Input/Output System (BIOS) settings that you can adjust. You can select to turn Num Lock on or off, and you can modify the startup order of the boot devices. In most cases, the only configuration option that you will need to change is the boot order.

Follow these steps to modify virtual machine BIOS settings:

1. In the Hyper-V Manager Virtual Machines pane, verify that the virtual machine state is Off, right-click the virtual machine, and select Settings.

2. On the Settings For page, select BIOS.

3. In the right pane, select Num Lock to ensure that it is enabled when you boot the guest operating system.

4. If you want to change the order of the boot devices, use the up and down arrows in the Startup Order section until it is configured as needed.

5. Click OK.

The default order in which boot devices are checked for a valid operating system or boot loader is as follows:

- CD
- IDE
- Legacy Network Adapter
- Floppy

If startup media is not found on the CD, the virtual machine will scan the virtual IDE bus channels for a bootable drive. A virtual machine cannot boot from a synthetic SCSI device because the synthetic device drivers are not available until the guest operating system boots.

Changing the Memory Setting

Based on changing performance needs that are driven by requirements such as servicing a larger user population or significant increase in workload transactions, you may need to adjust a virtual machine's memory setting. When revising virtual machine memory allocation, it is important to evaluate whether allocating additional memory is possible based on the physical memory installed in your Hyper-V server and the requirements of other virtual machines. Use the following steps to adjust the virtual machine memory setting:

1. In the Hyper-V Manager Virtual Machines pane, verify that the virtual machine state is Off, right-click the virtual machine, and select Settings.

2. On the Settings For page, select Memory in the Hardware section.

3. Enter the new memory value in megabytes.

4. Click Apply to save your modifications and then click OK.

Depending on the amount of memory installed in the physical server and the memory allocation for the parent partition, Hyper-V Manager will display the maximum memory available to allocate to the virtual machine. If you attempt to enter an allocation greater than the maximum available memory, Hyper-V will generate an error similar to the one shown in Figure 11-32.

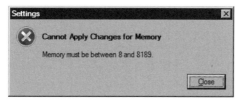

FIGURE 11-32 Virtual machine memory allocation error

NOTE Hyper-V does not support memory overcommitment or memory sharing. The sum of memory allocated to virtual machines must be less than the total memory installed in the physical server.

Changing the Processor Settings

As shown in Figure 11-33, there are several virtual machine processor settings that you can tune. Depending on the guest operating system that is installed in a virtual machine, you may be able to allocate and use up to four virtual processors to support workload requirements. You can also specify resource controls to balance processor resource usage among running virtual machines. In addition, you can limit processor functionality to run older operating systems such as Windows NT. In essence, limiting the processor functionality prevents a virtual processor from returning processor feature codes that older guest operating systems, such as Windows NT, do not support.

Use the following steps to adjust virtual machine processor settings:

1. In the Hyper-V Manager Virtual Machines pane, verify that the virtual machine state is Off, right-click the virtual machine, and select Settings.

2. On the Settings For page, select Processor in the Hardware section.

3. Modify the processor allocation, resources, and processor functionality as required.

4. Click Apply to save your modifications and then click OK.

MORE INFO In Chapter 2, "Hyper-V Overview," you can find the list of guest operating systems that Hyper-V supports, as well as the maximum number of virtual processors that can be allocated to each one. To learn more about tuning processor resource control settings, refer to the section titled "Understanding Processor Resource Control" in Chapter 7, "Hyper-V Best Practices and Optimization."

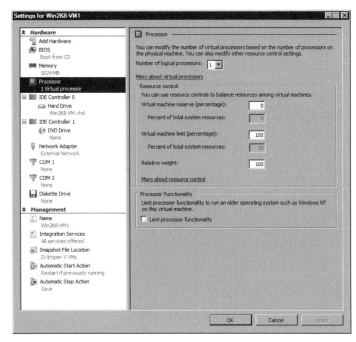

FIGURE 11-33 Virtual machine processor settings

Changing the Virtual Hard Disk Settings

The Hyper-V Manager New Virtual Machine Wizard allows the definition of only a single virtual hard disk during the creation of a new virtual machine. However, for most workloads, two or more virtual hard disks are required to separate the guest operating system files and application data files to achieve greater recoverability, security, and performance levels. A maximum of 260 virtual hard disks (four IDE and 256 SCSI) can be attached to a single virtual machine. In order to boot from a virtual hard disk, it must be connected to a virtual IDE controller. In addition, you can also boot a guest operating system that is connected using a pass-through disk. Pass-through disks allow a virtual machine to access a physical disk that is mapped directly to the Hyper-V server, but without a volume configured on it. Pass-through disks also allow you to exceed the 2040-GB limit of virtual hard disks.

> **MORE INFO** To learn how to configure pass-through disks, refer to Chapter 5, "Hyper-V Advanced Features."

Use the following steps to attach an additional VHD or pass-through disk to a virtual machine using a virtual SCSI controller:

1. In the Hyper-V Manager Virtual Machines pane, verify that the virtual machine state is Off, right-click the virtual machine, and select Settings.

2. If a virtual SCSI adapter is already installed in the virtual machine, you can use it to attach the new VHD and skip to step 4.

3. To install a new virtual SCSI adapter in the virtual machine, select Add Hardware in the Hardware section of the left pane, select SCSI Controller in the right pane, and then click Add.

4. In the left pane, select the new SCSI Controller component that was added in the Hardware section.

5. In the right pane, select Add to connect a new VHD to the virtual SCSI controller.

6. In the right pane, select one of the 64 locations to connect the new virtual hard disk using the Location drop-down box, shown in Figure 11-34.

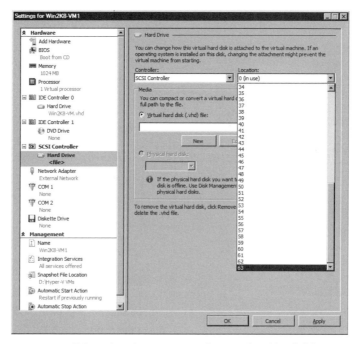

FIGURE 11-34 Select a location to connect the new virtual hard disk.

7. To create a new virtual hard disk to attach to the virtual SCSI controller, click New in the Media section of the right pane. The New Virtual Hard Disk Wizard will start and allow you to create a dynamically expanding, fixed size, or differencing virtual hard disk. After you complete the wizard, click Apply to save your modifications and then click OK.

8. If you want to specify an existing virtual hard drive, enter the fully qualified path to the folder where it is stored or click Browse to use Windows Explorer to navigate to the folder. After you are done, click Apply to save your modifications, and then click OK.

9. If you want to specify a pass-through disk, refer to the procedure defined in Chapter 5 to prepare the disk and connect it to the Hyper-V server. Then, select the pass-through disk from the Physical Hard Disk drop-down box in the Media section. After you are done, click Apply to save your modifications, and then click OK.

> **NOTE** If you do not find the pass-through disk in the Physical Hard Disk drop-down box, open the Disk Management snap-in and make sure that the disk is offline.

If you want to review the type, location, current size, and maximum size of a virtual hard disk, select Inspect Disk in the Hyper-V Manager Actions pane. A Windows Explorer dialog box will allow you to navigate to the location of the target virtual hard disk. After you select the virtual hard disk, a Virtual Hard Disk Properties dialog box will display the VHD details.

> **NOTE** For a general review of VHD types, refer to Chapter 2. If you need in-depth information concerning the use of differencing disks and other advanced virtual hard disk features, refer to Chapter 5.

Changing the Virtual DVD Drive Settings

When a new virtual machine is created, a virtual DVD drive is attached to the secondary virtual IDE channel. By default, the virtual DVD drive is not mapped to any media. Hyper-V allows up to four virtual DVD drives to be configured in a virtual machine (using all virtual IDE channels). Keep in mind that virtual machines must be powered off to add or remove virtual DVD drives.

In addition to not being mapped to any media, virtual DVD drives can map to physical CD/DVD drives or standard ISO 9660 images. There is one basic ISO image included with Hyper-V, Vmguest.iso, to support installation of Integration Services. If a virtual DVD drive is mapped to an operating system ISO image, the virtual machine can boot and install from the drive, resulting in a fast installation time because of the ISO image data access rate.

Use the following steps to create and attach an additional virtual DVD drive to a virtual machine:

1. In the Hyper-V Manager Virtual Machines pane, verify that the virtual machine state is Off, right-click the virtual machine, and select Settings.

2. To add a new virtual DVD drive, select the target virtual IDE controller (0 or 1) in the Hardware section of the left pane.

3. In the right pane, select DVD Drive in the IDE Controller section and then click Add.

4. In the DVD Drive section of the right pane, you have the following choices:
   - Select None if you do not want to immediately map the virtual DVD drive to a physical drive or ISO image.

- Select Image File and enter the fully qualified path to an ISO image.
- Select Physical CD/DVD Drive and then choose the physical drive from the drop-down menu.

5. After you are done, click Apply to save your modifications and then click OK.

Changing the Virtual Network Adapter Settings

A virtual machine is created with a single virtual network adapter. However, up to four legacy network adapters can be added to the virtual machine configuration. In addition, if Integration Services are installed in the guest operating system, you can add up to eight synthetic network adapters in the virtual machine. Hyper-V dynamically assigns a unique MAC address (by default within the 00-15-5D-xx-xx-xx range) to each virtual network adapter, enabling each adapter to connect independently to one of the available virtual networks.

> **MORE INFO** For more details on MAC address management in Hyper-V, refer to the section in Chapter 5 titled "Understanding MAC Address Pools."

As shown in Figure 11-35, Hyper-V supports three types of virtual networks: external, internal, and private. An external virtual network allows communication to external physical networks. An internal virtual network allows connectivity between virtual machines hosted on the same Hyper-V server, and with the Hyper-V server itself. A private virtual network allows connectivity only between virtual machines executing on the same Hyper-V server.

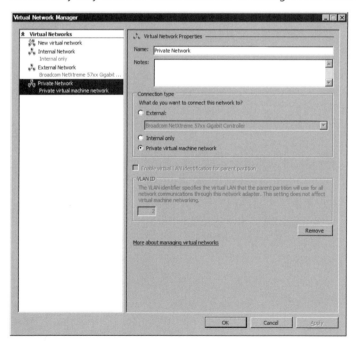

FIGURE 11-35 Virtual network options

For example, if you want to import multiple production servers into interconnected virtual machines executing on a single Hyper-V server without risking data transmission to the production network, use a private or internal network and connect each virtual machine to it using a virtual network adapter. If you must distribute the virtual machines across multiple Hyper-V servers, create an external virtual network connected to a physical network adapter on each of the Hyper-V servers. The physical network adapters should be connected to an isolated physical network to ensure that no data is transmitted across the production network. Then, connect each virtual machine to the external virtual network to allow network interconnectivity. Hyper-V supports an unlimited number of virtual networks to allow flexibility in the network connection configuration of virtual machines.

> **MORE INFO** You can learn more details about the external, internal, and private network data flow in Chapter 5.

In addition to adding or removing virtual network adapters and modifying the type of virtual network that a virtual network adapter connects to, you can also specify whether to assign a dynamic or static MAC address, and whether to enable and specify a virtual LAN identifier (VLAN ID).

> **MORE INFO** If you are interested in learning more about the VLAN implementation in Hyper-V, refer to Chapter 3, "Hyper-V Architecture," for Hyper-V networking architecture details, and refer to Chapter 5 for VLAN features and functions.

Use the following steps to create, attach, and modify additional virtual network adapters for a virtual machine:

1. In the Hyper-V Manager Virtual Machines pane, verify that the virtual machine state is Off, right-click the virtual machine, and select Settings.

2. To install a new virtual network adapter in the virtual machine, select Add Hardware in the Hardware section of the left pane.

3. In the right pane, you have the following choices, shown in Figure 11-36:

   - Select Network Adapter to install a synthetic virtual network adapter, and then click Add. Although you may be able to add a synthetic virtual network adapter, remember that the virtual machine can use this option only if Integration Services are supported for the guest operating system.

   - Select Legacy Network Adapter to install an emulated virtual network adapter, and then click Add.

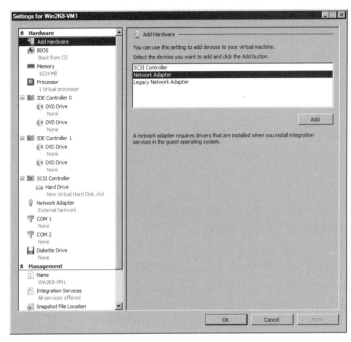

FIGURE 11-36 Selecting devices to add to your virtual machine

4. In the Network Adapter section of the right pane, select the virtual network to connect to using the Network drop-down box (see Figure 11-37).

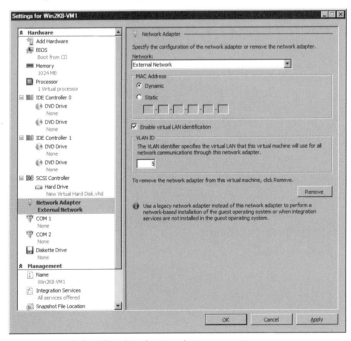

FIGURE 11-37 Select the virtual network to connect to.

5. Select whether to use a dynamic or static MAC address assignment. If you select Static, enter the MAC address.

> **NOTE** Ensure that the static MAC address is not already in use on the network. Otherwise, you will receive a duplicate MAC address error after the guest operating system boots.

6. Select Enable Virtual LAN Identification if you want to specify a VLAN ID, and then enter it in the VLAN ID section.

7. After you are done, click Apply to save your modifications, and then click OK.

Changing the Virtual COM Port Settings

There are two virtual COM ports available to enable a virtual machine to communicate through a named pipe. By default, the virtual COM ports are configured without any COM port connections. In general, a virtual COM port is attached to a named pipe to permit connection to a kernel debugger. You cannot connect a virtual COM port to a physical COM port on a Hyper-V server. Furthermore, the virtual COM ports cannot be removed from the virtual machine configuration.

Table 11-3 describes the virtual COM port connection settings that are available in Hyper-V.

TABLE 11-3 Virtual COM Port Connection Settings

SETTING	DESCRIPTION
None	This is the default setting for a new virtual machine, ensuring that no device is connected to a virtual COM port.
Named Pipe	This setting allows mapping a virtual COM port to a named pipe on the physical host or remote host connected to the same network.

Use the following steps to configure the virtual COM port settings:

1. In the Hyper-V Manager Virtual Machines pane, right-click the virtual machine and select Settings.

2. On the Settings For page (see Figure 11-38), in the Hardware section, select COM 1 or COM 2.

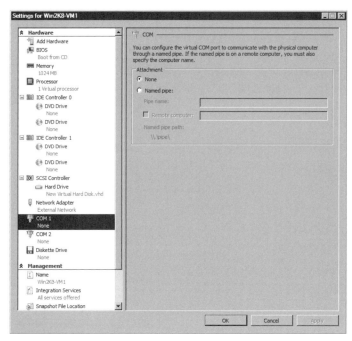

FIGURE 11-38 The Hardware section of the Settings For page

3. In the right pane, you have the following choices:

   - Select None if you do not want the COM port connected to any device.

   - Select Named Pipe and specify the pipe name.

4. Click Apply to save your modifications and then click OK.

Changing the Virtual Diskette Drive Settings

When a virtual machine is created, a single diskette drive is configured without any direct mapping to media. Like the virtual COM port components, the virtual diskette drive cannot be removed, and no additional floppy drives can be added to a virtual machine. A virtual floppy drive can be mapped only to a virtual floppy disk image (.vfd). Only a single virtual machine can be mapped to a writable virtual floppy disk image. However, multiple virtual machines can concurrently map and access a read-only virtual floppy disk. Hyper-V supports floppy disk images of 720 KB or 1.44 MB in size, but it will create images only in the latter format.

Use the following steps to change the virtual floppy drive mapping for a virtual machine:

1. In the Hyper-V Manager Virtual Machines pane, right-click the virtual machine and select Settings.

2. On the Settings For page, select Diskette Drive in the Hardware section.

3. In the right pane, you have the following choices:

- Select None if you do not want to immediately map to a floppy disk image.
- Select Virtual Floppy Disk (.VFD) File if you want to map to a floppy disk image. Then, enter the fully qualified path to an available floppy image file or click Browse to use Windows Explorer to locate the file.

4. Click Apply to save your modifications and then click OK.

> **NOTE** Hyper-V includes a single blank floppy disk image that you can find in %SystemDrive%\Users\Public\Documents\Hyper-V\Blank floppy disk.vfd.

Changing a Virtual Machine Name

If you mistype a virtual machine name or need it to conform to a new naming standard, follow these steps to rename the virtual machine:

1. In the Hyper-V Manager Virtual Machines pane, right-click the virtual machine and select Rename.
2. Enter the new name in the virtual machine Name field and then press Enter.
3. The new virtual machine name is immediately reflected in Hyper-V Manager.

Performing this action will change only the name of the virtual machine. The virtual machine configuration file, snapshot files, and saved state files all maintain persistent GUID-based names. The virtual hard disk name is also unaffected by the virtual machine name change.

> **NOTE** You can also change the virtual machine name in the virtual machine settings. On the Settings For page, select Name in the Management section and enter the new name in the right pane. You can also record notes about the virtual machine that are displayed in the Hyper-V manager when the virtual machine is selected.

Modifying Integration Services Settings

As described in Table 5-6 in Chapter 5, Hyper-V provides Integration Services for a variety of supported guest operating systems. To use Integration Services, you must first install them in the guest operating system. Even if the guest operating system supports a particular Integration Services component, you can modify the selection of services that are offered to a virtual machine to suit your operational requirements.

Follow these steps to configure the Integration Services offered to a virtual machine:

1. In the Hyper-V Manager Virtual Machines pane, right-click the virtual machine and select Settings.

2. On the Settings For page, select Integration Services in the Management section (see Figure 11-39).

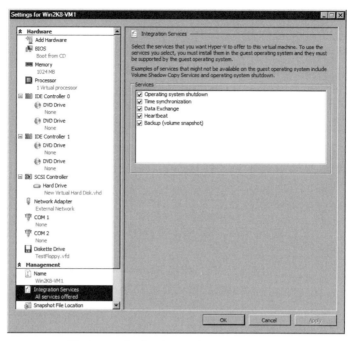

FIGURE 11-39 The Integration Services options

3. In the right pane, select or clear the offered Integration Services.

4. Click Apply to save your modifications, and then click OK.

> **BEST PRACTICES**   If you install an update to Hyper-V that provides a new version of Integration Services components, you should install them in each supported virtual machine to benefit from improvements made to device drivers and services performance.

Modifying the Snapshot File Location

By default, virtual machine snapshots are stored in %SystemDrive% \ProgramData\Microsoft \Windows\Hyper-V. However, Hyper-V allows you to specify a different storage location for each virtual machine.

Follow these steps to configure the location to store virtual machine snapshots:

1. In the Hyper-V Manager Virtual Machines pane, right-click the virtual machine and select Settings.

2. On the Settings For page, select Snapshot File Location in the Management section.

3. In the right pane, enter the fully qualified path to the folder or click Browse to use Windows Explorer to locate the folder.

4. Click Apply to save your modifications and then click OK.

As shown in Figure 11-40, after you take the first virtual machine snapshot, you are no longer allowed to change the snapshot file location.

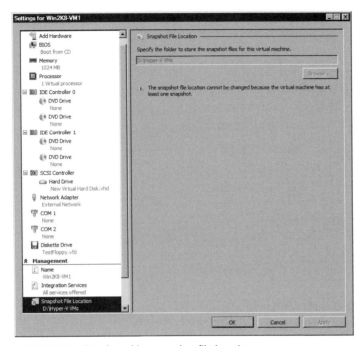

FIGURE 11-40 Virtual machine snapshot file location

> **MORE INFO** For more details on the implementation of virtual machine snapshots and how to create them in Hyper-V, refer to Chapter 5.

Modifying a Virtual Machine Automatic Start Action

By default, a new virtual machine is configured to start automatically when the Hyper-V server restarts if the virtual machine was running when the Hyper-V server was powered off. You can change the virtual machine automatic start action to do nothing or always start automatically. In addition, you can also specify a start action delay to reduce resource contention if multiple virtual machines restart automatically when a Hyper-V server is powered on. Follow these steps to change the virtual machine automatic start action settings:

1. In the Hyper-V Manager Virtual Machines pane, right-click the virtual machine and select Settings.

2. On the Settings For page, select Automatic Start Action in the Management section.

3. In the Automatic Start Action section, you have the following choices:

   - Select Nothing if you do not want the virtual machine to restart automatically.

   - Select Automatically Start If It Was Running When The Service Stopped to have the virtual machine automatically restart if it was in a running state when the Hyper-V server is powered-off.

   - Select Always Start This Virtual Machine Automatically if you want the virtual machine to restart regardless of its state when the Hyper-V server is powered off.

4. If you choose one of the automatic start actions, specify a startup delay if multiple virtual machines will restart concurrently. By default, the startup delay is 0 seconds, and all virtual machines configured in this manner will restart at (approximately) the same moment when the Hyper-V services are online.

5. Click Apply to save your modifications and then click OK.

> **NOTE** If you specify an automatic start delay for multiple virtual machines, ensure that you step the values for each one. For example, if you configure three virtual machines, specify an automatic start delay of 0 seconds for the first one, 20 seconds for the second one, and 40 seconds for the third one. Of course, you should adjust these values based on the startup time for each virtual machine. The actual values will also depend on whether or not the virtual machine restarts from a saved state.

Modifying a Virtual Machine Automatic Stop Action

You can also specify the automatic stop action for a virtual machine. The default action is to save the virtual machine state when the Hyper-V server is powered off. This option allows the virtual machine to restart from the saved state with the shortest delay. In this configuration, Hyper-V captures and stores the virtual machine state information, such as processor register data, and the current memory contents into files. The virtual machine state information is stored in a file named using the same GUID as the virtual machine configuration file, but with a .vsv extension. The virtual machine memory is stored in a binary file that is also named with the same GUID as the virtual machine configuration file, but with a .bin extension. The data contained in these two files is used to reload processor and memory contents during a quick and stateful restart of the virtual machine.

Follow these steps to change the virtual machine automatic stop action settings:

1. In the Hyper-V Manager Virtual Machines pane, right-click the virtual machine and select Settings.

2. On the Settings For page, select Automatic Stop Action in the Management section.

3. In the Automatic Stop Action section, you have the following choices:

   - Select Save The Virtual Machine State if you want state information saved to files when the Hyper-V server is powered off.

- Select Turn Off The Virtual Machine to power off the virtual machine when the Hyper-V Server is powered off.

- Select Shutdown The Guest Operating System if you have Integration Services installed in the virtual machine and you want the virtual machine to complete the shutdown process before the Hyper-V server is powered off.

4. Click Apply to save your modifications and then click OK.

You may want to avoid using the Turn Off The Virtual Machine option because this is equivalent to pulling the power plug on a physical computer and can result in data corruption.

BEST PRACTICES You should implement Quick Migration using Failover Clustering if you anticipate the need to move virtual machines between Hyper-V servers. Otherwise, use the Hyper-V import and export features to move virtual machines between Hyper-V servers.

MORE INFO For more information on Quick Migration and virtual machine import and export features, refer to Chapter 5 and Chapter 2, respectively.

 CAUTION It is not possible to move a virtual machine that is in a saved stated from Virtual Server 2005 R2 or Virtual PC to Hyper-V. It is also not possible to move a virtual machine that is in a saved state between Hyper-V servers that are based on different processor architectures, such as AMD-V and Intel VT. Although some virtual machine files, such as virtual hard disks (.vhd), are compatible between Virtual Server and Hyper-V and between Hyper-V servers, saved state files (.vsv, .bin) are incompatible.

MORE INFO For more information on the virtual machine migration process from Virtual Server 2005 R2 to Hyper-V, refer to Chapter 8, "Moving from Virtual Server 2005 R2 to Hyper-V."

Removing a Virtual Machine

Completely removing a virtual machine and associated files from a Hyper-V server requires two steps. First, you delete the virtual machine configuration information using the Hyper-V Manager MMC. This step does not delete any of the virtual machine files, except for the symbolic link that points to the virtual machine configuration file. This prevents mistakenly deleting virtual machine files from the Hyper-V server. If you are certain that you will no longer execute the virtual machine on the specific Hyper-V server, you have to manually delete all the associated files after deleting the virtual machine.

To delete a virtual machine from a Hyper-V server, follow these steps:

1. In the Hyper-V Manager Virtual Machines pane, right-click the virtual machine and select Delete.

2. After the symbolic link is deleted, the virtual machine name is no longer displayed in Hyper-V Manager Virtual Machines pane.

3. If you want to delete all of the virtual machine files, open Windows Explorer, navigate to the virtual machine folder location, and manually delete the files.

A virtual machine must be powered off or in a saved state before you can delete it from the Hyper-V Manager MMC.

> **NOTE**   Symbolic links to virtual machine configuration files are created in %SystemDrive% /ProgramData/Microsoft/Windows/Hyper-V/Virtual Machines. This is also the default folder in which Hyper-V stores virtual machine configuration files.

Installing a Guest Operating System

A virtual machine does not usually provide any useful service until it is configured with a workload that consists of an operating system and one or more applications. Installing an operating system in a virtual machine parallels the process performed for a physical computer. A virtual machine operating system can be installed using original media, an imaging tool, ISO images, or PXE-based installation. Table 11-4 lists the virtual machine requirements for each of these installation methods.

TABLE 11-4 Virtual Machine Guest Operating System Installation Options

SETTING	DESCRIPTION
Original Media	The virtual DVD drive must be mapped to the physical host drive containing the original media.
Imaging Tool	The virtual DVD drive must be mapped to the physical host drive containing a CD-based image. OR The virtual machine is created using a VHD that was prepared with the System Preparation tool (Sysprep).
ISO Image	The virtual DVD drive must be mapped to an ISO image file.
PXE-based Installation	The virtual machine must PXE boot to connect to Windows Deployment Services (WDS), to a physical to virtual (P2V) migration tool, or to another network-based installation service. This option is supported only by legacy virtual network adapters.

If an operating system must be installed from scratch, use an ISO image stored on a physical host drive when possible, instead of using original media. Installing an operating system from an ISO image mapped to the virtual machine DVD drive is much less time-consuming than installing from original media. In addition, if you intend to deploy the same operating system configuration repetitively, use the Sysprep tool to create a baseline VHD that you can copy and reuse to provision new virtual machines quickly and with minimal effort. The Sysprep utility prepares an operating system for distribution by resetting it to run the setup at the next boot, eliminating security identifier (SID) and machine name duplication issues that would otherwise arise. Sysprep should be used only after the operating system has been updated, Integration Services have been installed, and any baseline applications have been included in the configuration.

> **NOTE** The Windows Server 2008 compatible Sysprep tool is installed automatically and is found at %SystemDrive%\Windows\System32\Sysprep\Sysprep.exe.

The basic steps to install an operating system in a virtual machine using an ISO image file, assuming a single virtual DVD drive configuration, are as follows:

1. In the Hyper-V Manager Virtual Machines pane, right-click the virtual machine and select Settings.

2. On the Setting For page, select the virtual DVD drive in the Hardware section (see Figure 11-41).

FIGURE 11-41 Select the DVD drive used to install the guest operating system.

3. In the DVD Drive section of the right pane, select Image File and enter the fully quali-fied path to an ISO image file.

4. Click Apply to save your modifications and then click OK.

5. In the Hyper-V Manager Virtual Machines pane, right-click the virtual machine and select Start.

6. Click the virtual machine thumbnail to launch the Virtual Machine Connection application and connect to the virtual machine console.

7. After the virtual machine boots and begins the setup process, follow normal proce-dures to install the operating system (see Figure 11-42).

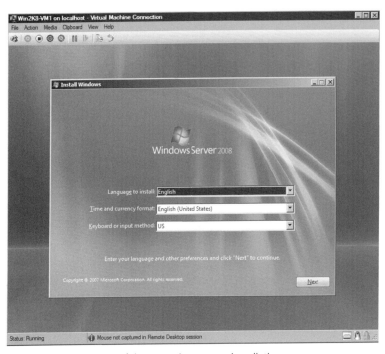

FIGURE 11-42 Beginning of the operating system installation

Installing Integration Services

After the virtual machine guest operating system configuration is complete, you should install Integration Services. Integration Services are a set of performance, integration, and function-ality enhancements that are installed in a guest operating system running in a virtual ma-chine. Virtual machine input/output (I/O) performance is significantly increased when virtual machine–specific driver updates replace standard guest operating system driver files for the mouse, keyboard, video, network, and SCSI controller components. Integration Services are updated from time to time, so it is important to incorporate these updates into your maintenance procedures and schedule to ensure that you are using the newest versions of the drivers as they become available.

Integration Services can be installed in a virtual machine by capturing the Vmguest.iso image file that contains Integration Services components and mapping it to the virtual DVD drive, or by scripting the installation.

Follow these steps to install Integration Services easily using the Virtual Machine Connection application to connect to the virtual machine:

1. In the Hyper-V Manager Virtual Machines pane, right-click the virtual machine and select Connect.

2. Log into the virtual machine using an account with local administrator credentials.

3. In the Virtual Machine Connection application Action menu, select Insert Integration Services Setup Disk (see Figure 11-43).

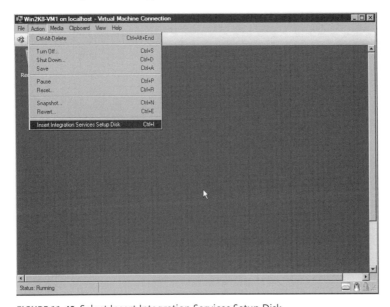

FIGURE 11-43 Select Insert Integration Services Setup Disk.

4. Select Install Hyper-V Integration Services in the AutoPlay dialog box (see Figure 11-44) and press Enter.

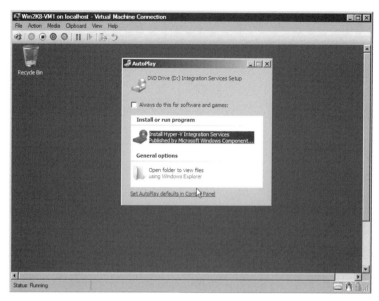

FIGURE 11-44 Select Install Hyper-V Integration Services

5. In the Upgrade Hyper-V Integration Services dialog box, click OK.

6. When prompted, click Yes to restart the virtual machine.

> **NOTE** The Vmguest.iso file that contains Integration Services is located on the Hyper-V server in the %SystemDrive%/Windows/System32 folder.

Controlling Virtual Machine State

Table 11-5 contains a list of options that Hyper-V provides to control and change the state of a virtual machine. In all cases, available options depend on the existing virtual machine state. It is critical to understand virtual machine state and transition paths in order to prevent corruption, data loss, or service interruptions caused by incompatibilities with applications or services running in the virtual machine. In order to change the state of a virtual machine, right-click the virtual machine in the Hyper-V Manager MMC and then select the appropriate action.

TABLE 11-5 Virtual Machine State Control Options

STATE	DESCRIPTION
Start	Power on the virtual machine.
	OR
	Turn on the virtual machine and restore it to the state that it was in when it was saved.

STATE	DESCRIPTION
Turn Off	Power off the virtual machine without saving any state information. This has the same effect as pulling a power plug on a physical machine.
Shut Down	Shut down the guest operating system, simulating a clean shutdown of a physical machine.
Save	Save the current state of the virtual machine to files (.vsv, .bin) and stop execution. This allows restoring a virtual machine to the condition that it was in when its state was saved.
Pause	Stop execution of the virtual machine, maintaining the current state of the memory.
Resume	Resume execution of the virtual machine from the exact state that it was in when paused.
Reset	Reset the virtual machine. This has the same effect as pressing the reset button on a physical machine.

For example, a virtual machine configured as a domain controller should not be placed in a saved state and later restored. Bringing an Active Directory database back online after being in saved state can cause database corruption and replication failures that can have severe consequences on the integrity of the Active Directory domain and forest. Typically, any application with temporal transactional dependencies should be very carefully managed to avoid critical data integrity issues caused by improperly suspending or turning off a virtual machine and bringing it back online after a significant period of time.

Updating Virtual Machines

Virtual machines should be included in update and maintenance procedures set up for physical machines. This ensures that the virtual machines have the latest set of security and nonsecurity updates. Update management can be handled several different ways: using CD-based update distribution with scripted installation, dedicated management tools like Microsoft Windows Server Update Service (WSUS), general-purpose tools such as System Center Configuration Manager (SCCM), or other comparable applications.

BEST PRACTICES Updating multiple virtual machines on a single Hyper-V server concurrently can affect the performance of the machines being updated, increasing the time it takes to install updates, as well as impacting on available resources for unaffected production workloads. To prevent performance problems from occurring, schedule your updates distribution to virtual machines running on the same Hyper-V server so that they are performed serially.

Performing Hyper-V Backup and Recovery

Windows Server 2008 provides a built-in backup solution called Windows Server Backup (WSB). Windows Server Backup uses the Volume Shadow Copy Service (VSS) to perform the normal backup and restore operations that you expect in an enterprise environment. In particular, WSB provides backup and restore support for the server operating system, volumes, folders, and files. In addition, WSB supports backup and restore operations for roles and applications that provide a VSS-compatible writer, including the Hyper-V role.

Installing Windows Server Backup

Windows Server Backup is a Windows Server 2008 feature, and therefore it is not installed by default. Follow these steps to install Windows Server Backup and configure it to support Hyper-V:

1. Open Server Manager and select Features in the left pane.

2. In the right pane of the Features Summary dialog box, click Add Features.

3. On the Select Features page of the Add Features Wizard (see Figure 11-45), expand Windows Server Backup Features.

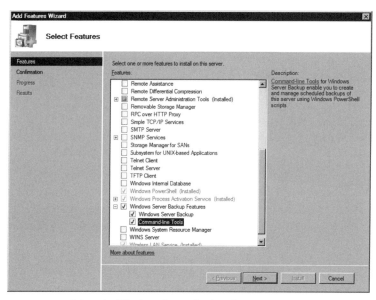

FIGURE 11-45 Select the Windows Server Backup Feature.

4. From the Windows Server Backup Features node, select Windows Server Backup. Optionally, you can also select Command-Line Tools.

5. After you make your selections, click Next.

6. On the Confirm Installation Selections page (see Figure 11-46), review your selections and then click Install.

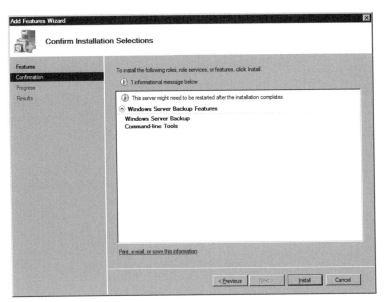

FIGURE 11-46 Review selections on the Confirm Installation Selections page.

7. On the Installation Results page, click Close.

Windows Server 2008 installs the Windows Server Backup MMC, the Wbadmin.exe backup command-line tool, and associated services. If you also select to install the Command-Line Tools for Windows Server Backup, you will be able to create and manage scheduled backups using Windows PowerShell scripts.

Configuring Windows Server Backup for Hyper-V Support

Windows Server Backup supports role and application VSS writers, but it does not have the ability to automatically import or register new VSS writers. Therefore, you must complete this step manually. In order to configure Windows Server Backup to support the Hyper-V VSS writer, you must modify the Windows Server Backup registry and register the Hyper-V VSS Writer GUID. You can perform these tasks using the Registry Editor or using a .REG file.

Determining the Hyper-V VSS Writer GUID

Before you can register the Hyper-V VSS Writer, you need to determine the Hyper-V VSS Writer GUID. The Volume Shadow Copy Service Administrative (VSSAdmin.exe) command-line tool can list VSS writers installed on the Hyper-V server as well as their associated GUID. Use the following steps to find the Hyper-V VSS Writer GUID with VSSAdmin:

1. Open a command prompt using the Run As Administrator option.

2. At the command prompt, type **VSSAdmin List Writers >C:\Temp\VSSWriters.txt**.

3. After a few seconds, the list of all VSS writers that are installed and registered with the VSS service are piped to the C:\Temp\VSSWriters.txt file.

4. Open the C:\Temp\VSSWriters.txt file and find the Hyper-V VSS Writer GUID by searching for the Microsoft Hyper-V VSS Writer string.

5. Verify that the Hyper-V VSS Writer GUID is 66841CD4-6DED-4F4B-8F17-FD23F8D-DC3DE.

Modifying the Registry Using the Registry Editor (REGEDIT)

Follow these steps to modify the registry using REGEDIT:

1. Open a command prompt using the Run As Administrator option.

2. At the command prompt, type **Regedit**.

3. In the Registry Editor, locate the following key:

   HKEY_LOCAL_MACHINE\SOFTWARE\Microsoft\Windows NT\CurrentVersion
   \WindowsServerBackup

4. If the key does not exist, right-click the HKEY_LOCAL_MACHINE\SOFTWARE\Microsoft \Windows NT\CurrentVersion key and select New, then select Key.

5. Type **WindowsServerBackup** as the name of the key and press Enter.

6. Right-click the WindowsServerBackup key, select New, and then select Key.

7. Type **Application Support** as the name of the key and press Enter.

   HKEY_LOCAL_MACHINE\SOFTWARE\Microsoft\Windows NT\CurrentVersion
   \WindowsServerBackup\Application Support

8. Right-click the Application Support key, select New, and then select Key.

9. Type **{66841CD4-6DED-4F4B-8F17-FD23F8DDC3DE}** as the name of the key and press Enter.

   HKEY_LOCAL_MACHINE\SOFTWARE\Microsoft\Windows NT\CurrentVersion
   \WindowsServerBackup\Application Support\{66841CD4-6DED-4F4B-8F17-
   FD23F8DDC3DE}

10. Right-click the {66841CD4-6DED-4F4B-8F17-FD23F8DDC3DE} key (see Figure 11-47), select New, then select String Value to create a REG_SZ string. Type **Application Identifier** as the value name, and set the value to **Hyper-V VSS Writer**.

> **IMPORTANT** Use caution when you modify the registry. Corrupting the registry can cause system instability and could cause the operating system to be unable to boot.

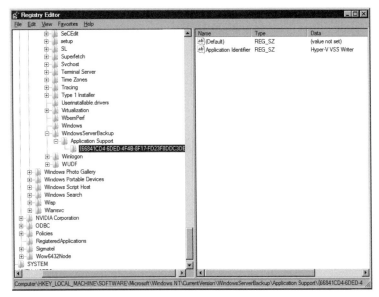

FIGURE 11-47 Select the key in the Registry Editor.

Modifying the Registry Using a .REG File

If you need to make the registry modification on multiple servers, or if you want to minimize errors, you can create a .REG file and import it into the Hyper-V server registry. You can create a .REG file using a standard ASCII text editor such as Notepad. If you have already made the registry modifications on a Hyper-V server, you can export the registry key and create a .REG file.

Follow these steps to create the .REG file by exporting it from an existing Hyper-V server registry:

1. Open a command prompt using the Run As Administrator option.

2. At the command prompt, type **Regedit**.

3. In the Registry Editor, locate and right-click the following key:

   HKEY_LOCAL_MACHINE\SOFTWARE\Microsoft\Windows NT\CurrentVersion
   \WindowsServerBackup

4. Select Export, enter a name for the .REG file, and then click Save.

5. Close the Registry Editor.

6. Open the .REG file and verify that it contains the following registry keys and values:

   Windows Registry Editor Version 5.00

   [HKEY_LOCAL_MACHINE\SOFTWARE\Microsoft\Windows NT\CurrentVersion
   \WindowsServerBackup]

   [HKEY_LOCAL_MACHINE\SOFTWARE\Microsoft\Windows NT\CurrentVersion
   \WindowsServerBackup\Application Support]

[HKEY_LOCAL_MACHINE\SOFTWARE\Microsoft\Windows NT\CurrentVersion
\WindowsServerBackup\Application Support\{66841CD4-6DED-4F4B-8F17-
FD23F8DDC3DE}] "Application Identifier"="Hyper-V VSS Writer"

After you create the .REG file, you can copy it to another Hyper-V server, install Windows Server Backup, right-click the .REG file, and select Merge to import the new keys into the Hyper-V server registry.

Windows Server Backup Considerations

You should be aware of the following factors when creating your Windows Server Backup plan for Hyper-V:

- You must back up the system drive to capture the Hyper-V configuration information and the default Authorization Manager store (%SystemDrive%\ProgramData \Microsoft\Windows\Hyper-V\InitialStore.xml).

- You cannot back up specific virtual machines; you can only back up Hyper-V server volumes.

- You must back up each volume that contains virtual machine files and data. Therefore, If you store a virtual machine configuration file on a volume separate from the virtual hard disk files, you must back up both volumes to be able to restore the virtual machine.

- When you perform a restore operation, you must select an application-based restore.

Restoring a virtual machine using Windows Server Backup is an all or nothing operation. You cannot restore individual virtual machine files, only the entire virtual machine. After a virtual machine's virtual hard disks are restored, you can attach them to another virtual machine (or the original virtual machine) and retrieve specific files.

> **NOTE**   Backup of online virtual machines is available only for guest operating systems that support the Integration Services Hyper-V VSS Writer component. Therefore, you can perform online backups of Windows Server 2008, Windows Server 2003, and Windows Vista. Windows 2000 Server and Windows XP virtual machines do not support Volume Shadow Copy Services online backups.

Backing Up a Virtual Machine Using Windows Server Backup

Follow these steps to configure the backup of a virtual machine using Windows Server Backup:

1. Open the Windows Server Backup console, shown in Figure 11-48. (You can select it from Administrative Tools.)

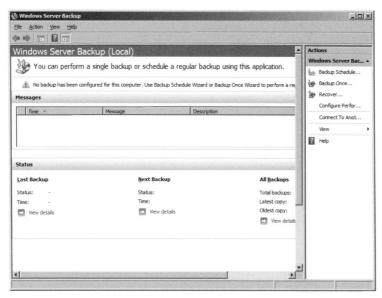

FIGURE 11-48 The Windows Server Backup console

2. In the Actions pane, select Backup Schedule.

3. On the Getting Started page of the Backup Schedule Wizard (see Figure 11-49), click Next.

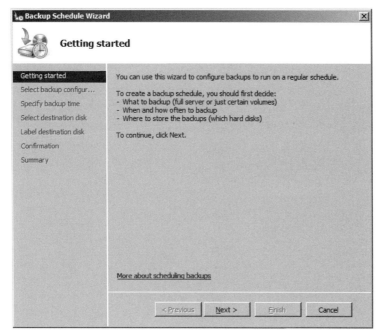

FIGURE 11-49 The Backup Schedule Wizard

4. On the Select Backup Configuration page (see Figure 11-50), select Custom and then click Next.

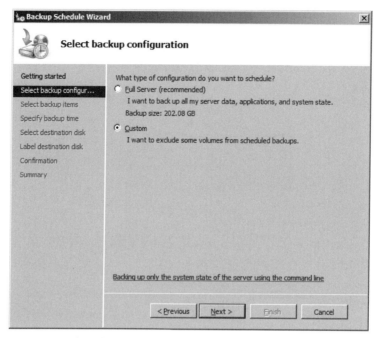

FIGURE 11-50 The Select Backup Configuration page

5. On the Select Backup Items page (see Figure 11-51), select the volumes that contain the virtual machine files. By default, system volumes are selected.

6. After you complete your selections, click Next.

7. On the Specify Backup Time page, you have the following choices, as shown in Figure 11-52:

   - Select Once A Day and specify the time to start the backup.
   - Select More Than Once A Day and specify multiple times to perform backups.

8. After you complete your selections, click Next.

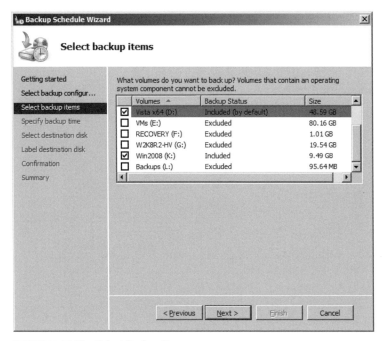

FIGURE 11-51 The Select Backup Items page

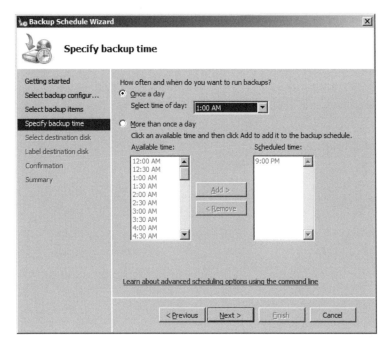

FIGURE 11-52 Specifying backup time

9. On the Select Destination Disk page (see Figure 11-53), click Show All Available Disks and then select a disk as the location to store your backups.

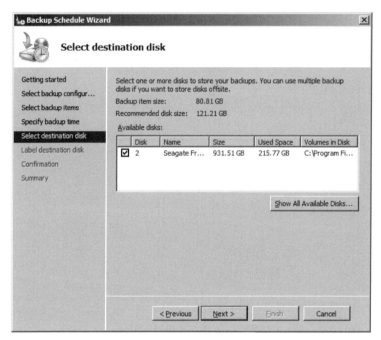

FIGURE 11-53 The Select Destination Disk page

10. After you complete your selections, click Next.

11. You may be presented with a warning that the selected disks will be reformatted and any existing volumes and data on it will be deleted. Click Yes to confirm your disk selections.

12. On the Label Destination Disk page (see Figure 11-54), click Next.

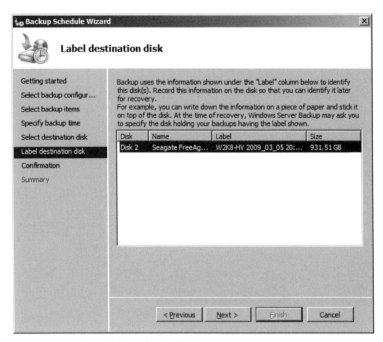

FIGURE 11-54 The Label Destination Disk page

13. On the Confirmation page, review your selections and click Finish.

14. On the Summary page, click Close.

15. Restart the Hyper-V server.

Restoring a Virtual Machine Using Windows Server Backup

Follow these steps to use Windows Server Backup to restore a virtual machine:

1. Open the Windows Server Backup console.

2. In the Actions pane, select Recover.

3. On the Getting Started page of the Recovery Wizard (see Figure 11-55), select This Server and then click Next.

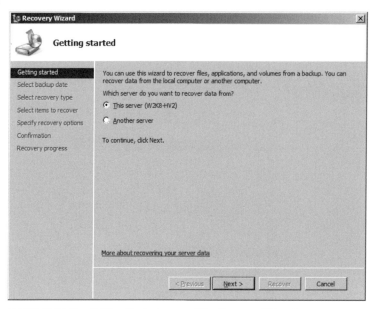

FIGURE 11-55 The Getting Started page of the Recovery Wizard

4. On the Select Backup Date page (see Figure 11-56), select from the available backups and then click Next.

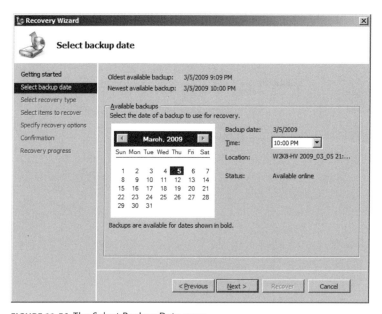

FIGURE 11-56 The Select Backup Date page

5. On the Select Recovery Type page (see Figure 11-57), select Applications and then click Next.

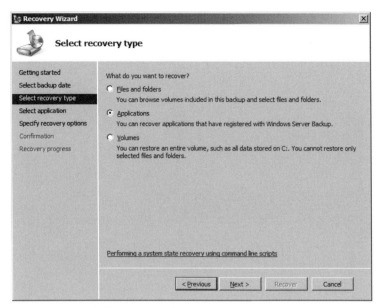

FIGURE 11-57 The Select Recovery Type page

6. On the Select Application page (see Figure 11-58), select Hyper-V.

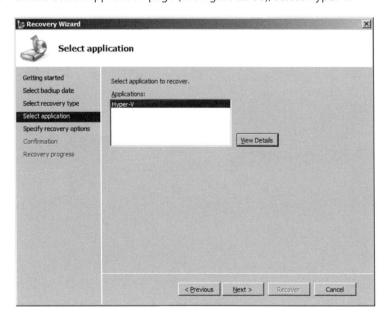

FIGURE 11-58 The Select Application page

7. Click View Details for a list of the virtual machines and Hyper-V configuration information that is captured in the backup. An example list of details is shown in Figure 11-59.

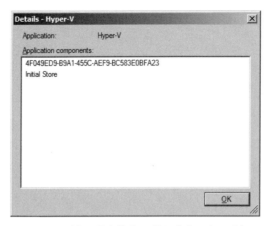

FIGURE 11-59 View Details for a list of virtual machines and configuration information

8. Click OK and then click Next.

9. On the Specify Recovery Options page, you have the following choices, as shown in Figure 11-60:

   ■ Select Recover To Original Location if you want to use the source location(s).

   ■ Select Recover To Another Location if you do not want to use the source location(s).

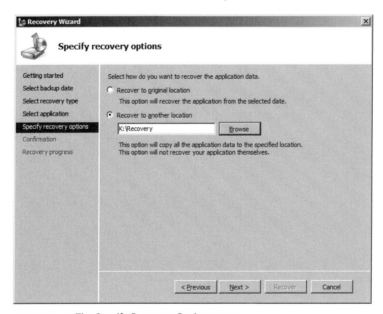

FIGURE 11-60 The Specify Recovery Options page

10. After you complete your selection, click Next.

11. On the Confirmation page (see Figure 11-61), review your selections and then click Recover.

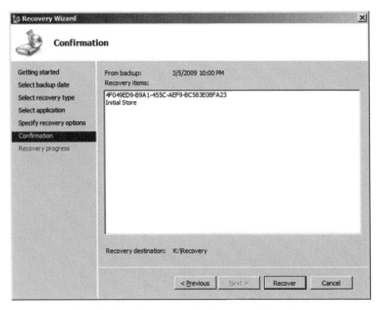

FIGURE 11-61 The Confirmation page of the Recovery Wizard

12. Windows Server Backup begins the recovery process and lists a status for each re-source that it is recovering, as shown in Figure 11-62.

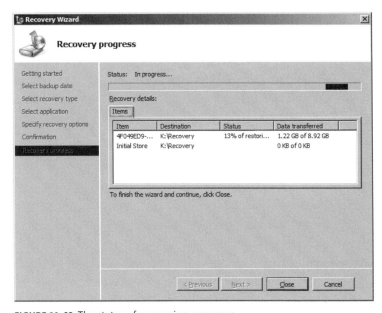

FIGURE 11-62 The status of recovering resources

13. When the restoration is complete (shown in Figure 11-63) on the Recovery Progress page, click Close.

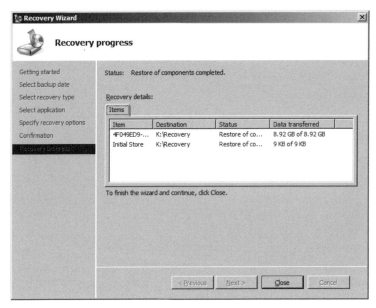

FIGURE 11-63 Close the Recovery Wizard when restoration is complete.

Monitoring Hyper-V Health and Performance

As described in Chapter 10, "Hyper-V Management Overview," you can monitor the health and performance of a Hyper-V server using the Reliability and Performance Monitor application that is installed by default with Windows Server 2008. Monitoring the performance of a Hyper-V server, virtual machines, and virtual machine workloads is a crucial aspect of maintaining your virtualized infrastructure. Monitoring performance data helps you do the following:

- Understand workload profiles and resource usage trends so that you can perform capacity planning.
- Determine how to tune resources to achieve better workload performance.
- Diagnose issues and identify problem components.

Standard performance tools such as the Performance Monitor and more sophisticated applications such as System Center Operations Manager 2007 can monitor the performance of virtualized resources as well as physical ones.

You should monitor your virtualized infrastructure using the same methods and procedures as you do in your physical environment. You can use physical workload performance data captured prior to migrating a physical server to a virtual machine to evaluate the change in performance. With this data, you can determine whether additional resources must be allocated to the virtual machine workload; whether it must be moved to a Hyper-V server with more powerful processors, more memory, and larger storage systems; and in very rare cases, whether the workload should be migrated back out of a virtual machine and onto a physical server.

MORE INFO To learn more about some of the prime performance counters that can help you to assess memory, processor, network, and disk performance, refer to the MSDN article "Measuring Performance on Hyper-V," available at *http://msdn.microsoft.com /en-us/library/cc768535.aspx*. Although it is focused on running Biztalk on Hyper-V, the information is broadly applicable.

Summary

You can manage a Hyper-V server locally or using a remote management workstation. You must configure the Hyper-V server and workstation before you can perform remote server management. The HVRemote script can be very useful to automate the configuration of the Hyper-V server and remote management workstation, especially in complex, multidomain or multiple workgroup scenarios. Use the Hyper-V Manager MMC to manage Hyper-V settings as well as virtual machines. Before you create a virtual machine, make sure that you define basic configuration settings. After you create a new virtual machine, you should tune the configuration of virtual components not specified at creation time before you install a guest operating system.

If you want to remove a virtual machine permanently, you must delete the associated files manually because these are not deleted automatically by Hyper-V. There are several methods to install an operating system in a virtual machine, but use ISO image files for higher performance when installing from media. Also, if repeated deployments are planned, use the Sysprep utility to prepare a VHD for duplication and fast provisioning of new virtual machines.

Install the Integration Services after the operating system configuration in order to enhance the virtual machine performance and functionality. Understand how to configure and use the Windows Server Backup to back up and restore virtual machines. You can back up an entire virtual machine using Windows Server Backup; however, you cannot back up individual virtual machine files. Finally, you can use the Reliability and Performance Monitor to evaluate the performance of your Hyper-V server and perform capacity planning as well as take preventive measures to ensure that there are sufficient physical resources available to support the virtual machine workloads.

Additional Resources

The following resources contain additional information related to the topics in this chapter.

- Knowledge Base article 952627, "Description of the Windows Vista Service Pack 1 Management Tools update for the release version of Hyper-V," available at *http://support.microsoft.com/kb/952627*

- Microsoft MSDN Web site, "Hyper-V Remote Management Configuration Utility," available at *http://code.msdn.microsoft.com/HVRemote*

CHAPTER 12

Server Farm Management

M anaging a farm of Hyper-V servers requires a single management solution that allows you to see the individual components of the server farm (hosts, virtual machines, library shares) and the consolidated set of resources in a single interface. System Center Virtual Machine Manager (SCVMM) 2008 is Microsoft's solution for managing a server farm. SCVMM provides the ability to view the Hyper-V server or the farm of Hyper-V servers to understand the performance and scalability issues that they host are experiencing. SCVMM also provides the ability to view all the virtual machines across all servers so that you can make load-balancing decisions. This chapter describes how to use SCVMM 2008 to manage a farm of Hyper-V servers.

Installing System Center Virtual Machine Manager 2008

Before you can understand how to use System Center Virtual Machine Manager 2008 to manage a farm of Hyper-V servers, you need to have an installation to work with. SCVMM 2008 consists of multiple components that work together to provide a single console interface.

The SCVMM components include:

- Virtual Machine Manager (VMM) server
- Virtual Machine Manager Administrator Console
- Virtual Machine Library
- Virtual Machine Manager Self-Service Portal
- Virtual Machine Manager database
- Virtual Machine Manager Windows PowerShell interface
- Virtual Machine Manager Reporting

The VMM server is the main building block that collects and manages the server farm information. The VMM Administrator Console is the user interface to the VMM server component and allows you to see and manage all the SCVMM resources. The VMM Library stores all of the objects used for provisioning new virtual machines. The Self-Service Portal provides a Web interface that allows a user to remotely manage virtual machines running on the server farm without needed to know which Hyper-V server they are running on. The VMM database provides important information about the server farm configuration, the available objects in the library, and monitoring data. The VMM Windows PowerShell interface is the underlying API that VMM server is based on, and it also provides a powerful scripting and automated management engine. VMM Reporting is the interface between SCVMM 2008 and System Center Operations Manager 2007 for performance resource optimization and management.

Installation Options

System Center Virtual Machine Manager 2008 can be installed with all components on a single server or with the individual components distributed to multiple servers, depending on load and requirements. Single server installations are recommended for up to 20 hosts, whereas distributing the components of SCVMM across multiple servers can support the tested limit of 400 hosts.

In either the single server or distributed installation approach, the VMM server, Administrative Console, Self-Service Portal, and Reporting interfaces require separate installation steps. The VMM Library and Windows PowerShell interfaces are required options for the VMM server installation. The VMM database can be installed automatically for you if you chose to use the SQL Server 2005 Express edition, or you can install SQL prior to installing SCVMM 2008.

Software and Hardware Requirements

In order to install SCVMM 2008 in any configuration (single server or distributed), first you must have a set of required software and hardware installed. For a single server installation, all the software prerequisites must be installed prior to the installation of SCVMM. For a distributed component installation approach, the individual component prerequisites must be installed prior to the installation of that component.

Software Requirements

Table 12-1 provides a breakdown of the software that is required for the single server installation and the software requirements for each component when installed in a distributed mode. The single server installation mode software requirements assume you want all SCVMM components on a single server, including integration with System Center Operations Manager.

TABLE 12-1 Software Requirements for Single Server or Distributed Component Installation Modes

INSTALLATION MODE	COMPONENTS INSTALLED	SOFTWARE REQUIRED
Single Server	Virtual Machine Manager (VMM) server	Windows Server 2008 x64 Standard, Enterprise, or Datacenter edition
	Virtual Machine Library	Microsoft .NET Framework 3.0
	Virtual Machine Manager Administrator Console	Windows PowerShell 1.0
	Virtual Machine Manager Self-Service Portal	Windows Automated Installation Kit (WAIK) 1.1 (required for P2V migrations)
	Virtual Machine Manager database	Local or remote SQL Server 2005 SP2 or SQL Server 2008 (Express, Standard, or Enterprise edition) installation
	Virtual Machine Manager Windows PowerShell interface	
	Virtual Machine Manager Reporting	Internet Information Server (IIS)
		Operations Manager 2007 SP1
		Operations Manager 2007 SP1 Reporting Server
		Operations Manager 2007 SP1 agent on all hosts you want to monitor
		System Center Virtual Machine Manager 2008 Management Pack for Operations Manager 2007 (required for PROTips)
Distributed Component	Virtual Machine Manager (VMM) server	Windows Server 2008 x64 Standard, Enterprise, or Datacenter edition
		Microsoft .NET Framework 3.0
		Windows PowerShell 1.0
		Windows Automated Installation Kit (WAIK) 1.1
	Virtual Machine Library	Windows Server 2008 x64 Standard, Enterprise, or Datacenter edition
		Windows Server 2003 (or R2) with SP2
	Virtual Machine Manager Administrator Console	Windows Server 2008 x64 Standard, Enterprise, or Datacenter edition
		Windows Server 2003 (or R2) with SP2
		Windows Vista SP1
		Windows XP SP2

INSTALLATION MODE	COMPONENTS INSTALLED	SOFTWARE REQUIRED
Distributed Component	Virtual Machine Manager Self-Service Portal	Windows Server 2008 x64 Standard, Enterprise, or Datacenter edition
		Windows Server 2003 (or R2) with SP2
		Internet Information Server (IIS)
	Virtual Machine Manager database	SQL Server 2005 SP2 Express, Standard, or Enterprise edition
		SQL Server 2008 Express, Standard, or Enterprise edition
	Virtual Machine Manager Reporting	Operations Manager 2007 SP1
		Operations Manager 2007 SP1 Reporting Server
		Operations Manager 2007 SP1 agent on all hosts you want to monitor
		System Center Virtual Machine Manager 2008 Management Pack for Operations Manager 2007
		SQL Server 2005 SP2 Standard, or Enterprise edition
		SQL Server 2008 Standard, or Enterprise edition

Hardware Requirements

The following tables provide the recommended hardware requirements for a single server installation and for distributed component installations based on the component installed.

Single Server Installation Hardware Requirements

A single server installation will require more processing and memory based on the number of managed hosts. A threshold of 150 managed hosts was used as an example of when additional hardware would be required. Table 12-2 provides the list of hardware requirements for a single server installation.

TABLE 12-2 Single Server Hardware Requirements

HARDWARE COMPONENT	MINIMUM RECOMMENDATION
Processor	Dual-processor, dual-core, 2 GHz (x64) or greater for managing up to 150 hosts Dual-processor, dual-core, 3.6 GHz (x64) or greater for managing more than 150 hosts
Memory	4 GB for up to 150 hosts 8 GB for more than 150 hosts
Hard drive space	50 GB (using a local default installation of Microsoft SQL Server 2005 Express Edition) 40 GB (using a remote SQL Server 2005 database) 80 GB (using the VMM server as a library server)
Network	1 Gigabit Ethernet

Distributed Components Hardware Requirements

Distributing components across multiple servers will provide the best performing and scalable SCVMM infrastructure. This will come at the cost of more hardware and systems to manage, though.

The main distributed component for the SCVMM infrastructure is the Virtual Machine Manager (VMM) server. This is a required component in the distributed SCVMM infrastructure. When scaling a VMM server to a large number of hosts, it is recommended that you install the database and library components on separate servers. Table 12-3 contains the minimum recommended hardware configuration for a VMM Server for up to and above 150 hosts.

TABLE 12-3 VMM Server Component Hardware Requirements

HARDWARE COMPONENT	MINIMUM RECOMMENDATION
Processor	Dual-processor, dual-core, 2 GHz (x64) or greater for managing up to 150 hosts Dual-processor, dual-core, 3.6 GHz (x64) or greater for managing more than 150 hosts
Memory	4 GB for up to 150 hosts 8 GB for more than 150 hosts
Hard drive space	50 GB (using a local default installation of Microsoft SQL Server 2005 Express Edition) for up to 150 hosts 50 GB for more than 150 hosts; distribute the SQL database and library share on other servers
Network	1 Gigabit Ethernet

Another important distributed component for the SCVMM infrastructure is the Administrative Console. This is a required component in the distributed SCVMM infrastructure. It is recommended to install the Administrative Console on the VMM server or on a remote administrative workstation, and it is required that the Administrative Console is installed on the VMM server to use SCVMM Reporting. Use the hardware recommendations in Table 12-4 if you need additional dedicated administrative consoles. Table 12-4 contains the minimum recommended hardware configuration for an administrative console for up to and above 150 hosts.

TABLE 12-4 Administrative Console Component Hardware Requirements

HARDWARE COMPONENT	MINIMUM RECOMMENDATION
Processor	Pentium 4, 2 GHz (x64) or greater for managing up to 150 hosts
	Single-processor, dual-core, 3.6 GHz (x64) or greater for managing more than 150 hosts
Memory	1 GB for up to 150 hosts
	2 GB for more than 150 hosts
Hard drive space	2 GB for up to 150 hosts
	4 GB for more than 150 hosts
Network	1 Gigabit Ethernet

The library server component provides storage for file-based objects that are distributed to Hyper-V servers (virtual machines, virtual hard disks, ISO images, scripts). The VMM server will have a library share by default, but there are situations in which you will want additional library share servers. For example, a dedicated library share for a VMM server that is managing more than 150 hosts allows the offloading of disk input/output. Another example is a Hyper-V server in a branch office location where you might want a library server installed locally to provide local library resources instead of transferring them over the wide area network (WAN). Library servers should be located as close as possible to the hosts on which they will provision virtual machines. This will result in multiple library servers in larger installations or environments where the hosts are distributed geographically.

Table 12-5 contains the minimum recommended hardware configuration for dedicated library servers.

TABLE 12-5 Library Server Component Hardware Requirements

HARDWARE COMPONENT	MINIMUM RECOMMENDATION
Processor	Single-processor, dual-core, 3.2 GHz (x64)
Memory	2 GB
Hard drive space	Varies based on the amount of content stored in the library share: ■ Virtual hard disks ■ Virtual floppy disks ■ ISO images ■ Scripts ■ Stored virtual machines
Network	1 Gigabit Ethernet

Self-Service Portal is an optional component that allows users to create and manage their own virtual machines or provides server administrators with the ability to remotely manage the operating system running on the virtual machines they own using a Web interface. The Web portal utilizes SCVMM 2008–defined user roles that determine the scope of the users' actions on their own virtual machines. In addition, the Web portal can be limited to manage only the virtual machines on a set of Hyper-V servers placed in a host group. Table 12-6 contains the minimum recommended hardware configuration for dedicated Self-Service Portal servers.

TABLE 12-6 Self-Service Portal Component Hardware Requirements

HARDWARE COMPONENT	MINIMUM RECOMMENDATION
Processor	Single-processor, dual-core, 3.2 GHz (x64) for up to 10 concurrent users Dual-processor, dual-core, 3.2 GHz (x64) for more than 10 concurrent users
Memory	4 GB for up to 10 concurrent users 8 GB for more than 10 concurrent users
Hard drive space	20 GB for up to 10 concurrent users 40 GB for more than 10 concurrent users
Network	1 Gigabit Ethernet for up to 10 concurrent users Dual 1 Gigabit Ethernet for more than 10 concurrent users

The Virtual Machine Manager database stores all VMM configuration information, library information, and job status information. The VMM database requires Microsoft SQL Server 2005 SP2 or newer. You can either specify a local or remote instance of an existing Microsoft SQL Server database or have the Setup Wizard install SQL Server 2005 Express Edition SP2 on the VMM server. Although VMM supports using SQL Server 2005 Express Edition SP2, it is recommended that you use SQL Server 2005 SP2 Standard or Enterprise edition for managing more than 150 hosts or integrating with Operations Manager 2007. Table 12-7 contains the minimum recommended hardware configuration for dedicated VMM database servers.

TABLE 12-7 Database Server Component Hardware Requirements

HARDWARE COMPONENT	MINIMUM RECOMMENDATION
Processor	Dual-processor, dual-core, 2 GHz (x64) or greater for managing up to 150 hosts
	Dual-processor, dual-core, 3.6 GHz (x64) or greater for managing more than 150 hosts
Memory	4 GB for up to 150 hosts
	8 GB for more than 150 hosts
Hard drive space	150 GB for up to 150 hosts
	200 GB for more than 150 hosts
Network	1 Gigabit Ethernet

The SCVMM 2008 Reporting component is an interface between a System Center Operations Manager 2007 installation and VMM Server. The System Center Operations Manager Reporting component can be an existing System Center Operations Manager installation, or if one does not exist, you can install a dedicated System Center Operations Manager infrastructure. Table 12-8 contains the minimum recommended hardware configuration for dedicated VMM Reporting servers.

TABLE 12-8 VMM Reporting Component Hardware Requirements

HARDWARE COMPONENT	MINIMUM RECOMMENDATION
Processor	Dual-processor, dual-core, 3.6 GHz (x64) or greater
Memory	4 GB or greater
Hard drive space	100 GB or greater
Network	1 Gigabit Ethernet

Step-by-Step Installation

In this section, we will perform a step-by-step installation of a single server SCVMM 2008 configuration. The steps will focus on the installation of SCVMM itself and will not address installing the prerequisites. Before you can start following these instructions, however, you will need to do the following:

- Enable the Windows PowerShell feature.
- Install the Windows Automation Installation Kit (WAIK) for Windows Server 2008.
- Install the Web Server (IIS) role (if you want a local self-service portal).
- Install SQL Server 2005 SP2 (recommended for managing a server farm).

Installing SQL Server 2005 SP2 on a different server than the VMM server will provide increased performance.

Evaluate the Prerequisite Configuration

Before you can start installing SCVMM 2008, you must ensure that the software and hardware prerequisites have been met. SCVMM 2008 has a Configuration Analyzer that you can use to check that everything you need is installed and properly configured. The SCVMM Configuration Analyzer is an add-on to the Microsoft Baseline Configuration Analyzer (MBCA) that provides the appropriate requirements for the MBCA to analyze and reports any configuration anomalies.

> **NOTE** Both the MBCA and the SCVMM 2008 Configuration Analyzer are available as downloads from the Microsoft Download Center at *http://www.microsoft.com/downloads /en/default.aspx*.

SCVMM 2008 Configuration Analyzer can be used to scan the local machine or a remote machine for installation prerequisites for each SCVMM role. Use the following steps to analyze the server to determine if all the prerequisites have been performed for SCVMM 2008 to be installed:

1. Click Start, click All Programs, click Virtual Machine Manager Configuration Analyzer, and then click Configuration Analyzer.

2. In the VMM roles and computer names area, specify the VMM roles you want to evaluate and enter the names of the computers you want to scan.

3. After you have specified all VMM roles or functions and the associated computer names, click Scan.

4. After the scan is completed, you will be presented with a report that provides details on any issues found. Before attempting to install VMM 2008, resolve these issues.

When you scan a remote computer, the SCVMM 2008 Configuration Analyzer uses the credentials that you logged on with, unless you specify different credentials in the Credentials area. The credentials for a remote computer must be those of a domain account that is a local administrator on the remote computer.

Installing the Virtual Machine Manager Server Component

To install SCVMM 2008 VMM server component, follow these steps:

1. Log on to the machine with domain administrator credentials.

2. Insert the SCVMM 2008 DVD and launch Setup.

3. On the splash screen shown in Figure 12-1, under Setup, click VMM Server. The VMM Setup will copy some temporary files needed for installation and then launch the installation wizard.

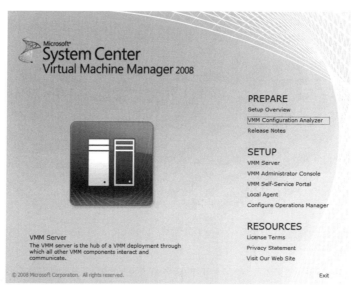

FIGURE 12-1 SCVMM 2008 installation splash screen

4. On the License Terms page, select the option I Accept The Terms Of This Agreement and click Next.

5. On the Customer Experience Improvement Program page, select an option and click Next.

6. On the Product Registration page, provide the User and Organization information and click Next.

7. On the Prerequisites Check page, verify that all of the prerequisites have been met and click Next. If you need to resolve a prerequisite, make the change and then return to the Prerequisite Check page and click Check Again.

8. On the Installation Location page, verify that the path is correct and click Next.

9. On the SQL Server Settings page, shown in Figure 12-2, provide the name of the server running SQL (or localhost for the local machine), select the SQL Instance, and provide the name of the existing database or check the box to create a new database. When you have selected all of the appropriate options, click Next.

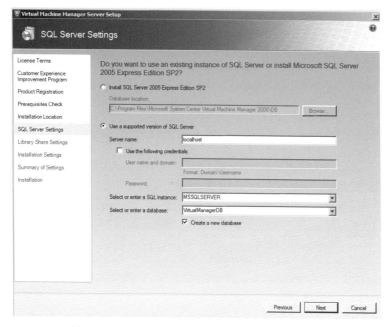

FIGURE 12-2 SCVMM 2008 SQL Server Settings page of the installation wizard

10. On the Library Share Settings page, select the option to create a new Library share and click Next.

11. On the Installation Settings page, shown in Figure 12-3, modify any of the default ports for the console, agents, or file transfer; change the VMM service account as desired; and then click Next.

> **NOTE** Make note of any port changes that you make because you will need those ports when installing additional components.

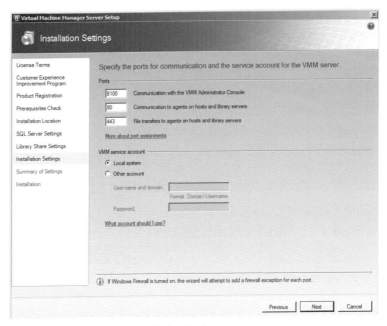

FIGURE 12-3 SCVMM 2008 Installation Settings page

12. On the Summary Of Settings page, review the settings you chose and then click Install to start the installation of the SCVMM 2008 VMM server component.

13. During the installation, you will see the status of each component being installed as well as the status of the entire installation. When the installation process is completed, you will receive an indication of a success or failure of the VMM server installation. When you are done reviewing the installation status page, click Close.

You can now proceed to the installation of the Administrative Console.

Installing Virtual Machine Manager Administrative Console

After you have the VMM server component installed, you can proceed to install the Administrative Console. The Administrative Console will be the primary interface that SCVMM administrators will use to manage the Hyper-V server farm.

To install the SCVMM 2008 VMM Administrative Console component, follow these steps:

1. On the splash screen for Virtual Machine Manager 2008 installation (shown in Figure 12-1), under the Setup heading, click the VMM Administrative Console option to start the installation.

2. The installation files will be copied to the server. On the License Terms page, select the option I Accept The Terms Of This Agreement and click Next.

3. On the Customer Experience Improvement Program (CEIP) page, make note of how to opt out of the CEIP and click Next.

4. On the Prerequisites Check page, verify that all of the prerequisites have been met and click Next. If you need to resolve a prerequisite, make the necessary changes, and then return to the Prerequisite Check page and click Check Again.

5. On the Installation Location page, verify that the path is correct and click Next.

6. On the Port Assignments page, modify the default ports for the console if desired and then click Next.

7. On the Summary Of Settings page, review the settings you chose and click Install to start the installation of the SCVMM 2008 Administrative Console component.

8. During the installation, you will see the status of each component being installed as well as the status of the entire installation. When the installation process is completed, you will receive an indication of a success or failure of the Administrative Console installation. When you are done reviewing the installation status page, click Close.

You can proceed to the installation of the Self-Service Portal component.

Installing Virtual Machine Manager Self-Service Portal

After you have the VMM Administrative Console component installed, you can proceed to install the Self-Service Portal. The Self-Service Portal will be the primary interface that administrators or end users will use to manage virtual machines they own that are running on the Hyper-V server farm.

To install SCVMM 2008 VMM Self-Service Portal component, follow these steps:

1. On the installation splash screen (shown in Figure 12-1), under the Setup heading, click the VMM Self-Service Portal option to start the installation.

2. The installation files are copied to the server. On the License Terms page, select the option I Accept The Terms Of This Agreement and click Next.

3. On the Prerequisites Check page, verify that all of the prerequisites have been met and click Next. If you need to resolve a prerequisite, make the necessary changes, and then return to the Prerequisite Check page and click Check Again.

4. On the Installation Location page, verify that the path is correct and click Next.

5. On the Web Server Settings page, verify the VMM server fully qualified domain name, modify the default ports for the Administrative Console if required, modify the port for the self-service console, and then click Next.

   If the default Web site is currently using port 80 and you did not modify the defaults, you will see the error shown in Figure 12-4. Either modify the Web port in use or configure a host header to continue to use port 80.

FIGURE 12-4 Self-Service Portal Web site port installation error

6. On the Summary Of Settings page, review the settings you chose and click Install to start the installation of SCVMM 2008 Self-Service Portal component.

7. During the installation, you will see the status of each component being installed, as well as the status of the entire installation. When the installation process is completed, you will receive an indication of a success or failure of the Self-Service Portal installation. When you are done reviewing the installation status page, click Close.

DIRECT FROM THE SOURCE

Hyper-V Updates

Bryon Surace, Senior Program Manager
Windows Virtualization

There have been some bug fixes and enhancements for Hyper-V since it was released. TechNet has a great resource that tracks all of the updates and when they are required in a single location; you can find it at *http://technet.microsoft.com /en-us/library/dd430893.aspx*.

Managing Hyper-V from an SCVMM 2008 server requires at least two updates:

- KB956589: To fix a communication issue between the SCVMM 2008 agent and the SCVMM VMM server

- KB956774: To fix a Background Intelligent Transfer Services (BITS) issue that prevents SCVMM Agent installation from failing

KB956774 should be installed on a Hyper-V server prior to attempting to add the host to SCVMM 2008. KB956589 needs to be installed on the Hyper-V server after the host is added to SCVMM 2008 and the agent is installed. Until you install KB956589, the Hyper-V server status will display as Needs Attention in SCVMM 2008 console.

Managing a Server Farm

Server farms are built to provide a consolidated set of resources that can be managed as a single resource. This allows scalability and ease of management. Managing a farm of Hyper-V servers with SCVMM 2008 requires planning to map the delegation abilities of the SCVMM 2008 to the management scenarios required. The most common scenarios where farms of Hyper-V servers will be required are data centers, test labs, common development environments, and virtual desktop infrastructures. Although each of these scenarios involves a pool of Hyper-V servers, the way they are configured and managed differ. The combination of the management scenario and the delegation requirements will drive the number of SCVMM 2008 servers that are required. Figure 12-5 shows the initial VMM Administrator Console page upon first launch. You can treat this as the blank canvas that you will customize to meet your management scenario requirements.

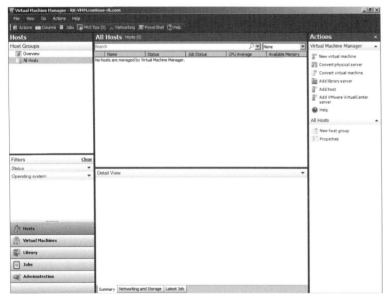

FIGURE 12-5 VMM Administrator Console

Types of Managed Hosts

SCVMM 2008 can manage hosts running Virtual Server 2005 R2 SP1, Hyper-V role on Windows Server 2008, Microsoft Hyper-V Server 2008, and ESX hosts (via Virtual Center). These hosts must be in the one of the following configurations:

- Windows Server–based hosts that are located in an Active Directory Domain Services (AD DS) domain that has two-way trust with the SCVMM 2008 server's Active Directory domain

- Windows Server–based hosts that are located in an Active Directory domain that does not have a two-way trust with the SCVMM 2008 server's Active Directory domain

- Windows Server–based hosts located on a perimeter network

- Windows Server–based hosts that are in a disjointed namespace, where the host's fully qualified domain name (FQDN) resolved from the domain name service (DNS) is not the same as the name obtained from Active Directory

- VMware ESX Server hosts located anywhere in your environment

NOTE To manage an ESX host, it must be currently managed by VMware Virtual Center. To manage the ESX host, you actually add the Virtual Center server, and all hosts managed by that server are added and automatically placed into host groups that match the hierarchy on the server. VMware ESX servers must remain within their parent host group or a child of that host group. If a new datacenter definition is subsequently added on the Virtual Center server, it appears as a new host group in SCVMM Administrative Console the next time the VMware VirtualCenter Server is refreshed.

Host Management

Before you can manage your first Hyper-V server, you must register it with the SCVMM 2008 VMM server component so that a VMM agent can be installed on the host. The agent receives instructions and commands from VMM server through the Administrative Console or the Windows PowerShell SCVMM commands and executes those on the Hyper-V server. These instructions can be anything from modifying the Hyper-V settings to creating and managing virtual machines.

Registering a Hyper-V server is a wizard-based process that you can start by clicking the Add Host action on the Actions menu. If the Hyper-V role is not already installed on a Windows Server 2008 server, the SCVMM agent installation process will enable it and reboot the server.

Grouping Hosts

By default, SCVMM only has a single host group called All Hosts. You can form logical groupings by creating new host groups. If you want to create groupings, you can organize host groups in a hierarchical fashion, for example, with parent host groups associated with children host groups. When you add a host to a VMM server that has multiple host groups, you can select to which host group the new host is added. You can modify host groups with hierarchical placement by using drag-and-drop capabilities.

Host groups have configurable properties, including general properties such as description, hardware reserves for a host (CPU percentage, memory, disk space, disk I/O per second [IOPS], and network capacity percentage), and the configuration of Performance Resource Optimization (PRO) tips. Host reserves are used in the virtual machine placement calculation to determine if there are enough hardware resources available to run a virtual machine.

NOTE Performance Resource Optimization in Virtual Machine Manager 2008 provides the ability to apply resource optimization for workload and applications within a virtualized environment. PRO requires integration between SCVMM 2008 and System Center Operation Manager 2007. Performance and health data is provided by PRO-enabled management packs in System Center Operation Manager 2007. Using this information, PRO can automatically or manually implement recommendations for minimizing downtime and accelerating time to resolution. These recommendations are called PROTips.

PRO configuration gives you the ability to enable or disable PRO for a host group, to define the minimum severity level of a tip (Critical only or Warning and Critical) that will be shown using the PROTips interface in SCVMM 2008, to determine how the tip should be implemented (manually or automatically), and to designate the severity level of tips that will trigger an implementation. If you have a hierarchy of host groups, child host groups can inherit the configurable properties from their parent host group.

SCVMM uses host groups as building blocks for its delegation model. Determining how you want to group hosts is usually driven by the management scenario. Since you can delegate only at the level of a host group in the SCVMM Administrative Console, how you place virtual machines on the hosts is also affected by your decision.

For example, if your servers (physical or virtual) are managed by function (Messaging, File, Print, Domain Controllers, and so on), and administration is segregated at the function level, then virtual machines must be grouped by function. SCVMM allows you to create groups of hosts and delegate administration at the group level. The smallest delegation you can have is a host group containing a single Hyper-V server with a single virtual machine.

Using the management by function approach requires you to assign the virtual machines to Hyper-V servers by function, and multiple functions should not be combined on a single Hyper-V server. If you manage by business group, then all the virtual machines for a specific business group must be contained on a set of Hyper-V hosts within a single host group.

For a management scenario such as a test lab, you may not manage by function or business group, but by project. In this type of scenario, you would create a host group and dedicate Hyper-V servers to a specific project and the virtual machines for that project would reside on those hosts. Typically in a test lab environment, you have a common pool of resources and all hosts can reside in a single host group.

For a management scenario such as a hosting virtual desktops for application compatibility purposes, you may require the virtual machines to be grouped by operating system version (Windows XP or Windows Vista) or by capabilities (32 or 64 bit).

For a management scenario such as a common development environment, you may require the virtual machines to be grouped by development project, by geography, or by special networking needs to get access to backend systems.

Delegating administrative access to the SCVMM console is done at the host group level and is applied to a user or group. If you want a user or group to be able to manage a set of hosts (and therefore all the virtual machines on those hosts), you create a new delegation user role. Creating that delegation is a wizard-based process from the Administration section of the SCVMM Administrative Console. The wizard is a simple three-step process:

1. Select the user or group of users to grant the delegation.

2. Select the scope of host groups and library servers for the delegation.

3. Create the delegation.

Figure 12-6 shows the Select Scope page of the wizard. You can see that host groups can be nested and that you can select the entire tree or any host group in the tree as part of the delegation. When you have delegated the hosts to the correct teams, each of those teams can manage their respective Hyper-V servers.

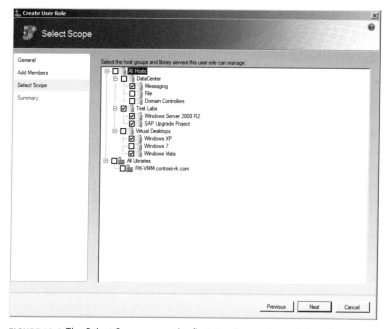

FIGURE 12-6 The Select Scope page, the first step in creating a delegation user role

Managing Host Properties

Each host has a set of properties that can be managed by right-clicking the host and selecting Properties. Available properties to manage include a host description, current availability for taking on additional virtual machine load (placement), registration status of virtual machines, host reserves, viewing the current hardware configuration (processor, memory, storage, floppy drives, network adapters, and CD/DVD drives), available virtual networks, default paths, remote console TCP/IP port, and a series of custom properties. Figure 12-7 shows the Host Properties dialog box.

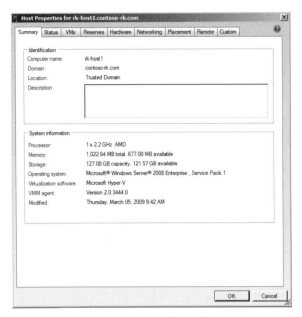

FIGURE 12-7 Hyper-V Host Properties dialog box

If a host needs to be serviced, the host can be removed from the active list of hosts in the server farm that are available for virtual machine placement. To do this, select the Status tab of the host properties and clear the option that says This Host Is Available For Placement. By doing this, the host is removed from the algorithm that determines the host ranking for virtual machine placement.

If you add a Hyper-V host to SCVMM, all of the currently registered virtual machines are automatically added to the SCVMM Administrative Console and are available to manage. If you deploy a new virtual machine using SCVMM 2008, it is automatically registered on the host. If there are virtual machines that you need to import into a Hyper-V host using SCVMM 2008, you must use the VMs tab in the Hyper-V host's properties to import the virtual machine. The import files must already be available on the Hyper-V storage.

To manage virtual networks on a Hyper-V server using SCVMM 2008, you must use the Networking tab in the Hyper-V host's properties to add or modify virtual networks. Clicking Add will allow you to define a new Private, Internal, or External virtual network connection and define a VLAN tag for the Hyper-V parent partition. To modify an existing virtual network, you select the virtual network and change any properties or type of virtual network. To remove an existing virtual network, select the virtual network in the list and click Remove.

To modify an existing default path to store a virtual machine on the Hyper-V server, or if you need to define a new alternate default path using SCVMM 2008, you must use the Placement tab in the Hyper-V server's properties to make these changes. The Placement tab allows you to browse the file system of the remote Hyper-V server and select an existing path to place virtual machines. If you need to create a new directory, you must select the Explore Directory option in the lower-left corner of the browse window.

To modify the TCP/IP port for the remote virtual machine connections on the Hyper-V server using SCVMM 2008, you must use the Remote tab in the Hyper-V server's properties to modify the port value. The default port value is 2179, but it can be changed to any port value in the range 1 to 65535.

Managing Host Networking

SCVMM 2008 allows you to migrate virtual machine between Hyper-V servers. In order for the migration to be successful and the virtual machine to communicate on the network, the virtual machine must be able to connect to the correct virtual network during migration. The best practice approach to making that work smoothly is to define the virtual networks connecting to the same subnets on all Hyper-V servers so that they have the same name (including capitalization). For example, if there is a physical network adapter connected to the 10.10.10.0 network on each Hyper-V server, you should create a virtual network on each host with the same name, such as External-10.10.10.0.

Host Networking View

SCVMM 2008 added a new feature to provide a graphical view of the networking configuration of the Hyper-V server. To access the network view, right-click a Hyper-V server in the SCVMM 2008 hosts view and click View Networking. You will see a graphical diagram of each virtual network on the host and the virtual machine attachments. Figure 12-8 is a view of a Hyper-V server that has two virtual machines that were created and connected to the same internal virtual network.

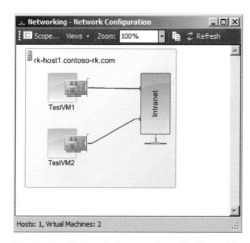

FIGURE 12-8 Network diagram view of a Hyper-V server

Managing SCVMM Using Windows PowerShell

David Ziembicki, Principal Consultant
Microsoft Consulting Services

System Center Virtual Machine Manager 2008 uses Windows PowerShell as the building block for all management actions. Anything you can do in the SCVMM 2008 user interface, you can script with Windows PowerShell. Many places in the SCVMM user interface will provide a button that you can click to see the Windows PowerShell the VMM server is about to execute so that you can copy/paste it for use in your own scripts for repetitive operations.

Microsoft has released three books that can help you learn the basics of Windows PowerShell:

- *Microsoft Windows PowerShell Step By Step* (Microsoft Press, 2007)

- *Windows PowerShell Scripting Guide* (Microsoft Press, 2008)

- *Windows PowerShell 2.0 Administrator's Pocket Consultant* (Microsoft Press, 2009)

Microsoft has also posted two online resources that will help you understand how Windows PowerShell can be used with SCVMM 2008 and provide example code that can quickly be leveraged. The two reference documents can be found at the following locations:

- "Managing Virtualization with SCVMM and PowerShell," available at *http://www.microsoft.com/downloads/details.aspx?displaylang=en&FamilyID= 0c3a871d-9e80-46dd-85bc-3f759f007416*

- "System Center Virtual Machine Manager 2008 Cmdlet Reference," available at *http://www.microsoft.com/downloads/details.aspx?familyid=58E79A68-CEA8- 4E73-840F-CDD8FEB9DE87&displaylang=en*

Self-Service Portal Management

SCVMM 2008 Self-Service Portal is designed for end users or server administrators to create and access virtual machines. To access the Self-Service Portal, you must create a self-service user role and add users as members of that role. Self-service users cannot manage the hardware properties of a virtual machine except for the virtual CD/DVD media connections. SCVMM Administrators can be made members of a self-service user role and use the Self-Service Portal to manage virtual machines, but they are limited to the permissions that are assigned to the self-service user role.

Configuration of the Self-Service Portal involves four steps. The first step is installing the portal (refer to the installation section entitled "Installing Virtual Machine Manager Self-Service Portal" earlier in this chapter for the installation steps). The second step is determining which Hyper-V servers should be dedicated Self-Service Portals to host virtual machines. The third step is creating a host group and moving all the Self-Service candidate Hyper-V servers to that host group. The forth step is creating a self-service user role that defines the following:

- Self-service role name
- Members of the role
- Permissions that the role members have
- Virtual machine creation rights
- Library shares that will be available to this role

Permissions for a self-service user involve the management of the state of the virtual machine and access rights. You can grant all or individual rights to the defined user role. The following permissions are available:

- **Start** Start virtual machines.
- **Stop** Stop virtual machines.
- **Pause and Resume** Pause and resume virtual machines.
- **Checkpoint** Create and manage snapshots.
- **Remove** Remove virtual machines.
- **Local Administrator** Grant local administrator rights on the virtual machines.
- **Remote Connection** Remotely connect to virtual machine.
- **Shutdown** Shut down virtual machines.

The virtual machine creation rights permission will allow the self-service user role members to create their own virtual machines. You can limit what predefined virtual machine templates they can use to create the virtual machines, and you can also define a quota value to each virtual machine the user deploys on a self-service host. Virtual machines count against the quota only if they are located on a host (running or not). If a user reaches their quota, they cannot power on any new virtual machines. Optionally, you can enable the quota to be shared across all users in the role. If you do this, then each running virtual machine counts to a global quota for that self-service role, regardless of who the virtual machine belongs to.

The library shares permission determines whether a user can store their virtual machine in a library or not. If the permission is enabled, you can select from the available library shares that the members of the self-service role can use. You cannot limit a subset of the members of a self-service role to a specific library share.

After you define all the permissions and the options, for a self-service user role, the members of the role can access the Self-Service Portal. Figure 12-9 shows the default window for the Self-Service Portal when a self-service role member has logged on with the assigned credentials.

FIGURE 12-9 Self-Service Portal member window

You can have multiple Self-Service Portals defined in a single server farm. A Hyper-V host can be a member of only a single host group, and a Self-Service Portal defines access by assigned host group. It is possible to define multiple self-service user roles against the same host group, allowing you to have different permissions or quotas for each host group.

Library Server Management

Library servers are the building blocks for provisioning new virtual machines. By default, a library server is created on the same server where the VMM server component is installed. You can create library servers on other servers throughout your infrastructure. When a virtual machine is provisioned from SCVMM 2008, it can be created from scratch, or you can utilize virtual machine templates from the library server to reduce the provisioning time. Figure 12-10 displays the default configuration of a library server installed on a VMM server. By default, the library contains only two blank virtual hard disks (VHDs): a 16-gigabyte (GB) dynamically expanding VHD named Blank Disk – Small, and a 60-GB dynamically expanding VHD named Blank Disk – Large.

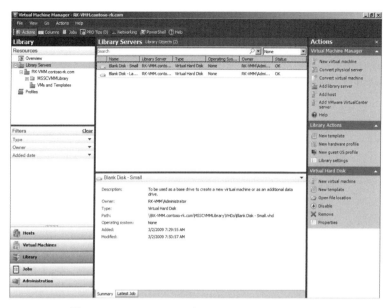

FIGURE 12-10 Library server management

Managing an existing library server consists of the following actions:

- Creating a new virtual machine template
- Creating a new virtual machine hardware profile
- Creating a new guest operating system profile
- Managing library files
- Managing the library settings

In addition to managing an existing library server, you also can create a new library server. Additional library servers should be created for each location that virtual machines will be provisioned to Hyper-V servers. You do not want virtual machines to be provisioned over a wide area network (WAN) link to a branch office or even across a fast link to another site. To eliminate the transfer of virtual machine files across slow links during virtual machine provisioning, create a library server in the remote location. You can do this directly on the Hyper-V server and reduce provisioning time.

Creating remote library servers will require that they are kept up to date with a central library server. Library servers are just file shares that hold file objects used during provisioning (virtual hard disks, virtual floppy disks, CD\DVD ISO images, scripts, configuration files, and so on). Any replication system that will allow you to replicate the contents of the share will work. It is best to use a tool that replicates only file changes instead of the entire file because of the size of the file objects.

Managing Virtual Machine Templates

Virtual machine templates are created from existing virtual machines or from virtual machines currently stored in the library. The existing virtual machine should first be prepared with Sysprep.exe so that it can be deployed with a unique security identifier (SID).

Creating a template is a multistep process that depends on the source that you select. If you select to use an existing template already stored in the library, the process involves five steps:

1. Select the source for the template.

2. Name the template.

3. Configure the hardware profile.

4. Configure the guest operating system profile.

5. Create the template from the selected options.

The template will be created on the same library server that the source template was selected from.

If the source is an existing virtual machine deployed on a Hyper-V server, the process involves seven steps:

1. Select the source for the template.

2. Name the template.

3. Configure the hardware profile.

4. Configure the guest operating system profile.

5. Select the library server to store the template.

6. Select the path in the library share to store the template.

7. Create the template from the selected options.

A common scenario is to create a template from a VHD in the library. Follow these steps to create a template from a VHD that has been prepared with Sysprep.exe and stored in the library:

1. In Library view, in the Actions pane, click New Template.

2. On the Select Source page, select Use An Existing Template Or Virtual Hard Disk Stored In The Library and then click Select.

3. In the Select Template Source dialog box, select the VHD that you want to use, click OK, and then click Next.

4. Enter a template name and description and specify the owner of the template. The template owner must have an Active Directory domain account.

5. On the Configure Hardware page, customize the hardware settings as needed, and then click Next.

    a. Modify the BIOS boot order for the VM (applicable to Hyper-V hosted guests only).

    b. Modify the number of processors required.

    c. Modify the amount of memory to allocate.

    d. Configure the virtual floppy mapping.

    e. Add a virtual DVD drive.

    f. Add a virtual hard disk to an IDE or SCSI controller.

    g. Configure one or more virtual network adapters.

    h. Configure how CPU resources are allocated and whether virtual machines are highly available.

    i. Specify if the virtual machines created from this template will be highly available.

6. On the Guest Operating System page, under General Settings section, configure the following settings:

    a. Computer name (use * to randomly generate a computer name)

    b. Local Admin password (use * to prompt for a password)

    c. Product Key

    d. Time Zone

    e. Operating System

7. On the Guest Operating System page, under the Networking section, configure the following settings:

    a. Domain membership

    b. Workgroup membership

8. On the Guest Operating System page, under the Scripts section, configure the following settings:

    a. **Answer File**   Specify a sysprep answer file to provide additional settings to the ones that the wizard will provide.

    b. **[GUIRunOnce] commands**   Specify any commands that you want to execute at first logon.

9. On the Guest Operating System page, when all settings have been modified, click Next.

10. On the Summary page, review all choices and then click Create.

After the template is created, you can manage the template by editing its properties. Figure 12-11 shows the Virtual Machine Properties dialog box for an existing template.

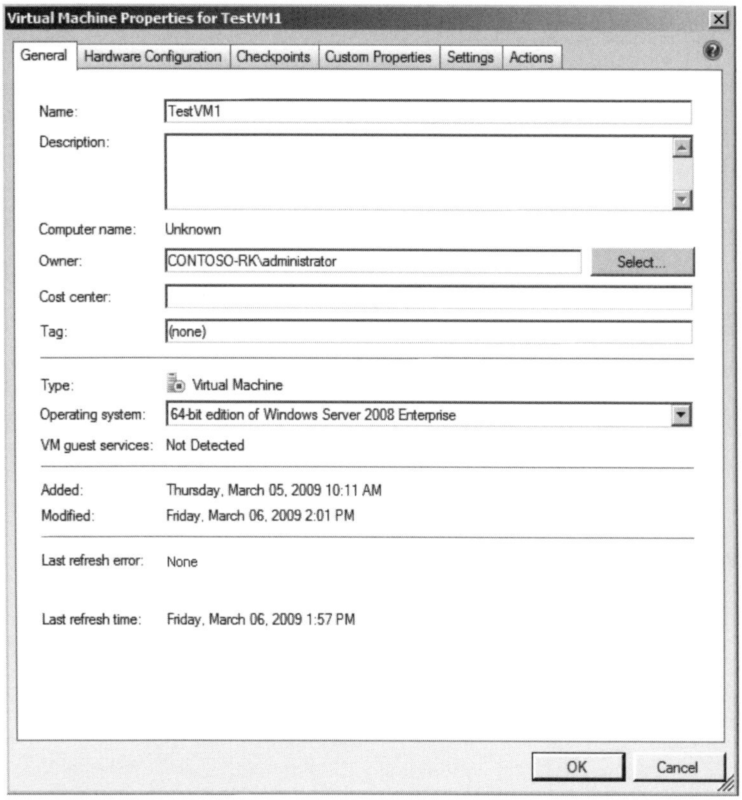

FIGURE 12-11 Virtual Machine Properties dialog box for an existing template

From the template Properties dialog box, you can edit the general properties, the default hardware configuration, the checkpoints that exist, the 10 custom properties, the quota and PRO settings, and the default actions when the Hyper-V server starts and stops.

Consider the following items before creating virtual machine templates from a source virtual machine:

- The virtual machine must be on a host managed by SCVMM 2008.
- The virtual machine will be prepared with Sysprep.exe and removed from the host during the process.
- The virtual machine must be running Windows XP or newer operating system.
- The administrator password on the virtual machine must be blank for the sysprep process to work.

NOTE If you do not want the source virtual machine to be removed from production to create a template, use the Clone option to clone the source virtual machine, do not connect it to the network, and use the clone to create the template instead.

NOTE If the template will be used to create virtual machines via the Self-Service Portal, the template properties must be edited and a value for the owner must be specified. Only the template owner—whether a user or a group assigned to the self-service policy—would be able to create, view, and manage virtual machines created with the template.

Managing Windows PowerShell Scripts in the Library

Storing Windows PowerShell scripts in the VMM Library allows you to view, edit, and run them from the Library view. In order to run Windows PowerShell scripts from the VMM Administrator Console, the machine the administrative console is installed on must have Windows PowerShell installed.

From the VMM Library you can view, modify, remove, or add a new Windows PowerShell script.

To add a Windows PowerShell Script to the VMM Library, follow these steps:

1. Create a Windows PowerShell script and save it with the .ps1 extension
2. Establish a network connection to the VMM Library server using \\Servername \MSVMMLIBRARY.
3. Copy the Windows PowerShell script to the folder or subfolder of the network share.
4. From Library view, select Refresh from the Library Server Actions menu.

To view or edit a Windows PowerShell script from the VMM Library, do the following:

1. In Library view, select the script that you want to view.
2. In the Actions pane, under Script, click View PowerShell Script.
3. This opens a copy of the script in Notepad for viewing.
4. If you edit the script, you must use Save As to save the modified script on the same share. The script will be added to the library during the next library refresh.

Running a Windows PowerShell script requires configuration of the PowerShell execution policy. By default, the policy is set to Restricted, which will not allow any Windows PowerShell scripts to run. You can use the Get-ExecutionPolicy cmdlet to determine your current execution policy.

There are four possible execution policies:

- **Restricted** No scripts can be run. Windows PowerShell can be used only in interactive mode.
- **AllSigned** Only scripts signed by a trusted publisher can be run.
- **RemoteSigned** Downloaded scripts must be signed by a trusted publisher before they can be run.
- **Unrestricted** No restrictions; all Windows PowerShell scripts can be run.

To run Windows PowerShell scripts from the VMM Library, you have two choices. The first choice is to sign the scripts and set the execution policy to AllSigned or RemoteSigned. The second choice is to not sign the scripts and set the execution policy to Unrestricted.

To set the current execution policy to Unrestricted, use the `Set-ExecutionPolicy` cmdlet with *Unrestricted* as the single passed parameter.

To run a Windows PowerShell script from the VMM Library when the execution policy is set correctly:

1. In Library view, select the script that you want to run.
2. In the Actions pane, under Script, click Run PowerShell Script to open a Windows PowerShell window and run the script.

Managing Hardware Profiles

Hardware profiles are created from scratch and stored in the library for use when provisioning virtual machines. A hardware profile, shown in Figure 12-12, consists of the following configuration:

- BIOS settings
- Processor settings (number and speed)
- Memory settings
- Floppy drive configuration
- Communication port configuration for COM1 and COM2
- IDE controller drive configuration
- SCSI controller drive configuration
- Network adapter configuration (number and type)
- CPU priority
- High availability configuration

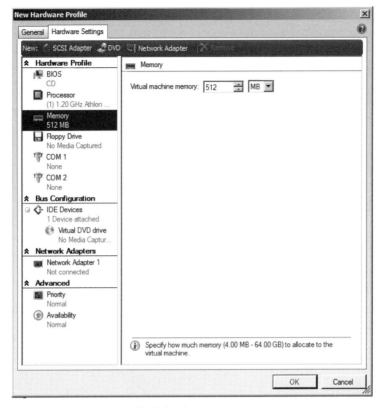

FIGURE 12-12 Hardware Profile dialog box

Managing Guest Operating System Profiles

Guest operating system profiles are used to define standard operating system settings that can be imported into a template to customize it. By creating guest operating profiles for the different operating systems you deploy, you can quickly define a standard approach to configuration. Figure 12-13 shows the guest operating system profile dialog box.

Guest operating system profiles allow you to configure the following options:

- Profile name
- Profile description
- Profile owner
- Guest operating system computer name
- Guest operating system organization information
- Guest operating system administrator password
- Guest operating system product key
- Guest operating system default time zone

- Guest operating system
- Guest operating system workgroup or domain membership
- Guest operating system custom sysprep answer file
- Guest operating system GUIRunOnce commands

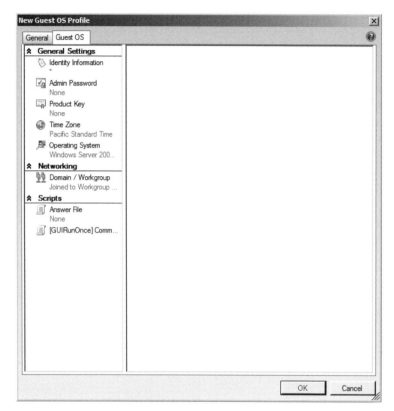

FIGURE 12-13 Guest Operating System Profile dialog box

Library Files Management

Library servers consist of a library network share that files can be downloaded from during virtual machine provisioning. For files to be used by SCVMM 2008, they must be added to the library share. This is done by copying the files to a library share on a library server and then refreshing the library share. When you copy files to an existing library share, the files are not visible or available for use until the next library refresh. The library automatically refreshes on a periodic schedule configurable by the administrator. The default refresh schedule is once an hour. You can also index the files immediately by refreshing the library share manually.

Use the following procedure to add files to an existing library share and then refresh the library share manually:

1. On the library server, copy the files to the library share where you want to store them.

2. In the SCVMM Administrator Console, select Library view.

3. In the navigation pane, expand Library Server and navigate to the library share that you copied the files to.

4. With the library share selected, in the Actions pane, under Library Share, click Refresh.

5. All files on the share are immediately indexed in Virtual Machine Manager and are available for use.

Virtual Machine Management

The SCVMM 2008 Administrator Console, shown in Figure 12-14, displays all the virtual machines that the SCVMM administrator or delegated administrator has access to, based on defined user role delegation. Each virtual machine will be displayed in the All Hosts center pane in list format, with the following information displayed by default:

- Virtual machine name
- Current status
- Job status
- Host the virtual machine resides on currently
- Virtual machine owner
- Current average CPU utilization percentage

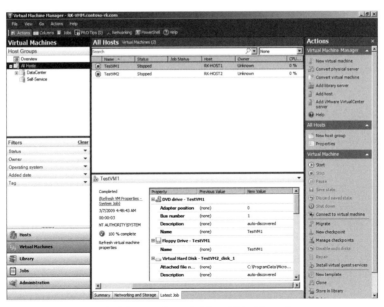

FIGURE 12-14 VMM Administrator Console Virtual Machines view

You can customize the information displayed in the columns by right-clicking the column header and selecting from the available column headings:

- Computer Name
- CPU Count
- Operating System
- Description
- VM Additions
- Added
- Modified
- Memory
- Disk Input
- Disk Output
- Network Input
- Network Output
- Disk Allocated
- Tag
- Cost Center
- Quota Points
- Availability
- Custom properties

Figure 12-14 shows the Actions menu (in the right pane) that displays the actions available for the currently selected virtual machine. Table 12-9 provides a list of all the available actions and a description of what the action performs.

TABLE 12-9 Virtual Machine Actions

ACTION	DESCRIPTION
Start	Power on or resume from saved state.
Stop	Power off.
Pause	Pause processor usage but memory usage stays the same.
Save State	Pause the virtual machine and save current memory and processing information to disk.
Discard Saved State	Delete the memory and processor information on disk so that the virtual machine will have to reboot from scratch.
Shut Down	Shut down the operating system using standard Windows API calls.
Connect To Virtual Machine	Start a remote desktop session with the virtual machine. If the virtual machine is not in the running state, an error will be displayed.

ACTION	DESCRIPTION
New Checkpoint	Take a snapshot.
Manage Checkpoints	Manage the current snapshot tree.
Install Virtual Guest Services	Install Hyper-V Integration Services. Only works for supported Windows operating systems.
New Template	Create a new template based on the selected virtual machine. The selected virtual machine cannot have any checkpoints.
Clone	Create a copy of the current virtual machine.
Store In Library	Save the state of the virtual machine and store it on the library server share.
Delete	Unregister the virtual machine from the Hyper-V server and the VMM Console.
View Networking	Display the current virtual network connections for the virtual machine.
Properties	Display the Properties dialog box so that the virtual machine properties can be managed.

Managing Checkpoints

SCVMM 2008 uses the generic term *checkpoints* to define the different technologies that Virtual Server, Hyper-V, and VMware ESX server use. For Hyper-V, a checkpoint refers to a snapshot. Snapshots are collections of saved state and virtual machine hardware configurations at points in time. Snapshots allow Hyper-V users to perform multiple "what-if" scenario tests and then return to the exact point in time where the virtual machine had been before the tests by applying a snapshot.

SCVMM provides the ability to manage checkpoints (snapshots). Select the virtual machine and select Manage Checkpoints from the Virtual Machine Actions menu to display the checkpoint management interface shown in Figure 12-15. The Checkpoint Management interface is a tab on the Virtual Machine Properties dialog box.

From this interface, you can create a new checkpoint, remove an existing checkpoint, restore the virtual machine to the point in time when the checkpoint was taken (apply a snapshot, in Hyper-V terms), and view the properties of the checkpoint. The Checkpoint Properties dialog box allows you to see the point in time when the checkpoint was taken and the hardware configuration of the virtual machine at that point in time.

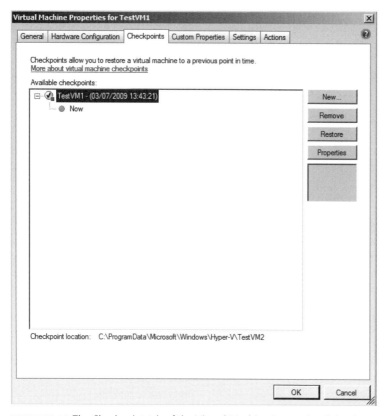

FIGURE 12-15 The Checkpoint tab of the Virtual Machine Properties dialog box

Cloning Virtual Machines

Cloning a virtual machine refers to the process of making a complete copy of an existing virtual machine and then placing that clone on an existing Hyper-V server or on an available library server. The clone process depends on the selection of the host or library placement option.

If you select to place the clone in a library server, the process involves five steps:

1. Name the clone.
2. Configure the hardware profile.
3. Select the library server.
4. Select the path to store the clone.
5. Create the clone from the selected options.

If you select to place the clone virtual machine on a Hyper-V server, the process involves six steps:

1. Name the clone.

2. Configure the hardware profile.

3. Select the host to place the clone.

4. Select the path on the host to store the clone virtual machine.

5. Select the virtual networks to use.

6. Create the clone virtual machine from the selected options.

Virtual Machine Properties Management

Each virtual machine has a set of properties that can be managed by right-clicking the virtual machine name and selecting Properties or by selecting Properties from the Actions menu. Virtual machine properties are broken down into a series of tabs: General, Hardware Configuration, Checkpoints, Custom Properties, Settings, and Actions. Figure 12-16 shows the General tab of the Virtual Machine Properties dialog box.

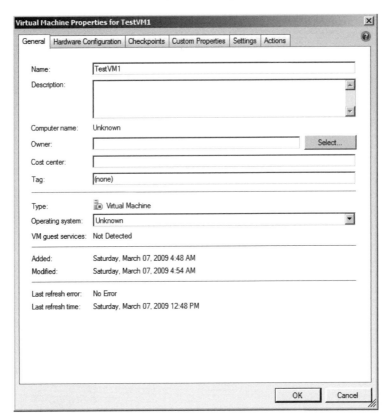

FIGURE 12-16 The General tab of the Virtual Machine Properties dialog box

General properties allow you to manage things like the virtual machine name, owner, and operating system. You can also view other properties such as when the virtual machine was added to the VMM Console, when it was last modified, and if integration services are loaded. Table 12-10 provides a description of each general property that can be managed.

TABLE 12-10 Virtual Machine General Properties

SETTING	DESCRIPTION
Name	Unique name of the virtual machine as seen by SCVMM. This does not have to be the computer name in the operating system, but it makes it easier to manage if it is.
Description	A description that you want to provide about the virtual machine.
Owner	The assigned owner of the virtual machine. This is the user that created the virtual machine by default, but it can be modified.
Cost Center	This is the cost center that you want to assign for reporting charge-back information on virtual machine usage.
Tag	Assign a tag to a virtual machine to enable filtering or grouping in the virtual machines view by tag. Any tag entered will be added to the tag filter list.
Operating System	Select the operating system that will be installed on the virtual machine.

The Hardware Configuration tab provides you with the commonly used hardware configuration options for creating a new virtual machine, template, or clone. Table 12-11 provides a description of each hardware configuration setting that can be managed.

TABLE 12-11 Virtual Machine Hardware Configuration

SETTING	DESCRIPTION
BIOS	Configure the startup order of the CD, IDE hard drive, PXE, and floppy devices. Also Enable/Disable Num Lock.
Processor	Processor configuration. Select the number, type, and speed of the processor.
Memory	Configure the amount of memory reserved.
Floppy Drive	Floppy drive configuration (none, physical, or virtual image).
COM1 – COM2	Communication port configuration for COM1 and COM2. No connection or a named pipe connection.
IDE Devices	IDE controller drive configuration. Virtual hard drives (size, type, controller port), virtual CD/DVD drives (none, physical, or virtual image).

SETTING	DESCRIPTION
SCSI Devices	SCSI controller drive configuration. Virtual hard drives (size, type, controller port).
Network Adapter	Network adapter configuration (connection, tag, VLAN, MAC address).
Integration Services	Integration services to offer the virtual machine (shutdown, time synchronization, data exchange, heartbeat, backup).
Priority	CPU Priority (high, normal, low, custom).
Availability	High Availability Configuration (enabled/disabled).

The Settings tab allows the configuration of quota and PRO configuration. Table 12-12 provides a description for each virtual machine settings option that can be managed.

TABLE 12-12 Virtual Machine Settings

SETTING	DESCRIPTION
Quota	Define the quota points for self-service portal usage tracking and charge back.
PRO	Configuration option to exclude the virtual machine from PRO implementations. This will prevent PRO from migrating a virtual machine.

The Actions tab allows the configuration of actions that happen to the virtual machine when the Hyper-V server starts and stops. Table 12-13 provides a description for each Action setting that can be managed.

TABLE 12-13 Virtual Machine Actions

SETTING	DESCRIPTION
Action When Physical Server Starts	Configure the action that is taken when Hyper-V server starts ■ Never Automatically Turn On The Virtual Machine ■ Always Automatically Turn On The Virtual Machine ■ Automatically Turn On The Virtual Machine If It Was Running When The Physical Server Stopped ■ Delay For Start In Seconds.
Action When Physical Server Stops	Configure the action that is taken when Hyper-V server stops ■ Save State ■ Turn Off The Virtual Machine ■ Shut Down The Guest Operating System

Hyper-V Cluster Management

SCVMM 2008 can manage Hyper-V host clusters of up to 16 nodes. To be a member of a Hyper-V host cluster, a node must be running Hyper-V and Failover Clustering.

Adding a Hyper-V Host Cluster

Adding a Hyper-V host cluster in SCVMM 2008 follows the same process as adding any other Hyper-V node. If SCVMM detects that a Hyper-V server is part of a cluster, it will display a dialog box, as shown in Figure 12-17. When you agree to add the host cluster, SCVMM will add all of the nodes of the cluster.

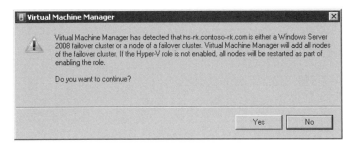

FIGURE 12-17 Cluster detection during the Add Host process

When the host cluster has been added to SCVMM 2008, it is shown in the host groups view as the name of the cluster with each node underneath. Figure 12-18 shows a cluster named RK-Cluster with two nodes, RK-HOST1 and RK-HOST2.

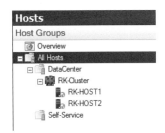

FIGURE 12-18 Host cluster in a host group

Managing a Host Cluster

Managing a host cluster using SCVMM 2008 is limited to a few actions. You can move a host cluster to a different host group, you can remove the host cluster from SCVMM and therefore remove all the nodes of the cluster, and you can modify the properties of the host cluster. You must perform any other management of the host cluster at the server or virtual machine level.

Moving a host cluster to another host group allows you to change the delegation model or the self-service model. Removing the host cluster of SCVMM is typically reserved for performing major maintenance or troubleshooting of the cluster and is very rarely done. The most common management task of a host cluster is managing the cluster properties.

Managing Host Cluster Properties

When you manage a Hyper-V host cluster, you manage the properties for the entire cluster. You do this by selecting the cluster you want to manage in the Hosts view and selecting properties from the Host Cluster menu in the Actions pane.

The Host Cluster properties allow you to monitor the status of cluster nodes, set the node failure reserve for the cluster, view the networks available in the cluster, view the shared storage assigned to the cluster and the free space available, and enable Physical Resource Optimization (PRO) for the cluster. Figure 12-19 shows the Host Cluster Properties dialog box.

FIGURE 12-19 Host Cluster Properties dialog box

On the General tab, the node failure reserve allows you to select the number of nodes of the cluster that will be used to handle node failures. If you select one, the cluster can survive a single node failure and still have enough resources to maintain all the virtual machines running. Each node of the cluster is evaluated based on the current virtual machine resource requirements. A single node failing would result in its virtual machines being migrated to other nodes in the cluster based on available resources. If there is no place for all the virtual machines to go in a single step migration, then the cluster is considered overcommitted. If a cluster will be placed in an overcommitted state by adding an additional virtual machine, the virtual machine placement will be blocked.

On the PRO tab, you can enable Performance Resource Optimization for the cluster and select the severity level at which the tips will be received. You can also enable PRO tips to be automatically implemented after they are received.

Summary

This chapter provided an overview of how System Center Virtual Machine Manager 2008 can be utilized to manage a farm of Hyper-V servers. You learned how to install a System Center Virtual Machine Manager 2008 single server or distributed component model so that you could scale properly to meet the server farm management needs. You also learned about host, library, Self-Service Portal, virtual machine, and host cluster management and configuration.

Additional Resources

The following resources contain additional information related to the topics in this chapter.

- System Center Virtual Machine Manager 2008, a resource that provides access to the product, technical, and installation information for System Center Virtual Machine Manager 2008, available at *http://www.microsoft.com/systemcenter /virtualmachinemanager/en/us/default.aspx*

- System Center Virtual Machine Manager 2008 Management Pack, a resource that provides information for System Center Virtual Machine Manager 2008 Management Pack, available at *http://www.microsoft.com/downloads /details.aspx?FamilyID=d6d5cddd-4ec8-4e3c-8ab1-102ec99c257f&displaylang=en*

- System Center Virtual Machine Manager System Requirements, a resource that provides detailed information on the hardware and software requirements for single server and distributed installation approaches, available at *http://technet.microsoft.com/en-us/library/cc764328.aspx*

- System Center Virtual Machine Manager 2008 Configuration Analyzer, a tool that allows you to analyze a server before or after SCVMM 2008 is installed to ensure that it is properly configured, which can be downloaded at *http://go.microsoft.com/fwlink/?LinkID=100597*

- Microsoft Baseline Configuration Analyzer (MBCA), a tool that is required for the SCVMM 2008 Configuration Analyzer to operate, which can be downloaded at *http://go.microsoft.com/fwlink/?LinkID=97952*

Hyper-V Backup and Recovery

In this chapter, you will learn about backup and recovery options that you can use in a Hyper-V server environment. In particular, you will gain an understanding of the Volume Shadow Copy Service (VSS), as well as how an enterprise-class application like System Center Data Protection Manager (DPM) 2007 SP1 leverages VSS to provide backup and recovery of local and remote Hyper-V servers and virtual machines. You will also learn how you can apply more traditional methods to back up virtual machines. Finally, you will find detailed procedures that guide you through the DPM 2007 SP1 installation and configuration process to support backup and recovery of Hyper-V server configuration information and virtual machines.

Backing Up a Virtualization Environment

A virtualization environment requires the same attention to backup planning as a physical environment, with additional focus on dependencies related to the virtualization layer. As opposed to a physical server whose internal system resource usage does not directly affect the performance of another physical server workload, a virtual machine shares a single set of physical hardware with other virtual machines, creating the potential for virtual machines to affect the performance and workloads of one another. Therefore, a Hyper-V server backup strategy must include a virtual machine backup schedule that has minimal affect on performance and application availability.

In addition, when dealing with a single physical server, the scope of a backup involves only the individual server. In a virtualized environment, the scope of a backup might include the Hyper-V server as well as one or more virtual machines. Therefore, a Hyper-V server backup strategy also has to balance the backup schedule for the virtual machines with that of the Hyper-V server.

In reality, the backup method is paramount to developing a successful strategy for a virtualized environment. If you can leverage the Volume Shadow Copy Service and the Hyper-V VSS writer interface to perform Hyper-V and virtual machine backups, you can implement a fairly straightforward backup strategy. However, if you have to use traditional backup methods for your virtualized environment, this will significantly increase the complexity of your backup strategy.

Understanding the Hyper-V VSS Writer

Generically, a VSS writer is an interface provided by an application to manage data and state information, ensure that pending data is flushed to disk, and ensure that the application is quiescent prior to initializing a volume shadow copy snapshot. This process is necessary to provide a consistent application state prior to performing a backup. In fact, Hyper-V provides a VSS writer that supports the backup of Hyper-V server configuration information and virtual machines.

Without a VSS writer, an application can still be backed up using VSS, but with some major drawbacks. In particular, application state consistency cannot be guaranteed, and therefore, neither can the backup. If a virtual machine were backed up in this manner, restoring the virtual machine using a VSS snapshot would be equivalent to turning off a virtual machine and then turning the machine back on, causing the loss of all state information for applications and services, as well as any data stored in memory.

In Hyper-V, the VSS writer is implemented in the Virtual Machine Management Service (VMMS) and offers the following functionality:

- Backup and recovery of Hyper-V server and all configuration settings
- Online backup of Windows Server 2003 or later version virtual machines when Hyper-V Integration Services are installed
- Offline backup of all supported virtual machine guest operating systems when Hyper-V Integrations Services are not installed
- Recovery of individual virtual machines to the same Hyper-V server or a different Hyper-V server

> **NOTE** Backing up the Hyper-V configuration information is of particular importance because it stores data such as the Hyper-V settings, virtual networks, registered virtual machines, and so on. Without this information, Hyper-V cannot operate, and neither can the virtual machines.

The Hyper-V VSS writer *does not* provide the following functionality:

- Online backup of Windows Server 2003 or later versions if Hyper-V Integration Services are not installed
- Online backup of virtual machines running operating systems other than Windows
- Online backup of virtual machines with FAT or FAT32 volumes
- Online backup of virtual machines with dynamic disks
- Online or offline backup of virtual machines with remote virtual hard disks
- Online or offline backup of virtual machines with an iSCSI provider loaded in the guest operating system and connected to remote iSCSI disks

DIRECT FROM THE SOURCE

Hyper-V VSS Writer Tools

Michael Michael, Architect
Virtual Machine Manager Team

To use the Hyper-V VSS writer, a VSS requestor is required. The Volume Shadow Copy Service SDK, available free from the Microsoft Download Center, contains two test applications that implement a VSS requestor interface. BETest and VShadow are excellent applications to highlight the functionality of the Hyper-V VSS writer and perform backup and recovery in a test environment.

Windows Server 2008 includes a command-line tool called DiskShadow, an application that uses the VSS application programming interface (API) to perform backups and shadow copies. DiskShadow is a complete VSS requestor that allows a user to enumerate all active VSS writers and their components, VSS providers, and shadow copies, or to perform a VSS writer-based shadow copy of a set of volumes. To use DiskShadow, you can execute a script or use a command-line interface. DiskShadow also has some advanced features you can use for such tasks as exposing a shadow copy to the local file system or reverting a volume to a shadow copy.

Windows Server 2008 also includes one more requestor that can be installed using the Windows Server Backup Features optional feature. Windows Server Backup can be configured to support backing up Hyper-V by registering the Hyper-V VSS Writer ID in the registry.

NOTE You can find more information about DiskShadow at *http://technet.microsoft.com /en-us/library/cc772172.aspx*. If you want to learn more about using Windows Server Backup, refer to Chapter 11, "Hyper-V Single Server Management."

VSS Components

Figure 13-1 shows the major components involved in the VSS backup process. Overall, the VSS service (\%SystemDrive%\Windows\system32\vssvc.exe) is the communications broker between the VSS requestor, the VSS writer, and the VSS provider.

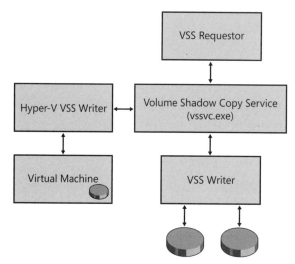

FIGURE 13-1 Volume Shadow Copy process components

The VSS requestor makes a request for the creation or restoration of a shadow copy; this is typically a backup application but is not exclusively so. The VSS requestor communicates with the VSS service to enumerate available VSS writers and obtain information from the target VSS writer regarding the data that must be backed up, as well as any specifics on how the data should be backed up. As mentioned in the sidebar titled "Direct from the Source: Hyper-V VSS Writer Tools," earlier in this chapter, Windows Server Backup is a VSS requestor. System Center DPM 2007 SP1 is also a VSS requestor. Other VSS requestors are available from independent software vendors (ISV) that develop backup or management software applications.

The VSS writer provides information through the VSS service to the VSS requestor concerning data to include or exclude from a shadow copy and how to back up the data. It also ensures that the data is in a consistent state prior to the shadow copy creation. The VSS writer is a component that is provided by an application or role, such as SQL Server, Exchange Server, or the Hyper-V role. Windows Server 2008 also provides a VSS writer for the NTFS file system. If an application does not have a VSS writer, a shadow copy can still be created; however, data consistency is not guaranteed. Data inconsistencies are caused by incomplete transactions within an application, resulting in data that has not been committed to disk. Therefore, VSS writer components are customized by application developers to ensure that all application data is committed and there are no outstanding writes before a shadow copy is created.

The VSS provider actually creates and maintains one or more shadow copies. The VSS service directs the VSS provider to create a shadow copy based on a request from the VSS requestor, and after the VSS writer directs the application to a quiescent state. Windows

Server 2008 includes a system software VSS provider. However, a storage solution vendor may develop a hardware-based VSS provider that is optimized for its storage solution system, and other solution vendors may implement more flexible, software-based VSS providers.

Hyper-V VSS Backup Process

The following is a step-by-step description of how the components pictured in Figure 13-1 interface to perform a Hyper-V VSS-based backup:

1. The VSS requestor (backup application) requests a list of VSS writers from the VSS service.

2. The VSS requestor selects the Hyper-V VSS writer and requests backup metadata that lists configuration and volume information.

3. The Hyper-V VSS writer gathers the metadata information and sends the information to the VSS service to provide to the VSS requestor.

4. The VSS requestor uses the metadata to select the configuration information, volumes, and virtual machines to back up.

5. The VSS service notifies the Hyper-V VSS writer to initiate preparation for shadow copy execution.

6. The Hyper-V VSS writer notifies target VMs to flush all buffers and caches, and when the flushing process is complete, informs the VSS service that it is ready.

7. The VSS service notifies the Hyper-V VSS writer to proceed into the commit shadow copy phase.

8. The Hyper-V VSS writer informs target VMs to quiesce all data, buffers, and caches, and then it temporarily freezes all write requests (reads are still valid).

9. The VSS service flushes the file system level buffer and freezes the file system.

10. The VSS service instructs the VSS provider to create the shadow copy (which takes only a few seconds).

11. The VSS provider responds to the VSS service that it has successfully created the shadow copy.

12. The VSS service unfreezes the file system and instructs the Hyper-V VSS writer to also unfreeze.

13. The Hyper-V VSS writer re-enables writes, and all pending write I/O operations are performed.

14. The VSS service verifies that all queued writes from all writers were successful.

15. If everything is nominal, the VSS service provides a shadow copy pointer to the VSS requestor.

16. The VSS requestor backs up the configuration and virtual machines from the shadow copy.

17. The VSS requestor saves a copy of the Hyper-V VSS writer metadata in an XML file for future restore operations.

Hyper-V VSS Writer Metadata Document

In order for the VSS requestor to use the VSS API to create a valid shadow copy, it requires detailed information concerning what should be included in the shadow copy, where the information is currently stored, and the volumes on which it resides. The mechanism that allows this information to be transferred from the VSS writers to the VSS requestor is the metadata document.

The Hyper-V VSS writer metadata document includes the following information:

- Hyper-V VSS writer GUID and friendly name
- Hyper-V configuration file information
- Virtual machine configuration and component file information
- Backup scenario supported for each virtual machine (online or offline)

The metadata document is actually a set of information gathered using the VSS and VSS writer APIs, and it is stored by the VSS requestor as an XML document for use in future restore operations. The XML document includes the following information:

- Identification section to identify the VSS writer that provided the metadata
- Restore method section that details how the restore should be performed and if a reboot will be required
- Online backup section that details all virtual machines that can be backed up in the online scenario
- Offline backup section that details all virtual machines that can be backed up in the offline scenario
- Hyper-V configuration section that details all the configuration files that should be backed up to restore the Hyper-V configuration

> **NOTE** The backup application, not the Hyper-V VSS writer, provides the backup granularity, whether it includes the entire volume on which virtual machines are stored or just the actual virtual machine files. The metadata document provides all required configuration and path information.

Using Traditional Methods to Back Up Hyper-V and Virtual Machines

If a VSS-based backup cannot be implemented in your environment, you can still use traditional backup methods to ensure that you can recover from a Hyper-V server or virtual machine failure. A traditional backup method uses a backup application that installs an agent in the operating system and copies data to an external storage device. Therefore, the traditional backup method can also be used for a virtual machine by installing the agent in the guest operating system. An important benefit is the ability to perform a backup while the virtual machine is online, although virtual machine performance will be affected by the backup. Additional benefits of an agent-based backup method are the more extensive granularity in choosing the backup set and the ability to allow the backup of data across the network, as well as the ability to restore individual backup data set files.

If you use an agent-based method to back up your virtual machines, you must ensure that your backup application or strategy includes all the files that make up the virtual machine configuration. A virtual machine consists not only of one or more data files that represent the virtual disks attached to the virtual machine, but also includes a configuration file (.xml) that maintains the virtual environment settings, resource allocation, and special features configuration of the virtual machine.

One of the drawbacks of the agent-based backup method is that the virtual machine must be online to be backed up. Therefore, if you have a virtual machine that is paused, that is in a saved state, or that is stored in a virtual machine library, an agent-based method fails to provide a useful backup strategy.

NOTE If one or more of your virtual machines is configured with iSCSI disks or remotely stored VHDs, the Hyper-V VSS writer cannot back up these virtual machines, and you will need to use an agent-based backup method to provide a recovery path.

Backing Up an Active Directory Domain Controller Virtual Machine

There are special considerations to take into account when defining a backup strategy for an Active Directory domain controller running in a virtual machine. Basically, Active Directory domain controllers should be backed up using only an application that properly interfaces with Active Directory during backup and restore operations. Because Active Directory is transactional in nature, the backup application must ensure that the data backup represents a consistent database state. By default, when restoring a domain controller, the backup application must modify the Active Directory database version to indicate that it was restored from backup and that it must acquire the latest updates from its replication partners.

In particular, Windows 2000 Server, Windows Server 2003, and Windows Server 2008 domain controllers use update sequence numbers (USNs) to track updates originating from the local domain controller. Each domain controller uses USNs to track the latest originating update it has received from each source replication partner, as well as the status of every other domain controller that stores a replica of the directory partition. When a domain controller is restored following a failure, it queries its replication partners for updates with USNs larger than the USNs in its records.

In addition to USNs, domain controllers keep track of source replication partner directory database identities through the invocationID attribute of the NTDS Settings object. When a domain controller is properly restored, the invocationID is reset and replicated to all domain controllers in the forest. Domain controllers in the forest also update their USNs to match the highest USNs of the restored domain controller. The combination of the new invocationID and the USN updates following a correct restore procedure allows replication to properly originate from the restored domain controller.

Both the Hyper-V VSS writer and agent-based backup applications developed to support Active Directory can be used to perform proper backup and restore operations of domain controllers.

 CAUTION You cannot use virtual machine snapshots to back up virtual machines that are Active Directory domain controllers. Reverting or applying a virtual machine snapshot will not update the invocationID or the USNs used by an Active Directory database. It is imperative that you use only *Active Directory–compatible* backup applications such as Windows Server Backup or System Center DPM 2007 SP1 to back up and restore *production* Active Directory domain controllers running in Hyper-V virtual machines.

MORE INFO Details about the way the replication system tracks directory changes, the process of recovery following a restore procedure, and the operating system changes that protect against inappropriate replication are described in the white paper titled "Backup and Restore Considerations for Virtualized Domain Controllers," available at *http://technet.microsoft.com/en-us/library/dd363545.aspx*.

Using VSS to Back Up Hyper-V and Virtual Machines

Using the Hyper-V VSS writer interface, backing up a Hyper-V infrastructure becomes more straightforward than using traditional backup methods. However, before implementing a VSS-based backup strategy, you must define the scenarios that exist in your Hyper-V infra-structure and ensure that your environment meets the requirements presented in Table 13-1. As mentioned earlier, the three basic Hyper-V–supported VSS backup categories include the following:

- Hyper-V configuration information
- Virtual machine online backup
- Virtual machine offline backup

TABLE 13-1 VSS-Supported Backup Scenarios

SCENARIO	REQUIREMENTS	VSS-SUPPORTED BACKUP
Hyper-V server	Windows Server 2008 Hyper-V or Microsoft Hyper-V Server 2008	Hyper-V configuration information
Windows Server 2003 or later versions	Virtual machine without remote or iSCSI VHDs Virtual machine with latest Integration Services installed	Virtual machine online backup
Windows Server 2003 or later versions without Integration Services	Virtual machine without remote or iSCSI VHDs	Virtual machine offline backup
Windows XP SP2 or later versions	Virtual machine without remote or iSCSI VHDs Virtual machine with latest Integration Services installed	Virtual machine offline backup
Windows XP SP2 or later versions without Integration Services	Virtual machine without remote or iSCSI VHDs	Virtual machine offline backup
Windows Server 2000 and earlier versions	Virtual machine without remote or iSCSI VHDs	Virtual machine offline backup
Non-Windows operating systems	Virtual machine without remote or iSCSI VHDs	Virtual machine offline backup

Only Windows Vista and later client operating systems, as well as Windows Server 2003 and later server operating systems, can be backed up without service interruption (online) using VSS. Earlier versions of Windows operating systems and non-Windows operating systems do not support the Volume Shadow Copy Service, and therefore have no mechanism to quiesce the system to guarantee data consistency.

After you have defined the various backup scenarios in your environment, you must determine the VSS-based backup application that you will use to protect your virtualization infrastructure. If you have only a few Hyper-V servers in your environment, you may be able to use Windows Server Backup, which is included in Windows Server 2008. If you are deploying or managing a larger Hyper-V server farm, then you should consider System Center Data Protection Manager 2007 SP1.

Using System Center Data Protection Manager 2007 SP1

System Center Data Protection Manager 2007 SP1 leverages VSS to allow you to perform Hyper-V server-level backups of virtual machines. With a Hyper-V server-level backup, you install a DPM agent only on the Hyper-V server, not on each individual virtual machine. Using this backup method, you can recover an entire virtual machine, rather than individual guest operating system or data files. Instead, this type of backup enables the equivalent of a bare-metal recovery for a virtual machine. DPM 2007 SP1 provides backup and recovery for the following Microsoft virtualization products:

- Windows Server 2008 Hyper-V
- Hyper-V Server 2008
- Virtual Server 2005 R2

> **NOTE** System Center DPM 2007 SP1 also provides backup and recovery for Windows Server 2008 and Microsoft applications such as Exchange Server 2007, SQL Server 2008, and Office SharePoint Server 2007. For more details, refer to *http://www.microsoft.com /systemcenter/dataprotectionmanager/en/us/default.aspx.*

Using DPM 2007 SP1, you can perform online backups of Hyper-V virtual machines with Integration Services and VSS support, as well as virtual machines running on Virtual Server 2005 R2 with Virtual Machine Additions and VSS support. When DPM 2007 SP1 performs an online backup of a virtual machine, it directs Hyper-V to pause the virtual machine, creates a shadow copy, and then directs Hyper-V to bring the virtual machine back online. DPM 2007 SP1 continues to process the shadow copy and can copy the backup data set to tape or to another DPM server without any further service interruption.

DPM 2007 SP1 also supports offline backups of non-VSS aware virtual machines. In order to perform an offline backup, DPM 2007 SP1 directs Hyper-V to transition the virtual machine into a saved state, creates the shadow copy, and then directs Hyper-V to bring the virtual machine back online. Using this offline backup process, the virtual machine service interruption is minimized.

If you need the ability to recover individual virtual machine files or want to provide backup and recovery of only a specific application running in a virtual machine, DPM 2007 SP1 supports the deployment of an agent to the guest operating system. In order to recover either the entire virtual machine or individual files, you can perform a Hyper-V server-level backup of a virtual machine in conjunction with backups of specific data using a DPM agent deployed inside the guest operating system. However, you should ensure that you do not schedule both types of backups during the same time period.

If you have DPM 2007 servers deployed in your current environment, you must complete the following major steps before you can successfully back up and recover Hyper-V configuration information and virtual machines using Hyper-V server-level backups:

- Update Hyper-V servers with KB956697 and KB959962
- Update virtual machine Integration Services
- Install DPM 2007 SP1
- Deploy DPM 2007 SP1 protection agents to Hyper-V servers
- Configure DPM 2007 SP1

KB956697 contains an update for the VMMS service that ensures that the Hyper-V VSS writer is recognized and properly used during VSS-based backups. KB959962 contains updated files for core Hyper-V components, including Integration Services. The updated Integration Services must be installed on supported virtual machines for successful DPM 2007 SP1 backups.

Updating Virtual Machine Integration Services

When you install KB959962 on a Hyper-V server, a new Vmguest.iso file is copied to the system. This file contains the updated version of Integration Services that you must install on each supported virtual machine that you want to back up using DPM 2007 SP1.

If you want to determine the version of Integrations Services that is installed in a virtual machine, follow these steps:

1. Open Hyper-V Manager, right-click the virtual machine, and select Connect.
2. Log into the guest operating system and open the Device Manager in the Control Panel.
3. Expand System Devices, right-click Hyper-V Volume Shadow Copy, and select Properties.
4. In the Hyper-V Volume Shadow Copy Properties dialog box, click the Driver tab.
5. As shown in Figure 13-2 on the following page, the Driver Version property reflects the Integration Services version number. In this case, 6.0.6001.18016 is the Integration Services version released with Hyper-V.
6. Click OK to close the dialog box.

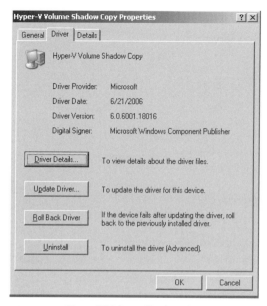

FIGURE 13-2 Hyper-V Volume Shadow Copy Properties dialog box

Follow these steps to install the new version of Integration Services in a virtual machine:

1. Open Hyper-V Manager, right-click the virtual machine, and select Connect.

2. Log into the guest operating system with an account that has local administrator credentials.

3. Click the Virtual Machine Connection application Action menu (shown in Figure 13-3) and select Insert Integration Services Setup Disk.

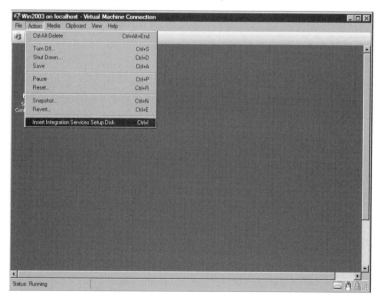

FIGURE 13-3 Virtual Machine Connection Action menu

4. Open Windows Explorer in the virtual machine and double-click the CD/DVD drive.

5. In the Upgrade Hyper-V Integration Services dialog box (shown in Figure 13-4), click OK to start the installation.

FIGURE 13-4 Upgrade Hyper-V Integration Services dialog box

6. In the Installation Complete dialog box, click Yes to restart the virtual machine.

7. After the virtual machine restarts, reconnect to it and verify that the Hyper-V Volume Shadow Copy Driver Version property is 6.0.6001.22334 or later.

8. Log out of the virtual machine and close the Virtual Machine Connection session.

Installing System Center Data Protection Manager 2007 SP1

You can obtain the DPM 2007 SP1 update as a free download from the Microsoft Web site at *http://technet.microsoft.com/en-us/dpm/dd296757.aspx*. Follow these steps to install the DPM 2007 SP1 update on all DPM 2007 servers that you want to use to perform Hyper-V server-level backups:

1. Ensure that you do not have any backup jobs in progress.

2. Double-click the DPM 2007 SP1 update.

3. On the Welcome page (shown in Figure 13-5), review the warnings, take any appropriate actions, and then click Next.

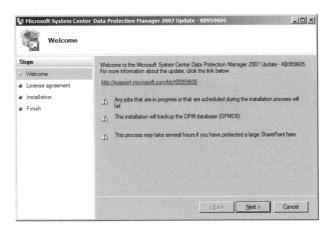

FIGURE 13-5 DPM 2007 SP1 Installer Welcome page

4. On the Microsoft Software License Terms page, review the information and then select I Accept if you agree with the license terms.

5. Click Next to begin the DPM 2007 SP1 installation (shown in Figure 13-6).

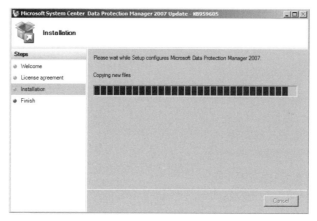

FIGURE 13-6 DPM 2007 SP1 installation in progress

6. On the Installation Success page (shown in Figure 13-7), click Close.

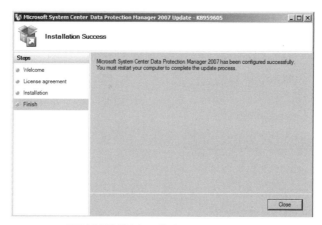

FIGURE 13-7 DPM 2007 SP1 Installation Success page

7. Click OK in the dialog box that prompts you to restart the Hyper-V server.

Enabling Local Data Protection in DPM 2007 SP1

Although not recommended, you can install DPM 2007 SP1 on a Hyper-V server and create local backups of the Hyper-V configuration and virtual machines. However, DPM 2007 SP1 will not allow you to back up the Hyper-V server configuration or any virtual machines until you enable Local Data protection. You can enable Local Data Protection using the DPM management shell by entering the following command:

```
Set-DMGGlobalProperty -AllowLocalDataProtection $true
```

If you want to disable Local Data Protection, enter the following command:

```
Set-DMGGlobalProperty -AllowLocalDataProtection $false
```

> **BEST PRACTICE** You should not use local DPM server backups as the only method to protect your Hyper-V server configuration, virtual machines, or DPM 2007 SP1 server data. In order to ensure a disaster recovery path resulting from a total loss of a Hyper-V server that is also running DPM 2007 SP1, you should save your backups to tape and store them at an offsite location, or back up the local server using an offsite DPM 2007 SP1 server, save backups to tape, and store them offsite in accordance with your management and security policies.

Deploying a DPM 2007 SP1 Protection Agent

Before you can perform Hyper-V server level backups of virtual machines, you must install a DPM protection agent on the server. After you install DPM 2007 SP1, it can enumerate servers that it can protect from your Active Directory and present them as targets for a DPM protection agent deployment. You can initiate the installation of a DPM protection agent through the DPM 2007 Administrator Console, as well as through Active Directory Group Policy and by using management tools such as System Center Configuration Manager 2007 or Systems Management Server 2003.

> **NOTE** Before you can deploy a DPM protection agent to a server, you may need to disable the Windows Firewall. After the protection agent is deployed, open TCP port 135 and specify the DPM protection agent file (Data Protection Manager\DPM\bin\MsDpmFsAgentCA.exe) as an exception in the Windows Firewall.

Follow these steps to initiate the installation of a DPM agent on a Hyper-V server using the DPM 2007 Administrator Console:

1. Open the DPM 2007 Administrator Console, select the Management task area, and then select the Agents tab as shown in Figure 13-8.

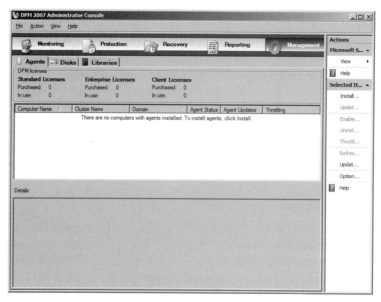

FIGURE 13-8 The DPM 2007 Administrator Console Management task area

2. In the Actions pane, select Install to launch the Protection Agent Installation Wizard.

3. On the Select Computers page, DPM 2007 SP1 displays a list of servers gathered from the Active Directory domain of which the DPM 2007 SP1 server is a member. This list of servers (shown in Figure 13-9) represents potential targets for a protection agent deployment.

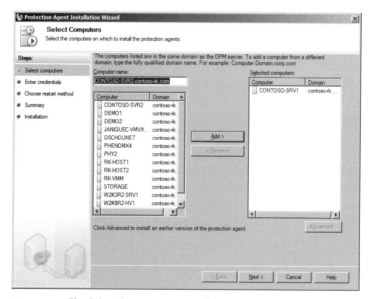

FIGURE 13-9 The Select Computers page of the Protection Agent Installation Wizard

4. Select the Hyper-V servers that you want to deploy a DPM agent to, and click Add to move them to the Selected Computers list. When you have completed your selections, click Next.

5. On the Enter Credentials page (shown in Figure 13-10), enter the user name and password for a domain account that is a member of the Domain Admins group for the selected servers, and then click Next.

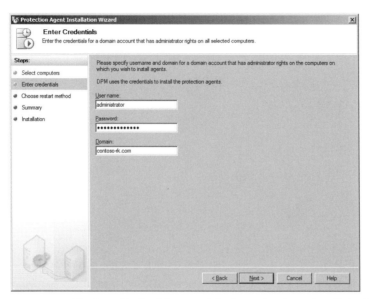

FIGURE 13-10 The Enter Credentials page of the Protection Agent Installation Wizard

6. As shown in Figure 13-11, DPM 2007 SP1 may display a warning that it could not identify whether the selected computers are clustered. After you review the information, click OK.

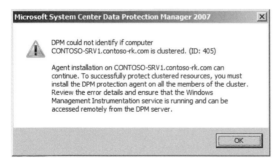

FIGURE 13-11 DPM 2007 SP1 clustered server warning

7. On the Choose Restart Method page (shown in Figure 13-12), you have the following choices:

- Select Yes. Restart The Selected Computers After Installing The Protection Agents, if you want the Hyper-V server to restart automatically after the DPM 2007 protection agent installation.

- Select No. I Will Restart The Selected Computers Later, if you want to restart the Hyper-V server manually after the DPM 2007 protection agent installation.

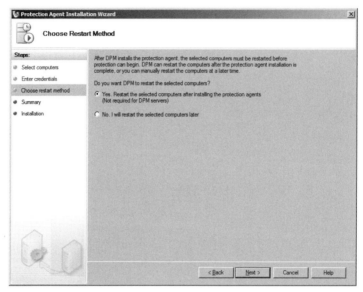

FIGURE 13-12 The Choose Restart Method page of the Protection Agent Installation Wizard

8. After you have completed your selection, click Next.

9. On the Summary page (shown in Figure 13-13), review your selections, then click Install.

10. On the Installation page, you can monitor the DPM protection agent installation progress. You can also close the Protection Agent Installation Wizard and monitor the installation progress in the DPM Administrator Console Agents view.

11. After the DPM protection agent installation completes (shown in Figure 13-14), click Close.

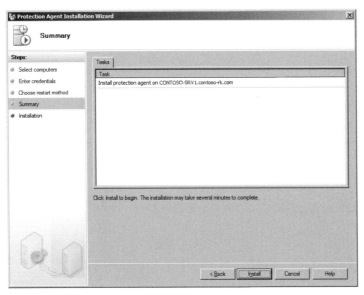

FIGURE 13-13 The Summary page of the Protection Agent Installation Wizard

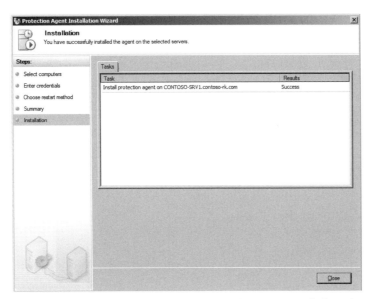

FIGURE 13-14 The Installation page of the Protection Agent Installation Wizard

12. In the DPM 2007 Administrator Console, on the Agents tab, click Refresh Information in the Action menu. If the DPM 2007 SP1 server successfully connected to the Hyper-V server DPM protection agent, the Agent Status will reflect a status of OK, as shown in Figure 13-15.

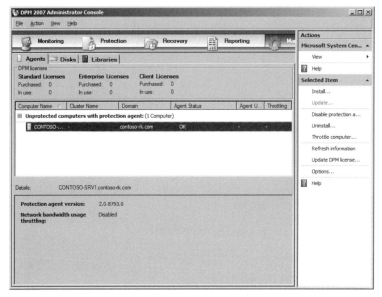

FIGURE 13-15 The DPM protection agent status in the DPM 2007 Administrator Console

Configuring a DPM 2007 SP1 Storage Pool

The next step in the configuration of DPM 2007 SP1 is the allocation of disks to create a storage pool. A DPM storage pool includes one or more dynamic volumes that are used exclusively to store DPM backup data sets. DPM 2007 SP1 will format the volumes, so any data previously stored will be lost. There are three types of disk storage that DPM 2007 SP1 can use:

- Direct Attached Storage (DAS)
- Storage Area Networks (SAN)
- iSCSI disk storage

Follow these steps to allocate dynamic volumes to create a DPM 2007 SP1 storage pool:

1. Open the DPM 2007 Administrator Console, select the Management task area, and then select the Disks tab, as shown in Figure 13-16.

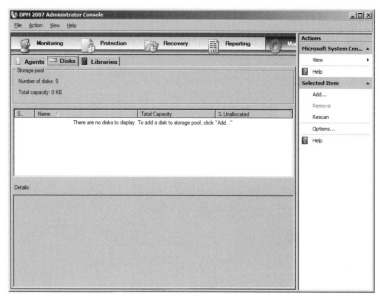

FIGURE 13-16 The DPM 2007 Administrator Console Disks tab

2. In the Actions pane, select Add.

3. In the Add Disks To Storage Pool dialog box (shown in Figure 13-17), you are presented with a list of available disks that DPM 2007 SP1 can use as a part of the storage pool. Select the disks that you want to add to the storage and then click Add. When you have completed your selections, click OK.

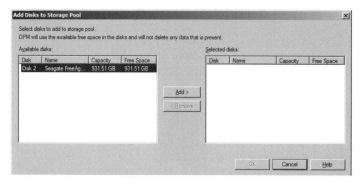

FIGURE 13-17 The Add Disks To Storage Pool dialog box

4. As shown in Figure 13-18, DPM 2007 SP1 may display a warning that the selected disks will be converted to dynamic disks and any existing volumes will be converted to simple volumes. After you review the information, click Yes.

FIGURE 13-18 DPM 2007 SP1 disk conversion warning

5. In the DPM 2007 Administrator Console, on the Disks tab, you will see a list of the disks added to the storage pool, as shown in Figure 13-19.

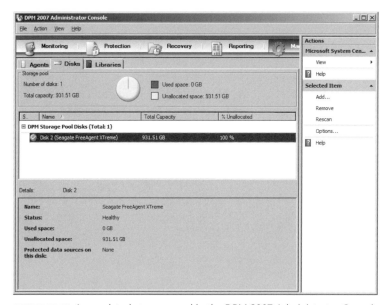

FIGURE 13-19 A populated storage pool in the DPM 2007 Administrator Console

Configuring a DPM 2007 SP1 Protection Group

After you configure a DPM 2007 SP1 storage pool, you must configure a protection group to perform Hyper-V server level backups of virtual machines. A protection group allows you to define all of the details of the backup, including the Hyper-V configuration information, virtual machines, and other resources that you want to include in the backup data set. You can also define the backup schedule, the backup retention range, the tape backup schedule (optional, but recommended), and recovery points.

Follow these steps to configure a DPM 2007 SP1 protection group:

1. Open the DPM 2007 Administrator Console and select the Protection task area, as shown in Figure 13-20.

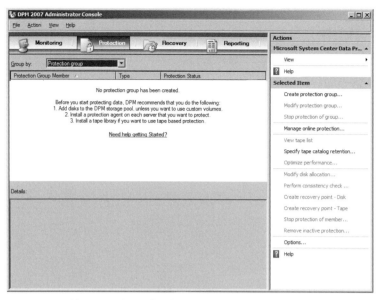

FIGURE 13-20 The DPM 2007 Administrator Console Protection task area

2. In the Actions pane, select Create Protection Group.

3. On the Welcome To The New Protection Group Wizard page (shown in Figure 13-21), review the information about protection groups and then click Next.

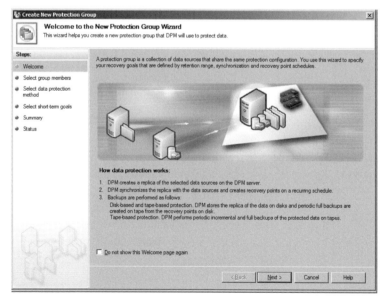

FIGURE 13-21 Welcome To The New Protection Group Wizard page

4. On the Select Group Members page, expand the target Hyper-V server entry and then expand the Microsoft Hyper-V entry, as shown in Figure 13-22.

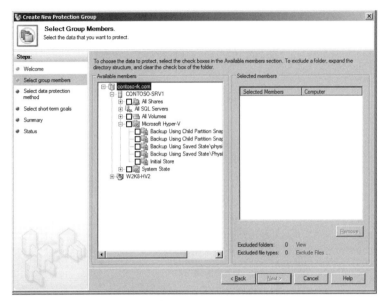

FIGURE 13-22 Select Group Members page

5. For each virtual machine running on the Hyper-V server, you can see the type of VSS-based backup that can be performed. Online backups are possible if Backup Using Child Partition Snapshot precedes the virtual machine name; offline backups are indicated by Backup Using Saved State. The Initial Store entry represents the Authorization Manager store for the Hyper-V server.

6. Select the virtual machines that you want to include in the protection group and the Initial Store, and then click Next.

7. On the Select Data Protection Method page (shown in Figure 13-23), enter a protection group name and select the protection method that will meet your backup strategy requirements. In this example, short-term protection to disks is selected, but a disaster recovery strategy should include long-term protection using tape backups.

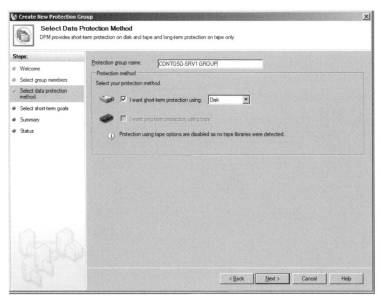

FIGURE 13-23 Select Data Protection Method page

8. On the Specify Short-Term Goals page, enter an appropriate retention range as shown in Figure 13-24. The default retention range is 5 days.

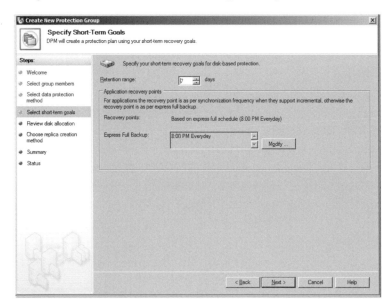

FIGURE 13-24 Specify Short-Term Goals page

9. After you have completed your selection, click Next.

10. On the Review Disk Allocation page (shown in Figure 13-25), click Modify to adjust the disk space allocation and ensure that you have enough space to support the backup data set, then click Next.

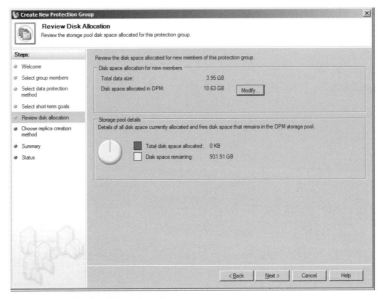

FIGURE 13-25 Review Disk Allocation page

11. On the Choose Replica Creation Method page (shown in Figure 13-26), you have the following choices:

   ■ Select Automatically if you want DPM 2007 SP1 to create the original replica by transferring the data across the network. If you select this option, you may also want to select Later and select a time with reduced network usage to begin transferring the data. After this selection, click Next.

   ■ Select Manually if you want to create a replica on the DPM 2007 SP1 server using removable media. If your Hyper-V server is connected across a slow wide area network (WAN), you may want to choose this option. After this selection, click Next.

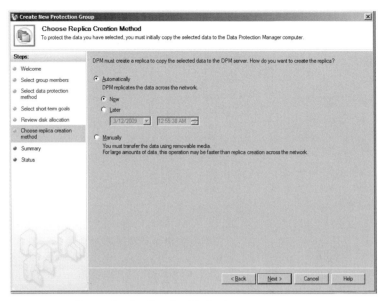

FIGURE 13-26 Choose Replica Creation Method page

12. On the Summary page (shown in Figure 13-27), review your selection, confirm that the information is accurate, and then click Create Group.

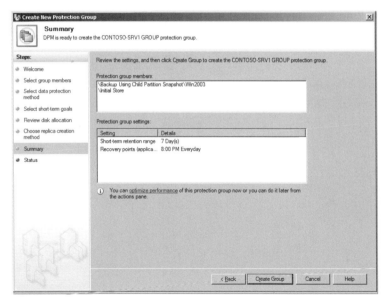

FIGURE 13-27 Summary page

13. On the Status page, you can track the progress of the protection group creation, as shown in Figure 13-28.

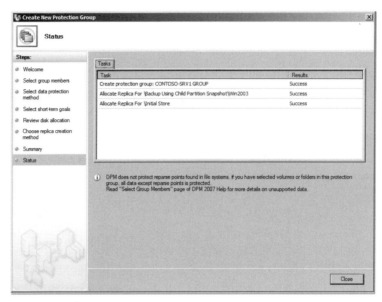

FIGURE 13-28 Status page

14. After the process is completed, click Close.

15. You can track the progress of the replica in the DPM 2007 Administrator Console, as shown in Figure 13-29.

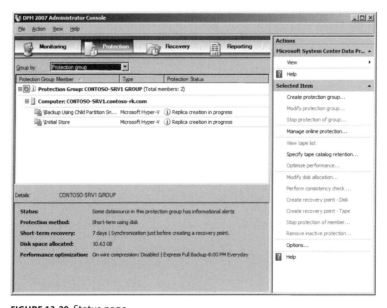

FIGURE 13-29 Status page

Recovering a Virtual Machine Using DPM 2007 SP1

After you configure a DPM 2007 SP1 protection group and one or more shadow copies of virtual machines are created, you have the ability to recover individual virtual machines. In order to do this, you must choose from available backup data and define whether to restore the data to the source location or to an alternate location.

Follow these steps to recover a virtual machine using DPM 2007 SP1:

1. Open the DPM 2007 Administrator Console and select the Recovery task area, as shown in Figure 13-30.

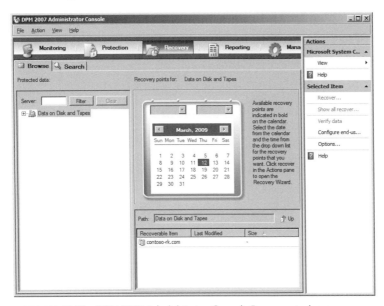

FIGURE 13-30 The DPM 2007 Administrator Console Recovery task area

2. In the left pane, expand Data On Disk And Tapes, the domain entry, the Hyper-V server entry, and the All DPM Protected Data entry, as shown in Figure 13-31.

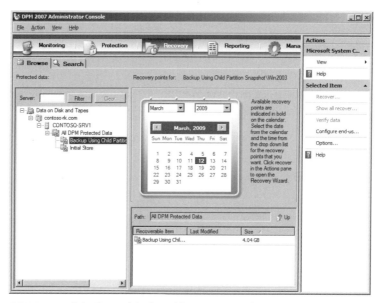

FIGURE 13-31 Selecting a virtual machine recovery point

3. In the left pane, select the virtual machine to recover and then select the date and time of the target recovery point in the middle pane.

4. In the middle pane, select the Recoverable Item and then select Recover in the Actions pane at right to launch the Recovery Wizard.

5. On the Review Recovery Selection page (shown in Figure 13-32), review the information for accuracy and then click Next.

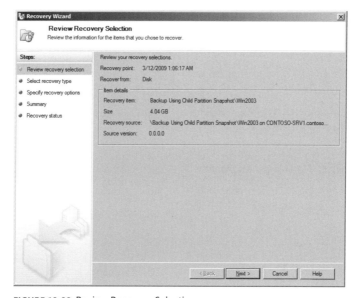

FIGURE 13-32 Review Recovery Selection page

6. On the Select Recovery Type page (shown in Figure 13-33), you have the following choices:

- Select Recover To Original Instance if you want to overwrite the files in the source directory during the recovery process.

- Select Copy To A Network Folder if you want to recover the files to a different location during the recovery process.

- Select Copy To Tape if you want to save the files to tape for shipment to an offsite location.

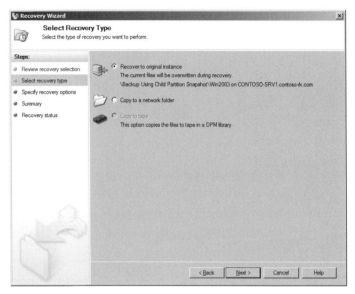

FIGURE 13-33 Select Recovery Type page

7. After you have made your selection, click Next.

8. On the Specify Recovery Options page (shown in Figure 13-34), you have the following choices:

- Click Modify to enable network bandwidth throttling and specify bandwidth limits during work and non-work hours.

- Select Enable SAN Based Recovery Using Hardware Snapshots if you are using a SAN with hardware snapshot functionality.

- Select Notification to have DPM 2007 SP1 send mails concerning the recovery process.

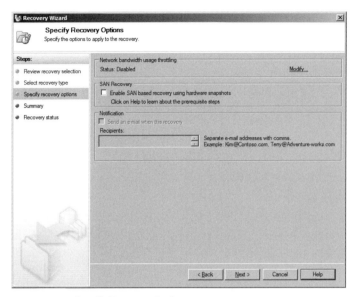

FIGURE 13-34 Specify Recovery Options page

9. After you have completed your selections, click Next.

10. On the Summary page (shown in Figure 13-35), review the information for accuracy and then click Recover to start the recovery process.

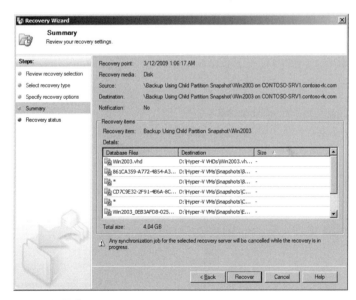

FIGURE 13-35 Summary page

11. On the Recovery Status page, you can track the recovery progress, as shown in Figure 13-36.

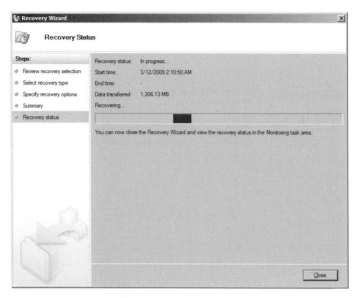

FIGURE 13-36 Recovery Status page

12. Click Close to return to the DPM 2007 Administrator Console.

13. In the DPM Administrator Console, click the Monitoring task area, click the Jobs tab, and then select Protection Group in the Group By list (shown in Figure 13-37).

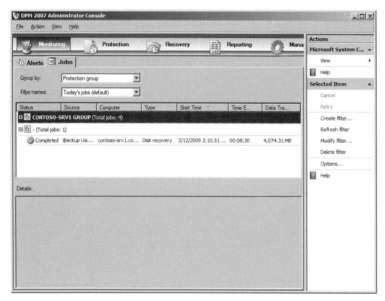

FIGURE 13-37 DPM 2007 Administrator Console Monitoring task area

14. Expand Total Jobs to monitor the recovery process.

15. If the recovery process completes successfully, a green check ball with a check mark will appear next to the associated job.

Summary

Hyper-V provides a VSS writer that allows applications like Windows Server Backup and System Center DPM 2007 SP1 to provide backup and recovery services for your virtualization infrastructure. VSS-based backup applications can greatly simplify and reduce the time needed to back up Hyper-V server configuration information and virtual machines using shadow copies. If Integration Services are available and installed in the virtual machine guest operating system, and VSS is supported, then the virtual machine can be backed up without service interruption (online backup). If the virtual machine guest operating system does not support VSS, service interruption is minimized by placing the machine in saved state while the shadow copy is quickly created (offline backup). If VSS-based backups of virtual machines are not possible, you can implement traditional backup methods using an agent installed in the guest operating system. A rigorous procedure must be followed to back up and restore Active Directory domain controllers in order to avoid collapsing the replication topology and corrupting the Active Directory database. Before you can use DPM 2007 SP1 to back up and recover Hyper-V servers, you must install specific updates on Hyper-V servers, install a new version of Integration Services on supported virtual machines, deploy DPM protection agents to Hyper-V servers, configure a DPM 2007 SP1 storage pool to store backup data sets, and configure one or more protection groups that define the backup targets, schedule, protection method, and retention time.

Additional Resources

The following resources contain additional information related to the topics in this chapter.

- Microsoft TechNet article, "How Volume Shadow Copy Service Works," available at *http://technet.microsoft.com/en-us/library/cc785914.aspx*
- Microsoft Web site, "Windows SDK for Windows Server 2008 and .NET Framework 3.5," available at *http://www.microsoft.com/downloads/details.aspx?familyid=F26B1AA4-741A-433A-9BE5-FA919850BDBF*
- Microsoft Web site, "What's New in DPM 2007 Service Pack 1," available at *http://www.microsoft.com/systemcenter/dataprotectionmanager/en/us/whats-new.aspx*
- Microsoft Web site, "What's New in Microsoft System Center Data Protection Manager 2007 Service Pack 1," available at *http://technet.microsoft.com/en-us/library/dd347836.aspx*

## CHAPTER 14

Server Migration Using System Center Virtual Machine Manager

System Center Virtual Machine Manager (SCVMM) 2008 is Microsoft's solution for migrating a physical server to a virtual machine or migrating a VMware virtual machine to the Microsoft platform. This is accomplished by migrating the physical server while it is powered on and operating, or by powering off the server and migrating it offline. Which option you choose is based on the operating system you are using and best practice guidance. This chapter will explain the migration options, the requirements, and the procedures for performing an online and offline physical to virtual conversion.

Migration Options

Migrating a server from the physical world to the virtual world can be beneficial when you are performing a server consolidation project of underutilized physical servers. But even though the servers might be underutilized, that does not mean you can afford to have extended downtime. System Center Virtual Machine Manager 2008 provides a physical to virtual (P2V) and virtual to virtual (V2V) server migration tool. This tool utilizes the Volume Shadow Copy Service (VSS) for online conversions as a way to minimize any downtime for operating systems that provide VSS support.

For operating systems that support VSS, a running server can take a VSS snapshot and transfer the information from that VSS snapshot without causing any downtime for the server. This is called an online P2V migration. For operating systems that do not support VSS snapshots, a different approach is required. These machines must be powered off and booted from a Windows PreInstallation Environment (WinPE) image. This image will allow unrestricted access to the server's hard disk to stream the hard disk data across the network to a newly built virtual machine. This is called an offline P2V migration.

Table 14-1 provides a breakdown of operating system support for offline P2V, online P2V, and V2V migrations.

TABLE 14-1 Migration Options

OPERATING SYSTEM	ONLINE P2V	OFFLINE P2V	V2V
Windows Server 2008 with Hyper-V role enabled	No	No	No
Windows Server 2008 without Hyper-V role enabled	Yes	Yes	Yes
Windows Server 2003 SP1 or later	Yes	Yes	Yes
Windows Server 2003 x64 Edition SP1 or later	Yes	Yes	Yes
Windows 2000 Server SP4	No	Yes	Yes
Windows Vista	Yes	Yes	Yes
Windows Vista x64	Yes	Yes	Yes
Windows XP SP2 or later	Yes	Yes	Yes
Windows XP x64 Edition SP2 or later	Yes	Yes	Yes

NOTE SCVMM 2008 physical to virtual migration does not support migrating Windows NT 4.0. If you need to migrate a physical Windows NT 4.0 server to Hyper-V, Microsoft provides the Virtual Server Migration Toolkit (VSMT). Using VSMT, you must first migrate the physical server to a virtual machine running on Virtual Server 2005 R2 SP1 then migrate the virtual machine to Hyper-V. Another choice is to use a third-party P2V migration tool that can migrate the Windows NT 4.0 physical server directly to Hyper-V.

MORE INFO For information on how to use VSMT to migrate a physical Windows NT 4.0 server to a virtual machine running on Virtual Server 2005 R2 SP1, refer to Chapter 10 of the "Virtual Server 2005 R2 Resource Kit" from Microsoft Press.

Migration Requirements

Performing a physical to virtual or a virtual to virtual migration requires the SCVMM system to understand the source server configuration, understand the target virtual machine capabilities, and know how to map that transition. This imposes a few requirements on the source system from a sizing and health perspective; it might require you to apply additional drivers or patches to the migration environment, for example; and it also requires you to confirm that certain communications paths are open.

Requirements on the SCVMM server and the target host for a P2V or V2V migration:

- For a P2V migration, the target host must be running Windows Server 2008 with the Hyper-V role installed, Microsoft Hyper-V Server 2008, or Virtual Server 2005 R2 SP1, and it must be managed by the SCVMM server that is performing the P2V migration.

- For a P2V migration, you may need to add some files to the internal SCVMM patch cache. The P2V wizard will tell you which updates are needed.

- For a V2V migration, a valid target host running Hyper-V must be available for placement of the new virtual machine.

Requirements on the source server:

- During an offline P2V conversion, drivers must be available for networking and storage interfaces on the source server so that WinPE can perform the transfer during the migration process. You may need to add drivers to the WinPE media for specific hardware on the source server.

- An offline P2V conversion requires the source machine to have at least 512 megabytes (MB) of physical memory.

- An offline P2V conversion requires the source server have an Advanced Configuration and Power Interface (ACPI) capable BIOS.

- The source server cannot have any bad sectors or the migration may fail. Run a disk maintenance tool (such as Chkdsk) on the source machine prior to migration.

- The source server must be in a workgroup environment, must be a member of the domain in which SCVMM is installed, or must be in a domain with which the SCVMM domain has an established two-way trust.

- The source server must be network accessible by VMM and by the Hyper-V server that it will be placed on.

Online Physical to Virtual Migration

Online P2V migrations are possible with almost every Windows operating system that Hyper-V and SCVMM 2008 support, except Windows 2000 Server. During an online migration, an agent is copied to the source server, a VSS snapshot is taken, and that VSS snapshot is transferred over the network to a newly created virtual machine on the Hyper-V server. When the copy is complete, the new virtual machine is modified to ensure that the correct hardware abstraction layer (HAL) and drivers load and that Integration Services are installed. During this process, the source physical server experiences only a slight performance impact caused by the snapshot creation and the network copy.

The P2V migration process uses a wizard to gather the required information, make decisions based on that information, and create the job that will be executed to perform the migration. The migration wizard for an online P2V migration involves the following steps:

1. Verify prerequisites (before you start the wizard).
2. Specify the source physical server.
3. Name the virtual machine.
4. Gather system information from the source physical server.
5. Modify the volume configuration.
6. Modify the processor and memory configuration of the migrated virtual machine.
7. Select the Hyper-V server for placement.
8. Select the path to place the virtual machine files.
9. Select the virtual network mapping for each network adapter.
10. Select additional properties like startup and shutdown actions.
11. Resolve any potential conversion issues.
12. Launch the conversion process.

During the actual migration job, the following actions are performed:

1. Create the new virtual machine.
2. Take a VSS snapshot of the source server.
3. Package the source machine VSS snapshot into VHD format and transfer to the target Hyper-V server.
4. Remove the agent from the source physical server.
5. Modify the virtual machine hardware.

DIRECT FROM THE SOURCE

Online P2V and Active Directory Domain Controllers

Gregoire Guetat, Program Manager
Directory Services Product Group

During the P2V conversion process, the new virtual machine and the physical domain controller must not be on at the same time, to avoid a USN rollback situation as described in Appendix A of the white paper "Running Domain Controllers in Hyper-V," found at *http://technet.microsoft.com/en-us/library/57eab7f4-3563-407f-8e4c-a87f908aa3c2*.

You should perform a P2V conversion of a domain controller in offline mode so that the directory data is consistent when the domain controller is turned back on. During P2V conversion, the virtual machine should not be connected to the network. The network interface card (NIC) of the virtual machine should be enabled only after the P2V conversion process is complete and verified. At this point, the physical source machine should be off. Do not bring the physical source machine back onto the network again before you reformat the hard disk.

The following steps will guide you through the conversion of a Windows Server 2003 server named PHYSICAL1 that is a member of the same domain as the SCVMM server.

1. In the SCVMM Actions menu, click Convert Physical Server.

2. On the Select Source page, shown in Figure 14-1, enter the name of the physical computer that you would like to convert, enter the credentials that have local administrative rights on the server, and then click Next.

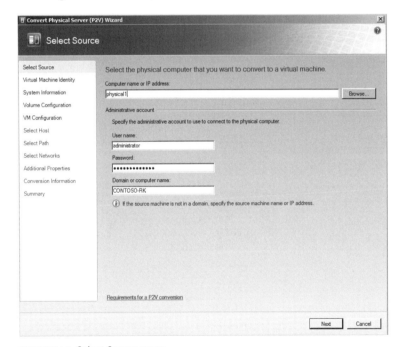

FIGURE 14-1 Select Source page

3. On the Virtual Machine Identity page, enter the virtual machine name, modify the virtual machine owner, enter a description if desired, and then click Next.

4. On the System Information page, shown in Figure 14-2, click Scan System to scan the physical server. When the scan is complete, the system information box at the bottom will display the operating system, the processor count, the hard drive information, and the network adapters. When you are done reviewing the system information, click Next.

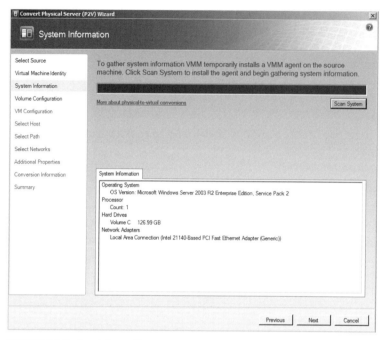

FIGURE 14-2 System Information page

NOTE During the Scan System step, VMM copies a tool called Vmmp2vagent.exe to the source machine. It is this tool that scans the system and transfers the system information back to the wizard. Vmmp2vagent also requests the VSS snapshot and transfers the snapshot during the conversion process.

5. On the Volume Configuration page, shown in Figure 14-3, make modifications to the hard drive type, size, and adapter to which the volume should be connected. You can increase the size of the hard disk at this point if the virtual machine needs more disk space. After you have made the appropriate changes, click Next.

6. On the Virtual Machine Configuration page, shown in Figure 14-4, you will see that it is possible to modify the number of processors and the amount of memory to assign to the new virtual machine. Make any required modifications, and then click Next.

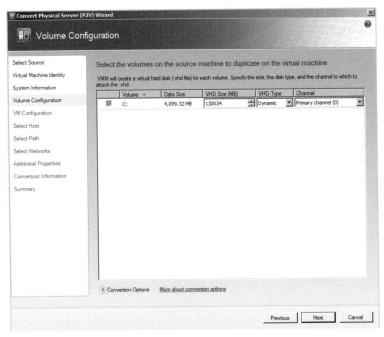

FIGURE 14-3 Volume Configuration page

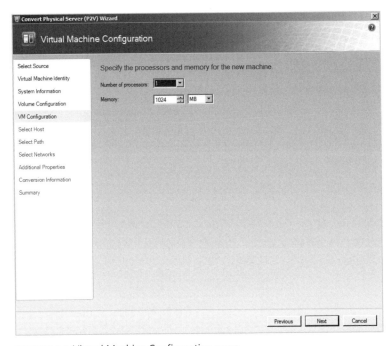

FIGURE 14-4 Virtual Machine Configuration page

7. On the Select Host page, shown in Figure 14-5, the available servers are ranked using intelligent placement. The recommended server will be at the top of the list. Select the Hyper-V server on which you want to place the new virtual machine and then click Next.

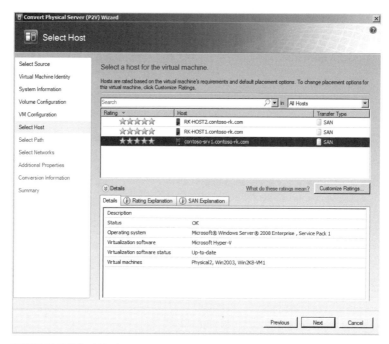

FIGURE 14-5 Select Host page

8. On the Select Path page, modify the path to store the new virtual machine in the desired location on the Hyper-V server and then click Next.

9. On the Select Networks page, select the virtual network connection binding that you want for the virtual machine or select the virtual machine to be in the Not Connected state to prevent unwanted network communications until you have verified everything is working correctly, and then click Next.

10. On the Additional Properties page, select the Automatic Stop and Start actions you prefer and then click Next.

11. On the Conversion Information page, review any open issues for the physical server, and then when you have completed your review and resolved these issues, click Next.

12. On the Summary page, shown in Figure 14-6, review the conversion settings and click Create to start the physical to virtual migration process.

> **NOTE** Clicking the View Script button in Figure 14-6 will display the Windows PowerShell script that SCVMM will run in the background to complete this migration task. Use this script as a way to quickly gain an understanding of how to write Windows PowerShell scripts that you can use to automate processes like P2V.

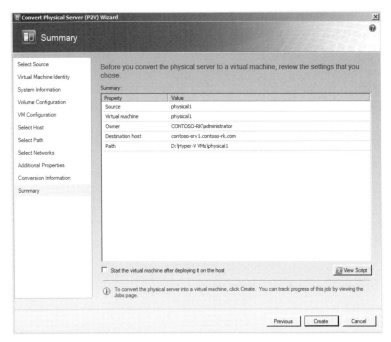

FIGURE 14-6 Summary page

13. During the conversion process, the Jobs window shown in Figure 14-7 is displayed. You can use it to track the progress of the conversion.

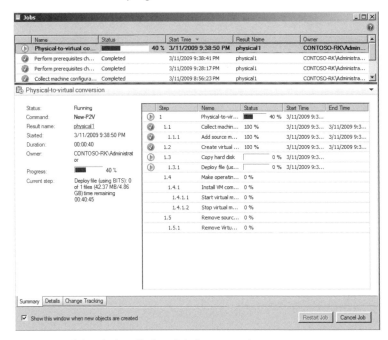

FIGURE 14-7 Jobs window displayed during conversion

14. When the job completes, the Jobs window will show success and provide information about the original physical server configuration property and the resulting property after the P2V conversion process, as shown in Figure 14-8.

15. When the job status says Completed, you can test the converted virtual machine to validate that it is operating as expected. If you attempt to start the virtual machine prior to the completion of the job, you risk causing the job to fail.

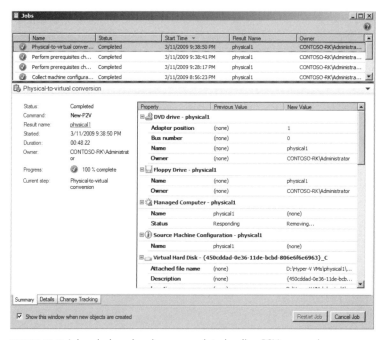

FIGURE 14-8 Jobs window showing a completed online P2V conversion

---

Making a P2V VM Highly Available

Tom Acker, Senior Support Engineer
Virtualization Support Team

During the placement process, if you select a Hyper-V server that is a node of a host cluster, you will be presented with the following dialog box, which will allow you to make the virtual machine highly available.

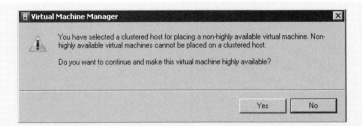

When you click Yes in this dialog box, no further configuration is necessary to make the machine a highly available virtual machine. The machine will appear in Failover Cluster Management as a managed highly available virtual machine.

Offline Physical to Virtual Migration

Although offline P2V migrations are possible for supported operating systems (refer to Table 14-1), only Windows 2000 Server *requires* the use of the offline conversion process. Windows 2000 Server does not support online P2V migrations because of the lack of VSS support in the operating system. Instead, during physical to virtual migration under Windows 2000 Server, the source physical server is booted into a WinPE environment while the disk is captured. Therefore, during a P2V migration when running Windows 2000 Server, there will be downtime, and users will be affected.

The offline P2V migration process uses the same migration wizard that the online process uses to gather the required information, make decisions based on that information, and create the job that will be executed to perform the migration. The migration wizard for an offline P2V migration involves the following steps:

1. Verify prerequisites (before starting the wizard).
2. Specify the source physical server.
3. Name the virtual machine.
4. Gather system information from the source physical server.
5. Modify the volume configuration.
6. Modify the IP address used for migration.
7. Modify the processor and memory configuration of the migrated virtual machine.
8. Select the Hyper-V server for placement.
9. Select the path to place the virtual machine files.
10. Select the virtual network mapping for each network adapter.
11. Select additional properties like startup and shutdown actions.
12. Resolve any potential conversion issues.
13. Launch the conversion process.

During the actual offline migration job, the following steps are required:

1. Collect the machine configuration via an agent.
2. Create the virtual machine.
3. Reboot the source server into WinPE.
4. Package the hard disk content into VHD format.
5. Stream the VHD across the network to the target Hyper-V server.
6. Power off the source server (optional).
7. Modify the virtual machine hardware.
8. Remove the agent from the converted virtual machine.

Offline P2V Prerequisites

In order to perform an offline P2V migration, you must make sure that certain requirements and configuration options are met. In order for the migration wizard to collect information about the source physical server during the scanning phase, SCVMM deploys a remote client to the server to gather the information. The installation for that client is a Windows 3.1 install package. You need to make sure that Windows Installer 3.1 is currently installed on the server to complete the scan step. Windows 2000 servers do not have Windows Installer 3.1 installed by default, so if you receive an error like the one shown in Figure 14-9, you must install the Windows 3.1 downloadable package update found as part of KB893803.

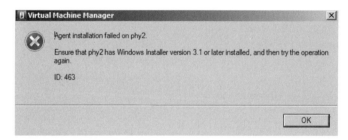

FIGURE 14-9 Windows Installer 3.1 Missing Windows Installer error message encountered during scan process

Gathering System Information

Gathering system information for a physical server is done so that the migration wizard can evaluate the current server. The evaluation looks for the following information:

- Hardware incompatibilities
- Software incompatibilities
- The migration method(s) available for the operating system (online or offline)
- System information

When the system scan is complete, a summary of system information is provided, as shown in Figure 14-10. If any known incompatibilities are discovered, they will be displayed and you will have the ability to address them and then return to the System Information page. Then you can click Scan System again to rescan the system for a reevaluation.

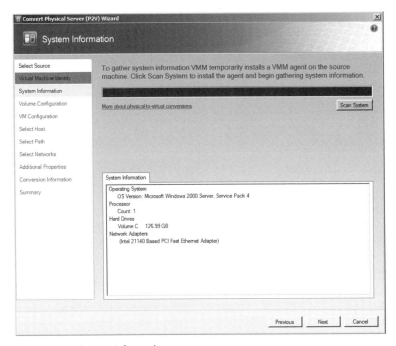

FIGURE 14-10 System Information scan

Modifying the Volume Configuration

The Volume Configuration page, shown in Figure 14-11, displays all the volumes found during the system scan. For each volume, it presents the drive letter identified, the current amount of used space, the recommended size of the virtual hard disk based on the current physical drive size, the recommended virtual hard disk type (which defaults to dynamically expanding), and the controller type and channel connection that is recommended to connect the volume. At this point you have the option to modify the size of the virtual hard disk that will be created, to change the type of virtual hard disk from dynamically expanding to fixed, and to select a different controller and channel to connect the volume to. You also have the option to clear the check box for a disk if you do not want to include it when the P2V migration is performed. Data drives that can be reconnected to the target virtual machine using pass-through or iSCSI connection without performing a migration of the contents are prime candidates to select not to migrate as part of the P2V process.

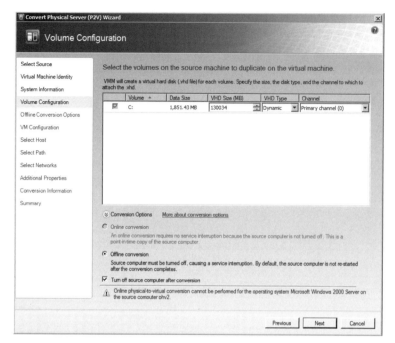

FIGURE 14-11 Volume Configuration page

Figure 14-11 also shows the Conversion Options that are available for this migration. If the physical server you are attempting to migrate meets the online P2V migration requirements, then the Online Conversion option will be available. Otherwise, only the Offline Conversion option will be available. You also have the option to turn off the source computer after conversion.

In Figure 14-11, you will notice the warning at the bottom of the page that indicates that the source machine is a Windows 2000 Server and that only offline conversion is available.

Modifying Offline IP Address

During the offline migration of a physical server, the server will be rebooted in WinPE so that the disks can be migrated. By default, it is assumed that WinPE will obtain a valid IP address using Dynamic Host Configuration Protocol (DHCP). If this is not possible, Figure 14-12 shows the options that are available to specify static IPv6 or IPv4 addresses that will used by WinPE. If you select to specify an IPv4 address, you will need to provide the IP address, the subnet mask, and the default gateway, as well as select the network adapter to bind that IP address information to, if multiple adapters exist.

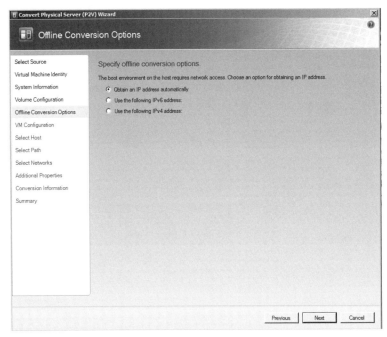

FIGURE 14-12 Offline IP Address Conversion Options page

> **NOTE** An update has been released to address some issues that you may encounter when performing offline conversions across subnets using private address ranges. Refer to Knowledge Base article KB959596, available at *http://support.microsoft.com/kb/959596*, for more information.

Modifying Virtual Machine Configuration

The Virtual Machine Configuration page shown in Figure 14-13 displays the options for modifying the processor and memory configuration of the migrated physical server. By default, the processor is set to the same number of processors as in the physical server, and the memory is set to the amount available in the physical server.

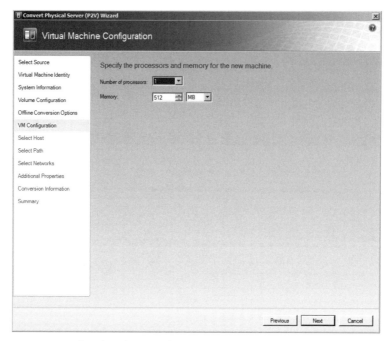

FIGURE 14-13 Virtual Machine Configuration page

For the processor, you have the option of increasing this value if the supported Hyper-V processor limit for the operating system is higher than the current value. For example, a Windows 2000 server is only supported in Hyper-V running on a single virtual processor. If you attempt to convert a Windows 2000 physical server that has two processors, the processor value will be set to 1. (Actually, the system scan step would catch this issue and highlight the incompatibility.)

For the memory, you have the option of increasing or decreasing the memory on the physical server. You might want to consider increasing the amount of virtual machine memory if the physical server has been frequently low on memory, or you might consider decreasing the amount of virtual machine memory if the physical server has regularly underutilized the available memory.

Selecting Host for Placement

The Select Host page shown in Figure 14-14 displays the results from the intelligent placement algorithm for all the hosts that are managed by the SCVMM server. The algorithm ranks the available hosts and makes a recommendation on the best host to select for the new virtual machine. You can accept the recommendation (the host on the top of the list), or you can optionally select any host in the list.

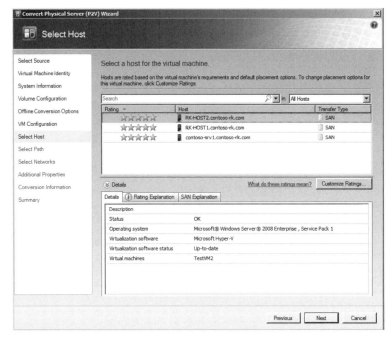

FIGURE 14-14 Select Host page

In the Details section at the bottom of the page, you can see the status, an explanation of the rating, and details on the transfer type of the selected server. The rating and transfer type explanations will provide information or details about what problems could occur if you select this server for the destination during the migration.

Selecting Storage Path

The Select Path page allows you to specify a location for the virtual machine files on the server that you selected. The default path is presented, and you have the option of clicking Browse to select an alternate path.

Selecting Networks

The Select Networks page shown in Figure 14-15 displays the network adapters discovered in the source physical server and allows you to select the virtual network that you want to bind the new virtual network adapter. You will be presented with available virtual networks based on the server selected on the Select Host page of the wizard.

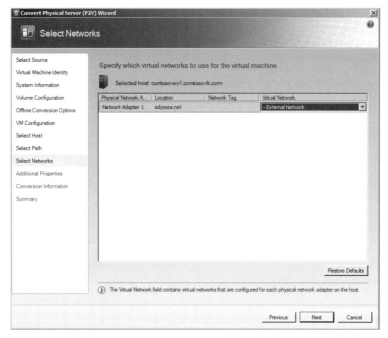

FIGURE 14-15 Select Networks page

Additional Properties

The Additional Properties page shown in Figure 14-16 displays the configuration options for defining what the virtual machine will do when the Hyper-V server starts and stops. The options are presented for selection using drop-down lists.

The options available for what the virtual machine will do when the Hyper-V server powers on are as follow:

- Never Automatically Turn On The Virtual Machine
- Always Automatically Turn On The Virtual Machine
- Automatically Turn On The Virtual Machine If It Was Running When The Physical Server Was Stopped

The default action is Never Automatically Turn On The Virtual Machine. If you select to automatically turn on the virtual machine, you have the ability to specify a delayed start time in seconds that will be used so that each virtual machine being started is started at a different time.

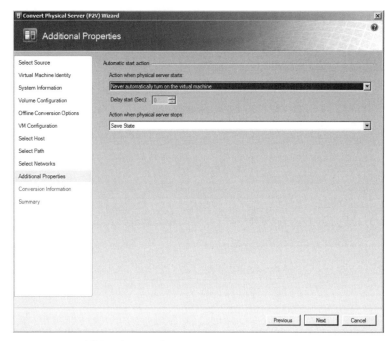

FIGURE 14-16 Additional Properties page

The options available for what the virtual machine will do when the Hyper-V server powers off are as follow:

- Save State
- Turn Off Virtual Machine
- Shut Down Guest OS

The default option is Save State.

Conversion Information

The Conversion Information page shown in Figure 14-17 displays the identified conversion issues you must resolve. This is where the P2V wizard will list the items that need to be fixed before you can proceed with an offline physical to virtual migration. Issues listed on the Conversion Information page could include missing drivers or hotfixes, lack of hardware resources, hardware resources on the physical server that will not exist in the virtual machine, and so on. If there are any issues identified, resolve the issues and then return to this page and click Check Again to rescan the source physical server to determine if the issues have been resolved. You should not attempt to proceed with the migration until all issues have been resolved, as shown in Figure 14-17.

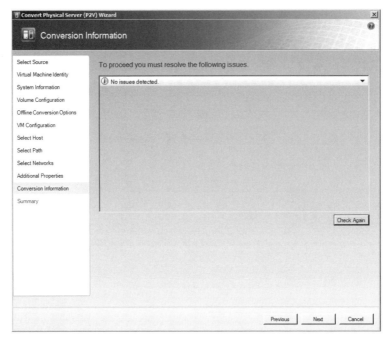

FIGURE 14-17 Conversion Information page

If the Conversion Information page identifies issues that require hotfixes or updates that must be applied during the migration, you will need to copy these files into the P2V Patch Import folder. Follow these steps to add the required files to the P2V patch folder:

1. Download the required packages indicated on the Conversion Information page from the Microsoft Web site. The packages will need to be renamed and possibly will need to be extracted.

   For example, an indicated patch might have the file name Windows2000-KB935839-x86-ENU.exe. You should rename it to something like KB935839.exe to meet the 8.3 naming convention requirements.

2. Copy the renamed packages into the folder C:\Program Files\Microsoft System Center Virtual Machine Manager 2008\P2V Patch Import.

If the Conversion Information page identifies issues with additional drivers that are required to perform the migration, you will need to copy the appropriate files into the Driver Import folder. Follow these steps to add the required files to the Drive Import folder:

1. Download the required drivers indicated on the Conversion Information page. If necessary, extract the drivers to get the raw driver files. Make sure to use drivers designed for Windows Vista or later operating systems because the version of WinPE used is based on Windows Vista.

2. Copy the raw driver files into the folder C:\Program Files\Microsoft System Center Virtual Machine Manager 2008\Driver Import.

Executing the Migration

When all the issues have been resolved and before you proceed, look at the details displayed on the Summary page (shown in Figure 14-18) to see what will happen during the migration. At this point you have the option to control what happens to the newly created virtual machine after the migration is complete—you can choose to start it or leave it powered off. You can also click View Script to view the Windows PowerShell command that will be used in the migration job.

Clicking Create will begin the process of creating the new virtual machine on the selected Hyper-V server and migrating the physical server contents.

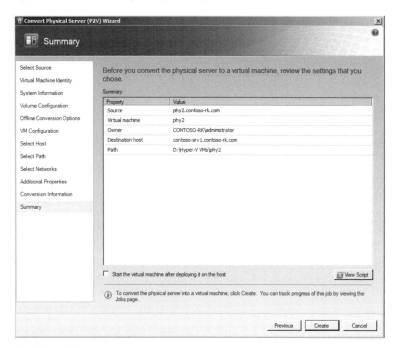

FIGURE 14-18 Summary page

Summary

This chapter provided an overview of System Center Virtual Machine Manager 2008 support for conversion of physical servers to virtual machines. You learned about the online and offline migration options that System Center Virtual Machine Manager 2008 supports and the prerequisites to use them. You also learned that for legacy operating systems like Windows NT 4.0 that SCVMM 2008 does not support, an alternative tool is available from Microsoft called Virtual Server Migration Toolkit, and other third-party tools are also available. You should select online P2V migrations whenever possible to reduce downtime of the physical servers during the conversion process, but offline P2V migrations are required for any Windows 2000 servers that you have in your infrastructure.

Additional Resources

The following resources contain additional information related to the topics in this chapter

- System Center Virtual Machine Manager 2008, a resource that provides access to the product, technical, and installation information for System Center Virtual Machine Manager 2008, available at *http://www.microsoft.com/systemcenter /virtualmachinemanager/en/us/default.aspx*

- System Center Virtual Machine Manager System Requirements, a resource that provides detailed information on the hardware and software requirements for single server and distributed installation approaches, available at *http://technet.microsoft.com/en-us/library/cc764328.aspx*

- System Center Virtual Machine Manager 2008 Configuration Analyzer, a tool that provides the ability to analyze a server before or after SCVMM 2008 is installed to ensure that it is properly configured, available for download at *http://go.microsoft.com /fwlink/?LinkID=100597*

- System Center Virtual Machine 2008 documentation, "P2V: Converting Physical Computers to Virtual Machines in VMM," available at *http://technet.microsoft.com /en-us/library/cc764232.aspx*

- Virtual Server Migration Toolkit 1.1, a set of tools that provides the ability to perform P2V migrations of Windows NT 4.0 computers. It is included in the Automated Deployment Services 1.1 update package, available for download at *http://www.microsoft.com/downloads/details.aspx?familyid=D99A89C9-4321-4BF6-91F9-9CA0DED26734&displaylang=en*

## CHAPTER 15

Server Monitoring with the Windows Server 2008 Hyper-V Management Pack for System Center Operations Manager 2007

This chapter contains information that you need to install, manage, and monitor Hyper-V servers using the Windows Server 2008 Hyper-V Management Pack for System Center Operations Manager 2007. The information presented in this chapter is based on a beta version of the Windows Server 2008 Hyper-V Management Pack, and thus you may see variations from what is presented here in the final release. The core of the chapter focuses on how the Windows Server 2008 Hyper-V Management Pack can assist you to centrally monitor the health and performance of your Hyper-V infrastructure.

Introducing the System Center Operations Manager 2007 Operations Console

The Windows Server 2008 Hyper-V Management Pack is an optional component that is imported onto a System Center Operations Manager 2007 Management Server, which controls access to the System Center Operations Manager 2007 database; manages the installation, configuration, and data collection for Operations Manager agents; and commits agent data to the database. The System Center Operations Manager 2007 Management Server provides a central management point that allows you to perform configuration tasks (deploy agents, create new tasks, and so on) and operations tasks (review and resolve alerts, monitor virtual machine state, and so on).

The System Center Operations Manager 2007 Operations Console includes five distinct workspaces: Monitoring, Authoring, Reporting, Administration, and My Workspace. The Monitoring workspace, shown in Figure 15-1, is the primary user interface to view and manipulate monitoring data. The monitoring data collected through System Center Operations Manager 2007 agents is compiled and processed to present state, alerts, events, performance information, and network device relationship diagrams. The Monitoring workspace also provides an interface to run predefined tasks against specified monitored devices.

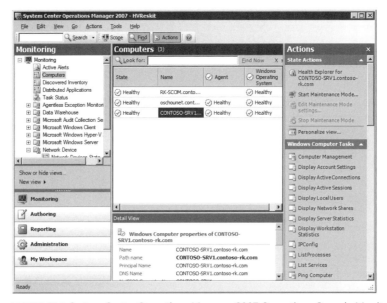

FIGURE 15-1 System Center Operations Manager 2007 Operations Console Monitoring workspace

System Center Operations Manager 2007 monitoring features are enhanced by importing application-specific Management Packs that define how a System Center Operations Manager 2007 Management Server collects, handles, and responds to data gathered from application instances. Some key items that a Management Pack defines are entities to manage (and their relationships), monitors, management rules, scripts, groups, data views, tasks, and a knowledge base that assists you to correct known application issues.

> **MORE INFO** Microsoft System Center Operations Manager 2007 R2 is the latest version of the management application. You can import the Windows Server 2008 Hyper-V Management Pack into System Center Operations Manager 2007 R2.

From the Monitoring workspace, you can use the Health Explorer (shown in Figure 15-2) to diagnose failures on monitored objects and act on error conditions. You can also run diagnostic or recovery tasks on demand, or you can configure tasks to run automatically when an alert is generated. The results of a diagnostic task are displayed when the state change event is highlighted.

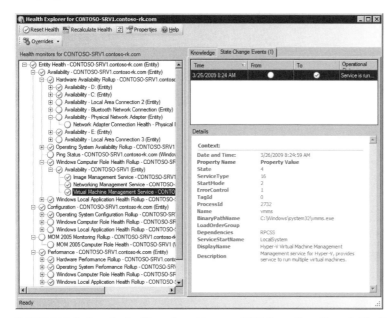

FIGURE 15-2 System Center Operations Manager 2007 Operations Console Health Explorer

Within the Monitoring workspace, you can also place a monitored object in maintenance mode. In maintenance mode, alerts, notifications, rules, monitors, automatic responses, state changes, and new alerts are suppressed at the agent. If a monitored object were to go offline for maintenance without being placed in maintenance mode, System Center Operations Manager 2007 would not receive the agent heartbeat, and as a result, it might quickly generate an overwhelming number of alerts and notifications.

> **BEST PRACTICE** It is recommended that you do not place a System Center Operations Manager 2007 server into maintenance mode. If you place it into maintenance mode, then alerts, notifications, rules, monitors, automatic responses, state changes, and new alerts generated on the Management Server will be suppressed. However, the Health Service on the System Center Operations Manager 2007 Management Server would continue to run. Therefore, alerts, notifications, rules, monitors, automatic responses, state changes, and new alerts from agent-managed computers would be processed and displayed as appropriate.

As shown in Figure 15-3, you can initiate maintenance mode by clicking Start Maintenance Mode in the Actions pane of the Monitoring workspace. You can configure maintenance mode for the selected monitored object only, or for the selected monitored object and the object that it contains. You can also specify the duration (in minutes) of the maintenance mode or schedule a time for the monitored object to be removed from maintenance mode.

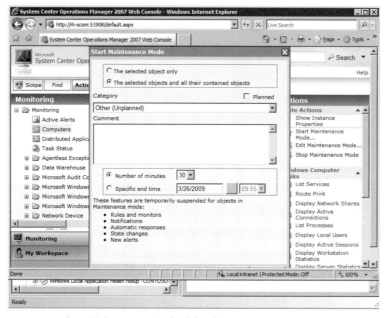

FIGURE 15-3 Start Maintenance Mode dialog box

The Authoring workspace, shown in Figure 15-4, allows you to create new computer groups, create and configure new rules and tasks, and assign rules to one or more computer groups.

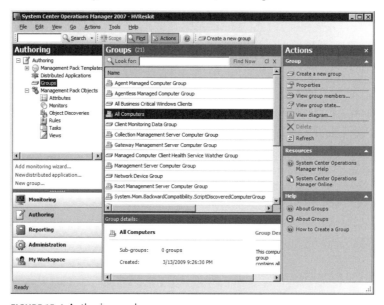

FIGURE 15-4 Authoring workspace

The System Center Operations Manager 2007 Reporting workspace, shown in Figure 15-5, is directly integrated into the Operations Console. For management packs without reports, there are generic reports that present data reflecting basic availability and performance parameters. With System Center Operations Manager 2007, multiple management groups can use a single reporting data warehouse. In addition, role-based security allows administrators to control report access through Active Directory security groups.

FIGURE 15-5 Reporting workspace

System Center Operations Manager 2007 configuration tasks are performed from the Administration workspace, shown in Figure 15-6. The Administration workspace is the primary user interface to configure and administer the System Center Operations Manager 2007 environment. Actions performed from the Administration workspace include discovering computer and network devices, deploying System Center Operations Manager 2007 agents, creating logical computer monitoring groups, and importing new management packs onto the System Center Operations Manager 2007 Management Server, to name just a few.

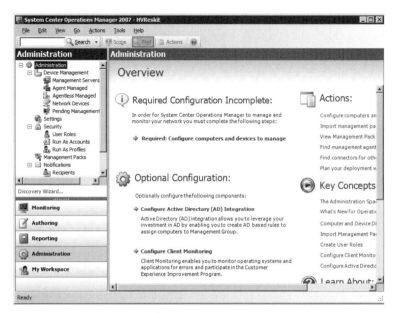

FIGURE 15-6 Administration workspace

My Workspace, shown in Figure 15-7, allows you to create custom views, save frequently used views and searches, and configure custom alert notification subscriptions.

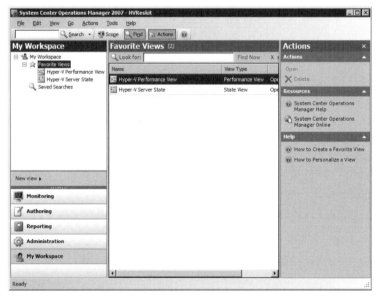

FIGURE 15-7 My Workspace in System Center Operations Manager 2007 Operations Console

System Center Operations Manager 2007 also provides a Web Console (shown in Figure 15-8) that allows access to the same Monitoring and My Workspace data available in the System Center Operations Manager 2007 Operations Console. The Web Console reflects the same layout as the Operations Console, including a fully functional Actions pane to execute tasks, as well as the ability to place monitored devices in maintenance mode. Furthermore, the Web Console provides an RSS feed that delivers alerts to Outlook 2007 or another RSS aggregator.

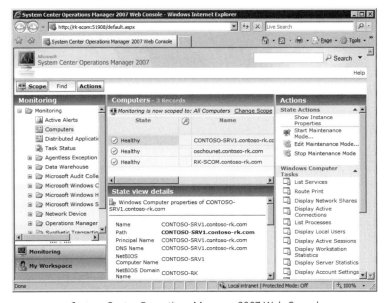

FIGURE 15-8 System Center Operations Manager 2007 Web Console

Windows Server 2008 Hyper-V Management Pack Features

The Windows Server 2008 Hyper-V Management Pack supports the following Hyper-V server editions:

- Hyper-V on the 64-bit edition of Windows Server 2008 Standard Edition
- Hyper-V on the 64-bit edition of Windows Server 2008 Enterprise Edition
- Hyper-V on the 64-bit edition of Windows Server 2008 Datacenter Edition

After you import and configure the Windows Server 2008 Hyper-V Management Pack on a System Center Operations Manager 2007 Management Server, you can use it to monitor the Hyper-V servers and virtual machine parameters listed in Table 15-1.

TABLE 15-1 Windows Server 2008 Hyper-V Management Pack Monitored Components

COMPONENT	DESCRIPTION
Hyper-V Server Health	Monitors Hyper-V server health using the Hyper-V services status, virtual machines health, and unresolved error and alerts generated by the Hyper-V services
Virtual Machine Health	Monitors drive space for dynamically expanding VHDs stored on the Hyper-V server
Virtual Networks	Tracks virtual networks, their type (external or internal), and the Hyper-V server associated with each virtual network

The Windows Server 2008 Hyper-V Management Pack includes the monitors listed in Table 15-2.

TABLE 15-2 Windows Server 2008 Hyper-V Management Pack Monitors

MONITOR	DESCRIPTION
Image Management Server	Monitors the state of the Image Management Service on the Hyper-V server. When the service is up and running, the state of the monitor is Healthy. When the service is not running, the state of the monitor is Critical. An alert is raised when the monitor changes from a healthy to an unhealthy state.
	Runs an automatic recovery task when the monitor changes to an unhealthy state. The recovery task attempts to restart the Image Management Service. If it is able to bring the service back up to a running state, the monitor returns to a Healthy state, and the alert is auto-resolved. If the recovery task is not able to restart the service, the monitor remains in a Critical state, and the alert remains unresolved.
Networking Management Service	Monitors the state of the Networking Management Service on the Hyper-V server. When the service is up and running, the state of the monitor is Healthy. When the service is not running, the state of the monitor is Critical. An alert is raised when the monitor changes from a healthy to an unhealthy state.
	Runs an automatic recovery task when the monitor changes to an unhealthy state. The recovery task attempts to restart the Networking Management Service. If it is able to bring the service back up to a running state, the monitor returns to a Healthy state, and the alert is auto-resolved. If the recovery task is not able to restart the service, the monitor remains in a Critical state, and the alert remains unresolved.

MONITOR	DESCRIPTION
Virtual Machine Management Service	Monitors the state of the Virtual Machine Management Service on the Hyper-V server. When the service is up and running, the state of the monitor is Healthy. When the service is not running, the state of the monitor is Critical. An alert is raised when the monitor changes from a healthy to an unhealthy state.
	Runs an automatic recovery task when the monitor changes to an unhealthy state. The recovery task attempts to restart the Virtual Machine Management Service. If it is able to bring the service back up to a running state, the monitor returns to a Healthy state, and the alert is auto-resolved. If the recovery task is not able to restart the service, the monitor remains in a Critical state, and the alert remains unresolved.
Hyper-V Virtual Drive Free Space	Monitors the amount of free space on the Hyper-V server disk that contains a dynamically expanding VHD. The state changes based on Warning and Error State Size parameter values. Although the parameters are configurable, the default values result in the following states:
	■ **Healthy** There is more than 2 GB of free disk space on the drive that stores the dynamically expanding VHD, or the VHD is not a dynamically expanding VHD.
	■ **Warning** There is less than 2 GB but more than 200 MB of free disk space on the drive that stores the dynamically expanding VHD.
	■ **Critical** There is less than 200 MB of free disk space on the drive that stores the dynamically expanding VHD.
Virtual Hardware Component Availability	Monitors and rolls up the health of virtual hardware components to the associated virtual machine.

The list of the Windows Server 2008 Hyper-V Management Pack monitors is available in the System Center Operations Manager 2007 Operations Console Authoring workspace, as shown in Figure 15-9.

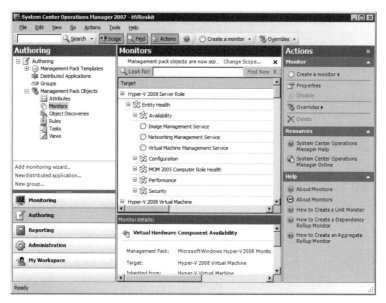

FIGURE 15-9 Operations Console Authoring workspace with list of Hyper-V Management Pack monitors

To view only the monitors included in the Windows Server 2008 Hyper-V Management Pack, follow these steps:

1. Open the System Center Operations Manager 2007 Operations Console and select the Authoring workspace.

2. In the left pane, expand the Authoring root, then expand Management Packs Objects, and select Monitors node.

3. In the center pane, under Monitors, select Change Scope.

4. In the Scope Management Pack Objects By Target(s) dialog box, select the Hyper-V targets, as shown in Figure 15-10.

5. After you have completed the selections, click OK.

6. In the center pane, under Monitors, the list of selected targets is displayed.

7. Expand the entries as desired to view the list of included monitors.

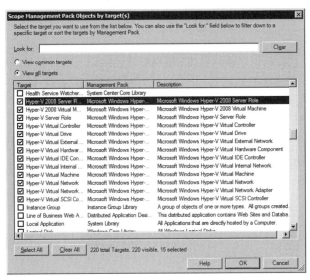

FIGURE 15-10 Scope Management Pack Objects By Target dialog box

Installing the Windows Server 2008 Hyper-V Management Pack

In preparation for the installation of the Windows Server 2008 Hyper-V Management Pack, you must verify that the prerequisites listed in Table 15-3 are completed in your environment.

TABLE 15-3 Windows Server 2008 Hyper-V Management Pack Prerequisites

PREREQUISITE	DESCRIPTION
Install System Center Operations Manager 2007 SP1	At minimum, you must install one System Center Operations Manager 2007 SP1 Management Server before you can import and use the Windows Server 2008 Hyper-V Management Pack.
Import Microsoft.Windows.Server. Library and Microsoft.Windows. Server.2008.Discovery Management Packs	It is essential to import version 6.0.6321.5 or later.
Update the System.Virtualization. Library and System.Hardware.Library Management Packs	The latest versions are included in the Windows Server 2008 Hyper-V Management Pack.

PREREQUISITE	DESCRIPTION
Install Integration Services on every virtual machine	If Integration Services components are not installed, System Center Operations Manager 2007 cannot monitor the heartbeat of the virtual machine and cannot accurately report the state of the virtual machine.

Executing the Windows Server 2008 Hyper-V Management Pack Installer Package

The files needed to import the Windows Server 2008 Hyper-V Management Pack onto the System Center Operations Manager 2007 Management Server are contained in an installer package (Windows Server 2008 Hyper-V Management Pack for Operations Manager 2007. msi). You must execute the installer package to extract its contents onto the file system before you can import the Management Pack.

> **NOTE** After it is released, the latest Windows Server 2008 Hyper-V Management Pack installer package will be available from the System Center Operations Manager 2007 Catalog Web site at *http://technet.microsoft.com/en-us/opsmgr/cc539535.aspx*.

Follow these steps to run and complete the execution of the Windows Server 2008 Hyper-V Management Pack installer package:

1. On the System Center Operations Manager 2007 Management Server, open Windows Explorer and then select the folder that contains the Windows Server 2008 Hyper-V Management Pack installer package (Windows Server 2008 Hyper-V Management Pack for Operations Manager 2007.msi).

2. Double-click the Windows Server 2008 Hyper-V Management Pack installer to begin the installation of the Management Pack files.

3. If a security dialog box is displayed, click Run.

4. In the License Agreement dialog box, select I Accept and then click Next.

5. In the Select Installation Folder dialog box, click Next.

6. In the Confirm Installation dialog box, click Install.

7. In the Installation Complete dialog box, click Close.

Importing the Windows Server 2008 Hyper-V Management Pack

After successful execution of the Windows Server 2008 Hyper-V Management Pack installer package, you can use the System Center Operations Manager 2007 Operations Console to import the Management Pack onto your System Center Operations Manager 2007 Management Server.

Follow these steps to import the Windows Server 2008 Hyper-V Management Pack onto a Management Server:

1. Open the System Center Operations Manager 2007 Operations Console and select the Administration workspace.

2. In the left pane, expand the Administration root and then select Management Packs (shown in Figure 15-11).

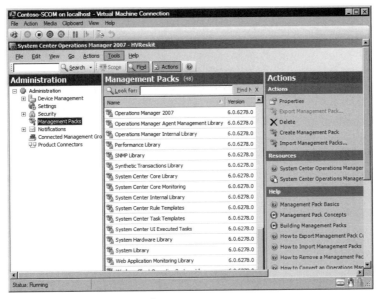

FIGURE 15-11 Management Packs pane

3. In the right pane, under Actions, select Import Management Packs.

4. In Windows Explorer, navigate to the folder that contains the Windows Server 2008 Hyper-V Management Pack files, select the System.Hardware.Library.mp, System. Virtualization.Library.mp, Microsoft.Windows.HyperV.2008.Discovery.mp, Microsoft. Windows.HyperV.2008.Monitoring.mp, and Microsoft.Windows.HyperV.Library.mp files, and then click Open.

5. In the Import Management Packs dialog box, click Import.

6. After the management packs have been successfully imported, click Close.

Verifying the Windows Server 2008 Hyper-V Management Pack Version

Because Management Pack updates are released from time to time to include patches or provide enhancements, you will need to verify the version of the Windows Server 2008 Hyper-V Management Pack imported into the System Center Operations Manager 2007 Management Server. Follow these steps to verify the Management Pack version information:

1. From the System Center Operations Manager 2007 Management Server, open the Operations Console.

2. In the left pane, under the Administration root, select Management Packs.

3. In the center pane, under Management Packs, locate the Microsoft Windows Hyper-V management packs.

4. Verify the version number displayed in the Version field.

Installing a System Center Operations Manager 2007 Agent

A System Center Operations Manager 2007 agent must be deployed to a Hyper-V server to monitor the Hyper-V service and the state of virtual machines. If you need to further monitor virtual machine health or application performance and health data (such as Microsoft Exchange Server), you must deploy an agent to the virtual machine and install application-specific Management Packs. If you do not install a System Center Operations Manager 2007 agent in a virtual machine guest operating system, the performance and health data that is collected is restricted to the information that is gathered from the Hyper-V server. Also, applications running in a virtual machine guest operating system are not monitored.

System Center Operations Manager 2007 provides an automated installation procedure to deploy agents to physical and virtual machines. Follow these steps to deploy agents to Hyper-V servers and virtual machines:

1. From the System Center Operations Manager 2007 Management Server, open the Operations Console.

2. In the left pane, open the Administration workspace.

3. In the left pane, expand the Administration root, then the Device Management node, and then right-click the Agent Managed node (shown in Figure 15-12).

4. From the menu, select Discovery Wizard.

5. On the Auto Or Advanced? page (shown in Figure 15-13), select Automatic Computer Discovery. This will scan an Active Directory domain for all Windows-based computers that are joined to the domain. If you would rather specify the types of devices to discover, you can select Advanced Discovery and choose how you want to narrow the search. After making your selection, click Next.

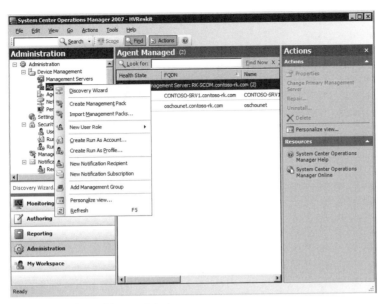

FIGURE 15-12 Agent Managed devices

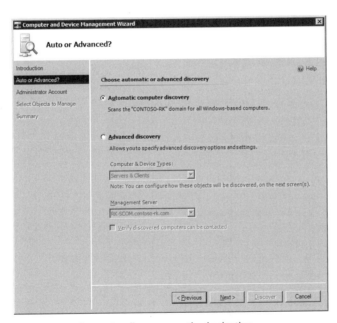

FIGURE 15-13 Computer discovery method selection

6. On the Administrator Account page (shown in Figure 15-14), select Use Selected Management Server Action Account and then click Discover.

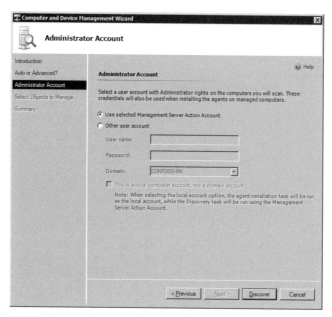

FIGURE 15-14 Administrator Account selection

7. After you click Discover, System Center Operations Manager 2007 provides a status of the discovery process, as shown in Figure 15-15.

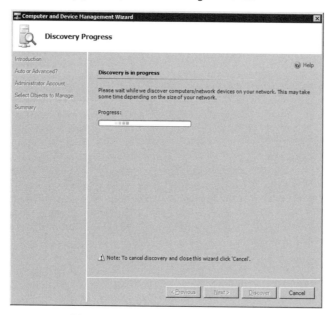

FIGURE 15-15 Discovery Process status

8. After the discovery process completes, on the Select Objects To Manage page, select the devices to which System Center Operations Manager 2007 should deploy an agent (shown in Figure 15-16), and then click Next.

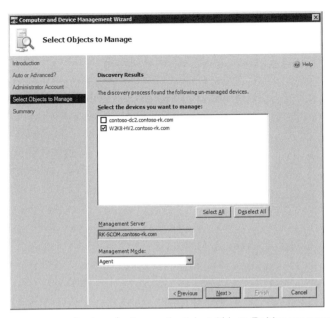

FIGURE 15-16 Device selection on the Select Objects To Manage page

9. On the Summary page, review the agent installation directory, specify the credentials that should be used to perform the agent installation (shown in Figure 15-17), and then click Finish.

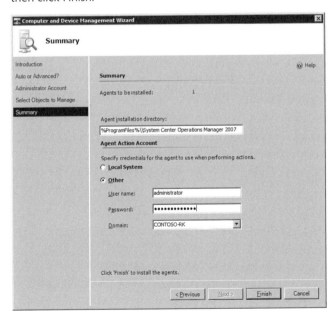

FIGURE 15-17 Account credentials selection

10. In the Agent Management Task Status dialog box, you can monitor the status of the agent installation.

11. After the agent installation completes, click Close.

> **IMPORTANT** By default, the Local System account is used as the agent action account. However, you can specify credentials for a domain or local account if you need to define a lower-privilege account to meet security policy requirements. Although this is possible, you must remember that some tasks cannot be executed using a low-privilege account, but instead require that the agent action account have administrative rights on the target Hyper-V server.

Monitoring Hyper-V Servers

Using System Center Operations Manager 2007, the Windows Server 2008 Hyper-V Management Pack, and System Center Operations Manager 2007 agents deployed on each Hyper-V server, you can leverage the Management Server—and specifically, the Operations Console— to centrally monitor the health of your Hyper-V infrastructure.

Hyper-V Server Monitoring Views

The System Center Operations Manager 2007 Operations Console provides several views to review and analyze health and performance monitoring data. Table 15-4 lists the views that are specific to a Hyper-V server and provides a description of the type of data presented in each view.

TABLE 15-4 Hyper-V Server Monitoring Views

TYPE	DESCRIPTION
Alert View	This view (shown in Figure 15-18) provides a list of alerts that are generated for monitored Hyper-V servers. By default, the Alert view displays the Hyper-V server name, the name of the component that generated the alert, the resolution state, the time stamp when the alert was created, and the age of the alert.
	If you select an alert, an Alert Details pane displays additional information including an alert description, a link to the product knowledge information for the alert, information about recovery tasks that are undertaken, causes for the alert, an alert summary, and available links to additional resources.

TYPE	DESCRIPTION
Server Role View	This view (shown in Figure 15-19) provides a list of Hyper-V servers that are being monitored, as well as the health status of the server. The health status is Green (healthy), Yellow (warning), or Red (critical) depending on the state of the Hyper-V services.
	If you select a Hyper-V server, a Details View pane displays additional server information.
Virtual Machine View	This view (shown in Figure 15-20) provides a list of virtual machines that are associated with monitored Hyper-V servers, as well as the health status of Hyper-V server physical disks that store virtual machine dynamically expanding VHDs. The health status is Green (healthy), Yellow (warning), or Red (critical) depending on the amount of free space on the disk.
	If you select a virtual machine, a Details View pane displays virtual machine information including the virtual machine GUID, virtual machine name, and virtual machine computer name.
Virtual Network View	This view (shown in Figure 15-21) provides a list of virtual networks that are associated with monitored Hyper-V servers.
	If you select a virtual network, a Details View pane displays virtual network information including the virtual network GUID, virtual network name, virtual network type, and associated Hyper-V server.

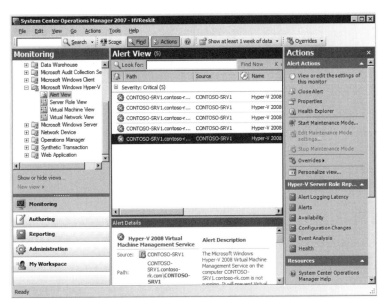

FIGURE 15-18 Hyper-V Alert View

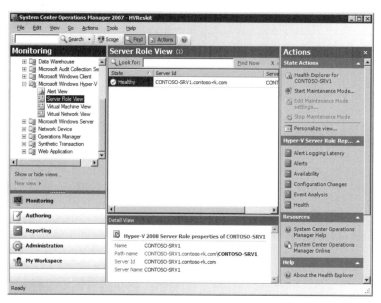

FIGURE 15-19 Hyper-V Server Role View

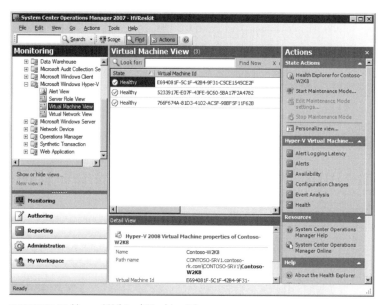

FIGURE 15-20 Hyper-V Virtual Machine View

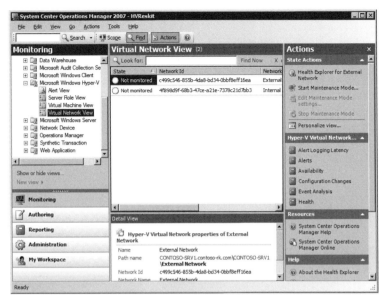

FIGURE 15-21 Hyper-V Virtual Network View

Standard Hyper-V Server Monitoring Views

Table 15-5 lists standard views that are available for any monitored component, although additional configuration may be required before data displays in these views.

TABLE 15-5 Hyper-V Server Standard Views

TYPE	DESCRIPTION
Alert View	This view displays alerts based on specific criteria such as alert severity, resolution state, and so on.
Diagram View	This view (shown in Figure 15-22) displays a graphical representation of the relationship between a Hyper-V server, associated virtual machines, and virtual component configuration.
Event View	This view displays the results of queries of event logs based on specific criteria defined in the event view properties.
Performance View	This view displays performance data collected from performance objects and counters defined for monitored devices.
State View	This view (shown in Figure 15-23) displays the health status of the monitored device.

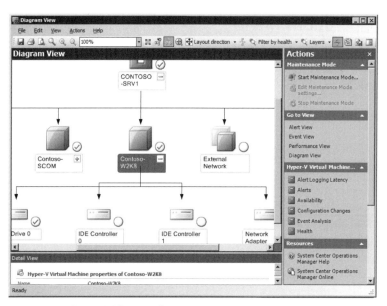

FIGURE 15-22 Hyper-V Diagram View

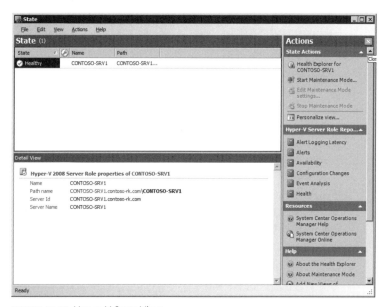

FIGURE 15-23 Hyper-V State View

System Center Operations Manager 2007 Health Explorer Tool

The System Center Operations Manager 2007 Health Explorer tool provides another means to review the health status of Hyper-V servers, state changes, and other critical issues. Figure 15-24 shows the Health Explorer for a Hyper-V server that experienced several instances of the VMMS service changing from a running state to a stopped state.

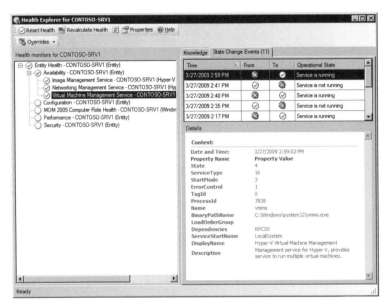

FIGURE 15-24 Health Explorer for a Hyper-V server

From within Health Explorer, you can view a history of recovery tasks that have run automatically, and you can examine the output from those tasks. If you need to perform troubleshooting, Health Explorer provides knowledge articles that contain explanations regarding the cause for state changes and associated alerts. As shown in Figure 15-25, information about diagnostic and recovery tasks that are performed to resolve issues is also defined.

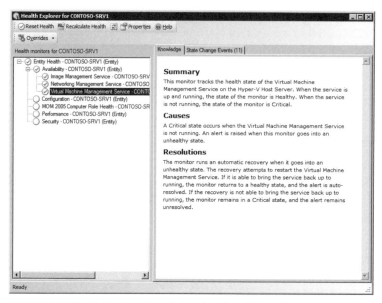

FIGURE 15-25 Health Explorer Knowledge data for a Hyper-V server

System Center Operations Manager 2007 Reporting

The Windows Server 2008 Hyper-V Management Pack does not currently include any Hyper-V–
specific reports. However, as shown in Figure 15-26, there are many default reports that you can
use to assess the performance of your Hyper-V infrastructure. In addition, you can design new
reports that capture only specific details needed for targeted performance assessments.

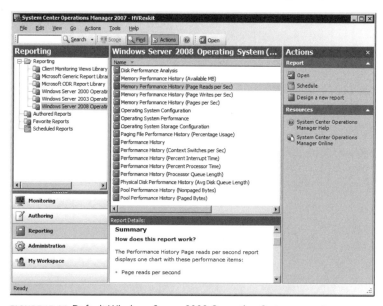

FIGURE 15-26 Default Windows Server 2008 Operating System reports

SQL Server Reporting is the foundation for System Center Operations Manager 2007 Reporting and is required to generate and view the reports. There is no special configuration required for default reports.

> **BEST PRACTICES** For all reports that require specification of a time period to generate graphical data, you should limit the time period to a reasonable span. The processing time needed for data-intensive reports depends on many factors, including System Center Operations Manager 2007 database size, System Center Operations Manager 2007 Management Servers, and the selected time period.

Summary

System Center Operations Manager 2007, in conjunction with the Windows Server 2008 Hyper-V Management Pack, provides a centralized health and performance monitoring solution for a Hyper-V infrastructure. Hyper-V servers, alerts, performance data, and relationship diagrams can all be monitored using the System Center Operations Manager 2007 Operations Console. The Windows Server 2008 Hyper-V Management Pack provides a set of monitors that allows you to assess the health of Hyper-V services and disk storage associated with dynamically expanding VHDs. In addition, you can use the reports provided by System Center Operations Manager 2007 to evaluate the performance of your Hyper-V infrastructure.

Additional Resources

The following resources contain additional information related to the topics in this chapter.

- Microsoft white paper, "Introducing Microsoft System Center Operations Manager 2007," available at *http://www.microsoft.com/systemcenter/operationsmanager/en/us /white-papers.aspx*

- Microsoft TechNet Web site, "Getting Started with Operations Manager 2007," available at *http://technet.microsoft.com/en-us/library/bb309673.aspx*

- Microsoft Web site, "Evaluate Microsoft System Center Operations Manager 2007 SP1 Today," available at *http://technet.microsoft.com/en-us/bb738014.aspx*

Hyper-V Management Using Windows PowerShell

Programmatically creating and managing virtual machines and server configuration has been an essential capability of Microsoft server virtualization solutions since the first release of Virtual Server 2005. With Virtual Server 2005, the interface was a Component Object Model (COM) application programming interface (API) that could be easily accessed using script or managed code. With Hyper-V, the strategy changed to utilizing the Windows Management Instrumentation (WMI) to standardize the calling interface and bring it in line with the strategic direction of other products. The use of WMI maintained the flexibility of using scripting or managed code to interact and manage virtual machines (VMs).

This chapter focuses on how to interface with the Hyper-V WMI API using Microsoft's new scripting standard, Windows PowerShell. We assume you have prior knowledge of and experience using Windows PowerShell, so the basics of PowerShell will not be discussed. The chapter will begin by explaining how to obtain access to the Hyper-V WMI classes using Windows PowerShell, and we'll introduce some basic scripts that will get you started. In the rest of the chapter, we will focus on how to use a Windows PowerShell library that has been developed internally by Microsoft and is available at *http://www.codeplex.com*. Although the library is not supported by Microsoft, it provides some great building blocks for creating and maintaining your Hyper-V infrastructure.

> **NOTE** All of the script development and examples developed for this chapter were done using Windows PowerShell 2.0 on Windows Server 2008 SP2 or Windows Server 2008 R2 operating system computers.

MORE INFO For more information on Windows PowerShell, you can reference the following books: *Windows PowerShell 2.0 Administrator's Pocket Consultant* (Microsoft Press, 2009), *Windows PowerShell Scripting Guide* (Microsoft Press, 2008), and *Microsoft Windows PowerShell Step By Step* (Microsoft Press, 2007).

Hyper-V Windows Management Instrumentation Classes

The Hyper-V WMI classes allow you to manage almost all aspects of the Hyper-V server and virtual machines. There are more than a hundred classes divided into 13 categories. Each class has read-only properties that can be easily queried to obtain status or the current configuration setting. Some classes have methods that allow you to modify and configure settings, hardware components, resources, and other aspects of the Hyper-V server or a virtual machine.

Table 16-1 provides a list of the Hyper-V WMI categories and a description of what each class allows you to configure, query, and manage.

TABLE 16-1 Hyper-V WMI Class Categories

CLASS CATEGORY	DESCRIPTION
BIOS	Read-only classes that allow you to determine information from the virtual machine BIOS.
Input	Classes for querying and managing the keyboard and mouse interfaces for virtual machines. Includes methods to control the keyboard and mouse.
Integration Components	Set of classes used to interact with the virtual machine Integration components. Allows you to query the state and manage the integration component settings.
Memory	Set of classes used to query the memory configuration of a virtual machine. Contains no methods to modify settings.
Networking	Set of classes used to query and manage the networking infrastructure of the Hyper-V server and virtual machines. Includes classes for virtual switches, switch ports, and network adapters.
Processor	Set of classes used to query and manage the virtual machine processor configuration. Allows you to interface with a single virtual processor or the pool of processors assigned to a virtual machine.
Profile Registration	Set of classes used to manage the global set of resources and components of a Hyper-V server.

CLASS CATEGORY	DESCRIPTION
Resource Management	Set of classes that allows a client to discover the valid range of default settings for a virtual resource. Provides the object to describe the minimum, maximum, default, and incremental values for the given resource's allocation.
Serial Devices	Read-only classes used to query the configuration of the serial controller and the two serial ports of a virtual machine.
Storage	Set of classes used to query and manage the storage objects. Storage objects consist of IDE and SCSI controllers, virtual hard drives, virtual floppy drives, and virtual CD/DVD media.
Video	Set of classes used to query and manage the emulated S3 video controller, the synthetic video adapter, and remote terminal services.
Virtual System	Set of classes used to query and manage the Hyper-V server, virtual machines, and components like snapshots.
Virtual System Management	Set of classes used to interface with system management interfaces and manage the ability to import and export virtual machines.

NOTE The virtualization WMI classes are described in more detail on the Microsoft Developer Network at *http://go.microsoft.com/fwlink/?LinkID=108564*.

Connecting to Hyper-V Windows Management Instrumentation

To interact with the Hyper-V server or virtual machines, you must establish a connection to the root virtualization namespace (*root\virtualization*) of the appropriate Hyper-V WMI class. For example, if you want to query the Hyper-V server to determine how many virtual machines are registered on the system, you need to connect to the *MSVM_ComputerSystem WMI* class.

Using Windows PowerShell, you utilize the Get-WMIObject cmdlet to connect to a specific class in the *virtualization* namespace. The following code obtains the connection to the virtualization namespace for the local computer using the *MSVM_ComputerSystem* class:

```
Get-WMIObject -class "MSVM_ComputerSystem" -namespace "root\virtualization"
-computername "."
```

This line will be part of every Windows PowerShell script that you write to interact with the Hyper-V WMI namespace. Depending on the action you are trying to perform, you will need to modify which class you need to interface with. After you obtain the connection, you can access the class properties directly and execute the class methods.

There are two primary ways to utilize this connection via script after you have obtained it. If you are a VBScript programmer, then you might be more comfortable with assigning the result of this connection to an object variable that you can reference. To do this, you add an object reference assignment at the beginning of the line:

```
$VM = Get-WMIObject -class "MSVM_ComputerSystem" -namespace "root\virtualization"
-computername "."
```

If you are a Windows PowerShell programmer, you will typically just pipe the output of this line into the next line by adding the pipe command at the end of the line:

```
Get-WMIObject -class "MSVM_ComputerSystem" -namespace "root\virtualization"
-computername "." |
```

If you execute the Get-WMIObject call listed above with a *Hyper-V WMI* class, you will get an object reference to the collection of the corresponding objects, and the output on the screen will be a list of the properties of each object. For example, if you use the *MSVM_ComputerSystem* class, you will get a dump of the parent and child partitions on the local server listing the standard set of properties for each partition. The following sample output shows a test machine parent partition. You can tell it is the parent partition because the *Caption* value is *Hosting Computer System*. If it were a virtual machine, the *Caption* value would be *Virtual Machine*.

```
PS C:\Users\Administrator> gwmi -class "MSVM_ComputerSystem" -namespace "root\
virtualization" -computername "."


__GENUS                         : 2
__CLASS                         : Msvm_ComputerSystem
__SUPERCLASS                    : CIM_ComputerSystem
__DYNASTY                       : CIM_ManagedElement
__RELPATH                       : Msvm_ComputerSystem.CreationClassName="Msvm_
ComputerSystem",Name="M4400R2"
__PROPERTY_COUNT                : 29
__DERIVATION                    : {CIM_ComputerSystem, CIM_System, CIM_
EnabledLogicalElement, CIM_LogicalElement...}
__SERVER                        : M4400R2
__NAMESPACE                     : root\virtualization
__PATH                          : \\M4400R2\root\virtualization:Msvm_ComputerSystem.
CreationClassName="Msvm_ComputerSystem",Name="M4400R2"
AssignedNumaNodeList            :
Caption                         : Hosting Computer System
CreationClassName               : Msvm_ComputerSystem
Dedicated                       :
Description                     : Microsoft Hosting Computer System
ElementName                     : M4400R2
EnabledDefault                  : 2
EnabledState                    : 2
```

```
HealthState             : 5
IdentifyingDescriptions :
InstallDate             :
Name                    : M4400R2
NameFormat              :
OnTimeInMilliseconds    :
OperationalStatus       : {2}
OtherDedicatedDescriptions :
OtherEnabledState       :
OtherIdentifyingInfo    :
PowerManagementCapabilities :
PrimaryOwnerContact     :
PrimaryOwnerName        :
ProcessID               :
RequestedState          : 12
ResetCapability         : 1
Roles                   :
Status                  :
StatusDescriptions      : {OK}
TimeOfLastConfigurationChange :
TimeOfLastStateChange   :
```

Querying the Local Hyper-V Server

When you have the connection to the Hyper-V WMI namespace using the *MSVN_ComputerSystem* class, you can interface with the Hyper-V server to request or set information. For example, if you wanted to get a listing of all virtual machines on the local Hyper-V server and only list a subset of the virtual machine properties, you would get the connection to the virtualization namespace, execute a query to get all the virtual machine objects, filter the properties you are interested in, and then display the properties.

The pure Windows PowerShell approach would result in the following code:

```
GWMI MSVM_ComputerSystem -namespace "root\virtualization" -computername "." |
where {$_.Caption -eq "Virtual Machine"} |
Format-List ElementName, Name, EnabledState
```

Note the switch from the full form of Get-WMIObject to the alias GWMI to shorten the line.

This Windows PowerShell script is getting a connection to the virtualization namespace and passing that object reference to a collection of objects. That collection is then passed to the conditional *where* statement to filter to only objects that have a caption parameter of *Virtual Machine*. That filtered collection is then passed to the *Format-List* function, and three parameters of the virtual machine objects (*ElementName*, *Name*, and *EnabledState*) are displayed.

Using the Windows PowerShell VBScript–like approach, the code would result in a slightly different format, but the end result would be the same:

```
$VMCol = GWMI -class "MSVM_ComputerSystem" -namespace "root\virtualization"
-computername "."


foreach ($VM in $VMCol)
{
     if ($VM.Caption -match "Virtual Machine")
     {

         write-host "================================="
         write-host "VM Name:  " $VM.ElementName
         write-host "VM GUID:  " $VM.Name
         write-host "VM State: " $VM.EnabledState
     }
}
```

In the VBScript-like approach, the collection of virtual machine objects is stored in a variable named *$VMCol*. That object is passed to a *For* loop so that the entire collection would be traversed looking for the objects that have a *Caption* value of *Virtual Machine*. If an object matched the caption comparison, then three parameters of that object are displayed on the screen.

 ON THE COMPANION MEDIA   On the book's companion media, in the \Chapter Materials\Scripts\Chapter 16 folder, you will find the PowerShell scripts discussed in this section. They are named Get-VMList.ps1 and Get-VMList_VBS.ps1, respectively.

Querying Remote Hyper-V Servers

Changing the script to query a remote computer is as simple as changing the *Computername* property in the Get-WMIObject script line of code. The following code obtains the connection to the virtualization namespace for a remote computer called REMOTESVR:

```
Get-WMIObject -class "MSVM_ComputerSystem" -namespace "root\virtualization"
-computername "REMOTESVR"
```

In order for the query to be successful, the user that is executing the Windows PowerShell script must have proper rights on the remote server.

Querying for a Specific Virtual Machine

So far we have shown how to get the list of virtual machines on a Hyper-V server using Windows PowerShell. Many times you want to specifically perform an operation on a specific virtual machine. In order to get the object reference back for a specific virtual machine, you need to modify the Get-WMIObject call to the class to filter to the specific virtual machine.

The filter process in Windows PowerShell works as follows:

1.   Specify or query for the virtual machine name.

2. Build a query to select only that virtual machine from the entire collection of virtual machines, using the virtual machine name.

3. Pass that query to the class using the *–query* option of the Get-WMIObject cmdlet.

4. Perform the action required on the virtual machine using the new object reference.

Let's build a script using this process. First we need to get the virtual machine name, and for simplicity we will just assign the name to a variable. The following line of code assigns a virtual machine named TESTSVR1 to a variable called *$VMName*.

```
$VMName = "TESTSVR1"
```

Next we need to build the query. The query language is very similar to T-SQL, so a standard *SELECT* statement will work. If you are using a variable name to build the query, you need to make sure that the query has the correct parentheses, or it will fail. The following code shows a query statement to select all the objects from the *MSVM_ComputerSystem* class, but it will filter the results to show only those that have an *ElementName* equal to the virtual machine name provided in the *$VMName* variable. The query is built as a string and assigned to a variable to make it easy use in the Get-WMIObject call. Note the use of double quotation marks around a single quotation mark to get the single quotation mark as part of the final string:

```
$query = "SELECT * FROM MSVM_ComputerSystem WHERE ElementName='" + $VMName + "'"
```

When you have created the query string, you can use it in a modified Get-WMIObject call to return an object reference to the specific virtual machine. Just add the *–query* option followed by the query string. The following code shows the *–query* option added to the Get-WMIObject call and the object reference is assigned to the *$VM* variable:

```
$VM = GET-WMIObject -query $query -namespace "root\virtualization" -computername "."
```

Now that you have the object reference to the virtual machine as *$VM*, you can reference any properties to retrieve values or you can call any available methods. To retrieve a property of the virtual machine, you reference the property directly using *$VM*.property syntax. The following code would retrieve the amount of time that the virtual machine has been powered on in milliseconds using the *OnTimeInMilliseconds* property value:

```
$VM.OnTimeInMilliseconds
```

To reference a method of the virtual machine, you would reference the method with all the required parameters. For example, if you wanted to request to start a virtual machine, you could use the method *RequestStateChange()* with a value of 2. The following code calls the *RequestStateChange* method and returns the result of the call to a variable that can be checked for status:

```
$Result = $VM.RequestStateChange(2)
```

If we combine the individual code lines into a Windows PowerShell script that checks if the virtual machine is currently powered off based on the value of the *OnTimeInMilliseconds* property and then requests to start the virtual machine with *OnTimeInMilliseconds* equal to 0, we would have the following code:

```
$VMName = "TESTSVR1"
$query = "SELECT * FROM MSVM_ComputerSystem WHERE ElementName='" + $VMName + "'"
$VM = GET-WMIObject -query $query -namespace "root\virtualization" -computername "."
if ($VM.OnTimeInMilliseconds -eq 0)
{
     $Result = $VM.RequestStateChange(2)
}
```

 ON THE COMPANION MEDIA   On the book's companion media, in the \Chapter Materials\Scripts\Chapter 16 folder, you will find the PowerShell script discussed in this section. The script is named StartVM.ps1.

Querying Multiple Classes

Sometimes an action you want to perform requires you to use more than one class to accomplish your goal. A good example is attempting to shut down a virtual machine. Although it would make sense that there would be a method as part of a virtual machine object that allows the shutdown of a virtual machine, it is not as simple as that. You can use the *RequestStateChange* method of a virtual machine to turn off a virtual machine, but shutting down a virtual machine is an action that the virtual machine guest operating system must initiate. The Hyper-V architecture has created an interface using the Integration Services installed in a guest operating system to initiate a controlled shutdown. Therefore, in order to shut down a virtual machine, you must follow this process:

1. Obtain access to the specific virtual machine object.
2. Obtain access to the *ShutdownComponent* of the virtual machine.
3. Call the *InitiateShutdown* method of the *ShutdownCompoment*.

The first step in the process was just covered in the previous section, so we will not go over that again. Let's start with the fact that we have the object reference to the specific virtual machine in the *$VM* variable.

To get access to the Integration Services *MSVM_ShutdownComponent* class of a virtual machine, you must write a query that obtains an object reference to that class using the virtual machine object reference. You can make the linkage using the *SystemName* property of the *MSVM_ShutdownComponent* class. The query string would result in the following line of Windows PowerShell code:

```
$query = "SELECT * FROM MSVM_ShutdownComponent WHERE SystemName='" + $VM.Name + "'"
```

After you have the query string created, you can use the *–query* option of the Get-WMIObject cmdlet to execute the query to retrieve the object reference to the *ShutdownComponent* of the specific virtual machine.

```
$Shutdown = GET-WMIObject -query $query -namespace "root\virtualization"
-computername "."
```

When you have the object reference to the *ShutdownComponent* of the virtual machine, you can call the *InitiateShutdown* method and request a shutdown to be attempted. The two parameters for the *InitiateShutdown* method are one that determines if the shutdown should be forced if something is preventing a normal shutdown call and one that is a user-defined string that describes the reason for the shutdown. This string will be logged with the shutdown event.

The following code shows the call to the *InitiateShutdown* method requesting a forced shutdown and providing a string that describes the reason:

```
$Result = $Shutdown.InitiateShutdown($true,"Shutting down due to data center move")
```

If you combine the process into a single Windows PowerShell script that is attempting to shut down a virtual machine named TESTSVR1 on the local Hyper-V server, you will have the following code:

```
$VMName = "TESTSVR1"

$query = "SELECT * FROM MSVM_ComputerSystem WHERE ElementName='" + $VMName + "'"
$VM = GET-WMIObject -query $query -namespace "root\virtualization"
-computername "."

$query = "SELECT * FROM MSVM_ShutdownComponent WHERE SystemName='" + $VM.name + "'"
$Shutdown = GET-WMIObject -query $query -namespace "root\virtualization"
-computername "."

$Result = $Shutdown.InitiateShutdown($true," Shutting down due to data center move ")
```

 ON THE COMPANION MEDIA   On the book's companion media, in the \Chapter Materials\Scripts\Chapter 16 folder, you will find the PowerShell script discussed in this section. The script is named ShutdownVM.ps1.

Modifying a Virtual Machine Setting

Modifying a virtual machine setting requires you to obtain access to the virtual machine configuration information, modify the setting, and then use the management service to implement the change. You may recall from Chapter 3, "Hyper-V Architecture," that this is required because all changes to a virtual machine's configuration must be requested by the Virtual Machine Management Service (VMMS) and must be made by the Configuration Component.

The following process is required to modify a setting of a virtual machine:

1. Get an object reference of the specific virtual machine.

2. Get an object reference to the current configuration settings of the virtual machine.

3. Modify the setting you want to change.

4. Get an object reference to *MSVM_VirtualSystemManagementService*.

5. Use the *ModifyVirtualSystem* method of the *MSVM_VirtualSystemManagementService* object and pass it the path of the virtual machine object and the modified configuration setting data object.

To demonstrate how to use this process to change a setting of a virtual machine, we will use an example of renaming a virtual machine. To rename a virtual machine, you will need the existing name and the new name you want to use:

```
$VMNameOld = "TESTSVR1"
$VMNameNew = "TESTSERVER1"
```

Next you need an object reference to the specific virtual machine:

```
$query = "SELECT * FROM MSVM_ComputerSystem WHERE ElementName='" + $VMNameOld + "'"
$VM = GET-WMIObject -query $query -namespace "root\virtualization"
-computername "."
```

Now you need to get an object reference to the configuration settings of the virtual machine. The *VirtualSystemManagementService* maintains this reference as an *Associator* class. Instead of using a *SELECT* query to get the reference to the *Associator* class, you must use a new query called *ASSOCIATORS OF* query. Finding the *Associators* of a virtual machine is done using a query statement of the format:

ASSOCIATORS OF {$VM}

where *$VM* is the object reference to the virtual machine.

To obtain access to a specific *Associator* class using an *ASSOCIATORS OF* query, you filter using the *WHERE* clause. The *Associator* class that has the virtual machine settings information is called the *MSVM_SettingsDefineState*. The following code provides an example of the *ASSOCIATORS OF* query string and the actual query to obtain the object reference to the virtual machine settings:

```
$query = "Associators of {$VM} WHERE AssocClass=MSVM_SettingsDefineState"
$VMSettings = GET-WMIObject -query $query -namespace "root\virtualization"
-computername "."
```

Now that you have the object reference to the virtual machine settings, you can access the virtual machine *ElementName* property and modify it by assigning a new value using the variable that has the new virtual machine name assigned:

```
$VMSettings.ElementName = $VMNameNew
```

This modifies the setting that currently is loaded in memory, but the change has not been written back to the virtual machine configuration .xml file. In order to make the change, we need an object reference to the *MSVM_VirtualSystemManagementService*. To get an object reference to the management service, you use the Get-WMIObject cmdlet and the class name *MSVM_VirtualSystemManagementService*.

```
$VMManagementService = GET-WMIObject -class "MSVM_VirtualSystemManagementService"
-namespace "root\virtualization" -computername "."
```

When you have the object reference to *MSVM_VirtualSystemManagementService*, you can use the *ModifyVirtualSystem* method to write the changes in memory back to the configuration file. The *ModifyVirtualSystem* method requires two input parameters: the path to the virtual machine configuration file and a string that represents the current *SystemSettingData* object in memory. The path to the virtual machine configuration file is a standard property of the virtual machine object, __PATH. In order to convert the *SystemSettingData* object in memory to a string, you must use the *GetText* function to perform the text serialization:

```
$Result = $VMManagementService.ModifyVirtualSystem($VM.__PATH,$VMSettings.GetText(1))
```

> **NOTE** Calling the *GetText* function using Windows PowerShell 1.0 requires you to get access to the raw object; this is accomplished using *psbase*. In PowerShell 1.0, you would have to use *$VMSettings.psbase.GetText(1)* in place of *$VMSettings.GetText(1)* in PowerShell 2.0.

Combining all the code into a single Windows PowerShell 2.0 script that will rename a virtual machine from TESTSVR1 to TESTSERVER1 results in the following code.

```
$VMNameOld = "TESTSVR1"
$VMNameNew = "TESTSERVER1"

$query = "SELECT * FROM MSVM_ComputerSystem WHERE ElementName='" + $VMNameOld + "'"
$VM = GET-WMIObject -query $query -namespace "root\virtualization" -computername "."

$query = "Associators of {$VM} WHERE AssocClass=MSVM_SettingsDefineState"
$VMSettings = GET-WMIObject -query $query -namespace "root\virtualization"
-computername "."

$VMSettings.ElementName = $VMNameNew


$VMManagementService = GET-WMIObject -class "MSVM_VirtualSystemManagementService"
-namespace "root\virtualization" -computername "."

$Result = $VMManagementService.ModifyVirtualSystem($VM.__PATH,$VMSettings.GetText(1))
```

 ON THE COMPANION MEDIA On the book's companion media, in the \Chapter Materials\Scripts\Chapter 16 folder, you will find the PowerShell script discussed in this section. The script is named RenameVM.ps1.

Using the Windows PowerShell Hyper-V Library

Unless you like to start from scratch, having a pre-existing library of Windows PowerShell functions that you can learn from and directly utilize is a great way to get started. Some Microsoft employees have worked together to develop a sample Windows PowerShell Hyper-V management library. The library is available on Microsoft's open source project Web site at *http://pshyperv.codeplex.com*. The information provided in this chapter is based on the 1.00b version of the library.

The library consists of a set of functions that allows you to manage the following components:

- Virtual machine configuration and state
- Virtual hard disks
- Virtual floppy disks
- Virtual CD/DVD images
- Virtual network adapters
- Virtual network switches
- Snapshots

In addition, the library has a series of helper functions that help optimize code reuse and maintain a consistent interaction with the functions.

Changing the Windows PowerShell Execution Policy

After you download the library, you will need to install it on your computer to make use of the available functions. Before you can install it, you need to modify your Windows PowerShell execution policy. To see your current execution policy setting, use the Get-ExecutionPolicy cmdlet. There are four possible execution policies:

- **Restricted**   No scripts can be run. Windows PowerShell can be used only in interactive mode.
- **AllSigned**   Only scripts signed by a trusted publisher can be run.
- **RemoteSigned**   Downloaded scripts must be signed by a trusted publisher before they can be run.
- **Unrestricted**   No restrictions; all Windows PowerShell scripts can be run.

The default execution policy is Restricted. To use the Hyper-V PowerShell management library, you need to load it in memory so all the functions are available. By default, it is not signed, so the only mode you can use it in is Unrestricted.

To set the current execution policy to Unrestricted, use the `Set-ExecutionPolicy` cmdlet in a Windows PowerShell command prompt, with *Unrestricted* as the single passed parameter:

```
Set-ExecutionPolicy Unrestricted
```

DIRECT FROM THE SOURCE

Creating Self-Signed Scripts

Mike Williams, Senior Consultant
Microsoft Consulting Services

When you are developing scripts, you have the option of creating your own self-signed certificate and signing scripts so they can run in the AllSigned execution policy on your local machine.

To create a self-signed certificate, use MakeCert.exe from the Microsoft .NET Framework or Platforms SDK. MakeCert allows you to create a local certificate authority on your local machine and then create a self-signed certificate using that certificate authority. The certificate can be secured with a private key password.

When you have the self-signed certificate, you can sign a script using the `Set-AuthenticodeSignature` cmdlet passing the script file to sign and the cert to use to sign it.

For more information and step-by-step procedures, run `Get-Help about_signing` from a Windows PowerShell prompt.

Loading the Library into Memory

After you change the execution policy, you can load the library into memory so the functions are available. To load the library into memory, use the following procedure:

1. Open a Windows PowerShell command prompt.
2. Change to the directory that contains the downloaded Hyper-V PowerShell management library.
3. Execute the following command:

   ```
   . .\hyperv.ps1
   ```

4. You should now be able to utilize the library functions. Test it by running the following function at the Windows PowerShell command prompt:

   ```
   Get-VhdDefaultPath
   ```

5. If the command executes with no errors and provides the default path for storing virtual hard disks on the Hyper-V server, then the library loaded correctly.

Using the Windows PowerShell Hyper-V Library   CHAPTER 16   **577**

Hyper-V PowerShell Management Library Functions

The Hyper-V PowerShell management library has four major categories of functions available to create Windows PowerShell scripts to manage virtual machines, virtual drives (disks, DVDs, and floppies), virtual networking, and snapshots. The functions include standard ones such as *get, set, add,* and *new,* as well as some Hyper-V specific ones such as *start, stop, remove, import, export,* and so on. In addition to directly usable functions, there are utility functions that make it easier to utilize the library. These functions provide the ability to test configurations, prompt a user to select from a list of values, select several things at one time, and format output.

The next few tables list the major categories of functions with a short description of what each function does. Refer to the management library documentation for a complete list of functions.

Table 16-2 provides a list of all the functions available in the library to manage virtual machines and describes what each function does.

TABLE 16-2 Virtual Machine Windows PowerShell Functions

FUNCTION	DESCRIPTION
Choose-VM	Allows the user to select virtual machines from a list
New-VM	Creates a new virtual machine
New-VMConnectSession	Launches a VMConnect session to a virtual machine
Get-VM	Returns a WMI object reference to a virtual machine
Get-VMBackupScript	Gets a script for backing up one or more virtual machines
Get-VMByMACaddress	Discovers a virtual machine from its MAC address
Get-VMJPEG	Gets a JPEG image of the current virtual machine screen
Get-VMSettingData	Returns the setting data object for the virtual machine
Get-VMMemory	Returns the amount of memory assigned to a virtual machine
Get-VMCPUCount	Gets the number and weighting of processors assigned to virtual machines
Get-VMProcessor	Gets active virtual processors and their load data
Get-VMDiskController	Gets an IDE or SCSI controller
Get-VMSerialPort	Returns information about serial ports
Set-VM	Sets the properties of an existing virtual machine
Set-VMState	Called by Start-VM, Stop-VM, and Suspend-VM functions to set the requested state
Set-VMMemory	Sets the amount of memory assigned to a virtual machine
Set-VMCPUCount	Sets the number of virtual processors assigned to virtual machines

FUNCTION	DESCRIPTION
Set-VMSerialPort	Maps serial ports on a virtual machine to named pipe
Add-VMSCSIcontroller	Adds a synthetic SCSI controller to a virtual machine
Remove-VM	Removes a virtual machine
Remove-VMSCSIcontroller	Removes a synthetic SCSI controller from a virtual machine
Export-VM	Calls the Hyper-V export process
Import-VM	Calls the Hyper-V import process
Shutdown-VM	Shuts down a virtual machine's operating system using the integration services shutdown interface
Start-VM	Starts a virtual machine or restarts a saved one
Stop-VM	Powers off a virtual machine without asking the operating system to shut down first
Suspend-VM	Puts the virtual machine into a saved state
Test-VMHeartBeat	Tests the responses from the heartbeat integration component

Table 16-3 provides a list of all the functions available in the library to manage virtual hard disks and briefly describes what each function does.

TABLE 16-3 Virtual Hard Disk Windows PowerShell Functions

FUNCTION	DESCRIPTION
New-VHD	Creates a new virtual hard disk file
Get-VMDriveByController	Gets the virtual hard drives attached to a controller
Get-VMDisk	Gets a list of virtual hard disk images in use
Get-VMDiskByDrive	Gets the virtual machine disk image attached to a drive
Get-VHDDefaultPath	Gets the default path used by Hyper-V for virtual hard disk files
Get-VHDInfo	Gets information about a virtual hard disk, such as its parent or size on disk
Add-VMDrive	Connects a virtual hard disk to a controller
Add-VMDisk	Mounts a virtual hard disk image into a drive
Add-VMNewHardDisk	Attaches a new virtual hard disk image to a new drive
Set-VMDisk	Changes the virtual hard disk image attached to a drive
Test-VHD	Tests that a virtual hard disk can be mounted and that any parent is mountable

FUNCTION	DESCRIPTION
Compact-VHD	Compacts a dynamic virtual hard disk file to save space on the server
Convert-VHD	Changes a virtual hard disk from one type to another
Expand-VHD	Expands the size of a virtual hard disk
Merge-VHD	Merges a child virtual hard disk with its parent to form a new disk
Mount-VHD	Mounts the virtual hard disk on the server
UnMount-VHD	Unmounts a previously mounted virtual hard disk from the server
Remove-VMDRIVE	Removes a virtual hard disk from a controller

Table 16-4 provides a list of all the functions available in the library to manage virtual networks and virtual network switches with a short description of what each function does.

TABLE 16-4 Virtual Networks and Network Switch Windows PowerShell Functions

FUNCTION	DESCRIPTION
Choose-VMExternalEthernet	Allows the user to choose a server network card
Choose-VMSwitch	Allows the user to choose a virtual switch
New-VMExternalSwitch	Creates a virtual switch connected to a server network card
New-VMInternalSwitch	Creates a virtual switch accessible to VMs and the server
New-VMPrivateSwitch	Creates a virtual switch accessible to VMs
New-VMSwitchPort	Defines a new port on a virtual switch
Get-VMSwitch	Returns information about virtual switches

Table 16-5 provides a list of all the functions available in the library to manage virtual machine snapshots with a description of what each function does.

TABLE 16-5 Snapshot Windows PowerShell Functions

FUNCTION	DESCRIPTION
Apply-VMSnapshot	Applies a snapshot to a virtual machine
Choose-VMSnapshot	Allows the user to choose a snapshot for a virtual machine
New-VMSnapshot	Creates a new snapshot of a virtual machine
Get-VMSnapshot	Gets information about snapshots of a virtual machine
Get-VMSnapshotTree	Formats the view of a virtual machine snapshots as a tree

FUNCTION	DESCRIPTION
Remove-VMSnapshot	Deletes a snapshot or tree of snapshots
Rename-VMSnapshot	Renames a snapshot
Update-VMSnapshot	Deletes a snapshot and creates a new one with same name

Managing Virtual Machines

You can use the functions for managing virtual machines as tools to create Windows PowerShell scripts that will allow you to accomplish a management task with less code than you would if you had to write your own. The following section provides two examples of how to combine the management library functions to create, modify, and remove virtual machines quickly.

Creating Virtual Machines

The Hyper-V PowerShell library comes with a function called *New-VM* that allows you to create a new virtual machine from a single line of Windows PowerShell code. The function takes two command-line parameters. Table 16-6 lists the parameter syntax for the *New-VM* function.

TABLE 16-6 *New-VM* Command-Line Parameters

SWITCH	PARAMETER	EXAMPLE
–name	Virtual machine name	–name "TestVM1"
–server	Remote server name	–server "Server1"

Only the virtual machine name parameter is required. If the server parameter is not provided, the local server is assumed by default. Creating a new virtual machine is as simple as typing the following line in a Windows PowerShell command prompt and pressing Enter:

```
New-VM "TestVM1"
```

You will notice that the *–name* parameter was not specified. The function is designed to assume that if there is only a single mandatory parameter, and only one parameter is specified on the command line, then the parameter provided is the mandatory parameter.

When you create a new virtual machine using the *New-VM* function, it only creates the virtual machine profile, registers the virtual machine with the Hyper-V server, adds one virtual processor, and configures the virtual machine with 512 megabytes (MB) of RAM. If you want to change the default values or if you want to add additional hardware to the virtual machine, then you must write the Windows PowerShell code to make those changes, or better yet, you can utilize the other library functions to make those changes.

For example, if you wanted to increase the default memory to 1 gigabyte (GB), increase the virtual processor count to 2, add a virtual hard disk to the primary IDE controller, add a virtual hard disk to an SCSI controller on port 3, mount a virtual DVD ISO image to the second port on the IDE controller, and add a network adapter and connect it to a virtual network, you would need to use the following functions from the library:

- *Set-VMMemory*
- *Set-VMCPUCount*
- *Add-VMDrive*
- *Add-VMDisk*
- *Add-VMNic*

Table 16-7 lists the function parameters for the *Set-VMMemory* function.

TABLE 16-7 *Set-VMMemory* Command-Line Parameters

SWITCH	PARAMETER	EXAMPLE
–vm	Virtual machine object reference	$VM
–server	Remote server name	–server "Server1"
–memory	Size of memory to set	–memory 1 GB

Table 16-8 lists the function parameters for the *Set-VMCPUCount* function.

TABLE 16-8 *Set-VMCPUCount* Command-Line Parameters

SWITCH	PARAMETER	EXAMPLE
–vm	Virtual machine object reference	$VM
–server	Remote server name	–server "Server1"
–CPUCount	Number of CPUs to assign	–CPUCount 2

Table 16-9 lists the function parameters for the *Add-VMDrive* function.

TABLE 16-9 *Add-VMDrive* Command-Line Parameters

SWITCH	PARAMETER	EXAMPLE
–vm	Virtual machine object reference	$VM
–server	Remote server name	–server "Server1"
–controllerID	Which controller to attach the drive	–controllerID 0
–lun	The controller port to attach the drive	–lun 3
–DVD	Switch that sets actions to be for a DVD drive instead of a virtual hard disk	–DVD
–SCSI	Switch that sets the controller type to SCSI	–scsi

Table 16-10 lists the function parameters for the *Add-VMDisk* function.

TABLE 16-10 *Add-VMDisk* Command-Line Parameters

SWITCH	PARAMETER	EXAMPLE
–vm	Virtual machine object reference	$VM
–server	Remote server name	–server "Server1"
–controllerID	Which controller to attach the drive	–controllerID 0
–lun	The controller port to attach the drive	–lun 3
–DVD	Switch that sets actions to be for a DVD drive instead of a virtual hard disk	–DVD
–SCSI	Switch that sets the controller type to SCSI	–scsi
–vhdpath	Path to where the virtual hard disk should be stored	"F:\VMs\TESTVM1\TEST.VHD"
	If no path is provided, the virtual hard disk is created in the default location.	"TEST.VHD"

Table 16-11 lists the function parameters for the *Add-VMNic* function.

TABLE 16-11 *Add-VMNic* Command-Line Parameters

SWITCH	PARAMETER	EXAMPLE
–vm	Virtual machine object reference	$VM
–server	Remote server name	–server "Server1"
–virtualswitch	Virtual switch to bind the virtual machine network adapter	–virtualSwitch "Internal Network"
–mac	Static MAC address to assign to the virtual machine	–mac "00155D010110"
–GUID	Switch that sets actions to be for a DVD drive instead of a virtual hard disk	–DVD
–legacy	Path to where the virtual hard disk should be stored	"F:\VMs\TESTVM1\TEST.VHD"
	If no path is provided, the virtual hard disk is created in the default location.	"TEST.VHD"

The following Windows PowerShell script provides an example of how to combine the required functions to modify existing settings and add a new configuration to a virtual machine immediately after creation:

```
$VMName = "TestVM2"


$NewVM = (New-VM $VMName)


Set-VMMemory $NewVM -memory 1GB
Set-VMCPUCount $NewVM -CPUCount 2
Add-VMDrive $NewVM 0 0
Add-VMDisk $NewVM 0 0 "Existingvhd.vhd"
Add-VMDrive $NewVM 0 1 -dvd
Add-VMDisk $NewVM 0 1 "Windows.iso" -dvd
Add-VMDrive $NewVM 0 3 -scsi
Add-VMDisk $NewVM 0 3 "Datavhd.vhd" -scsi


Add-VMNIC $NewVM (choose-VMSwitch) -virtualSwitch "Internal Network"
```

The script starts out by taking the virtual machine name TestVM2 and passing it to the *New-VM* function; the object reference to the new virtual machine is stored in the variable *$NewVM*. Each of the configuration functions used in the script are designed to take the virtual machine object reference as the first parameter. Although most configuration steps are a single function call, you will notice that adding a virtual hard disk or a DVD image to a virtual machine requires two calls. The first one to *Add-VMDrive* reserves the port for the actual addition of the disk using the *Add-VMDisk* function.

The *Add-VMDisk* and *Add-VMDrive* functions support both virtual hard disks and virtual DVD images. The *-dvd* parameter is used to notify the functions to perform the operations on a DVD instead of a virtual hard disk. The *-scsi* parameter is passed to the functions to inform them to perform the operation on a SCSI controller versus an IDE controller. The second and third parameters sent to the *Add-VMDisk* and *Add-VMDrive* functions specify the controller type and the port number that should be used during the operation.

The *Add-VMNic* function allows you to add a virtual network adapter to a virtual machine, configure the adapter, and optionally connect the adapter to a virtual network switch. If you do not specify the *-virtualswitch* parameter, the virtual network adapter is left in the disconnected state.

So in ten lines of Windows PowerShell code, you have created a new virtual machine, modified the amount of memory and the number of virtual processors it has, added an existing virtual hard disk to the IDE controller as the bootable disk, added an existing virtual hard disk to a SCSI controller as the data disk, and added a network adapter and connected it to a virtual network on the server.

 ON THE COMPANION MEDIA   On the book's companion media, in the \Chapter Materials\Scripts\Chapter 16 folder, you will find the PowerShell script discussed in this section. The script is named CreateVM.ps1.

Removing Virtual Machines

Removing virtual machines from local or remote Hyper-V servers is a single command-line operation using the *Remove-VM* function.

Table 16-12 lists the function parameters for the *Remove-VM* function.

TABLE 16-12 *Remove-VM* Command-Line Parameters

SWITCH	PARAMETER	EXAMPLE
−vm	Virtual machine object reference	$VM
−server	Remote server name	−server "Server1"
−wait	Switch to enable waiting until the function is complete before continuing	−wait

Using the *Remove-VM* function by itself allows you to specify a single virtual machine to remove, but you need to know the name of the virtual machine before running the function.

```
Remove-VM "TESTVM1"
```

If you combine the *Remove-VM* function with the *Choose-VM* function, you can create a single piped Windows PowerShell command line that will prompt the user with a list of the available virtual machines.

Table 16-13 lists the function parameters for the *Choose-VM* function.

TABLE 16-13 *Choose-VM* Command-Line Parameters

SWITCH	PARAMETER	EXAMPLE
−server	Remote server name	−server "Server1"
−multiple	Switch to enable the user to select multiple virtual machines from the list.	−multiple

If you provide no command-line parameter options, the *Choose-VM* function assumes the local Hyper-V server, and the user can select a single virtual machine from the list.

```
Choose-VM | Remove-VM
```

When you run this command line, a table of all the registered virtual machines will be presented, with a unique ID beside each one and a prompt asking "Which One?" Type the ID of the one you want to select and press Enter. When the user selects a virtual machine from the list, the virtual machine object reference is automatically passed to the *Remove-VM* function, and the *Remove-VM* function executes.

If you want to specify the server to choose the virtual machines from, then add the *−server* parameter and specify the server name. When you do this for the *Choose-VM* function, the

Remove-VM function automatically understands that the remove action needs to take place on the remote server.

```
Choose-VM -Server HVServer1 | Remove-VM
```

If you want to quickly remove all virtual machines from a server, you can combine the *Get-VM* library function and the *Remove-VM* function in a single piped command line:

```
Get-VM | Remove-VM
```

Use this combination *very* carefully. This will remove all the virtual machines from the local server and does not prompt or warn you that it is about to do so.

Managing Virtual Hard Disks

Creating new virtual hard disks using the Hyper-V PowerShell management library requires a single Windows PowerShell function, *New-VHD*. Table 16-14 lists the function parameters for the *New-VHD function*. *New-VHD* only has a single required parameter, *–vhdpath*, the path to the location where the virtual hard disk should be created.

TABLE 16-14 *New-VHD* Command-Line Parameters

SWITCH	PARAMETER	EXAMPLE
–vhdpath	Path to where the virtual hard disk should be stored	"F:\VMs\TESTVM1\TEST.VHD"
	If no path is provided, the virtual hard disk is created in the default location.	"TEST.VHD"
–size	Size of virtual hard disk	200GB
–fixed	Enables fixed type virtual hard disk	–fixed
–server	Remote server name	-server "Server1"
–parent	Path to parent virtual hard disk when creating a differencing disk	"F:\ParentDisks\BaseVHD.VHD"
–wait	Switch to enable waiting until the function is complete before continuing	–wait

Note if the *–parent* parameter is specified, the *–size* and *–fixed* parameters are ignored.

Following are some examples of how to use the command-line parameters. The first example creates a new 20-GB virtual hard disk in a specified location:

```
New-VHD "F:\VMs\NewDisk.vhd" -size 20GB
```

The second example creates a 200-GB fixed virtual hard disk in the default virtual hard disk location specified on the server and waits until the disk creation is complete before it passes control to the next line of the Windows PowerShell script.

```
New-VHD "NewDisk2.vhd" -size 200GB -fixed -wait
```

The third example creates a 40-GB child differencing disk from a specified parent that happens to be a syspreped version of Windows Server 2008 SP2.

```
New-VHD "NewChildDisk.vhd" -size 40GB -parent "F:\ParentDisks\SysprepWin2K8SP2.vhd"
```

The *New-VHD* function creates the virtual hard disk, but it does not connect the disk to a virtual machine. To attach the new virtual hard disk, you must use the *Add-VMDrive* and *Add-VMDisk* functions to make the connection, as demonstrated in the previous section.

Although it is acceptable to combine those functions in a single script and even possibly pipe them together to reduce the number of lines of code, if this is an action that you perform regularly, then it would be more efficient to have a single function to call that combines all of the actions. The function *Add-VMNewHardDisk* is provided to do just that. It incorporates the three functions *New-VHD*, *Add-VMDrive*, and *Add-VMDisk* together into a new function that requires a single line of Windows PowerShell code.

Add-VMNewHardDisk requires only a single parameter, the virtual machine object reference. If only the virtual machine reference is provided, *Add-VMNewHardDisk* creates a 127-GB dynamically expanding virtual hard disk in the default virtual hard disk location, with the name of the virtual machine, connected to the primary IDE controller on port 0.

Table 16-15 lists the function parameters for the *Add-VMNewHardDisk* function.

TABLE 16-15 *Add-VMNewHardDisk* Command-Line Parameters

SWITCH	PARAMETER	EXAMPLE
−vm	Virtual machine object reference	$VM
−size	Size of virtual hard disk	200GB
−fixed	Enables fixed type virtual hard disk	−fixed
−server	Remote server name	Server1
−parent	Path to parent virtual hard disk when creating a differencing disk	"F:\ParentDisks \BaseVHD.VHD"
−controllerID	ID for the controller to connect the virtual hard disk	0
−lun	Port on the controller to connect the virtual hard disk	3
−vhdpath	Path to where the virtual hard disk should be stored	"F:\VMs\TESTVM1 \TEST.VHD"
	If no path is provided, the virtual hard disk is created in the default location	"TEST.VHD"
−scsi	Specifies the controller is SCSI	−scsi

Following are some examples of how to use the command-line parameters for the *Add-VMNewHardDisk* function. The first example creates a new 20-GB virtual hard disk in a specified location and connects it to the IDE controller on port 0:

```
Add-VMNewHardDisk  -vm $VM -vhdpath "F:\VMs\NewDisk.vhd" -size 20GB
```

The second example creates a 200-GB fixed virtual hard disk in the default virtual hard disk location and connects it to the second SCSI controller on port 4:

```
New-VHD -vm $VM -vhdpath "NewDisk2.vhd" -size 200GB -fixed -controllerID 1 -lun 4 -scsi
```

The third example creates a 40-GB child differencing disk from a specified parent disk and by default connects it to IDE controller 0 on port 0:

```
New-VHD -vm $VM -vhdpath "NewChildDisk.vhd" -size 40GB -parent "F:\ParentDisks
\SysprepWin2K8SP2.vhd"
```

Managing Virtual Networks

Virtual networks are the network communication path for virtual machines. There are three types of virtual networks: external, internal, and private. External virtual networks are bound to physical network adapters in the Hyper-V server to allow the virtual machines to communicate on the physical local area network (LAN). Internal virtual networks allow virtual machines to communicate to the Hyper-V server they are running on, but not to any device on the physical LAN. Internal virtual networks are not bound to physical network adapters in the server. Private virtual networks allow virtual machines to communicate with other virtual machines connected to the same private virtual network, but not to the Hyper-V server or to any device on the LAN.

Creating Virtual Switches

When you create virtual network switches, the parameters and options you select are based on the type of the virtual network you are creating. The Hyper-V PowerShell management library has a separate function for each type of virtual network that can be created, and each function has different command-line parameters. Each function is described in the following tables, with examples of how to use the command-line parameters.

Table 16-16 lists the function parameters for the *New-VMExternalSwitch* function.

TABLE 16-16 *New-VMExternalSwitch* Command-Line Parameters

SWITCH	PARAMETER	EXAMPLE
–virtualswitchname	Name to assign to the new virtual switch	–virtualswitchname "External Net"
– ext	String that defines the server physical network adapter to bind to	"Broadcom"
	MSVM_ExternalEthernetPort object reference	Piped from choose-VMExternalEthernet
–server	Remote server name	–server Server1
–ports	Number of ports the virtual switch has	–ports 2048

The following two examples demonstrate how to use the *New-VMExternalSwitch* function and the command-line parameters. The first example creates an external virtual switch called "External Network" that is bound to the physical adapter whose name begins with "Broadcom" on remote server Host23, and the default number of ports is set to 2048.

```
New-VMExternalSwitch -virtualSwitchNameName "External Network" -ext "Broadcom"
-Server Host23 –ports 2048
```

The *–ext* parameter is treated as a search string. Any network adapter that contains the text "Broadcom" will match, so there is no need to know the entire network adapter string.

The next example shows how to use the *Choose-VMExternalEthernet* function to present the user with a list of physical network adapters on a server and pipe the selected adapter to the *New-VMExternalSwitch* function.

```
choose-VMExternalEthernet –Server Host23 | New-VMExternalSwitch -virtualSwitchNameName
"External Network" –ports 2048
```

Table 16-17 lists the function parameters for the *New-VMInternalSwitch* function.

TABLE 16-17 *New-VMInternalSwitch* Command-Line Parameters

SWITCH	PARAMETER	EXAMPLE
–virtualswitchname	Name to assign to the new virtual switch	–virtualswitchname "Internal Net"
–server	Remote server name	–server Server1
–ports	Number of ports the virtual switch has	–ports 2048

The following example illustrates how to use the *New-VMInternalSwitch* function parameters.

```
New-VMInternalSwitch -virtualSwitchNameName "Internal Network" -Server Host23
–ports 2048
```

Table 16-18 lists the function parameters for the *New-VMPrivateSwitch* function.

TABLE 16-18 *New-VMPrivateSwitch* Command-Line Parameters

SWITCH	PARAMETER	EXAMPLE
–virtualswitchname	Name to assign to the new virtual switch	–virtualswitchname "Internal Net"
–server	Remote server name	–server Server1
–ports	Number of ports the virtual switch has	–ports 2048

The following example illustrates how to use the *New-VMPrivateSwitch* function parameters.

```
New-VMPrivateSwitch -virtualSwitchNameName "Private Network" -Server Host23 -ports 2048
```

Deleting Virtual Switches

The Hyper-V PowerShell management library version 1.00b does not have a function for deleting a switch, but it is a simple process using the *DeleteSwitch* method of the *MSVM_VirtualSwitchManagementService* class. You can also use the *Choose-VMSwitch* function to obtain the object reference to the switch you want to delete.

The following code example demonstrates how to delete an existing virtual switch. You start by getting an object reference to the *MSVM_VirtualSwitchManagementService* class, then use the *Choose-VMSwitch* function from the library to select the virtual switch to delete, and finally use the *DeleteSwitch* method to delete the selected virtual switch.

```
$SwitchObj = Get-WMIObject -class "MSVM_VirtualSwitchManagementService" -namespace
"root\virtualization" -computername "."
$Switch = Choose-VMSwitch
$SwitchObj.DeleteSwitch($Switch)
```

Managing Snapshots

Snapshots are a core feature of Hyper-V for the developer and tester. They allow you to save the state and configuration of the virtual machine at a specific point in time and return to that point after making changes, so you do not have to worry about anything in the configuration, memory, or processes being lost. They are your own little time machines.

Having the ability to script the creation and management of snapshots can be important when testing automation in a scenario in which you might want to automate the creation of a snapshot before you make a change or install a new version of an application. You might also want to be able to revert to a previous snapshot in a repetitive what-if testing scenario.

The Hyper-V PowerShell management library has a collection of functions to manage snapshots easily. The following sections describe how to use the functions to create, apply, and remove snapshots.

Creating Snapshots

You create a new snapshot using the *New-VMSnapshot* function from the Hyper-V PowerShell management library. Table 16-19 lists the function parameters for the *New-VMSnapshot* function.

TABLE 16-19 *New-VMSnapshot* Command-Line Parameters

SWITCH	PARAMETER	EXAMPLE
–vm	Virtual machine object reference	$VM
–server	Remote server name	–server "Server1"
–note	Text string that is used to populate the notes field of a snapshot	–note "Test Note"
–wait	Switch to enable waiting until the function is complete before continuing	–wait

The following example illustrates how to use the *New-VMSnapshot* function command-line parameters:

```
New-VMSnapshot $VM –note "Before test begins" –Server Host1 –wait
```

This command line will create a snapshot for the virtual machine referenced in *$VM* object that resides on Host1, assign the note field to "Before test begins", and wait for the snapshot to complete before continuing to the next line of Windows PowerShell code.

Renaming Snapshots

The *New-VMSnapshot* function does not provide the ability to name the snapshot during creation. If you want to set or change the snapshot name, you must use the *Rename-VMSnapshot* function. Table 16-20 lists the function parameters for the *Rename-VMSnapshot* function.

TABLE 16-20 *Rename-VMSnapshot* Command-Line Parameters

SWITCH	PARAMETER	EXAMPLE
–vm	Virtual machine object reference	$VM
–server	Remote server name	–server Server1
–snapname	The name or object reference to an existing snapshot	–snapname "Snapshot14"
–newname	Text string to use as the new snapshot name	–newname "Snapshot before XYZ application install"

The following example illustrates how to use the *Rename-VMSnapshot* function command-line parameters:

```
Rename-VmSnapshot $VM -snapname (Choose-VMSnapshot $VM).ElementName -newname " Snapshot
before XYZ application install"
```

This command line will rename a snapshot for the virtual machine referenced in *$VM* object. Use the *Choose-VMSnapshot* function to prompt the user with a list of current snapshots of the virtual machine, obtain the *Elementname* of the snapshot selected, pass that as the existing snapshot name, and assign the new snapshot name "Snapshot before XYZ application install".

By default, snapshot names are based on the date and time that the snapshot was taken. Unless you know the snapshot name, using *Choose-VMSnapshot* will greatly simplify the process to get the snapshot name.

Applying Snapshots

When you have one or more snapshots for a virtual machine, you can use the *Apply-VMSnapshot* function to switch between snapshots. Table 16-21 lists the function parameters for the *Apply-VMSnapshot* function.

TABLE 16-21 *Apply-VMSnapshot* Command-Line Parameters

SWITCH	PARAMETER	EXAMPLE
–snapshot	Snapshot object reference	$Snap
–force	Forces the application of the snapshot even if the virtual machine is running	–force
–restart	Restarts the virtual machine after the snapshot has been applied	–restart
–wait	Waits until the snapshot is applied but does not restart it	–wait

The following example illustrates how to use the *Apply-VMSnapshot* function command-line parameters:

```
Choose-VMSnapshot $VM | Apply-VMSnapshot -force -restart
```

This command line will apply a snapshot for the virtual machine referenced in *$VM* object, using the *Choose-VMSnapshot* function to prompt the user with a list of current snapshots of the virtual machine. After the snapshot is selected, the snapshot will be forcibly applied, and the virtual machine will be restarted after the snapshot application is complete.

Removing Snapshots

When you have finished a series of what-if tests and the snapshots are no longer needed, it is a good idea to clean them up. The Hyper-V PowerShell management library provides a function to remove existing snapshots quickly. The function is called *Remove-VMSnapshot*, and Table 16-22 lists its function parameters.

TABLE 16-22 *Remove-VMSnapshot* Command-Line Parameters

SWITCH	PARAMETER	EXAMPLE
–snapshot	Snapshot object reference	$Snap
–tree	Switch to enable the removal of the snapshots in the tree branch below the snapshot being removed.	–tree

The following example illustrates how to use the *Remove-VMSnapshot* function command-line parameters:

```
Choose-VMSnapshot $VM | Remove-VMSnapshot -tree
```

This command line will remove a snapshot for the virtual machine referenced in *$VM* object, using the *Choose-VMSnapshot* function to prompt the user with a list of current snapshots of the virtual machine. The *–tree* option informs the *Remove-VMSnapshot* function to recursively call itself to remove all other snapshots from the current leaf down the tree branch.

Be very careful when using the *–tree* parameter. There are no prompts or warnings when you select a snapshot from the *Choose-VMSnapshot* function, so if you select the wrong snapshot and use the *–tree* parameter, you can quickly lose an entire tree of snapshots.

Summary

This chapter demonstrated how to interface with the Hyper-V WMI API using Windows PowerShell. The chapter explained how to obtain access to the Hyper-V WMI classes using Windows PowerShell, how to query the local and remote Hyper-V server for virtual machines, how to utilize multiple classes to gather information, and how to manage virtual machine settings using the native WMI classes. Although knowing how to write Windows PowerShell scripts from scratch is important, reusing scripts and functions that already exist can save you time. To demonstrate how powerful a library of functions can be, we introduced a Windows PowerShell library that was developed internally by Microsoft and is available at *http://www.codeplex.com*. Using the library functions, we covered the basics of managing virtual machines, virtual network switches, virtual hard disks, and snapshots. Although this library is not supported by Microsoft, it can be a valuable tool for creating and maintaining your Hyper-V infrastructure, allowing you to learn how the Hyper-V WMI classes work while saving valuable time.

Additional Resources

The following resources contain additional information related to the topics in this chapter.

- For more information about the Hyper-V WMI class reference, see the Microsoft Developer Network article "Virtualization WMI Provider," which describes the virtualization WMI classes in more detail and is available at *http://go.microsoft.com /fwlink/?LinkID=108564*

- Download the latest version of Hyper-V PowerShell Management Library at *http://pshyperv.codeplex.com*

- For more information about *Associators* and how to query them, refer to the Microsoft Developer Network article "ASSOCIATORS OF Statement," available at *http://msdn.microsoft.com/en-us/library/aa384793(VS.85).aspx*

- James O'Neill's Windows PowerShell blog is a great resource for more information about the Hyper-V PowerShell Management Library. O'Neill is the primary developer of the library, and his blog is available at *http://blogs.technet.com/jamesone*

Server Virtualization Scenarios

S erver virtualization projects fall into one of four main scenarios: data center, branch office, test lab, or software development. Each scenario has different considerations that affect how you design, manage, and operate the associated infrastructure. This chapter provides a description of each scenario and discusses what you should consider when you undertake a project that falls within one of these scenarios.

Data Center Scenario

Projects that focus on establishing a virtualized data center are typically driven by a data center that is short on resources and is affecting the business's ability to meet new capacity requirements or provide new services. Economic trends are also forcing companies to do more with less by reducing capital, management, and operational costs.

Host Design Considerations

Data center host designs are usually focused on maximizing the number of virtual machines per server to achieve the best consolidation ratio possible for the least cost. Most data center servers will have more processors, cores, memory, network connections, and storage than servers used in the other scenarios. Since data center virtualization servers usually host a higher number of virtual machines, it is highly recommended to utilize Hyper-V server failover clusters to provide high availability.

The decision to use rack-mount servers or blades will be based on your Hyper-V server capacity needs, the design of the blade, and the blade enclosure. Rack-mount servers can potentially provide more expandability and capacity than blade servers, but they do also require more space and power. Blade servers typically share a backplane that has a limited number of expansion slots that are shared across the blade enclosure, which limits the maximum throughput that the blade enclosure can achieve.

Network Considerations

In a data center scenario, network throughput and fault tolerance are key to ensuring high availability for the Hyper-V server and the virtual machines. As discussed in Chapter 7, "Hyper-V Best Practices and Optimization," each server should have a minimum of two network adapters: one that is reserved for parent partition communications and one for virtual machine communications. In a data center scenario, you will be consolidating a high number of virtual machines per server, and a single dedicated network adapter will not provide sufficient network throughput. Therefore, you will need additional network adapters to handle the virtual machine communication requirements. How many more you will need will be based on the combined network bandwidth requirements.

In addition to the network adapters that are used for server and virtual machine communications, in a data center scenario you will possibly also have network adapter requirements for the following:

- iSCSI
- Cluster communications
- Backup networks

If you use iSCSI-based storage, you will want to dedicate a minimum of one gigabit network adapter for iSCSI traffic. If you need fault tolerance using multiple paths to the iSCSI server, you will need two gigabit network adapters for iSCSI traffic. To obtain the best performance to the iSCSI server, you should consider using network adapters that support offloading the iSCSI communications in hardware.

> **NOTE** Network adapters that provide iSCSI offloading utilize software drivers from the network adapter manufacturer that understand that the iSCSI offloading has occurred. iSCSI offloading works for iSCSI connections established from the parent partition, but not from the child partitions. Child partitions cannot run the network adapter drivers that understand the iSCSI offloading implementation.

In a Windows Server 2008 failover cluster, an adapter can be enabled for cluster communication and client access. To ensure high availability of a cluster, each node should have two network adapters that cluster communications can use for primary and secondary communication paths. Failover cluster network traffic is lightweight and does not impact the network communication by a noticeable amount. It is acceptable to have cluster communications use the management network adapter, but it is not recommended to have cluster communications traffic use the iSCSI or virtual network adapters.

When you utilize host clustering in a data center environment, you will be migrating virtual machines between servers in planned and unplanned situations. Regardless of the situation, you want the virtual machine to maintain network connectivity when it migrates to another server. Because of the number of virtual machines on a Hyper-V server, you will typically require multiple virtual networks to serve the network I/O requirements. When you move a virtual machine between Hyper-V servers, the failover cluster will attempt to reconnect the virtual machine to the same virtual network GUID and then fall back to the virtual network name. If neither the GUID nor the virtual network name can be found, the virtual machine will be placed in a Not Connected state and you must reassign the virtual machine to an available network. If you follow best practices and standardize the virtual network names, then migrating from one Hyper-V server to another will allow for the networking to be automatically assigned, and the virtual machine will have network connectivity.

In a data center scenario, migrating virtual machines from one Hyper-V server to another could result in a virtual network becoming overloaded. Although you can manually rebalance the load between multiple virtual networks attached to the same subnet, allowing the system to do it automatically is a better approach.

Using network adapter teaming is one solution to this issue. Network adapter teaming allows different modes of operation:

- **Load balancing** Multiple physical network adapters act as a single network adapter to the system to load balance the network traffic.
- **Failover** Multiple physical network adapters in an active-passive configuration. The active node is sending and receiving traffic while the passive node is waiting to take over if the active adapter fails.
- **Aggregation** Multiple physical network adapters in an additive bandwidth configuration. When the first adapter becomes overloaded, the next network adapter starts transmitting-receiving traffic.

In order to ensure that the migration of a virtual machine from one host to another has minimal impact on the existing traffic while providing an automated way to balance the traffic, you can use the Load-Balancing network adapter teaming mode. This allows Hyper-V to see the multiple physical adapters as a single logical adapter. By providing Hyper-V with a single network adapter for virtual machine use, only a single virtual network is required. This minimizes management overhead for virtual network connections.

> **NOTE** Microsoft does not support network teaming—that is the responsibility of the network adapter provider. If you call Microsoft for support regarding a server that is in teaming mode, Microsoft might require you to break the team and remove the teaming software to troubleshoot the issue.

Using Load-Balancing network adapter teaming mode has one drawback—it combines all the traffic on a single network. Combining virtual local area networks (VLANs) and load balancing allows you to separate the traffic into different virtual subnets while using the same physical network connection.

High Availability Considerations

In a data center scenario, you are typically focused on maximizing the consolidation ratio of the Hyper-V servers so that you can minimize the number of required servers and capital costs. This results in Hyper-V servers running many virtual machines concurrently. If the server has a failure, all of the virtual machines would also fail, resulting in a large-scale outage. It is prudent to ensure that the server hardware and software provide the maximum uptime possible.

Although you can design your server systems for maximum uptime by using redundant components, failures still happen. Microsoft's Failover Clustering allows you to design a solution that provides planned and unplanned failover. Microsoft calls this a *Hyper-V server-level cluster* (also referred to as a *Hyper-V host cluster*). In a planned failure scenario, virtual machines running on one node of a server-level cluster can be migrated to another node. You might do this to perform maintenance on a cluster node or for workload-balancing purposes. In an unplanned failover scenario, if a cluster node fails suddenly, the virtual machine cluster resources are migrated to another node in the cluster, and the virtual machines are restarted from a powered-off state.

Windows Server 2008 Failover Clustering allows you to build 16 node Hyper-V clusters. Each node can actively run virtual machines. When designing a multimode cluster for a data center environment, you must make a decision about how the virtual machines will be placed in the event of a node failure. You can design for virtual machines from a failed cluster node to be spread across all remaining nodes in a load-balanced approach, or you can dedicate a cluster node and have all virtual machines fail to that node.

Hyper-V also supports virtual machine to virtual machine clusters for cluster-aware applications. Each node of a virtual machine cluster must reside on a different host cluster to be supported. When designing a host cluster to support a virtual machine cluster, the dedicated cluster node for failover is the best approach to ensure that a node failure does not result in multiple nodes of a virtual machine cluster residing on a single Hyper-V server cluster node.

Storage Considerations

In a data center scenario, servers are located in close proximity to each other. This allows the use of Storage Area Network (SAN) or Internet SCSI (iSCSI) technology to optimize the hard disk utilization and provide better performance. SANs allow disk input/output (I/O) to be spread across large numbers of disk spindles. By combining SAN with redundant arrays of independent disks (RAID) technologies, outages caused by loss of a disk drive can be minimized. The most common RAID levels used with SAN are RAID 5 and RAID 10. RAID 5 uses a minimum of three drive spindles and stripes the data across the spindles. RAID 5 protects against the loss of a single disk by storing parity bits that allow any missing data to be reconstructed. RAID 10 requires a minimum of four disks and combines striping and mirroring of disks to allow for the loss of a stripe set or mirror set without the loss of data. Other technologies used in a data center environment, such as host clustering, require shared storage to allow the virtual machines to be migrated quickly from one Hyper-V server to another without having to copy the virtual machines over the network.

iSCSI Configuration for Clusters

Justin Braun, Senior Microsoft Product Specialist
Compellent Technologies

SANs, like the Compellent Storage Center, provide the flexibility to choose the transport that best fits your data storage needs. Typically both iSCSI and Fiber Channel transports are supported and both are available from the same storage controllers simultaneously.

Although iSCSI Host-Bus Adapters (HBAs) can be used as the interface between your servers and the storage, Microsoft's iSCSI Software Initiator is a suitable alternative for your iSCSI connectivity and can use standard gigabit Ethernet ports that are commonly available on most servers today. iSCSI Software Initiator clusters require that you use Software Initiator version 2.0 or later.

On a Windows Server 2008 Failover Cluster, be sure to correctly configure persistent bindings and volume mounting in the Software Initiator to ensure that the iSCSI Software Initiator binds the volume(s) before the Cluster Service attempts to start. Failure to do so will result in the Cluster Service not being able to start, since the volumes are required cluster resources.

Today's SAN vendors provide tiered levels of storage and automated rules to migrate between the levels. There are usually three levels: Level 1 contains the fastest SCSI disks available (15,000 RPM drives), level 2 could contain SCSI disks that are not as fast (10,000 RPM drives), and level 3 could contain SATA disks that operate at a slower speed (7200 RPM). The storage in the first tier level is focused on providing the best I/O operation per second possible and should be used for clustering Hyper-V servers. In the second tier level, storage is focused on typical day-to-day operations for storing virtual machines, and in the third tier level, storage is focused on storing data that is not accessed frequently, such as virtual machines stored in the SCVMM library.

Backup Considerations

Backups of Hyper-V servers can be done from agents installed on the server, agents installed in the virtual machines, or agents installed in both locations. Windows Server 2008 provides the Volume Shadow Copy Service (VSS) to enable quick snapshots of volumes for backup purposes. VSS minimizes the downtime of the server during backup and provides interfaces for applications to create plug-ins that can properly inform the application to flush all changes from buffers and queue any additional writes while the snapshot is being taken. When the snapshot is finished, the plug-in is informed that it is safe to resume writing changes. Backups are typically stored on disk initially and then migrated to tape for offsite storage in a secure facility.

Backups in a data center scenario are usually performed from a central backup solution across the network. To ensure minimal impact to the production workloads, you should separate the backup network traffic from the production business traffic, using a separate network or a virtual local area network (VLAN). Providing this separation usually requires an additional network adapter in the Hyper-V server.

Treating a virtual machine like a physical machine results in backup agents deployed within the virtual machine. This allows for the application, files, and operating system state to be captured and restored like a physical server. It does not capture the configuration of the virtual machine, so if you need to restore the virtual machine on another host, you must create a new virtual machine, and then follow the procedures of the backup software. This means that you must maintain virtual machine configuration information separate from the virtual machine backup. One advantage of this approach is the ability to restore by file, directory, drive, application, or the entire machine.

In order to capture the virtual machine configuration and the backup of the virtual machine at the same time, you must:

- Use backup software that supports the Hyper-V VSS Writer.
- Install a backup agent on the Hyper-V server.
- Back up every volume that has the components of the virtual machine (configuration file, snapshots, and virtual hard disks).

One limitation of this backup approach is that the virtual machine must be restored before it is possible to mount the virtual hard disk and recover a file.

NOTE Windows Server Backup, which is included with Windows Server 2008, can back up the Hyper-V configuration, the virtual machine configuration, and the virtual machine files.

Management Design Considerations

Out of the box, management of a Hyper-V server is performed by the Hyper-V Manager Microsoft Management console (MMC), which is included with Hyper-V. The MMC is designed to manage a single Hyper-V server at a time. In a data center scenario, you will typically have many Hyper-V servers, so using the Hyper-V Manager MMC is not feasible. System Center Virtual Machine Manager (SCVMM) 2008 is Microsoft's solution to manage a pool of Hyper-V servers from a single console. The following sections discuss the design considerations for a SCVMM deployment in a data center scenario.

Deployment

SCVMM supports at least 400 servers and 8000 virtual machines per management console. For most organizations, a single management console can manage the entire data center virtualized infrastructure. If more than one data center exists, the management console should be placed in the data center that contains the most servers to minimize WAN traffic.

Although SCVMM ships with SQL Server 2005 Express Edition, data center scenario deployments should deploy SQL Server 2005 x64 Standard or Enterprise Edition. This eliminates the scalability limits of SQL Server 2005 Express Edition. All data and state is stored in the SCVMM 2008 database. To ensure easy recoverability of an SCVMM installation in a data center, SQL Server should not be installed on the same machine as the SCVMM Administration Console. If the Administration console hardware should fail, the recovery is a new installation of the SCVMM Administration Console pointing it at the existing SQL database during installation.

SCVMM will become the central administration and provisioning solution for your Hyper-V data center environment. To ensure the high availability of the data, the SCVMM database should be placed on a SQL server cluster and should be backed up nightly.

Library

Placement of library shares can affect the time to deploy a new virtual machine. By default, the installation of SCVMM creates a local library share. If this is the only library share created, all virtual machines will be deployed from this library over Background Intelligent Transfer Service (BITS) to the target server. Provisioning of virtual machines in a data center environment will result in increases to network traffic on the production network and will increase the time it takes to copy the template to the target server.

To speed up the provisioning of a virtual machine from the library and to reduce the effects on the production network, you have two options:

1. Utilize a dedicated network for all provisioning traffic.
2. Deploy library shares on the Hyper-V servers in the data center.

Deploying a dedicated network isolates the provisioning traffic but adds another network adapter requirement as well as network configuration complexity. Deploying additional library shares requires the replication of the library share data to each Hyper-V server and requires more disk space to be available to maintain a replica of the library files. If the library does not change much, placing the additional library shares on each Hyper-V server can drastically decrease the provisioning time. If the library does change on a regular basis, but few virtual machines are provisioned from the library, then the dedicated network would be the better option.

If multiple library shares are used within the data center, replication of the shares is required to ensure the most up-to-date version of the library shares is used. In the data center, a single library share should be used as the primary source. This should be the library share on the SCVMM server. Replication can be handled in multiple ways:

- Simple file copy
- Mirrored directories
- DFS-R
- Specialized replication software

Regardless of the option employed, it is very important that you make sure the replication is performed in a timely manner and the library shares are consistent.

Delegated Administration

SCVMM has two levels of administrators, the full administrator and the delegated administrator. The full administrator has complete unlimited control over all servers, virtual machines, and libraries in a SCVMM deployment. The delegated administrator can be limited to a set of servers contained in a host group or in specific library servers. Within those limited servers and library servers, delegated administrators have full control of all the virtual machines and objects in the library. A delegated administrator also has access to the SCVMM console, but access will be limited to the host groups, servers, and library servers they have right to administer.

For a data center environment, using delegated administrators will be driven by the IT organization structure and the administration requirements. If the IT organization uses a centralized approach to server management and all administrators support all servers, then a delegated model is not very useful. In distributed IT organizations, the delegated administration model can be very helpful to segregate management roles and management of specific servers, virtual machines, and libraries.

If a delegated administrator needs to manage a single Hyper-V server, you must create a host group and place the specific server in that host group. You also must create a new user role that is granted the delegated administration right and then add the delegated administrator to that user role.

Self-Service Web Portal

A self-service Web portal provides users with Web-based access to manage or create virtual machines across one or more Hyper-V servers. The portal can be policy controlled to limit a user's ability to manage or create virtual machines via the portal, but this does not restrict the user's ability to directly connect to the remote desktop service if enabled in the virtual machine. The self-service policy is applied to a host group and affects any Hyper-V server that is placed within that host group. A Hyper-V server cannot be a member of more than one host group at a time, so servers placed in a host group that has a self-service policy applied should be dedicated to Self-Service Portal use. In addition, the self-service Web portal should not be installed on the Hyper-V servers that you want to manage, but on the SCVMM server or a separate machine dedicated to providing the Self-Service Portal interface.

In a production data center environment, the Self-Service Portal is primarily used to provide users with the ability to remotely manage existing virtual machines using a Web interface without giving them delegated administration rights to the SCVMM Administration Console. This requires you to create one or more user roles that will limit the actions that members can perform. User roles can be created for server help desk members, application-focused administrators, location-based administrators, or any other type of administrator that needs access to administer only the virtual machine and not the host it is running on.

The user role is restricted from editing virtual machine configuration settings, but if allowed, the user can create new virtual machines and store virtual machines in a library and can stop, start, pause, shut down, checkpoint, and remotely manage virtual machines. These restrictions are placed on the user role to prevent members from increasing resource utilization of Hyper-V servers without prior approval.

Operational Considerations

In a data center environment, Hyper-V will be deployed on multiple servers in a single location with a higher density of virtual machines per server. This means that the loss of a single server can have major consequences. Although a host cluster will provide mitigation for a single server failure, ideally, if you knew about potential problems before they happened, you could move virtual machines proactively to reduce downtime.

System Center Operations Manager 2007 can help you proactively monitor your Hyper-V servers and the virtual machines running on the servers. Basic monitoring involves loading the management packs for Hyper-V, the Windows operating system management packs, and the management packs for the applications you are running. This configuration allows you to have monitoring, reporting, and alerting for the operating systems and applications running on the Hyper-V servers and the virtual machines. The management packs provide details on performance, input/output, memory utilization, processor utilization, and more. By using these features, the built-in rules will alert you to failures, oversubscription, and performance issues. You can even create custom rules to watch for specific situations.

By integrating System Center Operations Manager 2007 and SCVMM 2008, you can access an advanced feature called Performance Resource Optimization Tips (PROTips). You can configure PROTips manually, or you can configure it using predefined packs of rules and actions. The PROTips feature monitors the Hyper-V servers and virtual machines for specific resource and performance issues trends and will send an alert with a recommended action. You can configure PROTips to require the action to be implemented manually or automatically.

For example, PROTips provides automated monitoring of virtual machines to look for performance issues. If a performance issue is found, the PROTips recommendation might be to migrate a virtual machine to another server that has excess capacity. You can configure PROTips to provide an alert with the recommendation to migrate or to automatically migrate the virtual machine(s) experiencing performance issues to a new server that has the capacity to handle the required load.

In a data center with several large servers in close proximity, when you combine System Center Operations Manager 2007 to monitor the servers and virtual machines with SCVMM 2008 to manage them, you can utilize PROTips to monitor performance and resource utilization and to automate the migration of virtual machines between servers with minimal downtime.

Branch Office Scenario

A branch office can be defined as a remote location across a wide area network (WAN) connection that has limited local resources and typically no local administrative staff. Only critical services are typically provided locally; the general infrastructure and line-of-business services are provided from a data center location.

Designing a branch office virtualization solution involves minimizing the cost of the solution, making it easy to manage and monitor remotely, minimizing the WAN impacts, and providing a way to manage the system in the event of a WAN outage.

Host Design Considerations

Most branch office scenarios involve fewer than five virtual machines running on a single Hyper-V server. This configuration reduces the storage, processor, memory, and network connectivity requirements that a typical data center server would require. In addition, the Hyper-V server in a branch office scenario would not be migrating virtual machines between servers, so a fault-tolerant host cluster is not required, although some customers might implement this level of protection for key branch office locations.

Even with these limited requirements, focusing on availability and performance is still the recommended approach. This reduces the need for technical support onsite or in close proximity to the branch office location. Using an availability-focused approach can also reduce the downtime of the Hyper-V server or the virtual machines running in the child partitions.

A branch office Hyper-V server that will be supporting five virtual machines should have a minimum of a single quad-core processor with 8 gigabytes (GB) of RAM and internal hard disk storage. The Hyper-V server should still have a minimum of two network cards, one for Hyper-V management traffic and one for virtual machine traffic. The hard disks should be configured using fault-tolerant disk configuration with a redundant array of independent disks (RAID). A minimum of RAID 1 mirror for the operating system partition and RAID 1 for the virtual machine storage should be used to plan for disk failure. To improve performance, the virtual machine storage should use RAID 5 or RAID 10. Although RAID 0 (striping) can provide great performance, the loss of a hard disk results in the loss of the data on the stripe.

Management Considerations

Managing a Hyper-V server in a branch office location is really no different than managing a Hyper-V server in a data center location—the best method is to use SCVMM 2008 from a central location. WAN connectivity may be an issue in this decision, however, because the loss of the wide area network connection will prevent you from managing the Hyper-V server from the central SCVMM 2008 console. An alternate approach is to use the local Hyper-V Manager MMC console to manage the Hyper-V server and run virtual machines during times when the WAN connection is down.

Provisioning new virtual machines at a branch office location can be time-consuming if you attempt to do it over the WAN. To make this process more efficient, you can deploy an SCVMM library share on the Hyper-V server in the branch office location. This will allow the SCVMM 2008 console to provision virtual machines from the local library share and eliminate the need to copy the virtual machine files over the WAN link during provisioning. If the WAN link goes down, a new virtual machine can still be provisioned from the local library share using the Hyper-V Manager MMC console, although additional work may be required to copy and sysprep the machine. Only the virtual machine templates and supporting resource files should be deployed to the branch office library share to reduce space requirements and replication times.

Backup Considerations

In a branch office scenario with no local technical support or administrator, backup is typically managed from a central location. Using software such as System Center Data Protection Manager (SCDPM) 2007 Service Pack 1, you can back up the Hyper-V server and the virtual machines from a single agent installed in the parent partition. The storage of the backups is across the WAN in the central storage location by default. SCDPM uses delta replication to send only the bytes that have changed since the last backup, which reduces the amount of network traffic from the branch to the central backup server.

The alternative to backing up to a central server is to back up in the branch to a local storage location. The advantage of using this method is that the time to recover is much shorter; in addition, creating the backups and the restore process do not adversely affect WAN traffic. You can also back up and restore using the local method even if the WAN link is down.

You have two choices for local backup support: Windows Server Backup or SCDPM SP1. Windows Server Backup is included with Windows Server 2008 and simply needs to be configured to use the Hyper-V VSS writer; in this case, you would configure the backup to be made to local disk. SCDPM 2007 SP1 can be used by installing DPM and Hyper-V on the parent partition in the branch office. Using either backup method, additional disk space will be required in the branch office for backup storage. The disk space should be provided as separate volumes using spindles separate from the Hyper-V virtual machine storage, and they should be on a separate RAID controller for best performance.

Operational Considerations

Branch office locations do not have the same level of administrative and technical support as data center locations. Assuming that there are no local administrators or technical support personnel, it is important to design the branch office Hyper-V server to maximize remote maintenance and operations.

To provide remote maintenance when a hardware failure prevents the server from booting correctly, install a remote access or lights-out management board in the Hyper-V server. This will allow remote troubleshooting of hardware issues, but it requires a network connection, so plan for an alternative means of communication when the WAN is down; for example, set up the remote access board so it can use an alternate connection such as dial-up or DSL.

Hyper-V does not require the account with Hyper-V administrative authorization to be a local server administrator also. By default, only the local administrator has administrative access to Hyper-V to manage the configuration and local virtual machines. Additional accounts must be added to the security authorization store to allow non-administrators to be able to manage Hyper-V.

If the Hyper-V server experiences a failure of the management network adapter and the Hyper-V server cannot be accessed remotely, you need someone with the correct permissions available locally at the server console to save the state or power off the virtual machines so you can troubleshoot the problem. You can preconfigure an administrative account for use in emergency-only situations. The emergency administrative account would have the rights to launch the Hyper-V Manager MMC and manage the virtual machine state, provision new virtual machines, and remove virtual machines, but the account would not have the right to manage the operating system on the Hyper-V server or within any virtual machine. When the emergency is over, you can reset the password of the emergency account.

Test Lab Scenario

A test lab scenario involves investigating the functionality, performance, or viability of a proposed solution isolated from production environments for security or fault protection reasons. Every test should be considered a complete solution for the virtual machines needed to perform the test, not just for the machine on which the specific test is being performed. This allows you to consider any ramifications resulting from changes in the environment, and it also minimizes the impact of any actions taken during the test. Tests can range from those designed for short duration to those that can take months to complete.

When designing a test lab scenario, make sure that the Hyper-V hosts and the environment can be reconfigured and easily managed and that they can support fast provisioning and storing of test solutions; that you have remote access to the test machines; and that you can not only isolate the test environment from the production environment, but also from other running test solutions.

If your production environment uses Hyper-V, your test lab should also include duplicates of the production hardware for functional and performance testing verification, including host clustering configurations if they are used in production.

A test lab scenario will involve a minimum of one Hyper-V server and SCVMM 2008 to manage the environment, provide virtual machine provisioning, and allow for storage of virtual machines in the library.

Server Design Considerations

A test solution is defined as all of the virtual machines and resources that are required to perform and complete a single test case. Depending on the tests being performed, a test solution could share a set of common services (Active Directory, DHCP, DNS, firewalls, etc.), or each test solution could require these services provided as part of the set of provisioned virtual machines in the test solution. In other words, the number of virtual machines required per test will vary, and the test lab environment needs a pool of Hyper-V server systems to ensure that test solutions can be dynamically assembled as needed.

Test lab scenarios require the test to be provisioned and stored as a combined solution. Although it would be nice if every test could be provisioned on a single Hyper-V server, eventually, the size of a test solution will exceed the capacity of a single Hyper-V server. Depending on the type of test (functional versus performance), it might not be a good idea to provision the entire test on a single server because the limitations of the server performance could impact the test results.

When designing for a test lab scenario, it is best to design the Hyper-V server for an average-size test solution if it is practical based on cost. This allows the provisioning process and the network communications to be isolated to a single Hyper-V server, which also allows you to scale the number of Hyper-V servers in the test lab pool based on the number of test solutions that need to be running concurrently. Sizing the Hyper-V server based on the typical test solution involves defining the typical test solution, the number of virtual machines required, and the size of those virtual machines (memory, processor, disk space, network connections)—and then summing the resource requirements to determine the minimum host requirements.

Storage Considerations

Testing involves validating that the proposed solution functions and performs as designed. Functional testing requires a sufficient amount of storage space available to provision and operate the functional tests on the Hyper-V servers. Performance testing requires—at a minimum—the same storage space as functional testing, additional storage for capacity tests, and performance on par with the production environment. If the production environment uses SAN for storage, then the test lab environment should also have SAN storage. SAN storage also allows for the rapid addition of additional storage to Hyper-V servers based on the testing requirements.

Testing requires an iterative process in which you locate problems in the design, identify bugs in off-the-shelf products or internally developed software, and look for permissions or security problems. In any of these situations, you may want to save the current state of the test solution so that it can be recovered later, and you should have enough storage available to save the solution.

Two approaches are available for maintaining stored test solutions:

1. Store the saved virtual machines on the Hyper-V servers.

2. Store the saved virtual machines in the SCVMM library.

Either approach will require the appropriate amount of storage. For short-term storage, use the Hyper-V server. For long-term storage, you should use the SCVMM library. Since storage of the virtual machines in the SCVMM library potentially requires them to be copied over the network, it is best to use the library only when there you have storage space issues on the Hyper-V servers or if the virtual machines will be offline for a long period of time.

Network Considerations

If you can provision a test solution to a single Hyper-V server, then all communications can occur on the server using an internal or private virtual network. The virtual network can be provisioned at the same time you provision the test solution to the Hyper-V server, or you can provision virtual networks ahead of time and assign the test solution virtual machines. Any requirements for routing would require you to build a virtual machine with Routing and Remote Access Services (RRAS) to provide the routing between different virtual networks.

As discussed previously, test lab scenarios will eventually require you to provision a test solution across multiple Hyper-V servers in the test lab pool. This presents network communications issues, since the traffic should be isolated to a single test solution. Hyper-V provides a method to isolate traffic, but it requires manual configuration. Using port-based virtual local area networks (VLANs) or 802.1q (VLAN tagging), you can quickly configure isolated test segments between Hyper-V servers to each test solution.

Port-based VLANs require that you dedicate an entire network adapter to a single VLAN. This approach will limit the number of concurrent test solutions running on a Hyper-V server to the number of network adapters available for virtual networks. Using VLAN tagging, a single network adapter can support multiple VLANs. Each virtual machine can be configured to utilize a unique VLAN identification tag, isolating the traffic quickly and easily.

Establishing a set of VLAN ID tags for testing purposes ahead of time in the test lab and tracking which test solution they are assigned will allow you to quickly reconfigure virtual machines across servers to a specific VLAN ID isolating traffic. Reconfiguring the virtual machines in a test solution would require manually selecting the VLAN ID per virtual machine or writing a script that takes a list of virtual machines by server and then configuring that to the correct VLAN ID.

Management Considerations

Test lab environments are typically not managed by the same team that manages the production environment. Therefore we do not recommend that you manage the test lab environment with the same installation of SCVMM 2008 that you use to manage the production Hyper-V environment. In addition, the isolation of the test laboratory should prevent the production SCVMM 2008 from seeing the test lab Hyper-V servers.

The separate SCVMM 2008 installation to manage the test lab environment should include a central library share and a Self-Service Portal installation. The central library share should be the source for all prebuilt virtual machines and templates that will be provisioned in the test lab. Having prebuilt automated installs of OS and applications will reduce the time and effort required to get a test solution provisioned. Replicating the library share to each server in the test lab pool will allow you to provision virtual machines from the local Hyper-V server and will eliminate provisioning bottlenecks on the network.

Since multiple tests can be running on the pool of servers, it would not be practical to attempt to manage a test from the Hyper-V Manager because you get only a single server view at a time. Using the SCVMM Administrative Console creates the opposite problem—you would get a view of all the virtual machines at once, and you do not want to give the testers access to the Administrative console for security reasons. Using the SCVMM Self-Service Portal console is a perfect match. It provides a single view of all the virtual machines owned or assigned to a single user in a single view, regardless of which Hyper-V server the virtual machine is running on.

Utilizing the Self-Service Portal for a test lab scenario requires you to place the pool of Hyper-V servers into a host group for each installation of the Self-Service Portal. After you have the servers as members of the host group, you can create self-service user roles. User roles allow you to specify the scope of who is within the user role by user or group, to specify what actions a user role member can perform (Start, Stop, Pause, Resume, Checkpoint, Remove, Remote Connection, Shutdown, and Local Administrator Password configuration), to determine if the user role member can create virtual machines and the templates or library shares they can use, and to define the quota points they have available for deploying virtual machines.

For a test lab scenario, there will be different classes of users that will interact with the test environment:

- **Test creator**   Provisions the test solution
- **Tester**   Interacts with the virtual machines and performs the test actions
- **Developer**   Interacts with the virtual machines and troubleshoots software bugs
- **Support Engineer**   Provides expertise on specific product-related issues that arise in the test environment

Each class of user role is limited to the actions the specific role requires. For example, the test creator will need the right to create virtual machines, whereas the tester, developer, and support engineer role would not need this right.

After you have the Self-Service Portal and the user roles configured, the next issue you need to address is access to the Self-Service Portal. In today's environment of global companies, telecommuting, and use of contract labor, you cannot assume that everyone who will need to interact with the test lab will be at the physical location where the test lab resides, so you must provide for remote access to the test lab. You can assume that anyone who needs to connect to the Self-Service Portal will have access to the corporate network. These users may be sitting in an office, they may be connected through a virtual private network, or they may connect using a terminal services gateway. In order to provide the required access, you could simply expose the Self-Service Portal Web site on the edge of the lab environment via firewall and allow users remote access through a browser interface. In this case, you should secure the Self-Service Portal by using an SSL certificate to encrypt all communications.

Operational Considerations

Even though a test lab is not considered a production environment, operational issues in a test lab can adversely affect bringing a new application to production or quickly trouble-shooting an existing production system or application. Therefore, the test lab should be run like the production environment.

Deploy System Center Operations Manager 2007 to monitor the health of the Hyper-V servers. This will be a separate installation in the test lab specifically to manage the lab environment. Deploy System Center Operations Manager agents in the virtual machines when performing production-ready functional and performance testing to ensure there are no issues. Watch for performance issues during tests to determine if the configuration of the Hyper-V servers or other tests running in parallel on the same server or utilizing the same network is adversely affecting the test results.

Deploy a backup solution such as System Center Data Protection Manager to determine how long it will take to back up the solution. Perform restore testing to find out how long it will take to restore the solution from backup or after a disaster and to determine any challenges you may face in doing so. Backing up the SCVMM servers and the Hyper-V servers can also reduce the time it will take to reconstruct a test solution.

Use SCVMM checkpoints to minimize rework during tests. When you use checkpoints, you need to consider the virtual machine you are checkpointing as well as the potential rollback implications. If you checkpoint a server, perform a test, and then decide to revert to the previous point, you might create problems with your test environment. For example, the secure channel password for the server may have changed after you took the checkpoint. When you revert to the previous point, that password will not be consistent, and the server will have problems communicating with the Active Directory domain. Another example involves domain controllers—using checkpoints with domain controllers can result in update sequence number (USN) rollback and can cause serious issues with the stability of the Active Directory forest. When you use checkpoints, the best approach is to take a checkpoint of all the machines in the test solution at the same time. This allows you to revert the entire solution back to the same consistent point in time.

Alternative Use Considerations

Test labs perform a vital service by ensuring that solutions are properly tested before they are put into production or by troubleshooting the solutions after they are in production. If properly designed, test labs can also provide an important service during emergencies by acting as your disaster recovery site. Whether you use physical or virtual machines for your production environment, a test lab is a source of hardware that is configured the same or better than your production hardware. Designing the test lab to be repurposed quickly as a disaster recovery site during emergencies can save the expense of hardware for a dedicated disaster recovery site, optimize the use of the existing hardware, and allow the processes developed in the test lab for quickly provisioning machines to be implemented to good effect. By aligning your backup strategy with using virtual machines as the disaster recovery plan, you can quickly and easily use your test lab as your disaster recovery site.

When designing the test lab for use as a disaster recovery site, it is important to make sure the lab has the capacity required to convert it quickly to its alternative use. Different approaches exist to make the conversion effectively. One option is to have all the production virtual machines' backups replicated to a recovery server in the test lab. Then, during a recovery, all of the production machines would be restored into virtual machines running in the test lab. However, this will probably cause some problems with drivers and hardware abstraction layer (HAL) issues.

Another option is to have the backup process actually produce a virtual machine with the driver and HAL issues resolved. Then the recovery becomes simply a provisioning process of virtual machines to the pool of test lab Hyper-V servers. This option may require the deletion of existing test virtual machines to provide enough disk space, however.

A third option is to have the backup process produce a virtual machine and then predeploy those virtual machines to assigned Hyper-V servers in the test lab environment. The recovery process then requires you only to power off all of the virtual machines running test solutions and then power on the production virtual machines. In addition, you have to provision additional dedicated disk space on all Hyper-V lab servers.

Software Development Scenario

A software development scenario involves providing a virtual environment in which the software development workstation and the supporting systems are virtualized. Supporting systems, for example, could be Web servers, database servers, or directory services. Development environments can be isolated, or they can be on the production network if required for the backend systems access.

Designing for a software development scenario involves ensuring performance for code compilation, providing remote access to the development environment, providing for code repository, allowing teams of developers to collaborate, and isolating environments between project teams.

Host Design Considerations

Software development scenarios include Hyper-V servers with dedicated virtual machines for development workstations, dedicated code repositories for each project, and the supporting systems that are required. Some supporting systems such as databases are dedicated to a project team, and some supporting services such as Active Directory can be shared across projects. Software development environments do not typically involve on-going provisioning. When the development environment is set up for the project, it will usually exist for the entire project cycle.

When you are designing Hyper-V servers for virtualized software development workstations, performance is an important consideration. Compiling software is a process that makes intensive use of the processor and requires optimum disk performance. Virtual machines for software development should have a minimum of two virtual processors and 4 to 8 GB of RAM, and the physical disk storage system should utilize RAID 10 storage for performance and failure protection. This configuration will limit the number of development workstations that you can combine on a single Hyper-V server. A typical quad-processor, quad-core server could have a maximum of seven software development workstations running on it if the appropriate number of virtual processors are reserved. Supporting services and code repositories will require a minimum number of virtual machines for each project and can be placed on dedicated Hyper-V servers or distributed with the developer workstations.

Storage Considerations

Software development workstations experience high levels of disk I/O during compilation. Transitioning from dedicated physical workstations to virtualized development workstations combined on a single Hyper-V server can result in increased compilation times if the storage infrastructure is not properly designed. You can provide for optimum performance by utilizing SAN storage with a large number of spindles in a RAID 10 array.

Combining development teams from the same project or those that compile at the same time of the day will result in concentrated disk I/O. Combining development workstations from different projects or different time zones can help distribute the disk I/O more evenly throughout the day.

Network Considerations

Although it may be possible to combine all the workstations for a single software development project on a Hyper-V server, it is more likely that software development workstations from a single project will be distributed across Hyper-V servers. If software development projects require network traffic to be isolated, you will need to design the networking to allow for isolated segments between Hyper-V servers. As in the test lab scenario, VLANs can be used to accomplish this task.

Management Considerations

Developers will be primarily interacting with their virtualized software development workstation. This can be accomplished in two ways: the user can use a standard Remote Desktop client to directly connect to the machine, or they can use the Self-Service Portal feature of SCVMM. If the developer will be interacting with multiple software development workstation virtual machines, or with their personal workstation and virtual machines running support services, then it is better to utilize the SCVMM Self-Service Portal to provide a single console view of all of the virtual machines.

Summary

This chapter outlines four different server virtualization scenarios that are typically deployed in customer environments. Data center virtualization scenario design considerations include reducing the number of physical servers required to establish an operational infrastructure while sizing Hyper-V servers correctly, providing fault-tolerant solutions, creating reliable backup and restore procedures, and centralizing management and provisioning operations. Branch office scenario design considerations include setting up a single Hyper-V server to provide key services to a single location while designing for normal management, backup, and operations for WAN-connected and WAN outage situations. Test lab scenario design considerations include building an isolated test and validation environment while providing remote users access to the servers, ensuring that running tests affect each other minimally, and designing for alternate uses like disaster recovery. Software development scenario design considerations include ensuring that development workstations have the required compilation power and performance, as well as secure remote access, and that there are code repositories to provide secure storage of the source code.

Additional Resources

The following resources contain additional information related to this chapter.

- Infrastructure Planning and Design Guides provide direction on how to design different physical and virtual environments, available at *http://technet.microsoft.com/en-us/library/cc196387.aspx*

- Windows Server 2008 Security Guide providing recommendations on how to secure Windows Server 2008, including Hyper-V, available at *http://technet.microsoft.com/en-us/library/cc514539.aspx*

- Windows Server 2008 Failover Cluster, a TechNet article that provides an overview of failover clustering in Windows Server 2008, available at *http://technet.microsoft.com/en-us/magazine/2008.07.failover.aspx?pr=blog*

- Configuring SCVMM 2008 Self-Service Portal, online documentation that explains the configuration options for the Self-Service Portal, available at *http://technet.microsoft.com/en-us/library/cc956040.aspx*

- SCVMM TechNet TechCenter, centralized online technical documentation and support information on the SCVMM product family, available at *http://technet.microsoft.com/en-us/scvmm/default.aspx*

Virtual Desktop Infrastructure

The most common reasons that IT organizations adopt virtualization technologies such as Microsoft Windows Server 2008 Hyper-V are to address issues such as server sprawl, low server utilization, power and cooling problems, data center size, and IT budget reductions. Although still in the early stages of maturity, Virtual Desktop Infrastructure (VDI) is an area in which virtualization solutions are being tested and deployed to simplify end-user desktop provisioning and management, as well as to assist in the further reduction of IT budgets and operating costs.

Fundamentally, a VDI solution allows an organization to host virtual desktops on server farms within a data center and provide access to a virtual desktop from a variety of thin or rich clients, ranging from stateless terminal devices to full-fledged desktop or laptop computers. With VDI, the desktop operating system and applications are stored and executed on data center servers, and the user interface is presented on client devices by using a remote desktop protocol. Similar to a server virtualization infrastructure, a VDI solution is composed of a combination of hardware, virtualization software, and management tools that provide an end-to-end solution to provision, configure, and manage virtualized desktops.

The main objective of this chapter is to present you with an introduction to VDI concepts and areas in which VDI solutions are viable. Specifically, you will learn about the key attributes of a VDI solution, discover the two main types of virtualized desktops (static and dynamic), and find out about the major components that make up a VDI solution. Although VDI technology is not sufficiently mature to replace all user desktop environments, specific scenarios are prime candidates for a VDI implementation. After discussing these scenarios, the chapter concludes with an overview of current Microsoft VDI solutions.

Understanding Important VDI Attributes

IT departments have long been using different strategies to improve desktop management and minimize the complexity to provision, secure, update, back up, and recover end-user desktops, as well as to simplify the delivery, installation, and maintenance of applications required by various user communities. For example, Citrix and Microsoft Terminal Server solutions have been widely used to support centralized desktop services based around a single operating system instance. Although a terminal server–based architecture is an effective way to consolidate end-user desktops, it can introduce application compatibility issues as well as limitations to the users' ability to personalize or control their desktops. These problems are inherent both in the fact that with terminal services a single instance operating system is shared among multiple users, and that applications are running on a Windows server operating system rather than on a Windows client operating system. For these reasons and others, VDI technologies are evolving that leverage the benefits of virtualization technology to increase desktop deployment flexibility and centralize management of the end-user environment while providing the data security and manageability benefits of server-based desktop consolidation solutions.

Hardware-Independent Virtual Desktops

Many enterprises define standard server hardware configurations that allow them to minimize the number and complexity of server image builds and overall management processes in their environment. Although the same approach is often applied to user desktop hardware, it isn't uncommon for IT staff to maintain numerous desktop images that accommodate the diversity of deployed user systems that spans full desktops, laptops, and even more specialized devices such as tablet notebooks and smaller personal computing devices. In addition, because many enterprises implement a staggered hardware refresh cycle, IT staff must support legacy images to reload older systems and build additional images to support new hardware.

VDI eliminates much of this complexity by abstracting the underlying hardware from the workload (i.e., guest operating system and application stack) running in a virtual machine. Because a virtual machine presents a standard environment to the workload that is independent of the server hardware on which it is running and the client device used to access it, the number of images can be potentially reduced to a single base build containing a common set of services that can be used to quickly provision new virtual desktops.

Dedicated, Isolated, and Secure Virtual Desktops

The ability to encapsulate individual workloads in separate virtual machines (also referred to as partitions) allows virtual desktops to be dedicated to individual users. Because virtual machines can execute concurrently, each in their own isolated and secured partition, application errors and guest operating system crashes that occur within a specific virtual machine do not affect virtual desktops executing in other virtual machines. In addition, dedicated virtual desktops can be rebooted, powered on, and powered off without affecting any other users, delivering an experience that is equivalent to that of a physical desktop.

Dynamic Application Delivery and Configuration

Although not exclusive to VDI, separation of the application layer from the operating system further enables the single base image model for virtual desktops. Application virtualization with application streaming or server-hosted applications allows IT staff to decouple applications from the base image so that instead they can personalize virtual desktops using dynamic, on-demand delivery of applications based on user role and group membership.

There are two ways that applications can be separated from and dynamically delivered to a virtual desktop. In the first case, an application environment is installed on the virtual desktop to isolate applications running on the guest operating system. More specifically, the virtual environment is layered between the operating system and application stack. Virtualized applications are not installed on the guest operating system; instead, the code bits can be dynamically streamed and cached in the virtual environment as new portions of the application are needed. The virtual environment isolates each virtualized application from other applications, as well as the guest operating system, such that multiple versions of an application can run side by side without the prospect of conflict that could occur from installation of and modification to guest operating system resources. In the second case, the separation of the application layer is accomplished by hosting the applications on a terminal server and making them available to the virtual desktop. In this approach, applications are not streamed to or installed on the image of the virtual desktop, but rather are remoted from a terminal server to the virtual desktop, just as with a terminal server deployment to a traditional (physical) desktop.

Flexible Resource Allocation

When a physical desktop is no longer able to deliver the performance required to run its complement of applications because of resource limitations, two choices are available: upgrade one or more hardware components (e.g., memory, graphics, and/or processor) or replace the desktop with a more powerful system. In both cases, the end user will experience a disruption in daily activities that can range from several hours for a hardware upgrade to possibly weeks or months of operation with degraded performance until a new desktop is procured and deployed.

In a VDI implementation, allocation (or de-allocation) of resources to virtual desktops can be performed from the supply pool available on the physical server. Whereas the majority of physical desktops do not support the addition of hardware without powering off the system, "hot-add" technology is prevalent among server hardware, allowing expansion of server resources as capacity requirements grow. If a server or virtualization service requires a restart prior to recognizing new hardware, or the server does not have available capacity to allocate additional resources, virtual desktops can be rapidly migrated to other servers with available capacity.

Additionally, virtual desktop resource allocation can be individually modified as workload performance requirements change. This is true for basic resources such as memory and processors, as well as other virtualized resources such as network adapters, disk controllers, and storage devices. In some cases, dynamic resource allocation, which does not require the virtual machine to be paused or powered off, may be an option. For other resources, it may be required to power off the machine before new resources are allocated. However, the disruption to the end user is measured in minutes, rather than in hours or days.

Rapid Desktop Provisioning and Decommissioning

Provisioning or decommissioning a physical end-user desktop in a traditional environment is usually a manual process that may take days to complete. In a VDI environment, the process can take place in a matter of minutes. Essentially, provisioning a new virtual desktop involves the creation of a new virtual machine from a base image and deployment of the virtual machine to an existing server. At that point, the user is able to connect to the virtual desktop from a client device using a remote desktop protocol. The process to decommission a virtual desktop can be as simple as "unregistering" the virtual machine from the virtualization server and storing it in a library for archival purposes.

The reason that provisioning in a VDI environment can be accomplished so quickly is that a virtual machine is composed of just a few files that contain the virtualization configuration settings, guest operating system, applications, and data. The creation of a new virtual machine can be as basic as assigning storage for the new virtual machine, duplicating the file containing the end-user base image, configuring the virtual machine settings, deploying it to a virtualization server, and providing the user permissions to connect and access the virtual machine. There are many different VDI solutions available today that allow you to automate this process by pre-creating templates that define virtual machine and workload settings, optimizing the new virtual machine deployment based on up-to-date server performance and capacity data, or even by providing a policy-driven, self-service interface that allows users to instantiate their own virtual machines.

Rapid Desktop Migration

VDI solutions provide rapid desktop migration to support planned and unplanned hardware maintenance, and as a means to move virtual desktops to another server based on desktop performance requirements. In a physical desktop environment, even one where many personalization settings are network-based, migrating the desktop image to new hardware may require significant manual intervention and end-user downtime. In a VDI environment with centralized virtualization server farms and shared storage, as well as high-availability and load-balancing solutions, migrating a virtual desktop is a process that can be completely automated to minimize user downtime.

For planned hardware maintenance or performance upgrade migrations, VDI provides the option to save the virtual machine state (including memory and register states) into files, suspend execution, migrate the virtual machine to another server in the server farm, and resume execution. If the server farm is connected to shared storage such as a Storage Area Network (SAN), Network Attached Storage (NAS), or other similar infrastructure, the virtual desktop migration can be completed such that a user could reconnect to her virtual desktop within seconds and resume working where she left off. In the case of an unplanned hardware failure, VDI supports high-availability (HA) solutions that allow migration of virtual desktops to other server farm machines if the original server becomes unresponsive. In this case, the virtual machine state is not saved, but the virtual desktop can be reassigned to a new server that will allow the user to reconnect within minutes of the failure event.

Centralized and Secure Data Storage

One of the more problematic aspects of a physical desktop environment is the distribution of business data on potentially thousands of local hard drives. Of course, in most enterprises, file servers and policies are deployed to centralize, store, and secure data, but these measures do not guarantee that critical information won't be stored on a local hard drive or removable media. If there are also no reliable backups of the local storage devices, then there is the added risk of data corruption, loss of data, or data theft that can result in significant business impacts.

In a VDI environment, especially one that uses thin client devices, users can access their virtual desktops locally while data remains stored and secured in the data center (e.g., SAN or NAS). Without local storage devices, the risk of critical data corruption, loss, or theft at this level is eliminated.

Centralized Backups

Along with the problem of distributed data on traditional physical desktops comes the issue of local data backup. Because physical desktops may be located across many local area networks (LANs) and even wide area networks (WANs), a single, simple backup solution cannot be implemented. In fact, local storage is often not backed up at all because pushing thousands of users' data across LANs or WANs would certainly overwhelm most networks. In addition, some users may connect only occasionally to the corporate network, and entrusting the remote user with backup of their own data leads to haphazard results.

In a VDI environment in which the virtualization server farms and shared storage are centralized in a data center, the backup process can also be localized to the data center network. With server backup technology that supports snapshots, a method that captures only the changes in data rather than backing up all the data repeatedly, not only can the impact of performing backups on server performance be reduced, but the speed of backups can be improved, and the amount of data that has to be stored can be minimized.

Extensive Client Device Support

Whereas a traditional desktop environment usually requires the deployment of systems with a large number of components and complexity, a VDI environment provides an extensive choice of devices to connect an end user to a virtual desktop. For example, a VDI environment supports the deployment of thin client devices without a local client OS to users who perform a narrow set of tasks and do not need access to any local resources. It also supports connection from rich client devices (e.g., laptops) for mobile workers who require the ability to also work offline.

Thin clients that provide access to a virtual desktop with a minimal complement of components offer the biggest opportunity for high return on investment (ROI). Here are some of the benefits of thin client deployments that you can consider:

- Fractional power consumption, cooling, and space requirements
- Reduction in mean time between failures (MTBF) because of fewer components
- Reduction in touch-labor to perform replacements or swap out components
- Longer refresh cycle because of longer device life cycle
- Minimal configuration requirements

Of course, thin client deployments are strongly dependent on reliable, fault-tolerant networks and rigorous management of the VDI solution to ensure that users have high-quality, consistent access to their virtual desktops.

Identifying Major VDI Components

Just as for any technical implementation, the components used in a VDI solution are dependent on the functional requirements that it is intended to fulfill. A core set of components is common to every VDI solution; however, elements such as environment size, virtual desktop access requirements, application deployment strategy, management policies, budget restrictions, and a host of other considerations determine the complement of components used to implement an effective VDI solution. Figure 18-1 illustrates a simplified environment that includes the core VDI components and shows the decoupling of the base operating system, user settings, and applications that is possible with a dynamic VDI solution.

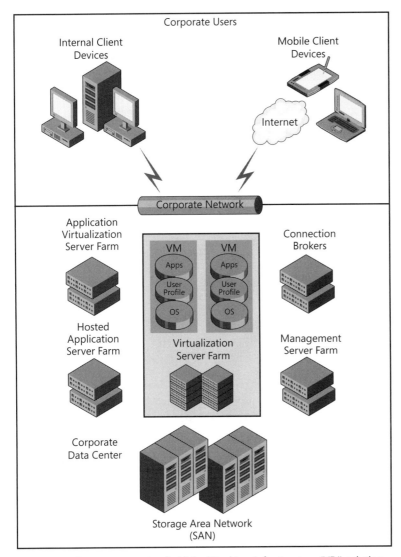

Corporate Users

Internal Client
Devices

Mobile Client
Devices

Internet

Corporate Network

Application
Virtualization
Server Farm

Connection
Brokers

VM
Apps
User
Profile
OS

VM
Apps
User
Profile
OS

Hosted
Application
Server Farm

Virtualization
Server Farm

Management
Server Farm

Corporate
Data Center

Storage Area Network
(SAN)

FIGURE 18-1 Core components of a Virtual Desktop Infrastructure (VDI) solution

Defining Static and Dynamic Virtual Desktops

One of the catalysts in defining the components of a VDI solution is the type of virtual
desktop that you intend to deploy. Therefore, it is important to understand the two principal
virtual desktop models: static and dynamic.

Static Virtual Desktop

A static virtual desktop is essentially a direct replacement of a physical desktop that runs in a persistent virtual machine and is dedicated to a particular user. The user can connect directly to the virtual desktop by using a remote desktop connection client. A static virtual desktop can consist of the guest operating system and installed applications, or it can make use of application virtualization and streaming for isolation and dynamic delivery of applications.

Dynamic Virtual Desktop

A *dynamic* virtual desktop is provisioned and assembled from a single master image and uses application virtualization and streaming as well as user profiles to deliver a personalized but nonpersistent virtual desktop to a user. User data storage can be persistent and stored on a virtual hard disk that is connected when the virtual desktop is initialized and disconnected when the virtual desktop is deactivated. User connections to dynamic virtual desktops are managed by a connection broker or desktop broker.

Core Virtualization Components

The core virtualization components are fundamental building blocks of any VDI solution. Included in this category are physical servers, virtualization software, and storage devices.

Physical Servers

One or more physical servers are required to host the virtualization software and virtual desktop execution, as well as optional application virtualization and VDI management services. Whereas a single server may be sufficient to support a base test environment, one or more server farms are required to provide high availability or fault tolerance, load distribution, and growth capacity for enterprise deployments.

Virtualization Software

Virtualization software, such as Virtual Server 2005 R2 and Hyper-V, supports the creation, isolation, and execution of concurrent virtual machines, allows the assignment and control of system resources, and enables implementation of advanced functionality such as high availability and fault tolerance. The choice of virtualization software can depend on the physical server architecture. For example, Virtual Server 2005 R2 is available to run on either 32-bit or 64-bit AMD-V or Intel VT processor platforms, whereas Hyper-V requires a 64-bit AMD-V or Intel VT processor platform.

Storage Devices

Storage devices provide the repository for virtual machine files that encapsulate virtual desktop configuration, a guest operating system, applications, data, and state information. Storage devices can range from Direct Attached Storage (DAS) for a single server implementation, to NAS for a small to medium server farm, and fiber-channel or iSCSI-connected SANs to support enterprise-class server farms.

Client Components

The core virtualization components provide the basic server infrastructure to host virtual desktops. The flip side of the equation is that an end user needs a device that allows him to remotely connect to his virtual desktop. Although the number and kinds of devices that can be used as virtual desktop clients continue to grow, they can generally be divided into two classes: rich client devices and thin client devices.

Rich Client Device

A *rich client* is generally a multipurpose desktop or laptop computer that can be used as a virtual desktop connection device, but that can also support working offline using local resources. A portable rich client device provides a best fit for mobile or specialized users, and its use in a VDI environment must be minimized to achieve the greatest management gains. A rich client device requires a local operating system and, at minimum, must be configured with a remote desktop client application to provide the user interface to the virtual desktop.

Thin Client Device

A *thin client* is a single-purpose device that contains the components necessary to connect to a virtual desktop and provide a rich user interface. A thin client device provides a best fit for any user who requires access to resources only through the virtual desktop, and without specialized graphical options. Because thin clients lack complex components, are easy to replace, have a small energy and physical footprint, and do not require a complete operating system, these devices are pivotal in a VDI implementation that seeks to simplify management and reduce long-term operation costs.

Application Virtualization Components

If each virtual desktop represents a static workload (guest operating system and installed applications), the combination of core virtualization and client components is sufficient to form a base VDI implementation that provides a one-to-one pairing between a user and a virtual desktop. However, this type of VDI solution has limited applicability and benefits, even as a preliminary proof of concept. Replacing thousands of physical desktops with virtual desktops without implementing solutions to reduce the operating system image instances, minimize application update and delivery processes, and address other costly management tasks does not maximize the long-term return on investment (ROI) potential of a VDI solution.

In fact, the implementation of a scalable and flexible VDI solution that can support hundreds or thousands of users with different application profiles requires the inclusion of additional components such as application virtualization and streaming, or server-based hosted applications in order to separate the delivery of applications from the base virtual desktop image. Without dynamic application delivery, you will not be able to minimize the number of managed virtual desktop images. If dynamic application virtualization delivery technologies are included within a VDI environment, however, you may be within reach of the goal of a single-base virtual desktop with centralized management and delivery of the guest operating system and applications based on dynamic user requirements.

Application Virtualization

Application virtualization technology consists of client and server components. The server components allow you to store and maintain application packages in a central repository and manage application delivery through policies that define how the applications are delivered to users. When an application requires updates, these can be applied a single time to the application package hosted on the central server and then distributed to users.

Client components are integrated into the virtual desktop to create an isolation environment that prevents the application from making permanent changes to local desktop resources such as system files and the registry. Applications can still read information from the local system registry and files, but writable versions of these resources are maintained inside the isolation environment. One of the main benefits of this approach is that multiple versions of an application can be executed in parallel without impeding each other.

Application Streaming

Application streaming helps to minimize the impact of latency introduced in an environment using application virtualization. Rather than sending all of the application code to the virtual desktop when it is first requested, only the portions of the code needed to start the application are streamed and cached in the isolation environment. As new portions of the application are needed, additional code is then streamed to the virtual desktop.

Application Hosting

Applications hosted on a terminal server can be dynamically provisioned to a virtual desktop, avoiding the installation and execution of an application on the virtual desktop. As with traditional terminal server environments where users access hosted applications from a physical desktop, virtual desktop users have access to hosted applications that are either integrated seamlessly into their virtual desktop or are accessible through a browser session. Similar to application virtualization, hosted applications are easily deployed, maintained, and decommissioned centrally from a data center location. In addition, since applications execute on a separate terminal server, more hardware resources are available to the virtualization server to accommodate additional virtual desktops.

Management Components

When transitioning from a physical desktop to a virtual desktop environment, it is essential that your management components allow you to effectively handle your virtualization environment as well as your physical infrastructure. A VDI solution (similar to a server virtualization solution) introduces areas that require additional or updated management tools. In particular, consider the following management components as vital elements of a VDI solution.

Integrated Management Console

In a VDI environment, you must concurrently monitor physical and virtual machines to track the overall health of the infrastructure, proactively plan for emerging resource or performance issues, and react to unplanned service interruptions. An integrated management console with role delegation is pivotal to monitoring, mapping, and displaying the interdependencies of virtual machines to the physical servers and storage devices, as well as to quickly communicate the status of the VDI environment at any point in time. Without an integrated management console, you would quickly become overwhelmed trying to make the connection manually between physical server and virtual machine status reported in separate management consoles. In addition, using an integrated management console with role delegation ensures that you can define policies and administrative assignments to a distributed administrative team, as is common in most IT organizations.

Connection Broker

A connection broker is the component in a VDI solution that provides the ability to dynamically connect a user to a virtual desktop. In a small-scale VDI deployment (e.g., fewer than 100 users), it is possible to dedicate a virtual desktop to a user as a replacement for a physical desktop. In such a scenario, virtualization servers are sized to support a set number of virtual desktops, and there is no requirement to dynamically shift resources between virtual desktops to maximize server utilization rates. However, for most VDI deployments that support hundreds or thousands of users without concurrent access or dedicated desktop requirements, a connection broker effectively directs the dynamic provisioning of virtual desktops, the assignment of virtual desktops to users, and the management of virtual desktop states (e.g., running, saved state, shut down) to maximize VDI resource utilization and minimize the number of core virtualization components deployed to support the environment.

Virtual Desktop Migration

In order to automate the migration of virtual machines between virtualization servers in a server farm, a VDI solution must include a management component that can analyze virtualization server load and performance data and make intelligent virtual desktop placement decisions that balance the goals of maximizing resource utilization and maintaining desktop resource requirements. Without an intelligent virtual desktop migration component, management of a dynamic virtual desktop environment is not feasible.

Virtual Desktop Repository

One of the challenges of large-scale VDI implementation is managing a sizable number of virtual desktop resources centralized in the data center. Whereas an integrated management console is the focal point to monitor active VDI resources, there is also a need for a repository to store and track inactive virtual desktop components such as virtual machine templates, configuration settings, virtual hard drives, and other virtual desktop building blocks. A virtual desktop repository should provide the ability to group, catalog, and quickly identify related resources, and should serve as the source from which new virtual desktops are provisioned.

Virtual Desktop Backup

Deploying virtual desktops on centralized servers gives you the ability to use a single backup solution to guard against data corruption and loss on virtualization servers as well as the virtual machines. For static virtual desktops that may have specialized applications installed, a snapshot-based backup component can be integrated into a VDI implementation to back up entire virtual machines, not just files that exist within virtual machines. If guest and server operating systems support it, a snapshot approach may be used to back up a virtualization server and all running virtual machines concurrently. If the virtual desktop guest operating system does not support a snapshot-based method, you have the option to use a traditional backup method, such as one that requires installation of an agent on the virtual desktop. For dynamic virtual desktops, one advantage when planning a backup method is that you need to back up only persistent user data and not the entire virtual machine.

Defining Common VDI Scenarios

Although VDI solutions do not represent a wholesale replacement strategy for all user desktop environments, specific scenarios do exist that can exploit VDI benefits. These scenarios share some common parameters, such as access to consistent workloads regardless of physical (e.g., office, hotel, and home) or geographical location, no need for local access to resources and data, and no need for dedicated or specialized graphical processing. As VDI and integrated management tools mature, additional physical desktop environments will become targets for VDI implementations and will enable organizations to create dynamic user environments that succeed in reducing long-term operational costs.

Offshore Development

An excellent example of a scenario that lends itself to a VDI solution is one that requires providing access to development or test resources to a new team that is located in a remote or offshore location. Using a traditional physical desktop deployment strategy, you would face delays bringing the team online because of the need to procure, load, and deliver individual physical desktops to the new location. In addition, you would probably encounter many logistical problems if you tried to remotely install and manage the systems without representation at the remote location, including difficulties with delivery and application of operating system and applications updates, ensuring that systems remain free of viruses and spyware, dealing with general hardware and software problems, and securing critical data.

In contrast, using a VDI solution, you can equip the new team with thin clients that require minimal configuration and management. The thin clients can connect to static virtual desktops running the full development or test environment. All management tasks, including provisioning, securing, and maintaining the virtual desktops, can be carried out locally by the IT staff. With VDI, initiating and dissolving remote teams can be accomplished quickly without having to worry about significant infrastructure at the remote location. The critical factor in this scenario is that network connectivity between the remote location and the VDI infrastructure must be reliable, fast, and redundant.

Call Centers, Help Desks, and Retail Branches

Other scenarios in which a VDI solution can be a practical choice include call centers, help desks, and retail branches where communities of users may work in shifts and use a shared set of applications and data. These users are also referred to as *task workers*. Shared characteristics of call centers, help desks, and retail branches are that task workers do not typically access all desktops concurrently, and they may not have dedicated work spaces, but they need to connect to a standard workload from any work space. Task workers may have access to sensitive information; therefore, the data that they use is often centralized and secured.

Deploying a thin client, dynamic VDI solution in these environments allows task workers to roam between work spaces and connect from any device to a common workload with access to the centrally stored data. For branches with high worker turnover, IT-related management tasks may require only creation (or suspension) of accounts and modifications to group memberships that provide access to the appropriate virtual desktop configuration. Additionally, this approach can help minimize the physical infrastructure deployed because virtual desktops can be assembled, activated, and deactivated based on real-time usage.

Microsoft VDI Solution Overview

Microsoft, in alliance with third-party vendors such as Citrix, provides a set of components that allow you to implement either a static or dynamic VDI solution. Microsoft's VDI solution shares many components with those used to implement a server virtualization infrastructure. Essentially, the Microsoft VDI solution builds on top of the same virtualization and management base, adding the specialized components for virtual desktop management.

Windows Server 2008 Hyper-V

In the Microsoft VDI solution, Microsoft Windows Server 2008 Hyper-V functions as the virtualization layer component. With hypervisor-based technology, Hyper-V is the core component that supports multiple, concurrent, isolated, secure partitions in which you can execute individual virtual desktops. Because of its integration with Windows Server 2008, it provides quick migration (with minimal downtime) of virtual desktops between Hyper-V servers using built-in failover clustering. With quick migration, virtual desktops are placed in a saved state prior to being moved and restarted on the new Hyper-V node within a minute. This is useful if a Hyper-V server requires planned maintenance or you need to rebalance the Hyper-V server load. The failover clustering support in Hyper-V also provides the ability to restart virtual desktops on a new Hyper-V node in case of an unplanned event, such as a hardware failure. Hyper-V supports a wide array of devices including SAN, NAS, DAS, and iSCSI, which allows it to be optimally configured to support small- or large-scale VDI deployments. In terms of client connections to virtual desktops, Hyper-V provides access through the Remote Desktop Protocol (RDP).

Windows Vista Enterprise Centralized Desktop

Although not a technology component, the Windows Vista Enterprise Centralized Desktop (VECD) encompasses the licensing options available to deploy Windows virtual desktops in a VDI environment. VECD defines licensing models for virtual desktops accessed through either traditional desktops or thin clients. Licenses are allocated on a device basis. A traditional desktop license requires an annual subscription in addition to Windows Software Assurance. A thin client license requires only an annual subscription that includes Windows Software Assurance. In either case, you can install an unlimited number of copies of Windows Vista Enterprise or downgrade operating systems, and you can access up to four concurrent running instances from a licensed device. The licenses apply to both static and dynamic virtual desktop architectures.

> **IMPORTANT**   You should thoroughly review the VECD licensing options based on your VDI architecture plans. VECD licensing details are available at *http://www.microsoft.com /windows/products/windowsvista/enterprise/benefits/licensing.mspx*.

Citrix XenDesktop

Citrix XenDesktop is instrumental in deploying a dynamic virtual desktop solution on an enterprise scale. XenDesktop works with Hyper-V and is composed of several components that work in tandem to deliver a personalized, on-demand virtual desktop to a user. Of core importance, the Desktop Delivery Controller (DDC) is the XenDesktop connection broker that identifies a user and dynamically assembles her virtual desktop. After the user is identified, XenDesktop can stream the operating system to the virtualization server environment, apply the user's profile to the operating system, and supply the user's applications through a policy-based, integrated application delivery technology such as Microsoft Application Virtualization, or remotely using Windows Server 2008 Terminal Services RemoteApp.

Remote Desktop Connection Broker in Windows Server 2008 R2

Max Herrmann, Senior Product Manager
Windows Server

In Windows Server 2008 R2, the new Remote Desktop Services role (previously called Terminal Services) includes a connection broker infrastructure that enables an end-to-end VDI solution for departmental environments. The new Remote Desktop Connection Broker extends the Session Broker capabilities already found in Windows Server 2008 and creates a unified administration experience for traditional session-based remote desktops as well as virtual machine-based remote desktops.

There are two key deployment scenarios supported by the Remote Desktop Connection Broker: persistent (permanent) VMs and pooled VMs. In the case of a persistent VM, there is a one-to-one mapping between a VM and a user. In other words, each user is assigned a dedicated VM that can be personalized and customized, and that preserves changes made by the user. Today, most early adopters of VDI deploy persistent VMs because they offer the greatest flexibility to the end user. In the case of a pooled VM, a single image is replicated as needed for each user. With a pooled VM, user state can be stored through profiles and folder redirection, but it does not persist after the user logs off. In either case, the Remote Desktop Connection Broker supports storage and deployment of the image(s) on Hyper-V servers.

In addition, the Remote Desktop Connection Broker provides an extensive set of APIs that allow creation of manageability and scalability extensions for the brokering solution. Specifically, extensibility points include the ability to create policy plug-ins (e.g., for determining the appropriate VM or VM pool), filter plug-ins (e.g., for preparing a VM to accept RDP connections), and resource plug-ins (e.g., for placing a VM on the proper server based on the server's load).

Microsoft Application Virtualization

Microsoft Application Virtualization (App-V) provides centralized storage and management of applications and on-demand, streamed delivery of applications to virtual desktops. An App-V client creates an isolation environment on the virtual desktop within which an application executes separately from other applications, eliminating any concerns about system instability caused by file versions or registry setting conflicts. App-V has the ability to stream only the portions of the code that are needed to start the application, providing additional portions based on actual user need. App-V can preserve application preferences in a file-based cache on the virtual desktop to speed up subsequent application launches, something that is useful for a static virtual desktop. In a purely dynamic environment, application and user preferences are reapplied each time the dynamic virtual desktop is assembled and delivered to an end user.

Windows Server 2008 Terminal Services RemoteApp

Windows Server 2008 Terminal Services RemoteApp is another option for a VDI solution to provide virtual desktop users with access to applications without embedding them into the virtual desktop image. In addition, RemoteApp is a solution for users who need access to one or more applications that are incompatible with the virtual desktop operating system. With this component, applications are installed and run remotely on Windows Terminal Services. In order to provide a seamless user experience, a RemoteApp-based application is launched by a user who clicks on an icon integrated into the virtual desktop or an entry in the Start menu. The icon may be linked to an RDP or Microsoft Installer (MSI) package that contains the instructions and parameters to launch an RDP session to the terminal server and invoke the application. When the connection is established, the application runs in a separate resizable window on the virtual desktop, side by side with local applications. File extensions can also be associated with a RemoteApp to launch a remote application automatically, ensuring that the user experience is identical to local programs.

System Center Virtual Machine Manager

System Center Virtual Machine Manager (VMM) is the management component that provides you with a single integrated console to manage your physical servers running Hyper-V and the virtual machines that they run. VMM provides functionality to provision virtual desktops and uses Intelligent Placement to determine the best Hyper-V server to deploy them. Intelligent Placement relies on the integration between VMM and System Center Operations Manager 2007, which is the source of performance data collected from existing Hyper-V servers. XenDesktop DDC also integrates with VMM to automate the deployment of virtual desktops on Hyper-V servers. In addition, VMM provides built-in functionality to perform a physical-to-virtual (P2V) migration of a disk image that enables transition from a physical to a virtual platform.

> **NOTE** You can learn more about System Center Virtual Machine Manager features in Chapter 12, "Server Farm Management," and Chapter 14, "Server Migration Using System Center Virtual Machine Manager."

System Center Data Protection Manager

System Center Data Protection Manager (DPM) is the management component that allows you to support Volume Shadow Copy Service (VSS) backups of active virtual desktops, provided that the guest operating systems are VSS-aware. For desktop operating systems that are not VSS-aware, DPM allows you to back up virtual desktops offline by shutting down or saving the state of virtual machines and then backing up the file set that constitutes a virtual machine.

> **NOTE** You can learn more about System Center Data Protection Manager in Chapter 13, "Hyper-V Backup and Recovery."

Summary

In this chapter, you were introduced to Virtual Desktop Infrastructure, which represents a combination of hardware, virtualization software, and management tools that provide an end-to-end solution to provision, configure, and manage virtualized desktops. You learned about key VDI attributes, and in particular how a VDI solution differs from a terminal services solution.

You also learned about the difference between static and dynamic virtual desktops, the components that integrate together to comprise a VDI solution, and some strategic scenarios that lend themselves to VDI implementation. An overview of the Microsoft VDI solution included Windows Server 2008 Hyper-V, VECD, System Center VMM and DPM, Windows Server 2008 Terminal Services, Application Virtualization, and Citrix XenDesktop and how each of these can contribute to support the creation of static and dynamic virtual desktop environments. It is important to consider that although VDI provides many benefits, including the ability to offer each user an isolated, dynamic, and personalized workload (client operating system and application stack), VDI technology is still in an emerging phase and does not yet represent a general desktop replacement solution.

Additional Resources

The following resources contain additional information related to this chapter.

- Microsoft Desktop Virtualization available at *http://www.microsoft.com/virtualization /solution-tech-desktop.mspx*

- Microsoft Application Virtualization available at *http://www.microsoft.com/virtualization /solution-tech-application.mspx*

- TS Remote App Step-by-Step Guide available at *http://technet.microsoft.com/en-us /library/cc730673.aspx*

- System Center Virtual Machine Manager 2008 available at *http://www.microsoft.com /systemcenter/scvmm/default.mspx*

- System Center Data Protection Manager 2007 available at *http://www.microsoft.com /systemcenter/dpm/default.mspx*

- Citrix XenDesktop available at *http://www.citrix.com/English/ps2/products /product.asp?contentID=163057*

- Microsoft Windows Vista Enterprise Centralized Desktop demonstration available at *http://www.microsoft.com/windows/products/windowsvista/enterprise/vecddemo /default.html*

- Microsoft Windows Vista Enterprise Centralized Desktop licensing available at *http://www.microsoft.com/windows/products/windowsvista/enterprise/benefits /licensing.mspx*

## CHAPTER 19

Server Virtualization Project: Envisioning Phase

Although it is often tempting to jump directly into the design and implementation of a problem solution, in all but the simplest environments, following a more rigorous project plan will help to ensure a successful server virtualization infrastructure deployment. The information in this chapter will guide you in identifying the specifics of the problem that led you to consider a virtualization project and will show you the steps involved in envisioning a server virtualization solution so that you can successfully put a plan into action.

Defining Server Virtualization Project Phases

There are five main project phases to complete prior to implementing a server virtualization solution in an enterprise production environment:

- **Envisioning**   The primary objectives of this phase include establishing a project vision statement, problem definition, project scope and preliminary budget identification, project team assignments, preliminary return on investment (ROI) analysis, and initial definition of project risks.

- **Discovery**   The primary objectives of this phase include the manual or automated compilation of current infrastructure hardware, software, and performance information in support of the project assessment phase.

- **Assessment**   The primary objective of this phase is the identification of physical servers that meet the requirements established for server virtualization, based on the information gathered during the project discovery phase.

- **Planning and Design**   The primary objectives of this phase include the development of the Hyper-V server infrastructure design, the overall virtualization solution components, the server workload consolidation plan, and the deployment, management, and operations plans.

- **Pilot**   The primary objective of this phase is the testing and verification of an appropriately scaled virtualization solution deployment that allows validation of the design and the deployment, management, and operations plans.

As you can see, each project phase has a very specific focus and set of deliverables. Envisioning will likely be the shortest phase of the entire project, but ultimately, it can have a great impact on the success or failure of the project.

What Is Envisioning?

Envisioning is the first step in a successful server virtualization project. During envisioning, an initial project team should focus on defining the vision behind the project; identifying the specific problems to solve with virtualization; establishing and obtaining consensus for the project scope; establishing the project team, roles, and responsibilities; and determining project risks. Your goal for the envisioning phase is to produce a set of deliverables that defines the project, helps justify the project, and establishes a preliminary budget for labor and resources. These deliverables will typically be the basis on which the project will be approved and will allow it to continue on to the next phase.

The envisioning phase is not about developing a specific solution to address the objectives of a project. Many projects fail because the project team conceptualizes a solution plan without really defining the scope of the project or the problems that need to be resolved. Typically, this results in one of two scenarios:

1. The solution is inadequate, it does not address all project requirements, and redesign efforts lead to an increase in project costs.

2. The solution is overdesigned, and budgeted funds are wasted to resolve problems that do not exist.

In both cases, time, resources, and budget are ineffectively used and the initial solution fails to fulfill the project requirements. It is up to an envisioning team to ensure that the driving factors of the project are well-defined and aligned with business priorities before moving on to problem solving. The envisioning team should also ensure that a server virtualization project is the best solution to the detailed problem set identified during the envisioning phase.

Identifying the Envisioning Team

The envisioning team should be composed of key management and technical architects who possess a sufficiently broad perspective on technical and business objectives and are empowered to act and develop the project. In the specific case of a server virtualization project, key team members should include management executive sponsors and architects of the server, network, management, and operations infrastructures.

The first two objectives of the envisioning team should be to define the project vision statement and define detailed problem statements that further drive the project.

Establishing a Vision

A vision statement defines the desired end state of your environment after the project is complete. Vision statements should be concise—typically, a single sentence, and never more than two paragraphs long. All team members should be involved when developing the vision statement to ensure that it is a shared vision and that it covers the intended goals. A good vision statement builds trust and focus between the team technical members and executive sponsors. Vision statements should also attempt to provide the team with positive motivation and offer context for decision making. Here are some sample vision statements:

- Adopt leading-edge virtualization technology that allows the business to be more agile, bring new products to the market faster, and increase revenue.

- Build a more efficient data center that provides higher availability, lower energy consumption, and more efficient use of resources while reducing capital expenditures.

DIRECT FROM THE SOURCE

The Importance of a Motivational Vision Statement

Teresa M. Lewandowski, PMP, Principal Project Manager
Microsoft Consulting Services

Having a vision statement that is motivational is particularly important during difficult projects. Since you can't always predict which projects might become difficult, it's safe to assume you'll need a strong vision statement for every project.

Not all projects are about saving lives or solving humanitarian issues, but each one should be undertaken for compelling reasons. Dig deep for those compelling business reasons during the envisioning phase and then take extra time if needed to articulate them in a way that will motivate team members throughout the project. The wording of the statement should be simple enough that it's easily remembered and can be repeated often. If you're clever enough to create a mantra of your vision statement, it can be turned into a project logo and later used on project documents, presentations, team shirts, or signage for the project team room.

Use your vision statement to bring each new project team member on board with the goal of having them own that vision, too. As the project progresses, there are sometimes obstacles that impede progress, such as uncooperative or territorial business units or passive resisters to change. There may also be organizational changes among stakeholders that appear to defuse the urgency or priority of the project in midstream. Especially when your project team is dispersed, virtual, and global, you will have little more than that strong compelling vision to keep the team focused and moving forward at times like these. If your team seems to be faltering or redefining their scope, use your vision statement as a tool to motivate and refocus them. Help them rise above the tactical and stay focused on the strategic purpose of their role and their importance to the success of the project.

When the project vision is established, the envisioning team can focus on defining detailed problem statements. Above all, the ability to design a proper solution strongly depends on the clear definition of the actual problems that need to be resolved in order to meet technical and business objectives.

Defining the Problem Statements

Defining the problems you are trying to solve with your server virtualization project also helps bring clarity to the vision and scope of the project. The problem statements should include both technical and business problems that you are experiencing within your company. By including both types of problems, you will ensure that all aspects of your business are considered during the planning and design phase.

Problem statements should include a description that identifies the problem in a quantitative manner. In this way, you will have more concrete criteria against which to measure the proposed solution and assess how the solution solves the stated problems. For example, instead of defining the problem as "Rack space is at a premium in the data center," you should define a measurable component that the problem statement can be evaluated against, such as "Currently only 10 percent of the rack space in the data center is open and available for expansion hardware." If the virtualization project increases the available rack space in the data center above 10 percent, you have addressed the problem. There is still one component missing to determine if you have really met expectations, however—a solution metric. In addition to stating the problem, you need to state a measurable target for the problem resolution. For this example, a measurable target could be defined as "Increase the open and available rack space in the data center to 25 percent of total rack space."

Table 19-1 provides a collection of sample technical problem statements and project metrics.

TABLE 19-1 Technical Problem Statements

PROBLEM STATEMENT	METRIC
Lack of available power—Data center has only 2 percent capacity remaining.	Increase the available power capacity in the data center to 25 percent.
Lack of available rack space—Data center has only 2,000 square feet of rack space remaining.	Increase the available rack space in the data center to 20,000 square feet.
Low server utilization—Average server utilization is 15 percent.	Combine workloads on servers to increase the average server utilization to 75 percent.
Legacy application compatibility—50 percent of legacy applications require an operating system that will not run on the latest hardware, requiring older hardware to be maintained.	Virtualize the workloads to eliminate the legacy hardware and support contracts.
Each standard physical server requires 2U of rack space.	Achieve a guest-to-host consolidation ratio of 16:1 for test/development servers and 10:1 for production servers to reduce rack space requirements.

Table 19-2 provides a collection of sample business problem statements and metrics.

TABLE 19-2 Business Problem Statements

PROBLEM STATEMENT	METRIC
Average time to procure and deploy a new server is two weeks. This delay results in lost return on investment.	Reduce the time required to add a new server to 24 hours.
Business continuity using physical servers results in twice the hardware costs of using virtual servers.	Reduce the hardware costs for business continuity to a maximum of 25 percent of the total hardware costs by using virtualized servers instead of physical servers.
Rebuilding servers during testing and development requires on average two hours when using automated deployment techniques.	Reduce the rebuild time for testing and development servers to less than 10 minutes.

Process for Defining Problem Statements

In order to assist in the definition of the technical problem statements for the server virtualization project, you should solicit input from different information technology teams across different geographies within your company. Remember that potentially different problems exist at every data center location and remote office, so do not overlook any part of your company. Remember also that you are looking for problems that should be in scope for the virtualization project.

Your internal customers are another source of problem statements. Talk to your business units or department heads to determine any business or technical problems they might be experiencing. Discuss issues that the development or testing teams are having with their environments. Talk to your operations teams to determine the top 10 operational problems they experience.

There are various ways you can collect problem statements. For examples, you can send direct e-mail messages to individuals, gather input during team meetings, use electronic surveys, or use a combination of methods. The goal is to collect as many problem statements as possible so that you can ensure that you are addressing key problems in the existing environment.

Setting Priorities

After you have collected all the problem statements and defined the project metrics, you need to determine which problems should be included in the scope of the planned project and which problems should be dealt with at a later time. To assist in that categorization, you should define a set of priorities and assign a priority to each problem statement. The simplest set of priorities includes High, Normal, and Low, but you could also use a more granular scale, if needed. For example, you can also define a scale between 1 (High) to 5 (Low).

You should get consensus on the priority to be assigned to each problem statement by holding a priority-setting meeting with the envisioning team. Group the problem statements from High to Low. If you find that you have a long list of problem statements, you can use the three (or more) levels of priority to divide the project into different phases to make it more manageable.

 ON THE COMPANION MEDIA   To assist in collecting problem statements, you will find a Microsoft Office Excel spreadsheet named Problem Statement JobAid.xls in the \Chapter Materials\Job Aids folder on the companion media. This spreadsheet has a single worksheet that contains the recommended information to collect.

Defining a Project Team

Every successful project can be attributed to having a great team of people performing the correct roles by working from a concise list of requirements and project scope. Defining a project team consists of establishing the required project roles and identifying the number of project team members needed for each role. In addition, the size of the team should be proportional to the size of the organization and the project. Therefore, smaller organizations may not find the need to implement all of the teams described in this section.

After the requirements and scope are defined, a project plan can be created during the planning phase that defines when the project team roles are required in relation to the project timeline. You will typically find that some roles are not required throughout the project or that a single person can perform multiple roles.

Identifying the Required Project Teams and Roles

Each server virtualization project is different, but typically a defined set of project teams and team roles are required in every virtualization project. Project teams and roles vary by the project phase. As a rule, every project needs a project manager for the entire length of the project. A tester may only need to be a dedicated member of the project team during the pilot phase, when the virtualization solution is ready to be tested against the requirements. However, a tester may be involved in key tasks during other project phases to ensure that testing requirements are taken into account.

Table 19-3 provides a list of the recommended project teams and descriptions for the roles that each team needs to fulfill for a successful server virtualization project.

TABLE 19-3 Project Teams

TEAM	DESCRIPTION
Steering Committee	Provides project direction and integration between the project teams, the stakeholders, and the executive sponsors.
Project Management Team	Manages the overall project, project schedule, project requirements, project budget, and project communications. Also manages expectations.
Architecture Design Team	Provides overall project subject matter expertise, manages project specification, manages project risk, defines and supervises building of project features, estimates the time and effort to complete each feature, and manages the subject matter experts.
Subject Matter Expert Team	Provides technical, business, and application experts who help define the project requirements and specifications, build project features, and define the test requirements.
Test Team	Develops testing strategy, plans, and procedures; manages the project issues; and conducts the testing.

TEAM	DESCRIPTION
Operations Team	Defines the disaster recovery strategy, tests the disaster recovery procedures, defines operational requirements and management procedures, and provides operational training.
Monitoring Team	Defines the requirements, procedures, and tool integration required to monitor the new virtualization infrastructure.

Identifying Team Roles

Each project team has a set of roles and responsibilities within the project. Teams can vary in size from a single person performing multiple roles to a multiperson team with one member assigned to each role on that team. Different people in your organization or people outside your organization can fill roles in a team. The key action is to find the right person to fill the role, ensuring the success of the project.

Steering Committee

The steering committee is the bridge between the executive sponsors, the stakeholders, and the project management team. The steering committee helps set the project scope and budgetary requirements. Financial and business decisions are brought to the steering committee for review and approval.

The committee membership usually contains the project manager, budget manager, business stakeholders, and the executive sponsor. Although the committee will meet regularly at the start of the project, typically once a week, after the project has met the strategic milestones, the committee meetings may reduce in frequency, perhaps to once a month.

During the steering committee meetings, the project manager provides project status, milestone status, and project risks. The budget manager provides the status on the project budget, ROI, and potential cost savings. The business stakeholders and executive sponsors provide updates on any business issues that could have an impact on the project.

Project Management Team

The project management team manages the entire project and is the main public face of the project. There are four primary roles in the project management team:

1. Project manager
2. Project scheduler
3. Budget manager
4. Communications manager

The key role within the project management team is the project manager. This individual is ultimately responsible for the project being completed on time and on budget. The project manager is directly responsible for managing the expectations of the project team, executive sponsors, and customers regarding project scope or requirements. This role also involves providing an overall project status report to management, managing any scope change requests, and approving any communications outside the team. The project manager also maintains an issue management system to ensure that project issues are tracked and reported.

The project scheduler maintains the project plan, provides status reports on project milestones to the project manager, manages any changes to the work tasks in the schedule, and manages the resource scheduling and resource requests. The project scheduler takes any approved scope changes from the project manager, modifies the project plan, and documents any impact such changes have on the plan for the team. In addition, the project scheduler is responsible for communicating any work tasks to team members and informing any new team members of their project commitments.

The budget manager creates and maintains the project budget for resources and labor, manages requests for any hardware or software, and provides the interface to the procurement department to approve any project invoices. The budget manager is in the approval workflow process for any project scope additions to address budget concerns and obtain budget approval before the additional scope is forwarded to the project scheduler.

The communications manager manages all project communications and satisfaction surveys and collects and distributes any reported issues. This role provides a single point of communication for the project team to increase efficiency. The communications manager works with business units and end users to inform them when servers will be unavailable during migration, based on the schedule that the project scheduler has negotiated. During larger projects, the communications manager distributes and compiles results from satisfaction surveys with customers and within the project team.

Architecture Design Team

The architecture design team provides the subject matter expertise for the overall project, produces the design functional specifications, identifies project risks, defines any features of the project, translates the design functional specifications into a list of tasks, and calls on application and business subject matter experts from the organization to assist when required. There are three primary roles in the architecture design team:

1. Lead project architect
2. Functional architect
3. Risk manager

The lead project architect participates in the virtualization project from start to finish. The person in this role provides the overall technical leadership and calls on functional architects and subject matter experts on an as-needed basis. The lead project architect is ultimately responsible for the technical solution developed for the virtualization project. Lead architects also define the overall project requirements and specifications. They merge specific functional requirements and specifications from the functional architects and subject matter experts to create the complete requirements and functional specification document deliverables.

Functional architects provide technical expertise for virtualization aspects of the project. Functional architects include, at a minimum, specialists in the following technical areas: networking, servers, storage, client, and security. These architects are the subject matter experts for these technical areas within the company, and they know the currently implemented architecture and undocumented customizations. Functional architects are responsible for developing the functional specifications for their areas of expertise, assisting in the estimation of time required to completion of project features, and aiding in the assembly of test and pilot environments.

The risk manager maintains the process for managing risk assessment during the project, tracks identified risks, provides status reports on the state of identified risks, and closes risks that have been mitigated. Depending on the project complexity, a risk management solution can vary from a simple Microsoft Office Excel spreadsheet to a more complicated workflow risk-management system with automated status-report generation. The risk manager may also be a member of the project management team to ensure the team remains aware of project risks and mitigations that directly affect the project schedule and budget.

Subject Matter Expert Team

The subject matter expert team is assembled from application and business experts specific to the servers and applications that are considered in scope for the project. The subject matter experts have specific knowledge about application daily operations, unique server configuration, application and business dependencies, and business operations. This information is required during specification creation, project feature definition, and testing. The unique knowledge these team members bring to the process is also used to determine server consolidation ratios as well as workload placement.

Test Team

The test team manages everything related to testing the proposed virtualization project implementation plan. It develops the test strategy, writes the procedures, assembles the test schedule and plans, and conducts the tests. There are three primary roles within the test team:

1. Test manager
2. Test engineer
3. Subject matter expert

The test manager supervises the testing strategy, the testing schedule, and the test engineers. The test manager's primary responsibility is to ensure that the testing methodology has a minimal impact on the testing schedule.

Choosing a Test Manager Is Crucial

Teresa M. Lewandowski, PMP, Principal Project Manager
Microsoft Consulting Services

The test manager is one of the most important roles to staff with the right person to ensure project success. You will need a strong and assertive personality to push back on schedule changes that reduce testing time for the sake of staying on schedule with pilot and deployment phases. The test manager also must have the respect of your architecture design team and your subject matter experts to ensure the quality of your migration approach. Although the test team isn't at full capacity until later in the project, you will minimize your risks if you have an experienced test manager involved in the discovery phase to define the hardware and resources required for the test environment and again during the planning and design phase to provide a detailed test plan. If the test manager is not a full-time team member during all phases of the project, it is essential that the project manager is the advocate for and represents the strategic importance of the testing tasks during his or her absence.

The test engineers are responsible for creating the test procedures, building the test environment, and performing the testing tasks. The subject matter experts are responsible for testing applications that require unique business and technical skills. This level of testing minimizes any application-specific issues.

Operations Team

The operations team focuses on the post-deployment operations strategy and management of the new virtualization infrastructure. Some people may believe that managing a group of virtual machines will be the same as managing the physical machines. However, virtual machine management must consider the effect of additional dependencies that do not exist when managing individual physical machines. For example, a physical server can be updated and rebooted with minimal to no impact on other physical machines. When running multiple workloads in Hyper-V, any update that requires reinitializing either the Windows hypervisor or the parent partition will affect every virtual machine running in a child partition on that server. Therefore, management and operation of Hyper-V server farms are crucial areas that require proper planning and risk mitigation.

Within the operations/management team, there are three primary roles:

1. Operations manager
2. Operations engineer
3. Training manager

The operations manager oversees the entire operations team, defines the operations and disaster recovery strategy, defines the management requirements, and assists in the creation of disaster recovery plans. The operations engineers are responsible for defining, creating, and testing the operations and disaster recovery plans and procedures. The training manager defines, creates, and delivers training for the new virtualization technology to the operations team.

Monitoring Team

The monitoring team has the responsibility to define the requirements, procedures, and tool integration needed to successfully monitor the new virtualization infrastructure. The monitoring team works closely with the architecture design team and operations team to ensure that any new tools required to monitor the new virtualization infrastructure can be integrated in the existing monitoring environment. In conjunction, they also work to define the appropriate monitoring components, rules, triggers, alerts, and any specialized code to develop, as well as any automated issue recovery procedures, problem workflow procedures, and report generation.

There are two primary roles in the monitoring team:

1. Monitoring manager
2. Monitoring engineer

The monitoring manager oversees the monitoring team and is responsible for the overall monitoring system. The monitoring engineers are responsible for defining, creating, and testing the monitoring system configuration, procedures, and report generation.

> **NOTE** The teams described in this section will vary in size based on the project size. Team members can perform multiple roles, and some team members may be only temporary. It is a best practice not to have the same members on both the architecture team and the test team. This allows the test team to provide an independent, unbiased evaluation of the technical solution.

Determining Project Scope

A clear project scope is the key to establishing a baseline of problem statements that will be addressed during the project. Problems that fall outside of the current project scope may be addressed in a subsequent project, or it may be agreed to postpone consideration of specific problems. This is commonly referred to as determining what is *in scope* and *out of scope* for a project. Maintaining a firm handle on project scope is crucial, because every time you add an item to the in-scope list, you potentially increase the required project budget and add new work items to the project schedule. If an item falls out of scope, you are potentially reducing the return on investment and not addressing a technical or business limitation in your environment. Defining project scope becomes a balancing act between creating a manageable project with high probability for success and positive business impact and minimizing the number of deferred issues.

Defining project scope is a three-step process. The first step involves deciding which of the collected problem statements are addressed with the project. The second step involves deferring or eliminating problem statements and setting project limitations that could be based on budget, technical matters, resource availability, schedule deadlines, business needs, and so on. Finally, the third step involves determining if the project scope necessitates a phased implementation.

Defining What Is In Scope

In order to clearly define project scope, problem statements must be detailed enough to allow development of project objectives. For example, stating "Only 2,000 square feet of data center rack space remains" does not establish if one or more data centers are affected, does not specify which data center has remaining space, and does not provide information that defines data center objectives. Here is a modified statement that enables project scope definition: "Existing physical servers in the Houston data center will be analyzed to determine the number of virtualization candidates and the amount of rack space square footage that would be recovered to support additional server-based projects." This more detailed problem statement indicates the Houston data center as a target, designates that rack space recovery through virtualization is requested, and defines recovered rack space as a project success measurement. The problem statement could be further refined to include a more specific amount of rack space square footage that could be recovered, providing an even more focused metric to use during project scope identification.

Defining What Is Out of Scope

Defining what problems are considered out of scope is also important to create a successful project plan. Defining out-of-scope items early in the project planning process allows you to refine assumptions and further clarify the objectives on which the project team will focus. An important component of project success is preventing scope creep—the tendency to add tangential problems to the project that may jeopardize the project schedule, budget, and on-time completion. Defining out-of-scope items can be based on various factors, including the following items:

- Server workload exclusions
- Applications exclusions
- Operating system exclusions
- Hardware exclusions
- Geographical exclusions
- Business exclusions based on legal concerns or pending mergers and acquisitions issues
- Time to test exclusions

Although specifically defining scope exclusions assists in narrowing the span of your server virtualization project, you should state clearly in your deliverables that items not included in the project scope are considered out of scope.

Vetting the Out-of-Scope List

Teresa M. Lewandowski, PMP, Principal Project Manager
Microsoft Consulting Services

Defining what is out of scope is equally important as defining what is in scope. Take great care to write an exhaustive list of everything deemed to be out of scope and then vet that list with your project stakeholders. Explicitly state that anything not listed as in scope is by default out of scope. Having the agreement of your project sponsor and your executive sponsor is only part of the task. You may find disagreement or lack of clarity among the other project stakeholders about what the project is going to accomplish within their span of control. This can be based on their own assumptions, their technical knowledge, or a presentation they've previously seen if they were involved in the project selection process. Use your Out-of-Scope list to bring all the stakeholders to the table in a discussion with the project sponsors to negotiate agreement from all parties. Remember that an equally important element of the scope definition is the "Conditions of Acceptance" to clarify the conditions under which the customer will accept the solution. This will serve to minimize any political fray later and will help your project team meet stakeholder expectations.

Determining Project Phases

Many server virtualization projects will include multiple implementation phases. For example, deployment and migration of data center servers should be completed in a separate phase from deployment and migration of branch office servers. Even though the end goals are similar, it is likely that they each will require different planning and tasks to resolve problems or address limitations specific to each environment. Defining project phases also allows you to reduce overall project complexity. Here are a few examples of the types of areas to consider when defining project phases:

- **Address low-hanging fruit first**   An early phase could involve virtualizing servers that can be migrated quickly and with minimal planning.
- **Hardware reuse**   If you are going to reuse hardware, you could define a phase that includes migration of the servers to be redeployed and a subsequent phase to address migration of servers that will be hosted on the redeployed hardware.

- **One business unit at a time** In order to reduce support issues and minimize the number of business units that are affected in the event of a deployment issue, you could define a separate phase for each business unit migration.

- **Geography** It is possible that resource constraints, regional project timelines, or other factors oblige you to define a geographically phased project.

There are many additional areas that you might consider, depending on the details of your project and particularities of your environment. It is important to realize that you should identify the driving factors in your environment early to understand the challenges you will face and help you construct a well-phased project plan.

Performing an ROI Analysis

During the envisioning phase, you should also perform a preliminary ROI analysis to assist you in the justification of the project costs based on business value derived from server virtualization. In order for an ROI analysis to yield useful results, it has to take measure of many different variables, including current infrastructure and operating costs, technology solutions, enterprise-specific metrics, growth predictions, and so on. The major areas of return that will probably be of most interest to you from the outset of a server virtualization project include lower operating costs, lower total cost of ownership (TCO), improvements in service, and improvements in the time required to bring new business processes online.

If you do not have an in-house method to perform an ROI analysis, you can download free tools like the Windows Integrated Virtualization ROI tool developed by Alinean. If you lack the expertise in your environment to perform an ROI analysis, engage knowledgeable consultants in this area to train you or assist you in performing a quick preliminary analysis that can be refined during the course of the project. It is important that you document the analysis, including all assumptions and their source, in addition to actual analysis results.

DIRECT FROM THE FIELD

Microsoft Integrated Virtualization ROI Tool

Tom Pisello, CEO
Alinean

The Microsoft Integrated Virtualization ROI Tool was developed independently by Alinean, the leading experts in IT Value Management and ROI/TCO analysis.

More than ever, CIOs and IT executives are required to prove the business value of IT spending. Although studies indicate that more than 90 percent of all IT purchases require ROI business cases for rationalization and justification, many companies are unable to quickly and credibly develop business cases for planned projects on their own.

To meet these challenges, Alinean has developed the most credible ROI/TCO analysis tools, competitive intelligence benchmarking, and best practices available. Offered exclusively through independent consulting partners and IT solution providers, Alinean research and tools deliver valued advice and independent validation—and most importantly—help IT professionals build credible business case plans for critical investment decisions.

Another key issue in IT today is that normal operating expenses consume far too much of the annual budget—leaving little room for innovative investments that can give the business a true game-changing competitive edge. To help address the lack of innovation spending, server virtualization is being considered and implemented in data centers as one way to drive operating costs lower and provide more in the budget for innovation.

The Virtualization Opportunity

Data center servers are notoriously underutilized. Most servers do not come close to peak operating capacity on any given day. Studies have shown that during a 24-hour period, less than 10 percent of the typical x86/x64 server computing capacity is used. Virtualization allows you to consolidate servers, increase utilization, and improve manageability. This can yield significant cost savings and benefits, including:

- Reduce server, storage, and networking costs
- Reduce increasing power, cooling, and facilities costs
- Improve IT productivity
- Reduce business risks
- Improve business agility

How Expensive Is a Data Center Server?

Considering typical server costs, each dual CPU server can average $9,000 per year in total direct ownership costs, a significant opportunity for potential savings.

The Business Case for Server Virtualization

Alinean estimates that implementing server virtualization can address the rising cost of ownership in the following ways:

- Consolidate server workloads, typically in the range of 8:1 to 15:1, resulting in:
  - A reallocation or retirement of existing servers and elimination of ongoing server maintenance and support costs
  - Avoidance of adding any (or as many) servers in the future to support growth
  - Elimination of not only the server but also related storage and networking costs for host bus adapters, network interface cards, and storage/network switch infrastructure
  - Reduction in growing power and data center space issues

- Reduce server provisioning to 1.5 hours per server with virtual environment (92 percent or more improvement)
- Reduce server administration workload from 60 percent to 90 percent less than current levels

As well as the direct savings, server virtualization can provide additional benefits, including driving business resilience, reducing disaster recovery (DR) time/risks, and improving availability by 80 percent.

The Windows Integrated Virtualization ROI tool helps partners and customers determine the consolidation benefits and TCO advantages of Microsoft's Integrated Virtualization as a key component of moving to Dynamic Core Infrastructure Optimization. The tool collects information about current production server, development/QA lab, desktop and application virtualization opportunities, and industry metrics. It then uses Alinean data and research to project the potential savings, service level and agility benefits, costs, and ROI for implementing various optimization strategies using the Microsoft Integrated Virtualization solutions. All research has been collected from the Alinean Value Base of IT spending metrics and from Microsoft product and pricing experts to reflect typical costs and savings for similar company type and size.

This professional business case reporting feature of the Alinean tool can help you with the following tasks:

- Justifying the value of each planned investment
- Improving collaboration with business units on IT investment decisions
- Streamlining ROI analysis, TCO benchmarking, and budgeting processes by 40 percent or more
- Making better investment decisions so that your enterprise can do more with less
- Proving and improving the value of IT to the organization

The Microsoft Integrated Virtualization ROI Tool can be used during a project envisioning and justification phase to create a detailed ROI analysis report (in Microsoft Office PowerPoint or Microsoft Office Word) that will take about half an hour to complete. You can find this essential planning tool at *http://www.microsoft.com /virtualization/ROItool*.

Identifying Risks

Risks cannot be avoided, but they can be mitigated. Before you can mitigate a risk, however, you have to identify it, assign a likelihood and impact, and document it. After you understand the risk, you can develop an approach to mitigate the risk. Identifying risks is a team process, so every member of the envisioning team should attend a risk identification brainstorming session. The focus of the brainstorming session should be to identify any risk that might affect the virtualization project. You should collect both technical and business risks to ensure that you have identified as many potential risks to the project as possible. For example, technical risks should include resource risks, design risks, solution risks, and assumption risks. Business risks include budgetary risks, project schedule risks, personnel risks, and other nontechnical risks. Examples of common risks that many projects share include the following:

- **Changing scope**   Scope changes have an impact on project schedule and budget.
- **Loss of key project team members**   Project members get reassigned to other projects, change jobs within the company, or leave the company to seek new employment.
- **Poor communication**   Poor communication among the project team members and between the team and those stakeholders outside the project can increase the possibility of incorrect assumptions and project shortfalls, resulting in customer satisfaction issues.
- **Impact on security**   Network security (blocked ports on routers and firewalls) can affect the automated discovery and inventory of servers, resulting in servers having to be inventoried by hand.
- **Funding changes**   Funding changes that reduce the project's budget can affect the scope and return on investment of the project.

The following list gives some examples of common risks that are specific to virtualization projects:

- **Change in operations processes**   Virtualization will mandate changes to existing processes and potentially increase operational costs.
- **"My server" syndrome**   Business units refuse to combine their servers with other business units, reducing the consolidation ratio that could be achieved.
- **Chargeback**   Consensus on a business unit chargeback model for virtualized servers cannot be reached, delaying the adoption and deployment of the virtualization solution in the environment.
- **Poor consolidation planning**   Baseline performance for the server hardware is not captured or used during consolidation planning, resulting in overutilization of the server hardware because inaccurate theoretical performance numbers are used instead of actual performance data.

Table 19-4 lists the attributes that should be collected for every risk that you document.

TABLE 19-4 Risk Attributes

ATTRIBUTE	DESCRIPTION
Risk ID	Numeric value that uniquely identifies a risk.
Probability	Likelihood that the risk will happen, specified as a numeric value from 1 through 100, where 1 is the lowest and 100 is the highest probability.
Description	Description of the risk.
Consequence	Result if the risk occurs. This includes technical, business, and financial consequences.
Mitigation Plan	Description of how to reduce or eliminate the impact of the risk on the project.
Impact	Effect of the risk if it occurs. Impact is specified as a numeric value from 1 through 10, where 1 has the lowest and 10 has the highest impact.
Owner	The individual who owns the risk and the risk mitigation plan.

 ON THE COMPANION MEDIA   To assist in collecting and tracking risks, you will find an Excel spreadsheet named Risk Management JobAid.xls in the \Chapter Materials\Job Aids folder on the companion media. This spreadsheet has a single worksheet that contains columns to collect the recommended risk attributes.

DIRECT FROM THE SOURCE

Ranking the Risks

Mike Williams, Senior Consultant
Microsoft Consulting Services

After you have identified the risks, you should rank them to determine the level of importance to the project. To do this, you take the probability (1 through 100) that you assigned the risk and multiply it by the defined impact (1 through 10). This will give you a number between 1 and 1,000. When you have this ranking, you can determine the order of importance for mitigation efforts.

Creating a Project Budget

After you have established a project scope, conducted an ROI analysis, and identified project risks, you can produce a preliminary project budget for the next two phases of the project: discovery and assessment. Data from these two phases are required to develop a detailed project budget and schedule. The preliminary project budget includes the following items:

- Labor budget for the discovery and assessment phases
- Hardware and software budget required to perform the discovery and assessment

The labor budget should include funding for a project manager, a lead architect, a project scheduler, a budget manager, and a functional architect. The hardware and software budget should include funds for one or more physical servers with the required specifications to perform the discovery tasks, discovery software tools, server operating system licenses, appropriate client access licenses (CALs), and potentially, a database license to store the collected data.

Summary

This chapter outlined the first phase of a server virtualization project: the envisioning phase. Envisioning is not about developing a server virtualization solution; rather, it is about understanding the current environment and the problems that exist in the environment that could be addressed with a server virtualization solution. The main tasks in the envisioning phase include developing a list of the problems in the environment and prioritizing them, assembling the project team, deciding what problems are in scope and out of scope, performing a preliminary ROI analysis, identifying and ranking project risks, and defining a preliminary budget to complete the discovery and assessment phases.

Additional Resources

The following resources contain additional information related to this chapter.

- Microsoft Solution Framework avaible at *http://www.microsoft.com/technet /solutionaccelerators/msf/default.mspx*
- Microsoft Integrated Virtualization ROI Tool available at *http://www.microsoft.com /virtualization/ROItool/default.mspx*

## CHAPTER 20

Server Virtualization Project: Discovery Phase

During the discovery phase of a server virtualization project, you are focused on collecting all the required information to define the remaining project phases. If you follow the recommendations discussed in Chapter 19, "Server Virtualization Project: Envisioning Phase," you will have an approved project scope that defines the geographic or business locations included in the project, the types of servers for which discovery data is required, and the types of servers excluded from consideration. Now the Architectural Design team or one or more subject matter experts can use this information to target the discovery data collection.

You will need to gather information in two steps during the discovery phase. The first step involves gathering data about any Active Directory forest and domains in the environment, including a network subnet to physical location mapping. When you have collected that information, you can proceed to the second step, which includes collecting the following information for each server:

- Hardware and software inventory

- Performance metrics

- Environmental information

This information is used in the project assessment phase to identify server virtualization candidates, group the candidates by predetermined parameters (application, location, hardware attributes, and so on), decide how best to combine candidate workloads, and produce a report that details the cost-savings for rack space, power, and cooling.

In this chapter, you will learn about the detailed information you need to collect to drive success in the next project phases. At the end of the chapter, there is a section titled "Automating the Discovery Process" that describes tools included on the resource kit companion media, downloadable from Microsoft, or available from other independent software vendors (ISVs) that you can use to automate the discovery process.

Collecting Baseline Information

Collecting data from Windows servers is typically performed remotely. This requires that the tool used to collect the information has proper credentials, typically an account that is a member of the server local administrators group. With the correct credentials, you can also collect server inventory and performance information.

Active Directory Forest Information

Although you can potentially specify the local administrative account on every server to collect inventory information, it is better to use a domain account. In order to determine which domain account to use and whether or not a single account can be used across multiple domains or forests, you need knowledge of the Active Directory forest and domain structure in the environment.

When collecting Active Directory forest information, you should include the forest name, the domain names that it contains, and the trusts that exist between forests and domains. This will allow you to create a map of the Active Directory forest infrastructure and trust relationships so that you can define the minimum number of user account credentials that will be required to retrieve server data.

Collecting Location Information

During the project planning and design phase, you determine the consolidation strategy, including which servers to migrate to the same Hyper-V servers in each location. In order to accomplish this, you need to create a list of locations as well as network subnets deployed in each location. This will allow you to assemble server inventory data by location and server consolidation groups.

When you have collected the network subnet and network subnet mask information for each location, create a table to compile the information. Table 20-1 provides an example of such a table.

TABLE 20-1 Location Information

LOCATION	SUBNETS	SUBNET MASK
Houston	10.10.10.0	255.255.255.0
	10.10.11.0	255.255.255.0
Atlanta	10.10.100.0	255.255.255.0
London	10.10.200.0	255.255.255.0

Two common ways you can get the subnet to physical location mapping are to ask your networking team or use information stored in Active Directory. The networking team will either have a network map that shows physical locations and associated subnets, or they will have this information documented in tabular form. Active Directory Site information is useful if the site-to-subnet mappings are up to date. Typically, companies use site names that represent the physical site location. You can obtain site location data and all the subnets that are assigned to a site from Active Directory. This information can be retrieved using the Active Directory Sites And Services Microsoft Management Console (MMC) or using a script. However, Active Directory Sites And Services only captures domain controllers that are mapped to a site, not all servers deployed at that site.

NOTE If a server or client computer is in a subnet that has not been entered in the Active Directory Sites And Services, that computer will be placed in the built-in container called Default First Site. When you query Active Directory for the site information for each server, you should verify that servers have not been placed in the Default First Site.

Collecting Inventory Information

To define the set of servers that are good candidates for virtualization, you must collect specific hardware and software information for each server. The hardware information that you need to collect includes processor type, memory configuration, number and type of network adapters, disk subsystem details, USB devices, and serial and parallel port devices. The software information that you need to collect consists of a list of installed applications as well as any updates, hotfixes, or service packs installed on the server. In addition, you need to inventory all the services running on each server. You will use this information and a set of rules or thresholds—described in Chapter 21, "Server Virtualization Project: Assessment Phase"—to determine which physical servers can be migrated to virtual machines running on Hyper-V servers.

Hardware Inventory

Table 20-2 provides a detailed list of hardware devices and settings that you should collect during a server hardware inventory. The major categories are Basic Input/Output System (BIOS), operating system, processor, memory, storage, network interface card, removable devices connected to USB interfaces, and devices connected to serial or parallel ports. This information is used mainly to build a virtualization candidate pool exclusion list.

TABLE 20-2 Recommended Information to Collect During Hardware Inventory

HARDWARE CATEGORY	INVENTORY INFORMATION
BIOS	Server manufacturer
	Model number
	Serial number
Operating System	Operating system
	Service pack
	Domain
	Server name
	Updates
Processor	Processor manufacturer (Intel, AMD)
	Processor model (Pentium IV, Opteron)
	Processor speed (in MHz)
	Number of processors
	Number of cores

HARDWARE CATEGORY	INVENTORY INFORMATION
Memory	Amount of physical memory
	Total number of memory sockets*
	Size of memory sticks*
	Number of free memory sockets*
Storage	Number of hard disks
	Total capacity of each disk
	File system type (FAT, NTFS)
	Partitions
	Basic or dynamic disk
	State (online or offline)
Network Adapters	Number of cards
	Maximum speed of each card
	Current speed of each card
	Manufacturer
	Special configurations (teaming, VLAN)
	Network settings per card
	■ IP Address
	■ Subnet mask
	■ Media Access Control (MAC) address
USB Devices	Any devices connected via USB
Parallel Port Devices	Any devices connected to the parallel port
Serial Port Devices	Any devices connected to the serial port

Optional information

You need BIOS information to identify the manufacturer and model of the server hardware. You will use this information later in the process to collect environmental information, such as the number of rack units (Us) the server required in the data center, along with its power-consumption rating and heat-dissipation rating.

You will use operating system information to group virtualization candidates by operating system release and service pack version. You can also use this as a validation of the operating system value that was published in Active Directory. In addition, collecting the domain and server name provides you with additional unique values that you will need to combine data.

You collect processor information to understand how the existing server compares to the capabilities of a Hyper-V virtual machine. Key information needed for the comparison includes the number of processors (sockets), number of processor cores, and the speed of the processor in MHz. You will use the processor manufacturer and model information to identify processor types in case the server is a candidate for reuse as a Hyper-V server but needs additional processors. The manufacturer and model information are also crucial to identify unsupported processors like Intel Itanium.

You need memory information to understand whether the current amount of memory in the physical server is the same as or lower than the 64-gigabyte (GB) limit of a Hyper-V virtual machine. You can collect optional information that identifies the number of free memory sockets in the server and the capacity of the existing memory sticks. You will use this information to determine the maximum amount of memory that the server can support without discarding any memory chips. The memory information is used to identify memory expansion capabilities in case the server is a candidate for reuse as a Hyper-V server but needs additional memory.

You will require storage information to understand the disk space requirements and issues that you may face when performing a migration from a physical server to a virtual machine. Hyper-V integrated drive electronics (IDE) virtual hard disks are limited to 127 GB in size, and Small Computer System Interface (SCSI) virtual hard disks are limited to 2.04 terabytes in size for a single disk. Collecting the number of disks in the physical server and the size of each one allows you to determine if any size limits may be exceeded. Collecting information about the partitions, file system type, and active state—and whether the disk is a dynamic disk or not—assists you in understanding issues related to physical-to-virtual (P2V) machine migration. For example, many P2V tools support the migration of basic disks, but some do not support the migration of dynamic disks.

You also need to collect network adapter information to compare the existing server adapter configuration to the capabilities of a Hyper-V virtual machine. Virtual machines can have a maximum of eight synthetic and four legacy Ethernet network adapters installed concurrently, and they do not support advanced features such as network adapter teaming. Physical Ethernet network adapters can also support multiple speeds (10/100/1,000/10,000 Mb/s). You can set an adapter to a specific speed or set it to auto-negotiate the speed. You need to document what speed the network adapter is currently configured at to appropriately size and configure the Hyper-V servers where servers are consolidated.

Therefore, you must collect information such as the number of network adapters in the server, the current and maximum interface speed of each adapter, the adapter manufacturer, and any details on special adapter modes such as teaming and Virtual Local Area Network (VLAN). You must also collect the TCP/IP settings (IP address, subnet mask, MAC address) from each adapter to understand what network connections exist so that you can define virtual networks on the Hyper-V servers that are connected to the same physical networks.

USB-connected devices on physical servers are typically special devices required by specific applications to function. For example, these include a USB smart-card reader for increased security or a USB flash key to store an encryption key. Hyper-V virtual machines support only keyboard and mouse USB-connected devices in pass-through mode. Therefore, collecting information on all USB-connected devices on a server will also assist you in determining if a server is an appropriate candidate for virtualization.

Parallel port devices on physical servers are not common, because most server manufacturers have stopped including parallel ports on their hardware. The Hyper-V virtual motherboard does not contain a parallel port, and therefore it cannot support any devices that require communicating over a parallel port interface. When you do find parallel ports on servers, you might find a hardware key that software applications use as a method of combating application piracy. Therefore, collecting information about any devices found to be connected through a parallel port will raise a flag that the physical server might have a hardware key or other special requirement that may exclude it as a virtualization candidate.

Serial port devices are common in branch office locations and some data centers that have rack-based uninterruptible power supplies (UPS). Some of these UPS devices use serial ports to communicate with the server to provide notifications of power loss events and battery power operation events.

Software Inventory

The goal of the software inventory is to compile a list of all the applications installed on the servers, including the version of each application, and a list of the currently installed updates, hotfixes, or service packs. Knowing what applications are loaded on servers allows you to make decisions concerning which machines should not be virtualized. In addition, knowing the application version and update-level version will help you group excluded servers into pools for homogeneous consolidation.

Table 20-3 provides a list of the software inventory information that you should collect for each server.

TABLE 20-3 Software Inventory Information

SOFTWARE CATEGORY	INVENTORY INFORMATION
Application	Name
	Vendor
	Version
	Service pack
Updates	Name
	Version
	Application association
Hotfixes	Name
	Version
	Application association

The application name tells you the recognizable name of the application or application suite. The application vendor provides you with the name of the company that publishes the application. The application version gives you information about which version(s) of the application is installed and lets you compare how many versions of an application you have installed in your environment. The service pack information tells you the latest consolidated set of updates installed on the server. The updates information indicates individual updates currently installed on the server. The hotfix information details any special updates installed on the server.

Services

A list of installed services on each server provides information you need to determine which services are currently started and actively using resources. Certain applications might be installed as services, so collecting this information can also help identify servers that may need to be excluded as virtualization candidates. Table 20-4 provides a list of the information that should be collected for each service installed on a server. The key values are the service name, startup mode, current state, and display name.

TABLE 20-4 Services Inventory Information

SERVICE CATEGORY	INVENTORY INFORMATION
Service	Name
	Service type
	Current state
	Caption*
	Description*
	Display name
	Path
	Started
	Startup mode
	Account name

Optional information

Considerations During Inventory

Teresa M. Lewandowski, PMP, Principal Project Manager
Microsoft Consulting Services

When planning how and when you're going to take the hardware and software inventory that you need for Hyper-V, there are a few things you may want to take into consideration. How current does your inventory need to be? How long will it take you to complete the inventory based on the size and complexity of your environment? If you need current and fresh data, but it takes you weeks or months to complete an inventory, what is likely to change over that time period? Some options you might consider are:

- Deploy multiple inventory collection systems globally that can capture a snapshot very quickly.

- Freeze your environment through the deployment phase.

- Keep the data fresh by establishing or integrating into a change control process and have the Hyper-V project tied into their approval process.

The data you collect must be usable, so watch for regional settings and language packs when performing a global inventory. Language packs will return error messages or prompts that require interpretation. Regional settings can return variations on the results—for example, in Germany and other European countries, a comma may be used in place of a decimal point.

Another risk to the accuracy of the inventory data is the presence of any ongoing projects that will be implementing or deploying new servers or applications during the server virtualization project. Request a high-level timeline from your project stakeholders to identify all current IT projects. You should use this information to develop your risk plan and note any such projects that will affect your assessment and deployment. One final suggestion is that you inquire about any performance tuning initiatives that will affect the environment but will be conducted more or less under the radar of any formal project or approval process.

Performance Monitoring

Monitoring the performance of your servers provides critical information about the workload performance that the physical server is supporting and provides insight into what performance issues might exist if the physical server is virtualized. Performance monitoring is the most time-intensive data collection task. To ensure that you have captured the peaks and lows of the performance signature for a server, you need to capture a representative sample of data over a long enough time span to provide you with accurate information.

When monitoring performance, you want to ensure that you capture data within a sufficient time span that allows it to capture events such as an end-of-the-month finance process, backup processes, any impact on performance from scheduled tasks, and any other impact on performance from normal application execution. Performance data should be captured for a minimum of one month so that all the monthly cycles of performance are captured. To minimize the impact of collecting performance data on the server, the data should be collected at a set interval, measured in minutes or seconds. For example, if you use Reliability And Performance Monitor to collect the data, using a five-minute interval instead of the default value of one second can result in obtaining a sufficient data sample while minimizing the data collection impact on the server.

Table 20-5 shows the monitoring parameters for the major categories of performance counters that should be monitored: processor, memory, network, and storage. Many of these parameters are performance counters embedded in the operating system that may require multiple instances to be collected. For example, on a multiprocessor server, you should monitor performance counters for all processor or core instances.

TABLE 20-5 Performance Monitoring Information

PERFORMANCE CATEGORY	MONITORING PARAMETERS
Processor	Total percent of processor time
	Percent of processor time for each processor instance
	Percent interrupt time
Memory	Available bytes of memory
	Pages per second
Network Interface (for each adapter instance)	Total bytes per second
	Bytes received per second
	Bytes sent per second
Logical Disk	Disk read bytes per second
	Disk write bytes per second
	Average disk bytes read per second
	Average disk bytes written per second

Processor monitoring is focused on the utilized percent of the processors in the server and the percent interrupt time. The percent of processor time tells you how much processing power the workloads on the server require over time. This information is collected for each processor or core instance. The percent interrupt time tells you how much time the processor is spending processing interrupts from devices and peripherals.

Memory performance monitoring gathers information on the available bytes and pages per second performance counters. Available memory bytes represent the amount of physical memory in bytes available for a process to request for allocation, or the amount of free physical memory. Pages per second is the rate at which pages are read from or written to the hard disk to resolve page faults. Because disk I/O is one of the slowest components in the system, understanding the level of pages per second supported by the storage subsystem is important to the assessment of how well a server will perform in a virtual machine.

Network performance monitoring gathers information on the total bytes that are sent and received per second on each network adapter. If you are consolidating several physical servers on the same Hyper-V server, you must analyze the cumulative network throughput of multiple, executing virtual machines as a function of time. This information will drive decisions to connect virtual machines across multiple virtual networks to balance the network workload across multiple host adapters.

Storage performance monitoring gathers information on the amount of data flowing between the memory and the disk subsystem. This is accomplished by using Logical Disk counters that provide real-time and average values for read and write operations to the physical disk. You must collect this information for each physical disk attached to the physical server.

> **NOTE**   Because of the volume of information that needs to be collected and the potentially large number of servers for which to collect performance data during the discovery phase of a virtualization project, it is not recommended to use a script as a collection mechanism. Instead, you should use a software application that is specifically designed to capture performance data and minimizes any server performance impacts that might skew the collected information.

Environmental Information

When collecting information during the discovery phase, one area that is easily overlooked is environmental information. Although it's not used in any decision making during the server virtualization project assessment or planning phases, it can be critical information to justify the project and demonstrate the cost reduction benefits of virtualization.

When you virtualize a physical server, you enable that physical server hardware to be repurposed or retired. If your data center or remote office locations are low on rack or floor space, or if the current level of power consumption prevents the expansion of servers at the rate that is required to support actual business growth, being able to retire or repurpose servers can be an extremely strategic benefit.

During the discovery process, you should collect information that identifies all the different server manufacturers and server models in your target environments, including the number of each model deployed. In addition, each rack-based server requires a certain amount of vertical space in the rack called a *Unit*, or *U*. The manufacturer product specifications should indicate how many Us a server requires in a rack. This can range from a 1-U server to as big as 10 Us. For server blades, you need to know how much rack space the enclosure requires in the rack and how many blades a rack typically holds. You need to take this data into account during the project assessment phase to ensure that you properly account for the rack space used by blade servers.

In addition to collecting rack space information, you also need to collect the power consumption information for each server model. Each server typically has a power supply rated to handle the load of a server that is fully expanded. The larger servers also have redundant power supplies. The manufacturer product specification should have the power-consumption rating listed in watts or kilowatts.

Rack-based servers have supporting peripherals such as disk storage cabinets, Keyboard-Video-Mouse (KVM) switches, network switches, and other rack-mounted devices that are no longer needed when the server is virtualized. Collecting this information will help you better estimate the total rack space or power consumption that can be eliminated if the virtualization project goals are fully realized. Unfortunately, automating the collection of information about supporting peripherals is not a simple task, so this can be a time- and resource-intensive task.

 ON THE COMPANION MEDIA   To assist you in collecting environmental information, you will find an Microsoft Office Excel spreadsheet named Potential Cost Savings JobAid.xls in the \Chapter Materials\Job Aids folder. This spreadsheet includes a worksheet called Cost Savings Details that contains the recommended environmental information to collect and some predefined calculations to assist in producing an environmental cost savings. A second worksheet is included that provides a summary view of the potential cost savings achieved by eliminating the supporting hardware.

Automating the Discovery Process

When collecting inventory, performance, and environmental data, you will want to automate the process as much as possible. You may already use tools in your environment that can assist in collecting the required data. For example, if you use an asset management system like System Center Configuration Manager (SCCM) or Systems Management Server (SMS), you can create queries that help you assemble the list of servers based on any predefined exclusion rules. You can also generate inventory data from these types of asset management systems.

If you have a server monitoring system like System Center Operations Manager (SCOM) or Microsoft Operations Manager (MOM) deployed in your environment, you can use the Virtualization Candidate report contained in the Server Virtualization management pack to help you determine which physical servers are candidates for virtualization.

If you do not currently use or do not have the budget to deploy these types of asset management systems or server monitoring solutions, then you can use scripts and other tools to help you collect the required discovery data.

Scripts

Included in this resource kit are sample scripts created to help you collect discovery data.

 ON THE COMPANION MEDIA The sample scripts are stored on the companion media in the \Chapter Materials\Chapter 20\Scripts folder.

Table 20-6 provides a list of the included scripts, a short description of each script, and the execution requirements or resulting output for a script. The scripts use different application programming interfaces (APIs) like Windows Management Instrumentation (WMI) and Active Directory Systems Interface (ADSI) to collect the data.

TABLE 20-6 Sample Data Collection Scripts

SCRIPT NAME	DESCRIPTION	REQUIREMENTS
GetDomains.vbs	Collects a list of domains within a forest	If you have multiple forests, you need to execute it in each forest using domain administrator–level credentials. Before use, you must modify the script to change the default domain name from Contoso.com to reflect your domain name.
GetSites.vbs	Collects the server-to-site mapping from Active Directory	You will be required to log on to a domain controller in the forest using domain administrator credentials and then execute GetSites.vbs. The script produces a comma-delimited file (.csv) with a line for each server containing the site name and the server name.
GetSubnets.vbs	Collects a list of subnets assigned to each Active Directory site	The script requires domain administrator–level credentials to execute. The GetSubnets.vbs script produces a .csv file with a line for each site containing the site name and the assigned subnets.

SCRIPT NAME	DESCRIPTION	REQUIREMENTS
GetComputers.vbs	Collects a list of computer accounts in the domain	The script requires domain administrator–level credentials to execute and must be executed in each domain. The GetComputers.vbs script produces a .csv file with a line for each computer containing the domain name, computer name, operating system, service pack version, and date when the computer account password was changed. Before use, you must modify the script to change the default domain name from Contoso.com to reflect your domain name.
GetSoftware.vbs	Collects a list of installed software from a server	The script requires local administrator–level credentials to execute and must be executed on each server. The GetSoftware.vbs script produces a .csv file with a line for each application containing the computer name, software application name, application publisher, and application version.
GetServices.vbs	Collects a list of installed services on a server	The script requires local administrator–level credentials to execute and must be executed on each server. The GetServices.vbs script produces a .csv file with a line for each service containing the computer name, the service name, the type of service, the current service state, the defined caption, the defined description, the display name, the path to the service executable, whether the service is started, the startup mode, and the name of the account used to execute the service.

General Purpose Tools

Using specialized tools to collect discovery data is a better approach than using scripts because they typically execute faster, although they may be harder to customize or combine data if multiple, dissimilar tool sets are used. Following are some general purpose tools that can be used to collect Active Directory and server information.

SystemTools Exporter Pro

SystemTools Exporter Pro is a SystemTools Software, Inc., tool that you can use to document the configuration of Active Directory and Windows servers deployed in small- to medium-size environments. Exporter Pro is designed to capture a wide range of information that includes:

- Active Directory objects (organizational units, groups, computer accounts, and so on)
- Machine software configuration (operating system, services, applications, and so on)
- Machine hardware configuration (processors, memory, network, disk space, and so on)
- Machine network configuration (TCP/IP, MAC address, and so on)
- Machine processes
- Machine applications
- Machine shares
- Machine local users and groups
- Security settings for files, shares, printers, services, and registry
- Files and directories
- Scheduled tasks
- User rights
- Account and audit policies
- Logged-on users

Exporter Pro can collect this data for any server or workstation in your environment, provided that you are running the tool in the context of an account with sufficient permissions and access rights to the data sources.

After you define the component data that you want to collect, Exporter Pro uses a combination of methods and protocols to retrieve information from Active Directory and directly from targeted machines including registry, WMI, and Active Directory queries. Exporter Pro provides predefined registry templates to capture installed software and updates information, and it has predefined WMI queries to capture machine-specific information including hardware, operating system, processes, event log information, and more. Exporter Pro also supports user-defined Active Directory queries. Exporter Pro saves the collected data into delimited output text files for export into any database or spreadsheet program to perform data analysis and produce reports.

> **NOTE** More information on SystemTools Exporter Pro can be obtained online at *http://www.systemtools.com/exporter/index.html*. A 30-day trial version is also available for download from the site.

Microsoft Active Directory Topology Diagrammer

The Active Directory Topology Diagrammer (ADTD), formerly named ADMAP, is a free tool that you can use to document various aspects of an Active Directory infrastructure. ADTD retrieves information from Active Directory using the Lightweight Directory Access Protocol (LDAP), Active Directory Services Interface (ADSI), and ActiveX Data Objects (ADO). Table 20-7 lists the Active Directory information that is captured with ADTD.

TABLE 20-7 ADTD Component Documentation List

ACTIVE DIRECTORY COMPONENT	DOCUMENTATION
Domain	Domain name
	Domain functional level
	Number of domain controllers (DCs)
	Domain controller details
	Name
	Operating system
	Service pack level
	Global catalog servers
	Number and types of trusts
	Number of user accounts
	Operations master role owners
	Schema version
Organizational Unit (OU)	OU hierarchy
	OU name
	Group Policy Object (GPO) links
Site	Site name
	Intersite topology generator (ISTG)
	Total number of DCs in each site
	Total number of subnets in each site
	Domain controllers in each site
	Global catalog servers in each site
	Subnets in each site
	IP and SMTP site links
	Replication connections within a site
	Replication connections between sites

ACTIVE DIRECTORY COMPONENT	DOCUMENTATION
Application Partition	Application partition name
	Total number of DCs that host the application partition
	Domain controllers that host the application partition

To use the ADTD, you need only to provide the name of a global catalog server in an Active Directory domain, choose the level of information desired, and enter the account name and password of an account with administrator credentials, if so prompted. By default, the information that ADTD gathers is logged to a file (ADTD.csv). However, a main benefit of this tool is that you can choose to have ADTD create Microsoft Visio 2003 (or later) diagrams of the data, including the Active Directory domain structure, OU hierarchy, application partitions, and site topology, links, and replication connections.

 ON THE COMPANION MEDIA You can download the single ADTD installation file, ADTD.Net Setup.msi, from *http://www.microsoft.com/downloads /details.aspx?familyid=cb42fc06-50c7-47ed-a65c-862661742764*. The ADTD installation procedure creates a directory to hold the ADTD binaries and documentation. An entry for ADTD is also created in the Programs menu.

Port Scanners

Port scanners can cycle through a range of IP addresses and attempt to connect to every standard port in an effort to identify servers and applications executing on a server. Port scanning success depends on the ability to interrogate all ports and the server or network not having mechanisms like firewalls built to prevent port scanning security intrusions. In addition, if a port scanner finds an IP address that has open ports, it must be able to identify the type of device (server, printer, network router, or other) that it has found. Although you can technically use this type of tool, the use of port scanners is not recommended to gather server information in your environment.

NOTE Port scanning is considered a security risk, and most organizations have policies against using these types of tools. If you need to use a port scanner, be sure to inform your networking management or security team before you use it.

IP/Subnet Sweeping

Although port scanning can be considered a security risk, most organizations are more lenient when it comes to scanning a subnet via a ping test, also known as ping sweep. The information from this type of scan can assist you in identifying assets that are not domain members or legacy assets that are no longer in use.

For a simple ping test across a subnet, you can use a port scanning tool—just be sure to do a "ping only" test as opposed to a port scan.

Discovery and Assessment Tools

Microsoft and third-party independent software vendors (ISVs) have developed tools that can assist in the discovery and assessment project phases.

Microsoft Assessment and Planning

Microsoft has released a tool in the Solution Accelerator line called Microsoft Assessment and Planning (MAP) Toolkit. The MAP Toolkit Solution Accelerator is a powerful inventory, assessment, and reporting tool that can inventory small or large IT environments without requiring installation of agent software on servers. MAP provides data and analysis features that can simplify the planning process for server migration to Windows Server 2008 and Windows virtualization technologies such as Windows Server 2008 Hyper-V and Virtual Server 2005 R2. MAP can also assist in the planning process to migrate desktops to the Windows Vista operating system and upgrade to Microsoft Office 2007.

MAP is implemented as a 32-bit or 64-bit Windows application that uses Microsoft SQL Server Express Edition or SQL Server 2005 Standard or Enterprise Editions to store collected data, as well as Microsoft Office Word and Microsoft Office Excel to generate reports. Figure 20-1 shows the main Assessments page of the MAP application. The Actions menu is divided into three sets of actions: Inventory, Reports And Proposals, and Useful Information. The Virtualization, Deployment, Security, Operations, and Product Information buttons are all links to more information that support the MAP solution accelerator.

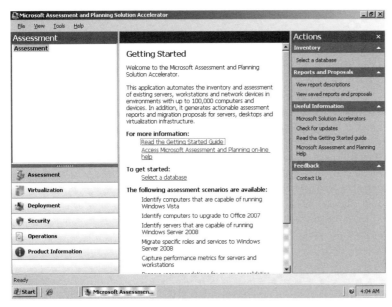

FIGURE 20-1 MAP startup page

Server Discovery Methods

MAP is able to identify servers using one or more discovery methods. The discovery methods make it easy for you to find the specific servers that are assessment targets. The discovery methods use automated processes to identify servers or allow you to specify servers through a batch mode or individually. MAP supports the following server discovery methods:

- **Directory Domain Services**   This method allows you to query a domain controller via the Lightweight Directory Access Protocol (LDAP) and select computers in all or specific domains, containers, or OUs. Computers that have not logged on for more than 90 days will not be inventoried.

- **Windows networking protocols**   This method uses the WIN32 LAN Manager APIs to query the Computer Browser service for computers in workgroups and Windows NT 4.0 domains. This method is limited to the servers listed in the computer browser service and can be affected by network firewalls.

- **File import**   Using this method, you can create a text file with a list of computer names to inventory. Each computer name should be listed on a new line, and the file should not use delimiters, such as comma, period, tab, and so on.

- **IP address range scan**   This method allows you to specify an IP address range. The wizard will then scan all IP addresses in the range and inventory only those computers.

- **Manual definition**   This method enables you to test and to inventory a few computers at a time by manually entering the computer names.

Inventory Methods

MAP uses multiple inventory methods to collect information about a computer or device. Three methods are used: WMI, Simple Network Management Protocol (SNMP), and Remote Registry.

WMI is required in all assessment scenarios to collect hardware, device, and software information from a remote server. The following server operating systems support WMI in a default installation:

- Windows Server 2008
- Windows Server 2003 or Windows Server 2003 R2
- Windows 2000 Server

SNMP is a network discovery protocol that allows you to collect or set network attached device attribute values remotely. By default, Windows operating systems do not enable the SNMP service. This inventory method is used if you select the option to generate reports listing all SNMP devices. Otherwise, this method is not used.

The Remote Registry service is used to find the roles installed on a server. It is also required for running the Performance Monitoring Wizard. This service is installed on Windows servers by default, but Windows Server 2008 does not start it by default.

The following conditions must exist for this inventory method to be successful:

1. The Remote Registry service must be started.
2. The Windows Firewall Remote Administration Exception must be enabled.
3. You must authenticate using local administrator–equivalent credentials.

MAP Operations

MAP follows a three-step process for server discovery and assessment. The first step involves selecting or creating the database used to store the inventory or performance data. The second step requires inventory and performance data collection. MAP provides a single wizard, the Performance Metrics Wizard, to perform this task. If a server has not been inventoried previously, the wizard will inventory the server prior to starting performance data collection. The last step is assessing the servers for virtualization candidates, performing consolidation planning, and producing analysis reports. MAP performs all of these actions using the Server Consolidation And Virtualization Wizard.

Creating the Database

When you install MAP, you can either point to an existing SQL 2005 database server or install SQL Server 2005 Express Edition on the MAP server. MAP can collect information from a single location where MAP is installed or from multiple locations across a wide area network (WAN), storing data in the specified database. MAP uses all the data in a single database to perform virtualization candidate assessment and consolidation planning. If you need to perform assessment or consolidation planning for each location individually, you must collect the data for each location individually and store it in a separate database for each location.

Performance Metrics Wizard

The Performance Metrics Wizard manages the process of remotely monitoring key disk, network, and CPU performance counters on remote servers. You choose the consolidation candidate servers to monitor by creating and importing a text file containing the computer names into the wizard. Performance monitoring is required to determine the placement of virtual machines within the virtualization infrastructure. The Server Virtualization And Consolidation Wizard completes the server placement analysis using the results of the Performance Metrics Wizard.

The Performance Metrics Wizard executes the following tasks:

- Performs an inventory of the monitored server
- Conducts detailed physical and logic disk performance counters monitoring
- Conducts detailed memory utilization monitoring
- Conducts detailed network utilization monitoring
- Conducts detailed processor utilization monitoring
- Conducts performance monitoring over a long time span

When you run the Performance Metrics Wizard, it requests a text file that contains all of the server names. The server name can be a host name, NetBIOS name, or the host fully qualified Domain Name System (DNS) name. After you provide the text file, the wizard requests the credentials to use for remote WMI calls. The user credentials must be a member of the local administrators group on the monitored servers. You can specify a single set of credentials to use for all servers or separate credentials for each server.

After you have provided account credentials, you must specify the time period to collect performance metrics. You configure this by specifying a date and time for completion. It is recommended to run the performance collection for a period of at least 30 days to collect representative server performance events.

Figure 20-2 shows the MAP dialog box that is displayed while the data collection is active. As you can see, MAP provides inventory, performance metrics collection, and report generation status.

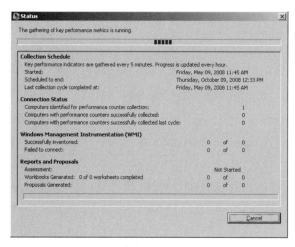

FIGURE 20-2 MAP status dialog box

The Performance Metrics Wizard generates a single Office Excel worksheet that provides a summary of the overall performance metrics collection and details for processor, network, physical disk, and logical disk utilization. In addition, it provides a connection statistic that documents the number of times that the MAP tool failed to communicate with the servers.

NOTE The MAP Server Virtualization and Consolidation Wizard features, functions, and output are described in Chapter 21, "Server Virtualization Project: Assessment Phase." For more information and to download MAP, refer to *http://www.microsoft.com/MAP*.

PlateSpin PowerRecon

PlateSpin, Ltd., produces a product called PowerRecon that is available in different versions, depending on the feature set that you need for your Hyper-V server virtualization project: PowerRecon Inventory Edition performs hardware and software inventory functions; PowerRecon Standard Edition adds performance monitoring to the inventory capability; and PowerRecon Standard Edition with Planning version adds consolidation assessment and planning to the Standard Edition. These PowerRecon versions are targeted for use in long-term server consolidation and data center optimization projects. PlateSpin also provides a PowerRecon Project Edition that includes all of the features found in the PowerRecon Standard Edition with Planning; this edition is designed for projects of limited duration.

NOTE Novell acquired PlateSpin, Ltd., in early 2008. Please note that the product names might be rebranded before this book is published. For more information on PowerRecon, refer to *http://www.platespin.com/Products/powerrecon/*.

PlateSpin PowerRecon is a sophisticated tool set for medium to large enterprises that provides an end-to-end analysis and consolidation planning software solution for server consolidation and virtualization projects. Specifically, PowerRecon offers the following key features:

- Hardware, software, and services inventory collection and reports
- Server and workload resource utilization collection and reports
- Workload consolidation and distribution planning and modeling

PowerRecon supports inventory and utilization data collection for Windows, Novell SuSE, RedHat, Sun Solaris SPARC, and other x86 operating systems.

Hardware, Software, and Services Inventory Collection and Reporting

PowerRecon can be deployed in a single instance or multi-instance configuration that supports inventory data collection ranging from small-scale, single location scenarios to enterprise-wide, geographically distributed scenarios. Each instance of PowerRecon can support up to 2,000 servers with the ability to aggregate the data collected by each PowerRecon server to a single, master location for centralized analysis and planning.

PowerRecon collects inventory data without requiring the installation of a software agent, instead gathering data through instrumentation that is built in to the supported operating system platforms. Hardware inventory data for each targeted server includes processor, memory, network, and disk resources. Software inventory data includes host operating system, installed and running applications and services, and installed service packs and updates.

Server and Workload Resource Utilization Collection and Reporting

PowerRecon can collect server and workload utilization information for any and all computers in its inventory. Utilization information is available to create charts and reports that allow analysis of server processor, memory, network, and disk space resource usage. PlateSpin provides a management pack to configure MOM 2005 to integrate with PowerRecon. The management pack activates all of the data counters required by PowerRecon and configures a five-minute monitoring interval.

PowerRecon comes with many predefined but customizable reports that document static hardware inventory data, deployed software and services, utilization metrics, and consolidation planning. Filters are also available to produce reports focused on specific server groupings and constrained resource utilization time periods.

Workload Consolidation and Distribution Planning and Modeling

PowerRecon includes a consolidation planning module that provides the ability to create consolidation scenarios with candidate workloads based on the server and workload utilization data gathered using PowerRecon. Consolidation scenarios can be constrained to include only specific workload types and resource utilization time periods for modeling purposes. Projected workload growth and variations can also be factored into consolidation scenarios.

Power Recon consolidation scenarios allow you to determine the minimum number of servers needed to consolidate a defined set of workloads or consolidation workload candidates and distribution across a defined set of servers. Server templates are defined for use in consolidation scenarios and model target virtualization hosts for workload distribution. PowerRecon provides several predefined server templates, or you can define new server templates configured to meet the standards defined in your environment. The information provided to define a server template includes the following general data:

- Server name, make, and model
- Total cost of ownership, rack unit requirements, and power consumption characteristics
- Host virtualization software (used to define the overhead associated with the virtualization system)

The following hardware configuration parameters and resource utilization limitations are also defined for each server template:

- Number of processors and speed
- Memory allocation
- Disk space allocation
- Total processor, memory, and disk space percentage thresholds
- Total disk operations and network bandwidth thresholds

You can configure server templates with different processor, memory, disk, and network bandwidth allocations and apply them to consolidation scenarios to determine the most cost-effective architecture that can support a defined workload set.

PowerRecon can generate summary and workload reports that contain the results from the consolidation scenarios, including comparisons of pre-consolidation utilization with post-consolidation projections, and workload distribution recommendations. PowerConvert, the PlateSpin tool that is used for physical-to-virtual machine conversions, integrates with PowerRecon to implement server consolidation plans and workload distribution recommendations.

Summary

This chapter outlines the discovery phase of a typical server virtualization project. The discovery phase focuses on collecting data required to support the assessment and planning and design phases. The data collected during the discovery phase is used to define servers that are good candidates for virtualization, and when virtualized, which combinations of server workloads to combine on Hyper-V servers for optimum resource utilization.

During the discovery phase, you collect information that includes Active Directory forests, domains, sites, and subnets, and you match that information to physical locations. You compile a list of servers that are within the target scope for the project. You collect hardware and software inventory information for each target server, as well as key performance counter information over a minimum period of 30 days, so that you can analyze peak, minimum, and average values for processor, memory, network, and storage utilization. You leverage the server hardware inventory data during the project assessment phase to determine how many server virtualization candidates have hardware specifications that allow them to be reused or redeployed as Hyper-V servers to offset capital investment. From the environmental information collected, you will be able to produce a benefits analysis report in the assessment phase that estimates the amount of rack space, power consumption, and heat dissipation that will be eliminated if target servers are virtualized.

In large environments, inventory, performance metrics, and environmental data collection automation is crucial. Therefore, you were also introduced to several Microsoft and third-party ISV software tools that can help you automate the discovery phase data collection.

Additional Resources

The following resources contain additional information related to this chapter.

- Microsoft Script Center, a resource that provides information about writing scripts to collect Windows computer information locally or remotely, available at *http://www.microsoft.com/technet/scriptcenter/default.mspx*
- Connecting to WMI on a Remote Computer, a resource that gives you instructions on how to connect to the WMI provider on a remote computer and query any WMI interface available, available at *http://msdn2.microsoft.com/en-us/library/aa389290.aspx*
- WMI Tasks for Scripts and Applications, a resource that has sample scripts for collecting data in different scenarios, available at *http://msdn2.microsoft.com/en-us/library/aa394585.aspx*
- Microsoft Assessment and Planning Solution Accelerator, a resource that includes detailed information about the MAP solution accelerator and related solution accelerators and also provides a link to download MAP itself, available at *http://www.microsoft.com/MAP*
- PlateSpin PowerRecon, a resource that provides a link to the PlateSpin home page, where you can get more information on the PowerRecon and PowerConvert tools, available at *http://www.platespin.com*

## CHAPTER 21

Server Virtualization Project: Assessment Phase

During the assessment phase of a server virtualization project, the architecture design team focuses on using the information collected during the discovery phase to determine which servers are good candidates for server virtualization. This involves analyzing the hardware, software, and performance data on a per-server basis against a set of defined limits. Hardware limits are defined by the virtual hardware available in the Hyper-V virtual machine. Performance limits are defined by the performance capabilities of a virtual machine. Currently installed software on a server can exclude a server for lack of vendor support for the application in a virtualized environment or performance requirements imposed by the application that exceed the established limits.

Identifying a Server Virtualization Candidate

You start the process of identifying server virtualization candidates with a list of physical servers that are in scope for the virtualization project. Using a set of hardware- and performance-based limits, you will place each physical server on the virtualization candidate list or you will exclude it from that list. Hardware limits are defined by the virtual hardware capabilities of a Windows Server 2008 Hyper-V virtual machine and physical hardware used for the Hyper-V server. These limits include the amount of memory, the number of processors, the maximum disk space, the number of network adapters required, and other special hardware requirements. Performance limits vary based on the configuration of the physical server being used as the Hyper-V server. The best values to use are those derived from actual tested performance of virtual machines running on the server. Evaluating a server using performance information also allows you to identify physical servers that have more resources than they need for the workloads they are running.

The process for identifying a virtualization candidate is really more about identifying physical servers that should be excluded from the virtualization candidate pool. The assumption is that any physical server remaining in the pool after the limits have been applied is a candidate for virtualization. This is a phased approach; you first determine exclusions based on hardware limits, then you determine exclusions based on performance limits, and finally you determine exclusions based on software application support. An exclusion triggered at any phase of the assessment immediately excludes a candidate from the pool.

Virtual Machine Hardware Limits

Windows Server 2008 Hyper-V virtual machines have a predefined set of hardware limitations. The one piece of virtual machine hardware that will change based on the server hardware is the processor. This is because of the architecture of Hyper-V and the fact that the processor is not emulated but exposed directly through to the virtual machine. Therefore, the virtual machine hardware will see the same processor that the server has installed. If the server has a 3.0-GHz physical processor, the virtual machine will have a 3.0-GHz virtual processor. Table 21-1 provides the hardware limits of the virtual machine.

TABLE 21-1 Virtual Machine Hardware Limits

HARDWARE FEATURE	MAXIMUM LIMIT
Number of processors	4
Processor speed (MHz)	Server processor speed
Memory	64 gigabytes
Number of network adapters	8 – Synthetic
	4 – Emulated
Number of disk controllers	2 – IDE
	4 – SCSI
Number of hard disk drives per controller	2 – IDE
	64 – SCSI

HARDWARE FEATURE	MAXIMUM LIMIT
Hard disk drive size (per drive)	2040 gigabytes – IDE or SCSI VHD
	256 terabytes – Pass-through (IDE or SCSI)
Total disk space	528.33 terabytes – IDE + SCSI VHD
	65 petabytes – Pass-through
Number of serial ports	2
Number of parallel ports	0

Assessing Hardware Limits

Hardware limits of virtual machines are used as the first layer of determining whether or not in-scope physical servers should be excluded from the server virtualization candidate pool. Hardware limits include basic components such as memory, disk space, processor, and network. More advanced or specialized limits include the presence of serial or parallel ports.

When performing the assessment process, you must evaluate the physical server against each virtual machine hardware limit. If the physical server fails any of the hardware limits tests, it is (typically) immediately excluded from the server virtualization candidate pool, and the assessment process should proceed with the next physical server. If the physical server passes all hardware limit tests, it should proceed to the next phase of assessment, performance thresholds.

Processor Hardware Limits

A Windows Server 2008 Hyper-V virtual machine has a processor hardware limit of four virtual processors. A physical server can have processors with one or more cores. A virtual processor is the logical equivalent of a physical processor core. Although this is a hardware limit, it is not a valid assessment to say that any physical server that has more than four processor cores should be immediately excluded from the server virtualization candidate pool. Processor consumption should be the driving assessment criterion for a physical server. It is possible to have a four- or eight-processor core server that has low processor consumption that falls under the defined hardware limit. Therefore, you should defer any assessment of processor limits until the performance assessment.

Memory Hardware Limits

A Windows Server 2008 Hyper-V virtual machine has a virtual hardware memory limit of 64 gigabytes (GB) of memory. Assessing the server based on the amount of physical memory installed ignores how much memory the server is actually consuming. This approach relies only on the hardware inventory information for the physical server to make a decision. Using this approach, if the physical server has more than 64 GB of memory installed, it would typically be excluded from the server virtualization candidate pool. Most servers deployed today do not effectively utilize all of the memory they have installed. Before a server is officially added to the excluded servers list, you should conduct a performance assessment to determine the peak amount of memory the server actually uses.

> **NOTE** Available memory on the server is a prime limiting factor for how many virtual machines can be running concurrently. To optimize the number of virtual machines that you can place on a Hyper-V server, you should reevaluate the memory allocation based on actual usage when a physical server is migrated to a virtual machine.

> **NOTE** Windows Server 2008 Standard edition has a physical server limit of 32 GB of memory. A virtual machine on a server running Windows Server 2008 Standard edition cannot achieve the 64 GB maximum allowed on a memory due to this limitation.

Network Adapter Hardware Limits

A Windows Server 2008 Hyper-V virtual machine has a virtual hardware limit of 12 active Ethernet network adapters: 8 synthetic adapters and 4 emulated adapters. Each Ethernet adapter can range from 10 megabits per second (Mbps) to 10 gigabits per second (Gbps). If a physical server under consideration requires more than 12 active network adapters in order to connect to more than 12 different networks, or if it requires more than 12 network adapters at the maximum speed that your network allows, the physical server should be excluded from the server virtualization candidate pool. If the physical server under consideration requires network adapters that are not Ethernet (for example, if they use token ring or other technology), the physical server should be excluded from the server virtualization candidate pool.

Disk Hardware Limits

Windows Server 2008 Hyper-V was designed to support very large hard disk configurations. A Windows Server 2008 Hyper-V virtual machine has two virtual hardware limits for hard disks that must be assessed. The first is the size of a single disk partition. A virtual hard disk (VHD) attached to a virtual IDE controller or a virtual SCSI controller has a maximum partition size of 2040 GB. With the addition of pass-through disks in Hyper-V, a Logical Unit Number (LUN) used as a pass-through disk has the 256-terabyte limitation of the NTFS file system. Therefore, if any single hard disk partition on the physical server is larger than 256 terabytes, the server cannot be virtualized.

The second is the total amount of disk space attached to the physical server. A virtual machine using VHD storage has a limit of 528.33 terabytes of disk space that can be attached. Using pass-through disks, a virtual machine has a limit of 65 petabytes. Therefore, if the physical server has more than 65 petabytes of disk space, the server cannot be virtualized.

Depending on your approach to virtual machine disk storage, VHD or pass-through disks, that option should be used to evaluate if the physical server exceeds the hardware limits of the virtual machine.

> **NOTE** Virtual disk controllers do not have features like RAID. If the source server has hard disks connected to hardware RAID controllers, they will be seen as the partitions and volumes exposed to the operating system and attached to SCSI or IDE controllers during the physical to virtual machine migration. If you want the performance from RAID, then you must ensure that the server disk subsystem where the VHD files are stored or the pass-through disk volumes are configured with hardware RAID.

Peripheral Port Hardware Limits

A Windows Server 2008 Hyper-V virtual machine has a virtual hardware limit of two serial communication ports and zero parallel communication ports. The serial ports are named pipes connections and are not direct connections to the physical ports on the Hyper-V server. Virtual machines cannot connect to devices plugged into the Hyper-V server's physical serial ports, but they can connect to software-based ports via the named pipes communication channels.

If the physical server has more than two *active* serial ports or if the serial ports require a specialized device to be plugged into the server's serial port, the server should be excluded from the virtualization candidate pool.

If the physical server has devices connected to any parallel ports, the server should be excluded from the virtualization candidate pool.

> **NOTE** Parallel ports are no longer supported because physical servers no longer have parallel ports included as part of the hardware. Parallel ports were mainly used for two purposes: locally attached printers and dongle devices for software piracy. Printers are now mostly network attached, and dongles are either USB based or not used any more.

Establishing Performance Thresholds

During the discovery phase, you collected performance data for memory, processor, disk, and network components. Although you can compare this data against the performance limits of a virtual machine, you should establish a set of thresholds within which a physical server must remain to be a candidate for server virtualization. The thresholds define the performance limits that a virtual machine can experience on average. If the physical server's average performance exceeds the thresholds that you set, the physical server should not be placed in the server virtualization candidate pool.

The performance thresholds for server virtualization candidates can be defined as a percentage of the available resources in a virtual machine or as an actual threshold value. If a percentage is specified, you must convert it to a value for use in the formulas. Thresholds such as processor speed and memory can be easily defined because they are fixed values. Thresholds for disk throughput are not as simple to define because there are so many variations based on how you configure the disk subsystem. Thresholds for network throughput are affected by the number of network adapters in the system. Table 21-2 provides some sample threshold percentages and respective values for single instances of hardware.

TABLE 21-2 Sample Virtual Machine Performance Thresholds

HARDWARE FEATURE	MAXIMUM LIMIT	THRESHOLD %	THRESHOLD VALUE
Processor speed (MHz)	Server processor speed (for example, 3000 MHz)	80	2400 MHz
Memory	64 gigabytes	N/A	64 gigabytes
Disk I/O	Server disk limit (for example, 200 MB/second)	70	140 MB/second
Network speed (per adapter)	700 Mbits/second	80	560 Mbits/second

When virtual machines need to scale to multiple instances of processors, disks, and network adapters, the thresholds need to be adjusted accordingly up to the maximum limit for each virtual hardware component. For example, a Hyper-V virtual machine can have up to four processors, so the maximum threshold value for processor is the threshold value for a single processor multiplied by four.

Virtual machine thresholds cannot exceed the physical hardware of the server. For example, a virtual machine can have a maximum threshold of 64 GB RAM, but if the Hyper-V server does not have 64 GB of RAM, it is not possible to run a virtual machine of that size.

IMPORTANT Since hardware performance changes rapidly and the configuration of the hardware that you are using can affect actual performance, you should establish a baseline for the selected server hardware for the maximum limits of the disk and network I/O. This will provide realistic values to use in your calculations and will result in better estimates.

Assessing Performance

Actual performance data for the processor, disk, and network are used as the second layer of to determine whether or not in-scope physical servers should be excluded from the virtualization candidate pool. The following sections for the processor, disk, and network provide guidance on how to assess performance limits and exclude servers that exceed the performance limit.

Processor Performance Assessment

When assessing a physical server to determine whether or not the processor requirements will exclude a physical server from the virtualization candidate pool, you must look at the processor utilization across the entire data collection window. Using the average value allows you to ignore peak values while making the virtualization candidate decision. Peak values become very important during the planning and design phase, however, as you combine workloads to determine the optimized placement of virtual machines on a host.

> **NOTE** Today's processors come with multiple cores and hyperthreading capabilities. Reference to a processor refers to a physical processor that has a single core, or it refers to the core of a multiple core processor. Hyperthreaded logical processors are not considered a separate processor for performance planning.

To determine the average processor consumption in megahertz (MHz) for each processor in the physical server, you need to know the average processor utilization, the speed of the physical server's processor, and the number of cores in the processor. After you have the average processor utilization for each processor or core in the physical server, you can sum the values to obtain the total average processor consumption:

Total Average Processor Consumption (MHz) =
SUM (physical server processor speed × each processor [or core's] average processor utilization)

When you have the total average processor consumption in megahertz for the physical server, you need to compute the total virtual machine processor threshold for the host.

Total Virtual Machine (VM) Processor Threshold (MHz) =
Single Processor Threshold (MHz) × four virtual processors

If the total average processor consumption is less than or equal to the total virtual machine processor threshold, the physical server is a candidate for virtualization. If the total average processor consumption is greater than the total virtual machine processor threshold, the physical server is exceeding the defined threshold and should not be added to the pool of virtualization candidates.

The following scenario provides an example. You have an older server running Windows 2000 Server on a dual-processor, 2000-MHz Intel Pentium IV server (single core). Processor 1 has an average utilization of 24 percent, and processor 2 has an average utilization of 29 percent. The total average processor consumption would be the sum of 24 percent multiplied by 2000 (0.24 × 2000 MHz) and 29 percent multiplied by 2000 (0.29 × 2000 MHz), which equals a total average processor consumption of 1060 MHz. Your new Hyper-V server is using 3.0-GHz (3000-MHz) processors, so your virtual machine threshold processor consumption equals 3000 MHz for a single processor virtual machine and 12000 MHz for a four-processor virtual machine. If the threshold percentage is 80 percent, the total virtual machine processor threshold value would be 9600 MHz. Using the defined logic, the total average processor consumption for the physical server (1060 MHz) is less than the total virtual machine processor threshold, so based only on processor performance consumption, this server would be added to the virtualization candidate pool.

Memory Performance Assessment

A Windows Server 2008 Hyper-V virtual machine has a memory virtual hardware limit of 64 GB of memory. During memory performance assessment, you compare the actual consumption of memory in the physical server to the memory performance threshold. This approach focuses on detecting physical servers that have more physical memory than they require, and depends on performance information that captures available bytes of memory data.

Most servers deployed today in customer environments do not effectively utilize all of the installed memory. This is typically due to standardized server configurations. Comparing the actual physical memory used on the server instead of the installed amount of memory can identify servers that do not fully utilize their memory resources.

Disk Performance Assessment

Hard disk performance is a key concern when assessing a virtualization candidate. Combining multiple disk workloads onto a single machine can have a great impact on disk performance. Proper planning of the disk subsystem and workload optimization is extremely important and will be covered in Chapter 22, "Server Virtualization Project: Planning and Design Phase."

Disk performance is measured in reads and writes (bytes per second). As part of the discovery phase, you collected the actual and average values for these two counters. To assess the performance of a server for exclusion from the virtualization candidate pool, you should use the average read and write values in bytes per second. Using peak values would potentially exclude too many servers based on a disk performance anomaly that occurred during the discovered data timeline.

Serial Attached SCSI (SAS) drives typically have a performance throughput of 90 megabytes per second (MB/second) per drive. Most servers use hardware RAID subsystems in which multiple hard disks are joined together to improve disk performance and provide data fault tolerance or drive failure protection. If you assume a minimum configuration of three disks for a RAID set, the combined performance of that RAID set would have the potential for 270 MB/second throughput.

To determine if the physical server exceeds the disk performance thresholds, you must compare the average disk read and write consumption in bytes per second on the physical server with the virtual machine disk read and write performance threshold that you established as a baseline for the server hardware performance.

If the total average disk read or write performance is less than or equal to the total virtual machine disk read or write threshold, the physical server is a candidate for virtualization. If the total average disk read or write performance is greater than the total virtual machine disk read or write threshold, the physical server is exceeding the defined threshold and should not be added to the pool of virtualization candidates.

Network Performance Assessment

During the discovery phase, you collected network performance data for send and receive operations in bytes per second for each network adapter. Assessing a physical server for exclusion from the virtualization candidate pool is based on the approach for assigning network resources and the speed of the network adapters in the Hyper-V server. A virtual machine connects to a virtual network, which is bound to a physical network adapter on the server. Because you can have one or more virtual machines connected to a virtual network, you can have one or more virtual machines sharing a single network adapter on the server. Gigabit Ethernet network adapters are the minimum recommended standard for the server.

In Chapter 3, "Hyper-V Architecture," you learned that a virtual network adapter has no coded performance limit. Because of the new architecture of Virtualization Services Client (VSC)/Virtualization Services Provider (VSP) and the VMBus, a virtual machine using integration components and a synthetic network adapter can achieve the limit of the physical network adapter. You also learned that each virtual machine can have up to 12 network adapters that can range from 10 Mbps to 10 Gbps.

To determine the total average network send and receive throughput in bytes per second for the physical server, you need to know the average network send and receive throughput in bytes per second for each network adapter. After you have the average network send and receive throughput in bytes per second for each network adapter in the physical server, you can sum the values to obtain the total average network send and receive throughput requirements for the candidate server:

Total Average Network Send Throughput (bytes per second) =
SUM (each network adapter average send throughput in bytes per second)

Total Average Network Receive Throughput (bytes per second) =
SUM (each network adapter average receive throughput in bytes per second)

Then you can obtain the total average network throughput:

Total Average Network Throughput (bytes per second) =
Total Average Send Throughput + Total Average Receive Throughput

When you have the total average network throughput in bytes per second for the physical server, you need to use it to compute the total virtual machine network throughput threshold for the Hyper-V server. This consists of the sum of the throughput for each virtual machine network adapter in bytes per second. This value will vary depending on the speed of network adapters in the Hyper-V server:

Total VM Network Throughput (bytes per second) =
SUM (each Network Adapter Throughput) (bytes per second)

If the total average network throughput of the candidate server is less than or equal to the total virtual machine network throughput, the physical server is a candidate for virtualization. If the total average network throughput is greater than the total virtual machine network throughput, the physical server is exceeding the defined threshold and should not be added to the pool of virtualization candidates.

> **NOTE** The practical limit for a single gigabit virtual network adapter is about 900 megabits per second. Assuming that the Hyper-V server has gigabit Ethernet adapters, the recommended performance threshold for a candidate server is 80 percent of that value, or 720 megabits per second for a single virtual network adapter.

> **NOTE** During the planning process, you will need to identify all candidates that have high network utilization and potentially dedicate a physical adapter and virtual network for their use. This can reduce the number of candidates that can be placed on a Hyper-V server, depending on the number of network adapters available in the server.

Assessing Application Support Limits

Application support limits are used as the third layer to determine whether or not in-scope physical servers should be excluded from the virtualization candidate pool. Not all applications are supported in a virtual machine environment. Some vendors might support their application in a virtual machine environment, but support only a specific vendor's implementation because of virtual hardware, performance, or other limitations.

During the discovery phase, software inventory information was collected for every server. This information is the base for you to work from to determine any application support issues. You first need to produce a list of unique software applications across the entire in-scope server list. This list should contain an entry for each different version or service pack revision of an application because vendors might require a certain version or service pack for virtualization support. After you have the list of unique software applications, applications can be eliminated from the list by determining whether or not they are supported by the vendor if used in a virtual environment.

Microsoft applications are the best place to start to reduce the list. Microsoft understood that application support would be a huge issue for virtualization technology and placed requirements in its Windows Server System Common Engineering Criteria early on to ensure that all new server-based applications that ship must be supported in a Microsoft virtualization environment unless a waiver is granted. The following applications are not supported in a virtualization environment.

- Microsoft Speech Server
- Microsoft Exchange 2007 Unified Messaging Role

All other Microsoft server applications are supported in virtual machines running on Hyper-V. Determining the support for the remaining third-party applications in the list requires you to visit the support Web sites for each product or to directly contact the vendor. Be sure to verify the version of the application supported and compare it to the inventory list.

When you have a list of applications not supported in Windows Server 2008 Hyper-V, you can exclude any server that is running those applications in production.

Using MAP for Assessment and High-Level Planning

Chapter 20, "Server Virtualization Project: Discovery Phase," provided an overview of the Microsoft Assessment and Planning (MAP) Toolkit and how to use the Performance Metrics Wizard to collect the inventory and performance data you need to perform an assessment. When you have all that data, you can use the information in the beginning of this chapter to exclude the servers based on pure hardware and software issues. After you exclude servers that exceed the server hardware configuration or run applications that cannot be virtualized, the next step is to assess the remaining servers based on the performance data for virtualization candidates, performing consolidation planning to figure out how many Hyper-V servers are needed and producing analysis reports.

In the earlier sections of this chapter, we talked about how to assess a physical server candidate manually using hardware, performance, and software approaches. MAP can perform the hardware and performance assessment from a single wizard called the Server Consolidation And Virtualization Wizard.

NOTE MAP does not currently assess software applications for vendor support or compatibility. To achieve this step, you can take the software inventory data and filter the list of potential candidates that MAP will assess from a hardware and performance perspective.

Virtualization Candidate Identification and Server Consolidation Scenarios

The Server Virtualization And Consolidation Wizard is used to complete a virtualization assessment and provide a high-level consolidation estimate based on a server hardware configuration that you provide. This wizard performs the following functions to complete the assessment:

- Consumes the inventory and performance monitoring data collected by the Performance Metrics Wizard

- Excludes servers from the candidate pool based on performance information

- Allows you to interactively provide a Hyper-V server configuration that will be used for consolidation placement

- Determines the number and placement of virtual machines on a Hyper-V server

- Provides detailed reports and proposals describing which servers can be virtualized and on which computers (Virtual Server 2005 R2 or Hyper-V) the consolidation process can be carried out

NOTE The consolidation planning that MAP performs with the Server Virtualization And Consolidation Wizard is intended to provide a high-level estimate of what consolidation might look like. It does not perform optimal placement of the virtual machines to minimize the number of servers required, nor does it validate that the servers you are attempting to consolidate are from the same location. In Chapter 22, you will learn more about the approach for detailed analysis.

Walking Through the Server Virtualization And Consolidation Wizard

When you run the Server Virtualization And Consolidation Wizard, the first page you will see is the Select Virtualization Technology page. It prompts you to define which virtualization technology you would like to use for server consolidation placement recommendations: Virtual Server 2005 R2 or Windows Server 2008 Hyper-V.

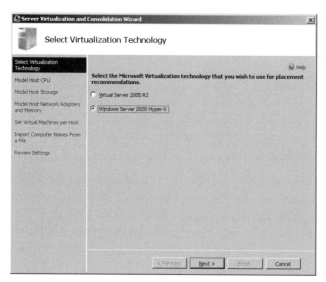

On the Model Host CPU page, the wizard requests the configuration of the host machine that you will be using for the consolidation. You specify the processor information: CPU type (Intel or AMD), CPU model, the number of physical processors, the number of cores per processor, the number of hyperthreads per core, the L2 and L3 cache sizes, and the front side bus speed of the server.

NOTE The Server Virtualization And Consolidation Wizard assumes that the hardware configuration you specify in the wizard will be used by all servers in this assessment and consolidation scenario. If you want to use a different hardware configuration, then you must run the wizard again using the same set of servers and specify a different configuration.

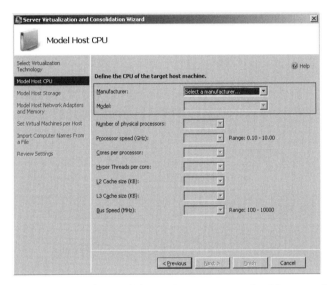

Next, open the Model Host Storage page. On this page, the wizard requests the storage configuration the host will use: disk type and speed, capacity per disk, RAID level, number of disks in the RAID level, and the cache size. The disk type and capacity that you specify will be used for each drive in the RAID array if you configure one.

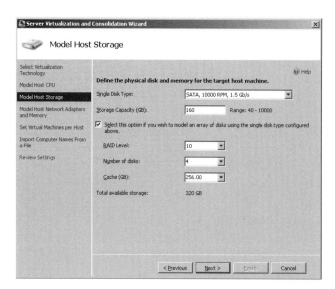

The last hardware information the wizard requests is the networking and memory configuration of the host, including network adapter speed, number of adapters, and amount of memory in gigabytes.

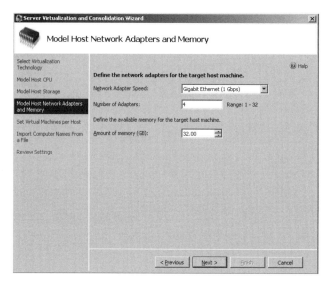

After you have defined the hardware, you can choose to have the maximum number of virtual machines placed on the host or select a fixed number on the Set Virtual Machines Per Host page. If you choose the maximum, the wizard will continue to add virtual machines until one of the hardware resources exceeds the threshold of the defined host configuration. If you select a fixed number, the wizard will not exceed that number even if there is capacity remaining on the server.

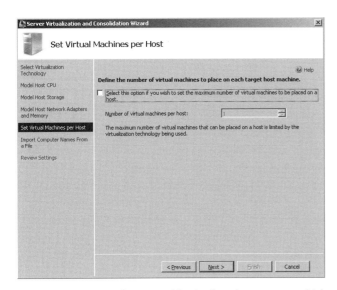

Now you are ready to provide the list of servers on which you want to run the assessment and consolidation process by providing a filename in the textbox on the Import Computer Names From A File page. The file should be in the same format that you used for the Performance Metrics Wizard, with one server per line.

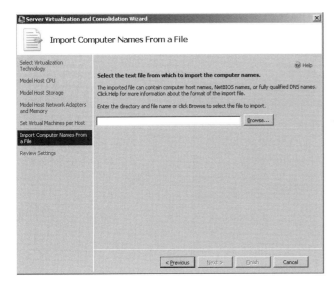

Let the Server Inventory Feature Find Your Servers for You

Jay Sauls, Senior Program Manager
Solutions Accelerators Core Engineering Team

For situations in which you may not have a complete list of server machine locations or aren't sure what's running on them, you can use the Server Inventory features in the MAP Toolkit to help you out. By choosing the Identify Servers That Are Capable Of Running Windows Server 2008 option in MAP, you can have the tool query Active Directory and run an IP address scan to get a comprehensive inventory of servers in your environment, including data on what kind of hardware those servers are running on and what roles they have installed. Using this list, you can then identify candidates for consolidation and build a list of machines for performance counter collection. At that point, you can run the Server Consolidation Wizard in the MAP Toolkit and get virtualization placement recommendations.

After you have provided all of the inputs required by the wizard, MAP uses the assessment and placement algorithms to determine which machines are virtualization candidates and then attempts to consolidate them on one or more hosts. The Status message box allows you to monitor the progress of the assessment.

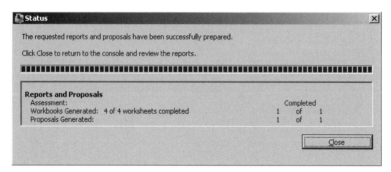

When the wizard is complete, it produces a Microsoft Office Excel spreadsheet that includes its virtualization candidate recommendations and host placement of the candidates and a Microsoft Office Word document that provides a prewritten customer proposal summarizing the consolidation results.

How Does Virtualization Guest Placement Work?

Jay Sauls, Senior Program Manager
Solutions Accelerators Core Engineering Team

There are two main stages of computing the virtualization guest placement recommendations in MAP. The first stage involves converting the measured utilizations of the physical machines to the equivalent utilization on the specified hypothetical host machine. For example, a 40 percent CPU utilization measured on a 2.4-GHz Intel Pentium 4 physical machine might be converted to a projected 8 percent utilization of a quad-core Intel Xeon 5300 series CPU specified for a virtualization host machine. These utilization conversions are performed using technology from the System Center Capacity Planner (SCCP) tool, which provides a library of hardware models. Using this technology, utilization of CPU, disk I/O, and network I/O is converted from the measured physical environment involving real machines to the projected utilization that would occur on the hypothetical host machine.

When equivalent resource utilizations have been computed for the host machine, the second stage of placement computation takes place. The following factors are taken into consideration to ensure that a host machine will have enough resources to handle guests:

- CPU
- Network I/O
- Disk subsystem I/O
- Memory
- Disk space

Additional checks are made to ensure that the virtualization environment can handle the guest operating system (for example, to make sure placement of an x64 guest operating system is not allowed on Virtual Server 2005).

The placement process begins by allocating a new hypothetical VM host machine (Host A). Then the most heavily utilized guest machine is assigned to Host A. The projected utilization of Host A with the guest machine on it is calculated by the SCCP engine. If the guest fits on the host without overutilization of any of the host resources, then the attempt is made to place the next-most-heavily utilized guest on Host A. This process is repeated until no additional guest machines are found that can be placed on the host. At that point, a new hypothetical host is allocated (Host B), and attempts are made to fit any remaining guests on Host B.

This process continues until all guests that can be fit on a host are placed and there are no unassigned guests left. Guests may fail to fit because they're unsuitable for the host or because the guest requires so many resources that even if the guest is placed on a host by itself, it still overwhelms the resources of the host.

Identifying Cost Savings

Assessing the positive cost and environmental impact of virtualizing servers by calculating the potential savings is a task that you do not want to overlook during the assessment phase. Every server you virtualize is a server available for a repurposed workload or for retiring to save on power, cooling, and space. You can use this information to justify the server virtualization project and demonstrate the cost benefits. The following sections detail the information that you will need to gather to calculate cost savings and return on investment (ROI) by hand.

> **NOTE** Microsoft has released a tool called the Virtualization ROI Tool to assist in automating this process. For more information and to access the tool, go to *http://www.microsoft.com/virtualization/roitool/default.aspx.*

Capital Cost Savings

After you have finished assessing which physical servers are candidates for virtualization, you can calculate the potential savings in capital costs. Capital costs include the cost of physical components like servers, switches, routers, racks, keyboard-video-mouse (KVM) devices, and disk systems. The major component in capital cost savings is the number of physical servers that will not have to be purchased in the future. When you virtualize existing physical servers, you obtain cost savings in two ways. The first is the elimination of the need to refresh that physical server at a future date. The second is the potential offset of purchasing physical servers for Hyper-V servers based on reusing existing equipment.

To calculate the future cost savings of not having to refresh a server, you need to know when that server was planned for refresh and the predicted cost for the refresh hardware. Companies generally have a two- to five-year refresh plan for servers, with the industry average being five years. Create a spreadsheet that has columns for the next five years and add a row for each virtualization candidate server. Place the cost savings for each virtualization candidate in the appropriate year. Now calculate the sum of the values in the columns to obtain an annual capital cost savings analysis for the next five years.

For virtualization projects in which you are not virtualizing existing physical servers but are looking to create new servers using virtualization, the calculation is slightly different. In this case, you would first determine the number of physical servers that you would be deploying and the cost for those servers; this will be the capital cost for physical deployment. Then you will need to establish the standard server configuration that you will deploy for each Hyper-V server and determine your purchase cost for that server. Next you would determine the number of Windows Server 2008 Hyper-V servers that you would need to host those same servers if they were virtualized. If you have not done the planning yet for those servers, you can assume a consolidation ratio to determine the number of required servers. Multiply the number of required servers by the cost for a standard Hyper-V server to obtain the virtualization deployment capital cost. Subtract the virtualization deployment capital cost from physical deployment capital cost to obtain the potential virtualization capital cost savings.

For a complete estimate, you actually need to take into account not just the servers, but also the supporting peripherals, such as disk cabinets, KVMs, network switches, and other rack-mounted devices that might be connected to the servers that would no longer be needed if the servers are virtualized. Unfortunately, collecting that information in an automated fashion is not a trivial task because these devices do not typically run an operating system, nor are they listed as objects in Active Directory.

If you want to include this information, you can take one of two approaches. The first approach is to make an estimate based on the number of servers that you are virtualizing. For KVM switches, if the standard KVM switch used in the data center is an eight-port model, assume that you will eliminate a KVM switch for every eight servers virtualized. You can use the same approach for network switches, using the number of switch ports in the calculation. Disk cabinet estimates in this approach are more problematic unless there are standards for server deployments—so that you know that every server model *X* was deployed with disk cabinet *Y*. An additional problem with this approach is you will not know the location where you will be eliminating a device.

The second approach requires you to perform a physical inventory for every server in the virtualization candidate pool to identify the attached peripherals that would be eliminated. The second option is more accurate and provides location information, but it takes longer and costs more.

After you decide which approach to use, you need to determine the standard purchase cost for each of these devices and the numbers of each that you will be eliminating on a location basis to calculate the potential cost savings in additional supporting peripherals.

Environmental Savings

During the discovery phase, you should have identified all the different server manufacturers and models. If you did not collect rack space usage and power consumption information for each server, you need to go to the manufacturer's Web site and obtain that information. When you have all this information for each different server manufacturer and model, you can calculate the environmental savings.

Rack Space Savings

The standard data center server rack is a rack 42 units (U) high. Servers typically range anywhere from 1U to 10U of rack space each. Therefore, the number of servers per rack will vary, but the number of units per rack is constant. For the rack space savings calculation, you can assume that all rack space is used in every rack. If the racks are not all completely full, your calculation for the number of racks that you will empty by virtualizing all the servers will actually be on the conservative side.

To determine the amount of rack space saved, just determine how many servers of each manufacturer you will virtualize, multiply that number by the rack space used by the servers, and then calculate the sum of those values. To determine the number of actual racks that you would free up in the data center, assuming the standard 42U rack, take the total rack space saved and divide by 42.

Power Consumption

Every server requires power to operate, and most servers operate on a 24-hour basis, 365 days a year (or you hope they do). Most servers are designed with a power supply that can provide power to the system if it is fully populated, and the power supply runs at only around 75 percent efficiency. It is usually a safe assumption to use the power supply rating in watts in your calculations.

To calculate the power consumption of each server, you also need to know the cost of a kilowatt-hour of electricity. Each location that you have servers at probably has a different cost per kilowatt-hour, so you need to collect those different values. In the sample calculations provided, an average value is used.

When you have the power consumption of each server's power supply, the number of servers, and the cost per kilowatt-hour for electricity, you can use a series of formulas to determine the total cost saved from virtualizing your candidate servers. The first formula is the total power consumed by a certain model server in a year (in kilowatt-hours) assuming continuous operation:

Power consumption per server per year (kilowatts) =
(watt rating of power supply × 365 × 24)/1000

After you have the consumption determined by server model, you can determine the total consumption by multiplying by the number of servers of that model that you are virtualizing and calculate the sum of those amounts:

Total power consumption per year (kilowatts) =
SUM (power consumption per server model × quantity of servers)

Now you have the total power consumption per year for the virtualization candidates in kilowatt-hours. To obtain the power consumption cost, multiply the total power consumption per year by the average cost per kilowatt-hour:

Total savings per year =
Total power consumption per year × average cost per kilowatt-hour

To provide an example of the potential power savings, assume that there are 500 servers in the virtualization candidate pool, each server has a power supply rating of 750 watts, and the cost per kilowatt hour is $.10:

Power consumption per server per year (kilowatts) = (750 × 365 × 24)/1000 = 6570

Total power consumption per year (kilowatts) = 6570 × 500 = 3,285,000

Total kilowatt savings per year = 3,285,000 × $.10 = $385,000

Cooling Costs

In addition to the power consumption of the servers during normal operations, servers also generate heat that must be dissipated. Because the servers run continuously, they generate heat continuously and therefore the cooling must be provided continuously. For simplicity in calculating cooling costs, you can assume that every watt of power consumed by a server generates one watt of heat that needs dissipating.

Engineers and scientists have not been able to design and produce a cooling system that is 100 percent efficient, so you should assume an efficiency percentage in the 60 to 70 percent range to be conservative. This means that if you need to dissipate 1,000,000 kilowatts of heat and your cooling system is 65 percent efficient, it will require 1,000,000/.65 or 1,538,461 watts of power for cooling.

Using the numbers from the previous 500 server example (3,285,000 kilowatts of annual power consumption and assuming one watt of power equals one watt of heat), there would be 3,285,000 watts of heat to dissipate. Assuming 65 percent efficiency for the cooling system, 5,053,846 watts of power would be required annually to cool the servers. At a cost of $.10 per kilowatt-hour, the savings would be $505,385 in cooling costs.

IMPORTANT   Do not forget to subtract the space, power, and cooling requirements of the Hyper-V servers from the potential savings numbers to obtain a more accurate prediction of real savings.

NOTE   The Microsoft Virtualization Return on Investment (ROI) tool available at *http://www.microsoft.com/virtualization/roitool/default.mspx* can help you assess the potential for environmental savings, but it does not use your actual virtualization candidates' server data to perform the calculation.

ON THE COMPANION MEDIA   To assist you in collecting cost savings information and producing a potential cost savings summary, you will find a Microsoft Office Excel spreadsheet named Potential Cost Savings JobAid.xls in the \Chapter Materials\ Job Aids folder. This spreadsheet has a single worksheet that contains the recommended information to collect and some predefined calculations to assist in producing a potential cost savings for servers and environmental items like power, cooling, and space. The spreadsheet does not take into account the space, power, and cooling of the new servers.

Summary

This chapter described how to approach the third phase of a virtualization project—the assessment phase. Assessment focuses on taking a list of potential virtualization server candidates and determining which servers should be removed from the candidates list based on hardware, performance, and supported software limitations. You learned how to set performance thresholds and how to use those thresholds to make exclusion decisions.

In order to minimize the effort to assess the performance data collected in the discovery phase, the chapter provided you with an example scenario using the Microsoft Assessment and Planning (MAP) solution accelerator Server Virtualization And Consolidation Wizard to perform the virtualization candidate assessment and consolidation planning. After you have processed all the servers, the remaining pool of virtualization candidates will be used in the next phase of the virtualization project, the planning and design phase. During this phase, you will take the high-level consolidation planning that the MAP tool provided and perform a detailed analysis and optimization of workloads.

In addition to learning how to assess a server for virtualization, you also learned how to use the virtualization and environmental information to calculate the savings in servers, space, power, and cooling.

Additional Resources

The following resources contain additional information related to this chapter.

- Windows Server System Common Engineering Criteria available at *http://www.microsoft.com/windowsserversystem/cer/default.mspx*

- Windows Server System software not supported within a Microsoft virtualization environment available at *http://support.microsoft.com/kb/897614*

- Microsoft Virtualization ROI Tool available at *http://www.microsoft.com/virtualization /roitool/default.aspx*

- Microsoft Assessment and Planning (MAP) solution accelerator available at *http://technet.microsoft.com/en-us/library/bb977556.aspx*

## CHAPTER 22

Server Virtualization Project: Planning and Design Phase

The server virtualization project planning and design phase consists of three main parts: determining Hyper-V server configuration requirements to support the migration of virtualization candidates, determining how to best consolidate the workloads of the virtualization candidates to maximize the number of virtual machines per Hyper-V server, and designing the overall solution requirements for the virtualization environment. The primary goal of server consolidation is to maximize the number of virtual machines hosted on each server. The number of virtual machines hosted on a physical server is called the *consolidation ratio*. The higher the consolidation ratio, the lower the capital cost of the virtualization infrastructure.

Server consolidation planning can be performed using two different strategies. The first strategy consists of defining Hyper-V server hardware specifications and then determining the consolidation ratio that can be achieved. The second strategy involves determining the desired consolidation ratio and then defining the required Hyper-V server hardware specifications. Table 22-1 identifies the key pros and cons for each strategy.

TABLE 22-1 Consolidation Strategies

CONSOLIDATION STRATEGY	PROS	CONS
Define hardware specifications and obtain the consolidation ratio	Ability to define standard configurations	Lower workload optimization
	Lower support costs	Lack of hardware configuration optimization

CONSOLIDATION STRATEGY	PROS	CONS
Define the consolidation ratio and obtain the hardware requirements	Higher consolidation ratio Higher workload optimization	Each server has a custom configuration Higher support costs More complicated planning process

The first strategy simplifies the planning process by defining Hyper-V server hardware specifications including the number of CPUs, amount of memory, amount of disk space, number of disks, number of network adapters, and speed of the network adapters. This provides a set of hardware constraints that you can use to perform workload optimization. Workload optimization then becomes a matter of determining the combination of virtualization candidate workloads that will maximize resource utilization without exceeding performance constraints. Although there are advantages to managing sets of standard Hyper-V servers, this strategy may not result in workload combinations that fully optimize resource utilization.

The second strategy centers on defining optimized workload combinations that drive Hyper-V server hardware requirements. Essentially, you begin by identifying a target consolidation ratio. For example, if you establish a target of hosting 20 virtual machines on a Hyper-V server, the consolidation ratio will be 20 to 1. During consolidation planning, you define sets of 20 virtualization candidates that provide the lowest resource utilization when their workloads are combined. The combined workload performance requirements define the Hyper-V server hardware requirements, including processor, memory, disk, and network interface card specifications. With this strategy, the principal benefits are achieving the required consolidation ratio target and Hyper-V server hardware configurations tuned to support defined workload combinations. However, Hyper-V server management can be more complex and potentially more costly using this method because you will be maintaining nonstandard hardware configurations.

As in most cases, choosing the best strategy for your environment consists of analyzing the tradeoffs and deciding which one allows you to best achieve your budget, business, and technical project goals. Predefining standard hardware configurations streamlines the configuration process and increases the likelihood of obtaining cost discounts from hardware vendors, but it does not always provide the optimum consolidation ratio and has a lower resource utilization margin. Predefining the consolidation ratio ensures an optimum hardware configuration to support workload requirements, but there is a prospect of increased capital and management costs. In this chapter, you will learn about the consolidation process using the first strategy, by establishing standard Hyper-V server hardware specifications and then planning to maximize the consolidation ratio in this type of environment.

Defining Hyper-V Server Configurations

Before you start the consolidation planning process, you must define Hyper-V server hardware configurations. The hardware configurations and their performance characteristics form the constraints that you must consider when you combine virtualization candidates in optimized consolidated workloads. During a server consolidation project, you will most likely virtualize physical servers in a range of locations with varying numbers of virtual machines on Hyper-V servers. To provide for variance in the consolidation ratio, you should establish a minimum of three standard Hyper-V server hardware configurations: a smaller-size server for locations such as branch offices, a medium-size server for medium office locations or small data centers, and a large-size server for major data center locations. Most small locations such as branch offices may typically have four virtualization candidates or less, a medium-sized office or small data center location may have 20 or more virtualization candidates, and a large data center could have hundreds or thousands of virtualization candidates.

Physical Requirements

Hyper-V server specifications can vary widely, since Microsoft Hyper-V supports a maximum of 192 virtual machines on each server. With the availability of quad-core 64-bit processors from Intel and AMD, storage area networks (SANs), 10,000 and 15,000 RPM Serial Attached SCSI (SAS) hard disk drives, and gigabit Ethernet, many different configurations are possible.

> **NOTE** Hyper-V supports the Intel and AMD x64 line of processors but not the Intel Itanium line of processors.

Even with the latest advances in server technology, processor or memory configurations of modern servers will naturally limit consolidation planning. Most enterprise servers range from single-processor to four-processor configurations with single, dual, or quad cores. For instance, a four-processor, quad-core server is maximized at 16 processor cores. In addition, memory limits on the latest types of servers are dependent on the memory speed selected. Slower memory allows you to use denser memory components. The typical memory ceiling is 128 gigabytes (GB), with a few systems able to achieve 256 GB of memory.

Table 22-2 provides a recommended minimum configuration for small, medium, and large Hyper-V categories. The configurations assume that virtual machines have a minimum of 1 GB of memory, another 1 GB of memory reserved for the parent partition, a minimum of one processor core reserved for the parent partition, one network adapter dedicated for parent partition communications, and one or more network adapters dedicated for virtual machine communications. Small category servers are recommended to have direct-attached storage (DAS) because of cost and management complexity. Medium and large category servers are assumed to be located in facilities that would benefit from shared storage capability of storage area networks.

TABLE 22-2 Recommended Minimum Server Hardware Configurations

SERVER CATEGORY	PROCESSOR	MEMORY	DISK	NETWORK ADAPTER
Small	1 dual- or quad-core	8 GB	DAS	2 x 1 gigabit Ethernet
Medium	2 quad-core	32 GB	SAN	5 x 1 gigabit Ethernet
Large	4 quad-core	64 GB	SAN	8 x 1 gigabit Ethernet

High-Availability Hardware Requirements

Moving from an environment with dedicated physical machines running individual applications and services to a set of consolidated workloads running in virtual machines that execute on a single server can raise the following questions:

- Are high-availability workloads likely candidates for virtualization?
- How do you guard against a hardware failure that can affect multiple virtual machines and hundreds or thousands of end users?
- How do you apply updates and service packs to a Hyper-V server without affecting running virtual machines and interrupting service to their end users?

Fortunately, Hyper-V supports a high-availability solution using Microsoft Windows Server 2008 that allows you to configure Hyper-V servers and virtual machines failover clusters. Hyper-V host clusters running on Windows Server 2008 support up to 16 nodes. Virtual machine clusters based on Windows Server 2003 support up to eight nodes in a cluster. If virtual machines use Windows Server 2008 as the guest operating system, failover clusters of up to 16 nodes are supported.

> **NOTE** Virtual machine clusters are only supported when each virtual machine cluster node is placed on a separate Hyper-V server. If multiple nodes of a virtual machine cluster exist on the same Hyper-V server, then those nodes are a single point of failure and eliminate the benefits of having a high-availability solution.

> **NOTE** Virtual machine clusters must use iSCSI for the shared disks in the cluster.

In order to create a Hyper-V host cluster, a minimum of two nodes must be used. Each node must be running Windows Server 2008 Enterprise edition or higher, as failover clustering is not included in the Windows Server 2008 Standard edition. After the nodes are installed and configured, one or more virtual machines can be manually or automatically failed across nodes. Using three or more nodes allows failover clustering to use a load-balancing method that ensures that a single cluster node does not become overburdened with failed-over workloads.

With the consolidation of multiple workloads on a single physical server, it is highly recommended that you use failover clustering to minimize service disruptions with the potential to affect a large end-user community. Even if most of your physical servers do not currently require a high-availability solution, you should evaluate which consolidated workloads require high-availability configurations in the planned virtualization infrastructure.

> **NOTE** For more information on host clustering capabilities and installation, refer to Chapter 5, "Hyper-V Advanced Features." You can also find a white paper on performing quick migrations using Hyper-V at *http://www.microsoft.com/windowsserver2008/en/us /high-availability.aspx.*

Consolidation Planning

Consolidation planning involves determining the number of Hyper-V servers required to support the candidate server workloads. The number of required Hyper-V servers depends on defined virtualization candidate groups. These groups can define physical location, administration and security strategy, and application constraints. After you have defined virtualization candidate groups, you can start the analysis process to determine the virtualization candidate workload combinations that generate the highest consolidation ratio. Then, when you have defined the workload combinations, you can look into which virtualization candidate hardware may be repurposed as Hyper-V servers.

DIRECT FROM THE SOURCE

Server Consolidation Planning

Mark Lunday, Project Manager
Microsoft Consulting Services

Server consolidation planning is a key element of project success; proper planning makes the difference between achieving well-defined goals or falling short and ending with dissatisfied customers. You must make sure to DOCUMENT ALL ASSUMPTIONS. Anything that is presumed to be fact—and anything that drives consolidation calculations—is vital to defending and understanding the budget derived from the planning efforts. Also, you should keep the business justification for the server consolidation project handy and refer back to it on a regular basis to keep the project goals and vision in sight.

Grouping the Candidates

Before you can start the workload analysis phase of consolidation planning, you must determine any grouping restrictions that affect the virtualization candidate pool. The virtualization candidate pool is the list of physical servers identified during the virtualization project assessment phase. Constraints that affect virtualization candidate groups include:

- Physical location
- Administration and security strategy
- Application

Physical location groups define the number of planned Hyper-V servers for each target location. Unless you consolidate sites as part of the virtualization project, you cannot combine affected workloads on the same server. Therefore, before you define location-based groups, make sure that you take into account any planned site consolidation. Because location information is obtained from the server data collection performed during the project discovery phase, site consolidation also must be reflected in that data.

Administration and security groups might be required if you want to implement server-based security instead of a virtual machine security strategy. Server-based security means that you create a global group in Active Directory for an administrative team, place that group in the local administrators group of the Hyper-V server, and then place only virtual machines on that server that the administrative group has the rights to manage. Although administration and security groups are technically feasible and commonly done, this results in less flexible use of the Hyper-V server resources and may increase the number of required Hyper-V servers. This also precludes implementing failover clusters between Hyper-V servers running virtual machines managed by different administration teams.

Using a virtual machine security strategy provides the most flexible configuration of the Hyper-V servers. However, it requires more complex configuration and management processes.

> **NOTE** Refer to Chapter 6, "Hyper-V Security," for a detailed discussion on how to secure access to Hyper-V servers and virtual machines.

Application groups might be required if you want to migrate servers running the same applications onto the same Hyper-V servers. You can also use the groups to define applications that should not be running on the same server for security or performance reasons. Application groups also can be applied in two different ways: dedicated or shared. The dedicated approach allows only virtual machines running a single application to be placed on a specific

Hyper-V server. The shared approach allows for a combination of virtual machines running different applications to be placed on a single server. The shared approach normally defines a limit to the number of combined applications.

Performing Workload Analysis

Workload analysis is the process of combining hardware and performance information for multiple virtualization candidates to attain the target hardware and performance thresholds for a Hyper-V server. To accomplish this, you must define thresholds for the Hyper-V server hardware configurations, collect the data for each virtualization candidates group, and perform specific calculations to determine the optimal combinations of candidates.

Establishing Thresholds

During the assessment phase of the virtualization project, you established a set of thresholds to determine whether a physical server was a good candidate for virtualization. The focus was to ensure that a virtualization candidate could have acceptable performance when migrated to a virtualized environment. During workload analysis, you need to set the thresholds for the entire Hyper-V server. These thresholds will also define reserved server resources. The reserved server resources will be used by a Hyper-V server to service local resource needs and as additional capacity for spikes in resource utilization.

Thresholds are defined for the four major components of a Hyper-V server: processor, memory, storage, and network. Table 22-3 provides a set of sample thresholds. For hardware components that can have multiple instances (processor, disk, and network), the values shown are for a single instance. Storage I/O is limited by disk performance and disk controller performance. The network interface performance is limited by the collision rate characteristics of the network and the driver configuration.

TABLE 22-3 Sample Hyper-V Server Performance Thresholds

HARDWARE FEATURE	THRESHOLD
Processor utilization	80% of maximum processing power
Physical memory utilization	80% of maximum physical memory
Disk I/O	75% of maximum disk controller throughput
Network I/O	80% of the maximum network adapter throughput

Benchmark Your Hyper-V Servers

Ken Durigan, **Architect**
Microsoft Consulting Services

The maximum values for disk and network throughput can vary widely, depending on manufacturer, driver quality, configuration, and type of technology. You should not perform any workload analysis based on assumed performance levels. It is a best practice to perform baseline benchmarks on the proposed hardware for Hyper-V servers to obtain realistic performance values. Using those values will provide a much better capacity planning capability than using theoretical maximum values.

After you have established the thresholds for the Hyper-V servers, you then determine the thresholds for each category of physical servers. Table 22-4 provides an example of thresholds for a small category server. The assumption for the hardware configuration of a small server is a single quad-core processor, 8 GB of memory, a single disk controller with a maximum throughput of 320 megabytes per second (MB/s), and a single dedicated gigabit Ethernet adapter for virtual machine use with a maximum throughput of 900 megabits per second (Mbps). Threshold values are calculated using the following formula:

Threshold Value = (Maximum Value × Quantity × Threshold Percentage) / 100

Maximum Value is the maximum performance value for a single instance of a component—for example, a 3.0-GHz processor. *Quantity* is the number of instances of a component that are available for virtual machine use—for example, the small category server has four processor cores, but one is reserved for parent partition processing, so three remain available for virtual machine use. *Threshold Percentage* is the performance threshold established to ensure that the parent partition maintains a resource reserve.

TABLE 22-4 Sample Small Server Category Threshold Values

THRESHOLD	THRESHOLD PERCENTAGE	MAXIMUM VALUE	QUANTITY FOR VIRTUAL MACHINE USE	THRESHOLD VALUE
Processor	80	3000 MHz	3	7200 MHz
Memory	80	8 GB	1	6.4 GB
Disk controller	75	320 MB/s	1	240 MB/s
Network adapter	80	900 Mbps	1	720 Mbps

Table 22-5 provides an example of thresholds for a medium category server. The assumption for the hardware configuration of a medium server is two quad-core processors (one core reserved for the parent partition), 32 GB of memory, two disk controllers with a maximum throughput of 320 MB/s each, and four dedicated gigabit Ethernet adapters for virtual machine usage with a maximum throughput of 900 Mbps each.

TABLE 22-5 Sample Medium Server Category Threshold Values

THRESHOLD	THRESHOLD PERCENTAGE	MAXIMUM VALUE	QUANTITY FOR VIRTUAL MACHINE USE	THRESHOLD VALUE
Processor	80	3000 MHz	7	16,800 MHz
Memory	80	32 GB	1	25.6 GB
Disk	75	320 MB/s	2	480 MB/s
Network	80	900 Mbps	4	2,880 Mbps

Table 22-6 provides an example of thresholds for a large category server. The assumption for the hardware configuration of a large server is four quad-core processors (two cores reserved for the parent partition), 64 GB of memory, four disk controllers with a maximum throughput of 320 MB/s each, and seven dedicated gigabit Ethernet adapters for virtual machine usage with a maximum throughput of 900 Mbps each.

TABLE 22-6 Sample Large Server Category Threshold Values

THRESHOLD	THRESHOLD PERCENTAGE	MAXIMUM VALUE	QUANTITY FOR VIRTUAL MACHINE USE	THRESHOLD VALUE
Processor	80	3000 MHz	14	33,600 MHz
Memory	80	32 GB	1	51.2 GB
Disk	75	320 MB/s	4	960 MB/s
Network	80	900 Mbps	7	5,040 Mbps

Data Preprocessing

After you have determined the threshold values for each server category and the virtualization candidate groups are identified, you can gather the required inventory and performance information and preprocess the data before workload analysis begins. Table 22-7 lists all the values that you need to assemble from the data collected during the discovery phase. Both inventory and performance data are required in order to calculate a comparison value to the threshold value. For example, processor performance counter data was collected as a percentage of processor time for each processor in the system. To transform that into a value that can be compared against the threshold, you must multiply the percentage of processor time for each processor by the processor speed in megahertz to obtain the actual megahertz consumed by each processor. Then you must sum all processor values to obtain the total processor megahertz consumed.

TABLE 22-7 Performance Categories and Parameters

PERFORMANCE CATEGORY	PARAMETERS
Processor	Processor speed in MHz
	Percentage of processor time for each processor instance
Memory	Available bytes of memory
	Total physical memory
Network (for each adapter instance)	Total bytes per second
Disk (for each physical disk)	Disk read bytes per second
	Disk write bytes per second

Recommended performance data collection intervals are every five minutes over a 30-day period. Although you could use all 8,640 values during workload analysis, it would lengthen the analysis time greatly. To simplify the analysis process and reduce the time it will take to perform what-if scenarios, you should average the data values. You can average the values over different time periods, but the recommended minimum is hourly and the recommended maximum is daily.

Workload Analysis Calculations

Workload analysis is performed separately for each group of virtualization candidates. The process involves combining multiple server workloads and comparing the combined workload to the resource thresholds. The thresholds you use are based on the server category required for the virtualization group you are analyzing. The workload resources analyzed are processor, memory, storage, and network.

The easiest way to combine workloads and compare them to the threshold values is to use the Microsoft Office Excel charting functionality or a custom SQL Reporting Services report, depending on how data is stored.

Using Microsoft Excel, you can create charts that graph performance over time for each workload using the stacked area chart type. Stacked area charts allow you to combine data from multiple series in an additive manner. This data is graphed against the reference threshold value to determine whether the combined workload resource utilization exceeds the defined threshold. Figure 22-1 shows an example of a two-dimensional stacked area chart for a processor workload over a 30-day period. In this example, the processor workload has been combined for four servers that would be migrated to a small server category. The chart shows that the threshold of 7400 MHz has not been exceeded by the combined workload.

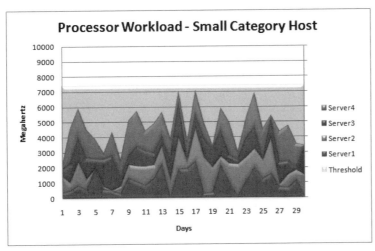

FIGURE 22-1 Stacked area chart example of processor workload from four servers

The workload analysis process involves selecting data from one server at a time and adding it to the proposed workload for a Hyper-V server. As you select candidate servers and add each one to the workload graph, the performance trend will show how the server workloads aggregate. As you add additional servers to the proposed workload, analyze each graph to determine if the threshold has been exceeded.

Figures 22-2, 22-3, and 22-4 illustrate the memory, disk, and network workload charts, respectively, for the same four server workloads featured in Figure 22-1. If you analyze each of these charts, you can see that the disk and memory workloads have exceeded the threshold values, but the network workload has not.

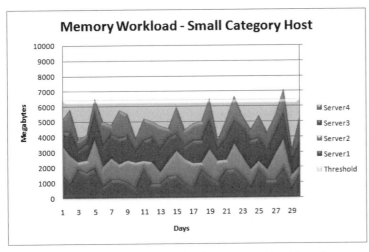

FIGURE 22-2 Stacked area chart example of memory workload from four servers

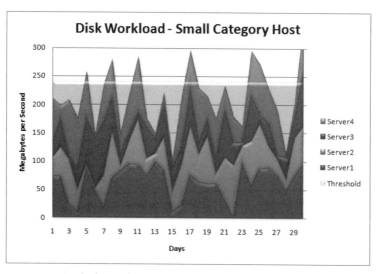

FIGURE 22-3 Stacked area chart example of disk workload from four servers

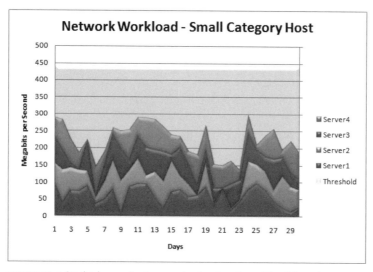

FIGURE 22-4 Stacked area chart example of network workload from four servers

If a performance threshold is exceeded, you have two options:

- Remove a server from the list to decrease the workload so that it is below the threshold and then define the set of servers that remain as a consolidation set, or

- Modify the selected servers to determine if a different set of servers would combine workloads in a more efficient manner.

To maximize the consolidation ratio for each server and obtain the optimal workload deployment, the second option should be pursued to cycle through possible server workload combinations. When you have determined that a specific server combination comes closest to defined thresholds without exceeding them, remove the servers from the virtualization candidates pool to analyze and assign the consolidated set to a Hyper-V server. Then repeat the analysis steps for the remaining pool of servers until all server workloads have been assigned to a Hyper-V server.

After you have completed a workload analysis for every server in every virtualization candidates group, you can determine the number of servers in each category that the virtualization project will require. This information will assist you in calculating a more accurate preliminary server hardware budget estimate.

 ON THE COMPANION MEDIA To assist you in performing workload analysis, you will find a Microsoft Excel spreadsheet in the \Chapter Materials\Job Aids folder named Workload Analysis JobAid.xls. This spreadsheet has multiple preformatted worksheets and stacked area graphs that allow you to enter server data averaged over a daily basis for processor, memory, storage, and network workloads. Each worksheet has a row for the threshold values and a row for each set of server data. You must edit the source data area for each chart after you enter the server data on each worksheet. Microsoft Excel 2007 allows you to select individual rows of data to chart. This provides you with a means to select servers for combined analysis easily.

Equipment Reuse

Consolidating server workloads into virtual machines can result in a large quantity of server hardware that can be repurposed in your environment. Depending on your server refresh life cycle, the reuse potential of the server hardware can vary. To determine the reusability of the hardware, you should perform an analysis of the inventory data collected during the discovery phase. Using the server category standards that you defined, analyze the server hardware inventory and identify servers that could be repurposed as Hyper-V servers. You also need to ascertain if only servers that match the server category specifications will be considered or if a server with a similar but not identical configuration is acceptable.

When analyzing the inventory data, you should first look for models of servers that match the models you plan to purchase. The servers in your inventory will probably not have all the required levels of components, but consider upgrading the servers at a cost less than purchase of a new server. When you have identified a list of possible reuse candidates by matching manufacturer models, analyze the inventory for servers that have or could have the equivalent of or better hardware specifications than the defined Hyper-V server categories.

After you have identified all possible reuse candidates, perform an analysis to compare the budget requirements associated with only purchasing new hardware to the budget requirements if you repurpose and upgrade existing server hardware as Hyper-V servers and purchase fewer new servers. This analysis will provide you with an estimate of the cost savings that you can achieve through equipment reuse.

Additional Design and Planning Tasks

Beyond performing server consolidation planning, a server virtualization project must also focus the planning and design phase to address operational changes that virtualization will introduce into an environment and the impact the changes may cause. A complete solution that can manage Hyper-V servers and virtual machines, monitor the health of the virtual environment, and address virtualization management issues is crucial to the operation of a healthy virtualization infrastructure.

Virtualization Infrastructure Management

Although Windows Server 2008 provides a Microsoft Management Console (MMC), called Hyper-V Manager, to administer the Hyper-V role and virtual machines, the interface is not designed for central management of a virtualization infrastructure that contains dozens, hundreds, or thousands of Hyper-V servers. In addition, the Hyper-V Manager console allows you to manage only a single Hyper-V server at a time. The Hyper-V Manager console is perfectly acceptable to manage up to about 10 Hyper-V servers. If your virtualization project will have more than 10 Hyper-V servers, or if you require advanced features such as a virtual machine library or advanced management features, you should investigate System Center Virtual Machine Manager 2008 (SCVMM).

For more detailed information on using the Hyper-V Manager MMC to manage Hyper-V, refer to Chapter 11, "Hyper-V Single Server Management." For detailed information on System Center Virtual Machine Manager 2008, installation instructions, and usage scenarios, refer to Chapter 12, "Server Farm Management," and Chapter 14, "Server Migration Using System Center Virtual Machine Manager 2008."

Virtualization Infrastructure Monitoring

With the Hyper-V role installed, a large set of performance counters are available to monitor Hyper-V server and virtual machine performance. However, the Windows Server 2008 Performance Monitor tool only allows you to monitor virtualization performance for a single Hyper-V server at a time. Although it is a very useful tool to gather performance data on a single Hyper-V server, which you may need from time to time, Performance Monitor does not provide a robust monitoring, reporting, and alerting solution for a virtualization infrastructure.

System Center Operations Manager 2007 (SCOM) provides a central console and an agent-based approach to monitoring, reporting, and alerting for Hyper-V servers and virtual machines. In addition, SCOM can monitor all the physical servers in your environment, allowing you to have a single console for both your physical and virtual environments. SCOM uses management packs to provide modular application-specific monitoring functionality. Microsoft provides a free management pack that monitors the virtual environment, including Hyper-V, Virtual Server 2005 R2 SP1, and SCVMM.

For more detailed information on using System Center Operations Manager 2007 as well as management pack installation and operations, refer to Chapter 15, "Server Monitoring with the Windows Server 2008 Hyper-V Management Pack for System Center Operations Manager 2007."

Virtualization Infrastructure Update Management

Windows Software Update Service (WSUS) and System Center Configuration Manager 2007 (SCCM) are Microsoft's premier solutions for update management. Although WSUS is an update management–only solution, SCCM provides additional features such as asset inventory and tracking and software deployment.

Designing an update management solution for a virtual environment has more complexities to consider than a traditional infrastructure. An update management solution for a virtual environment must account for the dependencies between Hyper-V server and hosted virtual machines. For example, it is essential that any update solution used within a virtualization infrastructure recognize when it is deploying updates to a Hyper-V server so that it does not cause an unnecessary reboot and downtime for the hosted virtual machines. Virtualization technologies such as snapshots introduce additional challenges for tracking the correct status of installed updates.

For more detailed information on how to adapt your current update management solution to support a virtualization infrastructure and to learn about key issues, refer to Chapter 12.

Virtualization Infrastructure Backup and Recovery

Backing up a virtual machine is slightly more complex than backing up a physical environment. You must be able to back up the Hyper-V server and each virtual machine. Because you might be backing up a virtual machine while other virtual machines are providing production services on the same Hyper-V server, you must design the backup solution to minimize the performance impact on running virtual machines.

When performing a backup of a Hyper-V server, you need to ensure that you back up the following information:

- Hyper-V server configuration settings
- Hyper-V server system state
- Hyper-V server file system

When performing a backup of a virtual machine, you need to ensure that you back up the following information:

- Virtual machine configuration settings
- Virtual machine system state
- Virtual machine volumes
- Virtual machine snapshot hierarchy
- Virtual machine differencing disk hierarchy

Backup Strategy

You have two primary choices for backing up a Hyper-V server and virtual machines in an online mode:

- Place a file-based backup agent on each computer (virtual machine and Hyper-V server) and back up across the network, or
- Perform a Volume Shadow Copy Service (VSS) snapshot of the Hyper-V server and virtual machines.

Using a local agent allows you to back up virtual machines as you do physical machines, but it places a performance overhead on the Hyper-V server while the backups are in progress, and there is generally no knowledge that the computer is a virtual machine. Hyper-V supports a VSS writer that allows you to back up the Hyper-V server and all virtual machines from a single agent running on the server. The Hyper-V VSS writer backup approach provides the best features of the other two approaches in one solution and is the preferred backup method.

> **IMPORTANT** An online backup of a running virtual machine can only be performed for guest operating systems with Integration Services (IS) installed, and it is restricted to guest operating systems that include the Volume Shadow Copy Service. The Backup Integration Services setting must also be enabled in the virtual machine configuration.

You can also back up virtual machines offline by shutting down or saving the state of virtual machines and backing up the files on the Hyper-V server. Backing up the powered-off or saved state files of the virtual machines provides a simple process, but it is not supported for some server roles such as Active Directory domain controllers.

Backup Applications

To use the VSS backup approach, your backup software must understand and use the Hyper-V VSS writer to take data-consistent backups with the Volume Shadow Copy Service. You need to update your existing backup software to obtain this new capability or possibly change backup software vendors to obtain this capability.

System Center Data Protection Manager 2007 (SCDPM) SP1 supports online and offline backup for Virtual Server 2005 R2 SP1 and Windows Server 2008 Hyper-V. For more detailed information on how to use SCDPM to back up your virtualization infrastructure, refer to Chapter 13, "Hyper-V Backup and Recovery."

Summary

This chapter focused on the planning and design phase of a virtualization project and its three major parts: defining Hyper-V hardware configurations, consolidation planning, and virtualization infrastructure solution planning. Consolidation planning was discussed based on a strategy of defining standard Hyper-V server hardware specifications and maximizing the virtualization consolidation ratio through optimization of workload combinations.

You learned how and why you should define different server configurations to match the various workload scales your environment may require. Using a strategy based on evaluation of actual performance thresholds, logical virtualization candidate groups, and simple formulas, you learned that consolidation planning, although possibly time-consuming, is critical and can be achieved successfully through a practical set of processes. You learned that when consolidation planning is complete, there are additional design and planning tasks that must be performed in order to develop a virtualization infrastructure solution that addresses and adapts management and operations processes to support Hyper-V servers and virtual machines.

Additional Resources

The following resources contain additional information related to this chapter.

- System Center Virtual Machine Manager 2008 available at *http://www.microsoft.com /systemcenter/scvmm/default.mspx*

- System Center Operations Manager 2007 available at *http://www.microsoft.com /systemcenter/opsmgr/default.mspx*

- System Center Configuration Manager 2007 available at *http://www.microsoft.com /systemcenter/configmgr/default.mspx*

- System Center Data Protection Manager 2007 available at *http://www.microsoft.com /systemcenter/dpm/default.mspx*

Server Virtualization Project: Pilot Phase

The pilot phase of a virtualization project focuses on validating the project planning and design. During this project phase, you need to develop the pilot objectives, identify the pilot scope, design the pilot architecture, develop a pilot plan, implement the pilot, and then evaluate its success.

Pilot Objectives

The pilot objectives should reflect key aspects of the project planning and design that must be validated prior to full production implementation of the virtualization infrastructure solution. From a high level, the pilot should focus on validating the migration, administration, management processes, and performance of the virtualized environment. Key aspects you will need to validate during a server virtualization project include the following:

- Hyper-V configuration
- Physical to virtual machine migration process
- Virtual machine provisioning process
- Administrative security model
- Update management process
- Backup and recovery process
- Hyper-V server performance

Depending on your particular server virtualization project scenario, you may have additional items to validate during the pilot phase. For example, if your project involves virtualization of a test and development environment, you would additionally validate the ability to deploy multiple virtual machines for a single test case, perform the test, and then store the virtual components back into a library for future use. In the case of a branch office virtualization project, you would add validation of policies and settings that secure virtual domain controllers. In a business continuity scenario, you would also validate the disaster recovery solution failover and failback processes. Fundamentally, validation of the technical solution and operational processes during the pilot phase ensures that the production deployment can deliver planned functionality and performance.

Pilot Scope

What makes developing a pilot plan challenging is that it must represent a scaled-down production deployment that validates the technical solution and operational processes without requiring the entire project scope to be completed. To accomplish this, the pilot scope should limit the locations and virtualization candidates to the minimum set that is required to validate the virtualization solution. All aspects of the design should be implemented (management, backup, administration, and so on), but the implementation does not have to include the full scale of the design. For example, to validate the physical to virtual machine migration process, you only need to perform a representative set of migrations—you do not need to migrate every server during the pilot phase.

Selecting Pilot Locations

During consolidation planning, physical location is used to create virtualization candidate groups that must be migrated to Hyper-V servers in the same location. A subset of these physical locations can also be used as targets during the pilot. By doing this, you can select the locations based on priority, complexity, size, proximity, or supportability. If the virtualization project involves central data center and remote office locations, the pilot scope should include one data center location and one remote location at a minimum.

Selecting pilot locations depends on the testing strategy. One strategy is to identify the locations that present worst-case scenarios. For example, the worst case can be defined as the location that has the slowest wide area network link, one that does not have a local technical support team, or the one that is logistically the hardest to reach. Using a worst-case strategy assumes that the locations selected will provide the toughest challenge during the pilot and allow the deployment team to validate the design as well as any risk mitigation plans. Not surprisingly, a worst-case pilot strategy can lengthen the pilot timeline, increase the number of pilot resources, and raise the pilot cost.

An opposite strategy is to focus on locations that minimize the pilot timeline and costs, reduce the logistics, and identify common issues. Therefore, you might select locations where technical support exists, smaller locations that can be fully migrated during the pilot, locations at which hardware already exists that can be used for Hyper-V servers, or remote locations that are close in proximity to a central location to reduce travel time and cost.

Selecting Virtualization Candidates

After you have identified the locations to use during the pilot, you should analyze the consolidation plan for each pilot location and identify the virtualization candidates that you will migrate. Each location will have one or more Hyper-V servers with an assigned group of virtualization candidates. Selection of candidates can be done at the host level or at the individual candidate level. Selecting a host selects all candidates assigned to that host. Selecting individual candidates might result in multiple Hyper-V servers needing to be deployed to obtain the designed workload optimization.

If you select individual virtualization candidates, focus on their unique value to the pilot. For example, select servers with different operating systems, different types of applications, various source hardware types (hardware manufacturer and configurations), and a range of performance characteristics. Following this approach will provide the ability to identify a larger number of potential issues during the pilot.

Pilot Architecture

Implementing the pilot requires the deployment of each virtualization solution architecture component: virtualization, administration, management, backup, fault tolerance, and monitoring. Microsoft has a product solution for each required component:

- Windows Server 2008 and the Hyper-V role provide virtualization and basic administration services.
- Microsoft System Center Virtual Machine Manager 2008 (SCVMM) provides advanced administration and management services.
- Microsoft System Center Data Protection Manager 2007 (DPM) SP1 provides backup services.
- Windows Server 2008 Failover Clustering provides fault tolerance services.
- Microsoft System Center Operations Manager 2007 (SCOM) SP1 provides monitoring services.

Each of these components integrates directly within an existing Active Directory domain infrastructure.

> **NOTE** The pilot phase recommendations presented here assume a Microsoft solution implementation. If you have other products that can provide the same functionality and are Hyper-V aware and compatible, then you can substitute those products. Substituting a non-Microsoft product might impact the integration and functionality of the pilot and increase the risk, however.

Figure 23-1 provides an architecture diagram of a data center implementation showing all the different solution components.

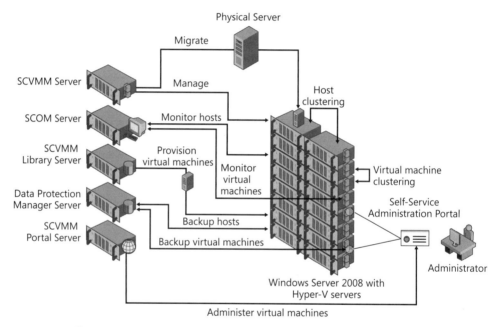

FIGURE 23-1 Pilot architecture

Planning the Pilot

A successful pilot project requires proper deployment, migration, and operational planning; communications within the project team and with the user community; an established project schedule with milestones, documented risks, and potential mitigation plan; and success criteria that will allow the project team to evaluate whether the pilot results validate the virtualization infrastructure design solution.

Creating a Deployment Plan

A deployment plan is the road map for deploying the pilot architecture. The pilot deployment plan focuses on deploying the architecture required to implement the pilot scope. As shown in Figure 23-1, the central data center architecture should include one or more Windows Server 2008 hosts running the Hyper-V role, at least one System Center Virtual Machine Manager 2008 server with the Self-Service portal option installed, a Microsoft Operations Manager 2007 SP1 monitoring console, and at least one System Center Data Protection Manager 2007 SP1 backup server. This provides the core Microsoft-supported architecture to host, provision, migrate, manage, monitor, and back up the pilot environment in the data center. Taking into account the pilot scope, you need to identify any additional data center or remote locations that need additional Hyper-V servers or other architecture services.

To ensure proper architecture installation, create a set of deployment procedures for verification during the pilot. The procedures should include the step-by-step instructions to install the basic architecture services and verify that they are operating correctly. Ensure that the instructions cover items such as service accounts, hardware and software system requirements, and operating system configuration information for each server.

Creating a Support Plan

Whereas the deployment plan focuses on the architecture that should be deployed for the pilot, the support plan focuses on the strategy and the team that will support the pilot while it is in operation. At a minimum, the support plan should answer the following questions:

- Will there be a separate team and special support phone number or process?
- Will support be limited to certain hours of the day or days of the week?
- How will global support be provided for international deployments?
- Will the pilot support team provide native-language speakers?
- What is the expected service-level agreement for response from the pilot support team?
- What is the escalation process if the pilot support team cannot resolve an issue?
- What is the rollback plan if a major issue is encountered during the pilot?

The support plan should be integrated into the development of the success criteria. Pilot support data should be analyzed to determine how service levels compare to historical operations for the migrated virtualization candidates. Data from pilot support cases should also be used to identify the top issues encountered, the problem resolutions, and any design or process change that can be used to eliminate or mitigate the issue for the production deployment.

Creating an Issue Tracking Plan

The pilot support team will be the primary interface for support calls. An issue tracking solution must be implemented and used to document and monitor issues, status, and resolutions throughout the pilot. For smaller projects, you may just use a Microsoft Office Excel spreadsheet. For larger, more complex projects that require coordination between multiple teams in various locations, an Issues Log Web part on a Microsoft Office SharePoint Server (MOSS) 2007 portal, Microsoft Visual Studio Team System, or a dedicated tracking tool are recommended. Table 23-1 provides a list of parameters that an issue tracking system should collect.

TABLE 23-1 Issue Tracking Parameters

ITEM NAME	ITEM DESCRIPTION
Issue Number	Unique number to track issue
Pilot Phase	The phase of the pilot in which the issue appeared
Date Issue Raised	The date the issue was submitted
Originator	The name or e-mail address of the issue originator
Issue Description	Detailed description of the issue
Pilot Impact	How the issue affects the pilot (resources, time, efficiency, scope, and so on)
Action	The actions that should be taken to resolve the issue
Action Owner	Who will be performing the recommended action
Due Date	When the action is due to resolve the issue
Status	Status of the issue (such as not started, under review, action in progress, and issue resolved)

In addition to collecting the issues, you should produce and review weekly reports that provide the status of the number of issues in each status category. You should also establish a set of thresholds and a process to generate alerts to ensure that issues are handled and show progress toward a resolution. For example, if an issue remains at *not started* for more than 10 days, it should generate an alert to the pilot project manager to contact the action owner and work on remedial action.

 ON THE COMPANION MEDIA   To assist in collecting and tracking issues, you will find an Excel spreadsheet in the \Chapter Materials\Job Aids folder called Issue Tracking JobAid.xls on the companion media. This spreadsheet has a single worksheet that contains columns to collect the recommended issue tracking attributes.

Using Microsoft Office SharePoint Server 2007 to Track Virtualization Pilot Success

Dave Hamilton, Architect
Microsoft Consulting Services

A good way to provide project visibility to management and the project team is to use Microsoft Office SharePoint Server 2007 during the pilot phase of the project to track issues and provide a dashboard for the pilot status. MOSS uses Web components called Web parts. Web parts are predefined modular Web interfaces that provide functionality such as document management, lists of information, calendars, task lists, and many more features. MOSS can be used to create a project portal providing document management for project documents, project task tracking, and metric reports using scorecards.

Using the Document Library Web part, you can store, track versions, and categorize project documents. Using the Project Tasks Web part, you can create a project plan complete with tasks, resource tracking, and Gantt charts. Using an Issue Tracking Web part, you can create a list to track issues throughout the project. By combining data from the Issue Tracking Web part and a Key Performance Indicator (KPI) List Web part, you can build a scorecard that contains a KPI status of the number of project issues categorized by the values in the issue status column (which include not started, under review, action in progress, and issue resolved).

Refer to the following video on Channel 9 on creating KPIs from SharePoint lists for more information: *http://channel9vip.orcsweb.com/ShowPost.aspx?PostID=214755.*

Developing a Migration Plan

The migration plan focuses on how to convert a physical server to a virtual machine with minimal service interruption to end users. The migration of physical machines to virtual machines has been greatly simplified with the introduction of tools that perform the physical to virtual (P2V) conversion in an automated fashion. System Center Virtual Machine Manager (SCVMM) 2008 is Microsoft's solution for P2V migration and virtual to virtual (V2V) machine migration from existing VMware virtual machines. In addition to Microsoft's tools, there are many third-party vendors that provide similar tools. PlateSpin (acquired by Novell in 2008), LeoStream, and Hewlett-Packard are a few examples of companies that provide third-party tools for automating migration, but others exist.

At minimum, a migration plan should address the following questions:

- Can an online migration of the physical server be performed, or does the process require server downtime?
- In what order will the physical servers be migrated?
- What are the migration dependencies?
- How will the migration process be monitored?
- How will the final cutover from the physical server be handled after the virtual machine has been tested?
- Will any special permissions be required to migrate a server?
- Will a new software license be required?
- Will an existing software license no longer be needed?
- Will the migrations be performed interactively or automated through scripts?
- What type of end-user notifications are required to migrate a server?
- Will the recovery process succeed if a deployment fails and a rollback is needed?

In addition, the migration plan should include developing a set of procedures that documents the migration process. The migration process should be validated during the pilot. Migration procedures should include step-by-step instructions to convert physical servers to virtual machines and verify that the virtual machine performance meets service level agreements.

Developing an Operations Plan

An operations plan provides the road map to changes in processes and procedures that are required for the new virtualization infrastructure. Changes will likely be needed in administration, update management, backup, disaster recovery, provisioning, and other areas.

At minimum, the operations plan should address the following questions:

- How do the following processes change?
  - Provisioning new hosts
  - Provisioning new virtual machines
  - Assigning permissions
  - Performing backups
  - Performing disaster recovery
  - Monitoring the virtualization components
  - Performing host and virtual machines updates
- Will virtual machines be backed up from the host agent or from agents loaded in the virtual machines?
- Will there be a separate administrative team to manage the Hyper-V servers?

- What changes to maintenance windows are required?
- Will automated workload balancing across hosts be used?
- What access does the help desk team need to virtual machines?
- Who has access to the System Center Virtual Machine Manager console?

The operations plan should identify all the areas that change, outline new processes, and provide detailed step-by-step procedures for validation during the pilot.

Developing a Training Plan

The training plan developed for a server virtualization pilot focuses on bringing administrators' skills up to date so that they can effectively manage the virtualization infrastructure. The training plan should identify the administrative team that will be responsible for the virtualized environment, their current skill levels, any training courses that they require to update their skills, and any new or adapted processes and procedures that they need to perform their administrative responsibilities. Ensure that both information technology department and business unit administrators are taken into account, especially if the business unit is managing the line of business (LOB) applications on the servers. Operation and management processes will generally be different for a virtualized server, so dispersing related information should be one of the highest training objectives.

The method you select for remote management of virtualized servers will affect the scope of the training plan. If the server administrator uses Remote Desktop to remotely manage the server, managing a virtualized server will be no different than managing a physical server in a traditional environment. If the Hyper-V VMConnect or System Center Virtual Machine Manager self-service portal interface is used, some level of training will probably be required.

Following is a list of common areas focused on in a training plan:

- Update management tools and processes
- Remote management tools and processes
- Monitoring tools and processes
- Backup tools and processes
- Disaster recovery processes
- New server provisioning process
- Application installation process
- Failover clustering process and management

Creating a Communications Plan

A communications plan can be one of the most important aspects of a pilot program. The plan focuses on how to communicate, whom to communicate with, when to communicate, and the information that should be communicated. More often than not, communication must be tailored to the target recipient group.

Effective communication to the pilot users or the end users who will be affected by the pilot is essential. You should not rely on a single communication method because users have different preferred ways of communicating. Combining e-mail messages, Web site postings, team meeting announcements, and other forms of communications ensures that the materials will be delivered in a timely manner regardless of the end user's preferred method of communication.

Properly targeting communications to the correct group of individuals also helps the credibility of the project. A balance must be achieved between ensuring that users and administrators receive communications and avoiding over-communicating, which can result in the user ignoring further communications. Categorize each communication and ensure that only the users in that category receive the communication.

Ensure that the communications happen in a timely manner. If possible, notices should be communicated at a minimum of two weeks in advance of any action. For example, users and administrators need a minimum of two week's notice that a physical server will be migrated. LOB application administrators should be scheduled at a minimum of two weeks in advance for operations verification following the migration of a server.

DIRECT FROM THE SOURCE

Targeting Your Communications

Will Martin, Senior Consultant
Microsoft Consulting Services

Users have different e-mail habits. Some diligently read every message received, others create rules to categorize their inbox, and others do not read anything unless it is directly addressed to them. There is no way to prevent a user from creating an inbox rule to delete any pilot communications, but there are ways to increase the potential for the message to be read.

Instead of sending a message to a distribution list that can be easily filtered in a rule, send all communications directly to each user. This approach personalizes the message and increases the potential for the message to get past any inbox filtering rule.

To accomplish this using Microsoft Office Outlook, you could write a Visual Basic for Applications script that uses the *ExchangeDistributionList* object to enumerate a distribution list, create a new message to each member of the distribution list, attach a standard rich text message, and then automatically send the message. Here is an example that you can use to customize your e-mail communications:

```
Dim oDL As Outlook.ExchangeDistributionList
Dim oEU As Outlook.ExchangeUser
Dim oAE As Outlook.AddressEntry
Dim oAEs As Outlook.AddressEntries
```

```
Set oDL As <address entry for the DL - can be passed to this routine as a
parameter>
Set oAEs = oDL.GetExchangeDistributionListMembers
For Each oAE in OAEs
    If oAE.AddressEntryType <> olExchangeDistributionListAddressEntry then
        Set oEU - oAE.GetExchangeUser
        <Script for sending email to the user goes here>
    Else
        <Recurse to run this script for embedded DLs>
    End If
Next
```

Another option is to use the Mail Merge feature of Microsoft Office Word 2007 to send to the individuals in the address list. You can personalize your e-mail so that individual addresses and names are included in your message.

For more help on using the *ExchangeDistributionList* object, refer to the MSDN Office Outlook 2007 developer's reference at *http://msdn2.microsoft.com/en-us/library /bb176360.aspx*. For more help on using the Mail Merge feature of Office Word 2007, search the Word 2007 Help system for "Mail Merge."

At minimum, communications should provide the following information to the target personnel:

- Overview of what is going to happen and why
- Benefit of the actions to the end user
- Timeline of the actions that will affect them
- Range of affected servers
- Range of affected services and applications
- Support process and contact information
- Escalation process

Documenting Risks

Evaluating and documenting pilot project risks allow you to develop mitigation plans and processes to maximize the success rate of the project. Business, technical, and resource risks should be captured, documented, reviewed, and acted on in a timely and consistent manner. The project risk list should be maintained and available to the entire pilot project team. Team members should be encouraged to raise new risks during the course of the project, but they also should assist in developing creative and effective solutions to eliminate or largely mitigate each risk.

Table 23-2 provides a list of required parameters that a project risk list should contain.

TABLE 23-2 Project Risk Items

ITEM	DESCRIPTION
Risk ID	Numeric value that uniquely identifies a risk
Risk Title	Descriptive title of the risk
Risk Description	Description of the risk
Consequence	Result if the risk occurs, including technical, business, and financial consequences
Probability	Measure of the likelihood that the risk will occur, typically indicated as a percentage or as a value from 1 through 10
Impact	Estimate of the adverse effects or magnitude of loss if the risk occurs, typically indicated as a value from 1 through 10
Mitigation Plan	Description of how to minimize or eliminate the risk with a series of tasks (If a mitigation plan is enacted, the project plan should be updated to reflect the tasks involved.)
Owner	The individual who owns the risk and the risk mitigation plan

Project risks should be maintained and updated in a manner that provides all project members and stakeholders easy access to the risk information. This can be accomplished by communicating to them through e-mail, by posting regular updates in a Microsoft Office Excel spreadsheet, or by using a Web interface such as is available in Microsoft Office Share-Point Server 2007.

 ON THE COMPANION MEDIA To assist in collecting and tracking risks, you will find an Excel spreadsheet called Risk Management JobAid.xls in the \Chapter Materials\Job Aids folder on the companion media. This spreadsheet has a single worksheet that contains columns to collect the recommended risk attributes.

Establishing Pilot Project Milestones

Pilot project milestones provide checkpoints at which to review the progress of the pilot. Milestones should be natural pause points that allow you answer the question, "How is the project doing?" Milestones vary by project, but they should always be used to measure progress toward the deployment and validation objectives. Therefore, every stage of a virtualization pilot project should have at least one milestone. You should not proceed to the next stage in a project if the previous stage's milestone has not been successfully completed (assuming the project stages are serial in nature). In addition, you should not proceed to a new project task until any task dependencies have been met. For example, if you are reusing physical servers for Hyper-V servers, you have a dependency on the successful migration of the physical server workload before you can rebuild it and repurpose it as a Hyper-V server. Therefore, one instance of a milestone could be the point in time when the last physical server workload has been successfully migrated.

In addition to deployment project milestones, validation milestones should be implemented at key points during the pilot timeline. For example, within the migration stage of the pilot project, you could establish a validation milestone after the first 10 percent of migrations have been completed. Before proceeding with the remaining 90 percent of planned migrations, you should verify that the pilot project processes and procedures are yielding the expected results and meeting objectives.

Establishing Success Criteria

Many projects are completed and considered a success without anyone ever really defining what success represents. Success criteria (sometimes called *conditions of satisfaction*) are measurable events or outcomes against which the project can be evaluated. Success criteria should be defined and agreed on with the executive sponsor before the project begins. This ensures that you can gather the right set of data points required to evaluate the success criteria of the project.

Measurability is the key aspect of establishing success criteria. For example, stating the project is a success if *the Hyper-V server has higher utilization* is not measurable. Restated to create a measurable success criterion, the requirement should specify that the project is a success if *the Hyper-V server has an average utilization of 50 percent or higher*.

Success criteria should be defined for each pilot project stage. You should also have success criteria for project objectives and goals. For example, if you have a goal that states "Reduce physical server capital costs by 20 percent," you will have to be able to show whether the project yielded the expected savings and met the goal.

Implementing the Pilot

During the actual pilot, you verify all virtualization project plans and designs through the implementation of a subset of the overall project scope. A scaled-down pilot implementation of the full-blown design allows you to ensure dependencies and potential issues are identified prior to the production deployment.

A pilot implementation is also a training opportunity for the production implementation team. If possible, staff the pilot implementation team with the identified key production implementation team members. This approach ensures that when the production begins, the key members of the implementation team have the necessary experience.

Ensure that the pilot implementation is using the same hardware as the planned production implementation. This allows identification of issues and validation of procedures using the actual hardware systems.

It is also important to understand the steps and actions taken during the pilot and the results and outcomes. You should implement a change management process using the management servers in order to track all changes to the environment. If a problem occurs, the change log will allow you to verify whether it is repeatable and develop a modified process to work around or mitigate the issue.

Measuring Project Success

During the pilot, you must collect data based on the defined success criteria that allows you to evaluate the project success. This task involves both qualitative and quantitative data collection. Quantitative data requires data collection using tools such as System Center Virtual Machine Manager 2008 and System Center Operations Manager 2007. By creating a report for each quantitative success criterion, you can quickly evaluate the project success and trends. Assessing trends can help you identify potential problem spots and allow you to take remedial action, such as conducting a root cause analysis, to determine how to reverse downward trends.

Qualitative data requires compilation of information using tools like SharePoint surveys, through which you can obtain user feedback concerning their experiences during the pilot implementation. Make sure to survey not only the direct pilot users but also any user who might have been affected by the pilot project based on items such as server downtime, poor performance, or help desk response time. Also, survey the pilot team to determine if they felt the project went smoothly or if they have suggestions to improve processes, procedures, or methods used during the pilot project.

Incorporating Lessons Learned

Inevitably, something will not go as planned during a pilot project, and either a risk mitigation plan is put into action, or another remedial action is taken to resolve the problem. At the end of the pilot phase, the project team should analyze the overall pilot experience, assimilate the information, and then modify project plans to prevent or mitigate similar problems during the production deployment. Modifications can take the form of changes to tasks in the project schedule, addition of project resources, changes to technical processes and procedures, or changes in project scope and objectives.

If the modifications are significant enough, an extension of the pilot or an additional pilot might be required to properly validate the changes and impacts to the project.

Summary

A server virtualization pilot project is a scaled-down deployment of the production implementation plan. The goal of a project pilot phase is to validate the virtualization infrastructure
design, processes, and procedures prior to a full production deployment. Before the pilot can
begin, pilot scope must be defined, and the pilot architecture must be available to deploy.
Planning a pilot requires the creation of individual plans and procedures for deployment,
support, migration, operations, and communications. You can increase project success by
creating an issue tracking process, developing a training plan, documenting project risks and
mitigation plans, establishing project milestones, and defining measurable success criteria.

When the pilot plans are ready, you can deploy the architecture and bring support processes online. You can then migrate the pilot virtualization candidates and collect quantitative
and qualitative data to evaluate against project success criteria. If the collected data shows
that the pilot project met or exceeded the success criteria, you can declare the pilot project
a success. If any issues arise during the pilot phase, you should incorporate mitigation plans,
remedial actions, and any lessons learned into the appropriate processes, procedures, and
objectives prior to undertaking the production deployment.

Additional Resources

The following resources contain additional information related to this chapter.

- Microsoft Outlook 2007 Developer Reference available at *http://msdn2.microsoft.com
  /en-us/library/bb177050.aspx*
- Infrastructure Planning and Design guides available at *http://go.microsoft.com/fwlink
  /?LinkId=100915*

Glossary

A

ACPI Advanced Configuration and Power Interface is an open specification that defines common interfaces for hardware recognition, power management, and hardware configuration.

ADSM Active Directory Service Marker, a subcomponent of Virtual Machine Management Service (VMMS) that provides registration and management of service connection points (SCP) in Active Directory.

agent A software application that provides remote functions and interfaces for another application.

AMD-V AMD's virtualization technology that provides hardware virtualization features that can be leveraged by software vendors to extend their virtualization solution architectures.

API Application programming interface.

application-level virtualization Virtualization approach that partitions and isolates applications from each other to prevent interaction or incompatibilities from occurring.

authorization store An xml file that maintains the authorization configuration for Hyper-V or SCVMM 2008.

B

BAT Block allocation table, a table of absolute sector offsets to the data blocks in the virtual hard disk header.

binary translation The emulation of one instruction set by another.

business continuity The strategy of defining and implementing a server and application solution that will resume services in a minimum amount of time in the event of a major disaster.

C

checkpoint The creation of a differencing disk as a way to provide rollback to a previous state of a virtual machine.

child partition A partition that is created by a hypervisor to run guest operating systems. It has access to synthetic and emulated hardware.

CIFS Common Internet File System is an application-layer network protocol that allows access to shared files, printers, and serial ports between nodes on a network.

clustering Using two or more servers connected to a shared disk system as single logical system for failure recovery.

cmdlet A command implemented by deriving a class from one of two specialized Windows PowerShell base classes.

CMS A single-user operating system, developed by IBM for the System/360 Model 67. It ran inside a virtual machine to deliver access to underlying system resources to each user.

collection An array of object references that can be enumerated.

COM (1) Component object model, a programming interface. (2) Communications port, refers to a serial port of the computer.

compact Process of removing empty sectors from a dynamically expanding virtual hard disk to reduce space used on the server.

conditions of satisfaction Measurable events or outcomes that a project can be evaluated against for success.

constrained delegation The ability to specify that a computer or service account can perform Kerberos delegation to a limited set of services.

CSCRIPT The command prompt–based VBScript processing engine.

D

DACL Discretionary access control list, which contains allow and deny access control entries for an object.

defragmentation A process used to ensure that files are stored as contiguous blocks on the hard disk, improving performance.

differencing disk A virtual hard disk that is an overlay to another virtual hard disk called a "parent" and that stores the disk writes. Differencing disks can have many overlay levels and a parent can have many "children" differencing disks.

disk geometry The combination of cylinders, heads, and sectors that define the capacity and configuration of a hard disk.

E

emulation The process whereby a virtual computer system or component performs in the same way as a physical computer system or component.

external network A virtual network bound to an adapter in the Hyper-V physical server.

F

FQDN Fully qualified domain name is the combination of the server name and the domain in which it resides.

For example, for a server named server1 in the domain contoso.com, the FQDN would be server1.contoso.com.

G

Gb/s Gigabits per second.

GB Gigabyte.

GHz Gigahertz.

GPA Guest physical address is the physical memory address space of the child partition.

guest The virtual machine being hosted by Virtual Server that is made up of the virtual hardware, operating system and installed applications.

guest operating system The operating system that executes in the virtual machine.

GUID Globally unique identifier is a type of identifier used in software applications to provide a unique reference number to an object.

GVA Guest virtual address is the virtual memory address space of the child partition.

H

HAL Hardware abstraction layer, a layer that is implemented in software to provide a standard interface to the hardware and hide differences from the operating system and applications.

HBA Host bus adapters, specialized disk controllers that provide high-speed connections between the host machine and the disk system.

heartbeat A signal emitted at regular intervals by a virtual or physical machine to indicate that it is responsive.

heterogeneous consolidation Combining different application workloads from multiple servers on a single server.

homogeneous consolidation Combining multiple server workloads for the same application on a single server.

host The physical server that is running Virtual Server 2005 R2.

host cluster A cluster of Hyper-V servers. Minimum cluster size is two nodes, maximum is 16 nodes.

host group A collection of hosts that are grouped together for administration, management, or security reasons.

host key (1) The key combination (by default, right Alt) that must be pressed when using Virtual Server to move keyboard and mouse focus from a guest operating system back to the host operating system. (2) The key combination (by default, Ctrl+Alt+Left Arrow) that must be pressed when using Hyper-V to move keyboard and mouse focus from a guest operating system back to the host operating system.

hosted virtualization Virtualization application that runs on top of an underlying host operating system like Windows Server 2003.

hypercall A special interface that provides access to computer instructions to an operating system running in a virtual machine. The operating system must be modified to use the hypercall instead of the standard interface.

hypervisor A virtual machine monitor implemented in software that can run directly on hardware or as a layer of an operating system.

I

IDE Integrated drive electronics is the hard and floppy disk interface that comes with almost every personal computer. The controller electronics are implemented on the hard disk itself.

in-scope A task, action, or object that is considered part of a project.

Intel VT Intel's virtualization technology that provides hardware virtualization features that can be leveraged by software vendors to extend their virtualization solution architectures

Integration Services A collection of services and software drivers that maximize performance and provide a better user experience within a virtual machine. Integration Services are only available for supported guest operating systems.

internal network A virtual network in Hyper-V that allows network communications between Hyper-V server and virtual machines, but not communications outside the Hyper-V server.

IOPS Input/output operations per second is a measure of how fast information is moving to and from a storage solution.

iSCSI SCSI protocols over IP networks. Technology that allows a remote server to present a portion of its storage space as a local SCSI disk.

ISO ISO files are images of CD or DVD disks that can be connected to the virtual CD/DVD drive of a virtual machine.

J

jumbo frames Packets that allow the default payload size of a packet to exceed the default Ethernet size of 1500 bytes and be as large as 9000 bytes.

K

KB Kilobyte.

Knowledge Base (KB) A library of official technical articles intended for anyone using or developing software for Microsoft products.

Kb/s Kilobit per second.

Keyboard, Video, Mouse (KVM) A device that allows you to share a keyboard, video, and mouse among multiple computers.

L

LBFO Load balancing and failover is a networking technology provided by ISVs to allow multiple physical network adapters to be configured so they look to the server like a single network adapter.

LDAP Lightweight Directory Access Protocol is an application protocol for querying and modifying directory services over TCP/IP. Standard defined by the Internet Engineering Task Force and defined in RFC 4510.

library A storage container for virtual machines, files, and templates in Virtual Machine Manager 2008.

live migration The migration of a virtual machine from one Hyper-V server to another Hyper-V server with no noticeable downtime.

logical processor The representation of a physical processor if single core or a physical core of a processor with multiple cores.

LUN Logical unit number is an address for a partition of a set of hard disks. The partition size can be any percentage of the disk array.

M

MAC Media access control is unique six-byte hardware address assigned to a network adapter so that any packet it sends can be returned.

Management Pack An extension to Microsoft Operations Manager that predefines rules, filters, performance counters, and alerts that should be monitored for a specific application or hardware.

maximum capacity The maximum percentage of a single processor (or core, if multicore) that can be consumed by a virtual machine.

maximum system capacity The maximum percentage of server resources that a virtual machine can consume.

Mb/s Megabits per second.

MB Megabyte.

MB/s Megabytes per second.

Merge The process of combining sectors from multiple differencing virtual hard disks to produce a single virtual hard disk with all changes.

MHz Megahertz.

N

NAS Network attached storage, a technology that allows disk systems to be directly attached to an IP network and accessed like a local disk.

native virtualization Virtualization approach that requires a processor to support virtualization-aware instructions to offload software processing.

NUMA Non-Uniform Memory Access is a processor architecture feature that provides faster access to memory that is locally attached to the processor so that is it tuned for performance.

O

operating system–level virtualization Virtualization approach in which a single operating system is abstracted to provide multiple isolated virtualized copies of the kernel, memory, and configuration. Only one copy of the operating system is ever running.

Options.xml Configuration file that contains the Virtual Server host configuration information, administration console settings, and binding information for physical network adapters.

out-of-scope A task, action, or object that is not considered part of a project.

P

P2V Physical to virtual is the process of migrating a physical machine to a virtual machine.

paravirtualization Virtualization approach in which the operating system requires modification to handle nonvirtualizable x86 instructions being supported between the virtual machine and the hypervisor via custom APIs called hypercalls.

parent partition Root partition of a hypervisor that controls access to the physical hardware.

partition A container for processes that is isolated from other containers and controlled by a hypervisor.

pass-through disk A physical disk on the server that is presented to the child partition as a virtual hard disk. The server cannot be using the disk resource.

PerfMon A performance monitoring application included with Windows 2000 and newer operating systems.

precompaction The process of running a tool that will clear any unused sectors in a virtual hard disk by writing zeros to the sectors.

private network A virtual network in Hyper-V that allows only virtual machine to virtual machine network communication.

PRO Performance resource optimization is the ability to utilize Virtual Machine Manager 2008 and Operations Manager 2007 to apply resource optimization for workload and applications within a virtualized environment.

PXE Pre-boot Execution Environment, a BIOS-enabled option to boot the computer from a network boot server, typically enabled by pressing F12.

Q

quiesce The process of flushing all memory and disk buffers to ensure that all transactions are complete before attempting a backup.

quorum disk The shared cluster disk on which configuration data is maintained in the quorum log, cluster database checkpoint, and resource checkpoints.

R

RAID Redundant array of inexpensive disks, a technology for combining hard disks together in a logical unit. There are different types of RAID that focus on availability and speed.

relative weight A numeric value assigned to a virtual machine that defines the importance of the virtual machine's access to resources versus another virtual machine. Virtual machines with higher relative weights obtain higher priority on resources.

reserved capacity The percentage of a single processor (or core if multicore) that is reserved for use by a virtual machine.

reserved system capacity The percentage of a total server processor (or core if multicore) capacity that is reserved for use by a virtual machine. This value cannot be larger than the maximum system capacity.

ring compression A method of executing multiple ring modes in a single ring mode of the physical processor.

RIS Remote Installation Service, a Windows application that provides remote boot and operating system installation across the network.

ROI Return on investment, the cost savings experienced from deploying a technology. The return is the total savings minus the cost of deploying and operating the new technology. Total savings would include capital, power, space, cooling, manpower, and time cost savings.

Rule Microsoft Operations Manager feature that defines events, alerts, and performance data to collect and establishes what to do with the information after it is collected.

S

SAN Storage area network is a technology that allows one or more computers to attach to a large array of disk drives and access defined blocks in independent or shared mode.

save state The process of saving the current memory, process, and disk configuration to files so that operation of a virtual machine can be quickly resumed. Similar to the concept of hibernating a computer.

SCP Service connection point is a feature that allows a service to register itself in Active Directory tied to the server that it is running on.

SCSI Small Computer System Interface.

SCVMM System Center Virtual Machine Manager, Microsoft's server application to manage one or more Hyper-V, Virtual Server 2005, and VMware ESX systems.

self-service portal A component of SCVMM 2008 that provides a Web-based interface for users to manage their virtual machines.

server consolidation The process of reducing the number of physical servers that are required to run a set of workloads by combining workloads on fewer servers.

server farm A collection of Hyper-V servers managed by a single SCVMM 2008 server.

side-by-side execution The ability of two applications to execute at the same time referencing different versions of the same dynamic link library (DLL).

SLA Service level agreement, a written definition of the expected service level that an organization managing a server would provide to the users. The agreement normally defines the levels and types of support and communications that are expected, as well as any adverse affects that will result if the levels are not reached or maintained.

slipstream The process by which you integrate drivers or updates into a Windows Image (WIM) to simplify the installation of the operating system.

snapshot A copy of the current hardware, software, process, memory, and disk state of a virtual machine that can be used to reset a virtual machine to a different state.

Snapshot Manager The Hyper-V component that manages virtual machine snapshots when the virtual machine is not running.

SPA System physical address is the physical memory address space of the physical computer.

SPL Single Port Listener for RDP is the feature within VMMS that manages the incoming connection requests from the virtual machine management client (Vmconnect.exe) and routes them to the appropriate worker process for handling.

SPN Service principal name, the information stored in Active Directory that defines a service running on a server and allows Kerberos authentication to the service.

state machine A machine that instantiates and manages the virtual machine, the state transitions, save and restore functionality, and snapshots.

support level An expected performance for support of a service, server, or application defined as a percentage value.

Sysprep A process and tool that allows you to remove the unique identity of a computer and reset it at next boot.

T

teaming The ability to have multiple network adapters act as one to provide higher throughput and failover. This is a network adapter manufacturer feature.

template A pre-defined virtual machine in the Virtual Machine Manager 2008 library server.

threshold A value selected to be a maximum or minimum limit target value.

U

UAC User Account Control is a feature of Windows Vista that forces all processes to run at a lower level of privilege by default and requires approval for any action needing a higher level of privilege before it will be executed. This feature is available to users with administrative privileges.

Undo disk A virtual hard disk in Virtual Server that stores all new writes so that the original virtual hard disk is not modified. When the virtual machine is powered off, you have the choice of committing all the writes in the Undo disk or discarding the writes and returning back to the state at power on.

unit (U) A standard for measuring the height of a rack mount device or rack.

user mode A process, service, or application that runs under the security context of a user account.

USN Update sequence number is a number assigned to an object in Active Directory that is used to track updates originating from a domain controller.

UUID An identifier that is used to provide a unique tracking number for an object.

V

V2V Virtual to virtual is the process of migrating a virtual machine of one format to another format.

VID Virtual infrastructure driver is a communications interface between the hypervisor and the parent partition using the hypercall API.

virtualization The abstraction of physical systems resources such that multiple logical partitions can be created to execute a heterogeneous set of operating systems, simultaneously on a single server.

virtualization candidate A physical server that meets all the requirements to be migrated to a virtual server.

VSC Virtualization service client.

VSP Virtualization service provider.

virtualization stack A collection of software components and virtual devices that work together to support the creation and management of virtual machines.

VFD Virtual floppy disk is the file-based representation of a physical floppy disk with full disk header and data storage.

VHD Virtual hard disk is a portable file-based representation of a physical hard disk with complete replication of a disk header structure.

VHDMount A Virtual Server utility that allows a server to mount a VHD file as a local disk for read and write operations.

VLAN Virtual local area network, a technology that provides multiple logical networks on a single physical cable.

VM (1) A virtual machine monitor developed by IBM for the System/360 Model 67. It created and controlled virtual machines. (2) Virtual machine, a computer that exists only in software.

VMBUS Virtual Machine Bus is a communications path for device and memory access between a child partition and a parent partition. A child partition cannot see communications from other child partitions.

VMC Virtual machine configuration, the file that holds the configuration information of the virtual machine (memory, hard disk, network adapters, BIOS settings, etc.) in Virtual Server 2005.

VMM (1) Virtual Machine Monitor, responsible for the creation, isolation, and preservation of virtual machine state, as well as the orchestration of access to system resources. (2) Virtual Machine Manager, the Microsoft solution to managing a farm of Hyper-V, Virtual Server 2005 R2, and VMware ESX virtualization servers.

VMMS Virtual Machine Management Service, a collection of components that work together to manage virtual machines.

VMNS Virtual Machine Network Service, the service that binds the virtual network to the physical network adapter in the host and allows traffic from the virtual machines to share the physical network adapter.

VMRC Client A Windows forms–based application that utilizes the VMRC protocol to remotely manage running virtual machines.

virtual floppy drive A software-based emulation of a 1.44-MB, 3.5" floppy drive.

virtual floppy disk A software-based representation of a 1.44-MB floppy disk.

Virtual Machine Additions A set of drivers and services installed in a virtual machine to provide better performance and enhanced user experience.

virtual machine library A collection of pre-built virtual machines accessible for modification and rapid deployment.

virtual memory The memory currently reserved for the virtual machine. Virtual memory can only be allocated from the server's available physical memory.

virtual network A network switch implemented in software that provides an unlimited number of ports for virtual machines to connect to and a single uplink port that can be bound to a physical network adapter in the server.

VSMT Virtual Server Migration Toolkit, an application that allows you to migrate a physical server to a virtual machine.

VSMM Virtualization stack memory manager.

VSS Volume Shadow Copy Service, the service available in Windows Server 2003 or newer operating systems that allows the server and any VSS-compatible applications to be quickly backed up without data loss.

W

WAIK Windows Automated Installation Kit is a software toolkit that assists in the creation of scripts and task sequences to create Windows OS images for automated deployment.

WIM Windows Image, the format used to transport all of the required files for installing a Windows operating system.

Windows PowerShell A new scripting language and command-line interface shell from Microsoft.

WinRM Windows Remote Management, Microsoft implementation of WS-Management Protocol, is a standard Simple Object Access Protocol (SOAP)–based, firewall-friendly protocol that allows hardware and operating systems from different vendors to interoperate.

WMI Windows Management Instrumentation is the set of interfaces that allows you to obtain hardware and software information about the local server.

WPM Worker Process Manager, which launches worker processes, maintains a list of all running worker processes, and provides change notifications to subscribers on the state of worker processes.

WSCRIPT The Windows form–based VBScript processing engine.

X

XML Extensible Markup Language (XML) is a general-purpose structured data format that facilitates the sharing of data across different information systems or applications.

Z

z/VM A current IBM virtualization product.

Index

A

P

X

About the Authors

JANIQUE CARBONE has been working in IT for over 15 years, specializing in enterprise infrastructure design and deployment projects. She is the coauthor of the *Microsoft Virtual Server 2005 R2 Resource Kit* (Microsoft Press, 2008) and writes articles focused on virtualization technology. After working for Microsoft Services for seven years, Janique founded the Infrastructor Group, which focuses on virtualization training and consulting. Janique is an MCSE and holds a B.S. and M.S. in Aerospace Engineering as well as an M.S. in Computer Science. She lives in Texas and shares life with her great husband, two wonderful children, and several lively dogs.

ROBERT LARSON is an Architect with Microsoft Consulting Services (MCS) and a subject matter expert on virtualization technologies. Robert is a regular speaker at TechEd and ITForum conferences on virtualization topics and has delivered multiple TechNet webcasts on Microsoft virtualization technologies. In addition to being the coauthor of the *Microsoft Virtual Server 2005 R2 Resource Kit*, he has authored or helped develop whitepapers for Microsoft on Hyper-V and Virtual Server 2005. Robert also writes articles on virtualization topics for Windows IT Pro magazine and VirtualizationAdmin.com. Robert has worked in the IT industry for over 20 years as engineer, outsourcer, and consultant. As an Architect for MCS, he assists customers and partners to plan and design data center and server consolidation projects involving virtualization. Robert has a master's degree in Computer Science. Robert lives outside Houston, Texas, with his lovely wife and two active children, and he enjoys basketball, scuba diving, and cooking. You can read his ramblings on virtualization and other topics on his blog at *http://blogs.technet.com/roblarson/default.aspx*.

What do you think of this book?

We want to hear from you!

To participate in a brief online survey, please visit:

microsoft.com/learning/booksurvey

...and enter this book's ISBN number (appears above barcode on back cover).

Tell us how well this book meets your needs—what works effectively, and what we can do better. Your feedback will help us continually improve our books and learning resources for you.

Thank you in advance for your input!

Where to find the ISBN on back cover

ISBN: 000-0-0000-0000-0

Example only. Each book has unique ISBN.

Stay in touch!

To subscribe to the *Microsoft Press® Book Connection Newsletter*—for news on upcoming books, events, and special offers—please visit:

microsoft.com/learning/books/newsletter